나혼자 끝내는 新토익

# LC+RC
# 1000제

실전 모의고사 **5**회

**나혼자 끝내는 新토익 LC+RC 1000제**

지은이 홍진걸 · 이주은 · 넥서스토익연구소
펴낸이 임상진
펴낸곳 (주)넥서스

초판 1쇄 발행 2017년 6월 5일
초판 10쇄 발행 2022년 4월 25일

출판신고 1992년 4월 3일 제311-2002-2호
10880 경기도 파주시 지목로 5
Tel (02)330-5500 Fax (02)330-5555

ISBN 979-11-5752-939-1 13740

www.nexusbook.com

나혼자 끝내는 新토익

# LC+RC 1000제

홍진걸·이주은·넥서스토익연구소 지음

## 실전 모의고사 5회

넥서스

대한민국 불변의 인기 키워드 중 최고는 토익이라 해도 과언이 아니다. 신(新)토익이 실시된 이후에도 토익에 대한 필요성은 여전하며 앞으로 공무원 시험까지 영역이 확대됨으로써 취업을 하는 데 있어서 토익은 꼭 필요한 시험이 되었다. 하지만 취업 준비하느라 바쁜 수험생들에게 언제까지나 토익만 강요할 수는 없다. 토익은 취업 준비에 있어 매우 중요한 요소지만 그만큼 가장 먼저 끝내야 하는 것이다.

토익 공부의 시작은 입문서나 기본서이겠지만 마지막 종점은 실전 문제집이다. 기본서와 전략서로 유형과 간단한 몸풀기를 연습했다면 정기 시험을 보러 가기 전 자신의 실력을 점검하고 최종 마무리하는 차원에서 가장 효과적인 실전서를 풀어 보는 일은 토익 학습 과정에서 참으로 중요하다. 시중에 워낙 좋다는 토익 교재들은 많다. 그러나 그중 가격적인 면에서 만족스럽고 최신 기출 유형을 잘 반영하며, 정답에 해설까지 포함되어 굳이 따로 해설집을 살 필요가 없는, 자신에게 가장 효율적인 책이 뭘지 생각하면 바로 답이 나올 것이다.

소위 쪽박달, 대박달이라는 말이 나올 정도로 정기 시험의 난이도는 꾸준하지 않고 수험자 자신의 컨디션이나 시험 환경에 따라 토익 점수가 달라질 수 있다. 이러한 외부 조건에 휘둘리지 않고 목표한 바를 단기간에 가장 효율적으로 끝내려면 뭐니 뭐니 해도 꾸준한 실력을 갖추는 것이다. 그러려면 무엇보다 이 책 저 책에 휘둘리지 않고 한 권을 끝까지 풀어 봐야 한다. 실전서 한 권을 시간을 정해 제대로 풀어본 후 틀린 문제나 어려운 부분을 꼼꼼하게 정리하고 확인한다면, 여러 권을 풀면서 토익 준비에 시간을 낭비하는 사람보다 훨씬 짧은 시간 안에 목표를 달성할 가능성이 높다.

신토익에서 수험생들이 가장 어려워하는 PART 7 삼중지문에 대해 특히 심혈을 기울여 실제 시험처럼 까다로운 문제를 수록하였다. 이로써 실전과 가장 비슷한 연습을 할 수 있도록 하였다. 마지막으로 이 책으로 공부하는 수험생 모두에게 지금 토익 공부가 단순히 고득점을 받는 데 그치지 않고 진정한 실용 영어 능력 향상을 위한 밑거름이 되길 바란다.

집필진 일동

# CONTENTS

# FEATURES

신토익을 반영한 5회 모의고사로 실전을 완벽 대비할 수 있습니다. 정기 토익 시험을 대비해서 실제 시험 환경과 같이 최종 마무리를 할 수 있습니다.

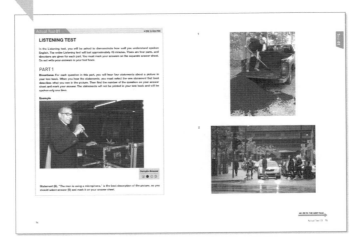

저자의 노하우가 담긴 쉽고 자세한

## 정답 및 해설

따로 해설집을 구매할 필요 없이 해설집을 수록하여 정답 및 해설을 확인하며 복습할 수 있습니다. 정답 키워드가 되는 부분을 표시하여 쉽게 정답을 찾고 이해할 수 있도록 구성하였습니다.

## 혼자서도 토익을 끝낼 수 있는 **1:1 코칭 & 부가 자료**

(1) 혼자 공부하면서 잘 이해되지 않거나 질문이 생겼을 때. "나혼토 1:1 코칭" 게시판이나 카카오톡을 활용하실 수 있습니다.

**LC:** 저자 이주은 ➡ 카카오톡 나혼토 1:1 코칭
카카오톡 ID: bkfellas

**RC:** 저자 홍진걸 ➡ 네이버 카페 나혼토 1:1 코칭 게시판
네이버 카페 cafe.naver.com/toeicway2

(2) **Listening** 받아쓰기 프로그램을 통해 복습을 하며 청취력을 향상시킬 수 있습니다. QR코드 또는 넥서스 홈페이지에서 이용할 수 있습니다.

MP3 바로 듣기
정답 자동 채점
받아쓰기 테스트

(3) 본문에 수록된 어휘 중에서도 특히 중요한 빈출 어휘 리스트와 이를 학습할 수 있는 온라인 테스트를 제공합니다.
www.nexusbook.com

## 쉽고 빠른 MP3 이용법 **콜롬북스 APP**

(1) 구글 플레이, 앱스토어에서 "콜롬북스" 어플 설치
(아래 QR코드 이용 또는 "콜롬북스"라고 검색해서 설치 가능)

(2) 넥서스 또는 도서명 "나혼자 끝내는 신토익 LC+RC 1000제" 검색(회원가입 필요 없음)

(3) 실전용, 복습용, 고사장 버전의 3종 MP3 다운로드

아이폰

안드로이드

2016년 5월 29일 정기시험부터 현재의 영어 사용 환경을 반영한 신(新)토익이 시행되었습니다. 전체 문항 수와 시험 시간은 동일하지만 각 파트별로 문항 수는 변화가 있으며 그동안 출제되지 않았던 그래프와 문자 메시지, 채팅, 삼중 지문 등 새로운 지문 유형과 문제가 출제됩니다.

## 신토익 시험의 구성

| 구성 | Part | Part별 내용 | 문항수 | 시간 | 배점 |
|---|---|---|---|---|---|
| Listening Comprehension | 1 | 사진 묘사 | 6 | 45분 | 495점 |
| | 2 | 질의 응답 | 25 | | |
| | 3 | 짧은 대화 | 39 | | |
| | 4 | 설명문 | 30 | | |
| Reading Comprehension | 5 | 단문 공란 채우기 | 30 | 75분 | 495점 |
| | 6 | 장문 공란 채우기 | 16 | | |
| | 7 | 단일 지문 | 29 | | |
| | | 이중 지문 | 10 | | |
| | | 삼중 지문 | 15 | | |
| Total | 7 Parts | | 200문제 | 120분 | 990점 |

## 신토익 이후 달라진 부분

❶ **Part 1**  문항 10개에서 6개로 감소
❷ **Part 2**  문항 30개에서 25개로 감소
❸ **Part 3**  문항 30개에서 39개로 증가, 〈3인 대화〉, 〈5턴 이상의 대화〉, 〈의도 파악, 시각 정보 연계 문제〉 추가
❹ **Part 4**  문항 30개로 기존과 동일, 〈의도 파악 문제〉, 〈시각 정보 연계 문제〉 추가
❺ **Part 5**  문항 40개에서 30개로 감소
❻ **Part 6**  문항 12개에서 16개로 증가, 〈알맞은 문장 고르기〉 추가
❼ **Part 7**  문항 48개에서 54개로 증가, 〈문자 메시지 · 온라인 채팅 지문〉, 〈의도 파악, 문장 삽입 문제〉,
     〈삼중 지문〉 추가

## 🔍 신토익 핵심 정보

| | | | |
|---|---|---|---|
| **Part 3** | 화자의 의도 파악 문제 | 2~3문항 | 대화문에서 화자가 한 말의 의도를 묻는 유형 |
| | 시각 정보 연계 문제 | 2~3문항 | 대화문과 시각 정보(도표, 그래픽 등)간 연관 관계를 파악하는 유형 |
| | 3인 대화 | 대화 지문 1~2개 | 일부 대화문에서 세 명 이상의 화자가 등장함 |
| | 5턴 이상의 대화 | | 주고 받는 대화가 5턴 이상으로 늘어난 대화 유형 |
| **Part 4** | 화자의 의도 파악 문제 | 2~3문항 | 담화문에서 화자가 한 말의 의도를 묻는 유형 |
| | 시각 정보 연계 문제 | 2~3문항 | 담화문과 시각 정보(도표, 그래픽 등)간 연관 관계를 파악하는 유형 |
| **Part 6** | 알맞은 문장 고르기 | 4문항 (지문당 1문항) | • 지문의 흐름상 빈칸에 들어갈 알맞은 문장 고르기 • 선택지가 모두 문장으로 제시되며 문맥 파악이 필수 |
| **Part 7** | 문장 삽입 문제 | 2문항 (지문당 1문항) | 주어진 문장을 삽입할 수 있는 적절한 위치 고르기 |
| | 문자 메시지 · 온라인 채팅 | 각각 지문 1개 | 2명이 대화하는 문자 메시지, 다수가 참여하는 온라인 채팅 |
| | 의도 파악 문제 | 2문항 (지문당 1문항) | • 화자가 말한 말의 의도를 묻는 문제 • 문자 메시지, 온라인 채팅 지문에서 출제 |
| | 삼중 지문 | 지문 3개 | 세 개의 연계 지문에 대한 이해도를 묻는 문제 |

# 나혼토 학습 스케줄

## 초급 수험자  기본서로 공부는 했지만 아직 700점 넘기가 힘들어요.

기본서로 공부를 했다고는 하지만 아직 실전 연습이 부족할 수도 있습니다. 실제 토익 시험을 보면서 시간이 부족한 경우가 많은데 이는 평소에 실전처럼 시간을 기록하며 연습을 하는 것이 중요합니다. 또한 어휘 실력이 부족한 시기이므로 온라인으로 제공되는 어휘테스트도 활용해 보세요. (www.nexusbook.com에서 어휘리스트, 어휘테스트 제공)

| 1일차 | 2일차 | 3일차 | 4일차 | 5일차 | 6일차 |
|---|---|---|---|---|---|
| Actual Test 1 문제 풀이 & 정답 확인 | Actual Test 1 LC 해설 확인 & 받아쓰기 | Actual Test 1 RC 해설 확인 & 어휘 복습 | Actual Test 2 문제 풀이 & 정답 확인 | Actual Test 2 LC 해설 확인 & 받아쓰기 | Actual Test 2 RC 해설 확인 & 어휘 복습 |
| 7일차 | 8일차 | 9일차 | 10일차 | 11일차 | 12일차 |
| Actual Test 3 문제 풀이 & 정답 확인 | Actual Test 3 LC 해설 확인 & 받아쓰기 | Actual Test 3 RC 해설 확인 & 어휘 복습 | Actual Test 4 문제 풀이 & 정답 확인 | Actual Test 4 LC 해설 확인 & 받아쓰기 | Actual Test 4 RC 해설 확인 & 어휘 복습 |
| 13일차 | 14일차 | 15일차 | | | |
| Actual Test 5 문제 풀이 & 정답 확인 | Actual Test 5 LC 해설 확인 & 받아쓰기 | Actual Test 5 RC 해설 확인 & 어휘 복습 | | | |

## 중급 수험자  감을 잡은 거 같은데 800점 전후로 왔다갔다 해요.

토익 공부도 좀 해보고 토익 시험도 2~3번 봤지만 여전히 점수가 잘 오르지 않는 경우입니다. LC는 실전 연습도 중요하지만 받아쓰기를 통해 다시 한번 복습해 보는 것이 좋습니다. RC는 각 파트별로 권장 풀이 시간에 맞춰 풀어보면서 취약한 부분이 어디인지 점검해 보세요.

| 1일차 | 2일차 | 3일차 | 4일차 | 5일차 | 6일차 |
|---|---|---|---|---|---|
| Actual Test 1 문제 풀이 | Actual Test 1 정답 및 해설 확인 | Actual Test 2 문제 풀이 | Actual Test 2 정답 및 해설 확인 | Actual Test 3 문제 풀이 | Actual Test 3 정답 및 해설 확인 |
| 7일차 | 8일차 | 9일차 | 10일차 | | |
| Actual Test 4 문제 풀이 | Actual Test 4 정답 및 해설 확인 | Actual Test 5 문제 풀이 | Actual Test 5 정답 및 해설 확인 | | |

## 고급 수험자  900점 이상을 목표로 하고 있지만 쉽지 않아요.

가끔은 정말 시험을 잘 봤다고 생각하지만 예상치 못한 곳에서 틀리는 문제가 있는 경우입니다. 한 번 틀렸던 문제들은 다시 틀리는 경우가 많으므로 꼭 다시 점검해 보세요.

| 1일차 | 2일차 | 3일차 | 4일차 | 5일차 |
|---|---|---|---|---|
| Actual Test 1 & 해설 | Actual Test 2 & 해설 | Actual Test 3 & 해설 | Actual Test 4 & 해설 | Actual Test 5 & 해설 |

# 나혼토 실력 점검

테스트가 끝난 후 각 테스트별로 점검해 보세요. 테스트별로 맞은 개수를 확인하며 실력이 향상됨을 체크해 보세요.

## 정답 확인 전

|  | 테스트 날짜 | 시험 소요 시간 | 체감 난이도 |
|---|---|---|---|
| Actual Test 01 |  |  | 상 　 중 　 하 |
| Actual Test 02 |  |  | 상 　 중 　 하 |
| Actual Test 03 |  |  | 상 　 중 　 하 |
| Actual Test 04 |  |  | 상 　 중 　 하 |
| Actual Test 05 |  |  | 상 　 중 　 하 |

## 정답 확인 후

|  | 맞힌 개수 | 환산 점수 | 총점 |
|---|---|---|---|
| Actual Test 01 | LC: |  | 점 |
|  | RC: |  |  |
| Actual Test 02 | LC: |  | 점 |
|  | RC: |  |  |
| Actual Test 03 | LC: |  | 점 |
|  | RC: |  |  |
| Actual Test 04 | LC: |  | 점 |
|  | RC: |  |  |
| Actual Test 05 | LC: |  | 점 |
|  | RC: |  |  |

* 환산 점수는 222페이지에 있는 환산 점수표를 이용해 주세요.

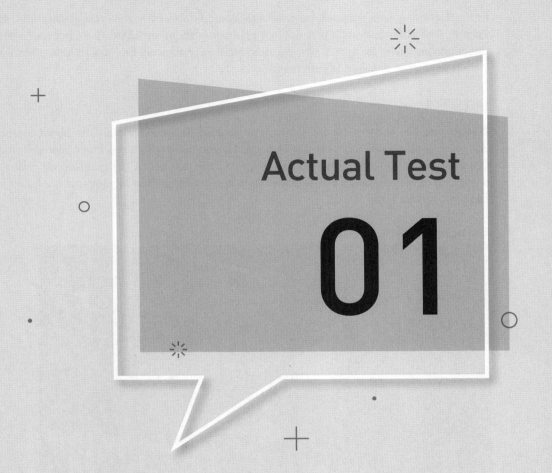

Actual Test

01

| 시작 시간 | : |
| --- | --- |
| 종료 시간 | : |

# LISTENING TEST

In the Listening test, you will be asked to demonstrate how well you understand spoken English. The entire Listening test will last approximately 45 minutes. There are four parts, and directions are given for each part. You must mark your answers on the separate answer sheet. Do not write your answers in your test book.

## PART 1

**Directions:** For each question in this part, you will hear four statements about a picture in your test book. When you hear the statements, you must select the one statement that best describes what you see in the picture. Then find the number of the question on your answer sheet and mark your answer. The statements will not be printed in your test book and will be spoken only one time.

**Example**

**Sample Answer**
Ⓐ ● Ⓒ Ⓓ

Statement (B), "The man is using a microphone," is the best description of the picture, so you should select answer (B) and mark it on your answer sheet.

1

2

GO ON TO THE NEXT PAGE ▶

**3**

**4**

5

6

GO ON TO THE NEXT PAGE ➤

# PART 2

**Directions:** You will hear a question or statement and three responses spoken in English. They will not be printed in your test book and will be spoken only one time. Select the best response to the question or statement and mark the letter (A), (B), or (C) on your answer sheet.

**7** Mark your answer on your answer sheet.

**8** Mark your answer on your answer sheet.

**9** Mark your answer on your answer sheet.

**10** Mark your answer on your answer sheet.

**11** Mark your answer on your answer sheet.

**12** Mark your answer on your answer sheet.

**13** Mark your answer on your answer sheet.

**14** Mark your answer on your answer sheet.

**15** Mark your answer on your answer sheet.

**16** Mark your answer on your answer sheet.

**17** Mark your answer on your answer sheet.

**18** Mark your answer on your answer sheet.

**19** Mark your answer on your answer sheet.

**20** Mark your answer on your answer sheet.

**21** Mark your answer on your answer sheet.

**22** Mark your answer on your answer sheet.

**23** Mark your answer on your answer sheet.

**24** Mark your answer on your answer sheet.

**25** Mark your answer on your answer sheet.

**26** Mark your answer on your answer sheet.

**27** Mark your answer on your answer sheet.

**28** Mark your answer on your answer sheet.

**29** Mark your answer on your answer sheet.

**30** Mark your answer on your answer sheet.

**31** Mark your answer on your answer sheet.

# PART 3

**Directions:** You will hear some conversations between two or more people. You will be asked to answer three questions about what the speakers say in each conversation. Select the best response to each question and mark the letter (A), (B), (C), or (D) on your answer sheet. The conversations will not be printed in your test book and will be spoken only one time.

32  Why is the man calling?
(A) To change an order
(B) To confirm a delivery time
(C) To cancel an event
(D) To make a complaint

33  What does the woman request?
(A) The man's credit card details
(B) The man's order number
(C) The man's full address
(D) The man's contact information

34  What does the woman say she will send the man?
(A) A coupon
(B) A menu item
(C) A complimentary meal
(D) A text message

35  What problem does the woman report?
(A) An elevator is broken.
(B) A repair person is unavailable.
(C) A file has been deleted.
(D) A staircase is blocked.

36  What does the man say he will do?
(A) Remove a blockage
(B) Send a repairman
(C) Locate an alternate exit
(D) Install a new elevator

37  What does the woman mean when she says, "it is almost noon"?
(A) The elevator will soon be needed.
(B) She has an important meeting to attend.
(C) Her lunch break is almost over.
(D) She is expecting some guests.

38  What is the man trying to do?
(A) Locate a place
(B) Repair a device
(C) Promote a product
(D) Listen to a radio

39  Why does the woman direct the man to Mildwater?
(A) It is famous.
(B) It is nearby.
(C) It offers a discount.
(D) It has been newly renovated.

40  What is the man told to do?
(A) Turn left at the light
(B) Call a taxi
(C) Drive to the next intersection
(D) Visit a local store

41  Why is the woman calling?
(A) To inquire about a survey
(B) To complain about a lost order
(C) To schedule a manufacturers meeting
(D) To ask about construction equipment

42  What does the man say he did a few days ago?
(A) Complete a survey
(B) Send some results
(C) Meet with Keith Baines
(D) Test a new item

43  What did testers not like about the new product?
(A) Its size
(B) Its price
(C) Its durability
(D) Its material

**GO ON TO THE NEXT PAGE**

44 What is the man shopping for?

(A) Some groceries
(B) A gift basket
(C) An electronic device
(D) Some office supplies

45 What does Sophia say about some items?

(A) They are currently on sale.
(B) They cannot be shipped out.
(C) They are out of stock.
(D) They can be found on a different floor.

46 What additional service does Sophia mention?

(A) In-store shipping
(B) Overnight delivery
(C) Free membership
(D) Gift wrapping

47 What are the speakers mainly talking about?

(A) Relocating an office
(B) Meeting for dinner
(C) Going to a movie
(D) Buying office supplies

48 What does the woman suggest the man do?

(A) Start packing up his belongings
(B) Grab some items from the lobby
(C) Take a break for a meal
(D) Work extra hours

49 What will the man probably do next?

(A) Turn off the light
(B) Put file folders in boxes
(C) Call a moving company
(D) Request some office supplies

50 Who most likely is the man?

(A) A restaurant owner
(B) An event organizer
(C) A financial supporter
(D) A radio broadcaster

51 What are the speakers mainly discussing?

(A) A new sports arena
(B) A fundraising event
(C) A store promotion
(D) A non-profit organization

52 Why does the man say, "How does that sound to you"?

(A) To request the woman's permission
(B) To provide another example
(C) To change the subject
(D) To advertise an upcoming event

53 What are the speakers discussing?

(A) Purchasing a concert ticket
(B) Acquiring a unique item
(C) Placing an ad online
(D) Organizing a musical performance

54 What problem is mentioned?

(A) Signed albums take time to arrive.
(B) The price of limited copies is very high.
(C) The store is not open for business yet.
(D) A potential birthday gift is out of stock.

55 What does the man suggest?

(A) Making an order online
(B) Delaying the date of an event
(C) Exchanging an item for a different one
(D) Purchasing an item at a different store

**56** What does the woman say she will do next week?

(A) Attend a conference
(B) Finish a product design
(C) Move to another city
(D) Have a job interview

**57** According to the conversation, what office duties does Marco handle?

(A) Requests for faxing documents
(B) Inquiries from customers
(C) Stocks of office supplies
(D) Travel arrangements

**58** What does Marco ask the woman to do?

(A) Return the next day
(B) Call her supervisor
(C) Make a payment
(D) Complete a form

---

**59** Why was the woman late?

(A) She had an earlier engagement.
(B) She went to the wrong place.
(C) She had to wait a long time for the train.
(D) She was preparing extra samples.

**60** What does the woman want to know about?

(A) Some samples for sale
(B) Directions to a workshop
(C) Some changes to a schedule
(D) The number of attendees

**61** What will the woman probably do next?

(A) Fetch some items
(B) Request some samples
(C) Find alternative transportation
(D) Purchase cosmetic products

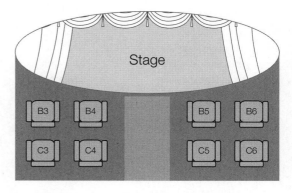

**62** What is the conversation mainly about?

(A) Locating a building
(B) Negotiating a deal
(C) Revising a seating chart
(D) Resolving a seating problem

**63** Look at the graphic. Which seat was the man originally assigned to?

(A) B4
(B) B5
(C) C4
(D) C5

**64** What does the man ask the woman to do?

(A) Check a theater ticket
(B) Move to another seat
(C) Request opera glasses
(D) Speak to his friend

GO ON TO THE NEXT PAGE

**Edmonton Building Directory**

| Office | Location |
|---|---|
| Dawson Dental Clinic | Suite 1022 |
| Jasmine Hair Shop | Suite 1013 |
| Silver Linings Counseling | Suite 2020 |
| LGB Construction | Suite 2023 |

**65** What is the purpose of the woman's visit?

(A) To meet with a client
(B) To see a therapist
(C) To deliver supplies
(D) To get a car repaired

**66** What does the man say about parking?

(A) It is for residents only.
(B) It must be paid in cash.
(C) It is free upon validation.
(D) It is currently unavailable.

**67** Look at the graphic. Which name of the office needs to be changed on the building directory?

(A) Dawson Dental Clinic
(B) Jasmine Hair Shop
(C) Silver Linings Counseling
(D) LGB Construction

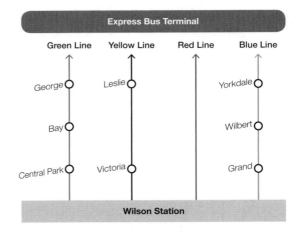

**68** Where does the conversation take place?

(A) On a bus
(B) In an office
(C) At a subway station
(D) In the street

**69** Look at the graphic. Which line does the woman suggest the man take?

(A) Green Line
(B) Yellow Line
(C) Red Line
(D) Blue Line

**70** Why is the man going to Boston?

(A) He is participating in a contest.
(B) He is buying a house.
(C) He is visiting his family.
(D) He is going on a business trip.

# PART 4

**Directions:** You will hear some talks given by a single speaker. You will be asked to answer three questions about what the speaker says in each talk. Select the best response to each question and mark the letter (A), (B), (C), or (D) on your answer sheet. The talks will not be printed in your test book and will be spoken only one time.

**71** Where is the talk taking place?

(A) At a fitness club
(B) At a medical center
(C) At a hotel
(D) At a factory

**72** What does the speaker say will happen in January?

(A) A branch office will be opened.
(B) A contract will be renewed.
(C) A busy season will begin.
(D) Membership fees will increase.

**73** What are the listeners asked to do?

(A) Look at some paperwork
(B) Introduce themselves to each other
(C) Go to another building
(D) Update their contact information

**74** What did the speaker do yesterday?

(A) She went to a pet store.
(B) She moved into an apartment.
(C) She worked overtime.
(D) She met with a client.

**75** What did the listener ask about?

(A) When the building was built
(B) Why a rental fee is expensive
(C) Whether pets are allowed
(D) Where parking is available

**76** Why does the speaker say, "you shouldn't miss this opportunity"?

(A) To encourage a positive decision
(B) To negotiate a contract
(C) To extend an invitation
(D) To present a different view

**77** What will cause traffic congestion tomorrow morning on the bridge?

(A) Change of signal lights
(B) Road expansion
(C) A musical event
(D) Some repair work

**78** What did the speaker say might affect the roadwork schedule?

(A) A change in the weather
(B) Traffic condition
(C) Work hours
(D) The ending of a concert

**79** What program are the listeners going to hear next?

(A) Local news
(B) A financial program
(C) Advertisements
(D) Weather forecast

**80** What is the main purpose of this message?

(A) To inform listeners of emergency exits
(B) To confirm listeners' appointments
(C) To talk about the reopening
(D) To announce that the facility is closed

**81** What should the listeners do if it is an emergency?

(A) They need to record their names and numbers.
(B) They need to visit on Monday.
(C) They need to call the number that was mentioned.
(D) They have to make an appointment.

**82** What should the listeners do to change an appointment?

(A) Visit the clinic
(B) Wait until the representative answers
(C) Talk to someone at an urgent care facility
(D) Leave a message

**GO ON TO THE NEXT PAGE**

**83** What is the purpose of the CEO's visit?

(A) To celebrate an anniversary
(B) To assign new tasks
(C) To inspect a facility
(D) To improve production capacity

**84** Why does the speaker say, "this isn't an official inspection"?

(A) To make preparations for an event
(B) To discuss an issue
(C) To reassure colleagues
(D) To acknowledge hard work

**85** What are the listeners asked to do?

(A) Attend a luncheon
(B) Host a welcome reception
(C) Join a factory tour
(D) Plan a retirement party

---

**86** Who is Emmanuel David?

(A) A fashion designer
(B) A radio host
(C) A magazine editor
(D) A manufacturing expert

**87** Why did Mr. David go to Cannes?

(A) To visit a client
(B) To view some designs
(C) To attend an event
(D) To open a production line

**88** What are listeners invited to do?

(A) Fill out a survey
(B) Enter a competition
(C) Inquire about the show
(D) Visit Mr. David's company

**89** What type of business does the speaker work for?

(A) A hospital
(B) A staffing agency
(C) A real estate agency
(D) A university

**90** What does the speaker imply when she says, "So please note that wait times can be long"?

(A) She wants to get a deadline extension.
(B) An investigation will be completed shortly.
(C) The listeners should return on another day.
(D) She hopes the listeners will be patient.

**91** According to the speaker, what is provided for listeners?

(A) Some refreshments
(B) Technical assistance
(C) Newspapers and magazines
(D) Some office equipment

---

**92** What is the purpose of the message?

(A) To review a follow-up report
(B) To announce new safety standards
(C) To set up new fire equipment
(D) To discuss ways to reduce costs

**93** Who most likely is the speaker?

(A) A building manager
(B) A facility inspector
(C) An accountant
(D) A real estate agent

**94** Why does the speaker want the listener to return his call?

(A) To purchase fire equipment
(B) To make some recommendations
(C) To re-inspect the facilities
(D) To give him a new report

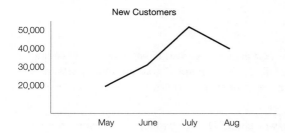

New Customers

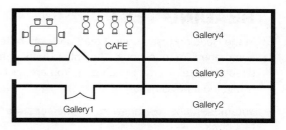

4th floor

**95** In what department does the speaker most likely work?

(A) Product development
(B) Purchasing
(C) Marketing
(D) Customer service

**96** According to the speaker, what happened in July?

(A) A package product was introduced.
(B) A branch location was added
(C) A department was reorganized.
(D) A business merger took place.

**97** Look at the graphic. When was the promotional event held?

(A) In May
(B) In June
(C) In July
(D) In August

**98** Who most likely is the speaker?

(A) A painter
(B) A university professor
(C) A museum guide
(D) A photographer

**99** Look at the graphic. In which gallery are the European paintings exhibited?

(A) Gallery1
(B) Gallery2
(C) Gallery3
(D) Gallery4

**100** What would listeners do if they are interested in the current exhibitions?

(A) Visit a bookshop
(B) Explore a website
(C) Watch a movie
(D) Attend a lecture

This is the end of the Listening test. Turn to Part 5 in your test book.

GO ON TO THE NEXT PAGE

# READING TEST

In the Reading test, you will read a variety of texts and answer several different types of reading comprehension questions. The entire Reading test will last 75 minutes. There are three parts, and directions are given for each part. You are encouraged to answer as many questions as possible within the time allowed.

You must mark your answers on the separate answer sheet. Do not write your answers in your test book.

# PART 5

**Directions:** A word or phrase is missing in each of the sentences below. Four answer choices are given below each sentence. Select the best answer to complete the sentence. Then mark the letter (A), (B), (C), or (D) on your answer sheet.

101 By decreasing the aircrafts' seating ------- in favor of more high-class accommodations, Banchster Airlines enhanced its profitability and its level of customer satisfaction.

(A) preparation
(B) intensity
(C) capacity
(D) aptitude

102 This meeting should be concluded ------- a promise not to reveal what was debated here.

(A) around
(B) above
(C) with
(D) until

103 ------- located at the highway exit, the new gas station will be opened by BMC Petroleum.

(A) Widely
(B) Conveniently
(C) Correctly
(D) Greatly

104 Before ------- with Ms. Goyal's public relations consultant, Mr. Kim wants to have a better understanding of the details of the agenda.

(A) consults
(B) to consult
(C) consulting
(D) consulted

105 The strategy workshop will open at 11 A.M. on Monday ------- will be followed by a meeting at 2:30, after which there will be a late lunch at 3:30.

(A) with
(B) either
(C) and
(D) such

106 The area licenser has ordered that until a written ------- has been approved by the building owner, no maintenance work can begin.

(A) judgment
(B) estimate
(C) guess
(D) suggestion

107 The new board of directors is soliciting ------- for human resources manager, treasurer and vice-president.

(A) to have nominated
(B) nominating
(C) nominations
(D) nominate

108 After Quantium made known its plans for a hostile takeover bid of AXT, the value of AXT stocks went up -------.

(A) expressively
(B) accidentally
(C) eagerly
(D) dramatically

**109** We have to keep all materials, printer components, desks and other ------- supplies in the basement warehouse.

(A) related
(B) achievable
(C) interested
(D) alike

**110** The head of the marketing department not only develops sales strategies, but is expected to take charge of ------- our services to prospective customers and to secure deals.

(A) promote
(B) promotes
(C) promoted
(D) promoting

**111** Among our nation's trade partner businesses, our new currency policies have ------- to stronger economies.

(A) contributions
(B) contributed
(C) contributing
(D) contribute

**112** The nation suffered a depression with inflation ------- rose steadily for over five years during the 1990s.

(A) they
(B) that
(C) when
(D) what

**113** Without having to worry about extensive paperwork and visits to the bank, the company's workers have the option of automatically transferring 5% of their monthly paychecks into special ------- accounts.

(A) saved
(B) save
(C) safely
(D) savings

**114** The personnel officers prepared a profile of each candidate which not only contained an analysis of their personality, but also listed a(n) ------- of their educational background and on-site experience.

(A) description
(B) mistake
(C) information
(D) attention

**115** Our summer barbecue was the most ------- of all the fundraisers our charity has conducted, with 24 groups participating over the whole weekend.

(A) successful
(B) delighted
(C) wealthy
(D) overall

**116** ------- the layout of the streets and parks was ideal for foot traffic, the board of directors selected the city as the place to hold their annual street festival.

(A) Because
(B) Unless
(C) More than
(D) Following

**117** A student who comes from a family whose wages are at the poverty rate or below ------- for special discounts on tuition fee, textbooks, and housing at my college.

(A) supplies
(B) equips
(C) arranges
(D) qualifies

**118** When new products are released, the old products tend to stay on the ------- for periods of two to five weeks.

(A) place
(B) sale
(C) advertisement
(D) market

GO ON TO THE NEXT PAGE

119 The special leasing rate is available ------- to workers of HJG Vehicle and their immediate family members.

(A) exclusionary
(B) exclusiveness
(C) exclusion
(D) exclusively

120 An editor always looks for errors and irregularities ------- an author's work.

(A) within
(B) while
(C) where
(D) wherever

121 TSD loan service strategy is ------- focused on small companies and personal accounts because it is a small-scale bank.

(A) primarily
(B) numerically
(C) originally
(D) initially

122 Beckhart Jewelers is currently ------- experienced, motivated and team-oriented managers for many new branch offices across the southern part of the province.

(A) looking
(B) seeking
(C) inquiring
(D) entering

123 The economic forum in Seoul will be the most extensive meeting of finance ministers ever ------- in Asia.

(A) referred
(B) stayed
(C) went
(D) held

124 One of the challenges a corporation faces is successful ------- of its products' identity to clients when operating in a foreign market.

(A) communicatively
(B) communicate
(C) communication
(D) communicated

125 The newly developed farm equipment has improved the ------- of farmers as well as the quality of their harvest.

(A) productivity
(B) measures
(C) instruction
(D) economics

126 ------- an executive in the International Operations Department at Saint & Co., Arshad Chowdhury last week became a member of the government's International Trade Advisory Committee.

(A) Often
(B) Once
(C) Now
(D) Soon

127 Because PNB Bank is ------- to announce a decrease in interest rates, investors are anxious for the press conference.

(A) expect
(B) expects
(C) expected
(D) expecting

128 In an attempt to rejuvenate the company's image, the head of Public Relations was asked to help create an ad campaign ------- the new corporate logo.

(A) featuring
(B) convening
(C) deserving
(D) accommodating

129 The store will ship them to you at half the ------- rate if you purchase over 100 dollars' worth of goods.

(A) duplicate
(B) numerous
(C) divided
(D) standard

130 The Justice Bureau office is required to ------- to all formal requests for official documents within 14 days.

(A) promise
(B) respond
(C) explain
(D) advise

# PART 6

**Directions:** Read the texts that follow. A word, phrase, or sentence is missing in parts of each text. Four answer choices for each question are given below the text. Select the best answer to complete the text. Then mark the letter (A), (B), (C), or (D) on your answer sheet.

**Questions 131-134** refer to the following letter.

To: All employees
From: Jonathan Smith
Date: June 19
Re: Remodeling the third floor of the building

From early next week, the remodeling of the marketing department, the third level of the building, will begin. -------- area will not be accessible to any employee including the marketing team members.
                    **131.**

Please be advised that there will be certain parts of the parking lot that are reserved for the construction equipment. The east side of the building, which is the Section C of the parking lot, will be closed during the entire construction process. In addition to Section C, there may be other parts of the lot that will be closed -------- for the use of heavy equipment.
                                                      **132.**

We strongly recommend that the employees avoid using their personal vehicles as much as possible. --------. We apologize for any inconvenience caused by this --------. Further information
              **133.**                                          **134.**
regarding the remodeling will be sent via e-mail as it gets closer to the construction date.

Jonathan Smith

131  (A) Either
     (B) These
     (C) This
     (D) Those

132  (A) temporal
     (B) temporary
     (C) temporarily
     (D) temporariness

133  (A) We encourage the usage of public transportation during this time period of remodeling.
     (B) Utilizing public transportation contributes to reducing carbon footprint.
     (C) There is enough space in the parking lot for all employees.
     (D) Employees are encouraged to park on the third floor during the construction period.

134  (A) closure
     (B) review
     (C) contract
     (D) proposal

**GO ON TO THE NEXT PAGE**

**Questions 135-138** refer to the following advertisement.

Best Price has been providing groceries and daily necessities to its customers for over 20 years. -------. We have recently added many new store ------- around the Georgia area in order to
135.                                                                              136.
provide the best products at the best prices.

We also plan to provide a wider variety of products and offer ------- hours of service. Our new
137.
service hours will be 24 hours in order to serve our customers best.

With the changes that have been made, we look forward to providing a quality service to our

customers. Further information on the changes, ------- the new locations and service hours, is
138.
available online: www.bestprice.com.

We look forward to serving you!

135 (A) Now we are expecting to be able to
       serve even more customers.
    (B) We have faced many difficulties and have
       therefore decided to close our store.
    (C) We plan to have a clearance sale this
       weekend.
    (D) Not many customers supported us
       despite our high-quality customer
       service.

136 (A) locations
    (B) information
    (C) products
    (D) research

137 (A) extended
    (B) limited
    (C) potential
    (D) resourceful

138 (A) have included
    (B) including
    (C) will include
    (D) is included

**Questions 139-142** refer to the following e-mail.

To: Frank Kane
From: Matthew Chung
Subject: Update to your catering inquiry

Thank you for choosing Chung's Catering! ------- it is true that we only provide catering service,
                                         **139.**
we can definitely work with an event company to satisfy your needs.

We know several event companies that have been working with us for a number of years. -------.
                                                                                      **140.**
The information regarding the event companies is attached in this e-mail. We guarantee that our

catering quality has always exceeded our customers' -------.
                                                    **141.**

Please note that we need at least a week of preparation prior to the event. We ------- happy to
                                                                               **142.**
meet you in person and discuss the details of your event as soon as possible.

Please contact us back with your convenient time and location for a meeting.

Regards,

Matthew Chung

---

139 (A) Therefore
    (B) While
    (C) Even
    (D) Until

140 (A) All of them provide the best quality
        service.
    (B) There are around 500 employees in each
        event company.
    (C) Event companies in this area specialize
        in holding small parties.
    (D) Our contract with Pine Event Planning
        ends this September.

141 (A) variations
    (B) expectations
    (C) relations
    (D) invitations

142 (A) would be
    (B) were
    (C) would have been
    (D) might be

GO ON TO THE NEXT PAGE

This is an estimate of the cost for the computer upgrade that Bronco Inc. requested on Jan 21.
After receiving the request, a team of experts from our company ------- a total of 45 computers at
**143.**
Bronco Inc.

After thorough inspection, the team decided that the total cost for the upgrade is going to be
$1,560. -------. We hope that you also feel $1,560 is a fair price for this -------.
**144.** **145.**

We also recommend that you ------- compare this price to other companies' estimates. We are
**146.**
confident with our pricing and also sure that you won't regret choosing us. Our company has
always tried to provide quality service at the appropriate price. We have taken great pleasure in
working with Bronco Inc. and look forward to hearing back from you.

If you feel that the price is fair, please let us know when to begin the upgrade procedure.

Sincerely,

Robin Park
CEO of Park & Ronson Technologies

---

**143** (A) are inspecting
(B) inspect
(C) will inspect
(D) inspected

**144** (A) The upgrade will be proceeded in a first-come, first-served basis.
(B) The computers need to be replaced with new ones right away.
(C) Our team is known for its honesty and fairness in these estimates.
(D) Professionals are not all satisfied with the new security program.

**145** (A) figure
(B) procedure
(C) problem
(D) connection

**146** (A) lately
(B) apparently
(C) actively
(D) decreasingly

# PART 7

**Directions:** In this part you will read a selection of texts, such as magazine and newspaper articles, e-mails, and instant messages. Each text or set of texts is followed by several questions. Select the best answer for each question and mark the letter (A), (B), (C), or (D) on your answer sheet.

**Questions 147-148** refer to the following notice.

## James' DVD Shop

192 Mentor Ave,
Willoughby, OH, 44094

Customer: Michael Han                                    ID#: 091928502
June 19

Dear Mr. Han,

This letter has been sent to you in order to notify you of the items that are currently overdue.

Our record shows that, on April 19th, you checked out two items, *Life on Mars* and *The Deep Sea*. The two items are some of the popular DVDs that our store has to offer in limited quantities. Therefore, many customers who have come to the store had to leave empty-handed because the items were not returned on time.

We ask you to return those items as soon as possible. The due date for the items was May 18th. Please be aware that there has been $60.00 worth of fines charged to your account due to the late return. The items must be returned to a staff member.

We hope you return the items as soon as possible and avoid any more fines charged to your account.

Regards,
James Hardwick
Owner of James' DVD Shop

---

**147** Why was the notice sent?

(A) To remind its customer that the requested items have arrived at the store
(B) To notify its customer that the store location has changed
(C) To advise its customer that the items may be defective
(D) To notify its customer that the items are overdue

**148** What can be inferred about the DVD store?

(A) It will hire Mr. Han as a clerk.
(B) The store doesn't have many popular DVDs.
(C) It will charge Mr. Han for the overdue items.
(D) It provides pick-up service.

**GO ON TO THE NEXT PAGE**

**Questions 149-150** refer to the following text message chain.

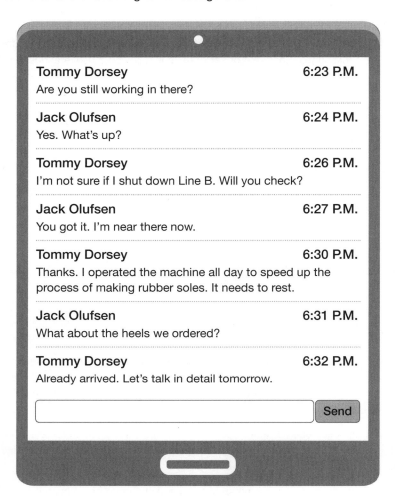

**Tommy Dorsey**      6:23 P.M.
Are you still working in there?

**Jack Olufsen**      6:24 P.M.
Yes. What's up?

**Tommy Dorsey**      6:26 P.M.
I'm not sure if I shut down Line B. Will you check?

**Jack Olufsen**      6:27 P.M.
You got it. I'm near there now.

**Tommy Dorsey**      6:30 P.M.
Thanks. I operated the machine all day to speed up the process of making rubber soles. It needs to rest.

**Jack Olufsen**      6:31 P.M.
What about the heels we ordered?

**Tommy Dorsey**      6:32 P.M.
Already arrived. Let's talk in detail tomorrow.

[ Send ]

**149** At 6:27 P.M., what does Mr. Olufsen mean when he writes, "You got it"?

(A) He will keep on operating some machine all day.
(B) He knows that meeting the deadline is important.
(C) He will make sure that Line B has been shut down.
(D) He agrees that working overtime is exhausting.

**150** For what type of business does Mr. Dorsey most likely work?

(A) A magazine publisher
(B) A hotel chain
(C) An airline company
(D) A shoe manufacturer

**Questions 151-152** refer to the following notice.

# Student Apartment Available for Rent

There are three student apartments available as of March 12th. The apartments are fully furnished and in a very clean condition. The apartments are only 5 minutes away from Georgia Institute of Technology and 15 minutes away from the University of Georgia by car. It's also located near the MARTA station, which lets students commute to their schools more easily. The apartments feature two bedrooms and two bathrooms. You are responsible for finding your own apartment mate. Also, you will be responsible for your own utilities including electricity, water, and telephone bill. For more information, please contact us at 404-182-5821.

**151** What is the purpose of the notice?

(A) To provide information regarding apartments for employees
(B) To advertise a house for sale
(C) To advertise apartments for students
(D) To inform students of the parking spaces

**152** What is stated about the apartments?

(A) How much monthly rent is going to cost
(B) What the average utilities cost is
(C) What kind of furniture is equipped
(D) How many rooms it has

**GO ON TO THE NEXT PAGE**

April 10
Janet Gould
20-15 Mewfield Rd SE,
Toronto ON  M2J 9W5

Dear Ms. Gould,

We are sorry to inform you that we won't be able to send out complimentary USB memory sticks we usually give out to our business partners around this time of year as our company is tightening the budget as much as we can due to the recent economic downturn.

However, we will be offering a small discount of 3% on purchases more than $500 to keep our customers satisfied. We are eager to keep our customers at the top of our priorities even during the hard times. Also, please keep in mind that all credit transfers from sales contracts must be completed by the 15th of every month as stipulated on contract terms. For any questions, please contact our customer services at 928-3037-1740.

Charlotte Brown
Assistant Manager, D&T Technologies
72 Casselman St, Everpool Bldg.
Toronto ON  M9X 4K2

**153** Why are there no complimentary items this year?
(A) Due to regulations enforced by the government
(B) Due to the company's monetary constraints
(C) Due to technical problems
(D) Due to the company's bankruptcy

**154** What has the company proposed as an alternative?
(A) Free repairs for the company's products
(B) Extension of product warranties
(C) Consultation visits by the company's technicians
(D) Discounts for purchases exceeding a certain amount

## Payments made easy now!

Have you been tired of having to go online every time you make a payment? Then, we are glad to tell you that we have fixed your problem!

Chase Bank has developed software that enables our customers to register for automated online payments for the enrolled period. Although you may have been able to sign up for automated online payments through each website, it is an unreliable, unorganized, and inconvenient process. Now you can register all your monthly payments all at one place!

The process is simpler than you would think. First, you should gather all the information about the companies to which you are making payments. The information must include: the company's name, address, account number, and the amount of payment. Once you have all of these ready, visit our website at www.chase.com/autopayments/register. This website will guide you through the rest of the process.

With this one enrollment, you will never have to worry about late payments and late penalties. Please be aware that this is a voluntary enrollment, and only customers who wish to be enrolled may sign up for the payment system. We hope you enjoy our new payment system!

If you have any questions, please contact our customer service team at 1-800-281-6821.

---

**155** To whom is this announcement addressed?

(A) Chase Bank customers
(B) Customers who have late fees
(C) Customers with disability
(D) VIP customers at Chase Bank

**156** What is mentioned about the payment system?

(A) It will cost them an annual enrollment fee of $20.
(B) Customers must be over 21 to sign up for the system.
(C) Customers can't withdraw from the system once they sign up.
(D) Every payment can be made at one place.

**157** Which one of the following is NOT one of the required information for enrollment?

(A) The amount of payment
(B) The company's address
(C) The company's phone number
(D) The company's name

GO ON TO THE NEXT PAGE

**Questions 158-160** refer to the following advertisement.

# Research Internship Position

The research department of Bliss Inc. has three positions open. The job requirements are an undergraduate degree in Mechanical Engineering, at least three years of work experience in a related field, and a recommendation letter. Applicants are expected to submit their applications by July 13th. The decision for the first round will be made within two weeks of submission. Once the first decision is made, selected applicants will be contacted for an interview at Bliss Inc.'s main building in Chicago. We wish you the best luck and hope to see you all at the interview.

**158** What kind of job will the accepted interns do?

(A) Marketing
(B) Profiling
(C) Researching
(D) Advertising

**159** Which of the following is NOT one of the job requirements?

(A) Applicants must have some work experience.
(B) Applicants must have a degree in a similar field.
(C) Applicants must be over 30.
(D) Applicants must obtain a recommendation letter.

**160** How long will it take to choose candidates for the first-round interview?

(A) Approximately 7 days
(B) Less than 2 weeks
(C) More than 2 weeks
(D) Precisely 3 weeks

**Questions 161-163** refer to the following article.

---

## Monthly News                                     July 19

---

The Grand La-dorque Museum will be opening on August 1, housing a collection of tens of thousands of pieces of art that span more than 400 years of human creativity in Canada. –[1]–. According to Alain Dorque, the museum founder, it will hold many of the Montreal collections and provide some of the greatest resources for the study of textiles, murals, and pottery. –[2]–. "My principle is to make works of art available to everyone in Canada and to inspire artists from all around the world," said Dorque. "I want this museum to be recognized as the world's leading place for art and to enrich the lives of people who visit and live in Canada." –[3]–.

To make this possible, he hired John Bowie, a young, prominent art professor at Montreal University as General Director. "I will make every effort to promote the museum and keep the public's interest up. –[4]–. Our website will be linked to social media such as Facebook, Twitter, and Instagram in a more visitor-friendly manner," said Bowie.

---

**161** What is NOT mentioned as a resource that the museum can offer?

(A) Woven fabric
(B) Wall painting
(C) Ceramics
(D) Architecture

**162** According to Mr. Dorque, why has he founded the museum?

(A) To improve people's lives through art
(B) To organize a campaign for the environment
(C) To attract more donors for a charity
(D) To sponsor artists for commercial purposes

**163** In which of the positions marked [1], [2], [3] and [4] does the following sentence best belong?

"For example, utilizing the online presence can be an option."

(A) [1]
(B) [2]
(C) [3]
(D) [4]

**GO ON TO THE NEXT PAGE**

**Questions 164-167** refer to the following letter.

February 28
From: John Marber
Marber Electronics
817 Hemphill Ave, Atlanta, Georgia 30332

To: Jason Kim
Everything Electronics
182 Wheisber's Road, Minnesota City, Minnesota 61725

Dear Mr. Kim,

I am truly sorry to inform you that I will not be able to attend the Spring Bi-Annual Engineers Convention. Spring had never been a busy season for our company, so I was sure that I would be able to attend the convention at the time I spoke to you on the phone. Unfortunately, our company is going through a listing process on the stock market, so most of our effort is dedicated to creating presentations for the investors and analyzing our company's growth over the past few years.
I regret that I must inform you of my cancellation on the convention, but I hope you understand. I definitely plan to attend the next convention in the fall. I am positive that nothing major will be going on during that time of the year. At the fall convention, we can discuss the joint program that we were going to discuss over the spring convention.

Again, I'm truly sorry and wish you the best of luck at the convention.

Sincerely,
John Marber
Marber Electronics

---

164 How often does the convention take place?

(A) Once a year
(B) Twice a year
(C) Once in every two years
(D) Three times a year

165 Why is Mr. Marber not able to attend the spring convention?

(A) His investors decided to withdraw a large amount of money from the company.
(B) He has to work on getting his company listed on the stock market.
(C) His flight was cancelled due to a severe weather condition.
(D) He forgot about another event that already had been scheduled at the same time.

166 When will Mr. Marber be able to meet Mr. Kim?

(A) He won't be able to meet Mr. Kim this year.
(B) He didn't specify his next available time in the letter.
(C) He is planning on meeting Mr. Kim at the fall convention.
(D) He suggested Mr. Kim meet him in Atlanta during the spring convention.

167 Why were they planning on meeting at the spring convention?

(A) They were going to introduce their families to each other.
(B) They wanted to launch a new product together.
(C) They were planning on discussing a cooperative project.
(D) They were the guest speakers at the spring convention.

Questions 168-171 refer to the following online chat discussion.

| | | |
|---|---|---|
| **William Ryan** [10:11 A.M.] | | Hello, guys. I just wanted to update you on the conference I attended in Bellaire last Friday. |
| **Abigail Tucker** [10:12 A.M.] | | How did it go? Anything we should know about? |
| **William Ryan** [10:13 A.M.] | | Due to travel delays, I was not able to attend the session featuring the panel discussion with the director of Houston Memorial Hospital. But the remaining presentations were very informative. |
| **Nathan Smith** [10:14 A.M.] | | How so? |
| **William Ryan** [10:16 A.M.] | | There was a speaker, Mr. Henry Spencer, who presented on the process of distribution, and I thought he could have a positive impact on our company. |
| **Nathan Smith** [10:18 A.M.] | | Since we sell medicaments in large quantities to retailers, I agree with William on that. |
| **Abigail Tucker** [10:20 A.M.] | | Me, too. Any chance we can invite him to the seminar held for our employees next Wednesday? |
| **Nathan Smith** [10:21 A.M.] | | Do you know his contact details? |
| **William Ryan** [10:23 A.M.] | | I have the conference booklet that contains his contact information. I will call him right after this. |
| **Abigail Tucker** [10:24 A.M.] | | Nice! Let us know about the results via e-mail. |

Send

**168** For what type of company does Mr. Smith most likely work?

(A) A general hospital
(B) A consulting company
(C) A hotel chain
(D) A medicine wholesaler

**169** What is indicated about Mr. Ryan?

(A) He gave a presentation at the conference.
(B) He missed one of the sessions.
(C) He has lived in Bellaire for years.
(D) He is dissatisfied with his business travel.

**170** What will Mr. Ryan most likely do next?

(A) Sign with a retailer
(B) Discuss with a director
(C) Hold a seminar
(D) Contact Mr. Spencer

**171** At 10:20 A.M., what does Ms. Tucker mean when she writes, "Me, too"?

(A) She expected the conference to be boring.
(B) She needs some informative lessons.
(C) She agrees with what Mr. Ryan said about a speaker.
(D) She will receive the results via e-mail.

GO ON TO THE NEXT PAGE

# H.S. Apparel Corporation

### A1206 Canary Wharf
### Tower Hamlets, East London
### www.hsapprel.co.uk

July 1

Ms. Zoe H. Carter
A21 West Wickham
Bromley, London
U.K.

Dear Ms. Carter,

Thank you for applying to work at H.S. Apparel. According to your résumé, I believe that you are qualified enough for the assistant position for the upcoming Fashion Design Conference held in London. – [1] –. We are very impressed by the career you have built in the fashion industry for years, not to mention your master's degree in Fashion Design from Parsons, New York, where you won many fashion prizes after graduation. – [2] –.

We would like to interview you sometime next week, although I myself am scheduled to fly to Paris next Thursday for an important business meeting with Hermme Shoes Inc. and will not be back in the office until July 10. – [3] –. If you are available to visit us for the interview before July 5, I would be happy to meet with you. If you are not, Ms. Shannon Wood, Manager of our HR Department, will be conducting the interview on behalf of H.S. Apparel. – [4] –. Please let me know the date and time that would be convenient for you.

Best regards,
Brandon Storm

**172** What is the purpose of the letter?

(A) To apply for a job position
(B) To build a partnership with a company
(C) To set a schedule for an interview
(D) To book an airplane ticket

**173** What is NOT mentioned in Ms. Carter's résumé?

(A) Her work experience
(B) Her educational background
(C) The prizes she earned
(D) The portfolio she made

**174** What can be inferred about Mr. Storm?

(A) He works for Hermme Shoes Inc.
(B) He lives in New York City.
(C) He will be on a business trip on July 8.
(D) He used to be a fashion designer.

**175** In which of the positions marked [1], [2], [3] and [4] does the following sentence best belong?

"Just for your information, she graduated from Parsons, too."

(A) [1]
(B) [2]
(C) [3]
(D) [4]

GO ON TO THE NEXT PAGE

Recruiter name: E&M Holdings
Contact name: Charles Robert, Personnel Director

If you are a Design Manager leading in your field of expertise, we would like to hear from you NOW. We are currently looking for an individual who is suitable for the role of Design Manager based within the E&M Holdings Team, one of the world's leading entertainment companies. Managing and leading the creative process within the company will be essential, and skill as the head coordinator supervising all creative projects will also be critical factors for the role.

**Requisite Qualifications**
- At least 5 years of experience in the field of Design
- Sociability with teammates
- Ability to produce excellent creative design
- Familiarity with PowerPoint, Photoshop, Illustrator, Excel
- Background in creating proposals and budgets
- Knowledge of Sales Marketing theory

Please submit all applications to charles@enmholdings.com including PDF samples of your work in the entertainment sector.

---

To: Charles Robert [charles@enmholdings.com]
From: Martha Robbie [robbiesworld@gmail.com]
Subject: Application for a job

I would like to inform you that I am highly interested in applying for the design manager position that you advertised in the November issue of *Global Fashion Design* magazine.

As you can see in my application form, I graduated in Graphic Design at the Cyber Art College two years ago, and have been working as an assistant graphic designer for Studio Grafico in Milan since then. With experience in managing two important projects for new clients, I have been playing an important role in the new products design department. Even though no one pressured me to do so, I voluntarily accepted extra responsibilities to increase my aptitude within the field.

Furthermore, I would like to add that I am a mature and industrious person despite my young age. Working hard with other people in challenging situations is something that I enjoy. I would appreciate if you seriously consider my application. In order to arrange an interview at your preferred time, please contact me at 647-491-8167.

Sincerely,
Martha Robbie

**176** Where is Charles Robert employed?

(A) At an architectural design firm
(B) At a design school
(C) At a magazine publisher
(D) At an entertainment company

**177** For which position is Martha sending in her résumé for?

(A) Magazine Journalist
(B) Assistant Graphic Designer
(C) Design Manager
(D) Personnel Director

**178** What is NOT essential for the job?

(A) A college diploma in the field
(B) Knowledge of marketing
(C) Former job experience in similar sectors
(D) Familiarity with teamwork and budgeting

**179** Why is Martha technically ineligible for the position?

(A) Because she is used to unexpected challenges.
(B) Because she refuses to take up extra responsibilities.
(C) Because she does not have enough experience.
(D) Because she has been an assistant graphic designer.

**180** Through which method does Martha want to arrange an interview?

(A) By mail
(B) By fax
(C) By phone
(D) Via SNS

GO ON TO THE NEXT PAGE

**Conference on Product Design**

Location: 4th main conference room at World Finance Building
Date and Time: July 5, 11:00-13:30
Participants:

-From Creative Center
Director: Henry Lambiris
Assistant: Jane Cox
Technical Adviser: Darryl Chandler

-From Moose Inc.
Management Director: Isaac Hodge
Marketing Manager: David East

-From Cannon Solicitors Office
Solicitor: Miles Cannon

Program Schedule:
| | |
|---|---|
| Strategy and Overview for New Product Designs | Jane Cox |
| The Outlook for the Global Market | Darryl Chandler |
| How to Conduct Successful Market Research | David East |
| How to Resolve Legal Issues | Miles Cannon |

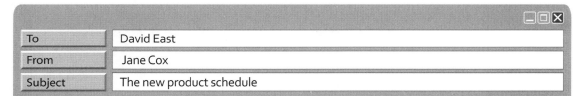

| To | David East |
|---|---|
| From | Jane Cox |
| Subject | The new product schedule |

Dear Mr. East,

We appreciate you giving your presentation at the meeting. It helped us gain better knowledge about the needs of the market and gave us more ideas about the direction of our new product, the Trebler Steel Mug. We are positive that this product is going to ensure us a large profit. We were informed by our product manager that the factory is on schedule and we will be able to produce the first batch of products in a few weeks if all goes well.

After the meeting, Mr. Cannon discussed with us about a possible change in the product's design. Regrettably, there has been a patent issue with the design, though we were able to avoid any lawsuits. In order for us to put our product in the market, we have to wait for the legal procedure to be settled which may require another four days in its entirety.

Frankly speaking, this is the main source of delay right now. Other things such as the pamphlet picture can be quickly modified depending on the legal outcome. We are hoping to put our new product on the market in the last week of next month. However, I would like to ask your opinion on this since we want to strategize for the holiday shopping season while taking into account Mr. Cannon's dealing with the patent office.

Also, for the planning of the next project, our director Henry Lambiris would like to discuss the details with you. Please let me know your preferred time, and I will arrange the meeting.

Best Regards,
Jane Cox

**181** What is the purpose of the meeting?

(A) To analyze customer comments on the old product

(B) To show the sales figures of the new product

(C) To talk about several issues with the new product

(D) To solve the legal problems with the new project

**182** What was the speech by the man working with the patent office?

(A) Strategy and Overview for New Product Designs

(B) The Outlook for the Global Market

(C) How to Conduct Successful Market Research

(D) How to Resolve Legal Issues

**183** What was the new problem the company faced after the meeting?

(A) The product line has been postponed for a while.

(B) Marketing desires to rearrange the date of sale.

(C) There is a legal issue about the product design.

(D) The package of the products needs to be changed.

**184** What is the result if the legal problem is severely delayed?

(A) Mr. Cannon will have to follow the original schedule of the factory.

(B) The initial date of sale will have to be adjusted.

(C) Mr. East has to explain the situation to Ms. Cox.

(D) They will scrap the product and start a new one.

**185** Which is correct based on the above agenda and e-mail message?

(A) The July 5 meeting was held on the 4th floor of the World Finance Building.

(B) The presentation about marketing research was given by Mr. Cannon.

(C) The legal issue might take another week to finalize.

(D) The director of Creative Center wants to talk with Mr. East.

# Mayland Event Planning Agency

As a full-service events agency, we know how to negotiate the best prices for venues, catering, florists and all other event services. We organize whole events from beginning to end, from strategic planning to finding venues, creating immense experiences and eventually fulfilling the needs of our clients.

Please be reminded that the following was added at the beginning of the year.
- On-site staff during events to ensure there are no hitches!
- Employee incentive trip (either one of two sites below to be rented)
  Call 241-494-3824.
- Annual educational meeting (either one of two sites below to be rented)
  Call 241-494-3822.

The two sites we are able to offer:
a) Rainbow Hilltop Garden (for up to 50 people) in Centiville City
b) Las Devillion Hotel (for up to 100 people) in Vegas City

For information on convention programs abroad, call 241-494-3820.

---

| E-Mail Message |
| --- |

| | |
| --- | --- |
| From: | Jack Vogel <jvogel@tomoda.engineers.com> |
| To: | Sophie Calvert <scalvert@lettemart.com> |
| Date: | October 8 |
| Subject: | Hiring Mayland |

Hello, Ms. Calvert.

I have a quick question about Mayland Event Planning Agency that you mentioned at Ms. Kinney's birthday party. As far as I remember, your colleagues were very satisfied with the services and it turned out they were quite motivated afterward. So I am considering hiring the agency for the upcoming holiday week as a way to help my employees be self-motivated for the rest of the year.

I also remember you said you had rented one of their sites. Some basic information as to what it was like would be really appreciated. And prices, also! We don't want to go beyond our budget.

Sincerely,
Jack Vogel
General Director, St. Louis office, Tomoda Engineering

| From | Sophie Calvert <scalvert@lettemart.com> |
|---|---|
| To | Jack Vogel <jvogel@tomoda.engineers.com> |
| Date | October 9 |
| Subject | [Re:] Hiring Mayland |

Hello, Mr. Vogel.

I am more than happy to help you on this. If memory serves me well, that was our 10th annual company picnic. Back then, I was not sure which agency to pick, because it was our first time to hire such an agency. Anyway, it turned out we chose the right one. We were delighted with the services they offered. Nearly 100 employees of our company seemed like they had the times of their lives. We didn't do much, but just followed their instructions in one of their sites offered. For your information, on-site staff will be there to assist you and check that everything is okay during the whole event. You will not be disappointed. I hope this helps.

Sincerely,
Sophie Calvert
Phone: (10) 463-392-7245
Executive assistant, Lette Mart

**186** Why did Mr. Vogel write an e-mail to Ms. Calvert?

(A) To ask for some advice on how to motivate employees
(B) To seek information about an event agency
(C) To suggest a better way to make profits
(D) To complain about the services an event agency offered

**187** What number will Mr. Vogel most likely call to reserve for his company event?

(A) 241-494-3824
(B) 241-494-3822
(C) 241-494-3820
(D) (10) 463-392-7245

**188** What is indicated about Mayland Event Planning Agency?

(A) Their annual educational meetings are free of charge.
(B) They do not provide convention programs outside the country.
(C) Their event services offered are comprehensive.
(D) They focus on strategic planning for hotel management.

**189** In which city was most likely Lette Mart event held?

(A) Centiville City
(B) Vegas City
(C) Mayland
(D) St. Louis

**190** What is NOT suggested about Mr. Vogel?

(A) He met Ms. Calvert at Ms. Kinney's birthday party.
(B) He wants his company to stay within a budget.
(C) He hired Mayland Event Planning Agency several times before.
(D) He is in charge of the St. Louis office.

**GO ON TO THE NEXT PAGE**

## Oaklane Community Center

www.oaklanecc.com

Dear Mr. or Madam,

A single grain of rice can tip the scale! This letter is to invite you to donate to Oaklane Community Center. Your contribution to a 26-mile marathon on 23rd March will be used for the purpose of building a day-care facility for single parents in Oaklane City.

The marathon event will be covered by a number of local newspapers, and more than 10,000 spectators are expected to join the event, which I am positive will also serve as a good marketing opportunity to promote your company.

The benefits for donors are as follows:

**Level 1 ($500)**: Letter of appreciation to be presented

**Level 2 ($1,000)**: Your company name to be listed on banners

Letter of appreciation to be presented

**Level 3 ($5,000)**: Interview of your company representative with local newspapers

Your company name and logo to be displayed on all promotional materials

At whichever level you choose to donate, you are the grain that tips the scale towards the future of single parents in Oaklane City.

*Manik Chaudhary*
Manik Chaudhary
Director, Oaklane Community Center

---

| E-Mail Message |
| --- |

| From: | Priti Doshi <pdoshi@nessonmobile.com> |
| --- | --- |
| To: | Manik Chaudhary <mchaudhary@oaklanecc.com> |
| Date: | March 2 |
| Subject: | Marathon Donation |

Dear Mr. Chaudhary,

Please be aware that Mr. Anton Bremen, our Promotion Director, will be attending the marathon event on March 23rd. We would like to contribute to the society where we belong, but it would be a win-win strategy if we also have an opportunity to promote our company at the same time. And please let me know if it is possible for Mr. Bremen to tour the Oaklane Community Center, especially the area where the day-care center will be constructed.

ps: Here I attached the digital copy of our company logo, as requested.

Priti Doshi

Assistant, Promotion Department, Nesson Mobile Inc.

## OAKLANE COMMUNITY CENTER MARATHON
### SUPPORTED BY NESSON MOBILE INC.

Saturday, March 23rd at 8:00 A.M.

Departing from Rockton Square, the Oaklane Marathon will run through some of your neighborhood. Police will be at major intersections to direct traffic.

The event benefits a local charity specifically; for the construction of a day-care facility in Oaklane Community Center. So join us along the route to support this meaningful event.

- Entertainment will be provided by a musical band that signed with the Oaklane Community Center.
- Homemade pancakes with blueberries, chocolate chips, coffee, juice and milk will be available free of charge.

For further information or to participate, call 458-231-57694 or visit www.oaklanecc.com/event/.

**191** What is the purpose of the letter?

(A) To invite local people to a sports activity
(B) To promote political campaigns
(C) To encourage donations from companies
(D) To inform employees of cultural events

**192** Who is most likely the beneficiary of the event?

(A) A 50-year-old single man with no kids
(B) A 28-year-old married woman with one girl
(C) A 31-year-old divorced woman with one boy
(D) A 40-year-old married man with two kids

**193** How much money did Nesson Mobile probably donate?

(A) $0
(B) $500
(C) $1,000
(D) $5,000

**194** What is suggested about Mr. Bremen?

(A) He works for Oaklane Community Center.
(B) He will be interviewed by local newspapers.
(C) He wishes to run the whole marathon course.
(D) He is a construction crew member.

**195** What is NOT true about the event?

(A) There will be a performance by a musical band.
(B) Marathoners will start from a square.
(C) Police will be dispatched to search vehicles.
(D) Some refreshments will be provided.

GO ON TO THE NEXT PAGE ▶

**Questions 196-200** refer to the following information sheet, e-mail and customer review.

## TLD Audio Inc.     TLD-21 Product Information

TLD-21 smaller, lighter but everything arranged to fit into the body!

Create more powerful sound beyond the scope of any other loudspeaker this size!

For small-venue sound reinforcement and stage-monitoring!

Compare with its previous model TLD-20!

| Model | TLD-20 | TLD-21 |
|---|---|---|
| Dimensions (H x W x D) | 510mm x 320mm x 320mm | 450mm x 290mm x 290mm |
| Color Options | Black, White | Black, White, Orange, Metallic Black |
| Power Rating | 1,000 Watts | |
| Frequency Range | 55Hz – 20,000Hz | 40Hz – 20,000Hz |
| Maximum SPL (Sound Pressure Level) | 126dB | 128dB |
| Net Weight | 14.8kg | 13.0kg |
| Shipping Weight | 16.3kg | 16.6kg |
| Price | $500 | $600 |

| | |
|---|---|
| From | Maria Kelson |
| To | Sales Team |
| Date | July 18 |
| Subject | TLD-21 model |

Everybody in the Sales Team:

I have just been informed by Mr. Daniel Horge from our Technical Team that there will be an update of the information sheet on TLD models. The current product information indicates that TLD-20 comes in only Black and White, while TLD-21 has two more options: Orange and Metallic Black. Mr. Horge said, however, that Metallic Black TLD-20 would also be on the market before the Christmas season this year, as customer demands build.

More importantly, correction will be made to Power Rating in the information sheet. After long and exhaustive experiments, it turned out that TLD-21 consumes more power than indicated on the sheet. It needs to be changed to 1,500 Watts. No change on TLD-20, though. I will make sure that a corrected version of the sheet will be supplied to you no later than the end of the month.

I would like you all to be aware of this update, since all TLD models will soon be displayed for sale at some of our stores.

Stay focused,

Maria Kelson

Sales Team Manager, TLD Audio Inc.

# TLD Audio Inc.

| Home | Product | Archives | Review | Contacts |

Purchaser Name: Jack Malone
Product:          TLD-21
Purchase Date:    July 19

I was not aware of the exact difference between TLD-20 and TLD-21. Many friends of mine recommended the latter, saying it is kind of a newer model, although the former was launched only half a year ago. Anyways, the only difference I had known was that 21 has more color options, and Metallic Black is a color I am fond of. So I was leaning toward buying the 21, and bam! The salesperson added that TLD-20 would also come in Metallic Black soon. I spent more than two hours at a store comparing those two models. But 21 looked noticeably smaller than 20, which led me to the conviction that it would fit better in my small room. So finally I bought the 21. After a couple of hours of checking out its sound quality at home, I found myself very satisfied with it. I still wonder what the other model would sound like, but if you are not sure which one to buy, always go with the newer. The newer the better, you can't fight the truth!

**196** According to the information sheet, what is NOT true about TLD-21 compared with the previous model?

(A) It offers a wider frequency range.
(B) It is lighter in a packing box.
(C) Its maximum sound pressure level is higher.
(D) It is more expensive.

**197** In the e-mail, the word "build" in paragraph 1, line 5, is closest in meaning to

(A) make
(B) increase
(C) deny
(D) impact

**198** What is stated about Ms. Kelson?

(A) She works in the Technical Team of TLD Audio Inc.
(B) She spent more than two hours figuring out the difference of two models.
(C) Metallic Black is her favorite color.
(D) She will see to it that the new version of the sheet will be supplied.

**199** How many colors of TLD-20 will be available for sale on Christmas Eve?

(A) 1
(B) 2
(C) 3
(D) 4

**200** Which of the features specified in the information sheet helped Mr. Malone decide to buy the newer model?

(A) Dimensions
(B) Color Options
(C) Frequency Range
(D) Maximum SPL

**Stop!** This is the end of the test. If you finish before time is called, you may go back to Parts 5, 6, and 7 and check your work.

## 잠깐!! 시작 전 꼭 확인하세요!

- 실제 시험과 같이 책상을 정리하고 마음의 준비를 하세요.
- 핸드폰은 잠깐 끄고 대신 아날로그 시계를 활용해 보세요.
- 제한 시간은 120분입니다. 제한 시간을 꼭 지켜주세요.
- 어렵다고 넘어가지 마세요. 가능하면 차례대로 풀어 보세요.

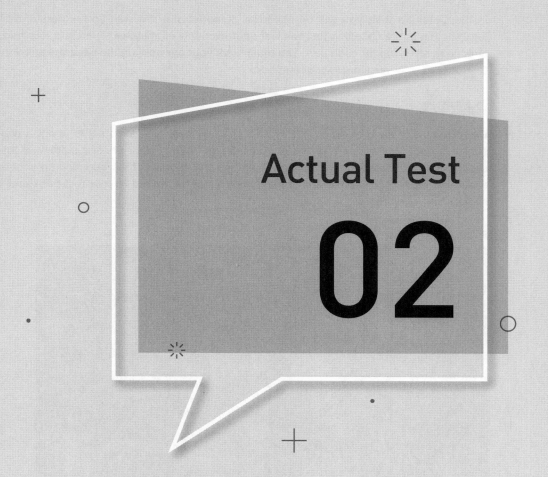

Actual Test

# 02

| 시작 시간 | : |
| 종료 시간 | : |

# LISTENING TEST

In the Listening test, you will be asked to demonstrate how well you understand spoken English. The entire Listening test will last approximately 45 minutes. There are four parts, and directions are given for each part. You must mark your answers on the separate answer sheet. Do not write your answers in your test book.

## PART 1

**Directions:** For each question in this part, you will hear four statements about a picture in your test book. When you hear the statements, you must select the one statement that best describes what you see in the picture. Then find the number of the question on your answer sheet and mark your answer. The statements will not be printed in your test book and will be spoken only one time.

**Example**

Statement (B), "The man is using a microphone," is the best description of the picture, so you should select answer (B) and mark it on your answer sheet.

1

2

**GO ON TO THE NEXT PAGE**

**3**

**4**

5

6

GO ON TO THE NEXT PAGE

# PART 2

**Directions:** You will hear a question or statement and three responses spoken in English. They will not be printed in your test book and will be spoken only one time. Select the best response to the question or statement and mark the letter (A), (B), or (C) on your answer sheet.

| | | | | |
|---|---|---|---|---|
| **7** | Mark your answer on your answer sheet. | | **20** | Mark your answer on your answer sheet. |
| **8** | Mark your answer on your answer sheet. | | **21** | Mark your answer on your answer sheet. |
| **9** | Mark your answer on your answer sheet. | | **22** | Mark your answer on your answer sheet. |
| **10** | Mark your answer on your answer sheet. | | **23** | Mark your answer on your answer sheet. |
| **11** | Mark your answer on your answer sheet. | | **24** | Mark your answer on your answer sheet. |
| **12** | Mark your answer on your answer sheet. | | **25** | Mark your answer on your answer sheet. |
| **13** | Mark your answer on your answer sheet. | | **26** | Mark your answer on your answer sheet. |
| **14** | Mark your answer on your answer sheet. | | **27** | Mark your answer on your answer sheet. |
| **15** | Mark your answer on your answer sheet. | | **28** | Mark your answer on your answer sheet. |
| **16** | Mark your answer on your answer sheet. | | **29** | Mark your answer on your answer sheet. |
| **17** | Mark your answer on your answer sheet. | | **30** | Mark your answer on your answer sheet. |
| **18** | Mark your answer on your answer sheet. | | **31** | Mark your answer on your answer sheet. |
| **19** | Mark your answer on your answer sheet. | | | |

# PART 3

**Directions:** You will hear some conversations between two or more people. You will be asked to answer three questions about what the speakers say in each conversation. Select the best response to each question and mark the letter (A), (B), (C), or (D) on your answer sheet. The conversations will not be printed in your test book and will be spoken only one time.

32  What type of product are the speakers discussing?

(A) Jewelry
(B) Clothing
(C) Furniture
(D) Appliances

33  What problem does the woman explain to the man?

(A) A product is faulty.
(B) A guarantee was not provided.
(C) A sales receipt was lost.
(D) A duplicate gift has been given.

34  What will the man probably do next?

(A) Locate an item
(B) Give a full refund
(C) Contact another store
(D) Order a different size

35  Why does the woman call the man?

(A) To discuss a report
(B) To invite him to a party
(C) To say she will be late
(D) To ask him for directions

36  What does the man offer to do?

(A) Request a delivery
(B) Arrange for a car
(C) Pick up an order
(D) Listen to a traffic report

37  What does the woman say she will do?

(A) Take a detour
(B) Make a payment
(C) Confirm a reservation
(D) Ask a coworker to help

38  Why does Stephanie want to change the meeting schedule?

(A) She needs to meet a deadline.
(B) She has another meeting to attend.
(C) She has to review some information.
(D) She will go on a business trip.

39  What does the man imply when he says, "But in the morning I'll be around here"?

(A) He is meeting with a client then.
(B) He will be very busy then.
(C) He is available then.
(B) He can't attend the meeting then.

40  What will the woman do next?

(A) Send an e-mail to a coworker
(B) Contact her boss
(C) Reserve a meeting room
(D) Discuss a schedule

41  What are the speakers discussing?

(A) An upcoming appointment
(B) A business location
(C) A store promotion
(D) An eyeglass prescription

42  Why is the woman behind schedule?

(A) A fax machine is out of order.
(B) A store has been busy.
(C) An employee is out sick.
(D) A doctor has not arrived yet.

43  What does the man say he will do?

(A) Go to a nearby store
(B) Make a phone call
(C) Return an item
(D) Review a document

**GO ON TO THE NEXT PAGE**

**44** Who most likely is the man?

(A) A newspaper editor
(B) A bus driver
(C) A real estate agent
(D) A phone operator

**45** Why did the woman mention Wilson Street?

(A) She wants to live close to her family.
(B) She does not want a big house now.
(C) She wants to work close to her home.
(D) She used to drive to work there.

**46** Why does the man say "Tell you what"?

(A) To provide detailed explanation
(B) To make a suggestion
(C) To confirm some information
(D) To recommend a business

---

**47** Why is the man at the local health center?

(A) To make a blood donation
(B) To collect some items
(C) To keep an appointment
(D) To volunteer for fund raising

**48** Where is the man instructed to go?

(A) To a restaurant
(B) To an office complex
(C) To a clinic
(D) To City Hall

**49** What does the man ask for?

(A) Directions to the clinic
(B) A changed address
(C) Some updated leaflets
(D) Assistance with a project

**50** What department does the man most likely work in?

(A) Production
(B) Sales
(C) Accounting
(D) Maintenance

**51** What problem does the man report?

(A) A repairperson did not arrive.
(B) Some machinery is damaged.
(C) A customer filed a complaint.
(D) Some supplies are running low.

**52** What does the woman ask the man to do?

(A) Submit an order form
(B) Use another machine
(C) Call an engineer
(D) Stop production

---

**53** What does the man request help with?

(A) Finalizing market research
(B) Setting up some meetings
(C) Preparing a presentation
(D) Updating a client database

**54** What does the woman say the marketing team has done?

(A) Evaluated competitors' campaigns
(B) Extended a project deadline
(C) Produced some new ideas
(D) Secured additional funding

**55** What will the man most likely do tomorrow?

(A) He will hire several experts.
(B) He will be promoted to a marketing director.
(C) He will rehearse his presentation.
(D) He will discuss marketing plans with coworkers.

**56** What department needs a new director?

(A) Sales
(B) Advertising
(C) Human Resources
(D) Planning

**57** According to the woman, what is the problem?

(A) She has missed a deadline.
(B) It is hard to find a qualified applicant.
(C) She does not want to relocate to a branch office.
(D) The new job doesn't meet the woman's expectations.

**58** What does the woman imply when she says, "Why didn't I think of that sooner"?

(A) She needs more time to finish her job.
(B) She has lost contact with her former coworker.
(C) She wants more information from the man.
(D) She completely agrees with the man's idea.

**59** What does the woman say will happen next week?

(A) A division will relocate.
(B) Two sales offices will be combined.
(C) New jobs will be advertised.
(D) Travel costs will increase.

**60** According to the woman, what is the man eligible for?

(A) A pay increase
(B) Paid vacation
(C) Transportation allowance
(D) Reimbursement for travel

**61** What does the man want to know more about?

(A) Working from home
(B) Financing for the commute
(C) Transferring to a new division
(D) Purchasing a new car

**62** Where do the interviewers most likely work?

(A) At a law firm
(B) At a travel agency
(C) At a newspaper
(D) At a financial institute

**63** What job requirement do the speakers discuss?

(A) Being on scene to cover stories
(B) Having editorial experience
(C) Speaking a foreign language
(D) Being professionally certified

**64** What will the woman most likely do next?

(A) Inspect some equipment
(B) Show a portfolio
(C) Meet some colleagues
(D) Provide references

**GO ON TO THE NEXT PAGE**

| ITEM | PRICE |
|---|---|
| 4X Smartphone | $300 |
| Plan 30 (monthly) | $40 |
| Insurance (monthly) | $10 |
| Bluetooth headset | $50 |
| TOTAL | $400 |

The Top 4 Semiconductor Sales Leaders

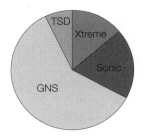

**65** Who most likely is the man?

(A) An engineer
(B) A repair person
(C) A sales clerk
(D) A tour guide

**66** What does the woman ask about?

(A) Cell phone plans
(B) Phone accessories
(C) Travel applications
(D) Methods of payment

**67** Look at the graphic. Which amount will be removed from the bill?

(A) $300
(B) $50
(C) $40
(D) $10

**68** What are the speakers mainly discussing?

(A) A business acquisition
(B) Company benefits
(C) Marketing strategies
(D) An annual report

**69** Why does the man say he is not sure about the proposal?

(A) Some information is inaccurate.
(B) He does not want to hire additional workers.
(C) A company's revenue has decreased.
(D) He is not familiar with a business deal.

**70** Look at the graphic. Where do the speakers work?

(A) GNS
(B) Sonic
(C) Xtreme
(D) TSD

# PART 4

**Directions:** You will hear some talks given by a single speaker. You will be asked to answer three questions about what the speaker says in each talk. Select the best response to each question and mark the letter (A), (B), (C), or (D) on your answer sheet. The talks will not be printed in your test book and will be spoken only one time.

**71** What kind of product is being demonstrated?

(A) A vacuum cleaner
(B) A coffee machine
(C) A steam cooker
(D) A juice maker

**72** What is special about the product?

(A) Its speed
(B) Its size
(C) Its price
(D) Its design

**73** What will happen at the end of the demonstration?

(A) A payment will be made.
(B) Certificates will be distributed.
(C) Drinks will be served.
(D) Complimentary books will be given.

**74** Why is the speaker calling?

(A) To discuss some maintenance work
(B) To schedule a visit
(C) To ask about a presentation
(D) To make a complaint

**75** When will the listener give a presentation?

(A) On Monday
(B) On Tuesday
(C) On Thursday
(D) On Friday

**76** What should Ms. Parker do if she has a question?

(A) Read a manual
(B) Speak to a coworker
(C) Call a repair shop
(D) Do research online

**77** What product is being advertised?

(A) An air conditioner
(B) A water purifier
(C) A compact car
(D) A mobile phone

**78** What is emphasized about the product?

(A) It is easy to use.
(B) It uses less fuel.
(C) It is affordable.
(D) It is a double seater.

**79** What can customers receive this month without charge?

(A) A sound system
(B) A gift card
(C) An extra battery
(D) A two-year warranty

**80** What department are the listeners probably working for?

(A) Sales
(B) Advertising
(C) Planning
(D) Personnel

**81** What does the speaker imply when he says, "don't worry about invoices"?

(A) Workers are supposed to rearrange invoices.
(B) Invoices are taken care of automatically.
(C) It is easy to operate a printing machine.
(D) A training session will be provided.

**82** What is the speaker going to teach next?

(A) How to fix a printer
(B) How to ship products
(C) How to find the inventory
(D) How to handle defective products

**GO ON TO THE NEXT PAGE** ➡

83 What is being celebrated?

(A) The opening of a restaurant
(B) The completion of renovation
(C) The success of a venture business
(D) The purchase of a facility

84 According to the speaker, who provided food?

(A) A local food establishment
(B) A financial contributor
(C) A town hall official
(D) A well-known author

85 What is mentioned about the newsletter?

(A) It is sent out weekly.
(B) It contains all staff information.
(C) It includes upcoming functions.
(D) It has a list of donors.

86 What is the woman waiting for?

(A) Her hotel room to be cleaned
(B) Her luggage to be retrieved
(C) Her itinerary to be printed out
(D) Her colleagues to arrive

87 What problem is being discussed?

(A) A factory inspection will be conducted.
(B) The woman has missed a connecting flight.
(C) A product presentation won't be successful.
(D) In-flight meals were not good.

88 Why does the woman say, "I know it is last minute"?

(A) To remind the listener to plan carefully
(B) To explain some changes in detail
(C) To apologize for an inconvenience
(D) To advise the listener to leave soon

89 Where does the speaker probably work?

(A) A film directors' association
(B) A publishing firm
(C) A movie company
(D) A community center

90 What does the speaker thank the employees for?

(A) The efforts to make a successful film
(B) A website that was launched successfully
(C) Good reviews from critics
(D) A successful conference that was held recently

91 Why does the speaker mention Joshua Lee?

(A) He will show volunteers what to do.
(B) He will meet reporters on behalf of the company.
(C) He will be away for volunteer service.
(D) He will be in charge of a branch office.

| Order Form | |
| --- | --- |
| ITEM | QUANTITY |
| Cookie Tray | 20 |
| Dozen Mini-Cupcakes | 100 |
| Fruit Tart | 50 |
| Classic Brownie | 150 |

92 Look at the graphic. According to the speaker, which quantity of the order form is probably incorrect?

(A) 20
(B) 100
(C) 50
(D) 150

93 What does the woman say she will do at 5 P.M.?

(A) She will give a demonstration.
(B) She will leave for the day.
(C) She will do some baking.
(D) She will create a cake recipe.

94 What is mentioned about the bakery?

(A) It sells baked goods online.
(B) It offers baking classes to the public.
(C) It specializes in custom-design cakes.
(D) Its hours of operation have changed.

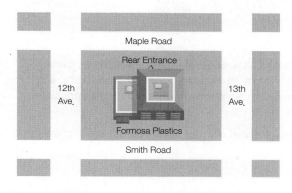

| Workshops | Date |
|---|---|
| Communication Skills | March 10 |
| Résumé Clinic | April 7 |
| Second Career Information | May 12 |
| Using Social Networking | June 9 |

95  What is scheduled to happen in two days?

(A) A street repair
(B) An annual event
(C) A corporate function
(D) A staff meeting

96  Look at the graphic. Which street will be blocked?

(A) Maple Road
(B) 12th Avenue
(C) 13th Avenue
(D) Smith Road

97  What are the employees advised to do?

(A) Use public transportation
(B) Participate in a local festival
(C) Allow more time for travel
(D) Finish their assignments early

98  Why is the speaker pleased?

(A) An event has been added.
(B) A center has been remodeled.
(C) A lot of participants have shown up.
(D) A famous author is giving a speech.

99  Look at the graphic. Which session has been canceled?

(A) Communication Skills
(B) Résumé Clinic
(C) Second Career Information
(D) Using Social Networking

100  What will happen after the morning session?

(A) Course materials will be provided.
(B) A tour will be given.
(C) A guest speaker will be introduced.
(D) Some food will be served.

This is the end of the Listening test. Turn to Part 5 in your test book.

**GO ON TO THE NEXT PAGE**

# READING TEST

In the Reading test, you will read a variety of texts and answer several different types of reading comprehension questions. The entire Reading test will last 75 minutes. There are three parts, and directions are given for each part. You are encouraged to answer as many questions as possible within the time allowed.

You must mark your answers on the separate answer sheet. Do not write your answers in your test book.

# PART 5

**Directions:** A word or phrase is missing in each of the sentences below. Four answer choices are given below each sentence. Select the best answer to complete the sentence. Then mark the letter (A), (B), (C), or (D) on your answer sheet.

**101** Ms. Bailey joined the firm only last August ------- is already doing much to increase productivity and to improve employee morale.

(A) or
(B) than
(C) and
(D) also

**102** A committee ------- of specialists and government officers will be talking about the country's economy and the effects of the newly established tax law on businesses.

(A) to be consisted
(B) consists
(C) consisting
(D) will consist

**103** Building & Construct Company ------- subcontracts the work to smaller companies who specialize in certain fields of construction owing to the high demand and wide range of its services.

(A) marginally
(B) prematurely
(C) uncommonly
(D) occasionally

**104** Mr. Thames' report contained too many ------- details, which made it hard to read.

(A) sufficient
(B) decreased
(C) prerequisite
(D) incidental

**105** The respective managers ------- the contact information should be delivered to are listed on this spreadsheet.

(A) where
(B) what
(C) whom
(D) whoever

**106** This year the sales figures were almost ------- to those recorded over each of the past two years.

(A) uniform
(B) equal
(C) fair
(D) even

**107** Eastern Electronic is expanding its ability to produce power in a cost-effective and environmentally friendly fashion ------- working with local representatives.

(A) during
(B) by
(C) so that
(D) because

**108** A fax machine is now a(n) ------- purchase for many lower income families thanks to a large supply in the market and a lowering in the price of the technology.

(A) comparable
(B) predictable
(C) affordable
(D) following

**109** The committee's report on security was highly ------- of school safety precautions.

(A) critical
(B) critic
(C) critics
(D) critically

**110** The company has ------- my contact information, so there will be no interruption in keeping in touch with me.

(A) update
(B) updating
(C) are updated
(D) updated

**111** A mobile manufacturer, Ettano, ------- its older models and introduce new ones early next year according to news reports.

(A) to discontinue
(B) have discontinued
(C) will discontinue
(D) discontinued

**112** Koben Motors earned the ------- ratings for comfort and safety in this year's Vehicle Satisfaction Evaluation.

(A) higher
(B) highest
(C) more highly
(D) most highly

**113** The new hotel website is ------- more useful to both our employees and visitors than the previous version.

(A) such
(B) very
(C) well
(D) much

**114** Applications for graduation during the summer semester must be submitted ------- July 31st or else you will have to wait until fall for your diploma.

(A) except
(B) between
(C) by
(D) on

**115** Beginning next Monday, items of memorabilia from this year's World Cup will ------- online.

(A) be sold
(B) selling
(C) have been sold
(D) have been selling

**116** The entire computer system at Veronne Shopping Mall went down on account of a blackout, but ------- people were able to use paper receipts to properly direct their orders.

(A) fortunately
(B) fortune
(C) fortunate
(D) fortunes

**117** Marcus Logan showed ------- ability in securing sales for the company, which resulted in his promotion, after two years of working for Swansea Co.

(A) exceptional
(B) multiple
(C) inclusive
(D) whole

**118** Archon sponsors an annual dinner for employees withdrawing from the workplace rather than holding individual ------- parties.

(A) retire
(B) retired
(C) retires
(D) retirement

**119** Because Mr. Carlo had been ------- late for work, he was reprimanded by his boss.

(A) consistently
(B) exactly
(C) sensibly
(D) steadily

**GO ON TO THE NEXT PAGE**

**120** Helen increased sales by nearly 20% ------- her time as sales manager of Emporio.

(A) upon
(B) into
(C) during
(D) about

**121** Hayter's lawnmower is renowned for its lightness as much as for its -------.

(A) reliability
(B) determination
(C) obligation
(D) confidence

**122** The company will be able to process shipments more efficiently ------- the construction of the new loading docks is complete.

(A) now that
(B) instead of
(C) usually
(D) regarding

**123** The two company's automobiles are ------- in terms of their performances, while they differ in their targeted customers.

(A) compare
(B) comparing
(C) comparison
(D) comparable

**124** A number of drive-through restaurant analysts have suggested ------- later on weekend nights due to the changing habits of consumers.

(A) closing
(B) were closed
(C) closed
(D) to close

**125** The road service vehicles must be constantly checked ------- they run the risk of being unable to properly clear the roads during extreme weather conditions.

(A) on account of
(B) besides
(C) either
(D) or else

**126** Only ------- with a degree in economics are eligible for the position.

(A) those
(B) whose
(C) which
(D) this

**127** The shopping mall decided to stay open 24 hours a day to better ------- its customers.

(A) provide
(B) offer
(C) reflect
(D) serve

**128** All employees are to refrain from using the elevators, and to move to the designated emergency exits in the event that the alarm -------.

(A) rings
(B) to ring
(C) be rung
(D) ringing

**129** Your purchase is covered by the company's limited warranty for a year from the date of -------.

(A) admission
(B) purchase
(C) membership
(D) owning

**130** Mr. Yeon expects that you will be able to craft a solution ------- the design flaw in the company's latest product.

(A) out
(B) about
(C) to
(D) over

# PART 6

**Directions:** Read the texts that follow. A word, phrase, or sentence is missing in parts of each text. Four answer choices for each question are given below the text. Select the best answer to complete the text. Then mark the letter (A), (B), (C), or (D) on your answer sheet.

**Questions 131-134** refer to the following advertisement.

Greetings from Greena's Accessories! Our shop has been assisting our customers to ------- their
**131.**
every household and fashion items for stylish living. You can expect a wide range of accessories
handcrafted by our professional artists.

We assure you that all the clerks at our store have the ------- skills to help you make the best
**132.**
decision on the items that you purchase. Excellent products and the workers are not the only
advantages that you will get from our store.

We have a guaranteed money back policy. -------. However, we are confident that you will not
**133.**
find a ------- store that will offer a better price than Greena's Accessories.
**134.**

Please visit our website for more information. We look forward to serving you at our store!

131  (A) create
     (B) decorate
     (C) clean
     (D) purchase

132  (A) necessarily
     (B) necessary
     (C) necessity
     (D) necessitating

133  (A) This is to ensure that customers get a
         refund when they find the same item for
         a cheaper price at a different store.
     (B) Customers are required to bring their
         receipts when claiming a refund.
     (C) This does not apply to discounted items,
         or any items that are not at the regular
         price.
     (D) It is important to stay within the price
         range when customers purchase their
         desired products.

134  (A) proper
     (B) single
     (C) precious
     (D) slight

**GO ON TO THE NEXT PAGE**

Questions 135-138 refer to the following letter.

Ronald Silbert
182 Louis St,
Atlanta, GA 30152

Dear valued customer,

First of all, we take great pleasure in having the opportunity to provide you with our best product, VUS 1025. Our company has been known for its thorough customer care system for decades now. This letter has been sent to help you better understand how to -------- the equipment that **135.** you purchased.

The product that you have received is one of the most sophisticated yet delicate machines that our company produces. In order to keep the machine working for many years, we recommend that you avoid using cloths with a ------- surface when cleaning the product. **136.**

-------. Any sort of spillage will result in serious damage. Although the condition of the equipment **137.** entirely depends on the individual owner's hands, we can confidently say that following the above instructions ------- the greatest enjoyment of the equipment. **138.**

Please provide us with your feedback in order to better understand our customers' needs.

135 (A) pick up
(B) care for
(C) put away
(D) give away

136 (A) rigorous
(B) smooth
(C) silky
(D) rough

137 (A) You do not have to clean the machine on a daily basis.
(B) The product you have purchased comes with a two-year warranty.
(C) Spraying water on the surface or using a damp sponge works best.
(D) Moreover, please keep in mind that the product is not waterproof.

138 (A) has ensured
(B) will ensure
(C) ensured
(D) to ensure

**Questions 139-142** refer to the following notice.

Recently, our Membership Services team has noticed that your membership ------- next month.
**139.**
We are sending this notification in order to help you not lose the special offers we exclusively
provide to our yearly members.

We hope that you previously received another notification about the remodeling of the lounge
area for the members. -------. In order to compensate for this -------, we will provide those who
**140.** **141.**
plan on traveling during this time of the month with a 15% discount on their flight tickets.

If you wish to be ------- in our membership service for the next year, please let us know as soon
**142.**
as possible. We hope that you do not miss out on the amazing deals that we have to offer for the
next year!

If you have any questions, please feel free to contact our customer care team.

139 (A) will have expired
(B) is expired
(C) expires
(D) expired

140 (A) The lounge area is equipped with sofas
and is decorated with Italian paintings.
(B) Members can wait in the lounge area
before their departure.
(C) Because of the renovation, the area will
be closed for the first and second week
of June.
(D) The approximate cost of renovation is
$1,000.

141 (A) inconvenience
(B) decision
(C) advantage
(D) usage

142 (A) excluded
(B) enrolled
(C) departed
(D) accounted

**GO ON TO THE NEXT PAGE**

Jan. 7th
Dan Cody
1825 Bally St.
St Louis, MO 39015

Dear Mr. Cody,

This letter has been sent to you in order to confirm the details of the inquiry that you have made. We would like to inform you that Mr. Casey has received your ------- for a personal meeting and
143.
agreed to spare 30 minutes just for you.

However, you must strictly observe the following instructions. Firstly, we insist that all the information regarding this meeting ------- to the assistant's e-mail, sleisng@pmail.com, at least 4
144.
days prior to the meeting. -------.
145.

Since Mr. Casey will be busy with the company's annual events, his only available times are Jan 12th at 10:00 A.M. and Jan 21st at 11:00 A.M. Please let us know which date and time is more ------- for you.
146.

For any information, please avoid contacting Mr. Casey directly. You can always reach me at 1-405-291-6281.

Regards,

Charlotte Tapager
Deputy Manager
SGLS Inc.

143 (A) dedication
(B) plan
(C) request
(D) presentation

144 (A) submits
(B) submitted
(C) be submitted
(D) submission

145 (A) Necessary information will be given to you by the end of next week.
(B) After reading the instructions, you need to send a confirmation letter in writing.
(C) Please be aware that Mr. Casey does not enjoy reading e-mails.
(D) Also, in case of cancellation, you must let us know two days in advance.

146 (A) consistent
(B) accustomed
(C) specified
(D) convenient

# PART 7

**Directions:** In this part you will read a selection of texts, such as magazine and newspaper articles, e-mails, and instant messages. Each text or set of texts is followed by several questions. Select the best answer for each question and mark the letter (A), (B), (C), or (D) on your answer sheet.

**Questions 147-148** refer to the following announcement.

---

### Dusten-Meryll Business Park

To all occupants of the Dusten-Meryll Business Park,

This announcement is to inform all the occupants that the superintendent office will be hosting a week-long campaign to raise awareness on the environmental benefits of recycling and to reduce the amount of garbage that is not properly recycled.

Please note that, starting on September 10th, occupants with the biggest improvement in recycling will be awarded with special treats ranging from snacks to office supplies at the end of the week-long campaign. Some helpful tips on reducing and properly disposing waste and general information on the environmental effects of recycling are available in leaflets at my office. Please feel free to come by and pick them up or to ask questions.

The results will be announced through the bulletin board in the lobby. Thank you.

Sincerely,

Joseph Baker
Director, Dusten-Meryll Business Park
1904 Pickle Rd,
Lewisburg, TN 37012
042-493-5987

---

**147** Why was the announcement made?

(A) To advertise a discount on office supplies
(B) To inform residents about waste pollution
(C) To ask for help in a voting campaign
(D) To offer details on a new environmental campaign

**148** Who most likely is Joseph Baker?

(A) Someone who works for an environmental organization
(B) Someone who oversees the business park
(C) A Lewisburg county official
(D) An occupant at the business park

**GO ON TO THE NEXT PAGE** ▶

**Questions 149-150** refer to the following text message chain.

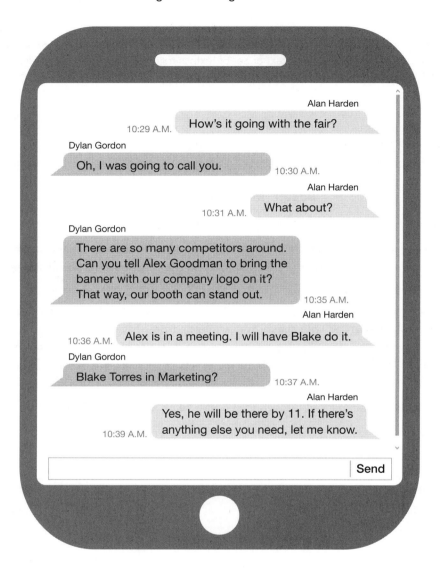

Alan Harden
How's it going with the fair?
10:29 A.M.

Dylan Gordon
Oh, I was going to call you.
10:30 A.M.

Alan Harden
What about?
10:31 A.M.

Dylan Gordon
There are so many competitors around. Can you tell Alex Goodman to bring the banner with our company logo on it? That way, our booth can stand out.
10:35 A.M.

Alan Harden
Alex is in a meeting. I will have Blake do it.
10:36 A.M.

Dylan Gordon
Blake Torres in Marketing?
10:37 A.M.

Alan Harden
Yes, he will be there by 11. If there's anything else you need, let me know.
10:39 A.M.

Send

**149** At 10:35 A.M., what does Mr. Gordon mean when he writes, "That way, our booth can stand out"?

(A) Their booth can be set up everywhere.
(B) They will successfully sponsor the fair.
(C) Their space can be easily noticeable.
(D) They will surpass people's expectations.

**150** Who most likely will bring the banner?

(A) Mr. Harden
(B) Mr. Gordon
(C) Mr. Goodman
(D) Mr. Torres

**Questions 151-153** refer to the following article.

Ms. Yvette Jenson began her successful clothing brand Herlings in a rather dingy and shabby attic at her parent's house in London after she had declared bankruptcy on her first clothing store in 1973. Risking too much in her first venture, her business had gone broke due to cash flow problems. Building on her years at the London Institute of Fashion, Ms. Jenson started her career by experimenting with scraps of cloth to fashion her own peculiar style of unique needlework designs. And though her first business ultimately failed, she had the entrepreneurial spirit to rebuild and create her new Herlings brand featuring a more refined look.

The Herlings line of clothing became gradually popular throughout the 1980s when its reputation grew through word of mouth. After a successful debut at the London Fashion Week, Herlings began to expand its brand across Europe. It caught the attention of the world after it received the Lyon Fashion Award for its animal-friendly faux fur, meticulous stitching, and high-end textiles.

With its rising presence in the industry, Herlings has been talked about by prominent fashion leaders and celebrities. While a branch store has not yet made it to the streets of Milano, many of the city's famous luxury brands seem to be on guard against the rising star. With the Herlings look becoming more vogue, rivals are starting to mimic her style. However, Herlings seems little concerned with the copycat issues as it continues to attract fans across Europe and beyond.

**151** What is true about Ms. Jenson?

(A) She was successful in her initial business startup.
(B) She made her debut in London.
(C) Her fashion design was in line with mainstream fashion.
(D) She acquired her degree in Paris.

**152** What is NOT stated as a characteristic of Herlings as a fashion brand?

(A) Excellent customer service
(B) Refusal to use real animal fur
(C) Sophisticated needlework
(D) Fine quality of textiles

**153** What are rivals to Herlings trying to do?

(A) Cut down on their prices
(B) Diminish Herlings' reputation
(C) Imitate Herlings' designs
(D) Employ its business strategies

**GO ON TO THE NEXT PAGE**

# Malderwood Public Libarary

72 Borian Drive
Heaton MS 10473
416-304-5716

Dear Mr. Montez,

This is to inform you that three items you borrowed on March 2nd are long overdue and that your account will be temporarily suspended starting tomorrow. Your late fee amounts to $7.00 ($0.50 per day) and it is strongly advised that you return those items as soon as possible to reactivate your library account. Here are the items you must return:

**Frontiers**
by Rosalie Granda
ISBN: 9781453209971

**The Marked Warrior**
by Nicholas Ainsworth
ISBN: 9341951203976

**Horses of Empire**
by Phillip Kent
ISBN: 9241051203842

154 Why was the notice sent?
(A) To announce that Mr. Montez won a prize
(B) To notify members of new book recommendations
(C) To remind Mr. Montez of his delayed books
(D) To announce changes in library policy

155 What can be inferred about the library?
(A) They will momentarily put Mr. Montez's account on hold.
(B) Mr. Montez donated hundreds of books to them.
(C) Mr. Montez requested some materials from the library.
(D) They will hold a special event to raise money for a charity.

**Questions 156-158** refer to the following e-mail.

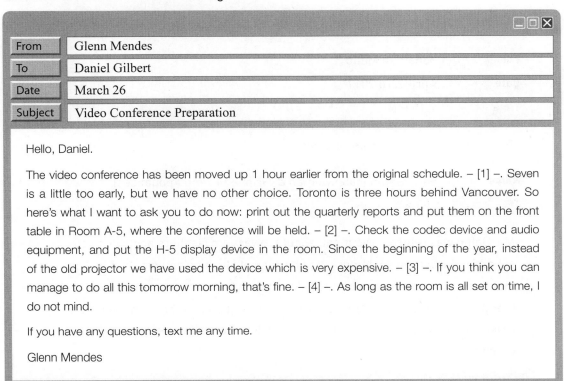

From: Glenn Mendes

To: Daniel Gilbert

Date: March 26

Subject: Video Conference Preparation

Hello, Daniel.

The video conference has been moved up 1 hour earlier from the original schedule. – [1] –. Seven is a little too early, but we have no other choice. Toronto is three hours behind Vancouver. So here's what I want to ask you to do now: print out the quarterly reports and put them on the front table in Room A-5, where the conference will be held. – [2] –. Check the codec device and audio equipment, and put the H-5 display device in the room. Since the beginning of the year, instead of the old projector we have used the device which is very expensive. – [3] –. If you think you can manage to do all this tomorrow morning, that's fine. – [4] –. As long as the room is all set on time, I do not mind.

If you have any questions, text me any time.

Glenn Mendes

**156** Why has the video conference schedule been changed?

(A) Mr. Mendes will be on a leave.
(B) There is a time difference.
(C) A room needs to be set up.
(D) Some equipment is missing.

**157** What will Mr. Gilbert NOT do for the video conference?

(A) Print out some reports
(B) Check audio equipment
(C) Move a display device
(D) Clean an old projector

**158** In which of the positions marked [1], [2], [3] and [4] does the following sentence best belong?

"So be careful when you handle it."

(A) [1]
(B) [2]
(C) [3]
(D) [4]

GO ON TO THE NEXT PAGE

**Questions 159-161** refer to the following memo.

| For | Jonathan Mallo |
|---|---|
| Date | April 23rd 2017 |
| Time | 2:15 P.M. |

The following message was received.

| Name | Sally Baffin (saleswoman at Grinnell Home Appliances) |
|---|---|
| TEL | 203-893-5248 |

Ms. Baffin was returning your call about the vacuum cleaners and mops you asked for earlier to supplement the shortage of cleaning equipment. She said that the vacuum cleaners with the 360° rotating feature are out of stock and that you should check out their website to find out about other items before you make another visit. For the mops, she said that they will be delivered by noon tomorrow.

| Taken by | Holly from Accounting |
|---|---|

**159** Who most likely is Mr. Mallo?

(A) An accountant
(B) A janitor
(C) A salesman
(D) An electrician

**160** What most likely is to happen when Mr. Mallo gets the message?

(A) He will return the vacuum cleaners.
(B) He will buy more mops.
(C) He will visit a website.
(D) He will call Grinnell Home Appliances.

**161** What can be inferred from the message?

(A) Mr. Mallo has visited the store before.
(B) Mr. Mallo knows Ms. Baffin personally.
(C) The vacuum cleaners are the latest models.
(D) The vacuum cleaners will be restocked this week.

**Questions 162-165** refer to the following online chat discussion.

| | | |
|---|---|---|
| **Daniel Brown** [11:24 A.M.] | | Good news! A shipment of monitors will be delivered this afternoon. |
| **Jennifer Lee** [11:25 A.M.] | | For real? What a quick delivery! |
| **Daniel Brown** [11:27 A.M.] | | I know! This is so amazing. I thought we would have to look for another manufacturer that can help us meet the deadline. |
| **Paul Pierce** [11:28 A.M.] | | So what do we do now? Exactly what time will it arrive? |
| **Daniel Brown** [11:31 A.M.] | | Mr. Robert Reece, who I spoke with on the phone informed me that the truck would be arriving around 4. So we have enough time to double-check the inventory before the shipment is unloaded. |
| **Paul Pierce** [11:32 A.M.] | | We should be careful this time. Last time, the number of keyboards didn't match the inventory list. |
| **Jennifer Lee** [11:34 A.M.] | | I can't agree with you more. But who's going to conduct the check, though? I have a meeting to attend this afternoon. |
| **Paul Pierce** [11:37 A.M.] | | I'll do it. After that, I'm going to speak with our subcontractor about the loss caused by their negligence. |
| **Daniel Brown** [11:38 A.M.] | | I appreciate that. So everything is on schedule, isn't it? |
| **Jennifer Lee** [11:39 A.M.] | | Pretty much. Alright, I have to go. Talk to you later. |

Send

**162** For what type of company does Mr. Brown most likely work?

(A) A company that sells computers
(B) A food delivery store
(C) A TV manufacturer
(D) A local radio station

**163** What was the problem with the previous delivery?

(A) Some items were delivered behind schedule.
(B) All items were way too expensive.
(C) The number of some items was incorrect.
(D) Most items were not properly packaged.

**164** Who will carry out the inventory check?

(A) Mr. Brown
(B) Ms. Lee
(C) Mr. Pierce
(D) Mr. Reece

**165** At 11:34 A.M., what does Ms. Lee mean when she writes, "I can't agree with you more"?

(A) She agrees with Mr. Pierce to some degree.
(B) She believes that the inventory list is not important.
(C) She no longer agrees with Mr. Pierce.
(D) She absolutely thinks that they should be careful.

**GO ON TO THE NEXT PAGE**

Questions 166-168 refer to the following announcement.

## Zenith Industries

The sales and accounting department at Zenith will be responsible for hosting the 60th anniversary of the company's foundation. Alongside some fine catering and get-together after work on Friday the 12th, which marks the 60th year since Zenith Industries Inc. has been in business, the company is planning on a special lecture on customer service for its employees.

The lecture will be given by Mr. Daniel Connery, a renowned expert in customer service and F2F sales. Mr. Connery has been travelling around Australia for 10 years to give lectures to countless salesmen and people in the service industry. He attained his master's degree at the Kentbury Institute of Business in 2004 after working as a regional director at Kyser Communications for 4 years. His lectures have been acclaimed by many as "practical" and based on realistic and helpful case studies along with some detailed explanation that gets right to the point.

The lecture will cover topics on dealing with customer complaints, maintaining a good relationship with customers, and effective communication skills. The seminar will be held on three separate time periods on Friday. Refer to the following schedule.

| 11:00 – 12:00 | Customer Complaints – How Do we Handle Them? |
|---|---|
| **Lunch** | |
| 14:00 – 15:15 | How to Keep Your Customers on Board for a Long Time |
| 15:30 – 17:00 | Communication Skills ABC |

166 What is the purpose of the announcement?

(A) To inform that work evaluation has been delayed
(B) To notify workers of a regular check-up
(C) To announce an upcoming performance evaluation
(D) To inform workers of an event featuring some lectures

167 What is NOT stated about Mr. Connery?

(A) He travels around the world to give lectures.
(B) He holds a master's degree from a business school.
(C) He has experience working in communications.
(D) His lectures mainly consist of case studies.

168 What is a topic covered by the lecture?

(A) Addressing your subordinates on misbehavior
(B) Keeping a lasting relationship with customers
(C) Strategies on winning business competition
(D) Ways to effectively advertise products online

Questions 169-172 refer to the following letter.

## Prestige Savings

182 Highland Road,
Phillandy, New Jersey 19293

November 17th

Dear Customer,

It is our pleasure to announce that our bank will be merging with Venture Capitals Ltd. on August 5th. From this merger, we are expecting to be able to provide a more stable service with wider variety of financial services. Moreover, we will be able to continue to provide our personal banking service as usual.

We have been trying our best to provide our customers with all the information regarding the changes that will be made on their accounts due to the merger. The changes will take effect on August 20th. Sometime before the 20th of August, all of our customers will receive a document through the mail sent from the bank with all the necessary information including the new bank locations, their personal bank account information, and some changes made to our online banking system.

Even after the merger, our priority is to serve our main customers: small to mid-sized businesses and personal customers. If you have any further questions, please feel free to contact our customer service representatives at 1-800-285-8592. You can also visit our website at www.vcltd. com/qa/merger for more information regarding the merger. Moreover, you are welcome to visit our current bank locations and ask any of the clerks about the merger.

Sincerely,
Charles Stanley
Senior Vice President
Prestige Savings

---

**169** By when will the customers receive information about the merger?

(A) As soon as the merger occurs
(B) On August 5th
(C) Before the 20th of August
(D) Later than the 20th of August

**170** Which one of the following is certain to change?

(A) Monthly maintenance fee
(B) Fund transfer fee
(C) Customers' account numbers
(D) Bank locations

**171** Which one of the following is NOT a method to learn about the merger?

(A) Visit the company's website
(B) Visit the current bank locations
(C) Write a letter to the company
(D) Call the customer service team

**172** How will the customers get the information packet?

(A) A customer representative will visit them door by door.
(B) They will receive it electronically.
(C) They will receive it by post.
(D) They won't receive it unless they request it.

**GO ON TO THE NEXT PAGE**

# Dasse Motors Inc.

124 Beachside Way
San Francisco, CA 95105
www.dasse.motors.com

February 17
Andrew G. Myers
J.P.A. Inc.
82 Maypole Street
San Jose, CA 95131

Dear Mr. Myers,

Working with J.P.A. Inc. for the past three years has been a delightful experience. – [1] –. We regret to inform you, however, that we at Dasse Motors no longer need your advisory services. – [2] –.

Our management has decided to head in a new business direction to avoid great loss in this sluggish economy. – [3] –. Since the professional business advisory services you have provided for our company are not suitable for the strategies we will map out, we have to cancel our contract with J.P.A Inc., although we take this chance to acknowledge the dedicated work you have done for us. – [4] –.

Indeed, we hope to remain on good terms with you and J.P.A. Inc. If the world economy bounces back and we need any services similar to what you have provided for us, we would definitely like to consider J.P.A. Inc. again.

Best regards,

Robert Anderson
CEO, Dasse Motors

**173** What most likely is J.P.A. Inc.?

(A) A motorcycle manufacturer
(B) A road construction company
(C) A business consulting firm
(D) A pharmaceutical company

**174** Why does Dasse Motors want to cancel the contract?

(A) The economic downturn is worldwide.
(B) The terms of the contract were unfair.
(C) New tax laws have become effective.
(D) Its competitors went bankrupt.

**175** In which of the positions marked [1], [2], [3] and [4] does the following sentence best belong?

"Its impact is so severe that we have seen a big gap between our actual and planned revenues."

(A) [1]
(B) [2]
(C) [3]
(D) [4]

GO ON TO THE NEXT PAGE

**Questions 176-180** refer to the following letter and survey.

Catherine Lim
9607 MacAllan Rd.
Albuquerque, NM 76051

Dear Ms. Lim,

I'm sending this letter because you have recently cancelled your subscription to *California Magazine*. We would appreciate a few minutes of your time to complete our customer satisfaction survey. The survey will help us improve the magazine, and give us a better understanding of our customers' needs.

As a former subscriber, your opinion is important to us. Should you choose to complete the survey, you will receive a *California Magazine* soccer T-shirt as our gift to you.

We would also like to encourage you to renew your subscription with a 30% discount on our already low subscription cost. Additionally, all new subscribers will be entered into a contest to win an all-expenses-paid trip to Italy.

Please contact me if you have any questions.

Sincerely,
Andy Son

---

## *California Magazine* Customer Satisfaction Survey

**1.** What is your overall satisfaction with the magazine?
_____ Very Satisfied
_____ Somewhat Satisfied
_____ Neutral
___✓___ Somewhat Dissatisfied
_____ Very Dissatisfied

**2.** How often do you read our magazine?
_____ Always
_____ Frequently
___✓___ Sometimes
_____ Rarely
_____ Never

**3.** Please rank numerically each part of the magazine in order of importance to you.
___4___ News
___1___ Tips And Tricks
___5___ Calendar of Events
___2___ Industry Trends
___3___ Featured Article

**4.** Rank the quality of the following items.
___4___ Writing
___2___ Layout
___1___ Photography
___3___ Cover Design

**5.** Why did you cancel your subscription?
_____ Subscription cost was too expensive.
___✓___ I found another publication that better suits my needs.
_____ I was not satisfied with the content.
_____ I prefer to buy *California Magazine* at a store.

**6.** Describe what you enjoyed about *California Magazine*:
*I enjoy traveling, so your stories about other countries were very interesting.*

**7.** What would you like to change about *California Magazine*?
*I wish you introduced more affordable travel options. All the trips you write about are so expensive!*

**8.** I would like to restart my subscription:
Yes ___✓___        No _____
If yes, when would you like to restart?
*September 1st*

**176** What is the main purpose of this letter?

(A) To introduce a magazine to Ms. Lim
(B) To warn Ms. Lim that her subscription expired
(C) To ask Ms. Lim to fill out a survey
(D) To request a subscription payment from Ms. Lim

**177** Who most likely is Andy Son?

(A) Salesperson
(B) Magazine writer
(C) Market researcher
(D) Travel agent

**178** What will Ms. Lim receive from *California Magazine* for doing the survey?

(A) Subscription discount
(B) Soccer T-shirt
(C) Trip to Italy
(D) Free magazine issue

**179** Which part of the magazine does Ms. Lim find the most interesting?

(A) Featured Article
(B) Calendar of Events
(C) Tips and Tricks
(D) Industry Trends

**180** What did Ms. Lim dislike about *California Magazine*?

(A) Subscription cost
(B) Photograph quality
(C) Cover appearance
(D) Trip affordability

GO ON TO THE NEXT PAGE

# Tripoli Security Services
## *Excellence, Credibility, Client-oriented*

Tripoli Security Services has been providing escort services to more than 3,000 high-profile clients ranging from A-list celebrities to high-profile politicians. At the top of our priorities are excellence, credibility and client-oriented service. All of our agents are certified bodyguards who are experts in multiple kinds of martial arts. They have also undergone a special training program here at Tripoli Security Services which addresses terrorism and emergency situations. Our business with clients is kept in strict confidentiality and our services are adjusted to the specific needs of our clients. Clients can choose from three types of service (Standard, Premium, VIP) which have different levels of security protection. Please contact our branches in the following areas or contact our customer service at cs_tripoli@gomail.com for information on rates and availability:

| **Los Angeles** | **California** | **Miami** |
|---|---|---|
| Tel) 238-583-4579 | Tel) 392-573-7923 | Tel) 296-482-8532 |
| *VIP services only | | *VIP and Premium services only |

---

| e-mail | |
|---|---|
| To | cs_tripoli@gomail.com |
| from | jolene_35@estellavin.com |
| Date | Aug. 29. 2016 |
| Subject | Business inquiry |

Hello,

I am a local wine producer and the chairwoman of the 2016 Bellingsly Wine Exposition Organizing Committee. With high-level officials and celebrities visiting to promote our expo, I have been concerned about the safety of our guests as we experienced for the first time unfortunate but minor security incident at the opening ceremony. To prevent such incidents from happening again, I would like to ask for your service from September 2nd to 12th. We will require all three types of security protection to accommodate all of our different personal requirements. We will also be requiring 5 limousines for transporting our guests to and from the airport.

Please reply to us by the end of the month to talk about business details. Thank you.

Jolene Hansen,
Estella Vineyard
Chairwoman of the 19th Bellingsly Wine Exposition Organizing Committee

181 What is suggested about Tripoli Security Services?

(A) It offers many kinds of martial arts training.
(B) It provides customers with protective guards.
(C) Its service focuses on national security secrets.
(D) It is trying to diversify into a new type of service.

182 Where is Ms. Hansen's event being held?

(A) Miami
(B) California
(C) Los Angeles
(D) Tripoli

183 Why does Ms. Hansen want the services of Tripoli Security Services?

(A) To preclude any further security issues
(B) To save on the event's budget
(C) To attract more guests than last year
(D) To show off to visitors

184 The word "addresses" in line 5 of the advertisement is closest in meaning to

(A) solves
(B) determines
(C) deals with
(D) confronts

185 What can be inferred from the e-mail?

(A) Ms. Hansen has never made use of security services.
(B) Ms. Hansen is working consecutive terms as the committee's chairwoman.
(C) Ms. Hansen has an acquaintance working at Tripoli Security Services.
(D) Ms. Hansen owns a bottling company.

GO ON TO THE NEXT PAGE

# The Croak Valley Cabin
41 Folks Road
Luitenburg, CS 461734
(353) 793-3520

Timothy Prasad,
317 Rollingside Street
Stoneland Way, Exober Province
(44) 248-3458

May 9th

Dear Mr. Prasad,

This letter is to inform you that we have processed the following reservation for you.

| Reservation Details | Payment Details | |
|---|---|---|
| Reservation code: RWYD-5DE3G | Total Amount: | 800.00 USD |
| Status: Confirmed | Deposit due at reservation: | 0.00 USD |
|     Family Room (Color: Blue) | Balance due: | 800.00 USD |
|     May 24 – May 26 (3 days) | | |
|     4 Persons | | |

Thank you for choosing the Croak Valley Cabin for your stay in Portroe. I have lived in Portroe my entire life. So, if you have questions about Portroe, please contact me via e-mail: kdillon@croakvalleycabin.com or call at (353) 793-3523. In case you want to change your reservation, please call our Reservation Desk at (353) 793-3525.

*Kevin Dillon, Cabin Owner*

---

| Kathlyn Prasad | 3:09 P.M. |
|---|---|

Hi, Dad. Sorry, but I'm afraid I can't go to the family picnic.

| Timothy Prasad | 3:11 P.M. |
|---|---|

What's wrong, honey?

| Kathlyn Prasad | 3:15 P.M. |
|---|---|

My best friend Sarah told me she would move to a different country with her family. So a bunch of friends of hers and I have decided to throw a farewell party for her, and I have to be there.

| Timothy Prasad | 3:16 P.M. |
|---|---|

I'm so sorry. Can't this wait, though?

| Kathlyn Prasad | 3:18 P.M. |
|---|---|

No, Dad. We only have time on May 25. Most of us are working part time.

| Timothy Prasad | 3:20 P.M. |
|---|---|

O.K, how about we go for family trip on your summer vacation, then? I've not yet paid a deposit for this cabin.

| Kathlyn Prasad | 3:21 P.M. |
|---|---|

You bet! Thanks, Dad.

| From | Timothy Prasad <tprasad@abcmail.com> |
| --- | --- |
| To | Kevin Dillon <kdillon@croakvalleycabin.com> |
| Date | May 21 |
| Subject | Family room reservation |

Dear Mr. Dillon,

I am so sorry, but I would like to make change to my booking from May 24 – May 26 to June 18 – June 20, since my daughter would not be able to join us.

I fully understand that it would be too much for you to hold the family room that I am booking this early. So I will put down 50% of the deposit on the room and contact your Reservation Desk for further details, as specified in Terms and Conditions on your website.

Best regards,
Timothy Prasad

**186** What is NOT stated in the letter?

(A) The color of the reserved room is blue.
(B) Mr. Prasad's will stay in a cabin for three days.
(C) Mr. Dillon has lived in Portroe his whole life.
(D) The number of Mr. Prasad's family members is 3.

**187** Why does Mr. Prasad want to change the schedule?

(A) Because his daughter will have to join a party.
(B) Because his daughter will move to a different country.
(C) Because he has already made full payment.
(D) Because Portroe is not a good place for him to visit.

**188** In the text message, the expression "You bet" at 3:21 P.M. is closest in meaning to

(A) Surprisingly
(B) Certainly
(C) Inevitably
(D) Warmly

**189** Which of the following numbers will Mr. Prasad most likely get to call?

(A) (353) 793-3520
(B) (44) 248-3458
(C) (353) 793-3523
(D) (353) 793-3525

**190** How much money will Mr. Prasad pay in advance?

(A) 0 USD
(B) 200 USD
(C) 400 USD
(D) 800 USD

GO ON TO THE NEXT PAGE

# MEMO

Date: Tuesday, February 23
To: All Employees
From: Jesse Henricks, General Director
Subject: Website Problem

I am aware that many of you have already reported the malfunction of our website since it was redesigned by a design agency we hired last month. I was informed by Mr. Perez in charge of the redesign, however, that certain errors can occur when the URL of a page is changed. Therefore, I assure you that this has nothing to do with the groundless rumor that we have been hacked.

There have been even attempts made by Mark Bennett of our technical team to provide faster Internet connection by deleting cookies that seems unnecessary, but it turned out they were equally unsuccessful. Hence, the same design agency will be called on tomorrow to solve the technical problem by the end of the week, and I assure that our website redesign will be successful and on time. Stay focused on work.

---

| | e-mail |
|---|---|
| **From** | Jamal Perez <jperez@ihcdesign.com> |
| **To** | Ben Knight <bknight@ihcdesign.com> |
| **Date** | February 23 |
| **Subject** | Mugen Engineers Service |

Ben,

I just received a call from Mr. Henricks, General Director of Mugen Engineers, regarding technical problems of their website which we redesigned on January 8. Sounded like a 301 redirection error occurred which hinders the process of forwarding an old URL to a new one. Mr. Perez asked me to come over for repairs, but as you know I am leaving for Canada for the annual conference early tomorrow morning and won't be back until the 26th of this month. Will you take care of this while I'm gone? I would really appreciate it.

ps: For your information, our warranty period has been extended to three months.

Many thanks in advance,
Jamal

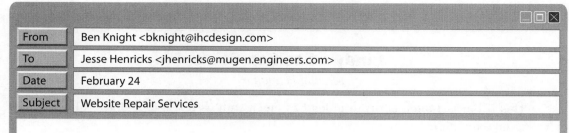

| From | Ben Knight <bknight@ihcdesign.com> |
| --- | --- |
| To | Jesse Henricks <jhenricks@mugen.engineers.com> |
| Date | February 24 |
| Subject | Website Repair Services |

Dear Mr. Henricks,

As per your request for repair services on your website we redesigned on January 8, I visited your company this afternoon, since my colleague, Mr. Perez, is away on a business trip. I wanted to meet with you to ask you a few things but was informed that you were also out of the office.

I examined your server and successfully fixed redirection errors which often occur when page URLs have changed. And I made sure that all tracking scripts are in place for a smooth transition.

I assume someone had removed necessary cookies, which seemed to be the main cause of the malfunction. The problems you had were not serious, although I recommend you prepare a backup that can be restored just in case. No extra charges are incurred according to our new policies.

Should you have any questions, you can contact either Mr. Perez or me on my cell phone: 973-465-3456.

Best regards,
Ben Knight

191 According to the memo, what statement is true?

(A) Mr. Bennett spread the rumor.
(B) Mr. Henricks works in the Technical Team.
(C) Mugen Engineers will hire a different design agency.
(D) Some believe that they have been hacked.

192 What is suggested about Mr. Perez?

(A) He caused the 301 redirection errors.
(B) He is in charge of Mugen Engineers.
(C) He designed the original website.
(D) He will be abroad until Friday.

193 In the second e-mail, the word "backup" in paragraph 3, line 2, is closest in meaning to

(A) support
(B) copy
(C) accumulation
(D) procedure

194 Why is Mr. Knight NOT charging the fees for repairs?

(A) Because technical errors occurred due to the buyer's own faults.
(B) Because errors always occur when a website is redesigned.
(C) Because services are offered within the warranty period.
(D) Because he is not legally authorized to do so.

195 Who is most likely to blame for the malfunction of the website?

(A) Mr. Henricks
(B) Mr. Bennett
(C) Mr. Perez
(D) Mr. Knight

GO ON TO THE NEXT PAGE

# Cindy's Fashion Store

*Moving is upon us!*

- This is our last-ditch effort to unload as much stuff as possible and avoid having to take it with us!
- Until the end of March, or while supplies last!
- Discounts for a huge selection of fashion jewelry and accessories!
- Expect to find tons of gold products at 20%, silver products at 30% and metal products at 50% off prices!
- Perfect location to stop in during your lunch break or to swing by after work!

---

Dear Ms. Priestly,

I came to buy a pair of earrings (HA-20) at your store, only to find your store is closed. My best friend Emily recommended this store. So I drove 20 miles to get here. How could you do this without any notice? When you read this, please contact me.

(241) 456-4576, nburrows@abcmail.com.

Nancy Burrows

---

| From | Cindy Priestly <cpriestly@cindy_priestly.fashion.com> |
|---|---|
| To | Nancy Burrows <nburrows@abcmail.com> |
| Date | March 24 |
| Subject | We are truly sorry. |

Dear Ms. Burrows,

Please accept our sincere apologies. We moved to re-open our store in Wilmington yesterday. In our haste to prepare tons of stuff, we forgot to post a notice on the door. Fortunately, Mr. Daryl Ross, our former manager, went back for lease termination and found your note.

Ms. Emily Hampshire, your friend, has been our regular customer for the past few years. She would drop by after work almost every day, and I remember several days ago she purchased exactly the same pair of silver earrings you mentioned in your note.

In order not to confuse customers, we will continue to offer the same discounts as specified in the Moving Sale advertisement until the end of March, although it is inevitable to change for certain items as follows:

- Necklaces, Pendants, Bracelets at 10% discounts, and
- Wedding Bands, Brooches at 15% discounts, whatever material they are made of.

Our new store will open in Wilmington on April 1. Feel free to visit! If you have any questions, please contact our new manager, Ms. Bridget Fowler, at (910) 876-1467 or visit www.cindy_priestly.fashion.com.

Sincerely,
Cindy Priestly, Owner

**196** Why did Cindy's Fashion Store hold a sales event?

(A) Because they wanted to make room for new inventory.
(B) Because they did not want to move too much stuff.
(C) Because they wanted to extend a lease for their property.
(D) Because they held a celebration for a new manager.

**197** According to the advertisement, what is stated as an advantage of Cindy's Fashion Store?

(A) Affordable product prices
(B) Tax-free benefits
(C) Friendly employees
(D) Easy accessibility

**198** What is suggested about Mr. Ross?

(A) He opened a store 20 miles away from Wilmington.
(B) He likes shopping after work.
(C) He found the note that Ms. Burrows wrote.
(D) He has recently been hired as a new manager.

**199** Who recommended Cindy's Fashion Store to Ms. Burrows?

(A) Ms. Priestly
(B) Ms. Hampshire
(C) Mr. Ross
(D) Ms. Fowler

**200** How much discount will get Ms. Burrows get for HA-20 earrings?

(A) 10%
(B) 15%
(C) 20%
(D) 30%

**Stop!** This is the end of the test. If you finish before time is called, you may go back to Parts 5, 6, and 7 and check your work.

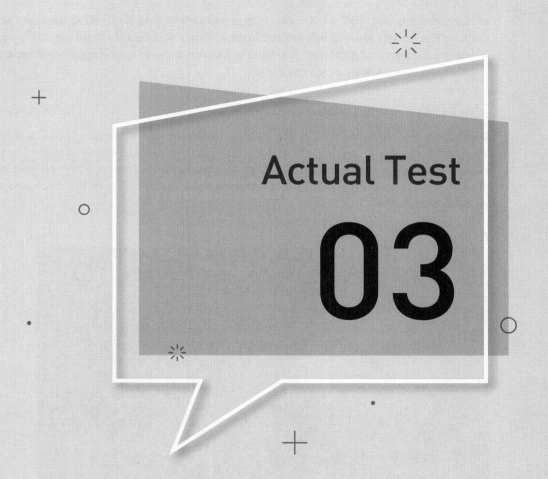

Actual Test

03

| 시작 시간 | : |
| 종료 시간 | : |

# LISTENING TEST

In the Listening test, you will be asked to demonstrate how well you understand spoken English. The entire Listening test will last approximately 45 minutes. There are four parts, and directions are given for each part. You must mark your answers on the separate answer sheet. Do not write your answers in your test book.

# PART 1

**Directions:** For each question in this part, you will hear four statements about a picture in your test book. When you hear the statements, you must select the one statement that best describes what you see in the picture. Then find the number of the question on your answer sheet and mark your answer. The statements will not be printed in your test book and will be spoken only one time.

**Example**

**Sample Answer**

Ⓐ ● Ⓒ Ⓓ

Statement (B), "The man is using a microphone," is the best description of the picture, so you should select answer (B) and mark it on your answer sheet.

1

2

GO ON TO THE NEXT PAGE ➤

3

4

**5**

**6**

GO ON TO THE NEXT PAGE ▶

# PART 2

**Directions:** You will hear a question or statement and three responses spoken in English. They will not be printed in your test book and will be spoken only one time. Select the best response to the question or statement and mark the letter (A), (B), or (C) on your answer sheet.

**7** Mark your answer on your answer sheet.

**8** Mark your answer on your answer sheet.

**9** Mark your answer on your answer sheet.

**10** Mark your answer on your answer sheet.

**11** Mark your answer on your answer sheet.

**12** Mark your answer on your answer sheet.

**13** Mark your answer on your answer sheet.

**14** Mark your answer on your answer sheet.

**15** Mark your answer on your answer sheet.

**16** Mark your answer on your answer sheet.

**17** Mark your answer on your answer sheet.

**18** Mark your answer on your answer sheet.

**19** Mark your answer on your answer sheet.

**20** Mark your answer on your answer sheet.

**21** Mark your answer on your answer sheet.

**22** Mark your answer on your answer sheet.

**23** Mark your answer on your answer sheet.

**24** Mark your answer on your answer sheet.

**25** Mark your answer on your answer sheet.

**26** Mark your answer on your answer sheet.

**27** Mark your answer on your answer sheet.

**28** Mark your answer on your answer sheet.

**29** Mark your answer on your answer sheet.

**30** Mark your answer on your answer sheet.

**31** Mark your answer on your answer sheet.

# PART 3

**Directions:** You will hear some conversations between two or more people. You will be asked to answer three questions about what the speakers say in each conversation. Select the best response to each question and mark the letter (A), (B), (C), or (D) on your answer sheet. The conversations will not be printed in your test book and will be spoken only one time.

**32** Why is the woman at the shop?

(A) To get video footage transferred
(B) To buy a DVD player
(C) To take a family video
(D) To purchase an instruction manual

**33** What problem does the man mention?

(A) The tape will be deleted.
(B) The warranty has expired.
(C) The video player is out of date.
(D) The sound can be unclear.

**34** What will the woman most likely do next?

(A) Purchase more video tapes
(B) Repair some items
(C) Search for new hardware
(D) Borrow some video equipment

**35** Who most likely is the man?

(A) A show organizer
(B) A ticket office clerk
(C) A musician
(D) A waiter

**36** What time does the woman buy tickets for?

(A) 5:00 P.M.
(B) 5:40 P.M.
(C) 6:00 P.M.
(D) 7:30 P.M.

**37** How much does the woman need to pay for the tickets?

(A) $200
(B) $300
(C) $400
(D) $500

**38** Where do the speakers mostly like work?

(A) At a fitness center
(B) At a library
(C) At a university
(D) At a travel agency

**39** What does the woman imply when she says, "All within just 10 minutes"?

(A) She needs to hire an assistant.
(B) She tries to exercise regularly.
(C) She thinks the task is impossible.
(D) She is interested in the man's opinion.

**40** What does the man offer to do?

(A) Reduce her workload
(B) Rearrange an office
(C) Employ more staff
(D) Revise the schedule

**41** Where most likely are the speakers?

(A) At a car repair shop
(B) At a car rental store
(C) At an airport
(D) At a factory

**42** What feature is the man looking for?

(A) Fuel efficiency
(B) Comfortable space
(C) Automatic transmission
(D) GPS navigation

**43** What will the woman most likely do next?

(A) Show the man another model
(B) Have a car inspected
(C) Take the man to the parking lot
(D) Ask a colleague to help the man

GO ON TO THE NEXT PAGE

**44** What are the speakers mostly discussing?

(A) Improving communication skills
(B) Migrating information to a database
(C) Dealing with customer complaints
(D) Transferring to another department

**45** What is Ms. Barret currently working on?

(A) A construction project
(B) A system upgrade
(C) A business presentation
(D) A product test

**46** What does the man suggest?

(A) Getting some assistance
(B) Speaking to a supplier
(C) Closing a business early
(D) Working extra hours

**47** What are the speakers talking about?

(A) The countries the man has been to
(B) The man's childhood
(C) The man's longtime interest
(D) The man's family traditions

**48** From whom did the man get the coins in his childhood?

(A) From his friend
(B) From his teacher
(C) From his parent
(D) From his neighbor

**49** What does the man suggest the woman do?

(A) Look at some rare items
(B) Help him collect coins
(C) Tell him about her hobby
(D) Go on a trip with him

**50** What is the woman's problem?

(A) An important document is missing.
(B) Some of her files have been deleted.
(C) A proposal has been rejected.
(D) A project is behind schedule.

**51** According to the man, what may be the cause of the problem?

(A) The woman got a virus on the computer.
(B) The woman downloaded a new program.
(C) The woman didn't upgrade her computer.
(D) The woman may be saving her files incorrectly.

**52** What does the woman ask the man to do?

(A) Help her locate her files
(B) Call a computer technician
(C) Look for a new program
(D) Check her software settings

**53** What is the man doing?

(A) He is writing a news article.
(B) He is collecting some post cards.
(C) He is making a reservation.
(D) He is reading customer feedback.

**54** Why does the woman say, "we should try the same"?

(A) To change a plan
(B) To make an excuse
(C) To agree with a suggestion
(D) To request some help

**55** What will the man do tomorrow morning?

(A) Discuss an idea
(B) Expand a product line
(C) Hold a special event
(D) Revise a budget plan

**56** Where are the speakers?

(A) In a greenhouse
(B) At a café
(C) At a flower shop
(D) In a garden

**57** What advantage is mentioned about the new equipment?

(A) It comes with a manual.
(B) It can be installed easily.
(C) It costs less on utilities.
(D) It has come down in price.

**58** According to the woman, what will happen later this year?

(A) Harvest yields will remain the same as last year.
(B) She will grow new plants indoors.
(C) The weather in the area will improve.
(D) The installation fee will increase.

---

**59** Where most likely do the speakers work?

(A) At a factory
(B) At a repair shop
(C) At a hardware store
(D) At a delivery service

**60** What caused the delay of the shipment?

(A) An overdue payment
(B) A technical problem
(C) An incomplete form
(D) A change in work schedule

**61** What will the man probably do next?

(A) Buy new machines
(B) Talk to a coworker
(C) Check a delivery
(D) Search for a repairman

| Company | Location |
|---|---|
| Avon Brochure | Dallas |
| Elddis | Houston |
| Wave Design | New Orleans |
| Vista Print | Phoenix |

**62** What type of event is the company organizing?

(A) A fundraiser
(B) A sporting event
(C) A seasonal sale
(D) A musical performance

**63** What is the woman concerned about?

(A) A reduced budget
(B) A scheduling conflict
(C) A shortage of employees
(D) A late delivery

**64** Look at the graphic. Which company will probably be hired?

(A) Avon Brochure
(B) Elddis
(C) Wave Design
(D) Vista Print

**GO ON TO THE NEXT PAGE**

| Argos Bedding | | |
|---|---|---|
| | | Order No. 8901 |
| Item | Quantity | Total Price |
| Blanket | 1 | $15 |
| Pillow | 1 | $50 |
| Pillowcase | 4 | $12 |
| Curtain | 2 | $80 |

**65** What is the man's problem?

(A) He cannot order an item online.
(B) He does not like what he purchased.
(C) He did not bring an original receipt.
(D) He received an incomplete order.

**66** According to the man, what happened during the move?

(A) An item was misplaced.
(B) Some movers arrived late.
(C) A truck broke down.
(D) Some furniture was damaged.

**67** Look at the graphic. How much money will the man be refunded?

(A) $15
(B) $50
(C) $12
(D) $80

| Schedule | |
|---|---|
| Stage 1 | Suites |
| Stage 2 | Ballroom |
| Stage 3 | Pools |
| Stage 4 | Building Exterior |

**68** What kind of company does the woman most likely work for?

(A) An architectural firm
(B) A hotel
(C) An apparel company
(D) A graphic design company

**69** What does the woman say about the ongoing project?

(A) She is dealing with some challenges.
(B) A client is very demanding.
(C) It is on the right track.
(D) A status report has been completed.

**70** Look at the graphic. What stage of the project will begin now?

(A) Stage 1
(B) Stage 2
(C) Stage 3
(D) Stage 4

# PART 4

**Directions:** You will hear some talks given by a single speaker. You will be asked to answer three questions about what the speaker says in each talk. Select the best response to each question and mark the letter (A), (B), (C), or (D) on your answer sheet. The talks will not be printed in your test book and will be spoken only one time.

71 Where most likely are the listeners?

(A) In a waiting room
(B) On a plane
(C) In a train station
(D) On a bus

72 What is the cause of the delay?

(A) Some passengers have not arrived.
(B) Some luggage is being loaded.
(C) A runway has been blocked.
(D) A flight has been overbooked.

73 What does the speaker say will happen?

(A) The weather will change.
(B) The plane will arrive on time.
(C) Some seats will become available.
(D) Some food will be provided.

74 Who most likely is the speaker addressing?

(A) Reception staff
(B) Food suppliers
(C) Sales people
(D) Store detectives

75 What will the listeners do this morning?

(A) Take inventory
(B) Receive training
(C) Visit a new store
(D) Watch a video

76 What will be provided for customers?

(A) A facility tour
(B) A free shuttle bus
(C) A discount coupon
(D) A welcome gift

77 Why is the speaker calling?

(A) To offer a position
(B) To explain a decision
(C) To request a document
(D) To schedule an interview

78 What does the speaker expect will happen soon?

(A) Assignments will be diversified.
(B) Funding will be increased.
(C) A contract will be renewed.
(D) Other positions will be available.

79 What does the speaker offer to do?

(A) Revise some regulations
(B) Examine a budget
(C) Keep a document on file
(D) Provide a reference

80 What happened this morning?

(A) A commercial building was sold.
(B) A new policy was announced.
(C) A public facility was reopened.
(D) A sports season began.

81 What is mentioned about the center?

(A) The opening date has been delayed.
(B) Parking is limited.
(C) Some areas are available for rent.
(D) A baseball game will be held.

82 What are listeners advised to do for more information?

(A) Look online
(B) Visit City Hall
(C) Call the station
(D) Check the newspaper

**GO ON TO THE NEXT PAGE**

**83** According to the speaker, what is the company trying to do?

(A) Reduce water consumption
(B) Save electricity
(C) Stop the use of plastic bags
(D) Implement carpooling

**84** What does the speaker mean when he says, "I understand your concerns"?

(A) He predicts that an initiative will fail.
(B) He knows why listeners have doubts.
(C) He does not like a suggested idea.
(D) He understands the details of a plan.

**85** What will the ICA customers receive for the next two months?

(A) Store credits
(B) Meal vouchers
(C) Free delivery
(D) Paper bags

---

**86** What is the main purpose of the meeting?

(A) To select a new supplier
(B) To analyze a competitor's product
(C) To go over survey results
(D) To publish a magazine

**87** What feature of the product is the most popular?

(A) A cooking time sensor
(B) A preprogrammed keypad
(C) A convection feature
(D) A multiple cooking mode

**88** Why does the speaker say, "which you wouldn't want to do in a regular microwave"?

(A) To give a comparison
(B) To criticize a competitor
(C) To make a suggestion
(D) To publicize a product

**89** Why does the speaker say, "Isn't it getting in shape"?

(A) To introduce a famous athlete
(B) To advertise dietary supplements
(C) To motivate listeners to exercise
(D) To satisfy consumer tastes

**90** According to the advertisement, what will happen during December?

(A) Special offers will be available.
(B) More classes will be added.
(C) Business hours will change.
(D) More instructors will be hired.

**91** What additional event is being mentioned?

(A) A competition
(B) A demonstration
(C) A concert
(D) A sale

---

**92** Who most likely is the speaker?

(A) A company president
(B) A publishing director
(C) A financial manager
(D) A sales representative

**93** What is the main purpose of the speech?

(A) To schedule future editorials
(B) To announce company layoffs
(C) To congratulate the employees
(D) To say farewell to colleagues

**94** What does the speaker say is happening in the industry?

(A) Publications are closing down.
(B) Employment opportunities are increasing.
(C) Financial aid is being offered.
(D) Conferences are being held.

**Results by the number of votes**

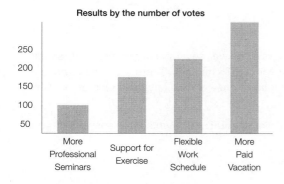

| Expense Report | | |
|---|---|---|
| **DATE** | **DESCRIPTION** | **AMOUNT** |
| November 8 | Air fare | $1000 |
| November 9 | Restaurant | $45 |
| November 10 | Accommodation | $220 |
| November 12 | Car Rental | $300 |

**95** Who is the speaker addressing?

(A) Office workers
(B) University professors
(C) Small business owners
(D) City officials

**96** According to the speaker, what happened last month?

(A) A company outing was held.
(B) A survey was given to employees.
(C) A new board member was appointed.
(D) A revised policy was introduced.

**97** Look at the graphic. Which suggestion will be accepted by the company?

(A) More professional seminars
(B) Support for exercise
(C) Flexible work schedule
(D) More paid vacation

**98** What is the purpose of the message?

(A) To request an original document
(B) To respond to an inquiry
(C) To accept a business proposition
(D) To reschedule a meeting

**99** Which department does the speaker probably work in?

(A) Sales
(B) Shipping
(C) Advertising
(D) Accounting

**100** Look at the graphic. Which expense needs to be confirmed?

(A) Air fare
(B) Restaurant
(C) Accommodation
(D) Car rental

This is the end of the Listening test. Turn to Part 5 in your test book.

GO ON TO THE NEXT PAGE

# READING TEST

In the Reading test, you will read a variety of texts and answer several different types of reading comprehension questions. The entire Reading test will last 75 minutes. There are three parts, and directions are given for each part. You are encouraged to answer as many questions as possible within the time allowed.

You must mark your answers on the separate answer sheet. Do not write your answers in your test book.

# PART 5

**Directions:** A word or phrase is missing in each of the sentences below. Four answer choices are given below each sentence. Select the best answer to complete the sentence. Then mark the letter (A), (B), (C), or (D) on your answer sheet.

**101** The investigation committee is pleased to announce that effective August 1st, Ms. Davis ------- her term as chancellor.

(A) is being started
(B) is started
(C) will be starting
(D) had been starting

**102** Many files ------- by the time the technicians discovered the failure in the computer system.

(A) had disappeared
(B) disappear
(C) will have disappeared
(D) are disappearing

**103** It was his 20 years of contributions to the field of chemistry that ------- him a lifetime achievement award from his colleague.

(A) achieved
(B) honored
(C) won
(D) took

**104** The survey indicates that it is still ------- through radio broadcasts that listeners first hear new pop songs despite the spread of digital technologies.

(A) predominated
(B) predominating
(C) predominantly
(D) predominant

**105** Cartech's engine parts are put through a ------- inspection procedure.

(A) withheld
(B) managerial
(C) founded
(D) stringent

**106** ------- student who is willing to volunteer for the local Community Service should apply as soon as possible.

(A) All
(B) Few
(C) Any
(D) Both

**107** The Honest Theater Co. recorded unprecedented revenues from ticket sales, and ------- more from advertising for the period ending April 30.

(A) even
(B) any
(C) very
(D) all

**108** Our chief developer Rick has extensive ------- of software architecture as well as years of experience in the field.

(A) ability
(B) opinion
(C) collector
(D) knowledge

109 To ensure a safe and reliable Internet service, Fibernet takes every possible ------- with its security systems.

(A) idea
(B) precaution
(C) rule
(D) entry

110 Juventa's ambition is to attain a(n) ------- as one of the top retailers in Asia through expansions into new territories.

(A) schedule
(B) order
(C) record
(D) position

111 Kapti Motors and Allyson entered into a joint project which should result in a ------- beneficial venture.

(A) precisely
(B) respectively
(C) mutually
(D) punctually

112 All of the region's qualified nurses are required ------- to the Nurse's Code of Ethics and Standards.

(A) adheres
(B) to adhere
(C) have adhered
(D) adhering

113 All of the signs were ------- orange and black when the restaurants first opened, but now they have gone for a more modern look.

(A) transferred
(B) alternated
(C) painted
(D) changed

114 Senator Robertson was straightforward and to the ------- during the debate when he spoke on automobile tariffs.

(A) spot
(B) feet
(C) point
(D) grade

115 While still maintaining a high level of customer satisfaction, subcontracting our customer services to an outside agency would ------- us to reduce expenditure.

(A) prefer
(B) inhibit
(C) keep
(D) enable

116 A shopping mall, a grocery store, a theater, and several restaurants are all ------- a ten-minute drive from Calhan Tower.

(A) onto
(B) within
(C) so that
(D) much as

117 When handing in ------- for reimbursement, a fully itemized list of your transactions during a business trip is required.

(A) receipts
(B) directions
(C) journeys
(D) procedures

118 The Personnel department manager is seeking experienced, qualified, team-oriented, and highly ------- employees to transfer to the new branch in Seoul.

(A) motivator
(B) motivate
(C) motivating
(D) motivated

119 *The Chronicler* is a monthly news magazine issued by Sloan Publishers, a ------- of Klain Media Group.

(A) category
(B) division
(C) separation
(D) selection

120 Because our company is ------- experiencing technical problems, there has been an interruption with the Internet connection.

(A) currently
(B) lately
(C) commonly
(D) ordinarily

GO ON TO THE NEXT PAGE

**121** ------- removing classified documents from the company's laboratory, you must have approval from both the department manager and the senior officer.

(A) Until
(B) Before
(C) During
(D) From

**122** With crucial industries such as mining and farming located in the region, the Department of Commerce wanted high-speed Internet access ------- the province.

(A) everywhere
(B) moreover
(C) throughout
(D) somewhat

**123** The Accounting Department processes all the receipts ------- have been collected from our salespeople.

(A) that
(B) when
(C) what
(D) then

**124** Our soccer team, ------- an advance to the final round, unfortunately failed to post a single win.

(A) nevertheless
(B) let alone
(C) in the event of
(D) contrary to

**125** Our restaurant will no longer be ------- credit cards for purchases under one dollar due to the higher service fees involved.

(A) renovating
(B) rendering
(C) running
(D) accepting

**126** Some parts of the stage remain ------- the curtains when viewed from the sides despite the best efforts of the organizers.

(A) down
(B) within
(C) behind
(D) over

**127** By reducing crime and persuading businesses to move into the region, the mayor, together with the city committee and local merchants, has done much to ------- the waterfront district.

(A) regain
(B) restart
(C) replace
(D) restore

**128** In order to improve customer satisfaction and attract new customers, Solina's website will be undergoing ------- changes.

(A) producing
(B) matured
(C) consumable
(D) substantial

**129** The latest reports indicate that the ------- of the nation's currency fell dramatically during the economic slump.

(A) expense
(B) worth
(C) fare
(D) value

**130** With ------- in over 25 countries, *Smart Machine* is one of South America's leading science and engineering publications.

(A) spectators
(B) subscribers
(C) participants
(D) witnesses

# PART 6

**Directions:** Read the texts that follow. A word, phrase, or sentence is missing in parts of each text. Four answer choices for each question are given below the text. Select the best answer to complete the text. Then mark the letter (A), (B), (C), or (D) on your answer sheet.

**Questions 131-134** refer to the following notice.

We are proud to announce that Mr. Jonson, the founder of VISN Inc., has ------- our invitation to **131.** give a speech on his early experiences as a young, successful entrepreneur.

We strongly encourage everyone to attend this event. Mr. Jonson is a well-regarded businessman ------- is considered to have innovated the portable electronics devices industry. **132.**

-------. **133.**

The event will start off with the speech by Mr. Jonson. Following the speech, many ------- invited **134.** by our conference from different industries will hold brief question and answer sessions where the attendants are allowed to ask questions regarding each industry.

As there will be food and beverages supplied, we need to know the exact number of attendants by the end of next week. Please fill out the application form if you wish to attend the event. If you have any questions about the event, please contact us at 1-285-462-2621.

131 (A) approved
(B) accepted
(C) accessed
(D) permitted

132 (A) what
(B) which
(C) who
(D) how

133 (A) His speech will include his personal experiences and the skills needed for being an entrepreneur.
(B) Creative thinking is essential for bringing both technological and economic developments.
(C) Running a business is the first step in gaining recognition from other people, including professionals.
(D) It is unfortunate that he decided to decline our offer, but we will find another candidate.

134 (A) represent
(B) representatively
(C) representatives
(D) representing

**GO ON TO THE NEXT PAGE**

To: Kevin Shawn
From: Jack Clinton
Date: June 11
Subject: Guest Speaker

This is an urgent e-mail regarding the guest speaker of the biannual event. The initial guest speaker, Mr. Steven Stamkos, is no longer available due to his severe medical condition. Since the guest speaker must be ------- at least three days before the event in order to print new flyers,
**135.**
we must work together to find a replacement speaker.

In order ------- a new guest speaker, we must keep in mind that he or she has to be a well-known
**136.**
figure in our industry. -------.
**137.**

I have one candidate in my mind. I thought Hugh Perry, the founder of Perry's Prints, would be an appropriate candidate for this job. He is ------- qualified in our industry and also has participated
**138.**
in one of the joint projects with our company. Please write me back on what you think of Mr. Perry as the guest speaker.

As it is an urgent issue, I expect you to write me back as soon as possible. If you do not wish Mr. Perry to be the new guest speaker, please list possible candidates for the job.

Regards,

Jack

135 (A) awarded
(B) transformed
(C) cleared
(D) appointed

136 (A) recruited
(B) recruits
(C) have recruited
(D) to recruit

137 (A) Guests must be reminded to remain seated quietly during the speech.
(B) A complimentary dinner will be provided to the guest speaker.
(C) Mr. Stamkos needs to submit his personal information, including contact details.
(D) Moreover, the person must be related to our company in some way.

138 (A) confidently
(B) wisely
(C) extremely
(D) mostly

---

### GBI Workers Protest in the Streets

There has been an incident where a number of GBI Inc. employees were blocking the entrance to the office of Oscar's on Brudwick Boulevard in Atlanta. -------. The conflict arose when the
**139.**
partnership company, Oscar's Inc., ------- its deal with GBI Inc. to supply 1,000,000 pieces of
**140.**
parts to GBI's most popular product.

Although it has been officially revealed that GBI Inc. has lost 3 million dollars from this incident, some experts have stated that the company probably lost a significantly larger ------- of revenue
**141.**
than 3 million dollars.

Although the protestors have been peacefully withdrawn, it has been ------- that the employees
**142.**
will continue to hold the protest until the issue is settled. The police department is having a hard time resolving the issue because Oscar's Inc. is not willing to reconsider taking the deal.

---

**139** (A) The reasons behind the incident remain unknown up to this day.
(B) This protest started due to the immoral business strategy of GBI's partnership company.
(C) Employees had to take responsibility for what they have done.
(D) Renovation of the office tower will begin next Tuesday.

**140** (A) called off
(B) made of
(C) participated in
(D) prepared for

**141** (A) amount
(B) number
(C) collection
(D) total

**142** (A) are reported
(B) reported
(C) reporting
(D) was reported

**GO ON TO THE NEXT PAGE**

**Questions 143-146** refer to the following memo.

To: Joe Zhang
From: Mike Hailey
Date: August 12
Re: Project Group Organization

This memo has been sent to notify you that the board has -------- your proposal for the project
143.
team.

Though the board was satisfied with your plan, it requested for specifics. Most importantly, the

-------- of each group member must be indicated in order to prevent any type of confusion. --------.
144.                                                                                        145.

The board recognizes your -------- to this project and also looks forward to seeing a successful
146.
outcome from it. Since the project is expected to bring in 20% of the company's revenue for this

quarter, the board has emphasized your role as the project leader.

Please submit another document with more details on your team and their roles. The board

wishes you the best luck and also appreciates your hard work for the company.

Regards,

Mike Hailey
Assistant to the Board

---

143 (A) rejected
(B) approved
(C) completed
(D) finalized

144 (A) responsibilities
(B) representations
(C) relationships
(D) knowledge

145 (A) Also, each group member must be
interviewed to test his or her abilities for
the task.
(B) You do not have to hand in any
documents or forms.
(C) Your team has to decide who should be
the project leader as soon as possible.
(D) As you have requested, this project will
not be related to the company.

146 (A) contributes
(B) contribute
(C) contributor
(D) contribution

# PART 7

**Directions:** In this part you will read a selection of texts, such as magazine and newspaper articles, e-mails, and instant messages. Each text or set of texts is followed by several questions. Select the best answer for each question and mark the letter (A), (B), (C), or (D) on your answer sheet.

**Questions 147-148** refer to the following e-mail.

| To | Mariko Inoue |
| from | Tomas Kang |
| Date | November 19 |
| Subject | Biannual Bonuses |

Ms. Inoue,

The employee evaluations must be turned in before the bi-annual bonuses can be determined. I would like to finish all the calculations before the executives' meeting next Tuesday. Please complete all the necessary documentation and turn in signed originals to me as soon as possible. Don't forget to keep copies of all evaluations for yourself.

Sincerely yours,
Tomas Kang
Senior Accountant

**147** What is the purpose of this e-mail?

(A) To respond to a letter received
(B) To request evaluation forms
(C) To request copied documents
(D) To send a résumé

**148** What does Tomas Kang ask Mariko Inoue to do?

(A) Sign all the receipts
(B) Make a copy of the minutes
(C) Rate her job performance
(D) Get permission for bonuses

**GO ON TO THE NEXT PAGE**

**Questions 149-150** refer to the following text message chain.

Kevin Murphy — 3:51 P.M.: Juliana, this seminar is taking longer than I expected. I need your help.

Juliana Harris — 3:52 P.M.: Okay, what do you want me to do?

Kevin Murphy — 3:54 P.M.: Meet my client and give him a little consulting on the financial services we offer.

Juliana Harris — 3:55 P.M.: What is his name? Anything else?

Kevin Murphy — 3:56 P.M.: That's it. His name is Lewis Hamilton. The details are on my desk.

Juliana Harris — 4:06 P.M.: Oh, he just opened his account today!

Kevin Murphy — 4:07 P.M.: Yes! If you have a question, text me any time.

Send

**149** For what type of business does Ms. Harris most likely work?

(A) A bookstore
(B) A bank
(C) A museum
(D) A hospital

**150** At 3:56 P.M., what does Mr. Murphy mean when he writes, "That's it"?

(A) He is requesting Ms. Harris to do nothing more.
(B) He expected that the seminar would finish earlier.
(C) He knows that Ms. Harris is busy at work.
(D) He will meet with his client as soon as possible.

# Tokyo Vehicle

Tokyo Vehicle, an automotive technologies company created in 1963, is celebrating its 50th anniversary!

The annual Tokyo Vehicle Dynamic Expo is designed to showcase the latest components and tuning tools relating to suspension, steering, braking, and handling technologies. All Equipment will be available for purchase at special introductory prices. The expo will be a one-day event presented jointly by Tokyo Vehicle and the National Technology Association.

The expo will be a family-friendly, relaxed and informative day exploring and showcasing HY transport options. In addition, you will have a chance to enter one of your rare cars into a contest for a chance to win a $10,000 gift certificate redeemable at any Tokyo Vehicle location.

When: August 30th
Time: 9:00 A.M. — 5:00 P.M.
Where: Tokyo Vehicle San Francisco Branch

The show is a manufacturing and engineering event, and will be attended by leading automotive and business leaders, technical experts, F&A professionals, and consultants.

Save $30 by reserving your ticket online! Visit www.tokyovehicle.com for reservation.

---

**151** What event is being announced?

(A) A trade show for vehicle equipment
(B) An opening of a new vehicle store
(C) An exhibition by a famous racer
(D) A registration for a driver's license test course

**152** What is NOT mentioned about the event?

(A) It is held once a year.
(B) There will be products for sale.
(C) Online tickets cost 30 dollars.
(D) A prize will be awarded.

**GO ON TO THE NEXT PAGE**

# Special Package
## Arizona Fitness Club

A membership at Arizone Fitness Club benefits your life. It's for your goals, your hopes, and your dreams. It's for your health! We believe one hour per day at our health club can positively affect the other 23 hours of your day.

We offer 600 conveniently located clubs across the US open up to 24 hours a day. Also, Arizona Fitness Club can be found in 30 countries, including Europe, South Africa, Korea, Canada, and we are still growing. Not only do you get to choose the classes and options that are right for you, you even get to select the payment plan that fits your budget.

Arizona Fitness Club is now offering special prices for new members until August 30. Get 30 % off and join our club today!

For more details about the benefits and our exercise facilities, please visit our website at www.azfitness.com or call 1-848-948-0082.

**153** What information is NOT provided in the advertisement?
(A) The number of branches in the US
(B) The price of the membership fee
(C) The discount rate for newcomers
(D) The club's main number

**154** What will happen after August 30?
(A) New members will pay the full amount.
(B) A flexible payment plan will no longer be available.
(C) Membership fees will be reduced by 30%.
(D) The club will expand its business in the US.

Mikel Hoffman
2760 S Street,
Sacramento, CA 79028

Dear customers,

Hollywood Video would like to express our thanks for your recent purchase. We hope you are satisfied with your new DV-576 player. Please accept this free DVD of *Super Race*, a movie starring Angelina Ahn, as a token of our gratitude.

We would also like to remind you that your purchase came with a three-year complimentary cleaning service. Having your DVD player cleaned professionally every six months will ensure that it will function properly for several years. Visit the nearest branch to get a complimentary service with the original purchase receipt.

Again, thank you for your purchase. If you have questions or concerns, please do not hesitate to contact Norman Misri, our technical support provider, at 1-847-928-9383.

Sincerely yours,
Pamposh Deewan
Sales Manager

**155** What is the purpose of this letter?

(A) To show appreciation
(B) To advertise a DVD player
(C) To announce a policy change
(D) To inform customers of special savings

**156** What does Hollywood Video offer for free?

(A) Movie ticket
(B) Service plan
(C) A DVD player
(D) Product delivery

**157** Who is Norman Misri?

(A) A movie actor
(B) A manager
(C) A sales manager
(D) A technician

**GO ON TO THE NEXT PAGE**

# Collaboration Agreement

Signed on July 22, 2017

The parties to the contract are:

Sagetalic Paper Company (491 Osnabruck Rd, Grand Forks, British Columbia) and the Institute of Pulp and Paper Industries at the University of Wellerman (93 Sir Grenoble Rd, Fraser Valley, British Columbia)

This contract is entered into on July 22nd, 2017 between Sagetalic Paper Company and the Institute of Pulp and Paper Industries. The following will be terms of the agreement on R&D collaboration.

1. The above parties have consented on a contract to form a cooperative relationship on an R&D project, the object of which is to develop an environmentally-friendly chemical product which will facilitate the paper pulping process.

2. The agreement will be in effect for the duration of 3 years or shorter should the parties come to a mutual consensus.

3. An initial investment of $100,000 will be made by the city government of Vancouver. Additional funding required during the project will be supplied by Sagetalic Paper Company. Withdrawal from the investment agreement will be dealt with legal measures.

4. Division of future profits from sales will be 3% for the city government of Vancouver, 27% for the Institute of Pulp and Paper Industries, and 70% for Sagetalic Paper Company for the first three years after the launch of the new product.

5. Technical findings or any relevant information gained during the project shall remain confidential. The violation of this term will result in the annulment of the project with the party responsible compensating for damages to the other relevant parties.

*Signatures*

_____                    _____
Sagetalic Paper Company                             Institute of Pulp and Paper Industries

---

**158** Who is responsible for the initial investment?

(A) The city government of Vancouver
(B) Sagetalic Paper Company
(C) University of Wellerman
(D) Donations by the steering committee

**159** What is NOT discussed in the agreement?

(A) Handling of technical information
(B) Legal representatives
(C) Distribution of future profits
(D) Duration of the project

**160** What is implied about the Sagetalic Paper Company?

(A) Its investment will be the smallest.
(B) It has been in business for twenty years.
(C) It will take the majority of the sales profit.
(D) It holds the sole right to the use of information.

**Questions 161-163** refer to the following e-mail.

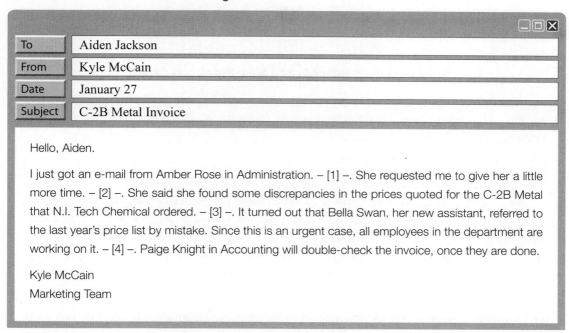

To | Aiden Jackson

From | Kyle McCain

Date | January 27

Subject | C-2B Metal Invoice

Hello, Aiden.

I just got an e-mail from Amber Rose in Administration. – [1] –. She requested me to give her a little more time. – [2] –. She said she found some discrepancies in the prices quoted for the C-2B Metal that N.I. Tech Chemical ordered. – [3] –. It turned out that Bella Swan, her new assistant, referred to the last year's price list by mistake. Since this is an urgent case, all employees in the department are working on it. – [4] –. Paige Knight in Accounting will double-check the invoice, once they are done.

Kyle McCain
Marketing Team

**161** What is the purpose of the e-mail?

(A) To explain why there has been a delay
(B) To announce the release of a new product
(C) To request help writing an invoice
(D) To place an order for metal materials

**162** In what department did the error take place?

(A) Administration
(B) Human resources
(C) Accounting
(D) Marketing

**163** In which of the positions marked [1], [2], [3] and [4] does the following sentence best belong?

"They don't match the price list issued early this month."

(A) [1]
(B) [2]
(C) [3]
(D) [4]

GO ON TO THE NEXT PAGE

August 1st

## Morning Foods Introduces a New Breakfast Cereal!

Faced with the demands of a busy day, some people choose convenience over nutrition when selecting their breakfast option. To give them a new choice, Morning Foods is introducing its new Sugar Crisp cereal, a convenient option with less than 150 calories per serving.

The Florida-based company issued a press announcement a few days ago promoting the national distribution of its newest breakfast cereal. The new cereal product will be displayed on the store shelves for sale all around the country starting August 3. Advertisements on major TV networks and radio stations will start in Chicago and Los Angeles one day before the national distribution date. Magazines and newspapers will run the ads at a promotional event in Las Vegas on the first date of sale.

This product launch marks the company's 5th new product line in the last two years. Additional new cereal lines launched during this period include Corn Chex, Cocoa Krispies, Fiber One, and Just Bunches. The group has been trying to supplement its established product lines with the new products to tackle decreasing sales. Sugar Crisp will be distributed primarily in the company's strategic markets of Chicago and Los Angeles sales have been traditionally strong.

**164** When is the new cereal scheduled to be available all across the nation?

(A) On August 1
(B) On August 3
(C) On August 4
(D) On August 5

**165** Where are printed advertisements scheduled to appear?

(A) Los Angeles
(B) Chicago
(C) Florida
(D) Las Vegas

**166** What is the reason for developing new cereals?

(A) Falling sales of existing products
(B) Sharp competition in the domestic market
(C) Unexplored potential in new strategic markets
(D) Finding a new top seller to rebrand the company

**167** What cereal has NOT been launched over the previous 24 months?

(A) Nut & Honey
(B) Corn Chex
(C) Cocoa Krispies
(D) Just Bunches

**Questions 168-171** refer to the following online chat discussion.

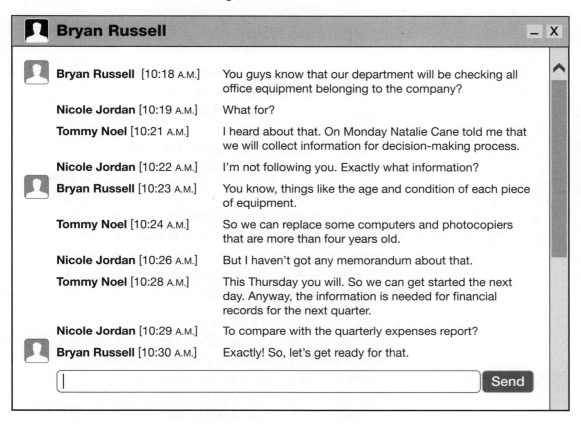

**Bryan Russell**       — X

| | |
|---|---|
| **Bryan Russell** [10:18 A.M.] | You guys know that our department will be checking all office equipment belonging to the company? |
| **Nicole Jordan** [10:19 A.M.] | What for? |
| **Tommy Noel** [10:21 A.M.] | I heard about that. On Monday Natalie Cane told me that we will collect information for decision-making process. |
| **Nicole Jordan** [10:22 A.M.] | I'm not following you. Exactly what information? |
| **Bryan Russell** [10:23 A.M.] | You know, things like the age and condition of each piece of equipment. |
| **Tommy Noel** [10:24 A.M.] | So we can replace some computers and photocopiers that are more than four years old. |
| **Nicole Jordan** [10:26 A.M.] | But I haven't got any memorandum about that. |
| **Tommy Noel** [10:28 A.M.] | This Thursday you will. So we can get started the next day. Anyway, the information is needed for financial records for the next quarter. |
| **Nicole Jordan** [10:29 A.M.] | To compare with the quarterly expenses report? |
| **Bryan Russell** [10:30 A.M.] | Exactly! So, let's get ready for that. |

Send

**168** To what department does Mr. Noel most likely belong?

(A) Marketing
(B) Sales
(C) Customer Service
(D) Accounting

**169** At 10:22 A.M., what does Ms. Jordan mean when she writes, "I'm not following you"?

(A) She thinks that Mr. Noel walks too fast for her to catch up.
(B) She cannot find the details about the equipment.
(C) She expects Mr. Noel to follow the company policies.
(D) She does not understand what information is needed.

**170** When will the information start being collected?

(A) On Monday
(B) On Tuesday
(C) On Thursday
(D) On Friday

**171** According to Mr. Noel, why is the information needed?

(A) To figure out what equipment needs to be replaced
(B) To take advantage of special tax benefits
(C) To carry the budget forward to the next quarter
(D) To compare with the quarterly expenses report

GO ON TO THE NEXT PAGE

## *Roxenne News*                    March 15

At a press conference on March 2, Liam Dolan, President of the M.E.S. Investors Corporation, announced the launch of the construction of Skyline World Theme Park in Oakland City, only 10 kilometers away from Roxenne. Mr. Dolan expressed his high hope that the massive project would improve the regional economy by attracting many business investors from areas around the city. –[1]–.

There are some voices of concern that the growing city may encroach on the surrounding areas. –[2]–. According to a survey, the majority of citizens in neighboring areas see this as a positive sign. "Many tourists will come. And this whole area will benefit in the long term," said Louis Klein, a Roxenne citizen. –[3]–.

A theme park is a huge attraction for entertainment, and rides and other events are for the enjoyment of large numbers of people. Experts agree that this will invigorate the local tourist industry. –[4]–. And although the revenue will be collected from admission tickets and parking fees, souvenirs, and food and beverage sales, advertising will be placed in a number of local newspapers, most of which are published by the companies based in the surrounding areas of the city.

**172** What does the article discuss?

(A) Business projects of an investment company

(B) Influences of a theme park on surrounding areas

(C) Tourist attractions selected by a magazine

(D) The rise and fall of an entertainment industry

**173** Why is the project welcomed by local citizens?

(A) It will enhance the security of their borders.

(B) It is designed to sustain the environment.

(C) It will help establish a free trade zone.

(D) It is expected to boost the regional economy.

**174** What source of income is NOT provided by Skyline World Theme Park?

(A) Admission tickets

(B) Parking fees

(C) Souvenirs sales

(D) Advertising fees

**175** In which of the positions marked [1], [2], [3] and [4] does the following sentence best belong?

"Nevertheless, there is no doubt that the theme park will stimulate the economy in neighboring areas."

(A) [1]

(B) [2]

(C) [3]

(D) [4]

GO ON TO THE NEXT PAGE

**Questions 176-180** refer to the following announcement and e-mail.

Dear valued customers,

It is with utmost pleasure that La Siesta, the one and only restaurant specializing in fusion Dominican cuisine in downtown Toronto, has recently welcomed Mr. Manuel Aritza as our new executive chef.

Mr. Manuel Aritza graduated from the Santo Domingo Culinary School in 1988 and furthered his study of cookery at the Finca Buen Vino School in Spain. His career began at a small diner back in his hometown Santo Domingo, where he enhanced his original and unique recipes which became so popular that the city designated him as its official chef. He immigrated to Canada just a month ago and has brought with him the zesty and exotic taste of Dominican dishes.

To commemorate our new captain, La Siesta is offering 10% discounts on all dishes except for the specials. We are also selling at a remarkably low price the wine so enthusiastically praised by Chef Aritza at just $10.99! Customers can also enter a congratulatory raffle whose winner will receive a $20 discount coupon and Chef Aritza's personal dining service.

To find out more about some of our new menu developed by Chef Aritza, please visit www.ollasiesta. com or contact the following people.

Customer Service                          Marketing Manager
Kelly Kalenzky <kelly_kal@ollasiesta.com>   Brandon Howe <bh7809@ollasiesta.com>

Sincerely,
La Siesta

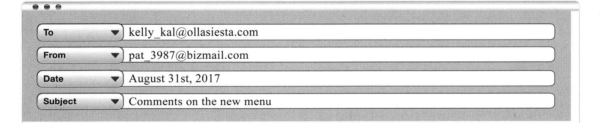

To        ▼  kelly_kal@ollasiesta.com
From      ▼  pat_3987@bizmail.com
Date      ▼  August 31st, 2017
Subject   ▼  Comments on the new menu

Hello,

I have recently dined at your fine restaurant which offers a unique cuisine at the heart of Toronto. Although I enjoyed our dinner, I cannot help but offer some comments that hopefully translate into positive improvement of the restaurant.

I was a little bit shaken by how hot and spicy the new menu presented by Chef Aritza was. La Siesta was, for me, a casual yet classy restaurant that offered somewhat modified and light dishes for everyone to enjoy. But most of the dishes we tried were so spicy that we ate only half of them while drinking through endless glasses of water. I assume that Chef Aritza's long experience in his home country is hard to get rid of but La Siesta needs to make small modifications to reduce its level of spiciness.

My husband and I very much enjoy dining at your restaurant and hope to continue our visits for years to come. Although I appreciate the new chef's enthusiasm, I hope that you take my comments into consideration.

Thank you.

**176** What is the purpose of the announcement?

(A) To introduce popular restaurants in Toronto

(B) To offer tips on cooking Dominican home recipes

(C) To tell of special events celebrating a new chef

(D) To advertise the opening of a new restaurant

**177** What does La Siesta specialize in?

(A) Dominican dishes

(B) Spanish dishes and wine

(C) Authentic Dominican cuisine

(D) Organic dishes

**178** To whom is the e-mail directed?

(A) A gourmet in Toronto

(B) A worker at La Siesta

(C) A business consultant

(D) A food critic

**179** Which of the following is NOT part of the commemorative events?

(A) Wine at a low price

(B) Raffle

(C) Discounts on some dishes

(D) Free dessert

**180** The word "modifications" in paragraph 2, line 6 of the e-mail is closest in meaning to

(A) adjustments

(B) eliminations

(C) blending

(D) sacrifices

GO ON TO THE NEXT PAGE

## Tesch Home Appliances

**40% reduction on some appliances! Only for Christmas week!**

**Ultra High Capacity Refrigerator — 40% OFF**
**Electric Range with Oven — 40% OFF**
**Stainless Steel Microwave — 40% OFF**
**65" Smart TV — 40% OFF**
**And discounts on more products**

For a limited time, we offer special prices for all customers. Get 40% off on our high quality home appliances. Our lowest prices are guaranteed! This incredible sale will begin on December 21 and end on December 27. Located next to Music Tango Store at the Conroe Shopping Center in Dallas, we are open every day from 8 A.M. to 9 P.M.

Nobody beats our service! We offer:
• Next-day free delivery on most orders* within the Dallas-Fort Worth Area
• Round the clock Monday-Saturday order placement and customer assistance
• A 60-day money back guarantee on all returned items
• In areas where we offer free delivery, we can also assist you with the installation of your appliances.
• Comprehensive in-store service and warranty**

*Subject to warehouse product availability.
**Additional fee applies.

---

To: d.perez@teschappliance.com
From: hansen8678@luxuraconstr.com
Date: December 22 17:05

Dear Mr. Perez,

I'm sending this e-mail on behalf of a Luxura Construction company. Our current apartment construction with 100 units is almost complete. Each unit will be equipped with basic appliances (refrigerator, washer, dryer and microwave). Your store comes highly recommended by some of my colleagues, and your current sale would certainly save me a great deal of money.

While I am definitely interested in purchasing all the necessary appliances from you, I must inform you that under our present construction schedule, we will be ready for appliance installation no earlier than January 5th. Given the size of my prospective order I would like to ask you to extend your discounted prices until that date. Please let me know if this would be possible.

I look forward to hearing from you!

ps: Our workers will install appliances so your installation service won't be needed.

Sincerely,
Eleanor Hansen
Luxura Construction

**181** What service does Tesch Home Appliances offer?

(A) Seven-days-a-week customer service
(B) Free product service and warranty
(C) Lowest prices in the Dallas-Fort Worth area
(D) Free delivery on every order

**182** According to the advertisement, why might an item not be delivered the next day?

(A) It should be delivered within the Dallas-Fort Worth Area.
(B) It was ordered on Saturday.
(C) It needs to be shipped overseas.
(D) It is out of stock at the warehouse.

**183** What will happen after Christmas week?

(A) All the orders will be delivered.
(B) The discount will be over.
(C) The construction will begin.
(D) The meeting will take place.

**184** Why is Ms. Hansen writing to Mr. Perez?

(A) To ask for special consideration
(B) To complain about delay in delivery
(C) To request technical assistance
(D) To cancel her order for some appliances

**185** What is suggested about the Luxura Construction company?

(A) It is in financial difficulties.
(B) Its headquarters is in Dallas.
(C) Its construction schedule has been changed.
(D) Its new apartment is located within the Dallas-Fort Worth area.

GO ON TO THE NEXT PAGE

The "wearables" industry is constantly filling the gap between technology and what we wear. Smart electronic devices like activity trackers or smart watches that can be worn on our body started as accessories, but are now blossoming into devices that are designed to monitor our health and support our lives in the form of the fabric of clothes or even a patch on our skin.

**Smart Watches**

With built-in GPS technology, smart watches provide tracking information like our movement and steps, and keep us posted on the calories we burn.

**Tech Fabric**

Tech fabric or fabric technology monitors not only biometric data on our body but also weather and ultraviolet ratings. Smart suits are expected to allow us to unlock our smart phones and replace our business cards digitally.

**VR Glasses**

Smart glasses are worn like a normal pair of glasses, but bio-sense technology embedded inside detects changes in our eyes for a safety purpose: the glasses warn drivers nodding off behind the wheel.

**Smart Patches**

Smart patches are designed to initiate calming exercises when heart and breathing rates show elevated levels of stress. When stress responses are sensed, they begin vibrating on our body to guide our breath to the restorative rhythm of our heart.

---

http://www.sttech.com/product

# 🎇 ST TECH

*Technology that sees imagination through your eyes*

| Home | Product | Archives | Review | Contacts |

**YL-100S Model**

◇ A variety of functions in one versatile frame! For outdoor activities, a series of waterproof models will start being released in April.

◇ The ST Tech sensor measures the movements of your eyes in a physiological fashion.

◇ Accelerometer system records the acceleration of your vibrating body.

◇ Gyroscope technology is applied to provide a reference direction in navigation systems that help find your position and plan the following routes.

◇ From the minute you wake up to the minute you go to bed, our state-of-the-art eyewear will see the world with you like your lifelong companion.

http://www.sttech.com/review

# ST TECH

*Technology that sees imagination through your eyes*

| Home | Product | Archives | Review | Contacts |

Name: Austin Gould
Model: YL-100S
Serial Number: GL205483A
Date of Purchase: January 10

Comments:

I bought YL-100S and found myself very satisfied with it. I have to drive to and from work every day and sometimes when I work overtime, I simply get exhausted. The other day I was up to my ears in work. While driving back home after work, I was so sleepy that my eyes were falling shut, but then my drive buddy alerted me, so I was able to avoid a car accident. Thanks to it, I can drive more comfortably and safely.

**186** For whom is the information most likely intended?

(A) Construction workers
(B) Fashion designers
(C) Tech-savvy consumers
(D) Professional athletes

**187** According to the information, who is most likely interested in Smart Patches?

(A) People who always forget their umbrella
(B) People who wish to know fashion trends
(C) People who easily get stressed out
(D) People who enjoy swimming every day

**188** In the online review, the word "exhausted" in paragraph 1, line 2 is closest in meaning to

(A) delighted
(B) forgetful
(C) very tired
(D) extremely sad

**189** What category does the product Mr. Gould purchased fall into?

(A) Smart watches
(B) Tech fabric
(C) VR glasses
(D) Smart patches

**190** What feature of YL-100S helped Mr. Gould to avoid a car accident?

(A) Versatile frame
(B) ST Tech sensor
(C) Accelerometer system
(D) Gyroscope technology

GO ON TO THE NEXT PAGE

# NEXOVA OFFICE FURNITURE & FITTINGS

*SHOP AT ANY NEXOVA STORE NATIONWIDE!*

## 30%OFF

ONE REGULAR
ITEM PRICED UNDER $400!
NOT VALID
FOR SHOPPING
ONLINE!

Coupon must be presented at the time of purchase. Offer not valid on custom clearance items. May not be combined with other coupons or associate discount. One coupon per item purchased. No reproductions. Merchandise total does not include shipping, handling, and taxes. Valid in US stores only until November 30.

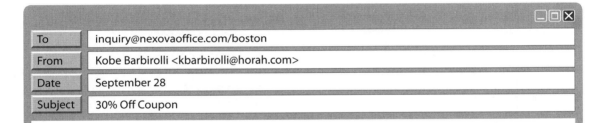

| To | inquiry@nexovaoffice.com/boston |
| --- | --- |
| From | Kobe Barbirolli <kbarbirolli@horah.com> |
| Date | September 28 |
| Subject | 30% Off Coupon |

Dear Sir or Madam,

I obtained a 30% off coupon issued by one of the Nexova stores in Los Angeles, but I would like to use it in your store, as our company has moved here to Boston.

The coupon says "ONE REGULAR ITEM PRICED UNDER $400," but I do not know what items you have available and their prices. I am interested in purchasing an office machine with which I can print papers out. As long as it serves the function, nothing else matters much at work. Would you please send me the price list of the products you have?

Kobe Barbirolli

# NEXOVA OFFICE FURNITURE & FITTINGS

*We sell only the highest quality products that fit your office needs.*

**Price List - valid until December 15**

- File Cabinet .................................................................$200.00
- Table...........................................................................$300.00
- Computer....................................................................$1,100.00
- Air Conditioner...........................................................$700.00
- Multi-Function Printer.................................................$300.00
- Telephone....................................................................$150.00
- Photocopy Machine.....................................................$5,500.00

**191** What is true about the 30% off coupon?

(A) It is valid on custom clearance items.
(B) It can be combined with other coupons.
(C) It excludes shipping charges.
(D) It can be used until the end of the year.

**192** What type of business is Mr. Barbirolli most likely in?

(A) Food service
(B) Transportation
(C) Publishing
(D) Aerospace

**193** In the e-mail, the word "matters" in paragraph 2, line 4 is closest in meaning to

(A) vanishes
(B) decreases
(C) is important
(D) is reimbursed

**194** What is suggested about Nexova Office Furniture & Fittings?

(A) It specializes in selling home furniture.
(B) It has a branch in Boston.
(C) It issues coupons valid worldwide.
(D) It was founded recently.

**195** What item will Mr. Barbirolli most likely purchase?

(A) File Cabinet
(B) Computer
(C) Multi-Function Printer
(D) Photocopy Machine

**GO ON TO THE NEXT PAGE**

# 🍽 Sawasdee Restaurant

### *AUTHENTIC THAI RESTAURANT*

We feature only the freshest taste in Thai food combined with a most relaxing atmosphere. Our experienced Thai native head chef will satisfy the taste buds of the most sophisticated gourmets!

> **Take-out Menu Available!**

🍽 **Lunch**   Monday – Friday 11:00 A.M. to 2:00 P.M.

🍽 **Dinner**   Tuesday – Saturday 5:00 P.M. to 10:00 P.M.
    Sunday & Monday 5:00 P.M. to 9:00 P.M.

Chili Sauce Chicken, Fried Fish Cakes, Peanut Sauce Chicken Wings, Dry Mushroom Curry, etc. You name it, we have it all!

1900 Berno Road
Ponewood, Stoberne Province
6426-3621
Just across Centralia Ave.

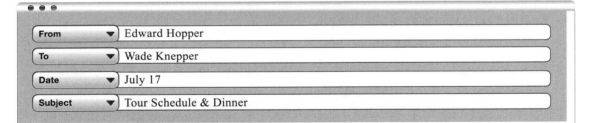

| From | ▼ | Edward Hopper |
|------|---|---------------|
| To | ▼ | Wade Knepper |
| Date | ▼ | July 17 |
| Subject | ▼ | Tour Schedule & Dinner |

Hello, Mr. Knepper.

As we talked on the phone, I will tell my boss, Mr. Robert Stone, that you are coming to take a tour of our factory on July 20. The tour is expected to start at 8 A.M. and we have lunch break at 12:00 P.M. After a one-hour break, the tour continues until it wraps up at around 6 P.M.

I heard that you love Thai foods. I know of a good restaurant in Stoberne Province, only 5 miles away from the factory. I am a regular customer there and have known their Head Chef, Mr. Chanchai, for a long time, but I will order the same dish as you.

Best regards,
Edward Hopper

# 🍴 Sawasdee Restaurant

Please take a few minutes to complete this form. Your feedback will help us learn what we are doing right and what we need more work on!

- How many in your party? __2__     Date: __July 20__
  ☐ Take out     ☐ Lunch     ☑ Dinner

- Your Age: ☐ Under 18     ☐ 19-35     ☑ 36 – 60     ☐ 60+          ☑ Male  ☐ Female

- The name of your server: __Jay Jones__

- What did you order? __Chicken Wings With Peanut Sauce & Thai Noodle Rolls__

| | | | | |
|---|---|---|---|---|
| - Quality of Food: | ☑ Excellent | ☐ Good | ☐ Fair | ☐ Poor |
| - Portion Size: | ☐ Excellent | ☐ Good | ☐ Fair | ☑ Poor |
| - Ease of Ordering: | ☐ Excellent | ☑ Good | ☐ Fair | ☐ Poor |
| - Service: | ☑ Excellent | ☐ Good | ☐ Fair | ☐ Poor |
| - Cleanliness: | ☑ Excellent | ☐ Good | ☐ Fair | ☐ Poor |
| - Overall Value: | ☐ Excellent | ☑ Good | ☐ Fair | ☐ Poor |

- Comment: _I came with a business partner, Edward, who recommended this place. After a tour that took all day, I was so hungry. The serving was a little small, although I have to admit that the food was really delicious. I think you should work on that._

- How did you learn about us?
  ☐ Newspaper     ☐ TV     ☐ Radio     ☑ Friend     ☐ Other: _____

**196** What is true about Sawasdee Restaurant?

(A) It specializes in Chinese cuisine.
(B) It is closed on weekends.
(C) It provides take-out service.
(D) It has many branches.

**197** What is suggested about Mr. Chanchai?

(A) He took a tour of a factory.
(B) He was born in Thailand.
(C) He is Mr. Hopper's boss.
(D) He posted an advertisement.

**198** According to the comment form, what needs to be improved at Sawasdee Restaurant?

(A) Quality of Food
(B) Portion Size
(C) Ease of Ordering
(D) Cleanliness

**199** Who most likely completed the comment form?

(A) Mr. Hopper
(B) Mr. Knepper
(C) Mr. Stone
(D) Mr. Jones

**200** What did Mr. Hopper most likely eat at Sawasdee Restaurant?

(A) Chili Sauce Chicken
(B) Fried Fish Cakes
(C) Peanut Sauce Chicken Wings
(D) Dry Mushroom Curry

**Stop!** This is the end of the test. If you finish before time is called, you may go back to Parts 5, 6, and 7 and check your work.

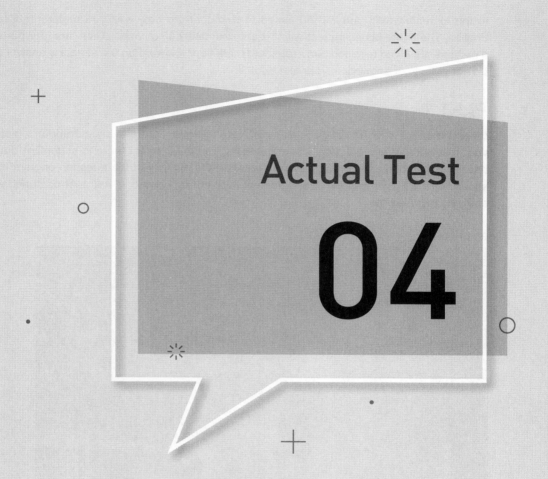

Actual Test

# 04

| 시작 시간 | : |
|---|---|
| 종료 시간 | : |

# LISTENING TEST

In the Listening test, you will be asked to demonstrate how well you understand spoken English. The entire Listening test will last approximately 45 minutes. There are four parts, and directions are given for each part. You must mark your answers on the separate answer sheet. Do not write your answers in your test book.

# PART 1

**Directions:** For each question in this part, you will hear four statements about a picture in your test book. When you hear the statements, you must select the one statement that best describes what you see in the picture. Then find the number of the question on your answer sheet and mark your answer. The statements will not be printed in your test book and will be spoken only one time.

**Example**

**Sample Answer**
Ⓐ ● Ⓒ Ⓓ

Statement (B), "The man is using a microphone," is the best description of the picture, so you should select answer (B) and mark it on your answer sheet.

**1**

**2**

**GO ON TO THE NEXT PAGE** ➡

3

4

**5**

**6**

GO ON TO THE NEXT PAGE

# PART 2

**Directions:** You will hear a question or statement and three responses spoken in English. They will not be printed in your test book and will be spoken only one time. Select the best response to the question or statement and mark the letter (A), (B), or (C) on your answer sheet.

**7** Mark your answer on your answer sheet.

**8** Mark your answer on your answer sheet.

**9** Mark your answer on your answer sheet.

**10** Mark your answer on your answer sheet.

**11** Mark your answer on your answer sheet.

**12** Mark your answer on your answer sheet.

**13** Mark your answer on your answer sheet.

**14** Mark your answer on your answer sheet.

**15** Mark your answer on your answer sheet.

**16** Mark your answer on your answer sheet.

**17** Mark your answer on your answer sheet.

**18** Mark your answer on your answer sheet.

**19** Mark your answer on your answer sheet.

**20** Mark your answer on your answer sheet.

**21** Mark your answer on your answer sheet.

**22** Mark your answer on your answer sheet.

**23** Mark your answer on your answer sheet.

**24** Mark your answer on your answer sheet.

**25** Mark your answer on your answer sheet.

**26** Mark your answer on your answer sheet.

**27** Mark your answer on your answer sheet.

**28** Mark your answer on your answer sheet.

**29** Mark your answer on your answer sheet.

**30** Mark your answer on your answer sheet.

**31** Mark your answer on your answer sheet.

# PART 3

**Directions:** You will hear some conversations between two or more people. You will be asked to answer three questions about what the speakers say in each conversation. Select the best response to each question and mark the letter (A), (B), (C), or (D) on your answer sheet. The conversations will not be printed in your test book and will be spoken only one time.

**32** Why is the woman concerned?

(A) She is out of town.
(B) She has something to do first.
(C) She is not ready for her interview.
(D) She has to pick up something from school.

**33** What does the woman ask the man to do?

(A) Pick up a friend
(B) Give her a ride
(C) Attend an interview
(D) Go to a school

**34** What will the man probably do next?

(A) Head to the subway station
(B) Deliver something
(C) Go to an interview
(D) Run to the school

**35** What are the speakers talking about?

(A) A popular pastime
(B) A new assignment
(C) An upcoming competition
(D) A nearby restaurant

**36** What is mentioned about a bakery?

(A) It has recently opened.
(B) It offers many kinds of bread.
(C) It has won a competition.
(D) It is conveniently located.

**37** What is Christine asked to do?

(A) Set up an interview
(B) Write an article
(C) Taste some food
(D) Take photographs

**38** What are the speakers mainly discussing?

(A) New marketing strategies
(B) A weekly meeting
(C) An employee schedule
(D) The office environment

**39** What type of company do the speakers work for?

(A) An interior design firm
(B) An architecture company
(C) A home appliances store
(D) An advertising agency

**40** What does the woman offer to do for the man?

(A) Show him to a room
(B) Make observations for him
(C) Draw a layout
(D) Help him with a project

**41** Why is the woman meeting the man?

(A) To open a savings account
(B) To invest in a mutual fund
(C) To discuss a job opportunity
(D) To seek financial support

**42** What is the woman asked to bring?

(A) A piece of identification
(B) A reference letter
(C) A copy of a contract
(D) An application form

**43** What does the woman say she will do?

(A) Duplicate an agreement
(B) Request documentation
(C) Pay for a purchase
(D) Review some information

GO ON TO THE NEXT PAGE

44 What are the speakers discussing?

(A) How to meet a deadline
(B) How to get some rest
(C) The man's vacation plan
(D) The woman's business itinerary

45 How long will the woman stay in Madrid?

(A) For two days
(B) For three days
(C) For nine days
(D) For two weeks

46 What does the man suggest?

(A) Leaving as soon as possible
(B) Working on the conference materials
(C) Getting some relaxation
(D) Calling off the business trip

47 What event are the speakers discussing?

(A) An award ceremony
(B) A retirement party
(C) A welcome reception
(D) A grand opening

48 What does the woman mean when she says, "The garden looks gorgeous though"?

(A) She would like more preparation time.
(B) She enjoys outdoor activities.
(C) She wants to have the event outdoors.
(D) She is talented at art and design.

49 What does the man suggest?

(A) Moving to a different location for another party
(B) Offering a variety of entertainment
(C) Hiring additional workers to do the gardening
(D) Installing some equipment outside

50 What is the man's problem?

(A) He is busy with the marketing team's work.
(B) No copy machine is available.
(C) He has misplaced some documents.
(D) A lunch break is almost over.

51 What does the woman imply when she says, "Lunch time will be over in about half an hour"?

(A) The man has to fix the copy machine.
(B) The man doesn't have much time left.
(C) The meeting will end in about half an hour.
(D) The man doesn't have time to attend the meeting.

52 What does the woman recommend to the man?

(A) Go to a print shop
(B) Bring some supplies
(C) Find out the hours of operation
(D) Call the third-floor staff

53 Where are the speakers?

(A) At an outdoor concert
(B) In a train station
(C) In an airport
(D) At a box office

54 What does the woman ask about?

(A) Available snacks
(B) Seat selection
(C) Ticket prices
(D) The ending time of the movie

55 What does the man suggest the woman do?

(A) Exchange tickets before the show
(B) Purchase tickets in advance
(C) Take the seats near the back
(D) Return at a later time

**56** What are the speakers mainly discussing?

(A) A progress report
(B) An employee evaluation
(C) A business trip
(D) An annual budget

**57** Why does the woman say, "Ms. Barry has been away on business"?

(A) To give the man permission
(B) To report a change in schedule
(C) To verify some information
(D) To offer a possible reason

**58** What does the woman suggest the man do?

(A) Talk to his supervisor
(B) Go on a business trip
(C) Train his employees
(D) Evaluate some employees' performance

**59** What is the man about to do?

(A) Analyze company earnings
(B) Combine two companies
(C) Give a presentation
(D) Interview potential employees

**60** Who will the man meet with?

(A) Company leaders
(B) Book publishers
(C) Rival executives
(D) Industry analysts

**61** What caused an increase in profits?

(A) Aggressive advertising
(B) Rearranging the company
(C) A diversified product line
(D) Workshops for employees

**62** Why is the man making a call?

(A) He wants decorations.
(B) He needs tickets to the concert.
(C) He needs a space for a show.
(D) He wants seating arrangements.

**63** What does the man want to know?

(A) The time of the show
(B) The size of the center
(C) The cost of the arrangements
(D) The number of samples

**64** What does the woman request?

(A) An arrangement over the price
(B) The man's e-mail address
(C) A map of the facility
(D) The types of ornaments

GO ON TO THE NEXT PAGE

| Choose the speed that suits your needs | | | |
|---|---|---|---|
| 15 Megabytes | 25 Megabytes | 50 Megabytes | 100 Megabytes |
| $70 | $80 | $100 | $150 |

**65** What feature of the plan is the woman looking for?

(A) Free online games
(B) Cancellation without a penalty
(C) Internet access on the move
(D) Multiple connection capability

**66** What does the man say about the plans?

(A) Prices vary according to the speed.
(B) His store offers the largest selection.
(C) No plan meets the woman's needs.
(D) Information can be viewed online.

**67** Look at the graphic. How much has the woman agreed to pay?

(A) $70
(B) $80
(C) $100
(D) $150

| Extension Number | |
|---|---|
| Information Desk | 120 |
| Printing Station | 130 |
| Lost and Found | 140 |
| Facilities | 150 |

**68** Where most likely is the conversation taking place?

(A) At an information desk
(B) At a printing shop
(C) In a rest room
(D) In a hotel lobby

**69** What is the man's problem?

(A) He cannot use a library card.
(B) He has misplaced something.
(C) He is lost at the library.
(D) He did not bring an ID card.

**70** Look at the graphic. Which extension number will the woman dial?

(A) 120
(B) 130
(C) 140
(D) 150

# PART 4

**Directions:** You will hear some talks given by a single speaker. You will be asked to answer three questions about what the speaker says in each talk. Select the best response to each question and mark the letter (A), (B), (C), or (D) on your answer sheet. The talks will not be printed in your test book and will be spoken only one time.

**71** What is this message about?

(A) Informing an applicant of a decision

(B) Encouraging an applicant to finish his form

(C) Reminding an applicant about the application deadline

(D) Advertising a company's products

**72** In what department did Mr. Hendricks apply?

(A) Web Design

(B) General Affairs

(C) Advertising

(D) Human resources

**73** How can Mr. Hendricks find the information needed?

(A) By requesting an interview

(B) By visiting the company

(C) By calling the relevant department

(D) By sending an e-mail to the human resources department

**74** What type of business is being discussed?

(A) A cocktail bar

(B) A coffee shop

(C) An art gallery

(D) A restaurant

**75** What will some customers receive this evening?

(A) Traditional desserts

(B) Free recipe books

(C) Complimentary drinks

(D) Discount coupons

**76** Why does the speaker say, "As a standalone restaurant inside the yacht club"?

(A) To emphasize a key characteristic

(B) To warn listeners of danger

(C) To propose a new dinner option

(D) To offer directions to a business

**77** Why is the sale being held?

(A) The mall is going out of business.

(B) Stores are unloading last season's products.

(C) The economy is on the rise.

(D) It is to celebrate the start of spring.

**78** When does the March sale begin?

(A) On the 20th

(B) On the 21st

(C) On the 23rd

(D) On the 26th

**79** Where can people get information about the sale?

(A) In a clothing store

(B) At the information booth

(C) At the center of the mall

(D) On a notice board

**80** Where most likely is the speaker?

(A) At a convention center

(B) At a hotel restaurant

(C) At an auditorium

(D) At a school's cafeteria

**81** What is mentioned about Michael Clare?

(A) He runs a small business.

(B) He has organized an awards ceremony.

(C) He was elected the best chef in the state.

(D) He has improved school lunch programs.

**82** What will happen after dinner?

(A) Ms. Wallace will make a speech.

(B) An election will take place.

(C) Some of the employees will play music.

(D) The principal will give his name and address.

GO ON TO THE NEXT PAGE

**83** What is being announced?

(A) A street shutting down
(B) A weather disaster
(C) A construction cleaning
(D) A major malfunction of the vehicle

**84** What has caused the problem?

(A) An overflow of water tank
(B) Road repairs
(C) A burst sewage pipe
(D) A detour route

**85** Who will be most affected by the incident?

(A) News reporters
(B) Local residents
(C) Construction workers
(D) City officials

---

**86** What is the topic of the meeting?

(A) Reducing expenses
(B) Promoting a new vehicle
(C) Reorganizing a company
(D) Implementing a new policy

**87** What does the speaker imply when he says, "which is unfortunately still unclear"?

(A) He hopes to get additional funding.
(B) He does not know when he will retire.
(C) He thinks a new product will not sell well.
(D) He is unsure when a product will be released.

**88** What does the speaker say he will do?

(A) Apply for a government grant
(B) Hold a press conference
(C) Meet with employees individually
(D) Consider a corporate merger

**89** What is the main purpose of the talk?

(A) To request feedback on revised regulations
(B) To describe plans for a pay raise
(C) To explain new work shifts
(D) To announce a new pay schedule

**90** When will the change take effect?

(A) May 1st
(B) May 30th
(C) June 1st
(D) June 25th

**91** How can listeners get more information?

(A) By speaking to their manager
(B) By reading a memo
(C) By visiting a website
(D) By checking their bank statements

---

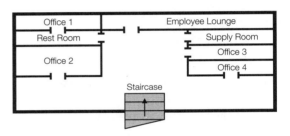

**92** What is the purpose of the message?

(A) To discuss a proposal
(B) To cancel an appointment
(C) To provide a reminder
(D) To request a floor plan

**93** What is the listener asked to do?

(A) Move to another building
(B) Leave the office early
(C) Meet the deadline
(D) Deliver the document

**94** Look at the graphic. Which office belongs to the speaker?

(A) Office 1
(B) Office 2
(C) Office 3
(D) Office 4

| Jelly Doughnut Shop | |
| --- | --- |
| Free Gift | Location |
| Sport Bottle | Bowles |
| Eco Bag | Rivers Mall |
| Key Holder | Lindbergh |
| Coffee Mug | Florissant |

**95** What is Jelly Doughnut Shop celebrating?

(A) A grand opening
(B) An anniversary
(C) A profitable year
(D) A local festival

**96** Look at the graphic. At which doughnut shop is the announcement being made?

(A) Bowles
(B) Rivers Mall
(C) Lindbergh
(D) Florissant

**97** How can listeners learn more about the promotion?

(A) By writing a customer review
(B) By asking an acquaintance
(C) By visiting a nearby store
(D) By checking an advertisement

| Monday Schedule | |
| --- | --- |
| 9:00 | Court hearing |
| 10:00 | |
| 11:00 | Marketing meeting |
| 12:00 | Lunch |
| 13:00 | |
| 14:00 | Strategy meeting |
| 15:00 | |
| 16:00 | Client consultation |

**98** Where most likely does the speaker work?

(A) At an employment agency
(B) At an accounting firm
(C) At a financial institute
(D) At a law firm

**99** Why does the speaker want to meet the listener?

(A) To handle a client complaint
(B) To discuss a hiring process
(C) To explain an increase in rent
(D) To get a project budget approved

**100** Look at the graphic. What time does the speaker want to meet with the listener?

(A) At 9:00 A.M.
(B) At 10:00 A.M.
(C) At 1:00 P.M.
(D) At 3:00 P.M.

This is the end of the Listening test. Turn to Part 5 in your test book.

GO ON TO THE NEXT PAGE

# READING TEST

In the Reading test, you will read a variety of texts and answer several different types of reading comprehension questions. The entire Reading test will last 75 minutes. There are three parts, and directions are given for each part. You are encouraged to answer as many questions as possible within the time allowed.

You must mark your answers on the separate answer sheet. Do not write your answers in your test book.

# PART 5

**Directions:** A word or phrase is missing in each of the sentences below. Four answer choices are given below each sentence. Select the best answer to complete the sentence. Then mark the letter (A), (B), (C), or (D) on your answer sheet.

101 Ms. Randall explained that she was not trained as a commercial refrigeration -------, though she has experience with industrial ovens.

(A) technicality
(B) technical
(C) technology
(D) technician

102 Any ------- transactions will be forwarded to the monitoring committee which supervises everything related to the finance industry.

(A) improper
(B) anxious
(C) extinct
(D) reserved

103 Mr. Castelli, the senior director, will ------- leadership to improve the abilities of the managers at the company.

(A) provide
(B) grant
(C) serve
(D) remain

104 Mr. Carmen spent the whole weekend reviewing the changes ------- for next year's budget.

(A) to propose
(B) proposes
(C) propose
(D) proposed

105 The change of address form for the driver's license and the postal service must be filled out ------- and mailed to different agencies.

(A) diversely
(B) jointly
(C) partially
(D) separately

106 Dr. Bella is a well-known psychologist with ------- laboratory experience on the subject of adolescent boy's behavior.

(A) extension
(B) extend
(C) extending
(D) extensive

107 Much of the exterior of the house is original, but a renovation company ------- the terrace two weeks ago.

(A) hired
(B) entered
(C) installed
(D) called

108 The researchers came up with a breakthrough that led them closer to making electronic displays ------- out of plastic.

(A) totaling
(B) totaled
(C) totally
(D) total

**109** One reason for the success of our company is that Eric likes to personally test every product -------.

(A) himself
(B) him
(C) his
(D) he

**110** Due to the plentiful rainfall the farmers had this year, they are anticipating that the harvest season will continue ------- at least another week.

(A) before
(B) for
(C) which
(D) than

**111** The CEO of Bandar Construction was invited to ------- a regional economic development symposium.

(A) arrive
(B) contain
(C) attend
(D) occur

**112** Rob Largo, the CEO of Tallarex, started his career by ------- in real estate.

(A) invests
(B) invested
(C) investing
(D) invest

**113** M & G company's special bonus will be distributed evenly ------- its departments.

(A) during
(B) after
(C) among
(D) toward

**114** The company's union and management were engaged in negotiations over the pay and ------- to be received in the following year.

(A) forces
(B) controls
(C) benefits
(D) interests

**115** You have to find somewhere to stay by Aug 12, ------- which time you will begin your work on our communications network.

(A) with
(B) on
(C) at
(D) across

**116** FTR Express has assured its clients that it ------- its delivery schedule despite the bad weather.

(A) meet
(B) meeting
(C) to meet
(D) will meet

**117** Responsible for ensuring a good relationship with our customers and a ------- working environment, Rooney is our Resident Manager.

(A) tender
(B) pleasant
(C) fragile
(D) confident

**118** The people of the region were surprisingly positive and calm ------- the recent tsunami.

(A) however
(B) prior to
(C) yet
(D) in spite of

**119** Right before he was ------- to work, Bailey's wife reminded him to take his phone with him.

(A) nearly
(B) about
(C) off
(D) close

**120** The regularly scheduled meeting will be ------- until next month in the event that the CEO holds the press conference tomorrow.

(A) expected
(B) postponed
(C) continued
(D) projected

**GO ON TO THE NEXT PAGE**

**121** The items will be sent through express mail if you choose goods ------- one of our various designers.

(A) from
(B) out of
(C) behind
(D) over

**122** We hope to have our new restaurant near the university open ------- Mar 31st so we can have the grand opening celebration right when students start the spring semester.

(A) among
(B) of
(C) by
(D) up

**123** ------- it went public ten years ago, Azien has been one of the hottest stocks on the market.

(A) Than
(B) How
(C) Since
(D) If

**124** The new head of Kabel sought to invigorate the flagging company ------- restructuring and streamlining its organization.

(A) through
(B) except
(C) above
(D) behind

**125** Walid has had to hire additional engineers and customer representatives with the ------- demand for its products.

(A) resolved
(B) increased
(C) involved
(D) approached

**126** New Smart kitchen counters should ------- be cleaned with a non-caustic, non-abrasive cleaner, which you can purchase through the website.

(A) nearly
(B) exactly
(C) only
(D) doubly

**127** The coffee chain store will be located in the commercial area ------- the newly built highway.

(A) along
(B) without
(C) among
(D) into

**128** The company's president would like all employees to cease their current projects, and ------- together on the release of our feature product.

(A) to work
(B) worked
(C) working
(D) works

**129** Our restaurant will close an hour earlier so as to reduce costs ------- students are leaving for their winter vacation.

(A) now that
(B) because of
(C) whatever
(D) however

**130** Keeping in regular touch with customers who have not used our services for a while is a highly recommended -------.

(A) practice
(B) resource
(C) plot
(D) reference

# PART 6

**Directions:** Read the texts that follow. A word, phrase, or sentence is missing in parts of each text. Four answer choices for each question are given below the text. Select the best answer to complete the text. Then mark the letter (A), (B), (C), or (D) on your answer sheet.

**Questions 131-134** refer to the following advertisement.

Spring is the time for picnics! The Santa Fe Bicentennial Park has just opened after a lengthy construction period. In order to show the city's appreciation to its residents for their patience during the time of construction, it has decided to offer 20% discount on the admission tickets just for Santa Fe residents. In other words, all Santa Fe residents are ------- for the discount!
**131.**

There is no other requirement to get the discounted price. -------. Residents are advised that the
**132.**
city is expecting a large number of visitors during the first two months. We are expecting that the entrance to the park ------- up to 40 minutes as there are only six ticket booths.
**133.**

If you have any questions regarding the park or the discounted rate, please email us at www. santafeparks.gov. We will ------- to all inquiries as quickly as possible, but we ask that you be
**134.**
patient with your inquiries as we get more than two thousand e-mails a day.

---

**131** (A) preferable
(B) alternative
(C) eligible
(D) selective

**132** (A) Residents will automatically receive discounted tickets at the booth.
(B) Discounts will only be given to those who have made donations.
(C) Residents over the age of 20 are required to present their ID.
(D) There will be a special performance at the park every Saturday.

**133** (A) had taken
(B) may take
(C) took
(D) taking

**134** (A) reply
(B) announce
(C) notify
(D) answer

**Questions 135-138** refer to the following memo.

To: Jacob Jarrio
From: Martin Geronimo
Re: Moving the Design Department

As you were notified a week ago, the design department ------- to the newly constructed building
**135.**
next to the current one. The new space assigned features a large-screen TV and new computers.

The ------- is scheduled to take place on the 1st of June. Although a professional moving
**136.**
company will be transporting all the heavy furniture and equipment, the employees are expected
to take care of their personal belongings. All the small items must be cleaned out two days prior
to the moving.

Although the new room may be smaller than the original one, there are many advantages that
the design department can enjoy. -------, the new room is located right next to the advertising
**137.**
department so that the two departments can work together more efficiently. In addition, the new
room is equipped with a brand-new air conditioning system. -------.
**138.**

135 (A) will be moving
   (B) did move
   (C) will have moved
   (D) was moved

136 (A) transition
   (B) transformation
   (C) preparation
   (D) application

137 (A) Thus
   (B) For example
   (C) Although
   (D) Moreover

138 (A) We are deeply concerned that our
      workers may not appreciate the change.
   (B) This would provide our workers with a
      better working environment.
   (C) The advertising department is
      responsible for installing the air
      conditioning system.
   (D) The estimated cost for a new air
      conditioning system is $200.

Dear Mr. Kwon,

We are sorry to hear that the product you have recently purchased from us is malfunctioning. We hope that your ------- with this single item does not affect your thoughts on our company in any way. We want to assure you that we will take care of the issue as quickly as possible.
**139.**

All you need to do is to enclose your defective item along with the form provided in this letter and send it to our customer care team. You can either request for a refund ------- a replacement.
**140.**

Please note that our company is ------- to meeting our customers' expectations and providing them with the best service possible. -------.
**141.**
**142.**

If you have any further questions or requests, please feel free to call our customer care team at 1-825-288-2836.

139 (A) disadvantage
    (B) pleasure
    (C) trial
    (D) dissatisfaction

140 (A) to
    (B) as
    (C) or
    (D) of

141 (A) decided
    (B) dictated
    (C) dedicated
    (D) divided

142 (A) We sincerely apologize for the defective product.
    (B) Please note that no refund is allowed.
    (C) Thank you for purchasing our product.
    (D) Your continuous support is recognized.

GO ON TO THE NEXT PAGE

**Questions 143-146** refer to the following e-mail.

To: John Adams
From: Kate Kuczynski
Date: Dec 2
Subject: Tax Reimbursement

Dear Mr. Adams,

I am sending you this e-mail to let you know that there are minor problems with your tax reimbursement process. Because the government ------- have changed since last year, we have
143.
to make a few adjustments on the document.

I understand that you indicated your daughter's tuition as a personal expense because it is a family matter. From this year, however, personal expenses over $10,000 cannot be considered for reimbursement. ------- marking it a personal expense, I suggest that you indicate it as an
144.
educational expense.

Also, for you to receive your ------- tax return, I recommend you submit a statement of expenses
145.
made with your company's credit card. -------.
146.

Please write me back as soon as possible with the information that I requested.

Thank you.

Sincerely,

Kate Kuczynski

143 (A) policies
(B) politics
(C) properties
(D) prepositions

144 (A) Unless
(B) Despite
(C) Because
(D) Instead of

145 (A) filled
(B) final
(C) full
(D) fine

146 (A) The tax reimbursement process usually takes one to two weeks.
(B) We are not certain whether you can receive your tax return or not.
(C) All of the people working in your company are eligible for a credit card.
(D) Those expenses for business matters can also be considered for a tax return.

# PART 7

**Directions:** In this part you will read a selection of texts, such as magazine and newspaper articles, e-mails, and instant messages. Each text or set of texts is followed by several questions. Select the best answer for each question and mark the letter (A), (B), (C), or (D) on your answer sheet.

**Questions 147-148** refer to the following schedule.

## Free Movie Festival for March

After the films begin at 8:00 P.M., people will no longer be able to enter the theater. Please remember that all attendants must be in the room before starting. In order to get your 30 points, you will be required to stay until the movie ends, which will normally only be for 2 hours. The following films will be the ones that are available this month.

### March

| SUN | MON | TUE | WED | THU | FRI | SAT |
| --- | --- | --- | --- | --- | --- | --- |
|  |  |  |  |  | 1 | 2 |
| 3 | 4 | 5<br>Believe It Or Not | 6 | 7<br>Man of Golden Titanium | 8 | 9 |
| 10 | 11 | 12<br>Seven Knights | 13 | 14<br>World War 2 | 15 | 16 |
| 17 | 18 | 19<br>Our Land | 20 | 21<br>Memorial Day | 22 | 23 |
| 24 | 25 | 26<br>Forest House | 27 | 28<br>The Catcher in the Rye | 29 | 30 |
| 31 |  |  |  |  |  |  |

*No service on National Holidays

**147** When will the viewers receive their points?

(A) About 10:00
(B) Right after 9:00
(C) At 8:00 sharp
(D) Around 6:00

**148** On which day will the theater be closed?

(A) March 5th
(B) March 12th
(C) March 21st
(D) March 26th

GO ON TO THE NEXT PAGE

Questions 149-150 refer to the following text message chain.

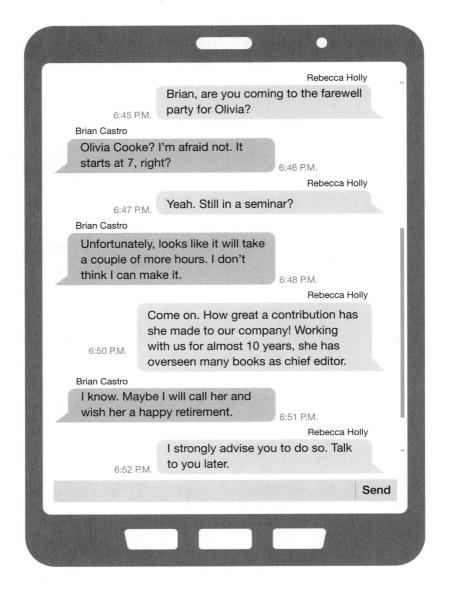

**Rebecca Holly**
6:45 P.M.
Brian, are you coming to the farewell party for Olivia?

**Brian Castro**
Olivia Cooke? I'm afraid not. It starts at 7, right?
6:46 P.M.

**Rebecca Holly**
6:47 P.M.
Yeah. Still in a seminar?

**Brian Castro**
Unfortunately, looks like it will take a couple of more hours. I don't think I can make it.
6:48 P.M.

**Rebecca Holly**
6:50 P.M.
Come on. How great a contribution has she made to our company! Working with us for almost 10 years, she has overseen many books as chief editor.

**Brian Castro**
I know. Maybe I will call her and wish her a happy retirement.
6:51 P.M.

**Rebecca Holly**
6:52 P.M.
I strongly advise you to do so. Talk to you later.

Send

**149** At 6:48 P.M., what does Mr. Castro mean when he writes, "I don't think I can make it"?

(A) He thinks that it is hard to throw a party for Ms. Cooke.

(B) He disagrees about whether Ms. Cooke has really made a contribution.

(C) He will not attend a seminar that lasts until 7 P.M.

(D) He does not think he will be able to join the party.

**150** For what type of company does Ms. Holly most likely work?

(A) A publisher

(B) A bank

(C) A grocery store

(D) A movie theater

## The World Traditional Clothing Museum

The World Traditional Clothing Museum, which has displayed over 300 clothes, is one of the most famous costume museums in the world. The museum is located in Seoul, Korea, and shows a particular focus on 16th and 17th centuries. The museum displays examples of many of the world's exceptional fashions, including Lord Peter's family collection of aristocratic garments. The Museum is open every day of the week except Monday. Tickets are $10 each for adults, $7 for seniors over 65 years old and $5 for each child.

151 What is the main attraction in the World Traditional Clothing Museum?

(A) Classic Jewelry
(B) Traditional Cosmetics
(C) Ethnic Attire
(D) Antique Furniture

152 How much would someone who is 82 years old have to pay?

(A) $5
(B) $7
(C) $10
(D) $11

## Seminar for Workers

According to employment experts, approximately 25% of the working population is involved with shift work one way or another. Studies show that if an individual is unable to manage shift work issues properly, he or she is more prone to suffering digestive problems, experiencing disruptive sleep patterns, and having higher accident rates.

This seminar will explain some basic tips and strategies to adapt both physically and socially to overcome the issues that arise from a shift work schedule. During the seminar, information on the nature of sleep and its stages, the role of biological clocks and circadian rhythms, improving health and safety, and reducing fatigue will be given.

**TUITION** $110.00

**SCHEDULE**
The following is an outline of the schedule, which could change and is dependent on the date of enrollment.

**LOCATION** Mirage Building

**DATE** February 17, 2017

**TIMES** 9:30 A.M. ~ 4:00 P.M.

For more information or to register for courses, please call our toll free number 1-871-758-6571. You can reach us by e-mail at personnel@creativepersonnel.com

**153** On February 17, 2017, what event will take place?

(A) A health examination
(B) A performance
(C) A meeting
(D) A lecture

**154** In the memo, what is mentioned as a side-effect of shift work?

(A) Not feeling the desire to exercise
(B) Higher frequency of changing jobs
(C) Becoming depressed
(D) Insomnia

**Questions 155-157** refer to the following e-mail.

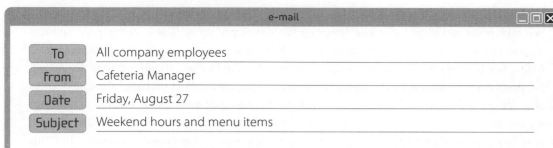

| | **Soups** | **Ice cream** | **Salad** | **Main Dishes** |
|---|---|---|---|---|
| | $3.99 | $3.99 | $4.99 | $5.99 |
| **Saturday** | *Corn | Strawberry | *House | Pizza |
| | Beef | Vanilla | Chicken | Lasagna |
| **Sunday** | *Vegetable | Chocolate | Cheese | *Veggie Sushi |
| | *Broccoli | Green Tea | *Fruit | Souvlaki |

**155** What is asked of the customers by the cafeteria manager?

(A) To quickly decide on the items they want
(B) To clean up after eating their meals
(C) To use the food court during the weekend
(D) To suggest menu items for the following week

**156** What will be available as a special combo deal on Sunday?

(A) Corn Soup and Vanilla ice cream
(B) Broccoli Soup and a Cheese Salad
(C) Green Tea ice cream and Veggie Sushi
(D) A Fruit Salad and Souvlaki

**157** Which food does NOT include lots of sodium?

(A) The House Salad
(B) The Green Tea Ice Cream
(C) The Chicken Salad
(D) The Lasagna

GO ON TO THE NEXT PAGE

**Questions 158-160** refer to the following information.

We take pride in the fact that our company has developed so well at a steady pace and has helped the national economy by providing jobs in many areas, especially in the technical fields. We have been the leading company among the trend of eco-friendly companies during the past two decades and have employed workers to not only collect garbage efficiently but to also operate high-tech incinerators in all areas to decrease pollution levels. For the sake of our society and the next generation, we have decided to invest in environment-related projects. Here is an overview of the structural changes that have been made in our organization since 1992 till now.

| Year | Work Force | Plant Sites | Annual Output ($mil) | Annual Output per Worker ($) |
|------|-----------|-------------|----------------------|------------------------------|
| 1992 | 72 | 3 | 1.4 | 9,747 |
| 1997 | 101 | 5 | 2.5 | 11,918 |
| 2002 | 143 | 6 | 2.7 | 13,334 |
| 2007 | 219 | 9 | 3.8 | 15,047 |
| 2012 | 278 | 11 | 4.5 | 16,719 |
| 2017 | 315 | 15 | 5.7 | 18,052 |

**158** How long has it been since the organization was established?

(A) 26 years
(B) 24 years
(C) 20 years
(D) 15 years

**159** What is mentioned in the passage and chart above?

(A) The size of the plants has remained the same due to economic issues.
(B) The number of employees has steadily risen.
(C) The company has been considerably reducing the number of employees.
(D) The yearly output has significantly decreased in 2002.

**160** What is true about the company?

(A) It will soon reach the limit of its growth potential.
(B) It will increase the size of its facilities.
(C) It will join with another company.
(D) It will invest more in environmental projects.

# MEMORANDUM

To: All Employees in Logistics Department
From: Zayn Jones
Date: August 9
Subject: Computerized System Inspection

A quick inspection of the computerized system in our department is scheduled for Tuesday, August 11. –[1]–. This month a number of technical problems have been reported regarding the Internet lagging at work, which is unusual because many of our employees have experienced Internet client error at the same time. –[2]–. We assume this somehow relates to the main server, the purpose of which is to share data and resources, and distribute work among multiple clients.

A message will pop up on your computer screen to instruct you to save all data you are working on before your computer is automatically disconnected. –[3]–. After the inspection, the main server will be restarted. –[4]–. Please be aware that there may be a single, brief loss of service before or after this happens. The maintenance is expected to take a couple of hours, and when it is completed, you may resume working.

**Test 04**

**161** What is stated as the cause of the technical problem?

(A) Negligent maintenance
(B) Main server error
(C) Internet provider's dishonesty
(D) Unexpected power outage

**162** What are employees advised to do?

(A) Conduct some maintenance on a server
(B) Sell some of the computers to clients
(C) Save necessary data before disconnection
(D) Distribute the work to avoid errors

**163** In which of the positions marked [1], [2], [3] and [4] does the following sentence best belong?

"Therefore, the chance of any individual computer causing this error is very low."

(A) [1]
(B) [2]
(C) [3]
(D) [4]

**GO ON TO THE NEXT PAGE**

# Vina Milk

July 13

Douglas Reece
B21 West Wickham
Bromley, London

Dear Mr. Reece,

We appreciate your efforts to contact us to ask about our products. It would be our pleasure to provide you with any type of milk whether it's skim, whole, homogenized, or butter milk. We have glass bottles (260ml, 500ml, 1000ml, 1800ml), cartons (200ml, 500ml, 1000ml, 1500ml), and plastic bottles (3000ml) as units of delivery to customers as well as bulk items for businesses. Not only can we supply sliced cheese and cream cheese in different types of packaging, but we also produce and export yogurt either plain or with organic fruit. A packet will be sent to you by express mail service, and it will contain a price list of our products as well as a catalog and an order form. Please fill out the form and send it back to us to receive our products. Feel free to ask us any questions that you may have and visit us on the web at www.vinamilk.com for more information. We hope to hear from you again.

Thomas Brett
Sales manager, Vina Milk

---

164 What was the purpose of this letter?

(A) To give basic product information to a possible client
(B) To confirm delivery on an order
(C) To notify the company about a package they received
(D) To ask about some figures

165 What is NOT an item Vina Milk provides based on the letter?

(A) Butter Milk
(B) Cheese Powder
(C) Homogenized Milk
(D) Yogurt

166 What can be inferred about Vina Milk?

(A) All products are imported from abroad.
(B) Over 10 different kinds of natural foods are sold in their stores.
(C) No chemical components are included in their yogurt.
(D) They usually deliver their products by mail.

167 How would an order be placed?

(A) By calling the sales manager of the company
(B) By sending in a survey after filling it out
(C) By filling out and returning the form that will be mailed
(D) By making arrangements personally with the manager

**Questions 168-171** refer to the following online chat discussion.

| | | |
|---|---|---|
| **Ethan Jeffrey** [9:21 A.M.] | | Hello, guys. Listen. As the market for accommodation in Old Brisbane has grown at an annual rate of 20 percent for the past 5 years, we should implement an aggressive marketing strategy. |
| **Anna Durbin** [9:22 A.M.] | | Are you referring to the opening of our new chain there? |
| **Ethan Jeffrey** [9:23 A.M.] | | Yes, I am. Any idea? |
| **Logan Kim** [9:26 A.M.] | | I think it is better to slow down. |
| **Ethan Jeffrey** [9:27 A.M.] | | What's that supposed to mean? |
| **Logan Kim** [9:30 A.M.] | | Investment is a double-edged sword, especially in Old Brisbane where there is a defined market, defined competitors and a typical way to run a business that has already been set. High risk, low return. |
| **Anna Durbin** [9:31 A.M.] | | I think I know what you are getting at. What is your suggestion, then? |
| **Logan Kim** [9:33 A.M.] | | With a limited budget, we should focus on a simple message like "We are cheaper than hotels," instead of putting a lot of money into marketing activities. |
| **Anna Durbin** [9:34 A.M.] | | I'm with Logan on this. |
| **Ethan Jeffrey** [9:35 A.M.] | | O.K., let's discuss this in detail at the weekly meeting. |

[ Send ]

**168** What type of business is Mr. Jeffrey most likely in?

(A) Restaurant
(B) Hostel
(C) General hospital
(D) Rental car

**169** Why does Mr. Jeffrey suggest an aggressive marketing strategy?

(A) There are no competitors in the market.
(B) It always guarantees high returns.
(C) The lodging market has grown steadily.
(D) He wants his company to be expanded.

**170** At 9:26 A.M., what does Mr. Kim mean when he writes, "I think it is better to slow down"?

(A) He wants Mr. Jeffrey to type slowly during the discussion.
(B) He thinks that it is not good to take an aggressive strategy.
(C) He expects that marketing plans will be very important.
(D) He knows that it takes a lot of time to prepare a meeting.

**171** What is indicated about Ms. Durbin?

(A) She lives in Old Brisbane.
(B) She will become a manager.
(C) She agrees to Mr. Kim's suggestion.
(D) She will hold a weekly meeting.

**GO ON TO THE NEXT PAGE**

*-June 1-*

# Extreme Sports World

Riding the rapids is a spine-tingling adventure created by only close encounters with Mother Nature. Waters that run through a mass of bubbles will fascinate those who love extreme outdoor sports. −[1]−. Indeed, rafting is an exciting sport of travelling down a river on a raft.

Although rafting can be an exhilarating experience for individual, it is considered an extreme sport and can be dangerous or even fatal. It also demands co-operation, for that reason. −[2]−. "It is very dangerous to go rafting on your own, especially without extensive knowledge of the river," said Noah Solti, a rafting guide of Wild Nature Travel Agency. "Many accidents occur on the river, mostly because of insufficient research and lack of preparation."

To prevent accidents from happening, wearing helmets and life vests is compulsory. −[3]−. And age restrictions are determined by the level of difficulty in rafting, as a high degree of physical stamina of participants is required. Plus, it is strongly recommended that those who try rafting bring some extra warm and dry clothes with them. −[4]−.

**172** What is the purpose of the article?

- (A) To provide necessary information about a sport
- (B) To explain how Mother Nature affects sports
- (C) To recommend a foreign travel agency
- (D) To announce a job opening for a rafting guide

**173** According to Mr. Solti, what is dangerous about rafting?

- (A) Diving for a spine-tingling adventure
- (B) Swimming through a mass of bubbles
- (C) Rafting alone without sufficient knowledge
- (D) Rafting through an exhilarating course

**174** What is determined by the level of difficulty?

- (A) Helmet sizes
- (B) Age limits
- (C) Weight of life vests
- (D) Number of rafting guides

**175** In which of the positions marked [1], [2], [3] and [4] does the following sentence best belong?

"Otherwise, they will feel bad in their wet clothes afterwards."

- (A) [1]
- (B) [2]
- (C) [3]
- (D) [4]

**GO ON TO THE NEXT PAGE**

# Expense Account Statement

Name: *Jake Ford*
For period ending: *May 8, 2017*

## Reimbursable Expenses Incurred
Hotel/Lodging: *$900.00*
Meals: *$200.00*
Tax: *$110.00*
Travel (air): *$900.00*
Personal Auto: _____ miles $_____
Other (itemized): *24 hours auto rental $72.00, cab fare $40.00*
Total Amount: *$2,222.00*

All the expenses were made in accordance with the company's policies, and I want to assure you that all the information stated above is true. Receipts are attached.

*Jake Ford*

---

To: Jake Ford
From: Josh Stoll, Accounts Payable
Subject: Expense Account Statement

According to company policies, it is clear that your statement shows how you overstepped the company's guidelines. $250.00 per night is the limit we put on all costs for compensation, but in total, you have spent $150.00 more than this limit.

Since the lodging expenses were unpredictable due to the fact that there was a convention and we were late in deciding to send you, the company understands that you did not have a wide range of choices. Nevertheless, if you wish to be compensated for the total amount of expenses, you will have to send in an RBSAE(Reimbursement Beyond Standard Allowable Expense), which will be attached to this memo. I would like you to hand in the form by next Friday to receive your full reimbursement for the expenses.

Regards,
Josh Stoll

**176** Why was the statement submitted?

    (A) To make a hotel reservation

    (B) To gain approval for a business trip

    (C) To arouse suspicion about the money that was spent

    (D) To be reimbursed for business travel expenses

**177** What area of expense exceeded the company's standard limit?

    (A) Food

    (B) Transportation

    (C) Accommodation

    (D) Parking

**178** For how many nights did Mr. Ford stay at the hotel?

    (A) Two nights

    (B) Three nights

    (C) Four nights

    (D) Five nights

**179** What is attached to the memo?

    (A) Several travel expense receipts

    (B) An employee's paycheck

    (C) An invoice listing deductions in pay

    (D) A form for supplementary expenses

**180** What is indicated about Mr. Ford's business trip?

    (A) He took part in a convention.

    (B) He drove his own car.

    (C) He was away for more days than allowed.

    (D) He stayed at more than one hotel.

GO ON TO THE NEXT PAGE

# World Airlines

## Annual Results (draft)

Alfred Sliva
October 21, 2017

### ■ SALES

Though World Airlines had a very promising start in the beginning of the year, there were several factors that made it a tough year for the entire airline industry. Due to fewer tourists visiting Asia and North America, there has been a drop in the number of passengers traveling to those areas. The industry was also negatively influenced by the difficulties that the European economies were experiencing. However, since World Airlines is still the biggest operator in Europe, it will probably maintain its lead and may even gain in profitability if that region recovers.

### ■ NEW ROUTES

High demand for most existing routes allowed the cargo division to achieve a great performance this year. In addition, new cargo routes turned out to be especially lucrative. These results have allowed the cargo division to help in increasing the company's overall results.

### ■ PERSONNEL

Unfortunately, the financial situation forced us to lay off 130 staff members. Though it was an incredibly hard decision, the company's survival depended on it. In addition, two of our 777 aircraft were removed from service due to old age.

---

e-mail

To: Alfred Sliva
From: Colin Raymond
RE: Annual Results

Hello, Alfred. I have read the draft of your report and would like to offer you some advice that may help you as you finalize your presentation to the board next month.

*Details: One method to make your presentation longer is to use numbers and statistics. Calvin can provide the monthly and quarterly passenger lines, and Erica can give you the freight numbers. Adding these figures will make your report more informative and substantial.

*Finances: Although no one likes hearing bad news, simply saying that we had a bad year does not exactly point out the problems. Add some numbers and compare it to our projections to see where we truly stand. Furthermore, we should discuss the severance provided for the workers who have lost their jobs. How bad was our situation?

**181** When is World Airlines expected to show a strong performance again?

(A) When they enter the Asia regional market
(B) After the economy recovers
(C) When they gain new passenger routes
(D) After they resolve their past issues

**182** Which division played a role in helping the company make some financial gains?

(A) Marketing
(B) Maintenance
(C) Accounting
(D) Shipping

**183** When will Mr. Sliva give a presentation?

(A) In September
(B) In October
(C) In November
(D) In December

**184** How did the financial situation of the company affect the staff members?

(A) 777 aircraft workers were unaffected.
(B) 130 employees lost their jobs.
(C) World Airlines cut down its amount of flights.
(D) Some staff members were relocated to other departments.

**185** What was NOT included in Colin's advice to Alfred?

(A) Ask Erica about the monthly and quarterly passenger numbers
(B) Team up with other members to lessen the amount of work
(C) Add more details to make the report longer
(D) Provide sufficient information on the layoffs

GO ON TO THE NEXT PAGE

*October 23*

# ✄ Montrae Weekly News ✄

The Internet is the most effective way for people to have their business found. Although websites are believed to demonstrate the company's credibility and qualification, they are not convenient for every kind of business owner. According to a survey conducted by Matrix Corporation, not a few owners waste a lot of money building a typical run-of-the-mill website. It turns out that more than 60 percent of business owners have not actively managed their website to promote their company or deal with business-related issues.

On the other hand, blogs are a good way to get people interested in or curious about business because they are appealing and have fresh content. They are a good, cheap alternative that allows small business owners to have a web presence. "You can update them at any stage and people can interact and leave comments any time," says Emma Dumont, Matrix Graphic Designer.

Ms. Rebecca Dayan, a consultant and representative of Matrix Corporation, will speak on how to use free blogs at C-5 Building in LaCrone Community Center in Montrae City on October 29.

Sophie Reynolds, Staff Writer

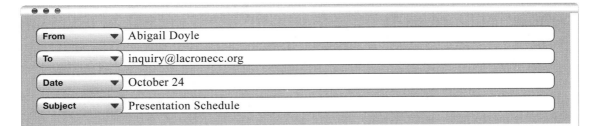

| From | ▼ Abigail Doyle |
| To | ▼ inquiry@lacronecc.org |
| Date | ▼ October 24 |
| Subject | ▼ Presentation Schedule |

Dear Sir or Madam,

While I was reading Montrae Weekly News, the article about blogs really interested me. I own a small bakery on Roxanne Avenue and haven't been able to afford to establish a website for it. But I've always had a thought that it would be nice to use the Internet to promote my business. The problem was money and time. For this reason, I believe the presentation will be really helpful and inspiring to someone like me. If you give me some schedule of the event, I would really appreciate it.

Sincerely,

Abigail Doyle

## LaCrone Community Center

### *Presentation: Utilization of Internet & Blog*
### *Sponsored by Matrix Corporation*

- 10:00 A.M. – 10:30 A.M.    Registration
- 10:30 A.M. – 11:00 P.M.    Brief Address by Mr. Michael Dylan, Community Center Chairman
- 11:00 A.M. – 12:00 P.M.    Internet Utilization
- 12:00 P.M. – 1:00 P.M.    Lunch at Community Center Dining Hall
- 1:00 P.M. – 2:30 P.M.    Blog for Your Business

For any questions you may have, call 642-3544 or e-mail at inquiry@lacronecc.org.

**186** What most likely is Matrix Corporation?

(A) A business consulting company
(B) An environmental NGO
(C) A film making company
(D) A magazine publisher

**187** In the article, the word "run-of-the-mill" in paragraph 1, line 8 is closest in meaning to

(A) ordinary
(B) significant
(C) modern
(D) hazardous

**188** Who will give the presentation of Blog for Your Business?

(A) Ms. Dumont
(B) Ms. Doyle
(C) Ms. Dayan
(D) Mr. Dylan

**189** What is suggested about Ms. Doyle?

(A) She has subscribed to Montrae Weekly News for years.
(B) She works for LaCrone Community Center.
(C) She does not have enough time to manage a website.
(D) She has always wanted to be a graphic designer.

**190** For whom is the schedule most likely intended?

(A) Global chain company CEOs
(B) Small business owners
(C) Labor union leaders
(D) International research institutes

**GO ON TO THE NEXT PAGE**

**Questions 191-195** refer to the following e-mail, message and web page.

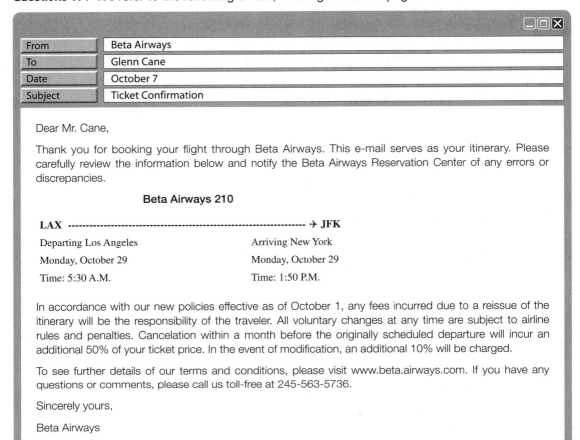

| From | Beta Airways |
|------|--------------|
| To | Glenn Cane |
| Date | October 7 |
| Subject | Ticket Confirmation |

Dear Mr. Cane,

Thank you for booking your flight through Beta Airways. This e-mail serves as your itinerary. Please carefully review the information below and notify the Beta Airways Reservation Center of any errors or discrepancies.

### Beta Airways 210

**LAX** ------------------------------------------------------------- ✈ **JFK**

| Departing Los Angeles | Arriving New York |
|------------------------|-------------------|
| Monday, October 29 | Monday, October 29 |
| Time: 5:30 A.M. | Time: 1:50 P.M. |

In accordance with our new policies effective as of October 1, any fees incurred due to a reissue of the itinerary will be the responsibility of the traveler. All voluntary changes at any time are subject to airline rules and penalties. Cancelation within a month before the originally scheduled departure will incur an additional 50% of your ticket price. In the event of modification, an additional 10% will be charged.

To see further details of our terms and conditions, please visit www.beta.airways.com. If you have any questions or comments, please call us toll-free at 245-563-5736.

Sincerely yours,

Beta Airways

---

# Telephone Message

**Caller:** Daniel Harding

**Contact:** 525-6764 (Ext. 8)

**For:** Glenn Cane

**Date:** Monday, October 8

**Time:** 1:05 P.M.

**Details:** Mr. Harding called to inform you of a possible schedule change of N.I.F. Conference. Only time will likely be changed, though. So if you have already booked a flight, you may want to change it. For details, you better call him on his cell phone because he said he'd leave early to check on our factory himself.

**Taken by:** Emma Dean

www.beta.airways.com/reservation/change

# BETA AIRWAYS INC.

*One of the world's largest airlines, offering domestic flights throughout the United States!*

| Home | News | Flight | Reservation | Contact |

Customer Name:  Glenn Cane

Reservation Number: 45B134C70

Plane Information:  Beta Airways 26

Date of Post:  October 9

**LAX** ------------------------------------------------------------------ ✈ **JFK**

Departing Los Angeles

Arriving New York

Sunday, October 28

Monday, October 29

Time: 11:30 P.M.

Time: 7:50 A.M.

I originally booked a flight that departs at 5:30 A.M. and arrives at 1:50 P.M., October 29. Due to change of my business schedule, however, I had to make modifications to my flight itinerary as input above. I would like to take the one that departs and arrives 6 hours earlier. I already checked and found that there are many flights available and will pay the additional fee of $20 incurred due to this change, according to your policies.

---

**191** What is the purpose of the e-mail?

(A) To inquire about new policies

(B) To confirm a reservation

(C) To recommend an airport

(D) To suggest a special offer

**192** In the e-mail, the word "booking" in paragraph 1, line 1 is closest in meaning to

(A) reserving

(B) staying

(C) recording

(D) calculating

**193** What is indicated about Mr. Harding?

(A) He will attend a conference on October 29.

(B) He took a message from Ms. Dean.

(C) He visited a factory on October 8.

(D) He works for an airplane company.

**194** What is the original price of the plane ticket Mr. Cane purchased?

(A) $20

(B) $40

(C) $100

(D) $200

**195** What can be inferred about the N.I.F. Conference?

(A) It is sponsored by Beta Airways Inc.

(B) It will be held in Los Angeles.

(C) It has been moved up several hours.

(D) It is held every other year.

**GO ON TO THE NEXT PAGE**

**Questions 196-200** refer to the following memorandum, e-mail and floor plan.

# Memorandum

To: Procurement Department Employees, IBS Corporation
From: Jay Brandon
Date: August 8
Re: Freight Elevator

It has been brought to my attention that some of the employees in the Procurement Department frequently use the freight elevator for personal reasons.

You are NOT to use the freight elevator, unless it is for a business purpose that is acceptable under the company's policies. The freight elevators are for transport of goods such as heavy equipment or supplies and therefore cannot serve other purposes. Please use the two passenger elevators near the entrance, which are designed to carry employees between building floors.

Lastly, the loading capacity of our freight elevator must not exceed 6,000 lbs. We have called the repairmen twice this month due to the malfunction caused by overloading.

---

| From | Blake DeWitt |
|------|--------------|
| To | Ethan Barber |
| Date | August 9 |
| Subject | Office Furniture |

Dear Mr. Barber,

I am so relieved to hear that you have the office furniture 16A-Type ready for shipment. I was very concerned that there may be some delay due to the problem with your subcontractor. I hope things will work out well and that they will stop the strike and get back to work.

Regarding the delivery, there is something you should be advised about. Yesterday, a memorandum was sent to all employees in my department regarding freight elevators. The elevator that you have always used in the ACE Building, the one next to the storage room on the 1st floor, is out of order. We called the repairmen, only to be told they would not be able to visit until next Monday. So when you deliver the furniture, I recommend that you take the other freight elevator.

Should you have any questions, please feel free to contact me any time.

Blake DeWitt, IBS Corporation

## ACE Building Plan 1st floor

| Elevator C | Office 102 | Office 101 | Elevator A | Information Desk |
|---|---|---|---|---|
| | Walkway | | | ⇔ Entrance |
| Elevator D | Storage Room | Office 103 | Elevator B | Security Office |

**196** According to the memorandum, what is stated as the cause of the elevator malfunction?

(A) Frequent use by passengers
(B) Excessive load of freight
(C) Negligent inspection by engineers
(D) Unexpected power outage

**197** What is suggested about Mr. Barber?

(A) He started his career as a successful architect.
(B) He drew a building plan for Mr. DeWitt.
(C) He advised Mr. Brandon on freight elevators.
(D) His subcontractor is undergoing a labor dispute.

**198** In the e-mail, the phrase "out of order" in paragraph 2, line 4 is closest in meaning to

(A) inefficient
(B) released
(C) manufactured
(D) broken

**199** What can be inferred about Mr. DeWitt?

(A) He broke an elevator when using it for personal reasons.
(B) He contacted repairmen to fix an elevator.
(C) He works in the Procurement Department.
(D) He used to work as an elevator engineer.

**200** What elevator will Mr. Barber use for delivery of 16A-Type furniture?

(A) Elevator A
(B) Elevator B
(C) Elevator C
(D) Elevator D

**Stop!** This is the end of the test. If you finish before time is called, you may go back to Parts 5, 6, and 7 and check your work.

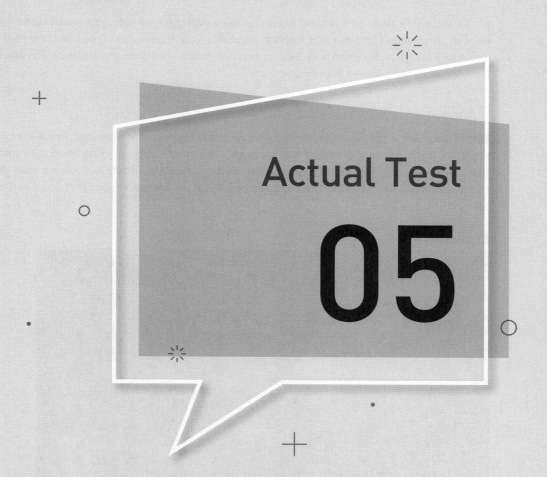

Actual Test

**05**

| 시작 시간 | : |
|---|---|
| 종료 시간 | : |

# LISTENING TEST

In the Listening test, you will be asked to demonstrate how well you understand spoken English. The entire Listening test will last approximately 45 minutes. There are four parts, and directions are given for each part. You must mark your answers on the separate answer sheet. Do not write your answers in your test book.

## PART 1

**Directions:** For each question in this part, you will hear four statements about a picture in your test book. When you hear the statements, you must select the one statement that best describes what you see in the picture. Then find the number of the question on your answer sheet and mark your answer. The statements will not be printed in your test book and will be spoken only one time.

**Example**

Sample Answer
Ⓐ ● Ⓒ Ⓓ

Statement (B), "The man is using a microphone," is the best description of the picture, so you should select answer (B) and mark it on your answer sheet.

**1**

**2**

**GO ON TO THE NEXT PAGE**

**3**

**4**

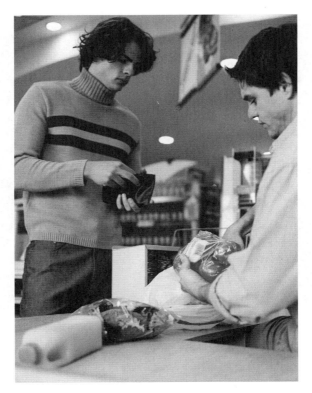

**5**

**6**

**GO ON TO THE NEXT PAGE** ➜

# PART 2

**Directions:** You will hear a question or statement and three responses spoken in English. They will not be printed in your test book and will be spoken only one time. Select the best response to the question or statement and mark the letter (A), (B), or (C) on your answer sheet.

| | | | |
|---|---|---|---|
| **7** | Mark your answer on your answer sheet. | **20** | Mark your answer on your answer sheet. |
| **8** | Mark your answer on your answer sheet. | **21** | Mark your answer on your answer sheet. |
| **9** | Mark your answer on your answer sheet. | **22** | Mark your answer on your answer sheet. |
| **10** | Mark your answer on your answer sheet. | **23** | Mark your answer on your answer sheet. |
| **11** | Mark your answer on your answer sheet. | **24** | Mark your answer on your answer sheet. |
| **12** | Mark your answer on your answer sheet. | **25** | Mark your answer on your answer sheet. |
| **13** | Mark your answer on your answer sheet. | **26** | Mark your answer on your answer sheet. |
| **14** | Mark your answer on your answer sheet. | **27** | Mark your answer on your answer sheet. |
| **15** | Mark your answer on your answer sheet. | **28** | Mark your answer on your answer sheet. |
| **16** | Mark your answer on your answer sheet. | **29** | Mark your answer on your answer sheet. |
| **17** | Mark your answer on your answer sheet. | **30** | Mark your answer on your answer sheet. |
| **18** | Mark your answer on your answer sheet. | **31** | Mark your answer on your answer sheet. |
| **19** | Mark your answer on your answer sheet. | | |

# PART 3

**Directions:** You will hear some conversations between two or more people. You will be asked to answer three questions about what the speakers say in each conversation. Select the best response to each question and mark the letter (A), (B), (C), or (D) on your answer sheet. The conversations will not be printed in your test book and will be spoken only one time.

**32** Where does the man work?

(A) At a real estate agency
(B) At a local tourist office
(C) At a radio station
(D) At a recruitment agency

**33** What does the man say about the special offer?

(A) It includes insertion into a website.
(B) It will expire soon.
(C) It is only for subscribers.
(D) It applies only to recruitment advertisements.

**34** What does the woman want to know about the advertisement?

(A) The word count
(B) The format
(C) The color
(D) The cost

**35** What is the man concerned about?

(A) Background noise
(B) An office closure
(C) Lack of daylight hours
(D) Insufficient light

**36** What does the woman suggest?

(A) Using a different office
(B) Working from home
(C) Finding a different employer
(D) Transplanting the trees elsewhere

**37** What does the man say he will do?

(A) Ask for information
(B) Leave the company
(C) Assemble a team
(D) Take on extra work

**38** Who most likely are the speakers?

(A) City officials
(B) Hiring agents
(C) Building contractors
(D) Telephone operators

**39** What are the speakers mainly discussing?

(A) A rough draft of a script
(B) An estimate for the roadwork
(C) A budget to prepare for bad weather
(D) A job interview for crew members

**40** What does Mr. Perez say he will do next?

(A) Hire temporary workers immediately
(B) Check the number of workers available
(C) Forward an e-mail to the woman's coworker
(D) Calculate the cost of the repairs

**41** Where does the woman most likely work?

(A) At a travel agency
(B) At a health clinic
(C) At a restaurant
(D) At an airline

**42** What does the man say he did a week ago?

(A) Returned from vacation
(B) Started a business overseas
(C) Made an appointment with a doctor
(D) Resigned from a job

**43** What does the man imply when he says, "I usually work until five"?

(A) He feels tired after work.
(B) He would like to take a day off.
(C) He is looking for a part-time job.
(D) He would prefer a later appointment.

**GO ON TO THE NEXT PAGE**

Test 05

**44** What is the woman asking the man to submit?

(A) Holiday destinations
(B) Confirmation of employment
(C) Revised contact information
(D) Vacation dates

**45** What has the woman recently done?

(A) Employ additional staff
(B) Take a vacation
(C) Post new regulations
(D) Organize a company outing

**46** What does the man say about his relatives?

(A) They live out of the country.
(B) They work at the same company.
(C) They will be taking some time off.
(D) They just started new jobs.

**47** Who most likely is the woman?

(A) A company executive
(B) A financial consultant
(C) A radio host
(D) A government official

**48** What goal does the woman discuss?

(A) Improving working conditions
(B) Easing the process of loan applications
(C) Creating job opportunities
(D) Refurbishing houses

**49** What does the man ask the woman about?

(A) A building initiative
(B) Construction suppliers
(C) Application forms
(D) An opening date

**50** What are the speakers mainly discussing?

(A) Attending a conference
(B) Going to France on business
(C) Constructing a factory
(D) Meeting with foreign investors

**51** What is happening today?

(A) A trip to the airport
(B) A tour of a facility
(C) A welcome dinner
(D) A conference call

**52** What are the speakers looking forward to?

(A) Hiring qualified employees
(B) Making a good investment decision
(C) Arriving in time for a conference
(D) Socializing with their clients

**53** What industry do the speakers most likely work in?

(A) Insurance
(B) Finance
(C) Advertising
(D) Construction

**54** Why does the man say, "I was preoccupied with the image editing"?

(A) To explain a new policy
(B) To offer an excuse
(C) To request some help
(D) To refuse an offer

**55** What is mentioned about the woman's presentation?

(A) An appealing image was used.
(B) It lacks creative advertising strategies.
(C) A change has not been included.
(D) Some more research will be needed.

**56** Where most likely are the speakers?

(A) At a storage facility
(B) At an airline check-in counter
(C) At a hotel reception desk
(D) At a bus terminal

**57** What does the woman want to do?

(A) Book a hotel room
(B) Drop off some papers
(C) Check out at a later time
(D) Return within a week

**58** What does the man ask the woman to do?

(A) Enter a room number
(B) Confirm her departure
(C) Pay a deposit
(D) Show her identification

---

**59** What are the speakers mainly discussing?

(A) Changing the leader of a project
(B) Applying for a business loan
(C) Building an office complex
(D) Acquiring a target company

**60** What is Miranda advised to do?

(A) Negotiate a contract in person
(B) Report to a new manager
(C) Provide written confirmation
(D) Reduce construction costs

**61** What does the man say he will do tomorrow?

(A) Visit a construction site
(B) Go on a vacation
(C) Meet new colleagues
(D) Relocate to another country

| Arrivals | | |
|---|---|---|
| **From** | **Status** | **Estimated Time** |
| Moscow | Canceled | 7:00 |
| London | Delayed | 10:40 |
| Munich | On Time | 14:00 |
| Philadelphia | On Time | 15:30 |

**62** Look at the graphic. Which city is Heidi traveling from?

(A) Moscow
(B) London
(C) Munich
(D) Philadelphia

**63** How did the man learn about the schedule change?

(A) By calling an airline
(B) From a colleague
(C) Through a travel agency
(D) By checking it online

**64** According to the woman, why should the speakers leave now?

(A) The snow caused slick road conditions.
(B) More snow is expected in the evening.
(C) Several roads have been closed.
(D) An outdoor event is being held.

**GO ON TO THE NEXT PAGE**

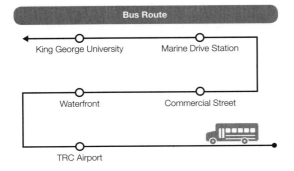

**Bus Route**

King George University — Marine Drive Station

Waterfront — Commercial Street

TRC Airport

**65** What does the woman ask the man about?

(A) Where to go shopping
(B) How much the bus fare is
(C) How to get to her destination
(D) When the next bus leaves

**66** Look at the graphic. Which stop will the woman get off at?

(A) Marine Drive Station
(B) Commercial Street
(C) Waterfront
(D) TRC Airport

**67** According to the man, how long does it take to walk to the shopping mall?

(A) 5 minutes
(B) 10 minutes
(C) 15 minutes
(D) 30 minutes

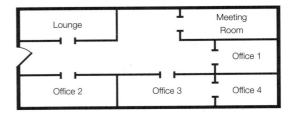

Lounge | Meeting Room

Office 1

Office 2 | Office 3 | Office 4

**68** What does the man say he will do tonight?

(A) Assign employees new tasks
(B) Design a building
(C) Attend a family function
(D) Prepare for a presentation

**69** Look at the graphic. Which office has been assigned to the man?

(A) Office 1
(B) Office 2
(C) Office 3
(D) Office 4

**70** What does the man ask the woman to do tomorrow?

(A) Hire a moving company
(B) Inform the sales staff of the assignments
(C) Attend an anniversary celebration
(D) Give a product demonstration

# PART 4

**Directions:** You will hear some talks given by a single speaker. You will be asked to answer three questions about what the speaker says in each talk. Select the best response to each question and mark the letter (A), (B), (C), or (D) on your answer sheet. The talks will not be printed in your test book and will be spoken only one time.

**71** What is being advertised?

(A) A cleaning company
(B) A refurbishment service
(C) A furniture shop
(D) A real estate agency

**72** How can customers receive a discount?

(A) By entering a discount code online
(B) By presenting a membership card
(C) By recommending a new customer
(D) By renovating at least three rooms

**73** According to the speaker, what will happen at the end of the week?

(A) A business will relocate.
(B) Additional services will be available.
(C) A special offer will end.
(D) A new design will be launched.

**74** What event is most likely being held?

(A) A book fair
(B) A movie preview
(C) A job fair
(D) An international conference on marketing

**75** According to the speaker, how often is this event held?

(A) Once a year
(B) Twice a year
(C) Three times a year
(D) Every three years

**76** To have a chance to win the presents, what should the listeners do?

(A) Call the number announced
(B) Buy mugs or bookmarks
(C) Come to the entrance
(D) Put their tickets in the drawing box

**77** What is the purpose of the message?

(A) To make a suggestion
(B) To postpone a meeting
(C) To confirm an order
(D) To ask a favor

**78** What does the speaker imply when he says, "the grand opening is in just seven days"?

(A) He needs to make fast decisions.
(B) He wants to reschedule an event.
(C) The listener should reserve a venue.
(D) A project is ahead of schedule.

**79** What most likely will the speaker do next?

(A) Send the listener some information
(B) Meet with an event planner
(C) Contact some suppliers
(D) Revise a budget plan

**80** Why is this year's booklist special?

(A) It is distributed free of charge.
(B) It is entering its twentieth year.
(C) It will be broadcast live on the radio.
(D) It is recommended by well-known authors.

**81** What will listeners hear next?

(A) An interview
(B) A news bulletin
(C) An award announcement
(D) An excerpt from a book

**82** Why should listeners call the station?

(A) To become a member
(B) To win a free book
(C) To purchase tickets
(D) To talk to a guest

**GO ON TO THE NEXT PAGE**

83 Where most likely does the speaker work?

(A) At an office supply company
(B) At a restaurant
(C) At a manufacturing plant
(D) At a delivery company

84 What is the problem?

(A) Some equipment is out of order.
(B) An invoice was sent incorrectly.
(C) A delivery vehicle is not available.
(D) Some orders haven't been filled.

85 What does the speaker mean when he says, "I just don't know what to do"?

(A) He cannot respond to an inquiry.
(B) He needs more training.
(C) The situation is very serious.
(D) More employees should be hired.

86 Who is this announcement intended for?

(A) Customers
(B) Chefs
(C) Waiters and waitresses
(D) Fishermen

87 Why is this announcement being made?

(A) To encourage listeners to sell more products
(B) To describe updates to the restaurant's menu
(C) To ensure safety precautions are followed
(D) To advertise a new restaurant

88 What would the listeners mention to the customers about today's special?

(A) It was imported from Belgium.
(B) Its price went up.
(C) It is fresh.
(D) It was caught in the Pacific.

89 Where is the speaker calling from?

(A) A post office
(B) A movie theater
(C) A travel agency
(D) A hospitality venue

90 What caused the problem?

(A) A telephone number was incorrect.
(B) A payment was not made.
(C) An e-mail account was inactive.
(D) An order form was misplaced.

91 What is the listener advised to do?

(A) Provide a receipt
(B) Make a call
(C) Review a contract
(D) Pick up tickets in person

92 Who most likely are the listeners?

(A) Career counselors
(B) Construction workers
(C) Potential investors
(D) Board members

93 What does the speaker imply when she says, "I know it's a tough call"?

(A) An increase in local tourism is expected.
(B) It will be a difficult decision for listeners.
(C) Construction noise will bother customers.
(D) There will be more job opportunities

94 What does the speaker suggest?

(A) Redesigning a website
(B) Hiring an industry expert
(C) Renovating a facility
(D) Moving to another location

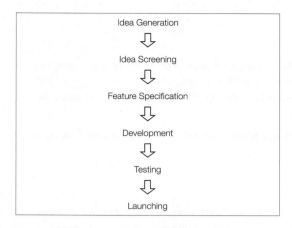

Not valid with already discounted group rates. Valid through March 31.

**95** What does the speaker say about the Silverstar 7?

(A) It was featured in a technology magazine.
(B) It has sold better than competing products.
(C) It has won a design award.
(D) It is the cheapest model on the market.

**96** According to the speaker, what do customers like about the new product?

(A) Its appearance
(B) Its price
(C) Its new function
(D) Its durability

**97** Look at the graphic. Which step has been added recently?

(A) Idea generation
(B) Idea screening
(C) Feature specification
(D) Development

**98** What kind of event is being organized?

(A) A retirement party
(B) A holiday party
(C) A promotion party
(D) A theme party

**99** Look at the graphic. Why is the speaker unable to use the coupon for the event?

(A) The coupon cannot be used with a group discount.
(B) The venue of the event has been changed.
(C) The restaurant went out of business.
(D) The event will take place after the expiration date.

**100** What does the speaker ask the listener to do?

(A) Buy a present
(B) Order invitation cards
(C) Bring a camera
(D) Hire a band

This is the end of the Listening test. Turn to Part 5 in your test book.

**GO ON TO THE NEXT PAGE**

# READING TEST

In the Reading test, you will read a variety of texts and answer several different types of reading comprehension questions. The entire Reading test will last 75 minutes. There are three parts, and directions are given for each part. You are encouraged to answer as many questions as possible within the time allowed.

You must mark your answers on the separate answer sheet. Do not write your answers in your test book.

# PART 5

**Directions:** A word or phrase is missing in each of the sentences below. Four answer choices are given below each sentence. Select the best answer to complete the sentence. Then mark the letter (A), (B), (C), or (D) on your answer sheet.

101　All the workers should be advised that the company website will be off-line from 1 to 5 P.M. on July 1st ------- regularly scheduled maintenance.

(A) in case
(B) in that
(C) due to
(D) while

102　Today's meeting with the foreign investors has been delayed a bit, but will start -------.

(A) shortly
(B) urgently
(C) nearly
(D) openly

103　You cannot receive a driver's license ------- proper documents.

(A) until
(B) upon
(C) along
(D) without

104　In case your computer malfunctions while under warranty, please contact our customer service department to inquire about a refund or -------.

(A) receipt
(B) complaint
(C) promotion
(D) replacement

105　Patricia has a tendency to speak so ------- that sometimes confirmation of her exact message is necessary.

(A) centrally
(B) nearly
(C) indirectly
(D) mutually

106　As professors report that their students are more refreshed after the rest, the introduction of a spring break at the university proved surprisingly -------.

(A) accessible
(B) abundant
(C) beneficial
(D) legible

107　The President will hold a press conference to answer any questions ------- his address concerning the national pension system.

(A) except
(B) upon
(C) following
(D) at

108　------- of the speakers at the workshop is our company's vice president, and the other is a government official from the Trade Department.

(A) The one
(B) Someone
(C) As one
(D) One

**109** We are now in negotiations with Transtel Communications over national ------- of our economic news program.

(A) distribution
(B) distributed
(C) distributor
(D) distribute

**110** Mr. Chase informed his children that he wanted them to pay for their last semester's tuition fee by ------- to prepare them for adulthood.

(A) yourself
(B) himself
(C) herself
(D) themselves

**111** Onita Residences is located in a quiet neighborhood complete ------- a tennis court, swimming pool, and fitness center.

(A) beside
(B) across
(C) from
(D) with

**112** Winter appliances such as heaters should undergo regular testing to ------- the life of the equipment.

(A) prolong
(B) enlarge
(C) endure
(D) persist

**113** Due to regularly scheduled maintenance, rides on the roller coaster have been halted ------- further notice.

(A) until
(B) onto
(C) next to
(D) except

**114** Because some of the material in the textbook was too -------, the professor skipped certain sections.

(A) repeat
(B) repetition
(C) repetitive
(D) repeating

**115** Because the company's conference included a presentation by a renowned motivational speaker, it was ------- attended.

(A) quite
(B) well
(C) some
(D) many

**116** Mr. Bode Miller was promoted to head chef after he ------- the restaurant's menu.

(A) had mastered
(B) masters
(C) has mastered
(D) is mastering

**117** The conditions in the contract appear to have been ------- by the managers in charge of it.

(A) misinterpreting
(B) misinterpretation
(C) misinterpreted
(D) misinterpret

**118** We would like to cater the company's event on Sunday, but unfortunately we ------- have appointments with three other parties that day.

(A) well
(B) already
(C) never
(D) soon

**119** Edouard Ferlet ------- some of the most popular jazz songs coming out of Paris in recent years.

(A) write
(B) writes
(C) written
(D) wrote

**120** Simply bring in five receipts ------- proof of purchase and we will offer a complimentary store bag.

(A) except
(B) off
(C) through
(D) as

GO ON TO THE NEXT PAGE

**121** It is advisable to bring along a mechanic ------- you are planning to purchase a used car from a private owner.

(A) so
(B) that
(C) due to
(D) if

**122** The agency enacted a series of environmental ------- in response to the public outcry after a toxic spill contaminated most of Lake Gurand.

(A) reformer
(B) reformed
(C) reformatory
(D) reforms

**123** Management and labor have ------- agreed on the terms of the contract after a series of heated negotiations and threats of a strike.

(A) finally
(B) yet
(C) soon
(D) since

**124** Your membership ------- covers admittance to all classes, use of lockers, and one free personal trainer session.

(A) fare
(B) worth
(C) fee
(D) tip

**125** The application ------- animated slides made the presentation more enjoyable and memorable.

(A) to
(B) of
(C) by
(D) at

**126** The firm started to replace its paper documents with digital files in the early 90s and ------- it has both saved money and reduced waste.

(A) now that
(B) in case
(C) otherwise
(D) therefore

**127** The company's president ------- a new financial director to oversee the company's accounting operations every three years.

(A) operates
(B) predicts
(C) appoints
(D) deposits

**128** Our director believes that the race for continuously improving our platform requires us to hire some program ------- for our wireless division.

(A) development
(B) developers
(C) develops
(D) developed

**129** A feasibility study is under way ------- extension of our fiber optic cables into more remote areas of the nation.

(A) for
(B) next
(C) onto
(D) while

**130** Please notify Mr. Farrington that the conference has been rescheduled ------- that investors from the foreign office can attend.

(A) concerning
(B) so
(C) since
(D) over

# PART 6

**Directions:** Read the texts that follow. A word, phrase, or sentence is missing in parts of each text. Four answer choices for each question are given below the text. Select the best answer to complete the text. Then mark the letter (A), (B), (C), or (D) on your answer sheet.

**Questions 131-134** refer to the following notice.

May is the time for the selection of the most valuable worker at IBS Inc. The nomination ------- takes place on the 27th of May. ------- who wish to apply for the title should fill out their
131.                                      132.
application form by the 13th.

-------. First, being selected as the most valuable worker of the year could be one of the
133.
strongest factors to promotion. Also, it guarantees a five-day vacation at any time of the year except for August and September.

The committee ------- employees who have shown not only their complete dedication to the
134.
company but also made a noticeable contribution.

Although getting the title has been proven to be very competitive, we encourage all employees' participation.

131 (A) proceeds
    (B) procedures
    (C) procedure
    (D) proceeded

132 (A) Those
    (B) Them
    (C) Anyone
    (D) They

133 (A) This title could be beneficial in several ways for many employees.
    (B) Employees may face numerous difficulties as a result of the title.
    (C) Employees must have worked at the company for at least 3 years.
    (D) So far, not many employees attended the event.

134 (A) returns
    (B) cares
    (C) considers
    (D) congratulates

**GO ON TO THE NEXT PAGE**

Test 05

### Another Hit by Director Griffin

Hines Griffin, one of the most respected directors in film industry, recently created another movie called *The Carousel*. -------. *The Carousel* deals with a ------- story of a medieval knight who
135.                               136.
participates in a tournament where a group of knights test their equestrian skills.

Carl Sergio plays Johann Favallet who competes in the tournament, not knowing of a secret plot against him. The movie adds dramatic ------- by keeping who is behind the staged tournament
137.
secret until the very end.

A notable feature of the film is that the writers show ------- skill in depicting the complexities of
138.
each of the characters in the tale.

The film is considered not only a big commercial hit but also a masterpiece of historical drama which is both true to history and entertaining to modern audiences.

135 (A) This new movie is expected to bring in more than 20 million viewers just in two months.
    (B) The director struggled to escape from many difficulties he faced.
    (C) *The Carousel* is highly criticized by the public for not conveying the reality.
    (D) At first, the actors of *The Carousel* were not pleased with the scenario.

136 (A) fascinating
    (B) fascination
    (C) fascinated
    (D) fascinates

137 (A) cynicism
    (B) criticism
    (C) effect
    (D) cause

138 (A) narrow
    (B) extensive
    (C) limited
    (D) excessive

**Questions 139-142** refer to the following e-mail.

Date: June 10
From: DVD Rentals
To: Harley Duncan
Subject: Overdue Items

Mr. Duncan, this e-mail is sent to notify you of the overdue DVDs that you rented a month ago.

-------. However, the items that you have rented are overdue by more than two weeks now. If you
139.

do not return ------- within the next two days, your current fine, $40, will be doubled to $80 as
140.

they are going to be considered lost.

We understand that you've contacted our store to extend the rental period for the items.

However, please note that another e-mail had been sent to let you know that those DVDs are not

------- for renewal.
141.

------- we would like to let you enjoy the DVDs for more than two weeks, the store policy is very
142.

strict, and it is also not fair for those who are waiting for those items.

Please return the DVDs as soon as possible in order to avoid the potentially large amount of fine

added to your account.

---

139 (A) If you are a silver member, you are
       exempt from paying the fine.
    (B) According to your list, you mostly rented
       horror movies.
    (C) The regular rental period for those DVDs
       is only two weeks.
    (D) A new policy will be added to our current
       store policy.

140 (A) that
    (B) their
    (C) them
    (D) it

141 (A) eligible
    (B) able
    (C) capable
    (D) exposed

142 (A) For example
    (B) Although
    (C) Therefore
    (D) In addition

GO ON TO THE NEXT PAGE

**Questions 143-146** refer to the following announcement.

To the members of the Board of Directors,

The annual company dinner for the Board of Directors ------- on the first Wednesday of May at
143.
6:00. The place for the event is going to be the ballroom of the Manhattan Hilton Hotel on 40th
Street.

-------, all the board members are welcome to invite up to three guests besides their family
144.
members. Please be aware that all the visitors must bring an ID as it is an exclusive meeting.

The gathering is designed to be the place and time for our board members to ------- their ideas
145.
on how to improve the company with other members. -------.
146.

We hope to see you all at the event. Please keep in mind that it is a formal event and so we
advise you to dress accordingly.

Thank you.

Sincerely,

Jacob Tyler
CEO of Earnst and Young Inc.

143 (A) will be held
(B) will hold
(C) was held
(D) has been held

144 (A) However
(B) As usual
(C) By contrast
(D) On the other hand

145 (A) force
(B) explain
(C) share
(D) understand

146 (A) People in our company do not get along
with each other very well.
(B) Also, it is meant to provide beverages
and dishes prepared by our fine culinary
staff.
(C) It is important to get advice from family
members in times of stress.
(D) You may not present your own personal
thoughts about the company.

# PART 7

**Directions:** In this part you will read a selection of texts, such as magazine and newspaper articles, e-mails, and instant messages. Each text or set of texts is followed by several questions. Select the best answer for each question and mark the letter (A), (B), (C), or (D) on your answer sheet.

**Questions 147-148** refer to the following e-mail.

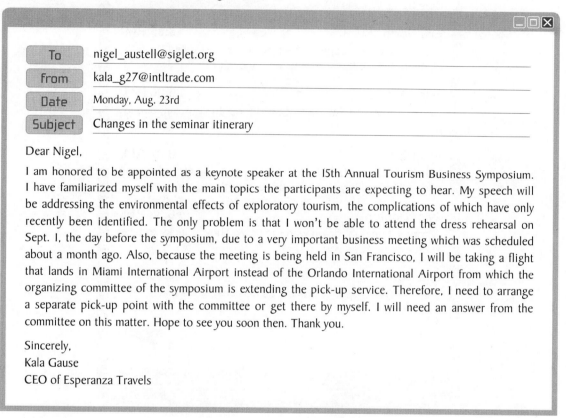

| To | nigel_austell@siglet.org |
|---|---|
| From | kala_g27@intltrade.com |
| Date | Monday, Aug. 23rd |
| Subject | Changes in the seminar itinerary |

Dear Nigel,

I am honored to be appointed as a keynote speaker at the 15th Annual Tourism Business Symposium. I have familiarized myself with the main topics the participants are expecting to hear. My speech will be addressing the environmental effects of exploratory tourism, the complications of which have only recently been identified. The only problem is that I won't be able to attend the dress rehearsal on Sept. 1, the day before the symposium, due to a very important business meeting which was scheduled about a month ago. Also, because the meeting is being held in San Francisco, I will be taking a flight that lands in Miami International Airport instead of the Orlando International Airport from which the organizing committee of the symposium is extending the pick-up service. Therefore, I need to arrange a separate pick-up point with the committee or get there by myself. I will need an answer from the committee on this matter. Hope to see you soon then. Thank you.

Sincerely,
Kala Gause
CEO of Esperanza Travels

**147** Why won't Ms. Gause be attending the dress rehearsal?

(A) She needs to visit her sick mother.
(B) She has a prearranged meeting.
(C) Her business is under investigation.
(D) She is on vacation in Miami.

**148** How will Ms. Gause get to the symposium venue from the airport?

(A) It is not determined yet.
(B) The organizing committee will send her a cab.
(C) She will hire a private driver.
(D) She is taking the train that stops at a nearby station.

**GO ON TO THE NEXT PAGE**

**Questions 149-150** refer to the following text message chain.

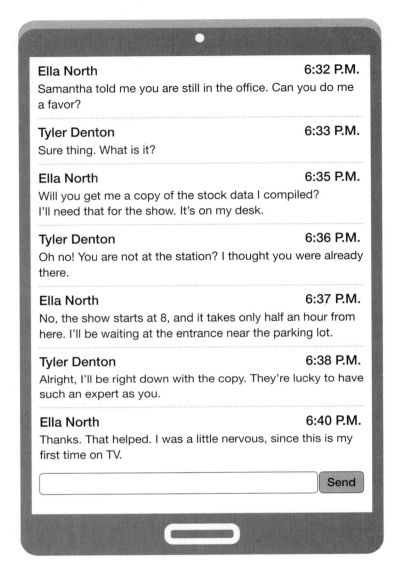

**Ella North**          6:32 P.M.

Samantha told me you are still in the office. Can you do me a favor?

**Tyler Denton**          6:33 P.M.

Sure thing. What is it?

**Ella North**          6:35 P.M.

Will you get me a copy of the stock data I compiled?
I'll need that for the show. It's on my desk.

**Tyler Denton**          6:36 P.M.

Oh no! You are not at the station? I thought you were already there.

**Ella North**          6:37 P.M.

No, the show starts at 8, and it takes only half an hour from here. I'll be waiting at the entrance near the parking lot.

**Tyler Denton**          6:38 P.M.

Alright, I'll be right down with the copy. They're lucky to have such an expert as you.

**Ella North**          6:40 P.M.

Thanks. That helped. I was a little nervous, since this is my first time on TV.

Send

---

**149** At 6:33 P.M., what does Mr. Denton mean when he writes, "Sure thing"?

(A) He is willing to assist Ms. North.
(B) He agrees that he needs to work overtime.
(C) He knows what Ms. North will ask for.
(D) He thinks that he should come along.

**150** Who most likely is Ms. North?

(A) A news anchor
(B) A security guard
(C) A policewoman
(D) A financial analyst

# Warehouse Clearance Sale

Forst Outdoor Supplies
94 East 29th Street
New York City, NY

Save big dollars on camping supplies at our off-season clearance sale from February 2nd to 10th. You can find top quality tents, sleeping bags, camp stoves and other camping gears made of durable materials. You can save 70% on all stock from last year's spring outdoor line while 50% discount will be available on first aid kits.

For parents who purchase child-safety products, we will be handing out complimentary outdoor socks for the whole family! Come and enjoy our blowout sale while it lasts!

**Test 05**

**151** How much can customers save on last year's stock?

(A) 20%
(B) 40%
(C) 50%
(D) 70%

**152** What do customers receive on purchasing child-safety goods?

(A) Additional discounts
(B) Coupons from a local store
(C) Portable speakers
(D) Socks for camping

GO ON TO THE NEXT PAGE

Questions 153-154 refer to the following announcement.

# Become a Certified Nutritionist!

18<sup>th</sup> Regular Briefing Session by the Nutritionists Association of Australia
Time: 10:00 A.M. - 1:00 P.M. (30-minute lunch break is scheduled at noon.)
Location: 29 Elmswood Avenue, Melbourne VIC 3205

Becoming a certified nutritionist has become ever more competitive and difficult as the profession grows in popularity and demand. Nutritionists are especially sought after by prestigious private schools, fitness centers and general hospitals at high salaries. Nutritionists are appreciated for their expertise in offering a healthy and oftentimes therapeutic diet for individuals with special dietary needs.

Join our 18<sup>th</sup> regular briefing session on becoming a certified nutritionist to learn new information on the registration process, the style and manner of examination and skills required. To participate in our session, you must register online at www.nsa.au. For the first 30 registrations, the association members will give individual career consultations for free! Be sure to check out our website for further information.

**153** What is the purpose of the announcement?

(A) To increase awareness on the importance of a balanced diet
(B) To advertise an upcoming event for aspiring nutritionists
(C) To give a warning on a recent outbreak of food poisoning
(D) To recruit a new nutritionist for a school cafeteria

**154** Who will receive free career consultation?

(A) People who register early enough
(B) People who apply for the consultation
(C) 30 students majoring in nutritional science
(D) The first 30 people who register online for the session

# Hagyes International Corporation

A4044 Cabot Circus,

Bristol, U.K.

– Home Appliances for Studio Apartment –

The compact size of our product can be fit anywhere in your home, which makes it different from others. –[1]–. The can dispenser capable of holding up to five cans provides easy access to cold drinks. The temperature control conveniently located at the top right inside helps easily adjust the temperature and keeps food fresh. –[2]–. Three shelves provide abundant space for organizing, and especially the top two are adjustable to fit your storage needs. –[3]–. Last but not least, our product passed the tests carried out by the world famous certification institute, Efficient Energy Lab. –[4]–. You can save money on utility bills without having to sacrifice convenience.

**155** What is being advertised?

(A) A refrigerator

(B) A microwave

(C) An oven

(D) An air conditioner

**156** What is special about the product?

(A) Small size

(B) Light weight

(C) Low price

(D) Lifetime warranty

**157** In which of the positions marked [1], [2], [3] and [4] does the following sentence best belong?

"Consequently, our product is entitled to the EEL mark affixed on it."

(A) [1]

(B) [2]

(C) [3]

(D) [4]

GO ON TO THE NEXT PAGE

## Silverton High School Event Calendar for May

| Date | Event |
|---|---|
| May 3rd–8th | **MID-TERM EXAM**<br>Students are reminded that they need to personally check with their teachers the room they will be taking the tests in since some are going through renovation and therefore unfit for use. |
| May 12th–14th | **BAKE-SALE**<br>The Parents' Committee is preparing a bake-sale to raise money to pay for medical bills of our beloved student, classmate, and friend, Lily Watson, who is recovering from a recent car accident at St. Mary's Hospital. Our principal, Mr. Bate, has personally pledged a $1,000 to the bake-sale! We wish all Silvertonians a yummy bake-sale! |
| May 25th | **CAREER DAY**<br>Silverton is happy to invite Mr. Strozier, a human rights activist, as the keynote speaker at this year's career day! Students will also be able to meet famous local celebrities like Ms. Jolly, and Mr. Nofrillsman and participate in career guidance counseling. Students are required to bring $1 for 108-page long booklets on career choices and aptitude tests. |

**158** What can be inferred about Silverton High School?

(A) Mr. Nofrillsman is a Silverton alumni.
(B) The school is refurbishing some classrooms.
(C) All the events are organized by the Parents' Committee.
(D) Career day booklets were provided by the district school board.

**159** What is the purpose of hosting a bake-sale?

(A) To celebrate the end of mid-term exams
(B) To commemorate the school's 38th anniversary
(C) To gather money for an injured student
(D) To increase students' cooking skills

**160** What is NOT true about the career day?

(A) A human rights activist will be a main speaker at the event.
(B) Local celebrities are coming to celebrate the event.
(C) Students can receive an informative booklet for a dollar.
(D) The principal will be participating as a counselor.

| To | d.forcier@cranmail.net |
|---|---|
| From | kelley.cs13@gertschmt.com |
| Date | Feb. 3rd, 2017 |
| Subject | Re] Heating system not working |

Dear Ms. Forcier,

We are sorry to hear that your heating system has been broken for the last two days. We also regret that we weren't able to repair your heater promptly as our services are not available on weekends. Since we registered your complaint the first thing this morning, our repairman will be visiting you at 3:00 P.M. to examine and fix your heater.

If our repairman concludes that the problem was caused by a product defect, we will be sure to install a new one at no charge and offer you a 40% discount on all our maintenance services ranging from pest control and spring-cleaning to refurbishing. Customers are reminded that to prevent water pipes from freezing. They can take simple precautions like insulating all their water pipes and setting the heater to operate a few times a day.

For more information on preventing heating problems and our services, please visit www.gertschmt. com.

Thank you.

Kelley Pakele
Customer services
Gertsch Building Maintenance

**161** What day was the e-mail read by a customer services representative?

(A) Monday
(B) Tuesday
(C) Friday
(D) Sunday

**162** What can be inferred about Ms. Forcier?

(A) She will sue the company for negligence.
(B) She will be visited by a repairman in the afternoon.
(C) She will call the company's headquarters.
(D) She will turn on the heater a few times.

**163** What will the customer receive if the product is found to be faulty?

(A) Free consultation on renovation plans
(B) Insulation for the water pipes
(C) Complimentary appointments for a spa treatment
(D) Lower prices on maintenance services

GO ON TO THE NEXT PAGE

To: Nolan Bostwick [nbcs@uptoncom.net]
From: Melinda Weist [mwgw@uptoncom.net]
Date: June 8th
Subject: On your suggestion

Dear Mr. Bostwick,

We thank you for your meaningful suggestion on the need for developing an alert system for groupware errors or shutdowns. You reported that a lot of our clients were calling customer service because of sudden disconnections which also carried the threat of data loss. Although your department was engulfed by numerous phone calls, you actively addressed the frustrating situation promptly and resourcefully. Your idea of an automatic warning system interlocking our server with the clients' was modeled by our engineers and is now waiting a pilot test.

As you know, the company greatly appreciates helpful contributions like the ones you have made and we express our gratitude and recognition by granting bonuses. Also, since your idea proved to be pivotal in improving our customer relations, we decided to give you a weeklong vacation to the Bahamas paid by the company in addition to the bonuses. You will also receive ten meal tickets to use at our cafeteria. As you have seen by the president's excitement and our employee's enthusiasm at last week's meeting, the whole company can't thank you enough for your contribution.

Excellent work, Mr. Bostwick!

**164** What job position is Mr. Bostwick most likely to have?

(A) A customer services representative
(B) A technician
(C) A marketing department employee
(D) A member of the executive board

**165** How far did the company work on Mr. Bostick's idea?

(A) Assessing its success
(B) Formulating sales strategies
(C) Coming up with additional examples
(D) Constructing a prototype

**166** What is NOT a part of reward given to Mr. Bostwick?

(A) Paid vacation to an exotic tourist destination
(B) Free meals at the company cafeteria
(C) Promotion to a higher position
(D) A bonus

**167** What can be inferred about Mr. Bostwick?

(A) He used to work as an engineer.
(B) He has met with the company's president.
(C) He is going to bring his family on the vacation.
(D) He has worked at the company for over a decade.

**Questions 168-171** refer to the following online chat discussion.

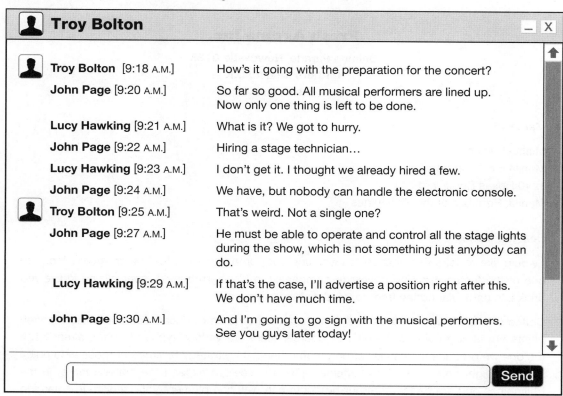

| **Troy Bolton** | _ X |
| --- | --- |

**Troy Bolton** [9:18 A.M.] How's it going with the preparation for the concert?

**John Page** [9:20 A.M.] So far so good. All musical performers are lined up. Now only one thing is left to be done.

**Lucy Hawking** [9:21 A.M.] What is it? We got to hurry.

**John Page** [9:22 A.M.] Hiring a stage technician…

**Lucy Hawking** [9:23 A.M.] I don't get it. I thought we already hired a few.

**John Page** [9:24 A.M.] We have, but nobody can handle the electronic console.

**Troy Bolton** [9:25 A.M.] That's weird. Not a single one?

**John Page** [9:27 A.M.] He must be able to operate and control all the stage lights during the show, which is not something just anybody can do.

**Lucy Hawking** [9:29 A.M.] If that's the case, I'll advertise a position right after this. We don't have much time.

**John Page** [9:30 A.M.] And I'm going to go sign with the musical performers. See you guys later today!

[ Send ]

**168** For what type of company does Mr. Bolton most likely work?

(A) A television manufacturer
(B) A lighting equipment retailer
(C) An event planning agency
(D) A radio station

**169** At 9:23 A.M., what does Ms. Hawking mean when she writes, "I don't get it"?

(A) She does not understand what Mr. Page said about hiring a stage expert.
(B) She cannot tolerate with a stage technician's behavior.
(C) She does not know how many musical performers will come.
(D) She did not expect stage technicians to be lined up.

**170** Who most likely will be hired?

(A) A master carpenter
(B) An orchestra conductor
(C) A beauty stylist
(D) A light board operator

**171** What will Mr. Page do next?

(A) Deal with a legal case
(B) Advertise a position
(C) Meet musical performers
(D) Hold a seminar

**GO ON TO THE NEXT PAGE**

# Fresh Aroma Inc.

**Shimna Parade, Newcastle BT33**
**Northern Ireland, U.K.**
**www.fresharoma.co.uk**

March 15

Michael Manoy
Manila F & B Corporation
1240 Roxas Boulevard
Manila, Republic of the Philippines

Dear Mr. Manoy,

I would like to take this chance to introduce our company. –[1]–. We, Fresh Aroma Inc., are one of the fastest growing beverage companies in Northern Ireland, specializing in brewed drinks, in particular coffee from roasted coffee beans.

Coffee seeds are imported by one of our agents from some African countries where coffee plants are largely cultivated. –[2]–. Of course, there are various types of coffee already but the one we produce tastes less strong than others. Our strategy is aimed at those who enjoy so-called light coffee with less caffeine. –[3]–. We seek to expand the coffee market in the Philippines and are certain that our products can well complement your service in enlarging your coffee market. It is in this respect that we wish to extend our interest in becoming a partner of Manila F & B Corporation, the city's biggest wholesaler of beverages.

Please find enclosed our company brochure which details the information you need to know about us. –[4]–. Should you have any questions, please do not hesitate to contact us by phone: (+44) 487-5610 or e-mail: hbohm@fresharoma.co.uk.

We look forward to your positive response.

Best regards,

Harry Bohm

President, Fresh Aroma Inc.

172  What is the purpose of the letter?

(A) To inquire about beverage products
(B) To explain how a product is made
(C) To express appreciation for a contract
(D) To suggest a business partnership

173  What is NOT true about Fresh Aroma Inc.?

(A) It is located in Northern Ireland.
(B) It produces brewed drinks.
(C) Its agent imports coffee seeds from Africa.
(D) It aims at strong coffee drinkers.

174  What is included with the letter?

(A) A revised contract
(B) A survey form
(C) A company booklet
(D) A coffee pot manual

175  In which of the positions marked [1], [2], [3] and [4] does the following sentence best belong?

"And then, they are dried and roasted to varying degrees."

(A) [1]
(B) [2]
(C) [3]
(D) [4]

GO ON TO THE NEXT PAGE

## Paris Fashion Week Highlights

June 3rd, 2017 — Ella Hewitt reporting from Paris

### Successful Debut of a Rising Designer

Designer Michael Huguenot exhibited an impressive collection of couture dresses during his debut in Paris on June 1st. Mr. Huguenot, a German native, mastered his sewing skills and cultivated a unique perspective on fashion design by operating his very own boutique "Narcisse" in Dijon for ten years. His hermit kingdom of sophisticated and delicate ball gowns drew popular attention after he opened his boutique on the streets of Paris. His love for nature is also well represented in his dresses which are made of faux furs and natural textiles that require minimum chemical processing. He was invited by the organizer of Paris Fashion Week, Ms. Austelle, after Chancellor of Germany donned his emerald mermaid dress. After his successful debut this week, he was approached by many brand name fashion groups like Dignement and Tolle. Industry observers are expecting him to collaborate with one of the fashion giants very soon.

---

To: Michael Huguenot [michug@tmail.com]
From: Van Gaudette [vgpersonnel@hmqw.fr]
Date: June 8th, 2017
Subject: Job Offer

Dear Mr. Huguenot,

We were thoroughly impressed with the confidence and mastery you presented at your debut during the Paris Fashion Week. It was our pleasure to have had conversation with you after the show. What a fine job you have done!

In hopes of setting higher standards of craftsmanship here at HMQW, we are inviting you to join us as designer. Should you be interested in our offer, please send us your portfolio, curriculum vitae, and a copy of birth certificate by June 14th. Upon reviewing your documents, we will request that you open a local bank account to help finalize our contract.

If you have further questions, you can contact Jean-Marie our human resources representative at 013-681-2017.

**176** What is true about Mr. Huguenot?

    (A) He worked as owner of a clothing store for a decade.

    (B) He finished his education in his home country.

    (C) His work relies on textiles that are heavily treated with chemicals.

    (D) He has attended as a participant at the Paris Fashion Week several times before.

**177** Who is Ms. Austelle?

    (A) An HMQW CEO

    (B) Editor for a fashion magazine

    (C) The Chancellor of Germany

    (D) Event planner

**178** When was Mr. Huguenot first approached by a HMQW representative?

    (A) June 1st

    (B) June 3rd

    (C) June 8th

    (D) June 14th

**179** What is NOT required of Mr. Huguenot in the job offer?

    (A) A copy of birth certificate

    (B) Portfolio

    (C) Proof of a valid health insurance

    (D) A résumé

**180** What will be specifically requested to help complete the hiring?

    (A) Visit the HMQW headquarters for an interview

    (B) Apply for a loan at a French bank

    (C) Set up an account at a local bank

    (D) Call the human resources department

**GO ON TO THE NEXT PAGE**

To | Grace Forest [grace29@cooks.com]
From | Roxanna Staedal [roxy_72@vortex.net]
Date | August 11th
Subject | Party Favors

Greetings, beloved cousin!

It has been ages since we last saw each other. Thank you for returning a prompt R.S.V.P. We are so glad that you can join my husband and little John in celebrating our newborn's christening. I just wanted to confirm your current address because party favors especially prepared for relatives are too delicate to be distributed at the church. Since we don't want any broken party favors, we decided ship them safely and directly to your house. Once I have your correct address, I can register it for shipment and give you the security code for retrieval of the parcel. I have your address from 6 months ago as 36 Trevorane Dr, Richville, ON M2O 8F5, correct? Please answer me as soon as you can. Thanks, and see you soon!

P.S.: Remember to follow the dress code as described in our invitations for a family portrait!

To | Roxanna Staedal [roxy_72@vortex.net]
From | Grace Forest [grace29@cooks.com]
Date | August 12th
Subject | Re: Party Favors

What a surprise! A party favor too delicate to be handled at church? I can't wait to find out what it is. And our family is all prepared to dress up for the event so there is no need to worry. We have a new address at 83 Sirenadine Street, Hamsherville, MB X3L 9V1. Daniel was transferred to a new branch upon his promotion about a month ago so the whole family had to come along. We are very excited to meet the new addition to the Staedal family. See you soon!

**181** What is the purpose of the first e-mail?

(A) To invite someone to a family event
(B) To verify if an address is correct
(C) To introduce a new shipping method
(D) To suggest a party theme

**182** What will Ms. Staedal do after confirming the correct address?

(A) Give her cousin the password to her online shipment account
(B) Send her cousin a verification code needed to receive the shipment
(C) Return party favors for replacements
(D) Go shopping for the family's outfits for the event

**183** What can be inferred about the christening?

(A) Guests can dress in whatever way they like.
(B) It is the first one for the Staedal family.
(C) Pre-ordered party favors were shipped broken.
(D) Relatives will congregate to take a photo shoot.

**184** What most likely happened during the last 6 months?

(A) Ms. Forest started working as a party planner.
(B) Ms. Staedal finished her product reviews on party favors online.
(C) Ms. Staedal became pregnant.
(D) Ms. Forest had to move to a new house in a different region.

**185** The word "distributed" in line 4 of the first e-mail is closest in meaning to

(A) apportioned
(B) produced
(C) planted
(D) elongated

## *Bellridge City Bulletin*     April 15

*Yoga has moved to the mainstream in the city!*

Longevity Yoga School will be moving to a new location at 16th Street Southwest on April 21, as the construction was completed last Friday. The opening will be early next month.

The new location provides a much larger parking space than the old one on Fellanie Road did. "The extra places were required to accommodate an increase in the number of learners," said Christopher Kane, the School Director. "There has been a growing awareness of health issues. The majority of citizens view yoga as something healthy and worthwhile." To meet increasing consumer demands, the School will add extra classes on Saturday and extend lesson hours during the workweek. Opening hours are 8 A.M. to 6 P.M., Monday to Friday, and 10 A.M. to 2 P.M., on Saturday.

Yoga, the Hindu philosophy, is known as a spiritual discipline in which people can learn to control their mind and body. Yoga exercises include breath control, simple meditation, and the adoption of specific bodily postures, all of which are widely practiced for health and relaxation.

Blake Hilton, Staff Writer

---

From: Jennifer Potter [jpotter@navelline.com]
To: Ella Thomas [ethomas@navelline.com]
Date: May 18
Subject: A-2 Powder

Hi, Ella.

How did the Fair go today? I was concerned because Ms. Hannah told me that she had received a text message from you that said you would be late for the Fair due to construction work on Franklin Road. I hope everything went okay. Ms. Hannah told me to help you with the marketing promotion on A-2 Powder. She said the powder should be advertised as the one that makes any face, dry or oily, look much smoother. I have found launching a new product really exhausting.

I heard you started learning Yoga. Can I join? Seriously, I need to get rid of my stress. It will also keep me in good shape, so I think it'll be worth it. If you just let me know the address, I will find the location myself and meet you in front of the building.

Jennifer

Marketing Team, Navelline Inc.

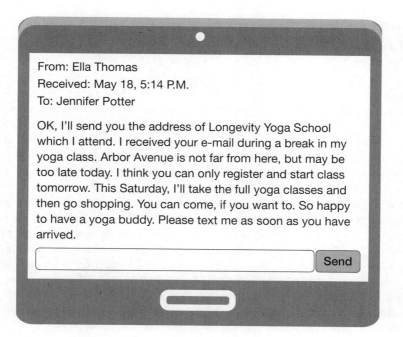

From: Ella Thomas
Received: May 18, 5:14 P.M.
To: Jennifer Potter

OK, I'll send you the address of Longevity Yoga School which I attend. I received your e-mail during a break in my yoga class. Arbor Avenue is not far from here, but may be too late today. I think you can only register and start class tomorrow. This Saturday, I'll take the full yoga classes and then go shopping. You can come, if you want to. So happy to have a yoga buddy. Please text me as soon as you have arrived.

Send

**186** According to the article, why did Longevity Yoga School move to a new location?

(A) The city council changed its development plan.
(B) The demand for yoga has grown in the city.
(C) The school decided to downsize its business.
(D) The original construction plan was abolished.

**187** What most likely is Navelline Inc.?

(A) A yoga teaching school
(B) A weekly magazine publisher
(C) An interior design agency
(D) A cosmetics selling company

**188** In the e-mail, the phrase "get rid of" in paragraph 2, line 1, is closest in meaning to

(A) relieve
(B) strengthen
(C) illustrate
(D) dismantle

**189** Where will Ms. Potter most likely meet Ms. Thomas?

(A) On 16th Street
(B) On Fellanie Road
(C) On Franklin Road
(D) On Arbor Avenue

**190** What can be inferred about Ms. Thomas?

(A) She has attended a yoga school for years.
(B) She has recently hired Ms. Hannah.
(C) She will be shopping after 2 P.M. on Saturday.
(D) She did not attend the Fair on May 18.

**GO ON TO THE NEXT PAGE**

## Dahir Local News                                          June 2

M.O.T. Contest aims to bring photographers together!

The M.O.T. Amateur Photographers Contest will be held in Mondetee Arts Center, Dahir on June 18. Amateur photographers from all around the world are expected to share their works and inspiration with other contenders.

Participation in the contest is free. Contenders may enter up to 3 photos in each category: Freedom and Love. The names of photographers are not displayed during voting, which means each photo is given an equal opportunity to be judged on its own merit. It is displayed the same number of times to voters as any other. "Our contest is unique because what matters here are the photos that will embody their creativity, not photographers' popularity or appealing to the public for votes," said Michael Derulo, the Contest committee chairman. It is widely known that the Contest's motto is 'Share the best shots

together.' "We congratulate photographers who have accomplished excellence and encourage others to keep up their artistic motivation. They freely express different points of view and thrive through competition," said Mr. Derulo.

For the M.O.T. Professional Photographers Contest held on the following day at the same location, however, the committee has prepared a special judging panel that comprises highly renowned industry professionals among gallery owners, editors, and acclaimed photographers.

The opportunity to submit works of art to one of the world's fairest photography contests will be available until June 16. Interested photographers will have a chance to win a $5,000 cash prize. Telephone number: 245-5670-3533 / Website: www.motawards.com.

---

From: Anthony Simon
To: inquiry@motawards.com
Date: June 11
Subject: Photography Entries

Dear Sir or Madam:

I have a question about the M.O.T. Amateur Photographers Contest. As far as I know, there are two different categories, "Freedom" and "Love," to which I can submit photos. My photos are prepared only for the "Freedom" category. What I do not know is the maximum number of the entries you accept for this category. I would like to submit as many as possible. If you kindly advise me on this, I would appreciate it.

Sincerely,

Anthony Simon

| From | ▼ Aaron Moody |
| To | ▼ Nate Fielder |
| Date | ▼ June 14 |
| Subject | ▼ Photography Contest |

Hi, Nate.

I heard you're up for the M.O.T. Professional Photographers Contest held next week. How's it going with the preparation? You know I'm pretty much into this kind of contest, but I will be busy by the time it's held. A very important meeting is scheduled on June 20 and 21. Sometimes I wish I were a professional photographer like you, so I would be able to take photos outdoors any time I want. If you win the prize, give me a big treat.

Best of luck!
Aaron

191 What is the purpose of the article?

(A) To explain why an arts center has been rented
(B) To promote a newly released camera
(C) To encourage photographers to join a contest
(D) To announce an important city plan

192 According to the article, what makes the M.O.T. Photographers Contest unique?

(A) Fair criteria for the selection
(B) Incomparably long history
(C) Well-trained committee members
(D) The greatest cash prize

193 Who are most likely NOT included in the special judging panel?

(A) People who own a famous art gallery
(B) People in charge of the final content of a newspaper
(C) People who take photographs professionally
(D) People who teach at a prestigious college

194 How many entries will Mr. Simon mostly likely submit?

(A) Three
(B) Four
(C) Five
(D) Six

195 When will Mr. Fielder participate in the M.O.T. Photographers Contest?

(A) On June 18
(B) On June 19
(C) On June 20
(D) On June 21

GO ON TO THE NEXT PAGE

# Mavern Tribune

April 15

More citizens purchase their furniture like tables, chairs, or desks at M & S Shopping Centre than anywhere else. It occupies 40 percent of the furniture market in the city, which is up 10 percent from last year. Named after the first letters of each of two co-presidents' last names, the M & S Shopping Centre started as a small retailer that sells only dining tables, but has now become the city's biggest shopping place.

What's more surprising is that the Centre appears to offer customers the best shopping experience. The March 15 issue of Mavern Tribune features the ratings and reviews of all furniture stores in Mavern, and the M & S Shopping Centre ranked No. 1 among them. "Some may say the news shouldn't be a surprise. We have always earned very high marks in every category except price, which is also considered quite reasonable when you think about our high quality raw materials," said Jack Smith, one of the co-presidents of the Centre.

However, a different opinion exists. Experts point out that any business can fail quickly. "For a large portion of shoppers, price matters when it comes to interior decoration. Only a minority of shoppers are willing to pay a premium for high quality. Price comes as first priority to the others," said Robert Wilson, a researcher of the L.I.H. Business Institute. Whether M & S Shopping Centre changes its business direction to reduce price or not, at least some of the efforts to reflect customers' opinion will seem inevitable.

Joshua Kloss, Staff Writer

---

From: Bryan Tanaka <btanaka@mscentre.com>
To: William Regan <wregan@mscentre.com>
Date: April 19
Subject: March issue of Mavern Tribune

Dear William,

Jane Foster in Marketing told me about the March issue of Mavern Tribune. The results turned out to be exactly the same as I had expected. I was aware that our products were a little too expensive in the market and kept reporting this issue to Alexander McArthur, but he was so stubborn that he wouldn't listen, unlike Jack Smith.

As mentioned in the Mavern Tribune, it is about the time for us to do something. To maintain high quality while meeting the financial challenges, I think we should be flexible with our partners, say, finding those who use slightly cheaper raw materials, if necessary. Another option is to issue discount coupons every month for a while, like Jane suggested, for the purpose of maintaining market share this quarter.

Let me know what you think.

Bryan Tanaka
Administration Team Leader, M & S Shopping Centre

# M & S SHOPPING CENTRE

All home furniture is available including

- Dining Tables
- Wicker Chairs
- Sofas
- Resin Chairs
- Sun Lounges
- Bar Stools

Starting this month May until the end of September, special discount coupons issued by M & S Shopping Centre each month may apply to any regular products!

To learn more about our rates, call us at 532-4653 during the business hours below or visit www. afcentre.com.

### Business Hours
Monday – Saturday: 9 A.M. – 7 P.M.
Sunday: 10 A.M. – 6 P.M.

**196** What is true about M & S Shopping Centre?

(A) It started business as a big wholesaler.
(B) Its market share increased by 10 percent this year.
(C) It sells only office furniture.
(D) It is the city's second largest shopping centre.

**197** According to the article, what is M & S Shopping Centre's least competitive feature?

(A) Price
(B) Product quality
(C) Delivery
(D) Warranty service

**198** Who most likely is Mr. McArthur?

(A) A co-president
(B) A marketing team member
(C) An administration team intern
(D) A subcontractor

**199** In the e-mail, the phrase "turned out" in paragraph 1, line 1 is closest in meaning to

(A) expected
(B) proved
(C) designed
(D) expired

**200** What can be inferred about Ms. Foster?

(A) She works with Mr. Tanaka in the same team.
(B) She has recently purchased Bar Stools.
(C) Her proposal has been accepted.
(D) Her salary is the highest in the company.

**Stop!** This is the end of the test. If you finish before time is called, you may go back to Parts 5, 6, and 7 and check your work.

# TOEIC® 점수 환산표

| 정답수 | Listening Comprehension | 정답수 | Reading Comprehension |
|---|---|---|---|
| 96-100 | 480-495 | 96-100 | 460-495 |
| 91-95 | 435-490 | 91-95 | 410-475 |
| 86-90 | 395-450 | 86-90 | 380-430 |
| 81-85 | 355-415 | 81-85 | 355-400 |
| 76-80 | 325-375 | 76-80 | 325-375 |
| 71-75 | 295-340 | 71-75 | 295-345 |
| 66-70 | 265-315 | 66-70 | 265-315 |
| 61-65 | 240-285 | 61-65 | 235-285 |
| 56-60 | 215-260 | 56-60 | 205-255 |
| 51-55 | 190-235 | 51-55 | 175-225 |
| 46-50 | 160-210 | 46-50 | 150-195 |
| 41-45 | 135-180 | 41-45 | 120-170 |
| 36-40 | 110-155 | 36-40 | 100-140 |
| 31-35 | 85-130 | 31-35 | 75-120 |
| 26-30 | 70-105 | 26-30 | 55-100 |
| 21-25 | 50-90 | 21-25 | 40-80 |
| 16-20 | 35-75 | 16-20 | 30-65 |
| 11-15 | 20-55 | 11-15 | 20-50 |
| 6-10 | 15-40 | 6-10 | 15-35 |
| 1-5 | 5-20 | 1-5 | 5-20 |
| 0 | 5 | 0 | 5 |

# Actual Test 1

## ANSWER SHEET

수험번호

응시일자 :　　　년　　　월　　　일

| 성명 | 한글 |
|---|---|
| | 한자 |
| | 영자 |

좌석번호

Ⓐ Ⓑ Ⓒ Ⓓ Ⓔ
① ② ③ ④ ⑤ ⑥ ⑦

확 인

### LISTENING (Part I~IV)

(답안 마킹란: NO. 1~100, 각 문항 A B C D)

### READING (Part V~VII)

(답안 마킹란: NO. 101~200, 각 문항 A B C D)

1. 사용 필기구 : 컴퓨터용 연필(연필을 제외한 사인펜, 볼펜 등은 사용 절대 불가)

2. 잘못된 필기구 사용과 〈보기〉의 올바른 표기 이외의 잘못된 표기로 한 경우에는 당 위원회의 OMR기기가 판독한 결과에 따르며 그 결과는 본인 책임입니다. 1개의 정답란 줄에 아래의 올바른 표기대로 정확히 표기하여야 합니다.

〈보기〉 올바른 표기 : ●　　　잘못된 표기 : ⊗ ◍ ◐

3. 답안지는 컴퓨터로 처리되므로 훼손하시면 안 되며, 상단의 타이밍마크(▮▮▮▮)부분을 찢거나, 낙서 등을 하면 본인에게 불이익이 발생할 수 있습니다.

4. 감독관의 확인이 없거나 시험 종료 후에 답안 작성을 계속할 경우 시험 무효 처리됩니다.

*서약 내용을 읽으시고 확인란에 반드시 서명하십시오.

본인은 TOEIC 시험 문제의 일부 또는 전부를 유출하거나 어떠한 형태로든 타인에게 누설 공개하지 않을 것이며 인터넷 또는 인쇄물 등을 이용해 유포하거나 참고 자료로 활용하지 않을 것입니다. 또한 TOEIC 시험 부정행위 처리 규정을 준수할 것을 서약합니다.

서 약

확 인

# ANSWER SHEET

# Actual Test 2

응시일자 : 년    월    일

수험번호

| 성명 | 한글 |
|---|---|
| | 한자 |
| | 영자 |

좌석번호

ⒶⒷⒸⒹⒺ
①②③④⑤⑥⑦

## LISTENING (Part I~IV)

| NO. | ANSWER | NO. | ANSWER | NO. | ANSWER | NO. | ANSWER | NO. | ANSWER |
|---|---|---|---|---|---|---|---|---|---|
| | A B C D | | A B C D | | A B C D | | A B C D | | A B C D |
| 1 | Ⓐ Ⓑ Ⓒ Ⓓ | 21 | Ⓐ Ⓑ Ⓒ Ⓓ | 41 | Ⓐ Ⓑ Ⓒ Ⓓ | 61 | Ⓐ Ⓑ Ⓒ Ⓓ | 81 | Ⓐ Ⓑ Ⓒ Ⓓ |
| 2 | Ⓐ Ⓑ Ⓒ Ⓓ | 22 | Ⓐ Ⓑ Ⓒ Ⓓ | 42 | Ⓐ Ⓑ Ⓒ Ⓓ | 62 | Ⓐ Ⓑ Ⓒ Ⓓ | 82 | Ⓐ Ⓑ Ⓒ Ⓓ |
| 3 | Ⓐ Ⓑ Ⓒ Ⓓ | 23 | Ⓐ Ⓑ Ⓒ Ⓓ | 43 | Ⓐ Ⓑ Ⓒ Ⓓ | 63 | Ⓐ Ⓑ Ⓒ Ⓓ | 83 | Ⓐ Ⓑ Ⓒ Ⓓ |
| 4 | Ⓐ Ⓑ Ⓒ Ⓓ | 24 | Ⓐ Ⓑ Ⓒ Ⓓ | 44 | Ⓐ Ⓑ Ⓒ Ⓓ | 64 | Ⓐ Ⓑ Ⓒ Ⓓ | 84 | Ⓐ Ⓑ Ⓒ Ⓓ |
| 5 | Ⓐ Ⓑ Ⓒ Ⓓ | 25 | Ⓐ Ⓑ Ⓒ Ⓓ | 45 | Ⓐ Ⓑ Ⓒ Ⓓ | 65 | Ⓐ Ⓑ Ⓒ Ⓓ | 85 | Ⓐ Ⓑ Ⓒ Ⓓ |
| 6 | Ⓐ Ⓑ Ⓒ Ⓓ | 26 | Ⓐ Ⓑ Ⓒ Ⓓ | 46 | Ⓐ Ⓑ Ⓒ Ⓓ | 66 | Ⓐ Ⓑ Ⓒ Ⓓ | 86 | Ⓐ Ⓑ Ⓒ Ⓓ |
| 7 | Ⓐ Ⓑ Ⓒ Ⓓ | 27 | Ⓐ Ⓑ Ⓒ Ⓓ | 47 | Ⓐ Ⓑ Ⓒ Ⓓ | 67 | Ⓐ Ⓑ Ⓒ Ⓓ | 87 | Ⓐ Ⓑ Ⓒ Ⓓ |
| 8 | Ⓐ Ⓑ Ⓒ Ⓓ | 28 | Ⓐ Ⓑ Ⓒ Ⓓ | 48 | Ⓐ Ⓑ Ⓒ Ⓓ | 68 | Ⓐ Ⓑ Ⓒ Ⓓ | 88 | Ⓐ Ⓑ Ⓒ Ⓓ |
| 9 | Ⓐ Ⓑ Ⓒ Ⓓ | 29 | Ⓐ Ⓑ Ⓒ Ⓓ | 49 | Ⓐ Ⓑ Ⓒ Ⓓ | 69 | Ⓐ Ⓑ Ⓒ Ⓓ | 89 | Ⓐ Ⓑ Ⓒ Ⓓ |
| 10 | Ⓐ Ⓑ Ⓒ Ⓓ | 30 | Ⓐ Ⓑ Ⓒ Ⓓ | 50 | Ⓐ Ⓑ Ⓒ Ⓓ | 70 | Ⓐ Ⓑ Ⓒ Ⓓ | 90 | Ⓐ Ⓑ Ⓒ Ⓓ |
| 11 | Ⓐ Ⓑ Ⓒ Ⓓ | 31 | Ⓐ Ⓑ Ⓒ Ⓓ | 51 | Ⓐ Ⓑ Ⓒ Ⓓ | 71 | Ⓐ Ⓑ Ⓒ Ⓓ | 91 | Ⓐ Ⓑ Ⓒ Ⓓ |
| 12 | Ⓐ Ⓑ Ⓒ Ⓓ | 32 | Ⓐ Ⓑ Ⓒ Ⓓ | 52 | Ⓐ Ⓑ Ⓒ Ⓓ | 72 | Ⓐ Ⓑ Ⓒ Ⓓ | 92 | Ⓐ Ⓑ Ⓒ Ⓓ |
| 13 | Ⓐ Ⓑ Ⓒ Ⓓ | 33 | Ⓐ Ⓑ Ⓒ Ⓓ | 53 | Ⓐ Ⓑ Ⓒ Ⓓ | 73 | Ⓐ Ⓑ Ⓒ Ⓓ | 93 | Ⓐ Ⓑ Ⓒ Ⓓ |
| 14 | Ⓐ Ⓑ Ⓒ Ⓓ | 34 | Ⓐ Ⓑ Ⓒ Ⓓ | 54 | Ⓐ Ⓑ Ⓒ Ⓓ | 74 | Ⓐ Ⓑ Ⓒ Ⓓ | 94 | Ⓐ Ⓑ Ⓒ Ⓓ |
| 15 | Ⓐ Ⓑ Ⓒ Ⓓ | 35 | Ⓐ Ⓑ Ⓒ Ⓓ | 55 | Ⓐ Ⓑ Ⓒ Ⓓ | 75 | Ⓐ Ⓑ Ⓒ Ⓓ | 95 | Ⓐ Ⓑ Ⓒ Ⓓ |
| 16 | Ⓐ Ⓑ Ⓒ Ⓓ | 36 | Ⓐ Ⓑ Ⓒ Ⓓ | 56 | Ⓐ Ⓑ Ⓒ Ⓓ | 76 | Ⓐ Ⓑ Ⓒ Ⓓ | 96 | Ⓐ Ⓑ Ⓒ Ⓓ |
| 17 | Ⓐ Ⓑ Ⓒ Ⓓ | 37 | Ⓐ Ⓑ Ⓒ Ⓓ | 57 | Ⓐ Ⓑ Ⓒ Ⓓ | 77 | Ⓐ Ⓑ Ⓒ Ⓓ | 97 | Ⓐ Ⓑ Ⓒ Ⓓ |
| 18 | Ⓐ Ⓑ Ⓒ Ⓓ | 38 | Ⓐ Ⓑ Ⓒ Ⓓ | 58 | Ⓐ Ⓑ Ⓒ Ⓓ | 78 | Ⓐ Ⓑ Ⓒ Ⓓ | 98 | Ⓐ Ⓑ Ⓒ Ⓓ |
| 19 | Ⓐ Ⓑ Ⓒ Ⓓ | 39 | Ⓐ Ⓑ Ⓒ Ⓓ | 59 | Ⓐ Ⓑ Ⓒ Ⓓ | 79 | Ⓐ Ⓑ Ⓒ Ⓓ | 99 | Ⓐ Ⓑ Ⓒ Ⓓ |
| 20 | Ⓐ Ⓑ Ⓒ Ⓓ | 40 | Ⓐ Ⓑ Ⓒ Ⓓ | 60 | Ⓐ Ⓑ Ⓒ Ⓓ | 80 | Ⓐ Ⓑ Ⓒ Ⓓ | 100 | Ⓐ Ⓑ Ⓒ Ⓓ |

## READING (Part V~VII)

| NO. | ANSWER | NO. | ANSWER | NO. | ANSWER | NO. | ANSWER | NO. | ANSWER |
|---|---|---|---|---|---|---|---|---|---|
| | A B C D | | A B C D | | A B C D | | A B C D | | A B C D |
| 101 | Ⓐ Ⓑ Ⓒ Ⓓ | 121 | Ⓐ Ⓑ Ⓒ Ⓓ | 141 | Ⓐ Ⓑ Ⓒ Ⓓ | 161 | Ⓐ Ⓑ Ⓒ Ⓓ | 181 | Ⓐ Ⓑ Ⓒ Ⓓ |
| 102 | Ⓐ Ⓑ Ⓒ Ⓓ | 122 | Ⓐ Ⓑ Ⓒ Ⓓ | 142 | Ⓐ Ⓑ Ⓒ Ⓓ | 162 | Ⓐ Ⓑ Ⓒ Ⓓ | 182 | Ⓐ Ⓑ Ⓒ Ⓓ |
| 103 | Ⓐ Ⓑ Ⓒ Ⓓ | 123 | Ⓐ Ⓑ Ⓒ Ⓓ | 143 | Ⓐ Ⓑ Ⓒ Ⓓ | 163 | Ⓐ Ⓑ Ⓒ Ⓓ | 183 | Ⓐ Ⓑ Ⓒ Ⓓ |
| 104 | Ⓐ Ⓑ Ⓒ Ⓓ | 124 | Ⓐ Ⓑ Ⓒ Ⓓ | 144 | Ⓐ Ⓑ Ⓒ Ⓓ | 164 | Ⓐ Ⓑ Ⓒ Ⓓ | 184 | Ⓐ Ⓑ Ⓒ Ⓓ |
| 105 | Ⓐ Ⓑ Ⓒ Ⓓ | 125 | Ⓐ Ⓑ Ⓒ Ⓓ | 145 | Ⓐ Ⓑ Ⓒ Ⓓ | 165 | Ⓐ Ⓑ Ⓒ Ⓓ | 185 | Ⓐ Ⓑ Ⓒ Ⓓ |
| 106 | Ⓐ Ⓑ Ⓒ Ⓓ | 126 | Ⓐ Ⓑ Ⓒ Ⓓ | 146 | Ⓐ Ⓑ Ⓒ Ⓓ | 166 | Ⓐ Ⓑ Ⓒ Ⓓ | 186 | Ⓐ Ⓑ Ⓒ Ⓓ |
| 107 | Ⓐ Ⓑ Ⓒ Ⓓ | 127 | Ⓐ Ⓑ Ⓒ Ⓓ | 147 | Ⓐ Ⓑ Ⓒ Ⓓ | 167 | Ⓐ Ⓑ Ⓒ Ⓓ | 187 | Ⓐ Ⓑ Ⓒ Ⓓ |
| 108 | Ⓐ Ⓑ Ⓒ Ⓓ | 128 | Ⓐ Ⓑ Ⓒ Ⓓ | 148 | Ⓐ Ⓑ Ⓒ Ⓓ | 168 | Ⓐ Ⓑ Ⓒ Ⓓ | 188 | Ⓐ Ⓑ Ⓒ Ⓓ |
| 109 | Ⓐ Ⓑ Ⓒ Ⓓ | 129 | Ⓐ Ⓑ Ⓒ Ⓓ | 149 | Ⓐ Ⓑ Ⓒ Ⓓ | 169 | Ⓐ Ⓑ Ⓒ Ⓓ | 189 | Ⓐ Ⓑ Ⓒ Ⓓ |
| 110 | Ⓐ Ⓑ Ⓒ Ⓓ | 130 | Ⓐ Ⓑ Ⓒ Ⓓ | 150 | Ⓐ Ⓑ Ⓒ Ⓓ | 170 | Ⓐ Ⓑ Ⓒ Ⓓ | 190 | Ⓐ Ⓑ Ⓒ Ⓓ |
| 111 | Ⓐ Ⓑ Ⓒ Ⓓ | 131 | Ⓐ Ⓑ Ⓒ Ⓓ | 151 | Ⓐ Ⓑ Ⓒ Ⓓ | 171 | Ⓐ Ⓑ Ⓒ Ⓓ | 191 | Ⓐ Ⓑ Ⓒ Ⓓ |
| 112 | Ⓐ Ⓑ Ⓒ Ⓓ | 132 | Ⓐ Ⓑ Ⓒ Ⓓ | 152 | Ⓐ Ⓑ Ⓒ Ⓓ | 172 | Ⓐ Ⓑ Ⓒ Ⓓ | 192 | Ⓐ Ⓑ Ⓒ Ⓓ |
| 113 | Ⓐ Ⓑ Ⓒ Ⓓ | 133 | Ⓐ Ⓑ Ⓒ Ⓓ | 153 | Ⓐ Ⓑ Ⓒ Ⓓ | 173 | Ⓐ Ⓑ Ⓒ Ⓓ | 193 | Ⓐ Ⓑ Ⓒ Ⓓ |
| 114 | Ⓐ Ⓑ Ⓒ Ⓓ | 134 | Ⓐ Ⓑ Ⓒ Ⓓ | 154 | Ⓐ Ⓑ Ⓒ Ⓓ | 174 | Ⓐ Ⓑ Ⓒ Ⓓ | 194 | Ⓐ Ⓑ Ⓒ Ⓓ |
| 115 | Ⓐ Ⓑ Ⓒ Ⓓ | 135 | Ⓐ Ⓑ Ⓒ Ⓓ | 155 | Ⓐ Ⓑ Ⓒ Ⓓ | 175 | Ⓐ Ⓑ Ⓒ Ⓓ | 195 | Ⓐ Ⓑ Ⓒ Ⓓ |
| 116 | Ⓐ Ⓑ Ⓒ Ⓓ | 136 | Ⓐ Ⓑ Ⓒ Ⓓ | 156 | Ⓐ Ⓑ Ⓒ Ⓓ | 176 | Ⓐ Ⓑ Ⓒ Ⓓ | 196 | Ⓐ Ⓑ Ⓒ Ⓓ |
| 117 | Ⓐ Ⓑ Ⓒ Ⓓ | 137 | Ⓐ Ⓑ Ⓒ Ⓓ | 157 | Ⓐ Ⓑ Ⓒ Ⓓ | 177 | Ⓐ Ⓑ Ⓒ Ⓓ | 197 | Ⓐ Ⓑ Ⓒ Ⓓ |
| 118 | Ⓐ Ⓑ Ⓒ Ⓓ | 138 | Ⓐ Ⓑ Ⓒ Ⓓ | 158 | Ⓐ Ⓑ Ⓒ Ⓓ | 178 | Ⓐ Ⓑ Ⓒ Ⓓ | 198 | Ⓐ Ⓑ Ⓒ Ⓓ |
| 119 | Ⓐ Ⓑ Ⓒ Ⓓ | 139 | Ⓐ Ⓑ Ⓒ Ⓓ | 159 | Ⓐ Ⓑ Ⓒ Ⓓ | 179 | Ⓐ Ⓑ Ⓒ Ⓓ | 199 | Ⓐ Ⓑ Ⓒ Ⓓ |
| 120 | Ⓐ Ⓑ Ⓒ Ⓓ | 140 | Ⓐ Ⓑ Ⓒ Ⓓ | 160 | Ⓐ Ⓑ Ⓒ Ⓓ | 180 | Ⓐ Ⓑ Ⓒ Ⓓ | 200 | Ⓐ Ⓑ Ⓒ Ⓓ |

확 인

1. 시용 필기구 : 컴퓨터용 연필(연필을 제외한 사인펜, 볼펜 등은 절대불가)

2. 정답은 필기구 사용과 〈보기〉의 올바른 표기 이외의 정답된 표기로 한 경우에는 답 위원회의 OMR기기가 판독한 경과에 따르며 그 결과는 본인 책임입니다. 1기개의 정답만 골라 아래의 올바른 표기대로 정확히 표기하여야 합니다.

   〈보기〉 올바른 표기 : ●      잘못된 표기 : ⊘ ⊗ ◍

3. 답안지는 컴퓨터로 처리되므로 훼손하시면 안 되며, 상단의 타이밍마크(▤▤▤)를 찢거나, 낙서 등 하면 본인에게 불이익이 발생할 수 있습니다.

4. 감독관의 확인이 없거나 시험 종료 후에 답안 작성을 계속할 경우 시험 무효 처리됩니다.

※ 서약 내용을 읽으시고 확인란에 반드시 서명하십시오.

본인은 TOEIC 시험 문제의 일부 또는 전부를 무단하거나 어떠한 형태로든 타인에게 공개하지 않을 것이며 인터넷 또는 이쇄물 등을 이용해 유포하거나 참고 자료로 활용하지 않을 것입니다. 또한 TOEIC 시험 부정 행위 처리 규정을 준수할 것을 서약합니다.

서  약

# ANSWER SHEET

# Actual Test 3

| 수험번호 | | | | |

| 좌석번호 |
| --- |
| Ⓐ Ⓑ Ⓒ Ⓓ Ⓔ |
| ① ② ③ ④ ⑤ ⑥ ⑦ |

| 성명 | 한글 | |
| --- | --- | --- |
| | 한자 | |
| | 영자 | |

응시일자 :     년     월     일

## LISTENING (Part I~IV)

| NO. | ANSWER | NO. | ANSWER | NO. | ANSWER | NO. | ANSWER | NO. | ANSWER |
| --- | --- | --- | --- | --- | --- | --- | --- | --- | --- |
| | A B C D | | A B C D | | A B C D | | A B C D | | A B C D |
| 1 | Ⓐ Ⓑ Ⓒ Ⓓ | 21 | Ⓐ Ⓑ Ⓒ Ⓓ | 41 | Ⓐ Ⓑ Ⓒ Ⓓ | 61 | Ⓐ Ⓑ Ⓒ Ⓓ | 81 | Ⓐ Ⓑ Ⓒ Ⓓ |
| 2 | Ⓐ Ⓑ Ⓒ Ⓓ | 22 | Ⓐ Ⓑ Ⓒ Ⓓ | 42 | Ⓐ Ⓑ Ⓒ Ⓓ | 62 | Ⓐ Ⓑ Ⓒ Ⓓ | 82 | Ⓐ Ⓑ Ⓒ Ⓓ |
| 3 | Ⓐ Ⓑ Ⓒ Ⓓ | 23 | Ⓐ Ⓑ Ⓒ Ⓓ | 43 | Ⓐ Ⓑ Ⓒ Ⓓ | 63 | Ⓐ Ⓑ Ⓒ Ⓓ | 83 | Ⓐ Ⓑ Ⓒ Ⓓ |
| 4 | Ⓐ Ⓑ Ⓒ Ⓓ | 24 | Ⓐ Ⓑ Ⓒ Ⓓ | 44 | Ⓐ Ⓑ Ⓒ Ⓓ | 64 | Ⓐ Ⓑ Ⓒ Ⓓ | 84 | Ⓐ Ⓑ Ⓒ Ⓓ |
| 5 | Ⓐ Ⓑ Ⓒ Ⓓ | 25 | Ⓐ Ⓑ Ⓒ Ⓓ | 45 | Ⓐ Ⓑ Ⓒ Ⓓ | 65 | Ⓐ Ⓑ Ⓒ Ⓓ | 85 | Ⓐ Ⓑ Ⓒ Ⓓ |
| 6 | Ⓐ Ⓑ Ⓒ Ⓓ | 26 | Ⓐ Ⓑ Ⓒ Ⓓ | 46 | Ⓐ Ⓑ Ⓒ Ⓓ | 66 | Ⓐ Ⓑ Ⓒ Ⓓ | 86 | Ⓐ Ⓑ Ⓒ Ⓓ |
| 7 | Ⓐ Ⓑ Ⓒ Ⓓ | 27 | Ⓐ Ⓑ Ⓒ Ⓓ | 47 | Ⓐ Ⓑ Ⓒ Ⓓ | 67 | Ⓐ Ⓑ Ⓒ Ⓓ | 87 | Ⓐ Ⓑ Ⓒ Ⓓ |
| 8 | Ⓐ Ⓑ Ⓒ Ⓓ | 28 | Ⓐ Ⓑ Ⓒ Ⓓ | 48 | Ⓐ Ⓑ Ⓒ Ⓓ | 68 | Ⓐ Ⓑ Ⓒ Ⓓ | 88 | Ⓐ Ⓑ Ⓒ Ⓓ |
| 9 | Ⓐ Ⓑ Ⓒ Ⓓ | 29 | Ⓐ Ⓑ Ⓒ Ⓓ | 49 | Ⓐ Ⓑ Ⓒ Ⓓ | 69 | Ⓐ Ⓑ Ⓒ Ⓓ | 89 | Ⓐ Ⓑ Ⓒ Ⓓ |
| 10 | Ⓐ Ⓑ Ⓒ Ⓓ | 30 | Ⓐ Ⓑ Ⓒ Ⓓ | 50 | Ⓐ Ⓑ Ⓒ Ⓓ | 70 | Ⓐ Ⓑ Ⓒ Ⓓ | 90 | Ⓐ Ⓑ Ⓒ Ⓓ |
| 11 | Ⓐ Ⓑ Ⓒ Ⓓ | 31 | Ⓐ Ⓑ Ⓒ Ⓓ | 51 | Ⓐ Ⓑ Ⓒ Ⓓ | 71 | Ⓐ Ⓑ Ⓒ Ⓓ | 91 | Ⓐ Ⓑ Ⓒ Ⓓ |
| 12 | Ⓐ Ⓑ Ⓒ Ⓓ | 32 | Ⓐ Ⓑ Ⓒ Ⓓ | 52 | Ⓐ Ⓑ Ⓒ Ⓓ | 72 | Ⓐ Ⓑ Ⓒ Ⓓ | 92 | Ⓐ Ⓑ Ⓒ Ⓓ |
| 13 | Ⓐ Ⓑ Ⓒ Ⓓ | 33 | Ⓐ Ⓑ Ⓒ Ⓓ | 53 | Ⓐ Ⓑ Ⓒ Ⓓ | 73 | Ⓐ Ⓑ Ⓒ Ⓓ | 93 | Ⓐ Ⓑ Ⓒ Ⓓ |
| 14 | Ⓐ Ⓑ Ⓒ Ⓓ | 34 | Ⓐ Ⓑ Ⓒ Ⓓ | 54 | Ⓐ Ⓑ Ⓒ Ⓓ | 74 | Ⓐ Ⓑ Ⓒ Ⓓ | 94 | Ⓐ Ⓑ Ⓒ Ⓓ |
| 15 | Ⓐ Ⓑ Ⓒ Ⓓ | 35 | Ⓐ Ⓑ Ⓒ Ⓓ | 55 | Ⓐ Ⓑ Ⓒ Ⓓ | 75 | Ⓐ Ⓑ Ⓒ Ⓓ | 95 | Ⓐ Ⓑ Ⓒ Ⓓ |
| 16 | Ⓐ Ⓑ Ⓒ Ⓓ | 36 | Ⓐ Ⓑ Ⓒ Ⓓ | 56 | Ⓐ Ⓑ Ⓒ Ⓓ | 76 | Ⓐ Ⓑ Ⓒ Ⓓ | 96 | Ⓐ Ⓑ Ⓒ Ⓓ |
| 17 | Ⓐ Ⓑ Ⓒ Ⓓ | 37 | Ⓐ Ⓑ Ⓒ Ⓓ | 57 | Ⓐ Ⓑ Ⓒ Ⓓ | 77 | Ⓐ Ⓑ Ⓒ Ⓓ | 97 | Ⓐ Ⓑ Ⓒ Ⓓ |
| 18 | Ⓐ Ⓑ Ⓒ Ⓓ | 38 | Ⓐ Ⓑ Ⓒ Ⓓ | 58 | Ⓐ Ⓑ Ⓒ Ⓓ | 78 | Ⓐ Ⓑ Ⓒ Ⓓ | 98 | Ⓐ Ⓑ Ⓒ Ⓓ |
| 19 | Ⓐ Ⓑ Ⓒ Ⓓ | 39 | Ⓐ Ⓑ Ⓒ Ⓓ | 59 | Ⓐ Ⓑ Ⓒ Ⓓ | 79 | Ⓐ Ⓑ Ⓒ Ⓓ | 99 | Ⓐ Ⓑ Ⓒ Ⓓ |
| 20 | Ⓐ Ⓑ Ⓒ Ⓓ | 40 | Ⓐ Ⓑ Ⓒ Ⓓ | 60 | Ⓐ Ⓑ Ⓒ Ⓓ | 80 | Ⓐ Ⓑ Ⓒ Ⓓ | 100 | Ⓐ Ⓑ Ⓒ Ⓓ |

## READING (Part V~VII)

| NO. | ANSWER | NO. | ANSWER | NO. | ANSWER | NO. | ANSWER | NO. | ANSWER |
| --- | --- | --- | --- | --- | --- | --- | --- | --- | --- |
| | A B C D | | A B C D | | A B C D | | A B C D | | A B C D |
| 101 | Ⓐ Ⓑ Ⓒ Ⓓ | 121 | Ⓐ Ⓑ Ⓒ Ⓓ | 141 | Ⓐ Ⓑ Ⓒ Ⓓ | 161 | Ⓐ Ⓑ Ⓒ Ⓓ | 181 | Ⓐ Ⓑ Ⓒ Ⓓ |
| 102 | Ⓐ Ⓑ Ⓒ Ⓓ | 122 | Ⓐ Ⓑ Ⓒ Ⓓ | 142 | Ⓐ Ⓑ Ⓒ Ⓓ | 162 | Ⓐ Ⓑ Ⓒ Ⓓ | 182 | Ⓐ Ⓑ Ⓒ Ⓓ |
| 103 | Ⓐ Ⓑ Ⓒ Ⓓ | 123 | Ⓐ Ⓑ Ⓒ Ⓓ | 143 | Ⓐ Ⓑ Ⓒ Ⓓ | 163 | Ⓐ Ⓑ Ⓒ Ⓓ | 183 | Ⓐ Ⓑ Ⓒ Ⓓ |
| 104 | Ⓐ Ⓑ Ⓒ Ⓓ | 124 | Ⓐ Ⓑ Ⓒ Ⓓ | 144 | Ⓐ Ⓑ Ⓒ Ⓓ | 164 | Ⓐ Ⓑ Ⓒ Ⓓ | 184 | Ⓐ Ⓑ Ⓒ Ⓓ |
| 105 | Ⓐ Ⓑ Ⓒ Ⓓ | 125 | Ⓐ Ⓑ Ⓒ Ⓓ | 145 | Ⓐ Ⓑ Ⓒ Ⓓ | 165 | Ⓐ Ⓑ Ⓒ Ⓓ | 185 | Ⓐ Ⓑ Ⓒ Ⓓ |
| 106 | Ⓐ Ⓑ Ⓒ Ⓓ | 126 | Ⓐ Ⓑ Ⓒ Ⓓ | 146 | Ⓐ Ⓑ Ⓒ Ⓓ | 166 | Ⓐ Ⓑ Ⓒ Ⓓ | 186 | Ⓐ Ⓑ Ⓒ Ⓓ |
| 107 | Ⓐ Ⓑ Ⓒ Ⓓ | 127 | Ⓐ Ⓑ Ⓒ Ⓓ | 147 | Ⓐ Ⓑ Ⓒ Ⓓ | 167 | Ⓐ Ⓑ Ⓒ Ⓓ | 187 | Ⓐ Ⓑ Ⓒ Ⓓ |
| 108 | Ⓐ Ⓑ Ⓒ Ⓓ | 128 | Ⓐ Ⓑ Ⓒ Ⓓ | 148 | Ⓐ Ⓑ Ⓒ Ⓓ | 168 | Ⓐ Ⓑ Ⓒ Ⓓ | 188 | Ⓐ Ⓑ Ⓒ Ⓓ |
| 109 | Ⓐ Ⓑ Ⓒ Ⓓ | 129 | Ⓐ Ⓑ Ⓒ Ⓓ | 149 | Ⓐ Ⓑ Ⓒ Ⓓ | 169 | Ⓐ Ⓑ Ⓒ Ⓓ | 189 | Ⓐ Ⓑ Ⓒ Ⓓ |
| 110 | Ⓐ Ⓑ Ⓒ Ⓓ | 130 | Ⓐ Ⓑ Ⓒ Ⓓ | 150 | Ⓐ Ⓑ Ⓒ Ⓓ | 170 | Ⓐ Ⓑ Ⓒ Ⓓ | 190 | Ⓐ Ⓑ Ⓒ Ⓓ |
| 111 | Ⓐ Ⓑ Ⓒ Ⓓ | 131 | Ⓐ Ⓑ Ⓒ Ⓓ | 151 | Ⓐ Ⓑ Ⓒ Ⓓ | 171 | Ⓐ Ⓑ Ⓒ Ⓓ | 191 | Ⓐ Ⓑ Ⓒ Ⓓ |
| 112 | Ⓐ Ⓑ Ⓒ Ⓓ | 132 | Ⓐ Ⓑ Ⓒ Ⓓ | 152 | Ⓐ Ⓑ Ⓒ Ⓓ | 172 | Ⓐ Ⓑ Ⓒ Ⓓ | 192 | Ⓐ Ⓑ Ⓒ Ⓓ |
| 113 | Ⓐ Ⓑ Ⓒ Ⓓ | 133 | Ⓐ Ⓑ Ⓒ Ⓓ | 153 | Ⓐ Ⓑ Ⓒ Ⓓ | 173 | Ⓐ Ⓑ Ⓒ Ⓓ | 193 | Ⓐ Ⓑ Ⓒ Ⓓ |
| 114 | Ⓐ Ⓑ Ⓒ Ⓓ | 134 | Ⓐ Ⓑ Ⓒ Ⓓ | 154 | Ⓐ Ⓑ Ⓒ Ⓓ | 174 | Ⓐ Ⓑ Ⓒ Ⓓ | 194 | Ⓐ Ⓑ Ⓒ Ⓓ |
| 115 | Ⓐ Ⓑ Ⓒ Ⓓ | 135 | Ⓐ Ⓑ Ⓒ Ⓓ | 155 | Ⓐ Ⓑ Ⓒ Ⓓ | 175 | Ⓐ Ⓑ Ⓒ Ⓓ | 195 | Ⓐ Ⓑ Ⓒ Ⓓ |
| 116 | Ⓐ Ⓑ Ⓒ Ⓓ | 136 | Ⓐ Ⓑ Ⓒ Ⓓ | 156 | Ⓐ Ⓑ Ⓒ Ⓓ | 176 | Ⓐ Ⓑ Ⓒ Ⓓ | 196 | Ⓐ Ⓑ Ⓒ Ⓓ |
| 117 | Ⓐ Ⓑ Ⓒ Ⓓ | 137 | Ⓐ Ⓑ Ⓒ Ⓓ | 157 | Ⓐ Ⓑ Ⓒ Ⓓ | 177 | Ⓐ Ⓑ Ⓒ Ⓓ | 197 | Ⓐ Ⓑ Ⓒ Ⓓ |
| 118 | Ⓐ Ⓑ Ⓒ Ⓓ | 138 | Ⓐ Ⓑ Ⓒ Ⓓ | 158 | Ⓐ Ⓑ Ⓒ Ⓓ | 178 | Ⓐ Ⓑ Ⓒ Ⓓ | 198 | Ⓐ Ⓑ Ⓒ Ⓓ |
| 119 | Ⓐ Ⓑ Ⓒ Ⓓ | 139 | Ⓐ Ⓑ Ⓒ Ⓓ | 159 | Ⓐ Ⓑ Ⓒ Ⓓ | 179 | Ⓐ Ⓑ Ⓒ Ⓓ | 199 | Ⓐ Ⓑ Ⓒ Ⓓ |
| 120 | Ⓐ Ⓑ Ⓒ Ⓓ | 140 | Ⓐ Ⓑ Ⓒ Ⓓ | 160 | Ⓐ Ⓑ Ⓒ Ⓓ | 180 | Ⓐ Ⓑ Ⓒ Ⓓ | 200 | Ⓐ Ⓑ Ⓒ Ⓓ |

# ANSWER SHEET

# Actual Test 4

수험번호

응시일자 :　년　월　일

| | 한글 | ⒶⒷⒸⒹⒺ |
|---|---|---|
| 성명 | 한자 | ①②③④⑤⑥⑦ |
| | 영자 | |

좌석번호

## LISTENING (Part I~IV)

| NO. | ANSWER |
|---|---|
| 1 | Ⓐ Ⓑ Ⓒ Ⓓ |
| 2 | Ⓐ Ⓑ Ⓒ Ⓓ |
| 3 | Ⓐ Ⓑ Ⓒ Ⓓ |
| 4 | Ⓐ Ⓑ Ⓒ Ⓓ |
| 5 | Ⓐ Ⓑ Ⓒ Ⓓ |
| 6 | Ⓐ Ⓑ Ⓒ Ⓓ |
| 7 | Ⓐ Ⓑ Ⓒ Ⓓ |
| 8 | Ⓐ Ⓑ Ⓒ Ⓓ |
| 9 | Ⓐ Ⓑ Ⓒ Ⓓ |
| 10 | Ⓐ Ⓑ Ⓒ Ⓓ |
| 11 | Ⓐ Ⓑ Ⓒ Ⓓ |
| 12 | Ⓐ Ⓑ Ⓒ Ⓓ |
| 13 | Ⓐ Ⓑ Ⓒ Ⓓ |
| 14 | Ⓐ Ⓑ Ⓒ Ⓓ |
| 15 | Ⓐ Ⓑ Ⓒ Ⓓ |
| 16 | Ⓐ Ⓑ Ⓒ Ⓓ |
| 17 | Ⓐ Ⓑ Ⓒ Ⓓ |
| 18 | Ⓐ Ⓑ Ⓒ Ⓓ |
| 19 | Ⓐ Ⓑ Ⓒ Ⓓ |
| 20 | Ⓐ Ⓑ Ⓒ Ⓓ |

(NO. 21~40, 41~60, 61~80, 81~100 each with ANSWER columns Ⓐ Ⓑ Ⓒ Ⓓ)

## READING (Part V~VII)

(NO. 101~120, 121~140, 141~160, 161~180, 181~200 each with ANSWER columns Ⓐ Ⓑ Ⓒ Ⓓ)

서 약

확 인

# ANSWER SHEET

# Actual Test 5

수험번호

응시일자 :   년   월   일

좌석번호

Ⓐ Ⓑ Ⓒ Ⓓ Ⓔ
① ② ③ ④ ⑤ ⑥ ⑦

| 성 명 | 한글 | |
|---|---|---|
| | 한자 | |
| | 영자 | |

확 인

## LISTENING (Part I~IV)

| NO. | ANSWER | NO. | ANSWER | NO. | ANSWER | NO. | ANSWER | NO. | ANSWER |
|---|---|---|---|---|---|---|---|---|---|
| | A B C D | | A B C D | | A B C D | | A B C D | | A B C D |
| 1 | Ⓐ Ⓑ Ⓒ Ⓓ | 21 | Ⓐ Ⓑ Ⓒ Ⓓ | 41 | Ⓐ Ⓑ Ⓒ Ⓓ | 61 | Ⓐ Ⓑ Ⓒ Ⓓ | 81 | Ⓐ Ⓑ Ⓒ Ⓓ |
| 2 | Ⓐ Ⓑ Ⓒ Ⓓ | 22 | Ⓐ Ⓑ Ⓒ Ⓓ | 42 | Ⓐ Ⓑ Ⓒ Ⓓ | 62 | Ⓐ Ⓑ Ⓒ Ⓓ | 82 | Ⓐ Ⓑ Ⓒ Ⓓ |
| 3 | Ⓐ Ⓑ Ⓒ Ⓓ | 23 | Ⓐ Ⓑ Ⓒ Ⓓ | 43 | Ⓐ Ⓑ Ⓒ Ⓓ | 63 | Ⓐ Ⓑ Ⓒ Ⓓ | 83 | Ⓐ Ⓑ Ⓒ Ⓓ |
| 4 | Ⓐ Ⓑ Ⓒ Ⓓ | 24 | Ⓐ Ⓑ Ⓒ Ⓓ | 44 | Ⓐ Ⓑ Ⓒ Ⓓ | 64 | Ⓐ Ⓑ Ⓒ Ⓓ | 84 | Ⓐ Ⓑ Ⓒ Ⓓ |
| 5 | Ⓐ Ⓑ Ⓒ Ⓓ | 25 | Ⓐ Ⓑ Ⓒ Ⓓ | 45 | Ⓐ Ⓑ Ⓒ Ⓓ | 65 | Ⓐ Ⓑ Ⓒ Ⓓ | 85 | Ⓐ Ⓑ Ⓒ Ⓓ |
| 6 | Ⓐ Ⓑ Ⓒ Ⓓ | 26 | Ⓐ Ⓑ Ⓒ Ⓓ | 46 | Ⓐ Ⓑ Ⓒ Ⓓ | 66 | Ⓐ Ⓑ Ⓒ Ⓓ | 86 | Ⓐ Ⓑ Ⓒ Ⓓ |
| 7 | Ⓐ Ⓑ Ⓒ Ⓓ | 27 | Ⓐ Ⓑ Ⓒ Ⓓ | 47 | Ⓐ Ⓑ Ⓒ Ⓓ | 67 | Ⓐ Ⓑ Ⓒ Ⓓ | 87 | Ⓐ Ⓑ Ⓒ Ⓓ |
| 8 | Ⓐ Ⓑ Ⓒ Ⓓ | 28 | Ⓐ Ⓑ Ⓒ Ⓓ | 48 | Ⓐ Ⓑ Ⓒ Ⓓ | 68 | Ⓐ Ⓑ Ⓒ Ⓓ | 88 | Ⓐ Ⓑ Ⓒ Ⓓ |
| 9 | Ⓐ Ⓑ Ⓒ Ⓓ | 29 | Ⓐ Ⓑ Ⓒ Ⓓ | 49 | Ⓐ Ⓑ Ⓒ Ⓓ | 69 | Ⓐ Ⓑ Ⓒ Ⓓ | 89 | Ⓐ Ⓑ Ⓒ Ⓓ |
| 10 | Ⓐ Ⓑ Ⓒ Ⓓ | 30 | Ⓐ Ⓑ Ⓒ Ⓓ | 50 | Ⓐ Ⓑ Ⓒ Ⓓ | 70 | Ⓐ Ⓑ Ⓒ Ⓓ | 90 | Ⓐ Ⓑ Ⓒ Ⓓ |
| 11 | Ⓐ Ⓑ Ⓒ Ⓓ | 31 | Ⓐ Ⓑ Ⓒ Ⓓ | 51 | Ⓐ Ⓑ Ⓒ Ⓓ | 71 | Ⓐ Ⓑ Ⓒ Ⓓ | 91 | Ⓐ Ⓑ Ⓒ Ⓓ |
| 12 | Ⓐ Ⓑ Ⓒ Ⓓ | 32 | Ⓐ Ⓑ Ⓒ Ⓓ | 52 | Ⓐ Ⓑ Ⓒ Ⓓ | 72 | Ⓐ Ⓑ Ⓒ Ⓓ | 92 | Ⓐ Ⓑ Ⓒ Ⓓ |
| 13 | Ⓐ Ⓑ Ⓒ Ⓓ | 33 | Ⓐ Ⓑ Ⓒ Ⓓ | 53 | Ⓐ Ⓑ Ⓒ Ⓓ | 73 | Ⓐ Ⓑ Ⓒ Ⓓ | 93 | Ⓐ Ⓑ Ⓒ Ⓓ |
| 14 | Ⓐ Ⓑ Ⓒ Ⓓ | 34 | Ⓐ Ⓑ Ⓒ Ⓓ | 54 | Ⓐ Ⓑ Ⓒ Ⓓ | 74 | Ⓐ Ⓑ Ⓒ Ⓓ | 94 | Ⓐ Ⓑ Ⓒ Ⓓ |
| 15 | Ⓐ Ⓑ Ⓒ Ⓓ | 35 | Ⓐ Ⓑ Ⓒ Ⓓ | 55 | Ⓐ Ⓑ Ⓒ Ⓓ | 75 | Ⓐ Ⓑ Ⓒ Ⓓ | 95 | Ⓐ Ⓑ Ⓒ Ⓓ |
| 16 | Ⓐ Ⓑ Ⓒ Ⓓ | 36 | Ⓐ Ⓑ Ⓒ Ⓓ | 56 | Ⓐ Ⓑ Ⓒ Ⓓ | 76 | Ⓐ Ⓑ Ⓒ Ⓓ | 96 | Ⓐ Ⓑ Ⓒ Ⓓ |
| 17 | Ⓐ Ⓑ Ⓒ Ⓓ | 37 | Ⓐ Ⓑ Ⓒ Ⓓ | 57 | Ⓐ Ⓑ Ⓒ Ⓓ | 77 | Ⓐ Ⓑ Ⓒ Ⓓ | 97 | Ⓐ Ⓑ Ⓒ Ⓓ |
| 18 | Ⓐ Ⓑ Ⓒ Ⓓ | 38 | Ⓐ Ⓑ Ⓒ Ⓓ | 58 | Ⓐ Ⓑ Ⓒ Ⓓ | 78 | Ⓐ Ⓑ Ⓒ Ⓓ | 98 | Ⓐ Ⓑ Ⓒ Ⓓ |
| 19 | Ⓐ Ⓑ Ⓒ Ⓓ | 39 | Ⓐ Ⓑ Ⓒ Ⓓ | 59 | Ⓐ Ⓑ Ⓒ Ⓓ | 79 | Ⓐ Ⓑ Ⓒ Ⓓ | 99 | Ⓐ Ⓑ Ⓒ Ⓓ |
| 20 | Ⓐ Ⓑ Ⓒ Ⓓ | 40 | Ⓐ Ⓑ Ⓒ Ⓓ | 60 | Ⓐ Ⓑ Ⓒ Ⓓ | 80 | Ⓐ Ⓑ Ⓒ Ⓓ | 100 | Ⓐ Ⓑ Ⓒ Ⓓ |

## READING (Part V~VII)

| NO. | ANSWER | NO. | ANSWER | NO. | ANSWER | NO. | ANSWER | NO. | ANSWER |
|---|---|---|---|---|---|---|---|---|---|
| | A B C D | | A B C D | | A B C D | | A B C D | | A B C D |
| 101 | Ⓐ Ⓑ Ⓒ Ⓓ | 121 | Ⓐ Ⓑ Ⓒ Ⓓ | 141 | Ⓐ Ⓑ Ⓒ Ⓓ | 161 | Ⓐ Ⓑ Ⓒ Ⓓ | 181 | Ⓐ Ⓑ Ⓒ Ⓓ |
| 102 | Ⓐ Ⓑ Ⓒ Ⓓ | 122 | Ⓐ Ⓑ Ⓒ Ⓓ | 142 | Ⓐ Ⓑ Ⓒ Ⓓ | 162 | Ⓐ Ⓑ Ⓒ Ⓓ | 182 | Ⓐ Ⓑ Ⓒ Ⓓ |
| 103 | Ⓐ Ⓑ Ⓒ Ⓓ | 123 | Ⓐ Ⓑ Ⓒ Ⓓ | 143 | Ⓐ Ⓑ Ⓒ Ⓓ | 163 | Ⓐ Ⓑ Ⓒ Ⓓ | 183 | Ⓐ Ⓑ Ⓒ Ⓓ |
| 104 | Ⓐ Ⓑ Ⓒ Ⓓ | 124 | Ⓐ Ⓑ Ⓒ Ⓓ | 144 | Ⓐ Ⓑ Ⓒ Ⓓ | 164 | Ⓐ Ⓑ Ⓒ Ⓓ | 184 | Ⓐ Ⓑ Ⓒ Ⓓ |
| 105 | Ⓐ Ⓑ Ⓒ Ⓓ | 125 | Ⓐ Ⓑ Ⓒ Ⓓ | 145 | Ⓐ Ⓑ Ⓒ Ⓓ | 165 | Ⓐ Ⓑ Ⓒ Ⓓ | 185 | Ⓐ Ⓑ Ⓒ Ⓓ |
| 106 | Ⓐ Ⓑ Ⓒ Ⓓ | 126 | Ⓐ Ⓑ Ⓒ Ⓓ | 146 | Ⓐ Ⓑ Ⓒ Ⓓ | 166 | Ⓐ Ⓑ Ⓒ Ⓓ | 186 | Ⓐ Ⓑ Ⓒ Ⓓ |
| 107 | Ⓐ Ⓑ Ⓒ Ⓓ | 127 | Ⓐ Ⓑ Ⓒ Ⓓ | 147 | Ⓐ Ⓑ Ⓒ Ⓓ | 167 | Ⓐ Ⓑ Ⓒ Ⓓ | 187 | Ⓐ Ⓑ Ⓒ Ⓓ |
| 108 | Ⓐ Ⓑ Ⓒ Ⓓ | 128 | Ⓐ Ⓑ Ⓒ Ⓓ | 148 | Ⓐ Ⓑ Ⓒ Ⓓ | 168 | Ⓐ Ⓑ Ⓒ Ⓓ | 188 | Ⓐ Ⓑ Ⓒ Ⓓ |
| 109 | Ⓐ Ⓑ Ⓒ Ⓓ | 129 | Ⓐ Ⓑ Ⓒ Ⓓ | 149 | Ⓐ Ⓑ Ⓒ Ⓓ | 169 | Ⓐ Ⓑ Ⓒ Ⓓ | 189 | Ⓐ Ⓑ Ⓒ Ⓓ |
| 110 | Ⓐ Ⓑ Ⓒ Ⓓ | 130 | Ⓐ Ⓑ Ⓒ Ⓓ | 150 | Ⓐ Ⓑ Ⓒ Ⓓ | 170 | Ⓐ Ⓑ Ⓒ Ⓓ | 190 | Ⓐ Ⓑ Ⓒ Ⓓ |
| 111 | Ⓐ Ⓑ Ⓒ Ⓓ | 131 | Ⓐ Ⓑ Ⓒ Ⓓ | 151 | Ⓐ Ⓑ Ⓒ Ⓓ | 171 | Ⓐ Ⓑ Ⓒ Ⓓ | 191 | Ⓐ Ⓑ Ⓒ Ⓓ |
| 112 | Ⓐ Ⓑ Ⓒ Ⓓ | 132 | Ⓐ Ⓑ Ⓒ Ⓓ | 152 | Ⓐ Ⓑ Ⓒ Ⓓ | 172 | Ⓐ Ⓑ Ⓒ Ⓓ | 192 | Ⓐ Ⓑ Ⓒ Ⓓ |
| 113 | Ⓐ Ⓑ Ⓒ Ⓓ | 133 | Ⓐ Ⓑ Ⓒ Ⓓ | 153 | Ⓐ Ⓑ Ⓒ Ⓓ | 173 | Ⓐ Ⓑ Ⓒ Ⓓ | 193 | Ⓐ Ⓑ Ⓒ Ⓓ |
| 114 | Ⓐ Ⓑ Ⓒ Ⓓ | 134 | Ⓐ Ⓑ Ⓒ Ⓓ | 154 | Ⓐ Ⓑ Ⓒ Ⓓ | 174 | Ⓐ Ⓑ Ⓒ Ⓓ | 194 | Ⓐ Ⓑ Ⓒ Ⓓ |
| 115 | Ⓐ Ⓑ Ⓒ Ⓓ | 135 | Ⓐ Ⓑ Ⓒ Ⓓ | 155 | Ⓐ Ⓑ Ⓒ Ⓓ | 175 | Ⓐ Ⓑ Ⓒ Ⓓ | 195 | Ⓐ Ⓑ Ⓒ Ⓓ |
| 116 | Ⓐ Ⓑ Ⓒ Ⓓ | 136 | Ⓐ Ⓑ Ⓒ Ⓓ | 156 | Ⓐ Ⓑ Ⓒ Ⓓ | 176 | Ⓐ Ⓑ Ⓒ Ⓓ | 196 | Ⓐ Ⓑ Ⓒ Ⓓ |
| 117 | Ⓐ Ⓑ Ⓒ Ⓓ | 137 | Ⓐ Ⓑ Ⓒ Ⓓ | 157 | Ⓐ Ⓑ Ⓒ Ⓓ | 177 | Ⓐ Ⓑ Ⓒ Ⓓ | 197 | Ⓐ Ⓑ Ⓒ Ⓓ |
| 118 | Ⓐ Ⓑ Ⓒ Ⓓ | 138 | Ⓐ Ⓑ Ⓒ Ⓓ | 158 | Ⓐ Ⓑ Ⓒ Ⓓ | 178 | Ⓐ Ⓑ Ⓒ Ⓓ | 198 | Ⓐ Ⓑ Ⓒ Ⓓ |
| 119 | Ⓐ Ⓑ Ⓒ Ⓓ | 139 | Ⓐ Ⓑ Ⓒ Ⓓ | 159 | Ⓐ Ⓑ Ⓒ Ⓓ | 179 | Ⓐ Ⓑ Ⓒ Ⓓ | 199 | Ⓐ Ⓑ Ⓒ Ⓓ |
| 120 | Ⓐ Ⓑ Ⓒ Ⓓ | 140 | Ⓐ Ⓑ Ⓒ Ⓓ | 160 | Ⓐ Ⓑ Ⓒ Ⓓ | 180 | Ⓐ Ⓑ Ⓒ Ⓓ | 200 | Ⓐ Ⓑ Ⓒ Ⓓ |

1. 시용 필기구 : 컴퓨터용 연필(연필을 제외한 사인펜, 볼펜 등은 사용 절대 불가)

2. 잘못된 필기구 사용과 〈보기〉의 올바른 표기 이외의 잘못된 표기로 한 경우에는 당 위원회의 OMR기기가 판독한 결과에 따르며 그 결과는 본인 책임입니다. 1개의 정답만 골라 아래의 올바른 표기대로 정확히 표기하여야 합니다.

〈보기〉 올바른 표기 : ●     잘못된 표기 : ⊘ ◑ ◓

3. 답안지는 컴퓨터로 처리되므로 훼손하지 안 되며, 성답의 타이밍마크(▌▌▌▌)부분을 찢거나, 낙서 등을 하면 본인에게 불이익이 발생할 수 있습니다.

4. 감독관의 확인이 없거나 시험 종료 후에 답안 작성을 계속할 경우 시험 무효 처리됩니다.

*서사와 내용을 읽으시고 확인란에 반드시 서명하십시오.

서     약

본인은 TOEIC 시험 문제의 일부 또는 전부를 유출하거나 어떠한 형태로든 타인에게 누설 공개하지 않을 것이며 인터넷 또는 인쇄물 등을 이용해 유포하거나 참고 자료로 활용하지 않을 것입니다. 또한 TOEIC 시험 부정 행위 처리 규정을 준수할 것을 서약합니다.

新 **토익!** 어떻게 시작해야 할지 몰라 망설이는 **초보 수험생**들을 위한

# 토익 초보·입문자 맞춤형 교재

나에게 **꼭 맞는**
**토익 책**은?

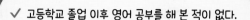

✓ 고등학교 졸업 이후 영어 공부를 해 본 적이 없다.

✓ 토익 시험이라곤 본 적이 없지만 신발 사이즈
   점수가 나올 거 같다.

✓ 혼자서 공부하기 힘들어 동영상 강의가 필요하다.

**YES**

초급자 맞춤형
동영상 강의 제공
총 24강

✓ 어느 정도 영어 공부는 해 왔지만 토익 공부는
   해 본적이 없다.

✓ 모의토익 시험에서 500점 정도는 나온다.

✓ 당장 토익 시험을 앞두고 있으며 750점 이상
   점수가 필요하다.

**YES**

나혼자 끝내는 신토익 스타트 LC+RC | 넥서스토익연구소 지음 | 2018년 1월 출간 | 404페이지
나혼자 끝내는 신토익 BASIC LC+RC | 원정서, 넥서스토익연구소 지음 | 2017년 12월 출간 | 352 페이지

# 新토익을 대비하는
# 가장 현명한 선택!

## • 나혼자 끝내는 新토익 실전서 •

신토익 LC+RC 5회분 ✚ 해설집

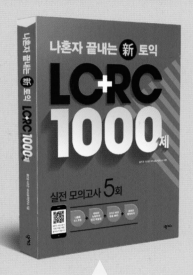

신토익 LC+RC 3회분 ✚ 해설집

실제 시험지가
봉투 안에 쏙~

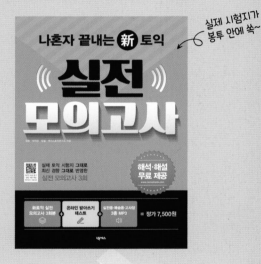

### 나혼자 끝내는 新토익
### LC+RC 1000제

✓ 한 권으로 끝내는 신토익 실전 모의고사 5회분 수록

✓ 해설집을 따로 구매할 필요가 없는
  LC+RC 합본 실전서

✓ 저자의 노하우를 담아 문제의 키워드를
  단숨에 파악하는 알짜 해설 수록

✓ 실전용 · 복습용 · 고사장 버전의 3종 MP3
  무료 다운로드(www.nexusbook.com)

### 나혼자 끝내는 新토익
### 실전 모의고사 3회분(봉투형)

✓ 실제 시험지 형태 그대로,
  신토익 실전 모의고사 3회분 수록

✓ 문제의 키워드를 단숨에 파악하는 알짜 해석 · 해설
  무료 다운로드(www.nexusbook.com)

✓ 실전용 · 복습용 · 고사장 버전의 3종 MP3
  무료 다운로드(www.nexusbook.com)

나혼자 끝내는 신토익 LC+RC 1000제 | 홍진걸·이주은 지음 | 2017년 6월 출간 | 364페이지

나혼자 끝내는 신토익 실전 모의고사 3회분 | 김랑·박자은·임철, 넥서스토익연구소 지음 | 2017년 7월 출간 | 144페이지

나혼자 끝내는 新 토익

LC+RC
1000제

실전 모의고사 5회
스크립트+정답 및 해설

나혼자 1:1 코칭 + 저자의 노하우가 담긴 해설집 + 3가지 버전 무료 MP3 + 온라인 받아쓰기

홍진걸·이주은·넥서스토익연구소 지음

넥서스

나혼자 끝내는 新 토익

# LC+RC 1000제

실전 모의고사 5회
스크립트+정답 및 해설

나혼토 1:1 코칭 + 저자의 노하우가 담긴 해설집 + 3가지 버전 무료 MP3 + 온라인 받아쓰기

홍진걸·이주은·넥서스토익연구소 지음

넥서스

## Actual Test 01

### 🎧 Listening Comprehension

본책 P14

**PART 1**

| | | | | | | | |
|---|---|---|---|---|---|---|---|
| 1 (C) | 2 (A) | 3 (D) | 4 (C) | 5 (C) | 6 (A) | | |

**PART 2**

| | | | | | | | | | |
|---|---|---|---|---|---|---|---|---|---|
| 7 (A) | 8 (B) | 9 (B) | 10 (C) | 11 (A) | 12 (B) | 13 (B) | 14 (B) | 15 (C) | 16 (B) |
| 17 (C) | 18 (A) | 19 (A) | 20 (A) | 21 (B) | 22 (B) | 23 (A) | 24 (C) | 25 (B) | 26 (C) |
| 27 (B) | 28 (C) | 29 (B) | 30 (B) | 31 (C) | | | | | |

**PART 3**

| | | | | | | | | | |
|---|---|---|---|---|---|---|---|---|---|
| 32 (A) | 33 (B) | 34 (D) | 35 (A) | 36 (B) | 37 (A) | 38 (A) | 39 (B) | 40 (A) | 41 (A) |
| 42 (B) | 43 (D) | 44 (B) | 45 (D) | 46 (A) | 47 (A) | 48 (C) | 49 (D) | 50 (D) | 51 (B) |
| 52 (A) | 53 (B) | 54 (D) | 55 (D) | 56 (D) | 57 (A) | 58 (D) | 59 (A) | 60 (D) | 61 (A) |
| 62 (D) | 63 (A) | 64 (B) | 65 (B) | 66 (C) | 67 (B) | 68 (C) | 69 (B) | 70 (D) | |

**PART 4**

| | | | | | | | | | |
|---|---|---|---|---|---|---|---|---|---|
| 71 (A) | 72 (C) | 73 (B) | 74 (D) | 75 (C) | 76 (A) | 77 (D) | 78 (A) | 79 (B) | 80 (D) |
| 81 (C) | 82 (D) | 83 (C) | 84 (C) | 85 (A) | 86 (A) | 87 (C) | 88 (C) | 89 (B) | 90 (D) |
| 91 (A) | 92 (D) | 93 (B) | 94 (B) | 95 (C) | 96 (A) | 97 (D) | 98 (C) | 99 (D) | 100 (A) |

### 📖 Reading Comprehension

본책 P26

**PART 5**

| | | | | | | | | | |
|---|---|---|---|---|---|---|---|---|---|
| 101 (C) | 102 (C) | 103 (B) | 104 (C) | 105 (C) | 106 (B) | 107 (C) | 108 (D) | 109 (A) | 110 (D) |
| 111 (B) | 112 (B) | 113 (D) | 114 (A) | 115 (A) | 116 (A) | 117 (D) | 118 (D) | 119 (D) | 120 (C) |
| 121 (A) | 122 (B) | 123 (B) | 124 (C) | 125 (A) | 126 (B) | 127 (C) | 128 (A) | 129 (D) | 130 (B) |

**PART 6**

| | | | | | | | | | |
|---|---|---|---|---|---|---|---|---|---|
| 131 (C) | 132 (C) | 133 (A) | 134 (A) | 135 (A) | 136 (A) | 137 (A) | 138 (B) | 139 (B) | 140 (A) |
| 141 (B) | 142 (A) | 143 (D) | 144 (C) | 145 (B) | 146 (C) | | | | |

**PART 7**

| | | | | | | | | | |
|---|---|---|---|---|---|---|---|---|---|
| 147 (D) | 148 (C) | 149 (C) | 150 (D) | 151 (C) | 152 (D) | 153 (B) | 154 (D) | 155 (A) | 156 (D) |
| 157 (C) | 158 (C) | 159 (C) | 160 (B) | 161 (D) | 162 (A) | 163 (D) | 164 (B) | 165 (B) | 166 (C) |
| 167 (C) | 168 (D) | 169 (B) | 170 (D) | 171 (C) | 172 (C) | 173 (D) | 174 (C) | 175 (D) | 176 (D) |
| 177 (C) | 178 (A) | 179 (C) | 180 (C) | 181 (C) | 182 (D) | 183 (C) | 184 (B) | 185 (D) | 186 (B) |
| 187 (A) | 188 (C) | 189 (B) | 190 (C) | 191 (C) | 192 (C) | 193 (D) | 194 (B) | 195 (C) | 196 (B) |
| 197 (B) | 198 (D) | 199 (C) | 200 (A) | | | | | | |

Actual Test 01   002 • 003

## PART 1

P14

**1** 미W
(A) He is getting off the truck.
(B) He is digging into the ground.
(C) **He is holding a tool.**
(D) He is collecting some leaves.

(A) 남자가 트럭에서 내리고 있다.
(B) 남자가 땅을 파고 있다.
(C) 남자가 도구를 잡고 있다.
(D) 남자가 나뭇잎을 모으고 있다.

어휘  get off 내리다   dig into ~을 파다   hold 잡다, 쥐다   collect 모으다, 수집하다

**2** 미M
(A) Some pedestrians are crossing the street.
(B) A bicycle is leaning against a railing.
(C) A man is locking up his bicycle.
(D) Several cars are parked along the street.

(A) 보행자들이 길을 건너고 있다.
(B) 자전거가 난간에 기대어 있다.
(C) 남자가 자전거를 잠그고 있다.
(D) 여러 차량이 도로를 따라 주차되어 있다.

어휘  pedestrian 보행자   lean 기대다   railing 난간   lock up 잠그다

**3** 영M
(A) She is stirring batter in the glass bowl.
(B) She is facing the kitchen cabinet.
(C) Some containers are filled with food.
(D) **Some vegetables are put on a cutting board.**

(A) 여자가 유리 그릇 안에 있는 반죽을 젓고 있다.
(B) 여자가 부엌 찬장을 향해 있다.
(C) 몇몇 용기에 음식이 가득 차 있다.
(D) 채소가 도마 위에 놓여 있다.

어휘  stir 젓다, 휘젓다   batter 반죽   cabinet 찬장   container 용기   cutting board 도마

**4** 미W
(A) There is a potted plant under the table.
(B) The lamps are being turned on.
(C) **The armchairs are placed next to each other.**
(D) Some frames are being taken off the wall.

(A) 테이블 아래에 화분이 하나 있다.
(B) 램프들이 켜지는 중이다.
(C) 안락의자가 나란히 위치해 있다.
(D) 몇몇 액자가 벽에서 떼어지는 중이다.

어휘  potted plant 화분   armchair 안락의자   take ~ off the wall ~을 벽에서 떼어내다

**5** 영M
(A) People are stretching both arms down to the ground.
(B) Lines are being painted on the floor.

(C) **A portable shelf is filled with sports equipment.**
(D) People are competing in a sports competition.

(A) 사람들이 양팔을 땅으로 뻗고 있다.
(B) 선이 바닥에 칠해지고 있다.
(C) 이동식 선반에 운동 기구가 채워져 있다.
(D) 사람들이 운동 경기에서 경쟁하고 있다.

어휘  portable 이동이 가능한   competition 경기, 경쟁

**6** 미W
(A) **An arched bridge spans a waterway.**
(B) The fountain is spraying water into the air.
(C) A boat is passing under the bridge.
(D) A tourist is taking a picture of the scenery.

(A) 아치형 다리가 수로 위에 걸쳐 있다.
(B) 분수대에서 공중으로 물을 뿜고 있다.
(C) 보트가 다리 아래로 지나가고 있다.
(D) 관광객이 풍경 사진을 찍고 있다.

어휘  arched 둥그렇게 구부린, 아치형의   span 걸치다   waterway 수로   fountain 분수   spray 뿌리다   scenery 경치

## PART 2

P18

**7** 미M
Where is your new apartment located?
(A) **It's right around the corner.**
(B) Some new supplies.
(C) Four hours from now.

당신의 새 아파트는 어디에 있어요?
(A) 바로 모퉁이 돌면 있어요.
(B) 새로운 물품들이요.
(C) 지금부터 4시간 후예요.

어휘  supplies 물품, 자재

**8** 영M
How much did wages increase this year?
(A) Between March and April.
(B) **By 10%.**
(C) At our headquarters.

올해 임금이 얼마나 증가했죠?
(A) 3월과 4월 사이요.
(B) 10퍼센트요.
(C) 우리 본부에서요.

어휘  wage 임금   headquarters 본부

**9** 미W
Who is taking the position of Mr. Russell?
(A) Ms. Kim is out of town.
(B) **He will stay with us for another year.**
(C) That would be too late.

누가 러셀 씨의 자리를 맡으시나요?
(A) 김 씨는 출장 중이에요.
(B) 그는 우리와 1년 더 일할 겁니다.
(C) 그건 너무 늦을 거예요.

어휘  position 일자리   out of town 출장 중인

**10** 미W
Can you give me a ride to the airport?
(A) At 10 o'clock every day.
(B) I didn't write it.
(C) **I left my car at home today.**

공항까지 절 태워 주실 수 있나요?
(A) 매일 10시에요.
(B) 제가 그걸 쓰지 않았어요.
(C) 오늘은 차를 집에 두고 왔어요.

어휘  give ~ a ride ~를 태워 주다

**11** 영M
When is a technician coming to replace the damaged parts?
(A) **Sometime this afternoon.**
(B) I saw a part of it in the morning.
(C) Put it over there.

손상된 부품을 교체하러 기술자가 언제 올까요?
(A) 오늘 오후 중이요.
(B) 제가 아침에 일부를 보았어요.
(C) 그걸 저쪽에 두세요.

어휘  technician 기술자   damaged 손상된   part 부품   fill in 기재하다

**12** 미W
I'm here for the convention today.
(A) At a hotel downtown.
(B) **Okay, please fill in this form first.**
(C) Whenever it is convenient for you.

오늘 있을 회의를 위해 왔습니다.
(A) 시내에 있는 호텔에서요.
(B) 네, 우선 이 서식의 빈칸을 채워 주세요.
(C) 언제든 당신이 편리한 시간에요.

어휘  convention (대규모) 대회[협의회], 회의   fill in 기재하다

**13** 미W
Is it okay if I leave early on Friday?
(A) It arrived this morning.
(B) **Yes, if you are all done.**
(C) Glad to hear that.

제가 금요일에 일찍 떠나도 괜찮을까요?
(A) 그건 오늘 아침에 도착했어요.
(B) 네, 당신이 모두 끝냈다면요.
(C) 그 말을 들으니 기뻐요.

어휘  done 다 끝낸, 완료된

**14** How long have you been taking yoga lessons?
미W
미M (A) In about two years.
(B) I started just last week.
(C) The class is the best one I have ever taken.

요가 수업을 얼마나 들으셨어요?
(A) 약 2년 후에요
(B) 지난주에 시작했어요.
(C) 제가 들은 수업 중 최고입니다.
어휘 yoga lessons 요가 수업

**15** Have you found the replacement parts for the computer?
미M (A) 20 dollars per month.
호M (B) It is too expensive.
(C) They're being installed now.

그 컴퓨터의 교체 부품은 찾으셨어요?
(A) 한 달에 20달러요.
(B) 그건 너무 비싸요.
(C) 지금 설치되는 중이에요.
어휘 replacement 교체 part 부품

**16** Don't forget to bring extra brochures for the meeting.
미W (A) Sure. I'll meet with him today.
미M (B) How many do you think we will need?
(C) Conference Room B.

회의를 위해 추가 책자를 가지고 오는 걸 잊지 마세요.
(A) 그럼요, 오늘 그 사람을 만날 거예요.
(B) 얼마나 필요할 거 같아요?
(C) 회의실 B요.
어휘 brochure 책자

**17** Do you know where the job is advertised?
미W (A) Yes, I like the new advertisement.
미W (B) I brought a copy of my résumé.
(C) You should go to the company's website.

그 일자리 광고가 어디에 실렸는지 아세요?
(A) 네, 전 새로운 광고가 좋아요.
(B) 제 이력서를 한 부 가져왔어요.
(C) 회사 웹 사이트에 가 보세요.
어휘 advertise 광고하다 a copy of 한 부

**18** May I see the expense report now?
호M (A) I turned it in to the financial manager.
미W (B) The budget is tight this month.
(C) To discuss a business proposal.

비용 보고서를 지금 볼 수 있나요?
(A) 제가 재무 부장에게 제출했어요.
(B) 이번 달 예산이 빠듯해요.
(C) 사업 제안서에 대해 논의하려고요.
어휘 expense 비용 turn in 제출하다 financial 재무의 tight 빠듯한 business proposal 사업 제안서

**19** How would you like your tea?
미W (A) With milk please.
미M (B) Thanks, it looks wonderful.
(C) It was a great experience.

차를 어떻게 해 드릴까요?
(A) 우유를 넣어 주세요.
(B) 고마워요, 아주 멋져 보이네요.
(C) 멋진 경험이었어요.

**20** When are you going to start working on this quarter's project?
미W (A) Kris will handle the task.
호M (B) You should've received it last week.
(C) We project around $500.

이번 분기 프로젝트 작업을 언제 시작하세요?
(A) 크리스가 그 일을 담당할 겁니다.
(B) 지난주에 이미 받으셨어야 했는데요.
(C) 500달러 정도 예상하고 있습니다.
어휘 handle 담당하다 project 예상하다

**21** Which factory produces these toys?
호M (A) Yes, it's going to be fun.
미M (B) The one in Riverdale.
(C) Probably next year.

어떤 공장에서 이 장난감들을 생산하죠?
(A) 네, 재미있을 거예요.
(B) 리버데일에 있는 공장이요.
(C) 아마도 내년이요.
어휘 produce 생산하다

**22** Why is the president holding a press conference this afternoon?
미M (A) Because it's the President Hotel.
호M (B) Maybe she is going to announce a merger.
(C) The press has been very positive about her.

사장님은 왜 오늘 오후에 기자 회견을 하세요?
(A) 그곳이 프레지던트 호텔이라서요.
(B) 아마 그녀는 합병 소식을 발표할 것입니다.
(C) 언론은 그에 관해 매우 긍정적이었습니다.
어휘 press conference 기자 회견 announce 발표하다 merger 합병 positive 긍정적인

**23** Ms. Winslow hasn't sent out the invitations to our customers yet, has she?
호M (A) No, but very few are going to show up anyway.
미W (B) The customs office is closed now.
(C) Actually she wasn't invited.

윈슬우 씨가 우리 고객들에게 초대장을 아직 발송 안 했죠, 그렇죠?
(A) 안 했어요, 하지만 올 고객은 거의 없을 거 같습니다.
(B) 세관 사무소는 현재 문을 닫았습니다.
(C) 실은 그녀는 초대되지 않았어요.
어휘 invitation 초청장 show up 오다 customs 세관

**24** The board will need a long time to make a final decision.
미M (A) Call him for directions.
미W (B) Within a month.
(C) I wonder why.

이사회는 최종 결정을 내리기 위해 긴 시간이 필요할 겁니다.
(A) 길 안내를 위해 그에게 전화하세요.
(B) 한 달 이내요.
(C) 왜 그런지 궁금하네요.
어휘 board 이사회 directions 길 안내

**25** How do you like your new accounting job?
미W (A) It should be done soon.
호M (B) I'm still working overtime to catch up.
(C) I applied online.

새로운 회계직은 어때요?
(A) 그건 곧 끝날 겁니다.
(B) 업무에 적응하느라 아직도 초과 근무를 하고 있어요.
(C) 전 온라인으로 지원했어요.
어휘 accounting 회계 catch up (뒤처져서 만회하기 위해) ~을 하다

**26** Should we drive to the theater or walk there?
미W (A) A new play.
호M (B) That's a good idea.
(C) My car is parked right here.

우리 극장에 차를 타고 갈까요 아니면 걸어갈까요?
(A) 새 연극이요.
(B) 좋은 생각이에요.
(C) 제 차가 바로 여기 있어요.
어휘 theater 극장 play 연극

**27** I'd like you to finalize the renovation project by July 2.
미M (A) Join us for our store opening.
호M (B) Okay, we'll do our best.
미W (C) He finished in last place.

당신이 리모델링 프로젝트를 7월 2일까지 마무리 지었으면 합니다.
(A) 저희 상점 개장식에 오세요.
(B) 네, 최선을 다하겠습니다.
(C) 그는 마지막으로 끝냈어요.
어휘 finalize 마무리 짓다 renovation 개보수 in last place 꼴찌로, 마지막으로

# PART 3

**28** 영M 미W

Mr. Stephenson won't be available for a conference call on Tuesday, will he?

(A) It will be available on the market soon.
(B) He came to speak on the issue.
**(C) No, but Ms. Pandora will take his place.**

스티븐슨 씨가 화요일 전화 회의를 할 시간이 안 되나요?
(A) 곧 시장에서 살 수 있게 될 거예요.
(B) 그는 그 문제에 관해 말하려고 왔습니다.
(C) 안 됩니다. 하지만 판도라 씨가 그를 대신하기로 했어요.

어휘 conference call 전화 회의  take one's place ~의 자리를 대신하다

**29** 미W 미M

Didn't you go to the festival yesterday?

(A) What time does it open?
**(B) I don't like crowds.**
(C) They play music in a band.

어제 축제에 안 가셨나요?
(A) 몇 시에 문을 열죠?
(B) 저는 붐비는 걸 싫어해요.
(C) 그들은 밴드에서 음악을 연주합니다.

어휘 crowd (한 곳에) 모인 군중

**30** 미W 영M

Would it be possible for you to fill in for Ms. Knight for a few days?

(A) Please fill out the application.
**(B) Not if it means another big project.**
(C) First thing tomorrow morning.

며칠 동안 나이트 씨를 대신해서 근무해 줄 수 있으세요?
(A) 신청서를 작성해 주세요.
(B) 다른 큰 프로젝트를 해야 하는 것이 아니라면요.
(C) 내일 아침 제일 먼저요.

어휘 fill in for ~를 대신하다  fill out ~을 작성하다  application 신청서

**31** 영M 미W

Don't you want to see the price estimate for the order?

(A) I have overestimated the production capacity.
(B) A large selection of goods.
**(C) Just leave it with my secretary.**

주문에 대한 가격 견적서를 보시지 않겠어요?
(A) 제가 생산력을 과대평가했어요.
(B) 다양한 상품들이요.
(C) 그냥 제 비서에게 남겨 두세요.

어휘 estimate 견적서  overestimate 과대평가하다  production capacity 생산력

---

Questions 32-34 refer to the following conversation. 영M 미W

M Good afternoon, I am calling about a pizza delivery I ordered from your website a few minutes ago. I ordered a pepperoni pizza, **32** but I want to add some toppings. Can I do that?

W Let me check the order. **33** Do you have an order number?

M Yes, it's 08994. I'd like to add extra cheese and jalapenos. And I'd also like a large soda please.

W Okay, no problem. Well, your total comes to 30 dollars now. **34** I'll send you a text message with the new amount and you can pay it to the delivery man.

남 안녕하세요. 몇 분 전에 당신의 웹 사이트에서 주문한 피자 배달에 관해 전화를 드렸는데요. 제가 페퍼로니 피자를 주문했는데, 몇 가지 토핑을 추가하고 싶어요. 가능할까요?

여 주문을 확인해 보겠습니다. 주문 번호가 있으신가요?

남 네, 08994번입니다. 전 치즈와 할라피뇨를 추가하고 싶어요. 탄산음료 큰 걸로도 원합니다.

여 네, 문제없습니다. 합계가 30달러로 보내 드릴 테니 수정된 금액을 배달원에게 지불해 주세요.

어휘 topping (음식 위에 얹는) 고명, 토핑  contact information 연락처  complimentary 무료의

**32** Why is the man calling?
**(A) To change an order**
(B) To confirm a delivery time
(C) To cancel an event
(D) To make a complaint

남자가 전화하는 이유는 무엇인가?
(A) 주문을 변경하려고
(B) 배달 시간을 확인하려고
(C) 행사를 취소하려고
(D) 불평을 하려고

**33** What does the woman request?
(A) The man's card details
**(B) The man's order number**
(C) The man's full address
(D) The man's contact information

여자가 요청하는 것은 무엇인가?
(A) 남자의 신용 카드 정보
(B) 남자의 주문 번호
(C) 남자의 완전한 주소
(D) 남자의 연락처

**34** What does the woman say she will send the man?
(A) A coupon
(B) A menu item
(C) A complimentary meal
**(D) A text message**

여자는 남자에게 무엇을 보낼 거라고 말하는가?
(A) 할인권
(B) 메뉴 항목
(C) 무료 식사
(D) 문자 메시지

---

Questions 35-37 refer to the following conversation. 미W 미M

W Hello. I'm calling to report that **35** one of the main elevators doesn't seem to be working. Can you send someone from the maintenance department to fix it please?

M Sorry for the inconvenience. **36** I'll send someone right away. Could you tell me the exact location of the elevator?

W Yes, it's the one next to Office 503. Will he be long? You know, **37** it is almost noon and **37** a lot of people will be going out to lunch soon.

M Don't worry. Someone will be there in a few minutes.

여 안녕하세요. 메인 엘리베이터 중 하나가 작동하지 않는 것 같아서 전화했습니다. 시설부에 있는 사람을 보내서 수리해 주실 수 있으세요?

남 불편을 드려 죄송합니다. 당장 사람을 보낼게요. 엘리베이터의 정확한 위치가 어디인가요?

여 503호실 옆에 있는 겁니다. 오래 걸릴까요? 아시다시피 거의 정오가 다 되어서 많은 사람들이 점심을 먹으러 나갈 거예요.

남 걱정 마세요. 몇 분 안에 수리하러 갈 겁니다.

어휘 exact 정확한  blockage 장애, 막힘  locate ~의 위치를 찾아내다  alternative 대체 가능한; 대안이 되는

**35** What problem does the woman report?
**(A) An elevator is broken.**
(B) A repair person is unavailable.
(C) A file has been deleted.
(D) A staircase is blocked.

여자가 전하는 문제점은 무엇인가?
(A) 엘리베이터가 고장 났다.
(B) 수리공이 올 수 없다.
(C) 파일이 삭제되었다.
(D) 계단이 막혔다.

매트프레이징  doesn't seem to be working → broken

P19

Actual Test 01  004 • 005

**36** What does the man say he will do?

(A) Remove a blockage
**(B) Send a repairman**
(C) Locate an alternate exit
(D) Install a new elevator

남자는 무엇을 하겠다고 말하는가?

(A) 장애물 치우기
**(B) 수리공 보내기**
(C) 다른 출구 찾기
(D) 새 엘리베이터 설치하기

**패러프레이징** send someone → Send a repairman

**37** What does the woman mean when she says, "it is almost noon"?

**(A) The elevator will soon be needed.**
(B) She has an important meeting to attend.
(C) Her lunch break is almost over.
(D) She is expecting some guests.

여자가 "거의 정오가 다 되어서"라고 말한 의미는 무엇인가?

**(A) 엘리베이터가 곧 필요하게 될 것이다.**
(B) 그녀가 중요한 회의에 참석해야 한다.
(C) 점심시간이 거의 끝나간다.
(D) 여자는 손님들을 기다리고 있다.

어휘 locate 위치를 찾다 inn 숙소 GPS 내비게이션 special deal 특가 상품 at this point 이 시점에서, 현재는 nearby 인근의, 가까운 곳의 intersection 교차로

**38** What is the man trying to do?

**(A) Locate a place**
(B) Repair a device
(C) Promote a product
(D) Listen to a radio

남자는 무엇을 하려고 하는가?

**(A) 장소 찾기**
(B) 전자 장비 수리
(C) 상품 홍보
(D) 라디오 듣기

**패러프레이징** locate the travelers' inn → Locate a place

**39** Why does the woman direct the man to Mildwater?

(A) It is famous.
**(B) It is nearby.**
(C) It offers a discount.
(D) It has been newly renovated.

여자가 남자에게 마일드워터를 알려 준 이유는 무엇인가?

(A) 유명하다.
**(B) 근처에 있다.**
(C) 할인을 제공한다.
(D) 새로 수리 보수되었다.

**40** What is the man told to do at the light?

**(A) Turn left at the light**
(B) Call a taxi
(C) Drive to the next intersection
(D) Visit a local store

남자는 무엇을 하라고 전달받았나?

**(A) 신호에서 좌회전하기**
(B) 택시를 부르기
(C) 다음 교차로까지 운전하기
(D) 지역 상점 방문하기

**패러프레이징** Go left at the traffic light → Turn left at the light

---

Questions 38-40 refer to the following conversation. 영M 미W

M Excuse me. ㊳ I'm trying to locate the travelers' inn that was advertised on the radio. I cannot seem to find it, and my GPS is not working.

W Actually there are two travelers' inns in town, West Point and Mildwater. Which one are you looking for?

M Well, I was looking for West Point because I heard on the radio that it offers special deals. But at this point, I think I'll go to whichever one is closest.

W ㊴ Mildwater is only a few minutes away by car. ㊵ Go left at the traffic light and you will see it.

남 실례합니다. 제가 라디오 광고에 나왔던 여행자 숙소를 찾고 있는데요. 그곳을 찾을 수 없을 것 같네요. 제 내비게이션이 안가고있어요.

여 사실 여행자 숙소가 두 개 있어요. 웨스트 포인트와 마일드워터요. 어디를 찾고 있죠?

남 라디오에서 특가 상품을 제공한다고 해서 저는 웨스트 포인트를 찾고 있었어요. 하지만 지금은 어디든 가장 가까운 곳으로 갈 생각이에요.

여 마일드워터가 차로 몇 분 밖에 안 걸려요. 신호등에서 좌회전하시면 보일 겁니다.

---

Questions 41-43 refer to the following conversation. 미W 미M

W Hello. This is Kimberly from the market research department. ㊶ Do you have the results of the questionnaires on our new bike helmet? I heard they were given out to sports equipment manufacturers last week.

M Hi, Kimberly. ㊷ I sent the results to your assistant, Keith Baines, about four days ago.

W Really? He said he didn't receive anything in the mail when I checked with him. Maybe they are lost.

M Don't worry. I have saved them on my computer. I'll send you those results by e-mail this time. ㊸ You may want to see how testers feel about the material of the helmet. Overall, they thought it was too hard and inflexible.

여 안녕하세요. 저는 시장 조사팀의 킴벌리입니다. 새 자전거 헬멧에 관한 설문 결과가 나왔나요? 지난주에 스포츠 장비 제조업체들에게 나눠줬다고 들었거든요.

남 안녕하세요, 킴벌리. 4일 전에 당신의 비서인 키스 베인즈에게 발송했는데요.

여 정말요? 제가 물어봤을 때 그는 우편물로 받은 것이 없다고 했으요. 잃어버린 것 같네요.

남 걱정 마세요. 제가 컴퓨터에 저장을 해 놓았어요. 이번에는 이메일로 당신에게 결과를 보내줄게요. 시험 사용자들이 헬멧의 재질에 대해 어떻게 느꼈는지를 보셔야 해요. 전반적으로, 재질이 너무 딱딱하고 신축성이 없다고 생각했거든요.

어휘 questionnaire 설문지 give out 배포하다 check with ~에게 묻다, 확인하다 material (성품의) 재질 inflexible 신축성이 없는 inquire 문의하다 schedule 일정을 잡다 durability 내구성

**41** Why is the woman calling?

**(A) To inquire about a survey**
(B) To complain about a lost order
(C) To schedule a manufacturers meeting
(D) To ask about construction equipment

여자가 전화하는 이유는 무엇인가?

**(A) 설문에 관해 문의하려고**
(B) 분실된 주문에 관하여 불만을 제기하려고
(C) 제조 회의의 일정을 잡으려고
(D) 공사 장비에 관해 물어보려고

**42** What does the man say he did a few days ago?

(A) Complete a survey
**(B) Send some results**
(C) Meet with Keith Baines
(D) Test a new item

## Questions 47-49 refer to the following conversation. (미W) (미M)

W Oh, ⓐ I thought you were done packing up. Do you think you can finish it by 7:30 tomorrow morning?

M What? Do they come right after we open the door at 7:00? Oh, well, I guess I have to stay here late tonight.

W Sorry to hear that. It didn't take me that long because there's not so much stuff to pack up in my office. Well, I can stop by later in the evening and give you a hand if you want. But first ⓑ why don't we go out and grab something to eat? It's already 6:30.

M Sounds great. I was about to take a break. ⓒ Let me just ask the supply department for more boxes, and we're ready to go.

여 짐 싸는 게 끝난 줄 알았어요. 내일 아침 7시 반까지 끝낼 수 있을 것 같아요?

남 뭐라고요? 그들이 우리가 7시에 문 열자마자 온다고요? 오늘 밤은 늦게까지 여기 있어야 하겠군요.

여 그 걸 듣게나 안됐군요. 제 사무실은 짐 쌀게 많이 없어서 그렇게 오래 걸리지는 않았어요. 원하시면 저녁때 제가 잠깐 들러서 도와줄 수 있어요. 그런데 우선 우리 지금 나가서 먹을 것 좀 사 오는 게 어때요? 벌써 6시 반이에요.

남 좋습니다. 막 쉬려던 참이었어요. 비품 부서에 박스를 더 요청만 하고 가도록 하죠.

어휘 be done 끝나다　pack up 짐을 싸다　grab something to eat 먹을 것을 사다　take a break 잠시 쉬다　belongings 짐　request 요청하다

**47** What are the speakers mainly talking about?
(A) Relocating an office
(B) Meeting for dinner
(C) Going to a movie
(D) Buying office supplies

화자들이 주로 이야기하고 있는 것은 무엇인가?
(A) 사무실 이사하기
(B) 저녁 식사하기
(C) 영화 보러 가기
(D) 사무용품 구매하기

**48** What does the woman suggest the man do?
(A) Start packing up his belongings
(B) Grab some items from the lobby
(C) Take a break for a meal
(D) Work extra hours

---

남자가 테스트 전에 했다고 말한 것은 무엇인가?
(A) 샘플 작성
(B) 결과 발송
(C) 키스 베인즈와 미팅
(D) 새로운 물품 테스트

**43** What did testers not like about the new product?
(A) Its size
(B) Its price
(C) Its durability
(D) Its material

새 제품에 대해 시험 사용자들이 좋아하지 않은 것은 무엇인가?
(A) 크기
(B) 가격
(C) 내구성
(D) 재질

## Questions 44-46 refer to the following conversation with three speakers. (미W) (영M) (영W)

W1 Welcome to ⓐ Shari's Gift Baskets. How may I help you?

M Well, ⓑ I'm looking for a gift basket to send to my client. I see a lot of flower arrangements here but do you also carry fruit baskets?

W1 Sorry, I'm not sure because I just started working here today. Let me ask my coworker. Hey, Sophia. Do you know if we have fruit baskets?

W2 Of course, we do. We have all kinds of edible arrangements, like fruit baskets and chocolate boxes too. ⓒ But they're on the second floor. Let me show you sir. Please follow me.

M Oh great. Thanks. By the way, do you know if there is a post office nearby? I need to mail the gift today.

W2 Actually, ⓓ you can use one of the shipping kiosks inside our store. They are located in front of the main entrance.

M That's perfect. Thank you very much.

여 사리즈 기프트 바스켓에 오신 걸 환영합니다. 무엇을 도와 드릴까요?

남 그런데 저는 제 고객에게 보낼 선물 바구니를 찾고 있어요. 여기 꽃다발은 많이 보이는데 혹시 과일 바구니도 취급하시나요?

여 죄송하지만 제가 오늘 일을 시작해서 잘 모르겠어요. 제 동료에게 물어볼게요. 소피아, 우리 과일 바구니도 있는지 알아요?

여 당연히 있죠. 과일 바구니와 초콜릿 박스 같은 먹을 수 있는 상품들도 다 있는데요. 그건 2층에 있어요. 제가 보여 드릴게요, 절 따라오세요.

남 이 좋네요. 고마워요. 그나저나, 이 근처에 우체국이 있는지 아세요? 제가 오늘 선물을 보내야 하거든요.

여 실은 자료 가게 안에 있는 배송 기기를 이용하시면 됩니다. 가게 입구 앞에 있어요.

남 아주 잘됐네요. 감사합니다.

어휘 carry (상품을) 취급하다　edible 먹을 수 있는　arrangement (여러 가지 물건을 조합한) 다발, 장식　kiosk 가판 기계　out of stock 재고가 없는　overnight 밤 사이의, 다음 날 도착하는

**44** What is the man shopping for?
(A) Some groceries
(B) A gift basket
(C) An electronic device
(D) Some office supplies

남자는 무엇을 쇼핑하고 있는가?
(A) 식료품
(B) 선물 바구니
(C) 가전 기기
(D) 사무용품

**45** What does Sophia say about some items?
(A) They are currently on sale.
(B) They cannot be shipped out.
(C) They are out of stock.
(D) They can be found on a different floor.

소피아는 일부 상품에 대해 뭐라고 하는가?
(A) 현재 할인 중이다.
(B) 발송될 수 없다.
(C) 재고가 없다.
(D) 다른 층에서 찾을 수 있다.

패러프레이징 on the second floor → on a different floor

**46** What additional service does Sophia mention?
(A) In-store shipping
(B) Overnight delivery
(C) Free membership
(D) Gift wrapping

소피아는 어떤 추가 서비스를 언급하는가?
(A) 상점 내 배송
(B) 익일 배달
(C) 무료 멤버십
(D) 선물 포장

여자가 남자에게 제안하는 것은 무엇인가?

(A) 짐 싸는 것 중단하기
(B) 로비에서 물건 가져오기
**(C) 잠시 쉬며 식사하기**
(D) 아근하기
**패러프레이징** grab something to eat → Take a break for a meal

**49** What will the man probably do next?

(A) Turn off the light
(B) Put file folders in boxes
(C) Call a moving company
**(D) Request some office supplies**

남자가 다음에 할 일은 무엇인가?

(A) 불을 끈다.
(B) 박스에 파일 폴더를 넣는다.
(C) 이삿짐 회사에 전화한다.
**(D) 사무용품을 요청한다.**

Questions 50-52 refer to the following conversation. 영M 미W

남 ⑤⁰ This is Roy Winstone from KSP Radio. ⁵¹ I heard that your restaurant is organizing a charity day to raise funds for homeless people.

여 Oh, hello, Mr. Winstone. Yes, that's right. ⁵⁰ We have planned a variety of activities for the event. There will be a sports game and a charity auction, and all the proceeds will be donated to Ryandale Shelter.

남 Actually, ⁵² I'd like to arrange an interview with you about the fund raiser. It's going to be broadcast on our radio show. How does that sound to you?

여 ⁵² Oh, that sounds great. I think the interview will bring in more people.

남 I'm sure it will. Well, is Thursday convenient for you?

남 저는 KSP 라디오의 로이 윈스톤입니다. 귀하의 식당에서 노숙자들을 위한 기금 모금을 위해 자선의 날을 준비 중이라고 들었습니다.

여 아, 안녕하세요. 윈스톤 씨. 네, 맞습니다. 저희는 그 행사를 위해 다양한 활동들을 준비했어요. 스포츠 경기와 자선 경매가 있을 것이고, 모든 수익금은 라이언데일 쉼터에 기부될 것입니다.

남 실은 그 기금 모금 행사에 관해서 당신과의 인터뷰 일정을 잡고 싶어요. 저희 라디오 쇼에 방송이 될 것입니다. 어떠신가요?

여 네, 좋습니다. 인터뷰가 사람들을 더 불러올 수 있을 것 같아요.

남 당연히 그럴 겁니다. 음, 목요일 시간이 괜찮으신가요?

**어휘** charity day 자선의 날  raise funds 기금을 모으다  homeless people 노숙자들  proceeds 수익금  broadcast 방송하다  fund raiser 기금 모금 행사  arena 경기장

**50** Who most likely is the man?

(A) A restaurant owner
(B) An event organizer
(C) A financial supporter
**(D) A radio broadcaster**

남자는 누구인가?

(A) 식당 주인
(B) 행사 주최자
(C) 재정 후원자
**(D) 라디오 방송자**

**51** What are the speakers mainly discussing?

(A) A new sports arena
**(B) A fundraising event**
(C) A store promotion
(D) A non-profit organization

화자들은 주로 무엇에 관해 이야기하는가?

(A) 새로운 스포츠 경기장
**(B) 기금 모금 행사**
(C) 상점 판촉행사
(D) 비영리 단체

**52** Why does the man say, "How does that sound to you"?

**(A) To request the woman's permission**
(B) To provide another example
(C) To change the subject
(D) To advertise an upcoming event

남자는 왜 "어떠신가요?"라고 말하는가?

**(A) 여자의 허락을 구하려고**
(B) 다른 예시를 제공하려고
(C) 주제를 바꾸려고
(D) 다가오는 행사를 홍보하려고

Questions 53-55 refer to the following conversation. 미W 미M

여 Hi. This is my first time here, but ⁵³ I know you carry a limited edition of *Never Let You Go* that's signed by the singer Luis Santos.

남 Yes, we do, but ⁵⁴ I'm afraid the signed albums are sold out at the moment. I can order non-signed ones if you would like, though it takes three to four days for them to arrive.

여 Oh, ⁵⁴ I was really hoping to have a signed copy to give to my friend for her birthday tomorrow. She is such a big fan of his.

남 All right. Then, let me see what I can do. I'll check online if our other locations have a signed CD. ⁵⁵ If they do, would you like to go over there and get it?

여 안녕하세요. 제가 오늘 여기 처음인데요. 선호스 루이스라는 가수가 사인한 〈Never Let You Go〉의 한정판을 판매하고 있는 걸로 알고 있어요.

남 네, 그렇습니다만 사인이 들어간 앨범들은 현재 매진되었어요. 원하신다면 사인이 없는 것을 주문해 드릴 수 있어요. 하지만 도착하는 데 3~4일 걸립니다.

여 꼭 사인이 들어간 앨범을 친구 선물로 주고 싶었거든요. 제 친구가 그 가수의 열렬한 팬이라서요.

남 알겠습니다. 그러면 제가 할 수 있는 일이 뭔지 보죠. 온라인으로 다른 매장에 사인이 들어간 앨범을 보유하고 있는지 알아볼게요. 넘은 게 있다면 가서 구매하시겠습니까?

**어휘** carry 취급하다  sold out 매진된  big fan 열렬한 팬  acquire 얻다  potential 잠재적인, 가능성 있는

**53** What are the speakers discussing?

(A) Purchasing a concert ticket
**(B) Acquiring a unique item**
(C) Placing an ad online
(D) Organizing a musical performance

화자들이 이야기하고 있는 것은 무엇인가?

(A) 콘서트 표 구매
**(B) 특별한 물건 주문**
(C) 온라인에 광고 올리기
(D) 음악 공연 기획

**패러프레이징** a limited edition → a unique item

**54** What problem is mentioned?

(A) Signed albums take time to arrive.
(B) The price of limited copies is very high.
(C) The store is not open for business yet.
**(D) A potential birthday gift is out of stock.**

Questions 59-61 refer to the following conversation. (영M) (미W)

M Good afternoon, Abigail. I missed you at the presentation on cosmetics this morning. Did you just arrive?

W ⑤⑨ Yes. I had a prior appointment, and it went on longer than I expected. It looks like there are already many people here at the workshop. I'm giving a makeup demonstration this afternoon and ⑥⓪ I want to be sure that I have enough samples to hand out.

M Yeah, the workshop is pretty full. There were more than 50 people at the morning session, and I have noticed more guests arriving since then.

W OK. I will certainly need more samples then. ⑥① I think I had better get some more from my car. See you in a bit.

남 안녕하세요, 애비게일. 오늘 아침 화장품에 관한 발표에서 당신을 못 봤어요. 지금 막 도착하셨어요?

여 네, 제가 선약이 있었는데 생각보다 오래 걸렸어요. 벌써 많은 사람들이 워크숍에 와 있는 것 같네요. 제가 오늘 오후에 화장 시범을 할 텐데 시범 줄에 쓸 샘플이 충분한지 확인하고 싶어요.

남 네, 워크숍은 거의 꽉 찼어요. 오늘 아침 발표에 50명 이상은 있었고, 그 이후로 더 많은 손님들이 도착하는 걸 봤거든요.

여 좋아요. 그럼 분명 더 많은 샘플이 필요하겠네요. 차에서 좀 더 가져오는 게 좋겠어요, 조금 후에 봐요.

어휘 miss (못 보거나 못 듣고) 놓치다, (만남을 안 두고) 지나치다　cosmetics 화장품　prior 이전의　give a demonstration 시범 설명을 하다　makeup 화장　hand out 배포하다　earlier engagement 선약　attendee 참석자　fetch 가지고 오다　alternative 대처할 수 있는

**59** Why was the woman late?
(A) She had an earlier engagement.
(B) She went to the wrong place.
(C) She had to wait a long time for the train.
(D) She was preparing extra samples.

여자가 늦은 이유는 무엇인가?
(A) 사전 약속이 있었다.
(B) 잘못된 장소로 갔다.
(C) 기차를 오래 기다려야 했다.
(D) 여분의 샘플을 준비하고 있었다.
패러프레이징 a prior appointment → an earlier engagement

**60** What does the woman want to know about?
(A) Some samples for sale
(B) Directions to a workshop
(C) Some changes to a schedule
(D) The number of attendees

---

어떤 문제가 제기되었는가?
(A) 사인이 된 앨범은 도착하는 데 시간이 걸린다.
(B) 한정판 앨범 가격은 매우 높다.
(C) 아직 매장이 영업을 개시하지 않았다.
(D) 생일 선물로 생각해 둔 것이 재고가 없다.
패러프레이징 sold out → out of stock

**55** What does the man suggest?
(A) Making an order online
(B) Delaying the date of an event
(C) Exchanging an item for a different one
(D) Purchasing an item at a different store

남자가 제안하는 것은 무엇인가?
(A) 온라인 주문하기
(B) 행사 날짜 연기하기
(C) 물건을 다른 것과 교환하기
(D) 다른 매장에서 물건 구입하기

Questions 56-58 refer to the following conversation with three speakers. (미W) (미M) (호M)

W Hi. My name is Dianne Rubinstein in product design. I'm here to get a copy of my proof of employment because I need to submit it before ⑤⑥ my job interview next week.

M1 Okay, let me see. Would you like to get a hard copy yourself or do you want us to send it to your potential employer?

W Please fax it to this number.

M1 All right. Just hold on a second. ⑤⑦ My colleague Marco handles fax services. Marco?

M2 Yes?

M1 Could you bring one of those fax request forms to Ms. Rubinstein?

M2 Sure... here you are. ⑤⑧ Fill out this form with what kind of document you want and where to send it. I think I can get it done by the end of today.

W Sounds great. Thank you. Do you have a pen?

여 안녕하세요, 저는 제품 디자인 부서의 다이앤 루빈스타인입니다. 제 재직 증명서를 한 부 받으러 왔는데요, 다음 주에 있을 취업 면접 전에 제출해야 해서요.

남1 알겠습니다, 한번 보죠. 복사본을 직접 받아 가시겠어요 아니면 저희가 재 고용주에게 보내 드릴까요?

여 이 번호로 팩스로 보내 주세요.

남1 좋습니다. 잠시만 기다리세요. 팩스 신청은 제 동료인 마르코가 처리하거 든요. 마르코?

남2 네?

---

**56** What does the woman say she will do next week?
(A) Attend a conference
(B) Finish a product design
(C) Move to another city
(D) Have a job interview

여자가 다음 주에 무엇을 할 거라고 하는가?
(A) 컨퍼런스 참석하기
(B) 제품 디자인 완성하기
(C) 다른 도시로 이사하기
(D) 취업 면접 보기

**57** According to the conversation, what office duties does Marco handle?
(A) Requests for faxing documents
(B) Inquiries from customers
(C) Stocks of office supplies
(D) Travel arrangements

대화에 따르면, 마르코는 어떤 사무 업무를 처리하는가?
(A) 팩스 서류 요청
(B) 고객 문의
(C) 사무용품 재고
(D) 출장 예약

**58** What does Marco ask the woman to do?
(A) Return the next day
(B) Call her supervisor
(C) Make a payment
(D) Complete a form

마르코는 여자에게 무엇을 하라고 요청하는가?
(A) 다음 날 다시 오기
(B) 상사에게 전화하기
(C) 돈을 지불하기
(D) 양식을 작성하기
패러프레이징 Fill out this form → Complete a form

---

남1 팩스 신청서를 한 부를 루빈스타인 양에게 좀 가져다주실래요?

남2 네, 여기 있습니다. 어떤 종류의 서류를 원하는지와 어디로 보낼지를 이 앙 식에 기입해 주세요. 제가 오늘까지는 처리할 수 있을 것 같아요.

여 좋습니다. 감사합니다. 펜 있으세요?

어휘 proof of employment 재직 증명서　hard copy 출력된 서류　potential employer 잠재 고용주　hold on 기다리다　request form 신청서　inquiry 문의　stock 재고

여자는 무엇에 대해 알고 싶어 하는가?
(A) 판매용 샘플들
(B) 워크숍까지의 길 안내
(C) 일정 변경
(D) **참석자의 수**

**61** What will the woman probably do next?
(A) **Fetch some items**
(B) Request some samples
(C) Find alternative transportation
(D) Purchase cosmetic products

여자가 다음에 할 일은 무엇인가?
(A) **물건을 가지고 온다.**
(B) 샘플을 요청한다.
(C) 다른 교통편을 찾는다.
(D) 화장품을 구입한다.

**패러프레이징** get some more → Fetch some items

Questions 62-64 refer to the following conversation and seat map. [미M] [미W]

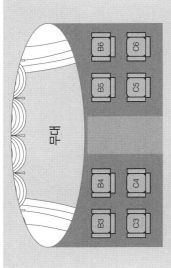

Stage

B3 B4 | B5 B6
C3 C4 | C5 C6

M Excuse me. ㉒ I'm afraid you might be sitting in my seat. I'm supposed to be in C4, by the aisle.

W Oh, let me check my ticket. ㉓ No, it says that I'm in C4.

M Why don't we take a look at yours? Hmm… I see the problem. ㉓ Your seat is right in front of me.

W Ah, that's right. Thank you. But if it's not too much trouble, ㉔ would you be willing to change seats with me? I just ran into an old friend of mine and she's going to be sitting in C3. I just hope to sit together with her.

W Okay, that's fine. Your seat is closer to the stage anyway.

**어휘** aisle 통로　if it's not too much trouble (보통 부탁할 때) 실례가 안 된다면　run into (우연히) ~를 만나다, 마주치다

**62** What is the conversation mainly about?
(A) Locating a building
(B) Negotiating a deal
(C) Revising a seating chart
(D) **Resolving a seating problem**

대화는 주로 무엇에 관한 것인가?
(A) 빌딩을 찾는 것
(B) 거래를 협상하는 것
(C) 좌석표를 수정하는 것
(D) **좌석 문제를 해결하는 것**

**63** Look at the graphic. Which seat was the man originally assigned to?
(A) **B4**
(B) B5
(C) C4
(D) C5

시각 자료를 보시오. 남자는 원래 어떤 좌석을 배정받았는가?
(A) **B4**
(B) B5
(C) C4
(D) C5

---

What does the man ask the woman to do?
(A) Check a theater ticket
(B) **Move to another seat**
(C) Request opera glasses
(D) Speak to his friend

**64** 남자는 여자에게 무엇을 해 달라고 하는가?
(A) 극장 표를 확인하는 것
(B) **다른 자리로 옮기는 것**
(C) 오페라 안경을 요청하는 것
(D) 남자의 친구와 이야기하는 것

**패러프레이징** change seats → Move to another seat

Questions 65-67 refer to the following conversation and building directory. [미M] [영M]

**Edmonton Building Directory**

| Office | Location |
|---|---|
| Dawson Dental Clinic | Suite 1022 |
| Jasmine Hair Shop | Suite 1013 |
| Silver Linings Counseling | Suite 2020 |
| LGB Construction | Suite 2023 |

W Hello. ㉖ I have an appointment with my therapist at 3 o'clock. I just parked at the garage and would like to know how I should pay for parking when I leave.

M Well, ㉖ visitors can use our garage for free if you get the parking slit validated and submit it when you leave. You should ask your therapist for that.

W Okay, I will. Thanks. And one more question. I don't see the name of the massage shop I go to on the building directory here. Do you know where I should go?

M Oh, yes. They just moved in a few days ago and we haven't changed the directory yet. ㉗ You can take the elevator and go to Suite 1013.

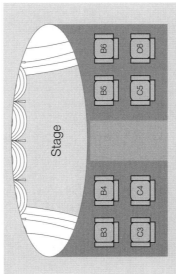

에드몬튼 건물 안내도

| 사무실 | 위치 |
|---|---|
| 도슨 치과 | 1022호 |
| 재스민 헤어숍 | 1013호 |
| 실버 라이닝 카운셀링 | 2020호 |
| LGB 건설 | 2023호 |

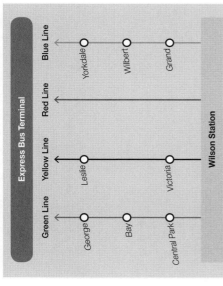

**Questions 68-70 refer to the following conversation and map.** 미W

미M

**Express Bus Terminal**

| Green Line | Yellow Line | Red Line | Blue Line |
|---|---|---|---|
| George | Leslie | | Yorkdale |
| Bay | | | Wilbert |
| Central Park | Victoria | | Grand |

**Wilson Station**

W Hi, Ryan. What are you doing here?

M Hey, Christine. I'm on my way to the Express Bus Terminal, but this station is very confusing. Under normal circumstances, I would definitely take the red line, but it's closed for repairs. Now I'm not sure which line I should take.

W Well, as you can see from the subway map, ⁶⁹ we are at Wilson Station right now. And if I were you, I would take this route to get to the bus terminal. It is not the express line ⁶⁹ but it has only two stops before you reach your destination.

M Yeah, it looks like it'll take me there in just about 15 minutes. Thank you for your help.

W No problem. Are you going on vacation?

M No, ⁷⁰ I'm going to Boston to attend a trade fair. I'll see you when I'm back.

W Okay. Have a nice trip!

---

안녕하세요, 라이언. 여기서 뭐하세요?

안녕하세요, 크리스틴. 전 지금 고속버스 터미널에 가는 길인데 이 역은 너무 혼란스럽네요. 평소 때라면 전 당연히 레드라인을 탔겠지만 지금 수리 때문에 폐쇄됐거든요. 어느 노선을 타는 게 좋을지 모르겠어요.

음, 이 지하철 노선도에서 보듯이 우리는 지금 윌슨역에 있어요. 그리고 제가 당신이라면 전 이 노선을 타고 버스 터미널에 가겠어요. 급행 노선은 아니지만 목적지에 도착할 때까지 역이 2개뿐이거든요.

네, 한 15분 정도면 거기 도착할 수 있을 것 같네요. 도와주셔서 고마워요.

별도. 휴가 가는 거예요?

아니요, 전 보스턴에 무역 박람회에 참석하러 가요. 돌아와서 봐요.

좋아요. 즐거운 여행 하세요!

**어휘** confusing 혼란스러운   under normal circumstances 보통 때라면   destination 목적지   fair 박람회   participate in ~에 참석하다   contest 대회

---

**68** Where does the conversation take place?
(A) On a bus
(B) In an office
**(C) At a subway station**
(D) In the street

대화는 어디서 일어나는가?
(A) 버스 안에서
(B) 사무실 안에서
**(C) 지하철역에서**
(D) 길거리에서

---

**어휘** building directory 건물 안내도   therapist 치료사, 마사지사   parking slit 주차권   validate 확인하다   resident 거주민   upon validation 확인이 된 경우에

---

**65** What is the purpose of the woman's visit?
(A) To meet with a client
**(B) To see a therapist**
(C) To deliver supplies
(D) To get a car repaired

여자의 방문 목적은 무엇인가?
(A) 고객을 만나려고
**(B) 테라피스트를 만나려고**
(C) 물품을 배달하려고
(D) 자동차를 고치려고

**테라피스트[치료]** have an appointment with my therapist → see a therapist

---

**66** What does the man say about parking?
(A) It is for residents only.
(B) It must be paid in cash.
**(C) It is free upon validation.**
(D) It is currently unavailable.

남자는 주차에 관해 뭐라고 하는가?
(A) 거주자만 사용할 수 있다.
(B) 반드시 현금으로 결제해야 한다.
**(C) 확인을 받으면 무료이다.**
(D) 현재 자리가 없다.

---

**67** Look at the graphic. Which name of the office needs to be changed on the building directory?
(A) Dawson Dental Clinic
**(B) Jasmine Hair Shop**
(C) Silver Linings Counseling
(D) LGB Construction

시각 자료를 보시오. 건물 안내도에서 어떤 사무실의 이름이 변경되어야 하는가?
(A) 도슨 치과
**(B) 재스민 헤어숍**
(C) 실버 라이닝 카운셀링
(D) LGB 건설

**69** Look at the graphic. Which line does the woman suggest the man take?

(A) Green Line
**(B) Yellow Line**
(C) Red Line
(D) Blue Line

시각 자료를 보시오. 여자는 남자에게 어떤 노선을 타라고 권하는가?
(A) 그린라인
**(B) 옐로라인**
(C) 레드라인
(D) 블루라인

**70** Why is the man going to Boston?

(A) He is participating in a contest.
(B) He is buying a house.
(C) He is visiting his family.
**(D) He is going on a business trip.**

남자는 왜 보스턴에 가는가?
(A) 그는 시합에 참석한다.
(B) 그는 집을 구입한다.
(C) 그는 가족을 방문한다.
**(D) 그는 출장을 간다.**

---

Questions 71-73 refer to the following talk. (호M)

Hello. My name is Marcus Franken, and **⑪** I am the head trainer at Highams Park Fitness Center. I am pleased to see you all here. You have been hired as personal trainers for **⑫** our busiest time of year, in January. This is when many people come to us to get fit after the holiday season. Since we have purchased a number of new exercise machines for our customers, I'm going to give you training on them first. I have a list of your names here. **⑬** When I call each one of your names, please introduce yourself to the others. And then we will move on to equipment demonstrations and some floor exercises.

안녕하세요. 저는 마커스 프랭컨이고 하이엄 파크 피트니스 센터의 책임 트레이너입니다. 이곳에서 여러분을 뵙게 되어 기쁩니다. 올해의 가장 바쁜 시기인 1월에 여러분은 모두 개인 트레이너로 채용되었습니다. 이때는 많은 사람들이 휴가 시즌 이후에 건강한 몸을 만들기 위해 우리를 찾아오는 시기입니다. 우리가 고객 들을 위해 새 운동 기계를 몇 개 구입했기 때문에 제가 먼저 그 기구들에 대한 교 육을 할 것입니다. 여러분의 명단이 여기 있는데요. 제가 각 이름을 호명하면, 자 기소개를 해 주시겠어요? 그 후에는 장비 시범과 몇 가지 바닥 운동으로 넘어가 도록 하겠습니다.

**어휘** get fit 건강한 몸을 만들다 a number of 수많은 demonstration 시범 floor exercise 마루 운동 renew 갱신하다 membership fee 회비 paperwork 서류-문서 업무

**71** Where is the talk taking place?

**(A) At a fitness club**
(B) At a medical center
(C) At a hotel
(D) At a factory

담화는 어디서 일어나는가?
**(A) 헬스클럽**
(B) 의료원
(C) 호텔
(D) 공장

**72** What does the speaker say will happen in January?

(A) A branch office will be opened.
(B) A contract will be renewed.
**(C) A busy season will begin.**
(D) Membership fees will increase.

화자는 1월에 무엇이 있을 거라고 말하는가?
(A) 지점이 오픈될 것이다.
(B) 계약이 갱신될 것이다.

---

(C) 바쁜 시기가 시작될 것이다.
(D) 회비가 오를 것이다.

**패러프레이징** our busiest time → A busy season

**73** What are the listeners asked to do?

(A) Look at some paperwork
**(B) Introduce themselves to each other**
(C) Go to another building
(D) Update their contact information

청자들이 하라고 요구받는 것은 무엇인가?
(A) 서류 보기
**(B) 자기소개하기**
(C) 다른 건물로 가기
(D) 연락처 업데이트하기

---

Questions 74-76 refer to the following telephone message. (영W)

Hi, Ms. Park. This is Debbie Ernst calling from Max Real Estate. **⑭** I'm getting back to you about the studio apartment that I showed you yesterday. **⑮** You asked if pets are allowed. And the answer is yes. I just talked to the landlord, and she said she had no issues with pets. Well, I think **⑯** you shouldn't miss this opportunity. **⑯** Let me know what you'd like to do. If you're interested, I'll prepare all the paperwork for the lease right away.

안녕하세요, 박 선생님. 저는 맥스 부동산에서 전화하는 데비 에른스트입니다. 제가 어제 보여드렸던 원룸 오피스텔에 관해 다시 연락드립니다. 애완동물이 허 용되는지 물어보셨죠. 된다고 합니다. 방금 집주인과 얘기를 했는데 애완동물은 문제가 없다고 하시네요. 음, 제 생각에는 이 기회를 놓치지 말아야 할 것 같아 요. 어떻게 하실지 알려 주세요. 만약에 관심이 있으시다면 즉시 임대에 필요한 서류를 모두 준비해 드리겠습니다.

**어휘** get back to ~에게 답신 전화하다 studio apartment 원룸 landlord 집주인 opportunity 기회 paperwork 서류 lease 임대 positive 긍정적인 negotiate 협상하다 view 견해

**74** What did the speaker do yesterday?

(A) She went to a pet store.
(B) She moved into an apartment.
(C) She worked overtime.
**(D) She met with a client.**

화자는 어제 무엇을 했는가?
(A) 애완동물을 가게에 갔다.
(B) 아파트로 이사 갔다.
(C) 야근을 했다.
**(D) 고객을 만났다.**

**75** What did the listener ask about?
(A) When the building was built
(B) Why a rental fee is expensive
**(C) Whether pets are allowed**
(D) Where parking is available

청자는 무엇에 대해 물었는가?
(A) 건물이 언제 지어졌는지
(B) 왜 임대료가 비싼지
**(C) 애완동물이 허용되는지**
(D) 어디에 주차를 할 수 있는지

**76** Why does the speaker say, "you shouldn't miss this opportunity"?
**(A) To encourage a positive decision**
(B) To negotiate a contract
(C) To extend an invitation
(D) To present a different view

화자는 왜 "이 기회를 놓치지 않아야 할 것 같아요"라고 말하는가?
**(A) 긍정적인 결정을 권하려고**
(B) 계약서에 대해 협상하려고
(C) 초대를 하려고
(D) 다른 견해를 제시하려고

어휘 commute 통근하다 ~bound ~행의 lane 차선 repainting 재도색 chance 가능성 be advised to ~하도록 권고되다 detour 우회하다 bustling 북적하는 concertgoer 콘서트 참석자들 venue행사 장소 in time for 시간에 맞춰 expansion 확장 make it 오다

**77** What will cause traffic congestion tomorrow morning on the bridge?
(A) Change of signal lights
(B) Road expansion
(C) A musical event
**(D) Some repair work**

내일 아침 교량 체증의 원인은 무엇인가?
(A) 교통 신호등 교체
(B) 도로 확장
(C) 음악 행사
**(D) 보수 작업**

패러프레이징 lane repainting → Some repair work

**78** What did the speaker say might affect the roadwork schedule?
**(A) A change in the weather**
(B) Traffic condition
(C) Work hours
(D) The ending of a concert

화자가 도로 작업 일정에 영향을 준다고 말한 것은 무엇인가?
**(A) 날씨 변화**
(B) 교통 상황
(C) 근무 시간
(D) 콘서트의 종료

**79** What program are the listeners going to hear next?
(A) Local news
**(B) A financial program**
(C) Advertisements
(D) Weather forecast

청자들이 다음에 들을 것은 무엇인가?
(A) 지역 소식
**(B) 금융 프로**
(C) 광고
(D) 일기예보

---

Questions 77-79 refer to the following radio broadcast. 미W

Hello, listeners, this is Armanda Ritz with the traffic report. Those who commute south bound on the Barnett Bridge should expect major delays tomorrow 77 due to lane repainting. 78 With at least a 10% chance of snow, the work will start from 8:00 A.M. and take the entire morning and end by noon. Commuters are advised to detour to Marine Drive or Dewdney Trunk Road. You should also expect another night time delay around Wilson Avenue since a big musical event is taking place at the Lincoln Convention Hall at 6:30 P.M. tomorrow. As the venue is always bustling, concertgoers are advised to start driving there at least half an hour earlier than usual if they want to make it in time for the event. This has been traffic with Armanda Ritz. 79 Dollar Sense with your financial consultant Wyatt Chen will be coming up next. I'll be back in 20 minutes.

---

Questions 80-82 refer to the following recorded message. 호M

Hello. You have reached the clinic of Dr. Barakat. 80 Our office is now closed for the observance of Memorial Day. 81 If this is an emergency, please call 911 or visit an urgent care facility near you. We will be open next Monday, the 25th, at 8:30 A.M. Our regular office hours are Monday through Friday from 8:30 A.M. to 6 P.M. 82 To make an appointment or to change it, or cancel your appointment, please record your name and phone number after the beep. We will contact you as soon as we can. Thank you.

안녕하세요, 바라카트 박사님의 병원으로 전화하셨습니다. 저희 병원은 현충일을 기념하여 오늘 진료하지 않습니다. 긴급한 상황인 경우 911로 전화하시거나 가까운 응급 처치 시설을 방문하세요. 다음 주 월요일인 25일 오전 8시 30분에 문을 엽니다. 평소 진료 시간은 월요일에서 금요일, 오전 8시 30분부터 오후 6시까지입니다. 예약을 하시거나 예약 변경을 하시려면 삐 소리 후에 이름과 전화번호를 남겨 주세요. 가능한 한 빨리 연락드리겠습니다. 감사합니다.

어휘 you have reached ~로 전화 연결되었다 observance 준수, 의식 Memorial Day 현충일 urgent 긴급한 record 녹음하다

**80** What is the main purpose of this message?
(A) To inform listeners of emergency exits
(B) To confirm listeners' appointments
(C) To talk about the reopening
**(D) To announce that the facility is closed**

이 메시지의 주된 목적은 무엇인가?
(A) 청자들에게 비상구를 알려 주려고
(B) 청자들의 예약을 확인하려고
(C) 재개업을 얘기하려고
**(D) 시설이 문 닫았음을 알리려고**

패러프레이징 Our office is now closed → the facility is closed

**81** What should the listeners do if it is an emergency?
(A) They need to record their names and numbers.
(B) They need to visit on Monday.
**(C) They need to call the number that was mentioned.**
(D) They have to make an appointment.

긴급 상황이면 청자들은 무엇을 해야 하는가?
(A) 이름과 전화번호를 녹음한다.
(B) 월요일에 방문한다.
**(C) 언급된 번호로 전화한다.**
(D) 약속을 한다.

---

청취자 여러분 안녕하세요, 교통 방송의 아만다 리츠입니다. 바넷 다리를 타고 남쪽으로 오시는 통근자들께서는 내일 차선 재도색 작업으로 인해 지체를 예상하셔야겠습니다. 눈이 올 확률이 최소 10퍼센트이기 때문에 작업은 아침 8시에 시작해서 오전 내내 작업해서 정오 전에 끝날 예정입니다. 통근자들은 마린 드라이브나 듀드니 트렁크 로드 쪽으로 우회하시기 바랍니다. 저녁 시간에는 윌슨 애비뉴 쪽에서도 또 다른 지체를 예상하셔야겠습니다. 큰 음악 행사가 내일 오후 6시 30분에 링컨 컨벤션 홀에서 열릴 예정이니까요. 그 장소는 항상 붐비기 때문에 콘서트 참석자들께서는 시간 내에 가시기 위해서는 최소한 30분 일찍 출발하시기 바랍니다. 지금까지 아만다 리츠였습니다. 화제가 되어 있는 와이어트 첸에 진행하는 달러 센스가 이어지겠습니다. 저는 20분 뒤에 다시 돌아오겠습니다.

**82** What should the listeners do to change an appointment?
(A) Visit the clinic
(B) Wait until the representative answers
(C) Talk to someone at an urgent care facility
**(D) Leave a message**

청자들이 예약을 변경하려면 어떻게 해야 하는가?
(A) 병원을 방문한다.
(B) 담당자가 답변할 때까지 기다린다.
(C) 응급 시설에 있는 사람과 얘기한다.
**(D) 메시지를 남긴다.**

패러프레이징 record your name and phone number → Leave a message

Questions 83-85 refer to the following excerpt from a meeting. 미M

Before we begin the managers' meeting, I have a very important announcement. Steve Daines, the new CEO, will be visiting our factory next Tuesday. **83** The purpose of his visit is to inspect the automation system we've recently installed throughout the factory. Since this upgrade involved large sums of money, he will probably want to see how efficiently the new system is operating. Now, this isn't an official inspection. **84** So, no special arrangements will be needed. **85** We'll have a lunch meeting with Mr. Daines that day and I expect all the managers to be there.

관리자 회의를 시작하기 전에, 매우 중요한 공지 사항이 있습니다. 새로운 대표 이사인 스티브 데인스 씨가 다음 주 화요일에 우리 공장을 방문할 것입니다. 그의 방문 목적은 우리가 최근에 공장 전체에 설치한 자동화 시스템을 점검하기 위한 것입니다. 이번 업그레이드에 많은 돈이 들었기 때문에 그는 새로운 시스템이 얼마나 효율적으로 작동되는지 보고 싶을 것입니다. 자, 이건 공식적인 검사가 아닙니다. 그래서 어떤 특별한 준비도 필요하지 않습니다. 우리는 그날 다인스 씨와 점심 미팅을 함께할 것이니 모든 관리자들은 참석해 주십시오.

어휘 inspect 점검하다, 검열하다 automation system (보통 공장의) 자동화 시스템 involve 수반하다, 관여시키다 official 공식적인 facility 시설물 production capacity 생산력 reassure 안심시키다 acknowledge 인정하다 luncheon 점심이 포함된 행사

**83** What is the purpose of the CEO's visit?
(A) To celebrate an anniversary
(B) To assign new tasks
**(C) To inspect a facility**
(D) To improve production capacity

대표 이사의 방문 목적은 무엇인가?
(A) 기념일을 축하하기 위해
(B) 새로운 업무를 배정하기 위해
**(C) 시설물을 점검하기 위해**
(D) 생산 능력을 향상시키기 위해

**84** Why does the speaker say, "this isn't an official inspection"?
(A) To make preparations for an event
(B) To discuss an issue
**(C) To reassure colleagues**
(D) To acknowledge hard work

화자가 "이건 공식적인 검열이 아닙니다"라고 말한 이유는 무엇인가?
(A) 행사의 준비를 하기 위해
(B) 문제에 대해 논의하기 위해
**(C) 동료들을 안심시키기 위해**
(D) 열심히 일한 것을 치하하기 위해

**85** What are the listeners asked to do?
**(A) Attend a luncheon**
(B) Host a welcome reception
(C) Join a factory tour
(D) Plan a retirement party

청자들은 무엇을 하라는 요청을 받는가?
**(A) 점심 행사에 참석할 것**
(B) 환영 파티를 열 것
(C) 공장 견학에 함께할 것
(D) 은퇴 파티를 계획할 것

패러프레이징 have a lunch meeting → Attend a luncheon

Questions 86-88 refer to the following radio broadcast. 영W

Today's interview will be with **86** Emmanuel David, the owner and main designer of Emmanuel Couture. Mr. David's rise to success has been phenomenal and last week, **87** he attended the industry's most prestigious Arts de la Mode award ceremony in Cannes where he was awarded Designer of the Year by the judges. Today, he will be talking about innovations in manufacturing technology that he has introduced into his production process which make his designer clothes more affordable for the general public. **88** Mr. David will also be available after the program to answer any of your questions. You can also contact us at www. kbp.com.

오늘의 인터뷰는 엠마누엘 꾸뛰르의 주인이자 메인 디자이너인 엠마누엘 데이비드와 함께할 것입니다. 데이비드 씨의 출세는 경이적이며 지난주 그는 칸에서 열리는 업계의 가장 권위 있는 이츠 데 라 모드 시상식에 참석하여 심사위원들이 뽑은 올해의 디자이너 상을 받았습니다. 오늘, 그는 대중들을 위해 디자이너 의류를 더 저렴한 가격으로 만들게 해 준, 생산 과정에 도입했던 제조 기술의 혁신에 관하여 얘기할 것입니다. 데이비드 씨는 또한 프로그램이 끝나고 질의응답도 하실 예정입니다. www.kbp.com으로 질문을 남겨 주세요.

어휘 couture 유명 디자이너 제품, 고급 여성복 rise to success 출세 prestigious 명망 있는, 권위 있는 award ceremony 시상식 award (상을) 수여하다 affordable (가격이) 알맞은 post 게시하다 host (방송 등의) 진행자 fill out 작성하다 enter a competition 경기에 참가하다[출전하다]

**86** Who is Emmanuel David?
**(A) A fashion designer**
(B) A radio host
(C) A magazine editor
(D) A manufacturing expert

엠마누엘 데이비드는 누구인가?
**(A) 패션 디자이너**
(B) 라디오 진행자
(C) 잡지 편집자
(D) 제조 전문가

**87** Why did Mr. David go to Cannes?
(A) To visit a client
(B) To view some designs
**(C) To attend an event**
(D) To open a production line

**Questions 92-94 refer to the following telephone message.** 호M

Hi, this is Kenneth Parker calling from the Office of Workplace Safety. I'm sure you reviewed the follow-up report I had sent to you 93 after we inspected your facilities the other day. As the report says, your building is meeting the overall safety standards that have recently been revised by the government. 92 However, I have added up some suggestions that I think will be of great help to you if you want to cut down on the cost of fire equipment such as sprinklers. I'll be available between noon and 5:00 P.M., so 94 call me back at 555-3291 and we can discuss that. Thank you.

안녕하세요, 저는 직장 안전청의 케네스 파커입니다. 며칠 전에 귀하의 시설물을 점검한 뒤에 제가 보낸 후속 보고서를 검토해 보셨으리라 믿습니다. 보고서에 나온 대로, 귀하의 건물은 최근 정부가 개정한 전반적인 안전 규정을 충족시키고 있습니다. 하지만 스프링클러와 같은 화재 장비의 비용을 줄이고 싶으시다면 도움이 될 만한 제안을 첨가했습니다. 낮 12시부터 오후 5시까지 시간이 가능하니 555-3291번으로 전화 다시 주시면 그것에 대해 얘기를 해 볼 수 있습니다. 감사합니다.

어휘 workplace 직장, 일터 follow-up 후속의 inspect 점검하다 meet the safety standards 안전 규정을 준수하다 revise 개정하다 add up 덧붙이다 cut down on 줄이다 set up 설치하다

92 What is the purpose of the message?
(A) To review a follow-up report
(B) To announce new safety standards
(C) To set up new fire equipment
**(D) To discuss ways to reduce costs**

메시지의 목적은 무엇인가?
(A) 후속 보고서 검토
(B) 새로운 안전 규정 발표
(C) 새로운 화재 장비 설치
**(D) 비용 절감 방법 의논**
패러프레이징 cut down on the cost → reduce costs

93 Who most likely is the speaker?
(A) A building manager
**(B) A facility inspector**
(C) An accountant
(D) A real estate agent

화자는 누구인가?
(A) 건물 관리인
**(B) 시설 점검자**
(C) 회계사
(D) 부동산 중개인

---

89 What type of business does the speaker work for?
(A) A hospital
**(B) A staffing agency**
(C) A real estate agency
(D) A university

화자는 어떤 종류의 업체에서 일하는가?
(A) 병원
**(B) 채용 업체**
(C) 부동산
(D) 대학
패러프레이징 Employment Agency → A staffing agency

90 What does the speaker imply when she says, "So please note that wait times can be long"?
(A) She wants to get a deadline extension.
(B) An investigation will be completed shortly.
(C) The listeners should return on another day.
**(D) She hopes the listeners will be patient.**

화자가 "그러니 대기 시간이 길어질 수 있다는 것을 알아 두세요"라고 말한 의도는 무엇인가?
(A) 그녀는 마감 연장을 받고 싶다.
(B) 조사는 곧 끝날 것이다.
(C) 청자들은 다른 날 다시 오는 게 좋다.
**(D) 그녀는 청자들이 인내심을 갖기 바란다.**

91 According to the speaker, what is provided for listeners?
**(A) Some refreshments**
(B) Technical assistance
(C) Newspapers and magazines
(D) Some office equipment

화자에 따르면 무엇이 청자들을 위해 제공되었는가?
**(A) 간식**
(B) 기술적인 도움
(C) 신문과 잡지
(D) 사무기기
패러프레이징 Some snacks and beverages → Some refreshments

---

데이비드 씨가 권에 갈 이유는 무엇인가?
(A) 고객을 방문하려고
(B) 어떤 디자인들을 보려고
(C) 행사에 참석하려고
(D) 생산 라인을 개시하려고

88 What are listeners invited to do?
(A) Fill out a survey
(B) Enter a competition
**(C) Inquire about the show**
(D) Visit Mr. David's company

청자들이 요청받은 것은 무엇인가?
(A) 설문 작성하기
(B) 대회에 참가하기
**(C) 프로그램에 관해 묻기**
(D) 데이비드 씨 회사 방문하기

---

**Questions 89-91 refer to the following announcement.** 미W

Good morning, everyone. Welcome to 89 Ultimate Employment Agency. We specialize in the placement of healthcare professionals from nurses to medical researchers. So if you're looking to make the most of your healthcare career, you've found the right company. Today, each one of you will have a consultation with our recruiters. After that, they will match your skills to the requests of the medical facility you'd be best suited for. I'd like to let you know that 90 our consultations for today are fully booked. 90 So please note that wait times can be long. 91 Some snacks and beverages are provided on the counter over there. Please help yourself while you wait. Thank you.

안녕하세요, 여러분. 얼티밋 채용 회사에 오신 것을 환영합니다. 우리는 간호사부터 의료 연구자까지의 의료 전문인의 취업을 전문으로 합니다. 그래서 당신이 의료 경력을 최대로 활용하고 싶으시다면, 딱 맞는 회사를 찾으신 겁니다. 오늘, 여러분 각각은 우리 채용관들과 상담을 하게 될 것입니다. 그 후에 여러분의 기술을 그대 가장 잘 맞는 의료 기관과 연결해 드릴 것입니다. 여러분께 오늘의 상담이 모두 예약되었음을 알려 드립니다. 그러니 대기 시간이 길어질 수 있다는 것을 알아 두세요. 간식과 음료가 저쪽에 있는 탁자에 제공되어 있습니다. 기다리시는 동안 드세요. 감사합니다.

어휘 specialize in ~을 전문으로 하다 placement (일자리) 취업, 일자리 consultation 상담 medical facility 의료 기관 be suited for ~에 맞다 book 예약하다 wait time 대기 시간 help oneself ~을 마음껏 먹다, 쓰다 refreshments 간식

**94** Why does the speaker want the listener to return his call?
(A) To purchase fire equipment
**(B) To make some recommendations**
(C) To re-inspect the facilities
(D) To give him a new report

화자는 왜 청자에게 전화를 다시 해 달라고 요청하는가?
(A) 화재 장비를 구입하려고
**(B) 몇 가지 추천 사항을 전달하려고**
(C) 시설을 재점검하려고
(D) 그에게 새로운 보고서를 주려고

---

Questions 95-97 refer to the following talk and graph. [영W]

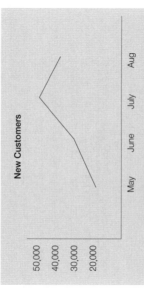

**New Customers**

Thank you for coming to ⑨⑤ the quarterly marketing meeting. First, I'd like to discuss how successful we have been in attracting new customers. Please take a look at the graph on page 3. Obviously, ⑨⑥ the most successful month was July because we launched our new Internet & TV package that month. As you know, about 50,000 people signed up for it. ⑨⑦ And the second highest increase occurred during the "referral bonus" promotion. I think it was a brilliant way of adding new customers. Okay, now, let's talk about the new advertising campaign for the next quarter.

---

---

**95** In what department does the speaker most likely work?
(A) Product development
(B) Purchasing
**(C) Marketing**
(D) Customer service

화자는 어떤 부서에서 일할 것 같은가?
(A) 상품 개발
(B) 구매
**(C) 마케팅**
(D) 고객 서비스

**96** According to the speaker, what happened in July?
**(A) A package product was introduced.**
(B) A branch location was added
(C) A department was reorganized.
(D) A business merger took place.

화자에 따르면, 7월에 무슨 일이 있었는가?
**(A) 결합 상품이 소개되었다.**
(B) 지점이 추가되었다.
(C) 부서가 개편되었다.
(D) 기업 합병이 일어났다.

**97** Look at the graphic. When was the promotional event held?
(A) In May
(B) In June
(C) In July
**(D) In August**

시각 자료를 보시오. 판매 촉진 행사는 언제 열렸는가?
(A) 5월
(B) 6월
(C) 7월
**(D) 8월**

---

Questions 98-100 refer to the following talk and museum map. [영M]

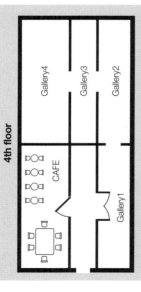

**4th floor**

CAFE

Gallery1

Gallery2

Gallery3

Gallery4

⑨⑧ This program includes a guided tour, which explores the highlights of the museum's collection. The tour will take about 90 minutes, and after the tour you can explore the exhibits on your own. There are many wonderful exhibits that are not included in this tour, so I highly recommend you see the exhibit of European paintings afterwards. ⑨⑨ It is on view in the gallery, which is located on the fourth floor next to the café. Check the museum's floor plans, and you'll locate it easily. ⑩⑩ If you'd like to learn more about our current exhibitions, there are excellent books in the bookstore.

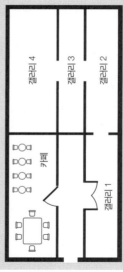

**4층**

카페

갤러리 1

갤러리 2

갤러리 3

갤러리 4

이 프로그램은 가이드가 딸린 견학을 포함하는데 미술관 전시품 중 주요 작품들을 둘러보게 됩니다. 견학은 90분가량이 걸리고 그 후에는 여러분 각자 전시품들을 둘러볼 수 있습니다. 견학에 포함되지 않는 훌륭한 전시품들이 많이 있기 때문에 저는 견학 후에 유럽의 그림 전시를 꼭 보실 것을 권해 드립니다. 4층 카페 옆에 위치한 갤러리에 전시되어 있습니다. 미술관의 안내도를 확인하시면 쉽게 찾을 수 있을 것입니다. 현재 열리고 있는 전시회에 대해 더 알고 싶으시다면 서점에 좋은 책들이 많이 있습니다.

**신규 고객**

5월 6월 7월 8월

**98** Who most likely is the speaker?
(A) A painter
(B) A university professor
(C) A museum guide
(D) A photographer

화자는 누구일 것 같은가?
(A) 화가
(B) 대학 교수
(C) 미술관 가이드
(D) 사진작가

**99** Look at the graphic. In which gallery are the European paintings exhibited?
(A) Gallery1
(B) Gallery2
(C) Gallery3
(D) Gallery4

시각 자료를 보시오. 유럽의 그림은 어느 갤러리에서 전시되는가?
(A) 갤러리 1
(B) 갤러리 2
(C) 갤러리 3
(D) 갤러리 4

**100** What would listeners do if they are interested in the current exhibitions?
(A) Visit a bookshop
(B) Explore a website
(C) Watch a movie
(D) Attend a lecture

청자들은 현재 전시회에 대해 관심이 있는 경우 무엇을 할 것인가?
(A) 서점을 방문한다.
(B) 웹 사이트를 살펴본다.
(C) 영화를 본다.
(D) 강연에 참석한다.

---

## PART 5

P26

**101 해석** 벤체스터 항공사는 좀 더 고급스러운 시설을 위해 비행기의 좌석 수를 줄여 수익성과 고객 만족도를 향상시켰다.
**해설** 문장을 빠르게 해석하면서 전체적인 의미에 부합하는 단어를 선택하는 문제이다. 비행기의 좌석을 줄여서 항공사의 수익성과 고객의 만족을 증가시켰다고 했으므로 전체적인 의미를 고려해 볼 때 가장 적절한 것은 (C)이다. seating capacity는 토익에 자주 나오는 복합 명사이므로 알아 두자. (B) 강렬함, 진동, 강도 / (D) 소실, 작성
**어휘** decrease 줄이다  seating capacity 좌석 수  in favor of ~에 찬성하여, ~을 위하여  high-class 고급의  accommodation 숙소, 시설  enhance 향상시키다  profitability 수익성  customer satisfaction 고객 만족도

**102 해석** 여기에서 논의되었던 것을 발설하지 않는다는 약속과 함께 이 회의를 끝내야 한다.
**해설** 의미상 알맞은 전치사를 선택하는 문제이다. 여기에서 토론되었던 것을 발설하지 말라는 약속과 함께라는 의미의 (C) with가 적절하다.
**어휘** conclude 끝내다  reveal (비밀 등을) 밝히다  debate 논의하다

**103 해설** BMC 페트롤럼 사는 고속도로 출구에 편리하게 위치한 새 주유소를 열 계획이다. (A) 경명위치에, 넓게 / (C) 바르게, 정확하게
의미상 알맞은 부사를 선택하는 문제이다. 세롭게 생긴 고속도로 업무 근처에 '편리하게' 위치한다는 의미의 (B)가 적절하다.
**어휘** exit 출구  gas station 주유소

**104 해석** 고용 씨의 홍보 자문가와 상담하기 전에 김 씨는 그 인건의 세부 사항에 대해서 더 잘 이해하고 싶어 한다.
**해설** 전치사 뒤에 알맞은 동사 형태를 고르는 문제로 동명사인 (C)가 가장 적절하다. before를 접속사로 보면 주절에 주어인 Mr. Kim이 번복되어 생략된 것으로, 원래 문장은 Before Mr. Kim is consulting with ~ 이다. 반면 앞에 주어가 없으므로 (A)는 올 수 없고, before 다음에 부사절을 쓸 수 없으므로 (B)도 알맞지 않다.
**어휘** consult with ~와 상의하다  public relation 홍보  have a better understanding of ~을 더 잘 알다  agenda 안건

**105 해석** 전략 워크숍은 월요일 오전 11시에 열릴 것이고 2시 30분에 휴회가 이어질 것이다. 그 후 3시 30분에 늦은 점심이 이뤄질 것이다.
**해설** 빈칸 앞뒤로 'will+동사원형'의 형태가 있는 것으로 볼 때 반접되는 등 위 접속사인 (C) and가 적절하며, such는 형용사 및 대명사로 쓸 수 있으며, either는 형용사, 대명사, 부사로 사용된다.
**어휘** A be followed by B A 다음에 B가 이어지다

**106 해설** 그 지역의 하가진는 빌딩 소유주로부터 서면 견적서가 승인될 때까지 어떤 보수 작업도 시작할 수 없다고 지시했다.
**해설** 의미상 빈칸 앞의 written과 어울리는 단어인 (B) estimate가 적절하다. written estimate는 '서면 견적서라는 뜻으로 토익에 자주 나온다.

---

**107 해석** 빈칸 앞의 solicit는 뒤에 to가 바로 올 수 없고 타동사로서 목적어를 바로 갖는다. 또한 nominate는 타동사로서 뒤에 바로 전치사 for를 취하지 않으므로 동명사인 (B)는 올 수 없다. 따라서 명사인 (C) nominations가 적절하다.
**어휘** board of directors 이사회  solicit 요청하다  nomination 지명, 추천  human resources 인사부  treasurer 회계원, 출납계원  vice-president 부사장

**108 해설** 판티엄 사가 ATX 사의 적대적 기업 인수 계획을 발표한 후에 ATX 사의 주가가 급격히 올랐다.
**해설** 선택지 중 주가가 올랐다는 표현과 가장 어울리는 부사 표현은 (D) dramatically이다. (A) 의미심장하게 / (B) 우연히, 못하지 않게 / (C) 열정적으로, 열심히
**어휘** make known 발표하다, 알리다  hostile takeover bid 적대적 기업 인수  value of stock 주가

**109 해석** 우리는 모든 자재와 프린터 구성 부품, 책상들과 그밖에 관련된 비품들을 지하 참고에 뒤야 한다.
**해설** 지하실의 참고에 옮겨서 넣어두는 것들과 '관련 있는' 것들과 각종 사무용품 등을 뒤야 한다는 내용으로 가장 적절한 어휘는 (A) related이다. (C) interested는 excited, attracted, impressed, amazed, frustrated처럼 사람을 수식하는 분사형이다. (D) 관계는 명사 앞에서 수식하는 것이 아니라 동사 뒤에서 서술된다. (B) 성취할 수 있는, 달성할 수 있는 / (C) 흥미를 가진 / (D) 시로 갖은, 비슷한
**어휘** material 자재, 재료  component 부품  supplies 공급품  basement warehouse 지하 참고

**110 해설** 마케팅 부서의 임무는 판매 전략을 개발할 뿐만 아니라, 자사의 서비스를 잠재 고객에게 홍보하는 것을 담당하고 계약을 따내야 한다.
**해설** 빈칸이 다음에 올수 있는 동사는 (동명사이므로 (D)가 답벗다. (A), (B)는 모두 동사로서 반칸에 올 수 없다. (C) promoted는 문서 형태로 전치사 소유격 our가 있으므로 받게일 수 없다.
**어휘** take charge of ~의 책임을 맡다  prospective customer 잠재 고객  secure 얻어내다, 획득하다  deal 거래

**111 해석** 국내 거래 협력 사들 중에서 우리의 새로운 통화 정책이 더 튼튼한 경제에 기여하고 있다.
**해설** have p.p. 형태의 현재완료 시제를 듣는 문제이므로 반칸에는 (B) contributed가 와야 한다. contribution은 보통 단수로 쓰이며 전치사 to와 어울리고 비슷한 어휘로 commitment, subscription 등이 있다. (A) 기여금, 공헌, 기고
**어휘** currency policy 통화 정책  contribute to ~에 기여하다

---

written consent(서면 동의서)와 함께 읽어 두자. (A) 편단, 심판, 재판 / (C) 추측 / (D) 암시, 연상, 제안
**어휘** licenser 하가자, 인가자  written estimate (서면) 견적서  building owner 건물 소유주  maintenance work 보수 작업

**112 해석** 1990년대에 그 나라는 5년 이상 꾸준히 상승하는 물가로 인한 경기 침체를 겪었다.

**해설** 주절의 동사는 suffered(로서 inflation 다음에 동사 rose기 또 나왔으 므로 빈칸은 주격 관계대명사 자리임을 알 수 있다. 따라서 정답은 (B) 이다. (C) when으로 관계대명사로 쓰일 경우 뒤에 완벽한 문장이 와야 하므로 빈칸 뒤에 주어가 없는 관계절은 답이 될 수 없다. (D) what으로 관계대명사가 선행사를 포함한 것으로, what=the thing which [that]으로 보면 된 다.

**어휘** depression 불경기, 불황 inflation 물가 상승 steadily 꾸준히

**113 해석** 많은 서류 작업이 은행 방문에 대한 걱정 없이 그 회사의 직원들로는 특 별 자동 예금 제도에 월급의 5퍼센트를 자동 이체할 수 있다.

**해설** 문장이 매우 길지만 빈칸의 앞뒤만 보면 쉽고 빨리 해결할 수 있는 문 제다. '저축 예금 계좌를 잊거나 못하는 savings account는 빈번히 의미로 자주 나오는 표현이므로 정답은 (D)이다. information으로 불가산 명사로 빈칸 앞에 관사나 소유격과 함께 쓰일 수 없다. 참 고로 each 뒤에는 단수 명사만이 못 온다.

**어휘** extensive 광범위한, 대규모의 paperwork 문서 업무 have an option 선택권이 있다 automatically 자동적으로 transfer 이체하 다 monthly paycheck 월급

**114 해석** 인사과 직원들은 각 지원자들의 인성 분석이 포함된 현장 프로필을 준비했 을 뿐만 아니라 그들의 학력과 현장 경험에 대한 설명을 리스트에 포함 시켰다.

**해설** 지원자의 학력과 현장 경험 앞에 동격의 전치사 of가 나온다. 뒤의 내용을 고 려해 볼 때 '설명, 기술'이라는 표현이 문맥상 적절하므로 정답은 (A)이다.

**어휘** personnel 인사과 officer 인사과 직원 candidate 후보자, 지원자 profile 개요, 신상 정보 educational background 학력 경험 personality 성격 experience 현장 경험

**115 해석** 주말 동안 24개의 단체가 참가한 우리의 여름 바베큐 파티는 우리 자 선 단체가 행해 온 지금까지의 모든 모금 행사 중에서 가장 성공적이었 다.

**해설** all the fundraisers (that) our charity has conducted가 현재완 료 시제이므로 과거부터 지금까지 해 온 모금 행사 중에서 가장 '성공 적이었다는 (A) successful이 문맥상 자연스럽다. (B) delighted는 감 정 유발 타동사로서 사람을 수식한다. 기뻐하는, 즐거워하는 (C) 부유한 / (D) 전우의, 총체적인

**어휘** fundraiser 모금 행사 charity 자선(단체) conduct 수행하다 participate 참가하다

**116 해석** 공원과 거리의 배치가 걸어서 가는 데에 이상적이었기 때문에 이사회는 그 도시를 연례 거리 축제를 개최할 장소로 선정했다.

**해설** 빈칸 뒤에 〈주어+동사〉절을 갖춘 절이 있으므로 빈칸에는 접속사가 와야 한 다. 따라서 (C)와 (D)는 제외된다. (B) Unless는 '만약 ~하지 않는다 면'이라는 의미로 문맥상 어색하다. 문맥상 인과 관계를 의미할 때 적절하므로, 이유를 의미하는 (A)가 적절하다.

**어휘** layout 배치, 설계 be ideal for ~에 대해 이상적이다 foot traffic 걸어서 통행하는 것 hold 개최하다 annual 연례의

**117 해석** 우리 학교에서는 가족의 수입이 반드시 수준이거나 그보다 낮은 학생 은 수업료의 교체해, 학교 기숙사에게나 특별 값의 자격을 얻는다.

**해설** 학교에서 일정 조건에 해당하는 학생에게 수업료의 교체해, 주거비에 특별 할인을 해 준다는 내용으로 '조건에 대한' 지격이 된다는 의미이므 로 빈칸 뒤에 전치사 for을 취하는 (D) qualifies가 적절하다. (B) 준비하 다, 갖추다 / (C) 배열하다

**어휘** poverty rate 빈곤 수준 tuition fee 수업료 housing 주거, 숙소

**118 해석** 신제품이 출시될 때 이런 제품들은 2~5주 동안 시장에 남아 있는 경 향이 있다.

**해설** 빈칸에 가장 자연스러운 명사는 (D)로, stay on the market(시장에 남아 있다)이란 의미로 자주 나오는 표현이므로 하나의 숙어처럼 외워 두 면 좋다. (A) 장소, 지점, 지역 / (C) 광고

**어휘** for periods of ~ 동안

**119 해석** 오직 HJG 비타클 사이 직원만이 특별 임대 요즘 작용을 받는다.

**해설** 특별 요즘을 특징들만 '독점적으로' 이용할 수 있다는 내용으로, 전치 사구 to workers를 수식하는 부사 (D)가 적절하다. 참고로 (A)와 (B) 는 도익에나 정답으로 된다이므로 이런 단어이다. (A) 배치하다 / 위한 / (B) 배타성 / (C) 제도, 배치

**어휘** leasing rate 임대 요즘 immediate family 직계 가족

**120 해석** 편집자는 항상 작가가 겨룬것에서 실수와 불규칙성들을 찾는다.

**해설** within으로 '(장소, 시간, 거리, 범위, 한계) 이내에'란 의미로 문맥상 작가 의 저술 내에서라는 의미가 자연스러우므로 (A)가 적절하다.

**어휘** irregularity 불규칙, 부정 이상 author 저자, 작가

**121 해석** TSD는 소규모 은행이기 때문에 맞춤 업무 전략으로 소기업이나 개인 계 좌에 주로 초점이 맞춰져 있다.

**해설** 동사 focus와 함께 '주로' ~에 초점을 맞춘다는 의미의 (A)가 일맞 ... (C) originally, (D) initially는 빈칸 앞뒤로 생반되는 내용이 나올 때 주로 사용한다. 예를 들어, '연례처럼에는 ~했다'라 시간이 지나다 ~했는' 식이다. (C) 숫자상으로

**어휘** be focused on ~에 집중되어 있다 personal account 개인 계좌 small-scale 소규모의

**122 해석** 백화점 주엘스 사는 현재 그 지방의 남부에 새로 생긴 지점들에 고용할 경험 있고 의욕 넘치며 팀워크 지향적인 관리자를 찾고 있다.

**해설** 회사에서 지점에 고용할 매니저를 '찾고 있다'는 내용이며, 빈칸 바로 뒤에 목적어가 있는 것으로 보아 타동사가 와야 하므로 (B)이 적절하다. (A) look은 전치사 for와 함께 '~을 찾다'라는 의미로 쓰이며, (C) inquire는 주로 자동사로 쓰여 '묻다, 알아보다'를 의미한다.

**어휘** loan 대출 be focused on ~에 집중되어 있다 personal account 개인 계좌 small-scale 소규모의

**123 해석** 서울에서 열리는 경제 포럼은 아시아에서 개최되는 재무장관 회의 중 에서 가장 대규모 회의일 것이다.

**해설** 아시아에서 '개최되는' 가장 영향력 있는 재무장관 회의라는 의미로 정 답은 (D)이다. (A) 조화하다, 관련되다

**어휘** economic 경제의 extensive 대규모의 finance minister 재무 장관

**124 해석** 해외 시장에서 영업을 할 때 기업들이 직면하는 도전들 중 하나는 제품의 특정에 관한 고객들과의 성공적인 의사소통이다.

**해설** 항공사와 전자사 사이에 올 수 있는 동사는 명사이다. 선택지 중에서 명사는 (C) communication밖에 없다. 의미상 기업이 직면하는 어려 움에 이어질 것은 성공적인 '의사소통'이라는 동격의 역할을 하는 명사 보어가 적절하다. 참고로 주어가 'one 아무E+단수 명사'일 때는 단수 취급 한다.

**어휘** challenge 도전 어려움 corporation 기업, 회사 face ~에 직면하 다 identity 개성, 독자성

**125 해석** 새롭게 개발된 농업 장비는 수확량의 절반이 아니라 농부들의 생산성 을 향상시켰다.

**해설** 새로 개발된 농업 장비 덕분에 절과 함께 향상된 것으로 (A)가 가장 적 절하다. A as well as B에서 A와 B는 모든 모범적으로 대등한 형태이 므로, 예를 들어, A가 명사이면 B도 명사여야 하고, A에 〈주어+동사〉 가 있다면 B에도 명사여야 한다. (B) 조치, 잇 표시, / (C) 지침, 지시

**어휘** equipment 장비 productivity 생산성 harvest 수확, 직물

**126 해석** 한때 사이트 사이 국제 운영팀 임명되었던 이세는 조두나는 지난주에 정부의 국제 무역 자문 위원회에 위원이 되었다.

**해설** 의미상 앞뒤로 부사를 선택하는 문제이다. 한때 회장이었던 사람이 지 난주에 자문 위원회의 회원이 되었다는 의미가 자연스러우므로 (B)가 정 답이다. once는 부사로만 아니라 접속사로도 쓰인다.

**어휘** executive 경영 간부(이사) advisory committee 자문 위원회, 고 문단

**127 해석** PNB 은행이 금리 인하를 발표할 것으로 예상되기 때문에 투자자들은 기자 회견을 염려한다.

**해설** expect는 5형식 동사로 〈expect+목적어+to부정사〉로 사용되며, 수동태로는 〈be expected to+동사원형〉으로 쓰이므로 (C)가 적 절하다. 〈be asked/invited, allowed, required, encouraged, instructed) to+동사원형〉도 함께 알아 둔다. 빈칸 앞에 is가 있기 때 문에 (A)는 쓸 수 없다.

**어휘** decrease 감소, 하락 interest rate 금리, 이율 investor 투자자 anxious 불안해하는, 염려하는 press conference 기자 회견

**128 해석** 회사의 이미지와 부정을 쇄신하기 위해 홍보 부장은 새 회사 로고를 특징으로 하는 광고 캠페인 제작에 원조를 요청했었다.

**해설** 회사의 이미지 개선을 위해 광고 캠페인을 만든다고 했는데, 어떤 광고 인지 수식하는 내용으로 가장 자연스러운 것은 (A)이다. feature는 '특...

**어휘** experienced 경험 있는, 숙련된 motivated 의욕 넘치는 team-oriented 팀워크 지향적인 branch office 지점, 지사 province 지방...

# PART 6

## [131-134]

P29

수신: 전 직원
발신: 조나단 스미스
날짜: 6월 19일
제목: 건물의 3층 리모델링

다음 주 초부터 3층에 있는 마케팅 부서의 리모델링이 시작될 것입니다. 마케팅 팀원을 포함한 모든 직원들은 ⑬ 이 지역에 접근할 수 없을 것입니다.

주차장의 특정한 곳에 건설 장비들이 들어갈 자리가 생깁니다. 이것 우측에 주차 시오. 주차장의 C구역인 건물의 동편은 전체 공사가 진행되는 동안 폐쇄될 것입니다. ⑬ 임시적 입니다. 구역뿐만 아니라, 주차장의 다른 곳들도 중장비 사용을 위해 ⑬ 일시적으로 폐쇄될 수 있습니다.

도로로 직원들이 차량 이용을 상당 것을 강력히 권고합니다. ⑬ 이 리모델링 기간 동안은 대중교통을 이용하기 바랍니다. 이 ⑬ 패쇄로 인해 야기된 는 모든 불편에 대해 사과드립니다. 리모델링에 관한 더 많은 정보는 공사 담재 가 다가오면 이메일로 보낼 것입니다.

조나단 스미스

**어휘** remodeling 건물 개보수   accessible 접근할 수 있는 include 포함하다 reserve (자리를) 따로 잡아 두다   heavy equipment 중장비   personal vehicle 개인 차량   inconvenience 불편 caused by ~에 의해 야기된 regarding ~에 관하여   via ~을 통해서

**131 해설** 빈칸 뒤에 단수 명사 area가 있으므로 (C) This가 적절하다. 뒤에 복 수 명사가 오는 (B) These나 (D) Those는 올 수 없다. (A) Either는 성반 접속사로 either A or B/A 또는 B 둘 중 하나의 의미이다.

**132 해설** 수동태 will be closed 뒤에서 수식하는 것은 부사이므로 정답은 (C) 이다. 부사는 동사의 앞이나 뒤에서 동사를 수식한다. (A)/(B), (D)는 각 각 형용사, 명사이므로 적절하지 않다.

**133 (A)** 이 리모델링 기간 동안은 대중교통을 이용하시기 바랍니다.
  (B) 대중교통을 이용하는 것은 탄소 배출량을 줄이는 데 기여합니다.
  (C) 주차장에 모든 직원들을 위한 충분한 공간이 있습니다.
  (D) 공사 기간 동안 직원들은 3층에 주차해야 합니다.

**해설** 빈칸에 적절한 문장을 고르는 문제이다. 빈칸 앞에서 직원들에게 개인 차량 이용을 상당 줄을 권한다는 내용이 나오므로 빈칸에는 개인 차량 대신에 이용할 수 있는 대안을 제시하는 것 적절하다. 따라서 리모델 링 기간 동안 대중교통을 이용하라는 (A)가 적절하다.

**어휘** usage 사용   utilize 이용하다   contribute 기여하다   carbon footprint 탄소 배출량

**134 해설** 문제에서 리모델링으로 인해 주차장의 일부가 폐쇄되기 때문에 직원들이 개인 차량을 가져올 수 없는 등의 불편에 대해서 사과하는 의미이므로 (A)가 적절하다. (B) 검토하다, (C) 계약 / (D) 제안

---

## [135-138]

베스트 프라이스 사는 20년 넘게 고객들에게 식료품과 생활필수품을 제공해 왔습니다. ⑬ 지금 저희는 더 많은 고객들에게 제공할 수 있기를 기대하고 있습니다. 저희는 최고의 가격에 최고의 제품을 제공하기 위해서 최근 조치가 이 지역에 다수의 새 지점들을 냈습니다.

저희는 또한 매우 다양한 제품들을 공급하고 ⑬ 연장된 영업시간을 계획합니다. 고객들에게 최상의 서비스를 제공하기 위해서 이제 저희는 24시간 영업으로 운영될 것입니다.

이러한 변화들로 저희는 고객들에게 양질의 서비스를 제공하기를 기대합니다. 새로운 지점과 영업시간을 ⑬ 포함하는 변화에 관한 더 많은 정보는 온라인 www.bestprice.com에서 이용 가능합니다.
귀하를 대면하기를 희망합니다.

**어휘** grocery 식료품   daily necessity 생활필수품   a wider variety of 매우 다양한   offer 제공하다   quality 품질의   extended 길어진, 늘어난

**135 (A)** 지금 저희는 더 많은 고객들에게 제공할 수 있기를 기대하고 있습니다.
  (B) 많은 어려움에 직면해 왔으며 이로 인해 매장을 접수하기로 했습니다.
  (C) 이번 주말에 참고 정리 세일을 할 예정입니다.
  (D) 뛰어난 고객 서비스에도 불구하고 많은 고객들이 지지하지는 않았습니다.

**해설** 빈칸 뒤에서 다수의 새로운 지점들을 냈다고 했으므로 더 많은 고객들에게 제공할 수 있기를 기대한다는 (A)가 가장 적절하다.

**어휘** clearance sale 참고 정리 세일

**136 해설** 빈칸 앞에 many가 있으므로 복수 명사가 와야 한다. 문맥상 장소를 나타내는 (A)가 적절하다. (D) 연구, 조사

**137 해설** 의미상 앞뒤 명사를 연결하는 문제이다. 고객들에게 최상의 서비스를 제공하기 위해 영업시간을 '연장한다'는 의미가 적절하므로 정답은 (A) 이다. (B) 제한된 / (C) 잠재적인 / (D) 수익이 좋은

**138 해설** 뒤에 명사구가 나왔기 때문에 빈칸에는 전치사가 알맞다. 선택지에서 전치사는 (B) including밖에 없다.

---

저희는 최고의 가격에 최고의 제품을 제공하기 위해서 장으로 섬다, 특색으로 삼다, 주요하게 등장하다[의 못으로 토의에 자주 출제되다, (B) (휘믿을) 소진하다, 소환하다 / (C) 반을 만하다, ~할 가 치가 있다 / (D) 수용하다

**어휘** in an attempt to ~하기 위하여   rejuvenate 다시 젊어 보이게 하다, ~을 활기를 도찾게 하다   corporate logo 회사 로고

**129 해석** 100달러 이상의 제품을 구입하면 매장에서 현재 배송료의 절반 가 격으로 배달해 줄 것이다.

**해설** 100달러 이상의 제품을 사면 '현재 요금의 절반의 기격으로 배달해 준다는 의미가 적절하므로 정답은 (D)이다. (A) 독같은, 사본의 / (B) 다수 의, 수많은 / (C) 분할된

**어휘** ship 수송하다   standard rate 표준 요금   goods 상품

**130 해석** 법무국 사무실은 14일 이내에 공식 서류에 대한 모든 공식적인 요청에 응답할 것을 요청받았다.

**해설** 어떠한 요청에 대해 '답하다'를 의미하며 전치사 to와 함께 쓰이는 (B) respond가 적절하다. (C) explain은 3형식 동사로서 (explain+목적 어+to+대상)이 함께이며, (D) advise는 5형식 동사로서 (advise+목적어+to+동사원형)의 형태로 쓰인다.

**어휘** Justice Bureau 법무국   respond to ~에 응답하다   formal 공식 적인   official document 공식 서류

## [139-142]

수신: 프랭크 케인
발신: 매튜 정
제목: 귀하의 출장 요리 문의에 대한 최신 정보

정소 케이터링을 선택해 주셔서 감사합니다. 저희는 오직 출장 요리 서비스만을
제공하기는 😊 하지만 고객님의 필요를 충족시키기 위해 회사와 함께
확실하게 이행을 수 있습니다.

저희는 수년간 함께 일해 온 여러 이벤트 회사를 알고 있습니다. 😊 그들은 모
두 최고의 우수한 서비스를 제공합니다. 이벤트 회사들에 관한 정보는 이메일에
첨부되어 있습니다. 저희 출장 요리 서비스의 질문 정보는 항상 😊 기밀 이
성이어드리고 확신합니다.

이벤트 전에 저희 고객님께서 일주일간의 준비가 필요하다는 것을 유념해 주세요. 고객님
을 직접 만나서 기능한 한 빨리 이벤트에 대한 세부 사항들에 대하서 의논하면 😊
좋겠습니다.

상담을 위해 고객님께서 편한 시간대와 위치를 알려 주세요.

매튜 정

어휘 catering 음식 공급업 inquiry 문의 definitely 분명히, 확실히 satisfy
충족시키다 attach 붙이다, 첨부하다 guarantee 보증하다, 보장하
다 exceed 넘다, 초과하다 preparation 준비 prior to ~ 이전에 in
person 직접 as soon as possible 가능한 한 빨리

**139 해설** 빈칸 뒤에 '주어+동사로 이루어진 절이 있으므로 빈칸은 접속사 자리
이다. 문맥상 '~의 반면에'라는 의미가 되어야 하므로 양보의 부사절을
이끄는 (B) While이 정답이다. (A)는 접속부사로 절속사가 아니라 부사
이기 때문에 문장을 연결할 수 없다. (C)는 명사, 대명사, to do, -ing,
전치사구, 부사구, 관형 앞에 위치한다. (D)는 '~할 때까지'를 뜻한다.

**140 (A) 그들은 모두 최고의 우수한 서비스를 제공합니다.**
(B) 각 이벤트 회사에는 약 500명의 직원이 있습니다.
(C) 이 분야의 이벤트 회사들은 작은 파티를 전문으로 합니다.
(D) 파인 이벤트 회사와의 계약은 9월에 끝납니다.

**해설** 빈칸 앞뒤로 이벤트 회사에 대한 내용이 나오므로 이와 관련된 내용이
나와야 한다. 이벤트 회사를 추천하는 것이므로 우수한 서비스를 제공
한다는 (A)가 가장 적절하다.

어휘 specialize in ~을 전문으로 하다

**141 해설** 의미상 알맞은 명사를 선택하는 문제이다. 적정 가격은 컴퓨터 업그레이
드 '기밀' 이상이라더라는 뜻으로 쓰이는 표현으로 (B) expectations가
정답이다. (A) 변화 / (C) 문제 / (D) 초대

**142 해설** 문맥상 과거의 내용이 아니라 앞으로 일어날 일에 대한 가정에 의미를
포함하고 있으므로 (A) would be가 적절하다. (B)는 과거 시제로 직
접되지 않으므로, (C)는 과거의 가정을 나타낸다. (D)는 현재의 가능
성을 나타낸다.

## [143-146]

이것은 1월 21일 브롱크 시가 요청했던 컴퓨터 업그레이드에 대한 비용 견적서
입니다. 이 요청을 받은 후에 저희 회사의 전문가 팀은 브롱크 시의 45개 컴퓨터
모두를 😊 검사했습니다.

전문가 팀은 철저한 검사 후에 업그레이드에 대한 총비용이 1,560달러라고 결
정했습니다. 😊 저희 팀은 이 견적서에서 정확함과 공정함을 알려자 있습니
다. 귀하께서도 1,560달러를 이 😊 절차에 대한 적절한 가격으로 보셨으면 합
니다.

저희는 또한 귀하께서 다른 회사의 비용과 이 비용을 😊 직접적으로 비교하기
를 권합니다. 저희의 비용 책정에 대해 자신하며 또한 자료를 선택한 것을 후회
하지 않으실 것입니다. 저희 회사는 항상 적절한 가격에 양질의 서비스를 제공하
기 위해 노력합니다. 저희 일의 질을 확인해 보시고 연락 기다리겠습니
다.

가격이 적절하다고 생각하시면 연체부터 절차를 시작할지 알려 주
십시오.

로버트 박 드림
파크 앤 로슨 테크놀로지 최고 경영자

어휘 estimate 견적서 request 요청하다 expert 전문가 thorough 철저한
inspection 검사 confident 확신하는, 자신감 있는 appropriate 적절한
pleasure 기쁨

**143 해설** 동사의 알맞은 시제를 고르는 문제이다. 1월 21일 요청을 받은 후에 검
사를 실시했고 그 견적서가 나왔는 내용이므로 과거 시제인 (D)가 적절하
다.

**144** (A) 업그레이드는 선착순으로 진행될 것입니다.
(B) 컴퓨터는 독시 서점으로 교체되어야 합니다.
**(C) 저희 팀은 이 견적서에서 정확함과 공정함을 알려자 있습니다.**
(D) 전문가들의 보인 프로그램에 전혀 만족하지 않습니다.

**해설** 빈칸 앞에서 팀에서 업그레이드의 비용을 1,560달러로 결정했다는 내
용이 나오고, 뒤에서도 이 비용이 타당하다는 것을 알리고 있다. 따라서 비
용에서 이 비용의 공정성을 알리는 것이 적절하므로 정답은 (C)이다.

어휘 first-come, first-served basis 선착순 fairness 공정성

**145 해설** 의미상 알맞은 명사를 선택하는 문제로, 적정 가격은 컴퓨터 업그레이
드 절차를 위한 것이므로 (B)가 적절하다. (A) 숫자 / (C) 문제 / (D) 연
관성

**146 해설** 문맥상 이 회사는 자사의 비용 책정이 적절하다고 보고 다른 회사의 비
용과 비교해 볼 것을 권하고 있으므로 (C) actively가 적절하다. (A) 최
근에 / (B) 분명히, 명백히 / (D) 점점 감소하여

## [147-148]

제임스 DVD

192 벤도 애비뉴
월레비 오하이오 44094

고객 마이클 한                          고객 번호: 091928502
6월 19일
한 씨에게

현재 연체된 대여품들을 귀하에게 알리기 위해 편지를 보냅니다. 😊

저희 기록에 의하면 4월 19일 귀하께서 (화성 생명체)와 (심해) 두 영화를 대여
했습니다. 이 두 영화는 저희 대여점이 제공하는 인기 있는 한정된 수량의 DVD
입니다. 따라서 DVD가 제때 반납되지 않으면 저희 가게에 방문하신 많은 고객
들은 반으로 가셔야 합니다.

저희 연체료 규정에 따라 이 DVD들을 빨리 반납해 주셔야 합니다. 두 DVD의 연
체료는 5월 18일까지였습니다. 두 DVD의 기본요금은 5월 18일까지였던 것을 알
려 드립니다. 😊 연체료 때문에 귀하의 계정에 더 많은 연체료가 청구되었으니 않
기를 바랍니다.

저희는 귀하가 가능한 한 빨리 반납해서 개정에 더 많은 연체료가 청구되지 않
기를 바랍니다.

제임스 하드웨
제임스 DVD 소유주

어휘 notify 알리다 currently 현재 overdue 기한이 지난 check out 대여
하다 quantity 양, 수량 empty-handed 빈손에 아무 소득 없이 due
date 만기일, 기한일 fine 벌금 charge 청구하다 account 계좌, 계정
specific 명확한, 특정한 defective 결함이 있는 hire 고용하다 clerk 점
원

**147 왜 이 통지서가 보내졌는가?!**
(A) 요청했던 품목이 대여점에 도착했다는 것을 알리기 위해
(B) 대여점의 위치가 바뀌었다는 것을 고객에게 알리기 위해
(C) 제품의 결함이 있을 수 있다고 고객에게 알리기 위해
**(D) 제품의 기한이 지났다고 고객에게 알리기 위해**

**해설** 지문의 첫 문장에 현재 연체된 물품들을 귀하에게 알리기 위해 보냈다
고 언급하였으므로 (D)가 알맞다.

**148 DVD 대여점에 유추할 수 있는 것은 무엇인가?**
(A) 한 씨를 점원으로 고용할 것이다.
(B) 대여점에는 인기 있는 DVD가 많지 않다.
**(C) 기한이 지난 품목에 연체료를 청구할 것이다.**
(D) 막달 서비스를 제공한다.

**해설** 연체가 되어서 한 씨 개정으로 연체료 60달러가 청구되었다고 하므로
정답은 (C)이다.

**[149-150]**

| 타미 도시 | 오후 6시 23분 |
| 아직 안네서 일하고 있어요? | |

| 잭 올름슨 | 오후 6시 24분 |
| 네, 무슨 일이요? | |

| 타미 도시 | 오후 6시 26분 |
| **149** 제가 라인 B를 정지시켰는지 확실치 않은데, 확인해 줄래요? | |

| 잭 올름슨 | 오후 6시 27분 |
| 문론 이죠. 지금 그 근처에 있어요. | |

| 타미 도시 | 오후 6시 30분 |
| 고마워요. **150** 그무 일담 제조 과정에 속도를 높이려고 기계를 하루 종일 작동시켰거든요. 좀 쉽게 할 필요가 있어요. | |

| 잭 올름슨 | 오후 6시 31분 |
| **150** 우리가 주문를 밀금인으? | |

| 타미 도시 | 오후 6시 32분 |
| 이미 도착했어요, 자세한 건 내일 얘기해요. | |

**어휘** shut down (기계를) 정지시키다  speed up 속도를 높이다  sole (신발의) 밑창  heel (신발의) 뒷굽  in detail 자세히

**149** 오후 6시 27분에 올름슨 씨가 "물론이지"라고 쓸 때 그 의도는 무엇이겠는가?
(A) 기계를 하루 종일 계속 작동시킬 것이다.
(B) 마감일을 맞추는 것이 중요함을 안다.
**(C) 라인 B를 확실히 정지시키겠다.**
(D) 초과 근무도 피곤하다는 것에 동의한다.

**해설** You got it은 방금 요청한 것을 하겠다는 표현이다. 오후 6시 26분에 타미 씨가 라인 B를 정지시켰는지 확실치 않은데, 확인해 줄 수 있느냐고 물었으므로 올름슨 씨는 라인 B를 정지했는지 확인하겠다는 의미로 썼음을 알 수 있다. 따라서 정답은 (C)이다.

**150** 도시 씨는 어떤 업종에서 근무하겠는가?
(A) 잡지 출판사
(B) 호텔 체인점
(C) 항공사
**(D) 신발 제조업체**

**해설** 오후 6시 30분에 타미 씨가 언급한 soles는 신발의 밑창 부분을 말한다. 또한, 오후 6시 31분에 올름슨 씨가 뒷굽에 대해 묻는 내용으로부터 이들이 신발 제조업체에서 일하고 있으므로 정답은 (D)이다.

**[151-152]**

### 임대 가능한 학생 아파트

3월 12일부터 사용 가능한 3개의 아파트가 있습니다. 아파트는 가구가 모두 갖추어져 있으며 매우 깨끗한 상태입니다. 아파트는 조지아 공과 대학교의 단 5분 거리에 있어 학생들이 쉽게 통학할 수 있습니다. **152** 아파트에는 2개의 침실과 2개의 욕실이 있습니다. 룸메이트도 직접 찾으셔야 합니다. 또한 전기, 수도, 전화 요금을 포함한 공과요금을 내야 합니다. 더 자세한 내용은 404-182-5821로 연락 주세요.

**어휘** for rent 임대용의  fully furnished 내부 일체의 institute 기관, 협회  commute 통근하다  feature 특징으로 삼다  utility 공공요금  electricity 전기  average 평균의  equip 갖추다

**151** 공고의 목적은 무엇인가?
(A) 직원 아파트에 대한 정보를 제공하기 위해서
(B) 주택 판매를 광고하기 위해서
**(C) 학생을 위한 아파트를 광고하기 위해서**
(D) 학생들에게 주차 공간을 알리기 위해서

**해설** 공고의 제목을 통해 학생들을 위한 아파트를 광고하는 것임을 알 수 있다. 방을 임대해 주는 것이지 집을 판매하는 것이 아니므로 (B)는 적절치 않다.

**152** 아파트에 대해 언급된 것은 무엇인가?
(A) 매달 임대료가 얼만인지
(B) 평균 공공요금은 얼만인지
(C) 어떤 가구가 갖추어져 있는지
**(D) 방이 몇 개가 있는지**

**해설** 공고문의 중간에 침실과 욕실이 2개씩 있다는 내용을 통해서 정답이 (D)인 것을 알 수 있다.

**[153-154]**

4월 10일
재스콤드
20-15 무불드 로드 동남쪽,
토론도 온타리오 M2J 9W5
굿드 씨께

**153** 최근의 경기 침체로 인해 저희 회사는 가능한 한 예산을 줄이려고 하고 있기 때문에 USB 메모리 스틱을 드릴 수 없어 유감입니다.

그러나 **154** 고객님을 만족시키기 위해 500달러 이상 구매하시면 3퍼센트 할인해 드립니다. 저희는 어려운 시기에도 고객들을 좌우선에 두려고 노력합니다. 또한, 모든 매매 계약의 제조 이래는 계약서에 명시된 대로 매월 15일까지 연묘되어야 한다는 점을 명심해 주십시오. 궁금한 점이 있으시면, 고객 서비스부 928-3037-1740으로 연락 주십시오.

실로 브라운
디엔티 테크놀로지 부팀장
72 캐슬로 스트리트 애버뉴 빌딩
토론토 온타리오 M9X 4K2

**어휘** complimentary 무료의  tighten 조이다  keep in mind 명심하다  credit transfer 체좌 이체  priority 우선 사항  downturn 침체  제조 이래  as stipulated 명시된 대로  contract term 계약 조건  enforce 실시하다  monetary 통화의  constraint 제약, 통치  alternative 대안  extension 확박  exceed 초과하다

**153** 올해에 무료 상품이 없는 이유는 무엇인가?
(A) 정부가 실시한 규정 때문에
**(B) 회사의 통화 제약 때문에**
(C) 기술자인 문제 때문에
(D) 회사의 파산 때문에

**해설** 최근 경기 침체로 회사가 예산을 줄이려고 애쓰고 있기 때문에 무료 보낼 수 없다고 하므로 정답은 (B)이다.

**154** 대안으로 회사가 제시한 것은 무엇인가?
(A) 회사 제품의 무료 수리
(B) 제품 보증 기간 연장
(C) 회사 기술자의 방문 상담
**(D) 특정 금액을 넘어서는 구입에 대한 할인**

**해설** 500달러 이상 구매하는 3퍼센트의 할인을 제공하겠다고 나와 있으므로 정답은 (D)이다.

**이제 결제가 쉬워졌어요!**

결제를 할 때마다 온라인으로 해야 해서 피곤하신 적이 있으셨나요? 그렇다면 지함이 귀하의 문제를 바로잡았었는걸 알려 드리게 되어 기쁩니다!

체이스 은행은 고객님이 등록된 기간 동안 온라인 자동 결제를 등록할 수 있게 해주는 소프트웨어를 개발하였습니다. 귀하께서 각각의 회사 웹 사이트를 통해서 온라인 자동 결제를 신청할 수 있을지라도 그것은 많은 수 없고 지저분적이지 않은 번거라 불편한 과정이나입니다. **156** 이제 귀하는 한 곳에서 모든 월 납부를 등록할 수 있습니다!

그 과정은 생각하시는 것보다 더 단순합니다. 첫째, 귀하에서 결제되는 회사에 대한 모든 정보를 모아야 합니다. 둘째, 회사의 이름, 주소, 계좌 번호, 결제 금액을 포함해야 합니다. 일단 귀하께서 이 모든 것을 준비하시면 저희 웹 사이트인 www.chase.com/autopayments/register로 방문해 주세요. 웹 사이트에서 나저지 과정을 안내해 줄 것입니다.

한 번의 등록으로 귀하는 체임이나 연체료를 걸코 걱정하지 않으실 것입니다. **157** 이것은 자발적인 등록이고 결제를 원하는 고객에 게만 이루어집니다. 저희 시스템에 등록하는 것을 선택하시면 언제든지 방문에 주세요, 웹 사이트이시나 나저지 과정을 안내해 줍니다.

질문이 있으시면 저희의 고객 서비스인 1-800-281-6821로 연락 주세요.

**어휘** payment 지불, 납입  fix 바로잡다, 수정하다  enable 가능하게 하다  register 등록하다  automated 자동화된  sign up 등록하다  unreliable 믿을 수 없는  unorganized 체계적이지 않은  inconvenient 불편한  gather 모으다  penalty 벌금  voluntary 자발적인  disability 장애  enrollment fee 입회비  withdraw 인출하다, 철회하다, 취소하다

**155** 이 광고는 누구에게 보내지는가?
(A) 체이스 은행 고객들
(B) 연체료가 있는 고객들
(C) 장애를 가진 고객들
(D) 체이스 은행의 VIP 고객
**해설** 후반부의 고객들에게 등록을 권장하는 내용을 통해서 이 안내문이 체이스 은행의 고객들에게 보내졌음을 알 수 있으므로 정답은 (A)이다.

**156** 납입 시스템에 대해 언급된 것은 무엇인가?
(A) 연간 등록비로 20달러가 든다.
**(B)2주 미만**
(C) 시스템에 등록하려면 고객은 21세 이상이어야 한다.
(D) 고객들이 일단 등록하면 그 시스템으로부터 취소할 수 없다.
**(D) 모든 결제가 한 곳에서 이루어질 수 있다.**
**해설** 두 번째 문단을 통해서 모든 납입을 한 곳에서 등록할 수 있다는 것을 알 수 있으므로 정답은 (D)가 알맞다.

**157** 다음 중 등록을 위해 요구된 정보가 이닌 것은 무엇인가?
(A) 납입액
(B) 회사 주소
**(C) 회사 전화번호**
(D) 회사 이름

**158 연구 인턴십 구인**

빌리스 사의 연구팀은 3개의 일자리에 구인을 합니다. **159** 저격 요건은 기계 공학이나 하위와 적어도 3년간의 관련 분야 직무 경험 추천입니다. 지원자들은 지원서를 7월 13일까지 제출해야 합니다. **160** 1단계 면접에는 서류 제출 2주 뒤에 이뤄질 것입니다. 1단계 결과가 나오면 선발된 지원자들은 시기로 연락이 올 것입니다. 당성에게 최고의 행운이 오기를 희망하면, 면접에서 받기를 바랍니다.

**어휘** position 위치, 자리  job requirement 저격 요건  undergraduate degree 학사 하위  recommendation letter 추천서  field 분야  applicant 지원자  application 지원서  submission 제출  selected 선발된  main building 본관  profiling 프로파일링  approximately 거의  precisely 정확히

**158** 선발된 인턴이 하는 일은 무엇인가?
(A) 마케팅
(B) 프로파일링
**(C) 연구**
(D) 광고
**해설** 제목을 통해서 연구구 인턴을 뽑는다는 것을 알 수 있으므로 (C)가 정답이다.

**159** 저격 요건이 아닌 것은 무엇인가?
(A) 지원자들은 직무 경험이 있어야 한다.
(B) 지원자들은 유사한 분야에서 하위를 가져야 한다.
**(C)지원자들은 30세 이상이어야 한다.**
(D) 지원자들은 추천서를 받아야 한다.
**해설** 두 번째 문장에서 저격 요건을 열거하고 있다. 지원자들은 직무 경험이 있어야 하며, 관련 분야 하위와 추천서가 있어야 한다고 했다. 지원자들이 30세 이상이어야 한다는 내용을 없으므로 (C)가 정답이다.

**160** 1차 면접지를 뽑는 데 얼마나 걸릴 것인가?
(A) 대략 7일
**(B)2주 미만**
(C) 2주 이상
(D) 정확히 3주
**해설** 1단계 결과는 서류를 제출한 지 2주 안에 결정되며 그 이후에 선발된 지원자들에게 면접을 위한 연락이 간다고 하므로 정답은 (B)이다.

**월간 뉴스**                                               7월 19일

캐나다에서 400년 이상 동안의 인류 창조성을 포괄하는 수만 개의 예술 작품을 수용하여 그랜드 다드르크 씨에 따르면 연구 지면도 제공하는 직물 전 박물,[1] **161** 박물관 설입자인 이왕 두드르크 씨에 따르면 연구 지면도 제공하는 직물 전 박물관,도저기 등이 위대한 예술에 다가설 수 있도록 하고, 전 세계의 예술가들에게 영감을 주는 것입니다.[2] "제 원칙으로 캐나다의 모든 사람들이 예술에 다가설 수 있도록 하고, 전 세계의 예술가들에게 영감을 주는 것입니다."라고 두드르크 씨는 말했다. **162** "저는 이 박물관이 시대에서 예술을 위한 앞서가는 장소로 인정받고 캐나다에 살거나 방문하는 사람들의 삶을 풍요롭게 했으면 합니다.[3]

이를 실현하기 위해서, 그는 모든드로 대하여 젊고 촉망 받는 예술과 교수 촌 교수 밑에서 서른 종의 이상을 보 해서 모든 노력을 할 것입니다. "제 박물관을 홍보하는 대중들이 높은 관심을 유지하기 위하여 모든 소셜 미디어 플랫폼으로 페이스북, 트위터, 인스타그램 같은 소셜 미디어에 링크를 둘 것입니다."라고 덧붙여 보어 시는 말했다.

**어휘** house 수용하다  span ~에 걸치다, ~을 포괄하다  founder 설립자  inspire ~에게 영감을 주다  mural 벽화  pottery 도자기  be recognized as ~로 인정받다  textile 직물  prominent 유명한  be linked to ~로 연결되다  enrich 풍요롭게 하다  in a more visitor-friendly manner 방문자들에게 보다 편리하게  principle 원칙  collections 수집물  fabric 직물  wall painting: 벽화(=mural), ceramic: 도자기(=pottery)

**161** 박물관이 제공할 수 있는 지면도 연급되지 않은 것은 무엇인가?
(A) 직물
(B) 벽화
(C) 도자기
**(D) 건축술**
**해설** 직물, 전, 벽화, 도자기 등이 위대한 연구 지면도 제공한다는 내용을 보며 여기서 직물에 포함되지 않은 선택지는 (D)임을 알 수 있다. Woven fabric: 직물(=textiles), wall painting: 벽화(=mural), ceramic: 도자기(=pottery)

**162** 드두르크 씨에 따르면 그는 왜 박물관을 설립하였는가?
**(A) 예술을 통해 사람들의 삶을 향상시키기 위해**
(B) 환경을 위한 캠페인을 조직하기 위해
(C) 자선단체를 위한 더 많은 기부자들을 모집하기 위해
(D) 상업적인 목적으로 예술가들을 후원하기 위해
**해설** 캐나다에 살거나 방문하는 사람들의 삶을 풍요롭게 했으면 내 문에서 살기 좋게 한다고 했으므로 (A)임을 알 수 있다.

**163** [1], [2], [3], [4]로 표시된 곳 중에서 다음 문장이 가장 적절한 곳은?
"예를 들어, 온라인 인자도를 활용하는 것이 하나의 선택이 될 수 있습니다."
(A) [1]
(B) [2]
(C) [3]
**(D) [4]**

**해설** 등록하기 위해 필요한 정보에는 회사 이름과 주소, 계좌번호와 납입액이 포함되어 한다고 본문에 나와 있다. 회사 전화번호는 연급되어 있지 않으므로 (C)가 정답이다.

**[168-171]**

| 윌리엄 라이언 [오전 10시 11분] | 안녕하세요. 지난 금요일 제가 참석했던 벨 래아 회의에 대해 새로 전해 줄 말이 있어요. |
| 애버게일 타커 [오전 10시 12분] | 그거 어떻게 됐어요? 우리가 알아둬야할 게 있나요? |
| | (168) 그 여행이 지연돼서, 휴스턴 메모리얼 병원 장비의 공개 토론이 있는 세션으로 참석할 수 없었어요. 하지만 나머지 발표는 성공히 유익했어요. |
| 윌리엄 라이언 [오전 10시 13분] | 어떻게 됐나요? |
| 나단 스미스 [오전 10시 14분] | 어떻게 말인가요? |
| 윌리엄 라이언 [오전 10시 16분] | 유통 과정에 대해 발표한 헨리 스페서라는 발표자가 있었는데, 저는 그가 우리 회사에 긍정적인 영향을 줄만한 사람이라고 생각했어요. |
| 나단 스미스 [오전 10시 18분] | (169) 우리가 다양한 약제품을, (171) 저도 그 점에 대해 알림 말에 동의해요. |
| 애버게일 타커 [오전 10시 20분] | 지도요: 다음 주 수요일에 직원들을 위한 세 미나에 그를 초청할 수 있을까요? |
| 나단 스미스 [오전 10시 21분] | 세부적인 그의 연락처를 알아요? |
| 윌리엄 라이언 [오전 10시 23분] | 그의 연락 정보가 있는 회의 책자를 가지고 있어요. (170) 이거 끝나고 바로 전화 걸게요. |
| 애버게일 타커 [오전 10시 24분] | 좋아요! 결과는 이메일로 우리에게 알려 주세요. |

어휘 travel delay (항공편 등의) 여행 지연 feature 특징으로 포함하다 panel discussion 공개 토론회 present on ~에 대해 발표하다 distribution 유통 medicament 약제품 in large quantities 다량으로 retailer 소매상, 소매업자 conference booklet 회의 책자

**168** 스미스 씨는 어떤 회사에서 근무하겠는가?
(A) 종합 병원
(B) 컨설팅 회사
(C) 호텔 체인점
(D) 약품 도매업체

해설 오전 10시 18분에 우리가 다양한 약제품을 소매상에게 판매한다는 내용으로 스미스 씨가 약품 도매업체에서 일하고 있음을 알 수 있으므로 정답은 (D)이다.

---

해설 박람회를 홍보하고 대중들이 높은 관심을 유지하기 위해 모든 노력을 할 것이라는 내용 다음에 온라인 인재들을 활용하는 예가 나오는 것이 자연스럽다. 특히 지문 마지막 문장에서 언급된 페이스북, 트위터, 인스타그램 같은 소셜 미디어는 온라인 인재들을 높이는 다양한 수단이 되므로 정답은 (D)이다.

**[164-167]**

2월 28일
발신: 존 매버
매버 일렉트로닉스
817 햄프 애비뉴, 애틀랜타, 조지아 30332

수신: 제이슨 킴
에브라임 일렉트로닉스
182 케이스퍼 로드, 미네소타 시티, 미네소타 61725

김 씨께

제가 (164) 연 2회 열리는 춘계 엔지니어 협의회에 참석할 수 없다는 것을 알리게 되어 정말로 유감입니다. 봄은 저희 회사에 결코 바쁜 시즌이 아니어서 전화로 귀하께 말했을 때 협의회에 참석할 수 있을 거라고 확신했습니다. 그래서 저희는 지금 투 (165) 유감스럽게도, 저희 회사는 주식 성장 과정을 진행하고 있습니다. 자료를 분석하는 과거 수년 동안의 저희 회사의 성장을 분석하는 지자들을 위한 발표를 만드는 과거 수년 데 힘을 쏟고 있습니다.

참석 취소를 알리게 되어 유감이지만 귀하께서 이해해 주시기를 바랍니다. 저는 그 기간 동안 중요한 일이 있지 않을 거라고 확신합니다. 저는 (166) 가을에 있을 협의회에서 우리가 봄 협의회에서 의논하려 했던 공동 프로젝트에 대해서 이야기 할 수 있을 것입니다. 다시 한번 진심으로 사과드리며 협의회에서의 성공을 빕니다.

존 매버
매버 일렉트로닉스

어휘 convention 협의회 unfortunately 유감스럽게도 go through ~을 겪다 listing (증권) 상장 stock 주식 be dedicated to ~에 전념(헌신)하다 analyze 분석하다 cancellation 취소 definitely 분명히, 틀림없이 positive 확신하는 joint 공동의, 합동의 withdraw 회수하다 severe 극심한 launch 출시하다 cooperative 협력하는

**164** 얼마나 자주 협의회가 개최되는가?
(A) 일 년에 한 번
(B) 일 년에 두 번
(C) 2년에 한 번
(D) 일 년에 세 번

해설 첫 문장의 Bi-Annual을 통해 협의회가 1년에 두 번 개최된다는 것을 알 수 있으므로 정답은 (B)가 정답이다.

**165** 매버 씨는 왜 봄 협의회에 참석할 수 없는가?
(A) 투자자가 회사로부터 많은 돈을 회수하기로 결정했다.
(B) 그의 회사가 주식 시장에 상장될 수 있도록 일해야 한다.
(C) 그의 비행기가 심각한 기상 상태 때문에 취소되었다.
(D) 그는 같은 시간에 이미 계획된 다른 행사를 맞추어졌다.

해설 편지의 내용을 보면 주식 성장 과정을 진행하고 있어 발표 준비와 자료 분석을 하느라 바빠므로 이번 협의회에 참석할 수 없다고 하므로 정답은 (B)이다.

**166** 언제 매버 씨가 김 씨를 만날 수 있을 것인가?
(A) 그는 올해 김 씨를 만날 수 없을 것이다.
(B) 그는 편지에 다음번에 기준한 시간을 말하지 않았다.
(C) 그는 가을 협의회에서 김 씨를 만나는 것을 계획하고 있다.
(D) 그는 봄 협의회 동안 애틀랜타에서 그를 만나려고 했다.

해설 봄에 있을 협의회에서 만나기로 했으나 매버 씨의 회사에서 일이 생겨 가을에 있을 협의회에서 만나 이번에 의논하려 했던 공동 프로그램에 대해서 이야기하자는 내용이므로 정답은 (C)가 맞다.

**167** 그들은 왜 봄 협의회에서 만나기를 계획했었는가?
(A) 서로에게 자기 가족을 소개하려 했다.
(B) 새 제품을 같이 출시하기를 원했다.
(C) 공동 프로젝트를 의논하기를 계획했었다.
(D) 봄 협의회에 만나기를 기대하고 있다.

해설 봄 협의회에서 의논하려 했던 공동 프로젝트를 가을에 의논하자고 하므로 공동 프로젝트에 대해 이야기하자는 내용이 적절하므로 정답은 (C)가 적절하다.

**169** 라이언 씨에 대해 알 수 있는 것은 무엇인가?
(A) 회의에서 발표를 했다.
**(B) 세션 중 하나에 참석하지 못했다.**
(C) 수년간 벨라루스에서 살았다.
(D) 총정에 대해 불만이었다.

**해설** 라이언 씨가 오전 10시 13분에 여행이 지연돼서, 휴스턴 메모리얼 병원장과의 공개 토론이 있는 세션은 참석할 수 없었다고 했으므로 정답은 (B)이다.

**170** 라이언 씨는 다음에 무엇을 할 것인가?
(A) 소매상과 계약한다.
(B) 현장에 도착한다.
(C) 세미나를 연다.
**(D) 스펜서 씨에게 연락한다.**

**해설** 오전 10시 23분에 라이언 씨가 "이가 끝나고 바로 전화해 볼게요"라고 했으므로 그는 채팅이 끝나자마자 스펜서 씨에게 전화할 것임을 알 수 있다. 따라서 정답은 (D)이다.

**171** 오전 10시 20분에 타카 씨가 "저도요"라고 쓸 때 그 의도는 무엇인가?
(A) 회의가 지루할 거라고 예상했다.
(B) 유익한 수업이 필요이다.
**(C) 라이언 씨가 발표자에 대해 한 말에 동의한다.**
(D) 결과를 이메일로 받을 것이다.

**해설** 오전 10시 18분에 스미스 씨가 "그 전에 대해 윌리엄 앞에 동의해요"라고 말했고, 그 다음에 바로 타카 씨가 "저도요"라고 했으므로, 그녀 역시 윌리엄 라이언의 앞에 동의한다는 의미임을 알 수 있다. 따라서 정답은 (C)이다.

---

**H.S. 어패럴 기업**
A1206 커네리 워프
타워 햄리츠, 이스트 런던
www.hsapprel.co.uk

7월 1일
조 에이치, 개타
A21 웨스트 위즘
브롬리, 런던
영국

개타 씨에게,

H.S. 어패럴에 지원하기 위해 지원해 주셔서 감사합니다. 귀하의 이력서로 보건대, 저는 귀하가 던지에서 곧 읽리는 패션 디자인의 회의에 받은 보건한 업무를 수행하기에 충분한 자격이 있다고 믿습니다. -[1]- 누국 파슨스에서 받은 패션 디자인 석사학위가 거기서 좋업 후 받은 패션 상들으로 말할 것도 없이 저희는 귀하가 수년간 패션계에서 쌓아온 경력에 깊은 인상을 받았습니다. -[2]-

저희는 귀하를 다음 주 중에 인터뷰하고 싶지만, 저는 에르메 슈즈 회사와 중요한 사안의 미팅으로 다음 주 목요일 파리로 가서 7월 10일까지는 사무실에 동이올 수 없습니다. -[3]- 귀하가 7월 5일 전에 인터뷰를 위해 방문하시는 것이 가능하다면, 제가 귀하를 만날 수 있을 것입니다. 만약 늦기 가능하다면, 저희 인사부 매니저인 새런 우드 씨가 H.S. 어패럴을 대표해서 면접을 진행할 것입니다. -[4]- 귀하에게 편한 날짜와 시간을 알려 주세요.

브랜드 스톰

**어휘** upcoming 다가오는, 곧 있을 impress 인상을 주다 build a career 경력을 쌓다 not to mention ~은 말할 것도 없고 master's degree 석사학위 fly to 비행기를 타고 ~로 가다 on behalf of ~을 대표해서 convenient 편리한

**172** 편지의 목적은 무엇인가?
(A) 구직 신청을 하기 위해
(B) 회사와 파트너십을 맺기 위해
**(C) 인터뷰 일정을 잡기 위해**
(D) 비행기 표를 예약하기 위해

**해설** 편지 말미에 7월 5일 전에 면접이 가능하면 직접 카타 씨를 만날 수 있을 것이고 그렇지 않으면 다른 사람이 면접을 담당할 것이라며 편한 날짜를 알려 달라고 하므로 정답은 (C)이다.

**173** 카타 씨 이력서에 언급되지 않은 것은 무엇인가?
(A) 업무 경력
(B) 학력 배경
(C) 받은 상
**(D) 그녀가 만든 포트폴리오**

**해설** 이력서 내용에는 패션계에서 쌓은 경력, 패션 디자인 석사학위 수상 경력 등이 언급되어 있지만 포트폴리오에 대해서는 언급되어 있지 않다. 따라서 정답은 (D)이다.

**174** 스톰 씨에 대해 알 수 있는 것은 무엇인가?
(A) 에르메 슈즈 회사에서 일한다.
(B) 누각 시에서 살고 있다.
**(C) 7월 8일에 출장 중일 것이다.**
(D) 패션 디자이너였었다.

**해설** 편지에서 "다음 주 목요일 파리로 가서 7월 10일까지는 사무실에 동이올 수 없습니다"라고 했다. 다음 문장에서 "귀하가 7월 5일 전에 인터뷰를 위해 방문하시는 것이 가능하다면, 제가 귀하를 만날로 갈 것이다"라는 것이므로 스톰 씨가 7월 8일에 출장 중일 것이다.

즉, 5일에 파리로 가서 7월 5일 이후에는 7월 10일까지는 출장 중인 것이므로, 스톰 씨가 7월 8일에 출장 중일 것이라는 (C)가 정답이다.

**175** [1], [2], [3], [4]로 표시된 곳 중에서 다음 문장이 가장 적절한 것은?
"그냥 참고로 알려드리면, 그녀도 파슨스를 졸업했습니다."
(A) [1]
(B) [2]
(C) [3]
**(D) [4]**

**해설** 인사부 매니저인 새런 우드 씨가 H.S. 어패럴을 대표해서 면접을 진행할 것이라는 문장 뒤에 그녀도 파슨스를 졸업했다는 말이 와야 자연스럽다. 그녀(she)라는 인칭명사를 받으려면 (D) [4]가 가장 적절하다.

## [181-185]

### 181 제품 디자인 회의

장소: 월드 파이낸스 빌딩 4번 주 회의실
날짜와 시간: 7월 5일, 11:00-13:30
참여자:
- 크리에이티브 센터
- 이사: 헨리 램버리스
- 보조자: 제인 쿡스
- 기술 고문: 데일 챈들러

- 무스 시
- 상무 이사: 이이작 호지
- 마케팅 부장: 데이비드 이스트
- 개드: 솔리시터스 오피스
- 변호사: 미랠즈 캐드

**프로그램 일정**
- 새 제품의 디자인에 관한 전략과 개선 ............ 제인 쿡스
- 세계 시장에 관한 전망 ............ 다릴 챈들러
- 성공적인 마케팅 조사 수행 방법 ............ 데이비드 이스트
                                              미랠즈 캐드

182 법적인 문제 해결 방법

수신: 데이비드 쿡스
발신: 제인 쿡스
재목: 새 제품 일정

이스트 씨에게

회의에서 당신의 발표에 감사드립니다. 그 발표는 저희에게 시장의 요구에 관한 더 나은 지식을 얻도록 해 주었고 저희의 새 제품 트레일러 스틸 마케팅 방향에 관한 더 많은 아이디어들을 주셨습니다. 저희는 이 제품의 저희에게 큰 수익을 가져다줄 거라고 확신합니다. 저희 제품 매니저에게서 공장이 일정대로 돌아가고 있고, 모든 것이 잘 진행되며 몇 주 내로 첫 번째 제품들을 생산할 수 있을 거라고 통보받았습니다.

회의 후에 캐드 씨가 제품 디자인을 약간 수정하는 것에 대해 저희에게 논의했습니다. 183 우리는상당히 많은 저희가 모두 소송을 피했으면 하는 문제가 있었습니다. 184 시장에 저희의 제품을 진출시키기 위해서 저희는 함법적인 절차가 승인되기를 기다려야 합니다. 그것은 전체 4일 정도일 것입니다.

솔직히 말하자면, 이것이 현재 지연에 주요 원인입니다. 램블릿 사진 검은 것은 저희는 다음 달 마지막 주시장에 저희의 새로운 제품을 내놓기를 기대하고 있습니다. 그러나 캐드 씨의 특정 사무실과의 협상 과정을 고려한 한편 저희는 휴일 쇼핑 시즌에 관한 전략을 재고할 현재기 때문에 당신의 의견을 묻고 싶습니다. 또한, 185 다음 프로젝트의 개발을 위해 저희 헤드 램버리스 이사님이 당신과 세부 사항에 대해 논의하고 싶어 하십니다. 당신이 선호하는 시간들을 알려 주시면 제가 회의를 잡겠습니다.

제인 쿡스

---

## [176-180]

모잡자 이름: 이엠엔 홀딩스
연락처 이름: 참소 로베르, 인사 부장

귀하께서 귀하의 전문 분야를 이끄는 디자인 매니저라면 저희는 '지금' 귀하로부터 연락을 받고 싶습니다. 저희는 현재 176 세계적인 선두 엔터테인먼트 회사 중하나인 이엠엔 홀딩스 팀에 가벼울 곳 177 디자인 매니저 자리에 적합한 한 사람을 찾고 있습니다. 회사 안에서 창의적인 과정을 관리하고 지원하는 것을 포함한 이 수이며 책임 코디네이터로서 모든 창의적인 프로젝트를 관리하는 것이 귀하의 주요 요소입니다.

**자격 요건**
- 178+ 177 디자인 분야에서의 최소 5년의 경험
- 178+ 팀 동료와의 사교성
- 훌륭하고 창의적인 디자인을 만드는 능력
- 파워포인트, 포토숍을 일러스트레이터, 엑셀 작업에 능숙함
- 178+ 제안 및 예산 작성 능력
- 178+ 판매 마케팅 이론에 관한 지식

엔터테인먼트 부문에서의 업무 PDF 샘플을 포함한 모든 지원서들을 charles@ enmholdings.com으로 제출해 주시오.

수신: 참소 로베르 [robbiesworld@gmail.com]
발신: 마샤 로비
재목: 일자리 지원

저는 귀하께서 (글로벌 패션 디자인) 잡지 11월 호에 광고한 177 디자인 매니저 자리에 지원하는 것에 굉장한 관심이 있다는 것을 알리고 싶습니다.

179 저는 2년 전에 사이베 아트 대학에서 그래픽 디자인 전공 학위를 보냈다시피 그 이후로 좋은 일자리에 있는 스트으로 그래픽 사에서 보조 그래픽 디자이너로 일하고 있습니다. 새로운 과 제품 디자인 부서에서 중요한 역할을 그래픽 디자인을 관리하는 경험과 함께 저는 새 제품 디자인 부서에서 두 개의 역을 담당했습니다. 비록 이후 두 저를 그렇게 하도록 강요하지는 않았지만 그 분야에서의 저의 소질을 높이기 위해 저 자발적으로 추가 책임을 맡았습니다.

게다가, 저는 나이임에도 불구하고 저는 성숙하고 근면한 사람이라고 알려 드리고 싶습니다. 어려운 상황에서 다른 사람들과 열심히 일하는 것은 제가 즐기는 것입니다. 귀하께서 진지하게 저의 자질을 검토해 주시면 감사드리겠습니다. 180 귀하가 선호하는 시간대에 면접을 잡으시려면 647-491-8167로 연락 주십시오.

마샤 로비 드림

---

### 176 참소 로베르는 어디에 고용되었는가?
(A) 건축 디자인 회사
(B) 디자인 학교
(C) 잡지사
**(D) 엔터테인먼트 회사**

해설 첫 번째 광고에서 세계적인 선두 엔터테인먼트 회사 하나라고 언급되어 있고, 참소 로베르는 그 회사의 인사 부장이므로 (D)가 알맞다.

### 177 마샤는 자신의 이력서를 어느 자리를 위해 보냈는가?
(A) 잡지 기자
(B) 보조 그래픽 디자이너
**(C) 디자인 매니저**
(D) 인사 부장

해설 광고에서는 디자인 매니저를 구하고 있고, 두 번째 이메일에서 마샤가 디자인 매니저에 관심이 있다고 말하고 있으므로 (C)가 정답이다.

### 178 그 일자리를 위해 필수적인 것이 아닌 것은 무엇인가?
**(A) 그 분야에서의 마사 학위**
(B) 마케팅 지식
(C) 유사 분야에서의 이전 직무 경험
(D) 팀워크와 예산 작성 일의 친숙성

해설 첫 번째 광고문에 나와 있는 자격 요건 항목에 (A)를 제외한 모두가 언급되어 있다.

### 179 왜 마사는 엄밀히 말해서 그 자리에 자격이 없는가?
(A) 예상치 않은 도전임 것이기 때문에
(B) 추가 책무를 맡는 것을 거부리고 있기 때문에
**(C) 충분한 경험을 갖지 않았기 때문에**
(D) 보조 그래픽 디자이너였기 때문에

해설 첫 번째 광고 자격 요건 항목에 최소 5년간의 경험이 필요하다고 했는데 마사는 스무도 그래피스 사에서 보조 그래픽 디자이너로 2년밖에 일하지 않았으므로 업무 경험이 부족하다. 따라서 정답은 (C)이다.

### 180 어느 방법을 통하여 마사는 인터뷰가 잡히기를 원하는가?
(A) 우편
(B) 팩스
**(C) 전화**
(D) SNS

해설 이메일 마지막 문장에 면접을 잡기 위해 전화로 연락해 달라고 언급되어 있으므로 (C)가 정답이다.

---

**어휘** expertise 전문 지식, 기술 currently 현재 individual 개인 suitable 적합한 leading 선두의 essential 필수적인 supervise 감독하다, 관리하다 critical 중요한 factor 요소 requisite 필요한 qualification 자격 sociability 사회성 familiarity 익숙함, 낯익음 sector 분야, 부문 pressure 강요하다 voluntarily 자발적으로 industrious 근면한 architectural 건축의) diploma 졸업장; 수료증 former 이전의 publisher 출판사 ineligible 자격이 없는, 부적격의 technically 엄밀히 따지면 영답히 take up 받아들이다, 시작하다

**어휘** advisor 고문  solicitor (법률 관련 자문을 주로 하는) 변호사  overview 개관  outlook 전망  resolve 해결하다  legal issue 법적 문제  ensure 보장하다  batch 무리, 한 회  regrettably 유감스럽게도  patent 특허  lawsuit 소송, 고소  procedure 절차  settle 해결하다  entirety 전체, 전부  frankly speaking 솔직히 말해  modify 수정하다  outcome 결과  strategize 전략을 짜다  take into account ~을 고려하다  sales figures 판매액  initial 처음의, 최초의  adjust 조정하다  scrap 폐기하다  finalize 마무리 짓다

**181** 회의의 목적은 무엇인가?
(A) 오래된 제품에 관한 고객들의 의견을 분석하기 위해서
(B) 새 제품의 판매 수치를 보여 주기 위해서
**(C) 새 제품에 관해 논의하기 위해서**
(D) 새 프로젝트에 관한 법적인 문제를 해결하기 위해서

**해설** 첫 번째 안건이 제품을 통해서 제품 개발에 관한 회의인 것을 확인할 수 있으므로 (C)가 정답이다.

**182** 특허와 관련해 법적인 절차를 타결하는 사람이 한 발표는 무엇인가?
(A) 새 제품의 디자인에 관한 전략과 검토
(B) 세계 시장에 관한 전망
(C) 성공적인 마케팅 조사 수행 방법
**(D) 법적인 문제 해결 방법**

**해설** 회의에 참여자는 프로그램 일정을 타결을 통해서 카드 씨가 준비한 것은 (D)임을 알 수 있다.

**183** 회의 후에 회사가 직면한 새로운 문제는 무엇인가?
(A) 잠시 동안 생산 라인이 연기되었다.
(B) 마케팅부가 판매 날짜를 다시 정기를 원한다.
**(C) 제품 디자인에 관한 법적인 문제가 있다.**
(D) 제품 포장이 바뀌어야 한다.

**해설** 이메일의 두 번째 단락을 통해서 회의 후에 카드 씨가 제품 디자인에 관한 특허 문제를 처리하고 있는 것을 확인할 수 있으므로 (C)가 정답이다.

**184** 법적 문제가 심각하게 지체된다면 어떤 결과가 생기는가?
(A) 카드 씨는 공장의 원래 일정을 따라야 할 것이다.
**(B) 판매 개시일이 조정되어야 한다.**
(C) 이스트 씨는 코스 씨에게 그 상황을 설명해야 한다.
(D) 그들은 그 제품을 폐기하고 새것을 시작할 것이다.

**해설** 법적인 절차가 되고 판매 날짜를 잡아야 하므로 판매 날짜가 오래 걸린다면 판매 날짜를 미뤄야 한다는 것을 알 수 있으므로 (B)가 정답이다.

**185** 회의 안건과 이메일의 정보에 근거해 옳은 것은 무엇인가?
(A) 7월 5일 회의는 월드 마인보스 빌딩의 4층에서 열렸다.
(B) 마케팅 조사에 관한 발표는 카드 씨가 하였다.
(C) 법적인 문제를 완료하기 위해서 1주일이 더 걸린다.
**(D) 크리에이티브 센터의 담당자는 이스트 씨와 얘기하기를 원한다.**

**해설** 이메일의 마지막 단락에서 크리에이티브 센터의 이사 헨리 램버리스가 이스트 씨와 논의할 것이라고 했으므로 (D)가 해당되므로 정답은 (A)이다.

---

발신: 소피 칼버트 (scalvert@lettemart.com)
수신: 잭 보겔 (jvogel@tomoda.engineers.com)
날짜: 10월 9일
제목: [회신] 메이랜드 고용

안녕하세요, 보겔 씨

이 문제 관련해서 도움을 드릴 수 있어서 정말 기쁩니다. 제 기억이 맞다면, 그게 처음 10주년 회사 소풍이었을 겁니다. 저희도 그런 대행사를 고용하는 게 처음이었기 때문에 어떤 업체를 골라야 할지 확신이 없었어요. 어쨌든, 저희가 찾고 있던 것으로 판명됐지요. 그들이 제공하는 서비스에 정말 즐거웠습니다. **188** 가의 100명 가까이 되는 저희 직원들이 행복한 시간을 보내는 것 같았어요. 저희가 딱히 한 건 없고, 그냥 그들이 제공된 장소 중 하나에서 그들이 도움을 주기 위해 한 일만 했으므로 참으로 이벤트 기간 내내 문제가 없도록 하고 도움을 줄 겁니다. 도움이 필요하면 장소 직원이 배치되어 있을 거예요. 절대 실망하실 일 없을 겁니다.

소피 칼버트
전화: (10) 463-392-7245
보자켓, 레타 마트

---

**[186-190]**

## 메이랜드 이벤트 기획 대행사

**188** 포괄적인 서비스를 제공하는 이벤트 대행업체로서, 저희는 장소, 음식 공급, 화원과 다른 모든 이벤트 서비스에 대한 최고의 가격을 협상하는 법을 알고 있습니다. **188** 저희는 이벤트의 시작부터 끝까지, 전문적 기획부터 장소를 물색하는 것까지, 저희 이벤트의 모든 것을 주관하여 엄청난 경험을 축적하여 왔으므로 굿각적으로 고개의 요구 충족시켜 드립니다.

올해 초부터는 아래의 사항들이 추가되었음을 알려드립니다.
- 이벤트 동안 문제가 발생하지 않도록 현장 직원 투입
**187** - 직원 교육 장려 여행 (아래 두 개의 장소 중 하나 대여)
전화: 241-494-3824
- 연례 회의 (아래 두 개 장소 중 하나 대여)
전화: 241-494-3822

저희가 제공해 드릴 수 있는 개의 장소.
a) 센터가 시에 위치한 레인보우 힐 전용(50명 인원까지)
**189** b) 베가스 시에 위치한 리스 데밸리오 호텔(100명 인원까지)

해오 회의 관련 프로그램에 대한 정보를 원하시면, 241-494-3820로 전화 주세요.

---

발신: 잭 보겔 (jvogel@tomoda.engineers.com)
수신: 소피 칼버트 (scalvert@lettemart.com)
날짜: 10월 8일
제목: 메이랜드 고용

칼버트 씨께,

**186** **190-A** 키니 씨 생일 파티에서 말씀하신 메이랜드 이벤트 기획 대행사에 대해 잠시 질문을 해 주셨습니다. 제가 기억하기로는, 당신 동료들이 서비스에 아주 만족했고 그 이후로 상당히 동기 부여가 된 걸로 아는데요. 그래서 남은 올해 동안 저희 직원들이 스스로 동기 부여가 될 수 있도록 다가올 이벤트를 연출로 위해 그 대행사를 고용할까 고려중입니다.

또한, 당신이 그들 장소 중 하나를 임대하셨다고 말씀하신 것으로 기억하는데요. **188** 저는 이벤트에 기본적인 정보를 요청하고 있으므로 정보를 얻기 위한 문의 메일임을 알 수 있다. 따라서 정답은 (B)이다.

**189** 어쨌거나 약간의 기본적인 정보를 주시면 정말 감사하겠습니다. 아, 그리고 **190-B** 예산을 초과하고 싶지는 않답니다.

**190-C** 총알 이사, 세인트루이스 지사, 토모다 엔지니어링
잭 보겔

---

**어휘** planning 기획  agency 대행사, 대행업체  full-service 포괄적인 서  비스를 제공하는  venue 장소  catering 음식 공급  florist (전문 지식원하는) 문제  immense 막대한  on-site 현장의  hitch (잠깐 지체하게 하는) 문제  incentive trip 보상 장려 여행  it turned out that ~라고 판명되다  go beyond budget 예산을 초과하다  delighted 매우 즐거운, 기쁜  me well 내 기억이 맞다면  annual 연례의  serves me well 매우 즐거운  have the time of one's life 즐거운 시간을 보내다

**186** 보겔 씨는 왜 칼버트 씨에게 이메일을 보냈는가?
(A) 직원들을 동기 부여하는 방법에 대한 충고를 얻으려고
**(B) 이벤트 대행사에 대한 정보를 얻으려고**
(C) 수익을 내는 더 좋은 방법을 제시하기 위해
(D) 이벤트 대행사가 제공한 서비스에 대해 불평하려고

**해설** 첫 번째 이메일에서 메이랜드 이벤트 기획 대행사에 대해 잠깐 질문한 게 있다며 기본적인 정보를 요청하고 있으므로 정보를 얻기 위한 문의 메일임을 알 수 있다. 따라서 정답은 (B)이다.

**187** 보겔 씨는 회사 이벤트를 위한 예약을 하기 위해 어떤 번호로 전화할 것인가?
**(A) 241-494-3824**
(B) 241-494-3822
(C) 241-494-3820
(D) (10) 463-392-7245

**해설** 첫 번째 이메일에서 직원들이 스스로 동기 부여가 될 수 있도록 다가올 연휴를 위해 그 대행사를 고용할까 고려 중이라는 내용으로 보아 직원들이 증진이나 동기 부여를 위한 이벤트를 생각하고 있음을 알 수 있다. 광고에서 이 이벤트 대행사가 제공하는 프로그램 중에 직원 보상 장려 여행이 여기에 해당되므로 정답은 (A)이다.

**188** 메이랜드 이벤트 기획 대행사에 대해 언급된 것은 무엇인가?

(A) 연례 교육 회의는 무료이다.
(B) 해외 회의 프로그램은 제공하지 않는다.
**(C) 제공되는 이벤트 서비스가 포괄적이다.**
(D) 호텔 경영을 위한 전략적 기획에 조언을 준다.

**해설** 광고에서 포괄적인 서비스를 제공하는 이벤트 대행업체로서 시작부터 끝까지 이벤트의 모든 것을 주관한다고 했으므로 정답은 (C)이다.

**어휘** comprehensive 포괄적인, 광범위한

**189** 래티 마트의 이벤트는 어느 도시에서 열렸겠는가?

(A) 센티빌 시
**(B) 배거스 시**
(C) 메이런트 시
(D) 세인트루이스 시

**해설** 두 번째 이메일에서 거의 100명 가까이 되는 래티 마트 직원들이 메이랜드가 제공한 장소에서 이벤트를 했었음을 알 수 있다. 광고에서 메이랜드가 제공하는 장소 중 100명까지 수용할 수 있는 장소는 배거스 시에 있으므로 정답은 (B)이다.

**190** 보렐 씨에 대해 암시되지 않은 것은 무엇인가?

(A) 그는 키니 씨와 생일 파티에서 캠버트 씨를 만났다.
(B) 그는 회사가 예산을 초과해서 지출하는 걸 원하지 않는다.
**(C) 그는 메이랜드 이벤트 기획 대행사를 전에도 몇 번 이용한 적이 있다.**
(D) 그는 세인트루이스의 지사를 책임지고 있다.

**해설** 첫 번째 이메일에서 키니 씨 생일 파티에서 만났음을 알 수 있고 또한 예산을 초과하고 싶지 않다고 했으며, 이메일 마지막에서 그가 지점이 세인트루이스가 지사의 총괄이사임을 알 수 있다. 이번에 그 대행사를 고용해 볼까 생각하고 있다고 했으므로 이전에는 이용해 본 적이 없음을 알 수 있다. 따라서 (C)가 정답이다.

---

**오크레인 시민문화회관**
www.oaklanecc.com

담당자 분께,

한 톨의 쌀이 저울을 기울게 하죠! 이 편지는 여러분이 오크레인 시민문화회관으로 시작하는 이벤트 대행업체로서 이벤트 대행업체로서 시작부터 끝까지 이벤트의 모든 것을 주관한다고 했으므로 정답은 (C)이다.

마일 마라톤 행사에 기부하시면 아는 오크레인 시의 한 부모 가정들을 위한 탁아소 건립에 사용될 것입니다.

마라톤 행사는 수많은 지역 신문이 취재할 것이고 10,000명이 넘는 관중들이 참여할 예정이므로 귀사를 홍보하기에도 좋은 마케팅 기회가 될 것이라 자신합니다.

기부자들을 위한 혜택은 다음과 같습니다:

**레벨 1 (500달러):** 감사장이 증정됩니다.

**레벨 2 (1,000달러):** 귀사의 이름이 현수막에 기재됩니다. 감사장이 증정됩니다.

**레벨 3 (5,000달러):** - 귀사의 대표자가 지역 신문의 인터뷰를 할 것입니다.
- 귀사의 이름과 로고가 모든 홍보 자료에 표시될 것입니다.

어떤 레벨을 기부하시든 2개에 관하는 오크레인의 한 부모들의 미래를 향해 저희을 기울게 할 그 한 톨의 쌀입니다.

마니 차우드레리
이사, 오크레인 시민문화회관

---

발신: 프라티 도시 (pdoshi@nessonmobile.com)
수신: 마니 차우드레리 (mchaudhary@oaklanecc.com)
날짜: 3월 2일
제목: 마라톤 기부
차우드레리 씨께,

저희 홍보 이사이신 언드 브레멘 씨가 3월 23일 마라톤 행사에 참석할 것임을 알려드립니다. 저희도 저희가 수한 사회에 기여를 하고 싶은데, 동시에 저희 회사를 홍보할 기회로 삼겠다는 이사회에 서로에게 좋은 전략이겠지요, 그리고 브레멘 씨가 오크레인 시민문화회관을 한번 둘러보는 것이 가능한지 알려주세요, 특히 탁아소가 건립될 지역에요.

주신 요청하신 대로, 저희 회사 로고 디자인 샘플 사본을 일부해 드립니다.

프라티 도시
비서, 홍보 부서, 넛슨 모바일

---

**오크레인 시민문화회관 마라톤 넛슨 모바일이 후원합니다.**
3월 23일 토요일 오전 8시

롯스턴 광장에서 출발하는 오크레인 마라톤은 여러분을 어려운 동네의 여러분 기부 지불 것입니다. 교통 정리를 위해 주요 교차로에 경찰이 경찰에 배치될 것입니다.

행사는 특히 오크레인 시민문화회관이 탁아소 건립을 위해 주요 지역 자선단체에 해 탁을 줄 것입니다. 그러니 길 따라 참여하셔서 이 뜻 깊은 행사를 지지해 주시기 바랍니다.

- 오크레인 시민문화회관과 계약된 음악 밴드에 의한 야흥이 있을 것입니다.

- 블루베리, 초콜릿 칩스, 커피, 주스, 우유와 함께 경쾌는 펜케이크가 무료로 제공됩니다.

자세한 정보를 원하시거나 참여하시고 싶으면 458-231-57694로 전화 주시거나 www.oaklanecc.com/event/를 방문하세요.

**어휘** A single grain of rice can tip the scale (속담) 한 톨의 쌀이 저울을 기울게 하다  donate 기부하다  contribution 공헌, 기여  day-care facility 탁아소, 어린이집  single parent 한 부 (배우자 없이, 혼자 아이를 기르는 사람)  spectator 관중  serve as ~의 역할을 하다  cover 취재하다  donor 기부자  letter of appreciation 감사장  promote 홍보하다  representative 대표자  display 표시하다, 진열하다  win-win strategy 서로 모두 이기는 전략  tour 둘러보다, (특정 지역을) 돌러보다  depart 출발하다  intersection 교차로  benefit ~에게 혜택을 주다  charity 자선 단체  beneficiary 수혜자  dispatch 보내다, 배치하다  free of charge 무료로

**191** 편지의 목적이 무엇인가?

(A) 지역 주민들을 스포츠 행사에 초대하기 위해서
(B) 정치 캠페인을 홍보하기 위해서
**(C) 회사들로부터의 기부를 장려하기 위해서**
(D) 직원들에게 문화 행사를 공지하려고

**해설** 편지에서 처음에 기부에 대한 내용이 나오고 10,000명이 넘는 관중들이 참여할 예정이므로 회사를 홍보하기에도 좋은 기회가 될 것이라는 내용으로 보아 회사들로부터 기부를 장려하기 위한 것임을 알 수 있다. 따라서 정답은 (C)이다.

**192** 누가 행사의 수혜자가 되겠는가?

(A) 아이가 없는 50세의 미혼 여성
(B) 한 명의 딸을 가진 28세의 기혼 여성
**(C) 한 명의 아들을 가진 31세의 이혼 여성**
(D) 두 명의 아이를 가진 40세의 기혼 남성

**해설** 편지에서 마라톤 기부금은 오크레인 시의 한 부모 가정들을 위한 탁아소 건립에 사용될 것이라고 하였으므로 행사는 한 부모(배우자 없이 혼자 아이를 기르는 사람)을 위한 탁아소 설립이 목적인 것을 알 수 있다. 선택지 중에서 아이가 있고 배우자가 없는 (C)가 정답이다.

[196-200]

## TLD 오디오 주식회사    TLD-21 제품 정보

더 작고, 더 가볍지만 모든 것이 다 들어간 TLD-21!
이 크기의 다른 어떤 스피커도 영역도 뛰어넘는 더 강력한 사운드!
작은 장소에서의 사운드도 증폭시킬 스테이지 모니터링!
이전 모델인 TLD-20과 비교하세요!

| 모델 | TLD-20 | TLD-21 |
|---|---|---|
| 크기<br>(높이 x 너비 x 길이) | 510mm x 320mm x 320mm | 450mm x 290mm x 290mm |
| **199** 색상 | 블랙, 화이트 | 블랙, 화이트, 오렌지, 메탈 블랙 |
| 전력 소요량 | 1,000 와트 | |
| 주파수 범위 | 55Hz ~ 20,000Hz | 40Hz ~ 20,000Hz |
| 최대 음압 수준 | 126dB | 128dB |
| 실제 무게 | 14.8kg | 13.0kg |
| **196** 배송 무게 | 16.3kg | 16.6kg |
| 가격 | 500달러 | 600달러 |

---

발신 마리아 젤슨
수신 영업 팀
날짜: 7월 18일
제목: TLD-21 모델

영업 팀원들께,

기술 팀이 다음 달 초 새로부터 TLD 모델의 정보지가 업데이트될 거라는 통보를 방금 받았습니다. 현재 제품 정보에는 TLD-200 블랙과 화이트만이 나와 있지만, TLD-21은 오렌지와 메탈 블랙이 추가 두 가지 선택 사항이 더 있다는 것을 **197** 닿으면 만큼 **198** 메탈 블랙 색상의 TLD-20도 올해 크리스마스 시즌 이전에 시장에서 볼 수 있을 거라 해요.

더 중요한 것은 정보지의 전력 소요량이 수정될 것이라는 것입니다. 첨차하고도 긴 실험 끝에, TLD-21은 정보지에 표기된 것보다 더 많은 전력을 소비하는 것으로 판명되었습니다. 1,500와트로 바뀔 것이고, TLD-20은 그대로입니다. **198** 제가 늦어도 이달 말까지는 여러분께 수정된 정보지가 제공되도록 할 것입니다.

우리 몇몇 상점에서는 모든 TLD 모델이 곧 진열될 것이나 여러분 모두 이번 업데이트에 대해 숙지하시길 바랍니다.

감사합니다.
마리아 젤슨
영업 팀 매니저, TLD 오디오 주식회사

---

http://www.tldaudio.com/review/notice

| 메인 화면 | 제품 | 자료실 | **평가** | 연락처 |
|---|---|---|---|---|

TLD 오디오 주식회사

구매자 이름: 잭 밀로
제품: TLD-21
구매 날짜: 7월 19일

저는 TLD-20과 TLD-21의 정확한 차이를 몰랐습니다. 더 최신 모델이라면서 후기를 추천했는데요. 전자도 불과 6개월 전에 출시됐죠 만요. 어쨌든, 제가 읽고 있었던 유용한 차이는 21이 더 많은 색상을 선택할 수 있다는 것이고, 분및 메탈은 제가 좋아하는 색이거든요. 그래서 21을 실기 마음이 기울었는데, 바로 그때 영상平이 TLD-20도 곧 메탈 블랙으로 나올 거라는 응을 덧붙였습니다. 두 모델을 비교하느라 가까워서 2시간 넘게 소비했습니다.

**200** 그런데 21이 20보다 화연하게 더 작이 보였고 제 작은 방에 제 맞출 거 같다는 화신으로 이어졌습니다. 그래서 결국 21을 샀지요 결에서 몇 시간 동안 음질을 화인해 보고 매우 만족했습니다. 다른 모델은 그런 면에서 어떤 소리일까 아직도 궁금하지만, 이제 이걸 설치 화신이 안 서면 항상 최신 걸로 가세요. 최신일수록 더 좋다는 건 진실? 그냥 받아들이세요.

---

**어휘** fit into ~안에 들어가게 맞다 body (스피커의) 본체 scope 영역, 범위 reinforcement 강화 dimension 크기, 치수 option 선택 사항 power rating 전력 소요량 frequency range 주파수 범위 SPL (Sound Pressure Level) 음압 수준 shipping weight 배송 무게 information sheet 정보지, 안내서 indicate 나타내다, 보여주다 build 쌓이다, 강렬해지다 exhaustive 철저한 experiment 실험 consume 소비하다 supply 공급하다, 제공하다 no later than 늦어도 ~까지 launch 출시하다 (신제품 등을) 출시하다 be fond of ~를 좋아하다 lean toward ~쪽으로 기울다 bam 강자기 (짧은 시간에) noticeably 화연하게, 눈에 띄게 conviction 화신

---

**196** 정보지에 따르면 이전 모델과 비교했을 때 TLD-20에 대한 사실이 아닌 것은 무엇인가?

(A) 더 낮은 주파수 범위를 제공한다.
**(B) 포장되었을 때 더 가볍다.**
(C) 최대 음압 수준이 더 높다.
(D) 더 비싸다.

**해설** 정보지에 보면, 배송 무게가 TLD-20은 16.3kg이고 TLD-21은 16.6kg이므로 TLD-21이 오히려 더 무겁다는 것을 알 수 있다. 따라서 정답은 (B)이다.

---

**197** 이메일의 첫 번째 단락, 다섯 번째 줄에 있는 build와 의미가 가장 가까운 것은?

**(A) 만들다**
**(B) 증가하다**
(C) 부인하다
(D) 충격을 주다

**해설** 이메일에서 build는 '~이 증가하다, 쌓여서 강렬해지다'의 의미이므로 정답은 (B)이다.

---

**193** 넷슨 모바일은 얼마만큼의 돈을 기부했겠는가?

(A) 0달러
(B) 500달러
(C) 1,000달러
**(D) 5,000달러**

**해설** 이메일에서 회사가 로고 디지털 사본을 첨부한다는 내용이 있는데 편지를 보면, 회사의 로고가 모든 홍보 자료에 해당을 받는 레벨은 레벨 30이다. 따라서 넷슨 모바일은 (D) 5,000달러를 기부하였을 것이다.

---

**194** 브라멘 씨에 대해 암시된 것은 무엇인가?

(A) 그는 오그레이의 시민문화회관을 위해 일한다.
**(B) 그는 지역 신문사와 인터뷰를 가질 것이다.**
(C) 그는 마라톤을 완주하기 원한다.
(D) 그는 건설 현장의 일부이다.

**해설** 이메일에서 어떤 브라멘 씨가 3월 23일 마라톤 행사에 참석할 것이라는 내용이 나온다. 즉, 레벨 3의 기부를 한 넷슨 모바일에서 홍보 이사는 브라멘 씨가 오는 것은 편지에 언급되어 있듯이 회사를 대표하여 지역 신문과 인터뷰하기 위함이므로 (B)가 정답이다.

---

**195** 다음 중 행사에 대하여 사실이 아닌 것은 무엇인가?

(A) 음악 밴드의 공연이 있을 것이다.
(B) 마라톤 참가자들은 광장에서 출발할 것이다.
**(C) 차량 검문을 위해 경찰이 배치될 것이다.**
(D) 악간의 다과가 제공될 것이다.

**해설** 공지에서 음악 밴드에 의한 여흥도 있을 것이라고 했으므로 (A)는 맞다. 또한, TLD-21은 정보지에 표기된 것보다 더 많은 전력을 소비하는 것으로 판명되었으므로 (B) 역시 맞다. 불 온체, 조롱된 치즈, 커피, 주스, 우유와 함께 제공에서 만든 빵케이크도 무료로 제공된다고 했으므로 (D) 역시 맞다. 경찰은 교차로에서 교통 정리를 위해 배치되는 것이지 차량 검문을 위해서 배치되는 것이 아니므로 (C)가 틀렸다.

**198** 젤슨 씨에 대해 진술된 것은 무엇인가?

(A) 그녀는 TLD 오디오 주식회사의 기술 팀에서 일한다.
(B) 그녀는 두 모델의 차이를 알아냈다고 2시간 넘게 소비했다.
(C) 메탈 블랙은 그녀가 좋아하는 색이다.
**(D) 그녀는 새 버전의 정보지가 제공되도록 할 것이다.**

**해설** 젤슨 씨가 쓴 이메일에서 늦게도 이들 알아지는 수정된 정보지가 제공
되도록 할 것이라고 했으므로 정답은 (D)이다.

**어휘** see to it that ~가 반드시 되도록 하다, 조치하다

**199** 얼마나 많은 색상의 TLD-20이 크리스마스이브에 판매 가능할 것인가?

(A) 1
(B) 2
**(C) 3**
(D) 4

**해설** 정보지를 보면, TLD-20의 색상은 블랙, 화이트 두 가지밖에 없다. 그
런데 이메일에서 메탈 블랙 색상의 TLD-20도 올해 크리스마스 시즌
이전에 시장에 출시될 거라는 내용으로 보건대, 크리스마스이브에 판매
가능한 TLD-20의 색상은 블랙, 화이트, 메탈 블랙으로 총 3개가 될
것이다. 따라서 (C)가 정답이다.

**200** 정보지에 명시된 것 중 어떤 특징이 말론 씨가 최신 모델을 사도록 하였는가?

**(A) 크기**
(B) 색상
(C) 주파수 범위
(D) 최대 음량 수준

**해설** 말론 씨가 작성한 고객 평가에서 TLD-20과 TLD-21 중에 무엇
을 살지 고민하다가 21이 20보다 휠씬하게 더 작아 보였고, 작은 방
에 더 맞출 거 같다는 확신으로 이어져서 결국 21을 샀다고 했다. 그
가 TLD-21을 사게 된 결정적인 이유는 크기 때문이다. 따라서 (A)
Dimensions가 정답임을 알 수 있다. 메탈 블랙이 좋아하는 색이라고
말하는 내용이 있다고 해서 혼동하면 안 되고 지문을 끝까지 읽어야
한다.

## 🎧 Listening Comprehension

**PART 1**

| | | | | | |
|---|---|---|---|---|---|
| 1 (A) | 2 (B) | 3 (C) | 4 (A) | 5 (D) | 6 (C) |

**PART 2**

| | | | | | |
|---|---|---|---|---|---|
| 7 (B) | 8 (C) | 9 (A) | 10 (B) | 11 (A) | 12 (B) | 13 (A) | 14 (A) | 15 (B) | 16 (C) |
| 17 (A) | 18 (C) | 19 (C) | 20 (B) | 21 (B) | 22 (A) | 23 (A) | 24 (C) | 25 (C) | 26 (B) |
| 27 (B) | 28 (A) | 29 (B) | 30 (A) | 31 (B) | 32 (B) | 33 (D) | 34 (A) | 35 (C) | 36 (A) |
| 37 (D) | 38 (C) | 39 (C) | 40 (D) | | | | | | |

**PART 3**

| | | | | | |
|---|---|---|---|---|---|
| 41 (D) | 42 (B) | 43 (A) | 44 (C) | 45 (C) | 46 (B) | 47 (A) | 48 (C) | 49 (C) | 50 (A) |
| 51 (B) | 52 (D) | 53 (C) | 54 (C) | 55 (C) | 56 (A) | 57 (B) | 58 (D) | 59 (A) | 60 (C) |
| 61 (A) | 62 (C) | 63 (A) | 64 (B) | 65 (C) | 66 (D) | 67 (B) | 68 (A) | 69 (C) | 70 (B) |

**PART 4**

| | | | | | |
|---|---|---|---|---|---|
| 71 (D) | 72 (A) | 73 (D) | 74 (A) | 75 (C) | 76 (B) | 77 (C) | 78 (B) | 79 (A) | 80 (A) |
| 81 (B) | 82 (C) | 83 (B) | 84 (A) | 85 (C) | 86 (B) | 87 (C) | 88 (C) | 89 (C) | 90 (A) |
| 91 (A) | 92 (B) | 93 (C) | 94 (D) | 95 (B) | 96 (A) | 97 (C) | 98 (C) | 99 (D) | 100 (D) |

## 📖 Reading Comprehension

**PART 5**

| | | | | | |
|---|---|---|---|---|---|
| 101 (C) | 102 (C) | 103 (D) | 104 (D) | 105 (C) | 106 (B) | 107 (B) | 108 (C) | 109 (A) | 110 (D) |
| 111 (C) | 112 (B) | 113 (D) | 114 (C) | 115 (A) | 116 (A) | 117 (A) | 118 (D) | 119 (A) | 120 (C) |
| 121 (A) | 122 (A) | 123 (D) | 124 (A) | 125 (D) | 126 (A) | 127 (D) | 128 (A) | 129 (B) | 130 (C) |

**PART 6**

| | | | | | |
|---|---|---|---|---|---|
| 131 (D) | 132 (B) | 133 (A) | 134 (B) | 135 (B) | 136 (D) | 137 (D) | 138 (B) | 139 (C) | 140 (C) |
| 141 (A) | 142 (B) | 143 (C) | 144 (C) | 145 (D) | 146 (D) | | | | |

**PART 7**

| | | | | | |
|---|---|---|---|---|---|
| 147 (D) | 148 (B) | 149 (C) | 150 (D) | 151 (B) | 152 (A) | 153 (C) | 154 (C) | 155 (A) | 156 (B) |
| 157 (D) | 158 (C) | 159 (B) | 160 (C) | 161 (A) | 162 (A) | 163 (C) | 164 (C) | 165 (D) | 166 (D) |
| 167 (A) | 168 (B) | 169 (C) | 170 (D) | 171 (C) | 172 (C) | 173 (C) | 174 (A) | 175 (C) | 176 (C) |
| 177 (A) | 178 (B) | 179 (D) | 180 (D) | 181 (D) | 182 (B) | 183 (A) | 184 (C) | 185 (A) | 186 (D) |
| 187 (A) | 188 (B) | 189 (D) | 190 (C) | 191 (D) | 192 (D) | 193 (B) | 194 (C) | 195 (B) | 196 (B) |
| 197 (D) | 198 (C) | 199 (B) | 200 (D) | | | | | | |

Actual Test
02

# PART 1

P56

**1** 미W
(A) **A worker is sawing some wood.**
(B) A worker is putting on a T-shirt.
(C) A worker is parking a truck.
(D) A worker is weighing some materials.

(A) 인부가 나무를 자르고 있다.
(B) 인부가 티셔츠를 걸치입고 있다.
(C) 인부가 트럭을 주차하고 있다.
(D) 인부가 자재의 무게를 재고 있다.

어휘 saw 톱질하다, 톱  weigh 무게를 재다

**2** 미W
(A) A woman is helping customers.
(B) **A woman is arranging a few articles of clothing.**
(C) A woman is polishing a wood floor.
(D) A woman is making a purchase.

(A) 여자가 고객들을 돕고 있다.
(B) **여자가 옷 몇 벌을 정돈하고 있다.**
(C) 여자가 나무 바닥에 광을 내고 있다.
(D) 여자가 물건을 사고 있다.

어휘 arrange 정리하다  article (옷) 한 벌  polish 광을 내다  make a purchase 구입하다

**3** 영M
(A) Some books are being organized.
(B) One man is standing on a ladder.
(C) **Several maps are hanging on the walls.**
(D) A couple is entering a store.

(A) 책들이 정돈되고 있다.
(B) 한 남자가 사다리에 서 있다.
(C) **여러 개의 지도가 벽에 걸려 있다.**
(D) 한 커플이 가게에 들어서고 있다.

어휘 ladder 사다리  enter 들어가다

**4** 미W
(A) Bicycles are stacked on top of each other.
(B) All the windows have the same shape.
(C) A sign with letters is taped on the ground.
(D) Metal fences are being dismantled.

(A) 자전거가 겹겹이 쌓여 있다.
(B) 모든 유리창이 같은 모양이다.
(C) 글자가 쓰인 표지판이 땅 위에 테이프로 부착되어 있다.
(D) 철제 담장이 해체되고 있다.

어휘 stack 쌓다  on top of ~의 위에  letter 글자  tape 테이프로 붙이다  dismantle 분해하다

**5** 영M
(A) People are racing in the ice rink.
(B) Children are playing basketball outdoors.
(C) The windows on the wall are being cleaned.
(D) **One man is kneeling with his hands up in the air.**

(A) 사람들이 스케이트장에서 경주를 하고 있다.
(B) 아이들이 야외에서 농구를 하고 있다.
(C) 벽에 있는 창문을 청소하는 중이다.
(D) **한 남자가 팔을 공중에 뻗은 채 무릎을 꿇고 있다.**

어휘 kneel 무릎을 꿇다  in the air 공중에

**6** 미W
(A) Some of the tables are occupied.
(B) A tree is being planted close to the building.
(C) **Fallen leaves are scattered all over the ground.**
(D) Some letters and numbers are being engraved on the wall.

(A) 테이블 중 일부는 사람이 있다.
(B) 나무가 건물 가까이에 심어 지고 있다.
(C) **낙엽이 땅 곳곳에 흩어져 있다.**
(D) 글자와 숫자가 벽에 새겨지는 중이다.

어휘 plant 심다  scatter 뿌리다  engrave 새기다

# PART 2

P60

**7** 미M
Where will the product demonstration take place?
(A) Yes, it's a nice place.
(B) **Check the e-mail I sent you.**
(C) The product is on sale now.

제품 시연회는 어디서 열리나요?
(A) 네, 그곳은 좋아요.
(B) **제가 보내 드린 이메일을 보세요.**
(C) 그 제품은 현재 할인 중입니다.

어휘 demonstration 시연회  take place 열리다, 발생하다  on sale 할인 중인

**8** 영M
Why has the seminar been rescheduled?
(A) It is scheduled to begin at noon.
(B) One of the largest seminars of this year.
(C) **So that more people can attend.**

세미나 일정이 왜 변경됐나요?
(A) 그건 정오에 시작될 예정입니다.
(B) 올해가 가장 큰 세미나 중 하나입니다.
(C) **더 많은 사람들이 참석할 수 있게 하려고요.**

어휘 reschedule 일정을 변경하다  attend 참석하다

**9** 미W
Do you want to take tomorrow off or next Monday?
(A) **Let me check my schedule.**
(B) I'm sure it's on now.
(C) She's going on a business trip tomorrow.

내일 쉬고 싶으세요 아니면 다음 주 월요일에 쉬고 싶으세요?
(A) **제 스케줄 좀 볼게요.**
(B) 지금은 켜져 있을 겁니다.
(C) 그녀는 내일 출장 갑니다.

어휘 take off 쉬다  go on a business trip 출장 가다

**10** 미W
How often should the credit report be updated?
(A) Please submit it by Monday.
(B) **At least once a week.**
(C) That's what they reported.

신용 보고서는 얼마나 자주 업데이트되어야 하죠?
(A) 그걸 월요일까지 제출해 주세요.
(B) **최소한 일주일에 한 번이요.**
(C) 그건 그들이 보고했던 겁니다.

어휘 credit report 신용 보고서  update 업데이트하다  submit 제출하다

**11** 영M
Which of the shifts is working today?
(A) **Alan's team is here this evening.**
(B) Three shifts a day.
(C) Trevor emailed them yesterday.

오늘 어느 교대조가 일하죠?
(A) **오늘 저녁은 앨런 팀입니다.**
(B) 하루에 세 개 조요.
(C) 트레버가 어제 그들에게 이메일을 보냈어요.

어휘 shift (특정 교대 근무를 하는) 교대조

**12** 미M
The printer needs more ink, doesn't it?
(A) It was printed pretty clearly.
(B) **Kate said she refilled it just this morning.**
(C) James Kim is our new manager.

그 프린터는 잉크가 더 필요하죠, 그렇죠?
(A) 아주 선명하게 인쇄되었습니다.
(B) **케이트가 바로 오늘 아침에 자기가 다시 채웠다고 했어요.**
(C) 제임스 김이 우리의 새 매니저예요.

어휘 pretty 아주 정도, 꽤  clearly 분명하게  refill 다시 채우다

**13** 영M
What is this video equipment for?
(A) I heard it's for tomorrow's conference.
(B) The rental fee is $30 per hour.
(C) **It is a big improvement from the last one.**

이 비디오 장비는 어떤 용도죠?
(A) **내일 회의에 쓸 거라고 들었어요.**
(B) 임대료는 시간당 30달러입니다.
(C) 예전 것에 비해 많이 좋아진 거죠.

어휘 equipment 장비  rental 임대  fee 수수료  improvement 향상

**14** Where can I get a city map?

[미W] (A) **There is an information center on Hamilton Street.**

[미M] (B) I'm leaving for Paris in a couple of days.

(C) Yes, I can.

시내 지도를 어디서 구할 수 있나요?

(A) **해밀턴 가에 정보 센터가 있어요.**

(B) 이틀 후에 파리로 떠날 거예요.

(C) 네, 할 수 있어요.

어휘 leave for ~로 떠나다  a couple of 둘의

**15** Doesn't the station stall accept credit cards?

[미W] (A) According to the installation schedule.

[영M] (B) **No, they only take cash.**

(C) It stops every thirty minutes.

역 매점은 신용 카드를 받지 않나요?

(A) 설치 일정에 따르면요.

(B) **안 받아요, 거긴 현금만 받아요.**

(C) 30분마다 정차합니다.

어휘 station stall 역 매점  accept 받아들이다  installation 설치

**16** What's the name of the travel agent you used last time?

[미M] (A) Throughout Europe.

[영M] (B) Next Wednesday.

(C) **I need to look it up.**

지난번 당신이 이용했던 여행사 직원의 이름이 뭔가요?

(A) 유럽 전역이요.

(B) 다음 주 수요일이요.

(C) **찾아봐야 합니다.**

어휘 travel agent 여행사 직원  throughout 전역에  look up 정보를 찾다

**17** You've canceled the newspaper subscription, haven't you?

[미M] (A) **No, I renewed it.**

[미W] (B) Yes, they are news articles.

(C) When you dropped off your prescription.

신문 구독을 취소하셨죠, 그렇죠?

(A) **아니요, 연장했는데요.**

(B) 네, 그건 뉴스 기사입니다.

(C) 당신이 처방전을 가져갔을 때요.

어휘 subscription 구독  renew 갱신하다, 연장하다  drop off 갖다 다, 가져오다  prescription 처방전 처방된 약

**18** Why is Mr. Kim going back to London?

[영M] (A) Why don't we leave on Monday?

[미W] (B) It was returned last week.

(C) **He has to follow up with his client.**

김 씨는 왜 런던으로 돌아가나요?

(A) 우리 월요일에 떠나는 건 어때요?

(B) 그건 지난주에 반송되었어요.

(C) **고객에 대한 후속 조치가 필요해요.**

어휘 go back 돌아가다  follow up 후속 조치를 취하다

**19** Don't you have a used copy of this book?

[미W] (A) Yes, I've made 20 copies.

[미M] (B) Please contact me if you have any questions.

(C) **No, not at the moment.**

이 책 중고책으로 갖고 있지 않나요?

(A) 네, 저는 20부를 복사했어요.

(B) 질문이 있으시면 저에게 연락 주세요.

(C) **아니요, 지금은 없습니다.**

어휘 used copy 중고책  at the moment 지금, 현재에

**20** Will you continue to work here or transfer to the Boston office?

[미W] (A) I don't think that's the right train.

[영M] (B) **I'm planning to move next month.**

(C) I can work until six.

여기서 계속 일하실 건가요, 보스턴 사무소로 옮기실 건가요?

(A) 그 기차가 아닌 것 같은데요.

(B) **다음 달에 옮길 계획입니다.**

(C) 여섯 시까지 일할 수 있어요.

어휘 transfer 옮기다, 전근 가다

**21** Let's have Sean edit this letter before we send it out.

[영M] (A) The letter A is not printed clearly.

[미W] (B) **He is away on vacation right now.**

(C) I think we should send them in first.

우리가 이 편지를 발송하기 전에 션이 편집하도록 합시다.

(A) A 글자가 명확하게 인쇄되지 않았습니다.

(B) **그가 지금은 휴가 중이라 없어요.**

(C) 그것들을 먼저 보내야 할 거 같아요.

어휘 edit 편집하다  letter 편지, 글자  send out 발송하다

**22** Excuse me, can I give you the package for Ms. Orser?

[미M] (A) **Yes, I was told to sign for him.**

[미W] (B) The packaging came out as expected.

(C) Usually it takes about two days to receive it.

실례지만 오서 씨에게 온 소포를 당신에게 드려도 되나요?

(A) **네, 제가 대신 사인하라고 들었어요.**

(B) 포장은 예상대로 나왔습니다.

(C) 보통 그것을 받기까지 2일 정도 걸려요.

어휘 package 소포  packaging 포장  as expected 예상대로

**23** You haven't reserved a flight to Hong Kong, have you?

[영M] (A) **No, but I'll call after lunch.**

[미W] (B) It was a long flight.

(C) Check your new itinerary please.

홍콩으로 가는 비행편을 예약하지 않았죠, 그렇죠?

(A) **하지 않았지만 점심 식사 후에 전화할 겁니다.**

(B) 그건 장거리 비행이었어요.

(C) 새로운 여행 일정표를 확인해 주세요.

어휘 reserve 예약하다  itinerary 여행 일정표

**24** Marlene said she would apply for a sales position at our Singapore office.

[미W] (A) Yes, my work is really interesting.

[미M] (B) It doesn't apply to Europe.

(C) **I heard Robin is being considered for it.**

말린이 우리 싱가포르 지사의 판매직에 지원할 거라고 하네요.

(A) 네, 제 일은 정말 재미있어요.

(B) 유럽은 해당하지 않아요.

(C) **그 자리는 로빈이 고려되고 있다고 들었는데요.**

어휘 apply for 지원하다, 신청하다  apply to 적용되다

**25** Why aren't we hiring those temporary workers again for the research?

[미W] (A) Please keep searching for cheap flights.

[영M] (B) Contemporary works are on display now.

(C) **They failed to meet our expectations last time.**

그 연구를 위해 임시직 직원들을 다시 고용하지 않는 이유가 뭐죠?

(A) 저렴한 비행편을 계속 찾아보세요.

(B) 현대의 작품들이 지금 전시 중입니다.

(C) **지난번에 그들이 우리의 기대에 못 미쳤거든요.**

어휘 hire 고용하다  temporary 임시직인, 임시의  contemporary 동시대의, 현대의  on display 전시 중인  fail to ~하지 못하다  meet one's expectation 기대에 부응하다

**26** How much will it cost to have the brochures delivered?

[미M] (A) To make it more attractive.

[영M] (B) **It depends on the location.**

(C) Yes, they arrived this morning.

책자가 배달되는 데 비용이 얼마나 들까요?

(A) 그걸 더 매력적으로 만들려고요.

(B) **지역에 따라 다릅니다.**

(C) 네, 그들은 오늘 아침에 도착했어요.

어휘 attractive 매력적인  location 지역, 위치

**27** Couldn't we postpone the conference until April?

[미M] (A) To the nearest shopping center.

[미W] (B) **The hotel charges cancellation fees.**

(C) Yes, the conference was a great success.

컨퍼런스를 4월까지 미룰 수 없을까요?

(A) 가장 가까운 쇼핑센터로요.

## PART 3

P61

**Questions 32-34 refer to the following conversation.** 미W 영M

W Hello. ㉜ I bought this coat here yesterday for my son's graduation. ㉝ However, my husband also bought him the same one. Can I return the item?

M Yes, of course. You can either have a full refund or choose another item of the same value.

W I will exchange it for something else. I like the jacket that is displayed in the window. ㉞ Do you have it in size 7?

어 안녕하세요. 제가 어제 여기서 제 아들 졸업 선물로 이 코트를 샀는데요. 그런데도 이이에게 같은 걸 샀어요. 제가 그걸 반품할 수 있을까요?

남 네, 물론입니다. 손님께서는 전액 환불을 받으실 수도 있고, 같은 금액의 다른 상품으로 고르실 수도 있습니다.

여 다른 걸로 교환할게요. 창가에 전열되어 있는 재킷이 마음에 드네요. 사이즈 7이 있나요?

어휘 graduation 졸업, 졸업식  display 진열하다; 진열품  full refund 전액 환불  exchange 교환하다  jewelry 보석류  appliance 가전제품  faulty 흠결함이 있는, 불완전한  guarantee (제품의) 품질 보증서  duplicate 똑같은, 사본의  locate 찾다

**32**
What type of product are the speakers discussing?
(A) Jewelry
**(B) Clothing**
(C) Furniture
(D) Appliances
화자들이 이야기하고 있는 제품의 종류는 무엇인가?
(A) 장신구
**(B) 의류**
(C) 가구
(D) 가전제품
패러프레이징 coat → Clothing

**33**
What problem does the woman explain to the man?
(A) A product is faulty.
(B) A guarantee was not provided.
(C) A sales receipt was lost.
**(D) A duplicate gift has been given.**
여자가 남자에게 설명하는 문제는 무엇인가?
(A) 제품에 결함이 있다.
(B) 품질 보증서가 제공되지 않았다.
(C) 판매 영수증을 분실했다.
**(D) 똑같은 선물을 받았다.**

**34**
What will the man probably do next?
**(A) Locate an item**
(B) Give a full refund
(C) Contact another store
(D) Order a different size
남자는 다음에 무엇을 할 것 같은가?
**(A) 물건을 찾는다.**
(B) 전액 환불을 해준다.
(C) 다른 상점에 연락한다.
(D) 다른 사이즈를 주문한다.

**Questions 35-37 refer to the following conversation.** 미W 미M

W Mark, this is Susan. I'm on my way to the bakery to pick up the cake we ordered for Richard's retirement party. But traffic on 10th Avenue is so bad that ㊱ I'm going to be late. I'm sorry.

M Oh, that's okay. Well, the party begins in an hour. Why don't I call the bakery and ㊲ see if they can deliver the cake to the banquet hall for us?

W I don't think they deliver. Actually, ㊲ Jeremy from the marketing department lives near the bakery. Let me call and ask him to pick up the cake.

여 마크, 수잔이에요. 리차드의 은퇴 파티에 쓸 케이크를 가지러 빵집으로 가는 중인데요. 10번가가 너무 막혀서 늦을 것 같아요. 죄송합니다.

남 아, 괜찮습니다. 음, 파티가 한 시간 후면 시작하네요. 제가 빵집에 전화해서 케이크를 연회실로 배달해 줄 수 있는지 알아볼까요?

여 거기는 배달이 안 될 거예요. 실은 마케팅 부서의 제레미가 그 빵집 근처에 살아요. 제가 그에게 전화해서 케이크를 가져오라고 부탁해 볼게요.

어휘 on one's way to (특정 장소로) 가는 중인  banquet 연회  directions 길 안내  arrange for 준비하다  detour 우회

**35**
Why does the woman call the man?
(A) To discuss a report
(B) To invite him to a party
**(C) To say she will be late**
(D) To ask him for directions
여자는 왜 남자에게 전화를 하는가?
(A) 보고서에 관해 이야기하려고
(B) 남자를 파티에 초대하려고
**(C) 늦을 거라고 말하려고**
(D) 남자에게 길을 물어보려고

---

**(B) 호텔이 취소 수수료를 부과합니다.**
(C) 네, 그 컨퍼런스는 매우 성공적이었어요.
어휘 postpone 미루다, 연기하다  charge 부과하다  cancellation fee 취소 수수료

**28**
I heard the office is staffed mainly with volunteers.
**(A) They are competent enough to handle the task.**
(B) Staff meetings are held on a regular basis.
(C) It's good to take part in voluntary services.
그 사무실은 주로 자원봉사자로 채워졌다고 들었어요.
**(A) 그들이 업무를 처리하기에 충분히 능숙히 있거든요.**
(B) 직원 회의가 정기적으로 열립니다.
(C) 자원봉사에 참가하는 것은 좋은 일입니다.
어휘 staff 직원을 제공하다, 직원으로 일하다  volunteer 자원봉사자  competent 유능한  staff meeting 직원 회의  on a regular basis 정기적으로  take part in 참가하다

**29**
Should I meet you by the entrance or wait for you in the reception area?
(A) No, not until 7 P.M.
**(B) Let's meet outside.**
(C) Would you like to make an appointment?
당신을 입구에서 만날까요, 로비에서 기다릴까요?
(A) 아니요, 오후 7시 이후에나요.
**(B) 밖에서 만납시다.**
(C) 약속을 잡으시겠어요?
어휘 entrance 입구  reception area 로비, 안내실, 접수처

**30**
How soon will I receive a response regarding my job application?
**(A) We'll call you within a week.**
(B) Your contact information.
(C) No, it'll be too late by then.
제 지원에 대해서 얼마나 빨리 답을 받을 수 있을까요?
**(A) 저희가 일주일 내로 전화하겠습니다.**
(B) 당신의 연락처요.
(C) 아니요, 그때쯤이면 너무 늦습니다.
어휘 response 답, 응답  contact information 연락처, 연락 정보

**31**
I'm sorry, but there is no more space at the Bristol warehouse.
(A) No, it'll be delivered soon.
**(B) I actually asked about the one in Greenville.**
(C) Just a few miles off the main road.
죄송하지만 브리스톨 창고에는 공간이 더 이상 없습니다.
(A) 아니요, 그건 곧 배달될 거예요.
**(B) 전 그린빌에 있는 창고에 대해서 물었는데요.**
(C) 큰길에서 몇 마일 떨어진 곳이에요.
어휘 warehouse 창고  main road 큰길

**36** What does the man offer to do?
(A) Request a delivery
(B) Arrange for a car
(C) Pick up an order
(D) Listen to a traffic report
남자가 제안하는 것은 무엇인가?
(A) 배달 요청하기
(B) 차 준비시키기
(C) 주문품 가져오기
(D) 교통 방송 듣기

**37** What does the woman say she will do?
(A) Take a detour
(B) Make a payment
(C) Confirm a reservation
(D) Ask a coworker to help
여자가 무엇을 하겠다고 말하는가?
(A) 우회하기
(B) 지불하기
(C) 예약 확인하기
(D) 동료에게 도움 요청하기

**38** Why does Stephanie want to change the meeting schedule?
(A) She needs to meet a deadline.
(B) She has another meeting to attend.
(C) She has to review some information.
(D) She will go on a business trip.
스테파니가 회의 일정 변경을 요청한 이유는 무엇인가?
(A) 마감을 맞춰야 한다.
(B) 다른 회의에 참석해야 한다.
(C) 어떤 정보를 검토해야 한다.
(D) 출장을 갈 것이다.

패러프레이징 go over the figures → review some information

**39** What does the man imply when he says, "But in the morning I'll be around here"?
(A) He is meeting with a client then.
(B) He will be very busy then.
(C) He is available then.
(D) He can't attend the meeting then.
남자가 "하지만 오전에는 여기에 있을 거예요"라고 말한 의도는 무엇인가?
(A) 그때 고객을 만날 것이다.
(B) 그때 매우 바쁠 것이다.
(C) 그때 시간이 된다.
(D) 그때는 회의에 참석할 수 없다.

**40** What will the woman do next?
(A) Send an e-mail to a coworker
(B) Contact her boss
(C) Reserve a meeting room
(D) Discuss a schedule
여자는 다음에 무엇을 할 것인가?
(A) 동료에게 이메일 보내기
(B) 그녀의 상사에게 연락하기
(C) 회의실 예약하기
(D) 일정 상의하기

Questions 38-40 refer to the following conversation. 영M 미W

M Kimberly, I just heard that Stephanie scheduled the marketing meeting for Thursday. Is that right?

W Oh, she just called and said that the sales figures for the last quarter came in this morning. ⑧ She still has to go over the figures, so she asked me to change the meeting time to Friday.

M I will be out of town on a business trip on Friday afternoon. But in the morning I'll be around here. Could you call Stephanie and ⑩ set the time before noon? No problem. She is on her way to work right now. ⑪ I'll talk to her when she comes in.

남 킴벌리, 방금 들었는데 스테파니가 마케팅 회의 시간을 목요일로 잡았다면서요. 그런가요?

여 아, 그녀가 방금 전화해서 지난 분기 매출액 내역이 오늘 이침에 들어왔다고 했어요. 그녀는 아직 그 수치를 검토해야 하거든요. 그래서 회의를 금요일로 변경해 줄 것을 요청했어요.

남 금요일 오후에 제가 출장을 가요. 하지만 이침에는 여기에 있을 거예요. 스테파니에게 전화해서 정오 전에 시간을 잡을 수 있어요?

여 문제없어요. 지금 그녀는 출근하는 중이에요. 오는 대로 얘기할게요.

어휘 sales figure 매출액 go over 검토하다 out of town 출타 중인 on one's way to 오는 중인

**41** What are the speakers discussing?
(A) An upcoming appointment
(B) A business location
(C) A store promotion
(D) An eyeglass prescription
화자들은 무엇에 관해 이야기하는가?
(A) 다가오는 약속
(B) 업체의 위치
(C) 상점 판촉 행사
(D) 안경 처방전

**42** Why is the woman behind schedule?
(A) A fax machine is out of order.
(B) A store has been busy.
(C) An employee is out sick.
(D) A doctor has not arrived yet.
왜 여자는 일정보다 뒤처졌는가?
(A) 팩스기가 고장 났다.
(B) 가게가 바빴다.
(C) 직원이 이파서 결근했다.
(D) 의사가 아직 도착하지 않았다.

Questions 41-43 refer to the following conversation. 미M 미W

M ⑪ My eye doctor faxed a prescription for some reading glasses to this optical store about an hour ago, and I was wondering if I could pick up the order now. My name is Benjamin Coleman.

W Let's see... Yes, here's the order for your eyeglasses, but I'm afraid they're not ready yet. ⑫ We've had such a busy day today, so we're a little behind schedule. I'm sorry, but could you come back in an hour?

M No problem. ⑬ I was going to check out the bookstore next door. So, I'll just do that now and come back later.

남 제 안과 의사가 한 시간 전에 이 안경점으로 독서용 안경 처방전을 팩스로 보내셨대요. 지금 주문한 것을 가져갈 수 있을까 해서요. 제 이름은 벤자민 콜먼입니다.

여 한번 볼게요. 네, 여기 당신의 안경 주문서가 있는데 안타깝게도 아직 준비가 다 되지 않았네요. 오늘 저희가 무척 바빠서 일정보다 조금 지연이 되었습니다. 죄송하지만 한 시간 후에 다시 와 주시겠어요?

남 문제없습니다. 제가 옆이 서점을 둘러보려고 했었거든요. 서점을 둘러보고 이따가 다시 오겠습니다.

어휘 eye doctor 안과 의사 prescription 처방전 optical store 안경점 behind schedule 일정보다 뒤처진 check out (물건, 공간 등을) 살펴보다 upcoming 다가오는 promotion 판촉 행사 be out sick 아파서 결근하다 return 돌아오다, (물건을) 반납하다, 환불하다

**43** What does the man say he will do?
(A) Go to a nearby store
(B) Make a phone call
(C) Return an item
(D) Review a document
남자는 무엇을 할 것이라고 하는가?
(A) 근처 상점에 가기
(B) 전화하기
(C) 물건을 환불하기
(D) 서류를 검토하기
패러프레이징 check out the bookstore next door
→ Go to a nearby store

**44** Who most likely is the man?
(A) A newspaper editor
(B) A bus driver
(C) A real estate agent
(D) A phone operator
남자는 누구인가?
(A) 신문 편집자
(B) 버스 운전사
(C) 부동산 중개인
(D) 전화 교환원

**45** Why did the woman mention Wilson Street?
(A) She wants to live close to her family.
(B) She does not want a big house now.
(C) She wants to work close to her home.
(D) She used to drive to work there.
여자가 윌슨 가를 언급한 이유는 무엇인가?
(A) 가족 가까이에 살고 싶어 한다.
(B) 지금은 큰 집을 원하지 않는다.
(C) 집 근처에서 가까이 일하기를 원한다.
(D) 예전에 운전해서 거기에 출근하곤 했다.

**46** Why does the man say "Tell you what"?
(A) To provide detailed explanation
(B) To make a suggestion
(C) To confirm some information
(D) To recommend a business
남자는 왜 "이렇게 하죠"라고 말하는가?
(A) 자세한 설명을 제공하려고
(B) 제안을 하려고
(C) 몇몇 정보를 확인하려고
(D) 업체를 추천해 주려고

Questions 44-46 refer to the following conversation. 미W 영M

W Hello. I saw an ad for apartment in the newspaper this
morning and I was wondering if they are still available
for rent.

M **44** Most of them are for sale, but we do have some for
rent. Is there anything specific you have in mind?

W There are four of us in my family so I need an apartment
with two bedrooms at least. Not only that, **45** it would be
great to have a place on Wilson Street where my office
is. I hate driving a long distance to work.

M I see. Tell you what, **46** if you give me your contact
number, I'll get back to you right after I check the rental
listings for the area on the computer.

여 안녕하세요. 오늘 아침 신문에 실린 아파트 광고를 봤는데요 아직 임대하기
능한지 궁금합니다.
남 대부분은 매매지만 일부는 임대를 합니다. 구체적으로 마음에 두고 있는
게 있으신가요?
여 저희 가족이 4명입니다. 그래서 최소한 침실 2개짜리가 필요해요. 게다가
제 사무실이 있는 윌슨 가에 집을 얻으면 좋겠네요. 장거리 운전해서 출근
하는 건 싫거든요.
남 알겠습니다. 이렇게 하죠. 저에게 전화번호를 알려 주시면 제가 컴퓨터로 그
지역에 임대 나온 것들을 본 후 바로 전화 드리겠습니다.

어휘 ad 광고 for rent 임대요 specific 구체적인 tell you what 이렇게 하
는 게 어떨까요 rental listing 임대(나올) 리스트 real estate agent 부동
산 매매 중개인

**47** Why is the man at the local health center?
(A) To make a blood donation
(B) To collect some items
(C) To keep an appointment
(D) To volunteer for fund raising
남자는 왜 지역 보건소에 있는가?
(A) 헌혈을 하려고
(B) 어떤 물건들을 수집하려고
(C) 약속을 지키려고
(D) 모금 활동에 지원하려고

**48** Where is the man instructed to go?
(A) To a restaurant
(B) To an office complex
(C) To a clinic
(D) To City Hall
남자가 가라고 전달받은 곳은 어디인가?
(A) 식당
(B) 사무실 단지
(C) 병원
(D) 시청

**49** What does the man ask for?
(A) Directions to the clinic
(B) A changed address
(C) Some updated leaflets
(D) Assistance with a project
남자가 요청한 것은 무엇인가?
(A) 병원까지의 길 안내
(B) 변경된 주소
(C) 갱신된 전단지
(D) 프로젝트 관련 도움
패러프레이징 some of the new leaflets → Some updated leaflets

Questions 47-49 refer to the following conversation. 미M 미W

M Hello. **47** I have received a leaflet about blood donations.
It says that I should sign up here at the local health
center. Is there someone I can talk to about it?

W My apologies. **48** We had to change the venue to the
Holmes Clinic on Main Street. We did print additional
leaflets, but obviously some of the old ones are still
around.

M That is not a problem. My office is just opposite the
clinic, so I will go there at lunchtime. **49** By the way,
could I take some of the new leaflets to pass around to
my colleagues at work?

남 안녕하세요. 제가 헌혈에 관한 전단지를 받았는데요. 이곳 보건소에서 등록
해야 한다고 쓰여 있더라고요. 그것에 대해 제가 상담할 수 있는 분이 계신
가요?
여 죄송합니다. 저희가 그 장소를 메인 가에 있는 홈스 클리닉으로 변경해야만
했어요. 저희가 분명 추가 전단을 인쇄했는데, 예전 것 중 일부가 분명 아직
도 돌아다니고 있는 것 같네요.
남 괜찮습니다. 제 사무실이 그 병원 바로 맞은편에 있어서, 점심시간에 그곳에
갈게요. 그런데, 제 직장에 있는 제 동료들에게 나눠줄 새 전단지를 좀 가져갈
수 있을까요?

어휘 leaflet (광고나 선전을 위한) 전단 blood donation 헌혈 sign up 등록
하다 health center 보건소 my apologies 죄송합니다 venue 장소
main street 시내 중심가 additional 추가의 어떤이 obviously 분명히,
명백히 pass around (여러 사람이 보도록) ~을 돌리다 colleague 동료
register 등록하다 collect 수집하다 fund raising 모금 활동, 지금 조달
directions 길 안내 updated 업데이트된, 갱신된

Questions 50-52 refer to the following conversation. 영M 미W

M Hello, Ms. Cogger. ⑤⓪ This is Quinn in the production department. ⑤① I'm calling about a problem with the router equipment. It seems pretty serious and I think it needs to be repaired right away.

W Okay, could you tell me which router is not working properly?

M It's the one in production section four. I think its cutting mechanism is malfunctioning.

W Well, I will send an engineer immediately. But in the meantime, ⑤② you should shut down that particular production line so no more products are affected. Can you do that straightaway?

남 안녕하세요, 코거 씨. 저는 생산 부서의 퀸입니다. 라우터 장비의 문제 때문에 전화했는데요. 상태가 꽤 심각해 보여서 지금 바로 수리해야 할 것 같습니다.

여 네, 어떤 기계가 제대로 작동하지 않는지 알려주시겠어요?

남 4번 생산 구역에 있는 것입니다. 기계의 절삭 장치가 제대로 작동하지 않는 것 같아요.

여 음, 제가 즉시 엔지니어를 보낼게요. 그렇지만 그 동안에 그 생산 라인은 즉시 단어주셔서 더 이상 제품에 영향을 미치지 않도록 해주셔야 해요. 지금 즉시 할 수 있죠?

어휘 router equipment 흠을 파는 기계 mechanism 기계 장치 malfunction 제대로 작동하지 않다 shut down (기계 등을) 정지시키다 particular 특정한 straightaway 즉시 file a complaint 불만을 제기하다 run low 고갈되다, 떨어져 가다 supplies 물품

50 What department does the man most likely work in?
(A) Production
(B) Sales
(C) Accounting
(D) Maintenance

남자는 어느 부서에서 일하고 있겠는가?
(A) 생산
(B) 영업
(C) 회계
(D) 수리 보수

51 What problem does the man report?
(A) A repairperson did not arrive.
(B) Some machinery is damaged.
(C) A customer filed a complaint.
(D) Some supplies are running low.

남자가 보고한 문제점은 무엇인가?
(A) 수리공이 도착하지 않았다.
(B) 몇몇 장비가 손상되었다.
(C) 고객이 불만을 제기했다.
(D) 몇몇 물자의 재고가 떨어지고 있다.

52 What does the woman ask the man to do?
(A) Submit an order form
(B) Use another machine
(C) Call an engineer
(D) Stop production

여자가 남자에게 요구하는 것은 무엇인가?
(A) 주문서 제출하기
(B) 다른 기계 사용하기
(C) 엔지니어에게 전화하기
(D) 생산 중단하기

패러프레이징 shut down that particular production line
→ Stop production

Questions 53-55 refer to the following conversation. 미M 미W

M Ms. Anyon, do you have time to help me? ⑤③ I'm sorting out the media and marketing proposals that I'm presenting to Astoria Trust for their new ad campaign. And I want to make sure I didn't miss anything important.

W Yes, I'd be glad to help. I heard that ⑤④ the marketing team has come up with some excellent ideas. If you can convince Astoria Trust that our proposals are more effective than those of our competitors, I'm sure they will choose us.

M I really hope so. ⑤⑤ Tomorrow I'm going to have a final meeting with the marketing staff and rehearse my presentation.

남 애넌 씨, 저를 좀 도와줄 시간이 있으세요? 제가 아스토리아 트러스트의 새 광고 캠페인에 대해 발표할 때 사용할 미디어와 마케팅 제안서를 분류하고 있는데요, 중요한 자료를 빠뜨리게 없는지 확인하고 싶어서요.

여 네, 기꺼이 도와 드릴게요. 제가 듣기로는 마케팅팀이 아주 훌륭한 아이디어를 내놓았다고 하던데요. 우리의 제안이 경쟁업체 것보다 더 효율적이라고 아스토리아 트러스트를 납득시킬 수 있다면 그들은 분명 우리를 선택할 거예요.

남 정말 그랬으면 좋겠어요. 내일 저는 마케팅팀과 최종 회의를 갖고 제 발표를 리허설할 거예요.

어휘 sort out 구분하다 come up with (의견이나 해결책, 아이디어 등을) 제안하다, 내놓다 convince 납득시키다 finalize 마무리 짓다 evaluate 평가하다 secure 확보하다 funding 자금, 재정 지원 expert 전문가 promote 승진시키다

53 What does the man request help with?
(A) Finalizing market research
(B) Setting up some meetings
(C) Preparing a presentation
(D) Updating a client database

남자가 도와 달라고 요청하는 것은 무엇인가?
(A) 시장 조사 마무리
(B) 몇몇 회의 준비
(C) 발표 준비
(D) 고객 자료 업데이트

54 What does the woman say the marketing team has done?
(A) Evaluated competitors' campaigns
(B) Extended a project deadline
(C) Produced some new ideas
(D) Secured additional funding

여자는 마케팅팀이 무엇을 했다고 말하는가?
(A) 경쟁업체들의 캠페인 평가
(B) 프로젝트 기한 연장
(C) 몇 가지 아이디어 양산
(D) 추가 자금 확보

패러프레이징 has come up with some excellent ideas
→ Produced some new ideas

55 What will the man most likely do tomorrow?
(A) He will hire several experts.
(B) He will be promoted to a marketing director.
(C) He will rehearse his presentation.
(D) He will discuss marketing plans with coworkers.

남자는 내일 무엇을 할 것인가?
(A) 몇 명의 전문가를 고용할 것이다.
(B) 마케팅 부장으로 승진할 것이다.
(C) 그의 발표를 리허설할 것이다.
(D) 동료들과 마케팅 안에 대해 논의할 것이다.

## Questions 56-58 refer to the following conversation. 영M 미W

M Miranda, ⑤ have you found anyone for the sales director position yet?

W I'm afraid not. I have received dozens of applications from Human Resources over the last couple of weeks, but ⑤ I haven't found anyone who's qualified. The position requires someone with three years of experience in sales and promotions, but no one has matched up to that.

M Hmm... ⑤ Why don't we get in touch with Sandra Shin then? Since she left us four years ago, she's been working in the field in South Carolina, and she told me over the phone last week that she wanted to return here to Florida.

W Why didn't I think of that sooner? ⑤ She would be a perfect fit for the job. I'll give her a call right away.

**어휘** dozens of 수십의 application 지원서 qualified 자격이 있는 match up to ~에 부합하다 get in touch with ~와 연락하다 perfect fit 안성맞춤인 것 relocate 이주하다 lose contact with ~와 연락이 끊기다 former 예전의

---

**56** What department needs a new director?
(A) Sales
(B) Advertising
(C) Human Resources
(D) Planning

어떤 부서에서 새로운 부장이 필요한가?
(A) **영업부**
(B) 광고부
(C) 인사부
(D) 기획부

**57** According to the woman, what is the problem?
(A) She has missed a deadline.
(B) **It is hard to find a qualified applicant.**
(C) She does not want to relocate to a branch office.
(D) The new job doesn't meet the woman's expectations.

여자에 따르면 무엇이 문제인가?
(A) 여자는 마감을 놓쳤다.
(B) **자격을 갖춘 후보자를 찾기가 어렵다.**
(C) 여자는 지점으로 전근가기를 원치 않는다.
(D) 새로운 일이 그 여자의 기대와 맞지 않는다.

**58** What does the woman imply when she says, "Why didn't I think of that sooner"?
(A) She needs more time to finish her job.
(B) She has lost contact with her former coworker.
(C) She wants more information from the man.
(D) **She completely agrees with the man's idea.**

여자가 "제가 왜 진작 그 생각을 못 했을까요"라고 말한 의도는 무엇인가?
(A) 그녀는 업무를 끝내기 위해 시간이 더 필요하다.
(B) 그녀는 전 동료와 연락이 끊겼다.
(C) 그녀는 남자로부터 더 많은 정보를 원한다.
(D) **그녀는 남자의 생각에 전적으로 동의한다.**

---

## 59

What does the woman say will happen next week?
(A) **A division will relocate.**
(B) Two sales offices will be combined.
(C) New jobs will be advertised.
(D) Travel costs will increase.

여자는 다음 주에 무엇이 있을 거라고 말하는가?
(A) **부서가 이전될 것이다.**
(B) 두 개의 영업소를 하나로 합칠 것이다.
(C) 새 일자리들이 광고될 것이다.
(D) 여행 비용이 증가될 것이다.

패러프레이징 will be moving to the new offices → relocate

## 60

According to the woman, what is the man eligible for?
(A) A pay increase
(B) Paid vacation
(C) **Transportation allowance**
(D) Reimbursement for travel

여자에 따르면, 남자는 무엇에 대한 자격이 있는가?
(A) 임금 인상
(B) 유급 휴가
(C) **교통 보조금**
(D) 출장 경비 현금

패러프레이징 some transportation subsidies → Transportation allowance

## 61

What does the man want to know more about?
(A) Working from home
(B) **Financing for the commute**
(C) Transferring to a new division
(D) Purchasing a new car

남자는 무엇에 대해 더 알고 싶어 하는가?
(A) 재택 근무하는 것
(B) **통근에 대한 비용 지원받는 것**
(C) 새로운 부서로 옮기는 것
(D) 새 차를 사는 것

---

## Questions 59-61 refer to the following conversation. 미W 미M

W Adrian, I wanted to speak to you about the upcoming company merger. ⑤ Your sales division will be moving to the new offices in Braintree next week, and I realize that it is a long way for you to travel to and from work.

M Yes, Braintree is almost two hours' drive away from where I live, which I believe will be a problem for me.

W Speaking of which, ⑥ you're entitled to some transportation subsidies according to the revised budget. In other words, the company can provide you with an annual railroad pass if you want.

M Oh, that sounds great. I'd definitely prefer to commute by train once we move to Braintree. ⑥ Could you give me details on how to sign up for that?

여 에드리언, 다가오는 회사 합병에 관련해 당신에게 얘기가 있어요. 당신의 영업부가 다음 주에 브레인트리에 있는 새 사무실로 옮기 되는데, 당신이 회사로 출퇴 근하기에는 먼 거리더군요.

남 네, 브레인트리는 제가 사는 곳에서 차로 거의 두 시간 거리인데 저한테는 저런트리 문제가 될 것 같아요.

여 그래서 말인데요, 수정된 예산안에 따르면 당신은 교통 수당을 받을 자격이 있어요. 다시 말해서, 원하신다면 회사가 일 년에 철도 승차권을 제공할 수 있다는 뜻이죠.

남 오, 그거 정말 좋네요. 브레인트리에 옮기 후에는 당연히 기차로 출퇴근하는 것이 좋습니다. 어떻게 그것을 신청할 수 있는지 알려주시겠습니까?

**어휘** merger 합병 realize 깨닫다, 알아차리다 travel to and from 출퇴근하다 revised 개정된 수정된 budget 예산안 be entitled to ~할 자격이 있다 transportation subsidy 교통 수당 commute 출퇴근하다, 통근하다 combine 결합하다, 합치다 allowance 수당 reimbursement 상환 finance 자금을 대다 transfer 이동하다, 전근 가다

Questions 62-64 refer to the following conversation with three speakers. 미M 호M 미W

M1 Thank you for agreeing to have an interview with us on such short notice, Ms. Gardner. [62] I'm Jeff Flake, the hiring manager at the Huntsville Times.

M2 And I'm Mike Lee, [62] the chief editor of the newspaper.

W Nice to meet you Mr. Flake and Mr. Lee.

M1 Well, we found your résumé very impressive. You seem to be a desirable candidate for a news reporter. But [63] we'd like to know how you feel about spending a lot of time in the field, covering stories. As you know, many reporters spend little to no time in an office.

W Yes, I understand that I would need to travel a lot to be on location for events. But that is no problem.

M2 Okay, did you bring your portfolio, Ms. Gardner?

W Yes, I did.

M2 Good. [64] Why don't you show us some of your work?

W [64] Sure, the file's right here on my laptop.

남1 갑작스러운 통지에도 면접에 응해 주셔서 감사합니다 가드너 씨. 저는 한 츠빌 타임즈의 채용 부장인 제프 플레이크입니다.

남2 그리고 저는 이 신문사의 편집부장인 마이크 리입니다.

여 만나서 반갑습니다 플레이크 씨 그리고 리 씨.

남1 저희는 당신의 이력서가 매우 인상 깊다고 생각했어요. 뉴스 기자로서 매 우 탐나는 후보자인 것 같아요. 그런데 저희는 당신이 현장에서 많은 시간 을 보내며 기사를 취재하는 것에 대하여 어떻게 느끼시는지 알고 싶어요. 아 시다시피, 많은 기자들이 사무실 안에서 시간을 거의 혹은 아예 보내지 못하거든요.

여 네, 시간을 취재하기 위해 현장에 가야 하는 일이 많다는 것은 알고 있습니 다. 그렇지만 그건 문제가 되지 않습니다.

남2 그렇군요, 포트폴리오는 가져오셨나요, 가드너 씨?

여 네, 그렇습니다.

남2 좋아요, 저희에게 당신이 썼던 기사를 좀 보여주시겠어요?

여 네, 파일이 바로 제 노트북 컴퓨터에 있습니다.

**62** Where do the interviewers most likely work?

(A) At a law firm
(B) At a travel agency
**(C) At a newspaper**
(D) At a financial institute

면접관들은 어디에서 일할 것 같은가?

(A) 법률 회사에서
(B) 여행사에서
**(C) 신문사에서**
(D) 금융 기관에서

**63** What job requirement do the speakers discuss?

**(A) Being on scene to cover stories**
(B) Having editorial experience
(C) Speaking a foreign language
(D) Being professionally certified

어떤 자격 요건에 대해 화자들은 이야기하는가?

**(A) 취재를 위해서 현장에 있는 것**
(B) 편집 경력이 있는 것
(C) 외국어를 하는 것
(D) 전문 자격증을 갖추는 것

패러프레이징 spending a lot of time in the field → Being on scene

**64** What will the woman most likely do next?

(A) Inspect some equipment
**(B) Show a portfolio**
(C) Meet some colleagues
(D) Provide references

여자는 다음에 무엇을 할 것 같은가?

(A) 기기를 점검한다.
**(B) 포트폴리오를 보여준다.**
(C) 동료들을 만난다.
(D) 추천서를 제출한다.

어휘 on (such) short notice 갑작스러운 통보 desirable candidate 탐나는 후보 cover 취재하다 on location 야외촬영하는 portfolio 작품집 on scene 현장에 있는 editorial 편집의 certified 자격증을 갖춘 chief editor 편집부장

Questions 65-67 refer to the following conversation and invoice. 영M 미W

| ITEM | PRICE |
| --- | --- |
| 4X Smartphone | $300 |
| Plan 30 (monthly) | $40 |
| Insurance (monthly) | $10 |
| Bluetooth headset | $50 |
| TOTAL | $400 |

M [65] Okay, so will that be all? A new smartphone and upgrade your data plan to Plan 30?

W Well, I just have one more question. [66] Is it possible for me to pay my bills online or even on my mobile phone? My job requires a lot of traveling, so I'm not always home when the bill comes.

M Yes, actually you can do both. All you need to do is set up an online payment account on our website. As for your smartphone, just download and install our mobile application.

W Okay, that's very convenient. [67] But I don't think I need a new Bluetooth headset. I'll just use my old one.

M [65][67] All right. I'll remove that item from your bill.

| 상품 | 가격 |
| --- | --- |
| 4X 스마트폰 | 300달러 |
| 30 요금제 (매월) | 40달러 |
| 보험(매월) | 10달러 |
| 블루투스 헤드셋 | 50달러 |
| 총액 | 400달러 |

남 좋습니다. 그럼 이게 전부죠? 새 스마트폰과 데이터 요금제를 플랜 30으로 업그레이드하는 거죠?

여 어, 질문이 하나 더 있는데요. 제가 요금을 온라인이나 혹은 제 휴대폰으로 결제하는 것이 가능할까요? 제 일이 출장이 많아서 고지서가 올 때 항상 집에 있는 게 아니라서요.

남 네, 사실 둘 다 가능합니다. 저의 웹 사이트에서 온라인 결제 계정만 만들어 주시면 돼요. 그리고 스마트폰에는 그냥 저희 모바일 앱만 다운로드 받고 설치해 주시면 됩니다.

여 알겠어요. 매우 편리하네요. 그런데 새 블루투스 헤드셋은 필요가 없을 것 같아요. 그냥 예전 것을 쓸래요.

남 알겠습니다. 그 상품은 계산서에서 빼겠습니다.

어휘 plan (휴대 전화, 인터넷 등의) 요금제  install 설치하다  application (스마트폰의) 앱  convenient 편리한  remove 제거하다  method 방법

**65** Who most likely is the man?
(A) An engineer
(B) A repair person
(C) A sales clerk
(D) A tour guide
남자는 누구일 것 같은가?
(A) 기술자
(B) 수리공
(C) 판매 사원
(D) 투어 가이드

**66** What does the woman ask about?
(A) Cell phone plans
(B) Phone accessories
(C) Travel applications
(D) Methods of payment
여자는 무엇에 대해 질문하는가?
(A) 휴대 전화 요금제
(B) 휴대 전화 액세서리
(C) 여행 앱
(D) 지불 방법

**67** Look at the graphic. Which amount will be removed from the bill?
(A) $300
(B) $50
(C) $40
(D) $10
시각 자료를 보시오. 어떤 금액이 계산서로부터 빠질 것인가?
(A) 300달러
(B) 50달러
(C) 40달러
(D) 10달러

---

Questions 68-70 refer to the following conversation and pie chart.
미W 미M

**The Top 4 Semiconductor Sales Leaders**

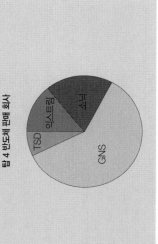

W 68 John, have you seen the acquisition proposal yet? Our company is considering buying TSD.

M I haven't read it yet. I just got back from a client meeting. What does it say?

W Take a look at this chart. It shows the top 4 semiconductor sales leaders for the last quarter. If we acquire TSD, we will definitely extend our market share. But we still wouldn't be the biggest company in the industry.

M That's right. However, 69 70 I'm not sure buying the company would be the right move because we're already the second biggest and I heard TSD's profits fell by 20% last year. Plus, as you can see from the chart, Xtreme is not a threat to us yet.

W Well, you've certainly got a point there. We should talk more about it at the board meeting next week.

탑 4 반도체 판매 회사

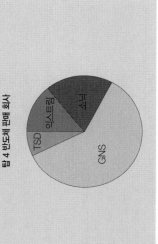

어휘 acquisition 인수  semiconductor 반도체  acquire 인수하다  extend 넓히다

**68** What are the speakers mainly discussing?
(A) A business acquisition
(B) Company benefits
(C) Marketing strategies
(D) An annual report
화자들은 무엇에 관해 이야기하는가?
**(A) 기업 인수**
(B) 회사 복리 후생
(C) 마케팅 전략
(D) 연례 보고서

**69** Why does the man say he is not sure about the proposal?
(A) Some information is inaccurate.
(B) He does not want to hire additional workers.
**(C) A company's revenue has decreased.**
(D) He is not familiar with a business deal.
남자는 왜 제안에 대해 확신이 없다고 하는가?
(A) 일부 정보가 부정확하다.
(B) 그는 추가로 일꾼들을 고용하고 싶지 않다.
**(C) 한 회사의 수입이 감소했다.**
(D) 그는 기업 거래에 대해 익숙하지 않다.
패러프레이징  profits fell by 20% → revenue has decreased

**70** Look at the graphic. Where do the speakers work?
(A) GNS
**(B) Sonic**
(C) Xtreme
(D) TSD
시각 자료를 보시오. 화자들은 어디서 일하는가?
(A) GNS
**(B) 소닉**
(C) 익스트림
(D) TSD

---

여 죠, 인수 제안서 보셨어요? 우리 회사가 TSD를 인수하는 것을 고려 중이에요.

남 아직 읽어보지 못했어요. 지금 방금 고객과 회의를 마치고 돌아왔거든요, 뭐라고 쓰여 있던가요?

여 이 차트를 한번 보세요. 이것은 지난 분기에 가장 반도체 판매가 높았던 4개의 회사를 보여주고 있어요. 만약 우리가 TSD를 인수하면, 당연히 시장 점유율을 확대할 수 있어요. 하지만 여전히 업계에서 가장 큰 회사가 되지는 못합니다.

남 맞아요. 하지만 전 이 회사를 사는 게 옳은 결정인지 모르겠어요. 왜냐하면 우리는 이미 두 번째로 큰 회사이고 TSD의 수익이 작년에 20퍼센트 감소했다고 들었어요, 게다가 차트에서 알 수 있듯이 익스트림은 아직 우리에게 위협이 못 되거든요.

여 음, 당신 말에 확실히 일리가 있네요. 다음 주에 있을 이사회에서 이것에 대해 더 이야기해 보는 게 좋겠어요.

P65

Questions 71-73 refer to the following demonstration. 영W

If you enjoy fresh fruit juice but don't have enough time to make it every morning, ⑰ try our new juicer, the Rocher. ⑫ This incredible juicer makes fresh drinks in no time. And thanks to the Quick Clean function, it can also be cleaned in just one minute. Today, ⑬ we will provide every participant here with a drink recipe book at the end of the demonstration. You can make various cocktail fruit drinks and healthy vegetable drinks at home. ⑬ Don't forget to pick up a complimentary copy on your way out. Okay, now let's get started.

여러분이 생과일주스를 즐기긴 하는데 매일 아침 만들 시간이 충분치 않다면, 저희의 새로운 주서기인 로셔를 사용해 보세요. 이 놀라운 주서기는 신선한 음료를 순식간에 만들어 냅니다. 그리고 빠른 세척 기능 덕분에 일 분 안에 세척할 수 있습니다. 오늘 시연이 끝날 때에 여기 있는 모든 참석자에게 음료 레시피 책을 제공할 겁니다. 집에서 다양한 칵테일 과일 음료와 건강한 채소 주스를 만드실 보실 수 있습니다. 나가시는 길에 잊지 말고 무료 레시피 책을 가져가세요. 자, 그럼 이제 시작하겠습니다.

여휘 juicer 주스기, 즙 짜는 기계   incredible 믿을 수 없는, 엄청난   in no time 즉시   demonstration 시연, 시범 설명   complimentary 무료의   payment 지급, 납부   certificate 증서, 증명서   distribute 분배하다

**71** What kind of product is being demonstrated?
(A) A vacuum cleaner
(B) A coffee machine
(C) A steam cooker
**(D) A juice maker**

시연되는 제품은 무엇인가?
(A) 진공청소기
(B) 커피 기계
(C) 스팀 요리기
**(D) 주스기**

**72** What is special about the product?
**(A) Its speed**
(B) Its size
(C) Its price
(D) Its design

제품에 관해 특별한 점은 무엇인가?
**(A) 속도**
(B) 크기
(C) 가격
(D) 디자인

**73** What will happen at the end of the demonstration?
(A) A payment will be made.
(B) Certificates will be distributed.
(C) Drinks will be served.
**(D) Complimentary books will be given.**

시연이 끝날 때 무슨 일이 있을 것인가?
(A) 돈을 지불한다.
(B) 증명서가 교부된다.
(C) 음료가 제공된다.
**(D) 무료 책자가 제공된다.**

패러프레이징 a complimentary copy → Complimentary books

---

Questions 74-76 refer to the following telephone message. 호M

Hello. This is Chuck from the maintenance department calling for Alice Parker. It's 1:30 P.M. on Monday. ⑭ The light bulbs you reported have been replaced and they work fine now. I know that you also wanted to have the projector in the conference room fixed. So I arranged a visit from the manufacturer. They told me that the repair would be complete before ⑮ your presentation scheduled for Thursday. But if it takes more time, you can alternatively use the projector in the auditorium. ⑯ Contact me at extension 313 if you have any questions. Thank you.

안녕하세요. 저는 유지 관리부의 척이고 앨리스 파커 씨에게 메시지 남깁니다. 현재 월요일 오후 1시 30분입니다. 알려주셨던 전구는 교체되었고 이제 잘 됩니다. 회의실에 있는 프로젝터 역시 수리를 요청하신 것으로 아는데, 제가 제조업체 방문 약속을 잡아놓았습니다. 그들 말로는 목요일로 예정된 발표 전에는 수리가 완료될 거라고 합니다. 그러나 수리에 시간이 더 필요하게 되다면 강당에 있는 프로젝터를 대신 쓰셔 됩니다. 다른 궁금한 점이 있으시면 내선 313으로 제게 연락 주세요. 감사합니다.

여휘 maintenance department 유지 관리부   light bulb 전구   report 신고하다, 보고하다   replace 교체하다   alternatively 그 대신에   projector 영사기   manufacturer 제조업체   auditorium 강당   extension 내선   do research 조사하다

**74** Why is the speaker calling?
**(A) To discuss some maintenance work**
(B) To schedule a visit
(C) To ask about a presentation
(D) To make a complaint

화자가 전화를 거는 이유는 무엇인가?
**(A) 수리 업무에 관해 이야기하려고**
(B) 방문 일정을 잡으려고
(C) 발표에 관해 질문하려고
(D) 불평을 하려고

**75** When will the listener give a presentation?
(A) On Monday
(B) On Tuesday
**(C) On Thursday**
(D) On Friday

청자는 언제 발표를 하는가?
(A) 월요일
(B) 화요일
**(C) 목요일**
(D) 금요일

**76** What should Ms. Parker do if she has a question?
(A) Read a manual
**(B) Speak to a coworker**
(C) Call a repair shop
(D) Do research online

질문이 있다면 파커 씨는 어떻게 해야 하는가?
(A) 사용설명서를 읽는다.
**(B) 동료에게 이야기한다.**
(C) 수리점으로 전화한다.
(D) 온라인으로 조사한다.

---

Questions 77-79 refer to the following advertisement. 미M

⑰ Toto Motors is delighted to unveil its latest lightweight vehicle, the Bravo 2. This sporty compact model is ideal for those who travel around the city. ⑱ It has extremely low gas consumption even in heavy traffic. And the streamlined design means that you can move around town quickly. And because it runs on diesel, you spend less money for more mileage. ⑲ This month only, Toto Motors is offering free air conditioning and an inbuilt multi-disc CD player with all models purchased. Check out the offers on www.toto.com and book a test drive today.

토토 모터스의 최신 경량 경차, 브라보 2를 소개하게 되어 기쁩니다. 이 스포티한 소형 모델은 시내 주행을 하는 사람들에게 이상적입니다. 이 차는 차가 막힐 때에도 기름이 아주 적게 듭니다. 그리고 날렵한 디자인은 시내를 빠르게 이동할 수 있음을 의미합니다. 또한, 디젤 차량이기 때문에 주행 거리는 더 길면서 돈이 덜 듭니다. 이달 한 달만, 토토 모터스는 구매된 모든 모델에 무료 에어컨과 내장형 멀티디스크 CD 플레이어를 제공합니다. www.toto.com에서 이 혜택을 확인하시고, 오늘 시승을 예약하세요.

여휘 delighted 아주 기뻐하는   unveil 드러내다, 발표하다   lightweight 경량의   vehicle 경차   sporty 빠르고 날렵한   compact 작은   ideal 이상적인   extremely 극히, 극도로   gas consumption 가스 소모량   streamlined 유선형의, 날씬한   mileage 주행 거리   inbuilt 내장된, 내장형   test drive 시승(하다)   water purifier 정수기   affordable 가격이 적당한   double seater 2인승   warranty 품질 보증

**77** What product is being advertised?
(A) An air conditioner
(B) A water purifier
**(C) A compact car**
(D) A mobile phone

광고하고 있는 제품은 무엇인가?
(A) 에어컨
(B) 정수기
**(C) 소형차**
(D) 휴대폰

**패러프레이징** lightweight vehicle → A compact car

**78** What is emphasized about the product?
(A) It is easy to use.
**(B) It uses less fuel.**
(C) It is affordable.
(D) It is a double seater.

제품에 관하여 강조하고 있는 것은 무엇인가?
(A) 사용하기 쉽다.
**(B) 보다 적은 연료가 소모된다.**
(C) 가격이 적정하다.
(D) 2인승이다.

**패러프레이징** extremely low gas consumption → uses less fuel

**79** What can customers receive this month without charge?
**(A) A sound system**
(B) A gift card
(C) An extra battery
(D) A two-year warranty

이번 달에 고객들이 무료로 받게 될 것은 무엇인가?
**(A) 음향 장치**
(B) 상품권
(C) 여분의 배터리
(D) 2년 보증

**패러프레이징** an inbuilt multi-disc CD player → A sound system

---

**Questions 80-82** refer to the following instructions. 호M

Good morning, everyone. Thanks for attending the staff training on ⑧ our online ordering system. I'm Ernie Stevens and I'll be your instructor for the next five sessions. As you already know, ⑧ a huge number of our orders are made online, so it's essential that you process them with accuracy. On the upper left hand side of your screen, you will see an "Orders" category. If you click on it, you will see the orders received in chronological order. However, you have to rearrange them by size so the larger orders can be seen at the top. We do that because larger orders usually take an extra day to be shipped. Oh and... don't worry about invoices. ⑧ They will be printed automatically when the process is complete. Now, ⑧ let me show you how to check the stock of the requested products.

여러분 안녕하세요. 온라인 주문 시스템에 관한 직원 교육에 참석해 주셔서 감사합니다. 저는 어니 스티븐스이며 앞으로 다섯 번의 수업을 할 강사입니다. 아시다시피, 엄청나게 많은 수의 주문이 온라인에서 이루어지고 있기 때문에 그 주문을 정확하게 처리하는 것이 필수적입니다. 화면 왼쪽 위를 보시면 '주문'이라는 항목이 보이실 겁니다. 그것을 클릭하시면 시간 순서대로 주문을 받은 것을 볼 수 있습니다. 하지만 여러분은 그것들을 크기별로 재배열해서 더 큰 주문들이 위에 보이게 해 주셔야 합니다. 그렇게 하는 이유는 더 큰 주문들은 보통 배송되는 데 하루가 더 걸리기 때문입니다. 오 그리고, 송장은 걱정 마세요. 절차가 끝나면 자동으로 인쇄가 되니까요. 그럼 이제 요청된 제품의 재고를 확인하는 방법 보여 드리겠습니다.

**어휘** instructor 강사  session 수업  huge 엄청난  essential 필수적인  process 처리하다  accuracy 정확성  chronological 시간 순의  rearrange 재배열하다  upper 위쪽의  category 항목  invoice 송장  personnel 인사과  inventory 재고  defective 결함이 있는  stock 재고

**80** What department are the listeners probably working for?
**(A) Sales**
(B) Advertising
(C) Planning
(D) Personnel

청자들은 어떤 부서에서 근무하겠는가?
**(A) 영업부**
(B) 광고부
(C) 기획부
(D) 인사부

**81** What does the speaker imply when he says, "don't worry about invoices"?
(A) Workers are supposed to rearrange invoices.
**(B) Invoices are taken care of automatically.**

---

(C) It is easy to operate a printing machine.
(D) A training session will be provided.

화자가 '송장은 걱정 마세요'라고 말한 의미는 무엇인가?
(A) 직원들이 다시 송장을 분류해야 한다.
**(B) 송장은 자동으로 처리된다.**
(C) 프린팅 기계를 작동시키는 것은 쉽다.
(D) 교육이 제공될 것이다.

**82** What is the speaker going to teach next?
(A) How to fix a printer
(B) How to ship products
**(C) How to find the inventory**
(D) How to handle defective products

화자가 다음에 가르칠 것은 무엇인가?
(A) 인쇄기 고치는 법
(B) 물품 발송하는 법
**(C) 재고 찾는 법**
(D) 결함 있는 제품 처리하는 법

**패러프레이징** check the stock → find the inventory

---

**Questions 83-85** refer to the following announcement. 영W

Welcome, everyone. ⑧ We are very pleased that you could join us for tonight's ceremony to celebrate the grand reopening of the newly renovated Dionside Town Hall. First, I would like to extend my gratitude to those who have made donations to support the renovation project. Thanks to your generosity, all of the windows and doors have been replaced. And we were able to install a new heating system for the entire building. Now, please feel free to look around. Take your time and join us for a small buffet in the main hall, ⑧ where food has been provided by a local restaurant. Finally, don't forget to sign up for our monthly newsletter ⑧ which details all the upcoming events taking place at the Town Hall.

환영합니다 여러분. 감사하게 보수된 디온사이드 타운 홀의 재개장을 축하하기 위한 오늘 저녁 행사에 함께해 주셔서 기쁩니다. 먼저, 이 보수 프로젝트를 지원하기 위해서 기부해 주신 모든 분들께 감사를 전하고 싶습니다. 여러분의 후한 기부 덕분에, 모든 창문과 문이 교체되었습니다. 그리고 건물 전체를 위한 새로운 난방 장치를 설치할 수 있었습니다. 이제 편하게 함께하실 둘러보세요. 천천히 보시고 그 메인 홀에 준비된 간소한 뷔페에 함께해 주세요. 지역 식당에서 제공한 음식이 마련되어 있습니다. 마지막으로, 타운 홀에서 열릴 다가올 모든 행사에 대한 상세한 정보가 담긴 월간 소식지를 잊지 말고 신청하세요.

**어휘** extend one's gratitude 감사를 전하다  donation 기부금  generosity 후함, 관대함  heating system 난방 장치  sign up for 신청하다  newsletter 소식지  detail 상세히 다루다  upcoming 다가오는, 곧 있을  official 공무원 관리  function 행사

**83** What is being celebrated?

(A) The opening of a restaurant
**(B) The completion of renovation**
(C) The success of a venture business
(D) The purchase of a facility

축하하고 있는 것은 무엇인가?
(A) 식당의 개장
**(B) 리모델링의 완료**
(C) 벤처 기업의 성공
(D) 시설의 구매

**84** According to the speaker, who provided food?

**(A) A local food establishment**
(B) A financial contributor
(C) A town hall official
(D) A well-known author

화자에 따르면, 누가 음식을 제공했는가?
**(A) 지역 식당**
(B) 재정 기부자
(C) 시청 공무원
(D) 유명한 저자

패러프레이징 a local restaurant → A local food establishment

**85** What is mentioned about the newsletter?

(A) It is sent out weekly.
(B) It contains all staff information.
**(C) It includes upcoming functions.**
(D) It has a list of donors.

소식지에 관하여 언급된 것은 무엇인가?
(A) 매주 발송된다.
(B) 모든 직원 정보를 포함한다.
**(C) 다가오는 행사들을 포함한다.**
(D) 기부자들의 명단이 있다.

패러프레이징 upcoming events → upcoming functions

**86** What is the woman waiting for?

(A) Her hotel room to be cleaned
**(B) Her luggage to be retrieved**
(C) Her itinerary to be printed out
(D) Her colleagues to arrive

여자는 무엇을 기다리고 있는가?
(A) 호텔방이 청소되기를
**(B) 짐을 되찾기를**
(C) 여행 일정이 인쇄되기를
(D) 동료들이 도착하기를

**87** What problem is being discussed?

(A) A factory inspection will be conducted.
(B) The woman has missed a connecting flight.
**(C) A product presentation won't be successful.**
(D) In-flight meals were not good.

어떤 문제점이 이야기되고 있는가?
(A) 공장 검열이 진행될 것이다.
(B) 여자는 연결 항공편을 놓쳤다.
**(C) 상품 발표가 성공적이지 못할 것이다.**
(D) 기내 식사가 좋지 않았다.

---

Questions 86-88 refer to the following telephone message. [미W]

Hi, Michael. It's Carol. I'm in a tough situation right now. ⑧ The airline lost my luggage and the model of our new 3D printer. I've been waiting for 3 hours now but nothing has been found yet. Honestly, I don't expect the airline to find either my luggage or the prototype anytime soon, considering the poor service I've had so far. ⑧ The thing is, my presentation is scheduled for tomorrow morning and I don't think I can make much of an impression without a prototype. ⑧ Perhaps it would be best if you fly in here yourself with a backup model. | know it is last minute, but I don't have much choice.

안녕하세요, 마이클. 캐롤이에요. 제가 지금 좀 곤란한 상황에 처했어요. 저 항공사가 우리 신상품의 3D 프린터의 시제품을 항공사에서 분실했어요. 제가 3시간째 기다리고 있는데 아직 아무것도 찾지를 못했어요. 솔직히 제가 지금까지 받은 형편없는 서비스를 감안하면, 항공사에서 제 짐이든 시제품이든 곧 찾을 거라고는 생각이 안 들어요. 문제는 저의 발표가 내일 아침으로 잡혀 있는데 시제품이 없이는 발표에서 좋은 인상을 줄 수가 없을 것 같아요. 아무래도 당신이 직접 여분의 시제품을 가지고 이곳으로 와 주시는 것이 제일 좋을 것 같아요. 지도 갑작스럽다는 건 알지만 선택의 여지가 별로 없네요.

어휘 model 견본, 시제품 prototype 시제품 last minute 막판 retrieve 되찾다 inspection 검열 inspection 검열 considering ~을 감안할 때 in-flight 기내의

---

**88** Why does the woman say, "I know it is last minute"?

(A) To remind the listener to plan carefully
(B) To explain some changes in detail
**(C) To apologize for an inconvenience**
(D) To advise the listener to leave soon

여자가 "지도 갑작스럽다는 건 알지만"이라고 말한 이유는 무엇인가?
(A) 청자에게 신중하게 계획할 것을 상기시켜 주기 위해
(B) 변경 사항을 자세히 설명하기 위해
**(C) 불편에 대해 사과하기 위해**
(D) 청자에게 빨리 떠나라고 권하기 위해

---

Questions 89-91 refer to the following excerpt from a meeting. [호M]

Good afternoon, everyone. Thanks for attending our last marketing meeting before ⑧ we release our new mystery movie, *The Strange Wizard*, this Saturday. I'm glad to tell you that ⑨ more than 20,000 tickets were sold through advance reservations. I'm sure it will be a great success, and ⑩ it's all because of your selfless dedication and hard work. I really appreciate it. Now, there's one last thing I need to ask of you. On the eve of the release date, we'll be holding a press preview in our auditorium and more than 30 reporters will show up. So I need volunteers to make arrangements for that. ⑨ Joshua Lee has the list of what needs to be done, so those who are willing to give a hand, please go see him by the end of the day. Thank you.

여러분 안녕하세요. 우리의 새로운 미스터리 영화 (이상한 마법사)를 이번 토요일에 개봉하기 전 가지는 마지막 마케팅 회의입니다. 사전 예약으로 2만 장 이상의 표가 팔렸다는 것을 알려 드리게 되어 기쁩니다. 분명히 큰 성공을 거두리라 확신하고 그 여러분이 열심히 헌신적으로 일해준 덕분입니다. 진심으로 고맙습니다. 이제, 여러분의 도움이 필요한 마지막 한 가지 있어요. 개봉 전날 우리는 강당에서 언론 시사회를 가질 예정인데 30명 이상의 기자들이 참석할 것입니다. 그래서 그 행사 준비를 위한 자원봉사자가 필요합니다. 조수아 리가 해야 될 일에 대한 목록을 가지고 있으므로 도움을 주고 싶으신 분들은 오늘 퇴근 전까지 가서 만나시기 바랍니다. 감사합니다.

어휘 release 개봉하다 advance 사전의 selfless 자신을 돌보지 않는 dedication 헌신 press preview 언론 시사회 auditorium 강당 give a hand 도와주다 association 협회 on behalf of ~을 대신해서

---

**89** Where does the speaker probably work?

(A) A film directors' association
(B) A publishing firm
**(C) A movie company**
(D) A community center

화자는 어디에서 근무하는가?
(A) 영화감독 협회
(B) 출판사

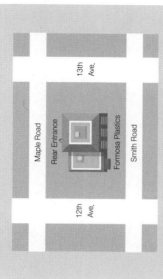

(C) It specializes in custom-design cakes.
(D) Its hours of operation have changed.

빵집에 대해 무엇이 언급되었는가?
(A) 빵을 온라인으로 판매한다.
(B) 대중에게 제빵 수업을 제공한다.
(C) 주문 제작 케이크를 전문으로 한다.
(D) **영업 시간이 변경되었다.**
패러프레이징 our business hours → Its hours of operation

**Questions 95-97** refer to the following announcement and city map. (9M)

Attention, Formosa Plastics employees. I'd like to remind you that 95 the Annual Westlake Marching Festival will be held in two days. Bands and performers will be marching in a parade through the city streets. 96 Please keep in mind that the street in front of the rear entrance of our building will be closed from 7 A.M. until 12 midnight. The other streets around the building will remain open but traffic congestion is expected because of the festival. 97 So please allow extra time for your commute on that day.

---

(C) 영화사
(D) 지역 자치 센터

**90** What does the speaker thank the employees for?
(A) **The efforts to make a successful film**
(B) A website that was launched successfully
(C) Good reviews from critics
(D) A successful conference that was held recently
화자가 직원들을 칭찬하는 이유는 무엇인가?
(A) **성공적인 영화를 만들기 위한 노력**
(B) 성공적으로 시작된 웹 사이트
(C) 비평가들로부터 받은 호평
(D) 최근에 개최된 성공적인 회의
패러프레이징 your selfless dedication and hard work → The efforts

**91** Why does the speaker mention Joshua Lee?
(A) **He will show volunteers what to do.**
(B) He will meet reporters on behalf of the company.
(C) He will be away for volunteer service.
(D) He will be in charge of a branch office.
화자가 조슈아 리를 언급하는 이유는 무엇인가?
(A) **그가 자원봉사자들에게 할 일을 보여 줄 것이다.**
(B) 그가 회사를 대표해 기자들을 만날 것이다.
(C) 자원봉사 관계로 자리를 비울 것이다.
(D) 지점의 책임을 맡게 될 것이다.

**Questions 92-94** refer to the following recorded message and order form. (9W)

| Order Form | |
| --- | --- |
| ITEM | QUANTITY |
| Cookie Tray | 20 |
| Dozen Mini-Cupcakes | 100 |
| Fruit Tart | 50 |
| Classic Brownie | 150 |

Hello. This message is for Robert Garcia. Mr. Garcia, it is Catherine calling from Sweet Flour Bake Shop. I'm calling to confirm your monthly order before I start baking. 92 You ordered ten times more mini-cupcakes than you usually do. I thought it was a typo so I corrected the number to 10 dozen as usual. Please give me a call if that is not okay. 93 I'll wait until 5 P.M. before I bake them. Oh, by the way, 94 our business hours have changed. Our hours on Mondays are now from 1 P.M. to 8 P.M., and the other days remain the same.

---

| 주문서 | |
| --- | --- |
| 상품 | 수량 |
| 상자 쿠키 | 20 |
| 미니 컵케이크 12개 | 100 |
| 과일 타르트 | 50 |
| 클래식 브라우니 | 150 |

안녕하세요, 로버트 가르시아에게 메시지를 남깁니다. 가르시아 씨, 저는 스위트 플라워 베이크 숍의 캐서린입니다. 빵을 굽기 전에 당신의 월간 주문을 확인하려고 전화했는데요. 평소보다 미니 컵케이크를 열 배나 더 주문을 하셨더군요. 오타라고 생각되어 제가 수량을 평소대로 열 두 개짜리 열 묶음으로 고쳤습니다. 만약에 이게 맞지 않다면 전화를 주세요. 저녁 5시까지 기다렸다가 빵을 굽도록 하겠습니다. 오, 그리고 영업 시간이 변경되었습니다. 매주 월요일 영업 시간이 이제부터는 오후 1시에서 8시까지이고 다른 요일은 그대로입니다.

어휘 typo 오타 dozen 열 두 개짜리 묶음 business hours 영업 시간 leave for the day 퇴근하다 specialize in ~을 전문으로 하다 custom-design 주문 제작

**92** Look at the graphic. According to the speaker, which quantity of the order form is probably incorrect?
(A) 20
(B) **100**
(C) 50
(D) 150
시각 자료를 보시오. 화자에 따르면 주문서의 어떤 수량이 부정확할 것 같은가?
(A) 20
(B) **100**
(C) 50
(D) 150

**93** What does the woman say she will do at 5 P.M.?
(A) She will give a demonstration.
(B) She will leave for the day.
(C) **She will do some baking.**
(D) She will create a cake recipe.
여자는 오후 5시에 무엇을 할 것이라고 하는가?
(A) 시연회를 할 것이다.
(B) 퇴근할 것이다.
(C) **빵을 구울 것이다.**
(D) 케이크 레시피를 만들 것이다.

**94** What is mentioned about the bakery?
(A) It sells baked goods online.
(B) It offers baking classes to the public.

포모사 플라스틱 직원 여러분, 잠깐만 주목해 주세요. 이틀 후에 연례 행사인 웨스트리
이크 시가 향토 축제가 열립니다. 밴드와 공연자들이 도르를 가로질러 퍼레이드
행진을 하게 될 텐데요, 우리 건물 후문 앞의 도로도 아침 7시부터 차정까지 폐
쇄된다는 것을 기억해 주세요. 건물 주변의 다른 도로들은 열려 있겠지만 축제
로 인해 교통 체증이 예상됩니다. 그러니 그 다용에는 통근 시간을 여유 있게 가
지십시오

**어휘** march 시가 행진하다　keep in mind that ~을 기억하다　rear
entrance 후문　traffic congestion 교통 체증　commute 통근　
function 행사

**95** What is scheduled to happen in two days?
(A) A street repair
**(B) An annual event**
(C) A corporate function
(D) A staff meeting

이틀 후에 무엇이 있을 것인가?
(A) 도로 공사
**(B) 연례 행사**
(C) 기업 행사
(D) 직원 미팅

**96** Look at the graphic. Which street will be blocked?
**(A) Maple Road**
(B) 12th Avenue
(C) 13th Avenue
(D) Smith Road

시각 자료를 보시오. 어떤 도로가 폐쇄될 것인가?
**(A) 메이플 도로**
(B) 12번가
(C) 13번가
(D) 스미스 도로

**97** What are the employees advised to do?
(A) Use public transportation
(B) Participate in a local festival
**(C) Allow more time for travel**
(D) Finish their assignments early

직원들은 무엇을 할 것을 권고받는가?
(A) 대중교통을 이용할 것
(B) 지역 축제에 참여할 것
**(C) 이동에 더 많은 시간을 잡을 것**
(D) 업무를 일찍 끝낼 것

**패러프레이징** allow extra time for your commute → Allow more
time for travel

---

Questions 98-100 refer to the following talk and schedule. 호M

| Workshops | Date |
|---|---|
| Communication Skills | March 10 |
| Résumé Clinic | April 7 |
| Second Career Information | May 12 |
| Using Social Networking | June 9 |

98 I'm very pleased that so many of you have signed up
for the employment services workshops our center offers. I'd like to
inform you of a change in our schedule. 99 The workshop
scheduled for June 9 has been canceled at the request of
the guest speaker. However, we do have a session next
month in May. As indicated in the program, each workshop
includes lunch, 100 so sandwiches and coffee will be
provided after the morning session.

| 워크숍 | 날짜 |
|---|---|
| 의사소통 기술 | 3월 10일 |
| 이력서 클리닉 | 4월 7일 |
| 제2의 직업 정보 | 5월 12일 |
| 소셜 네트워킹의 활용 | 6월 9일 |

이렇게 많은 분들이 저희 센터가 제공하는 고용 지원 서비스 워크숍에 등록해
주셔서 기쁩니다. 이력서 클리닉에 관한 오늘의 수업을 시작하기 앞서, 일정 변
경 사항에 대해 알려 드리겠습니다. 6월 9일로 잡혀 있는 워크숍은 초청 연사의
요청으로 취소되었습니다. 그러나 다음 달인 5월에는 수업이 있습니다. 프로그
램에 명시된 대로, 각 워크숍에는 점심이 포함되어 있어서 아침 수업 후에는 샌
드위치와 커피가 제공될 것입니다.

**어휘** sign up for 등록하다, 신청하다　employment services 고용 지원 서비
스　at the request of ~의 요청으로　show up 오다, 나타나다　course
material 수업 자료

**98** Why is the speaker pleased?
(A) An event has been added.
(B) A center has been remodeled.
**(C) A lot of participants have shown up.**
(D) A famous author is giving a speech.

왜 화자는 기뻐하는가?
(A) 행사가 추가되었다.
(B) 센터가 보수되었다.
**(C) 많은 참가자들이 왔다.**
(D) 유명한 작가가 연설을 할 것이다.

**99** Look at the graphic. Which session has been canceled?
(A) Communication Skills
(B) Résumé Clinic
(C) Second Career Information
**(D) Using Social Networking**

시각 자료를 보시오. 어떤 워크숍이 취소되었는가?
(A) 의사소통 기술
(B) 이력서 클리닉
(C) 제2의 직업 정보
**(D) 소셜 네트워킹의 활용**

**100** What will happen after the morning session?
(A) Course materials will be provided.
(B) A tour will be given.
(C) A guest speaker will be introduced.
**(D) Some food will be served.**

아침 수업 후에는 무슨 일이 있을 것인가?
(A) 수업 자료가 제공될 것이다.
(B) 견학이 제공될 것이다.
(C) 초청 연사가 소개될 것이다.
**(D) 음식이 제공될 것이다.**

**패러프레이징** sandwiches and coffee will be provided
→ Some food will be served

# PART 5

P68

**101 해석** 베일리 씨는 겨우 지난 8월에 회사에 들어와서 생산성을 늘리고 직원들의 사기를 향상시키기 위해 이미 많은 일을 하고 있다.

**해설** 문장의 주어는 Ms. Bailey이며 빈칸은 joined the firm ~과 is already doing ~의 두 개의 동사구를 연결하고 있다. 따라서 빈칸은 접속사 자리이고, 문맥상 '그리고'의 의미인 (C)가 적절하다.

**어휘** join a firm 회사에 들어가다  productivity 생산성  employee morale 직원들의 사기

**102 해석** 전문가들과 정부 관료들로 구성된 위원회는 그 나라의 경제가 기업에 새롭게 설립된 세금법의 영향에 대해서 이야기할 것이다.

**해설** 문장의 동사는 will be talking about이기 때문에 빈칸에는 형용사 역할을 하는 현재분사가 와야 하며 동사형인 (B), (D)는 올 수 없다. 빈칸 뒤 '구성된'이라는 의미로 사용되어서 수동태인 ~형을 만드로써 해석되므로 정답은 (C)이다.

**어휘** committee 위원회  specialist 전문가  newly established 신설의  tax law 세금법

**103 해석** 빌딩 앤 컨스트럭트는 그 사업이 높은 수요와 다양한 서비스 범위 때문에 대체적으로 건설의 특정 분야를 전문으로 하는 작은 회사들에게 그 일을 하도급을 줄것이다.

**해설** 문장의 동사는 subcontracts로 현재 시제이다. 선택지 중에 현재 시제일 때 쓸 수 있는 부사로 usually, normally, regularly, often, always, generally, typically 등이 있다. 따라서 정답은 (D)이다.

**어휘** subcontract 하도급을 주다  specialize in ~을 전문으로 하다  certain 확실한, 어떤  owing to+명사 ~ 때문에  demand 수요

**104 해석** 타임즈 씨의 보고서는 부수적인 세부 사항들이 너무 많이 포함되어 있어서 읽기 어렵다.

**해설** 임워의 형용사를 선택하는 문제로, 보고서가 읽기 어렵다는 것은 부수적인 세부 사항들이 많아서라는 것이 적절하다. 따라서 정답은 (D)이다. (A) 충분한 / (B) 줄어드는 / (C) 전체의

**어휘** incidental 부수적인  complete 완벽한

**105 해석** 그 연락처를 전달받아야 하는 각각의 담당자들이 이 스프레드시트에 열거되어 있다.

**해설** 선행사가 사람이고 빈칸 뒤의 목적어가 없으므로 목적격 관계 대명사 (C) whom을 써야 한다; where는 관계부사로 뒤에 완전한 문장이 와야 한다. what은 선행사를 포함해서 the thing that의 의미이기 때문에 답이 될 수 없다. 복합관계대명사인 whoever는 문장에서 명사절이나 부사절의 역할을 하고 선행사를 갖지 않는다.

**어휘** respective 각자의, 각각의  contact information 연락처

**106 해석** 올해 매출액은 과거 2년 동안의 각각 기록된 매출액과 거의 같았다.

**해설** 올해와 과거 2년 동안의 매출액을 비교하고 있으므로 두 개를 비교해 같다는 의미의 (B)가 가장 알맞다. equal로 뒤에 전치사 to가 붙어 지 주 사용되며, 이와 비슷하게 superior, inferior도 전치사 to가 뒤에 붙는다. 빈칸 뒤의 those는 대명사로서 their sales figures와 비교하기 위해서 사용되었다. (A) 확실한 / (C) 공평한 / (D) 양이 균등한, 편평한

**어휘** sales figure 매출액  recorded 기록된

**107 해석** 이스턴 일렉트로닉 사는 지역 담당자들과 일을 함으로써 비용 효율적이고 환경 친화적인 방식으로 전략을 생산할 수 있는 능력을 확대시키고 있다.

**해설** 빈칸은 전치사의 자리로서 뒤에 〈주어+동사〉가 오는 부사절 접속사 (A) during 뒤에는 기간이나 시기를 나타내는 명사만 올 수 있다. (D)는 올 수 없고 ~함으로써 해석되므로 정답은 (B)이다.

**어휘** expand 확대하다  produce power 전략을 생산하다  in (a) ... fashion ~ 방식으로  cost-effective 비용 효율적인  environmentally friendly 환경 친화적인

**108 해석** 시장에서나 대형 공급과 기술 하락 덕분에 요즘 가장 저렴하게 구입 가능한 상품이다.

**해설** 비교급 강조 표현으로 much, even, far, still, a lot 등이 있으며, very는 주로 형용사나 부사를, well은 동사나 분사를 수식해 준다. 따라서 정답은 (D)이다.

**어휘** affordable 알맞은  thanks to ~ 덕분에  large supply 공급  lowering 하락

**109 해석** 그 위원회의 보이에 관한 보고서는 혹고 국가 예방책에 대해 매우 비판적이었다.

**해설** 형용사를 보어로 취하는 be동사가 있기 때문에 빈칸에는 형용사 와야 한다. 이외에도 형용사를 보어로 취하는 2형식 동사에는 appear (to be), become, feel, look, prove (to be), remain (to be), seem (to be), smell, sound, taste, turn out (to be) 등이 있다. 선택지에서 유일한 형용사는 (A)뿐이므로 (A)가 정답이다. (B) 비판으로, 이율이슬라하게

**어휘** commission 위원회  security 보안  critical 비판적인  safety precautions 안전 예방책

**110 해석** 그 회사는 나의 연락처를 업데이트함으로써 나와 연락하는 데 어떤 방해도 없을 것이다.

**해설** have p.p. 형태이 현재완료 시제를 묻는 문제로 받는데는 p.p. 형태인 (D) updated가 와야 한다. update는 타동사로서 뒤에 목적어를 갖는다.

**어휘** contact information 연락처  interruption 중단, 방해

**111 해석** 뉴스 보도에 따르면 모바일 제조사 애매코는 구형 모델을 중단하고 내년 초부터 세 모델을 소개할 것이다.

**해설** 문장에 동사가 없기 때문에 빈칸에 반드시는 동사가 들어가야 한다. 내년 초부터라는 표현이 있기 때문에 미래 시제인 (C)가 적절하다.

**어휘** manufacturer 제조업체  discontinue 중단하다  introduce 소개하다

**112 해석** 그랩 모터스 사는 올해 민족도 평가에서 편리함과 안전성 측면에서 최상점급을 받았다.

**해설** 두 가를 비교하는 경우 비교급, 세 개 이상을 비교하는 경우 최상급을 사용하며, 비교 대상은 대부분 than을 사용하다, 최상급으로 우리글로 '여러 개 중에'라는 뜻이며, 자주 사용되는 표현으로 have ever p.p. 형태의 현재완료 경험 용법이나 〈of+복수 명사/중에서〉, 〈in+장소〉, 그 뒤에 형용사 available, possible, ever 등이 있다. 올해의 차량 만족도 평가의 편리함과 안전성 측면에서 가장 높은 등급을 받았다는 의미이므로 (B)가 적절하다.

**어휘** earn 획득하다  rating 순위, 평가  safety 안정성  evaluation 평가

**113 해석** 그 새로운 호텔 웹 사이트는 우리의 직원들에게 이전의 버전보다 훨씬 더 유용하다.

**해설** 비교급 강조로 much, even, far, still, a lot 등이 있으며, very는 주로 형용사나 부사를, well은 동사와 분사를 수식해 준다. 따라서 정답은 (D)이다.

**어휘** previous 이전의  version 판, 형태

**114 해석** 졸업 신청서가 여름 학기 동안 7월 31일까지 제출되어야 한다. 그렇지 않으면 당신은 하위를 가을까지 기다려야 할 것이다.

**해설** ~까지를 의미하는 전치사는 until과 by가 있으며, by는 무언가를 제출할 때 마감 가능을 나타내는 것을 의미한다. 전치사 on은 요일이나 날짜 앞에 사용된다.

**어휘** application 지원서, 신청서  semester 학기  graduation 졸업  diploma 졸업장, 수료증

**115 해석** 다음 주 일요일부터 올해 월드컵 기념품이 온라인을 통해 팔릴 것이다.

**해설** 온라인상에서 기념품이 판매된다 의미이기 때문에 적절하므로 정답은 (A)이다. 조동사 will 다음에는 동사원형이 나와야 하기 때문에 sell selling은 답이 될 수 없다. have been sold는 수동태이기는 하나 지금부터 미래까지 판다는 미래완료가 아니라 다음 주부터 판다는 의미이기 때문에 답이 될 수 없다.

**어휘** memorabilia 기념품

**116 해석** 비디러 쇼핑몰의 전체 컴퓨터 시스템은 정전 때문에 중단되었다. 그러나 사람들은 운 좋게 그들의 주문을 작성이 다를 수 있는 종이 부서에에 사용할수 있었다.

**해설** 빈칸 뒤에 완전한 문장이 오기 때문에 〈주어+동사+목적어〉가 있는 완벽한 문장이기 때문에 빈칸에 들어갈 수 있는 동사는 문장 전체를 수식해 주는 부사밖에 없다.

선택지 중에서 부사는 fortunately밖에 없으므로 정답은 (A)이다. (B)은 제산 / (C) 운이 좋은

**어휘** go down 중단되다 on account of ~ 때문에 blackout 정전 receipt 영수증 direct 지도하다, 지시하다

**117 해석** 마커스 로건은 회사를 위해 매출을 확보하려 틱월한 재능을 보여 줘서 결국 스앤지 사에 일사한 지 2년 만에 승진하였다.

**해설** 빈칸 뒤에 ability와 자연스럽게 어울리고, 매출을 확보하려 '틱월한' 재능을 보여 승진을 할 수 있었다는 의미가 적절하므로 (A)가 정답이다. (D) whole에는 the, a(n), 소유격이 오며 (C) inclusive는 토에서라 담으로 줄 앞에는 적이 없으므로 참고한다. (B) 다수의 / (C) ~이 포함된

**어휘** exceptional secure 확보하다, 지키다 sales 매출 result in 그 결과 ~하다

**118 해석** 일본 스는 개인의 은퇴 기념 파티를 열기보다 오히려 직정에서 은퇴하는 직원들을 위해 연간 만찬을 후원한다.

**해설** 빈칸 뒤에 명사가 와서 반간에 명용사가 오는 것으로 처리하기 쉽지만 retirement party는 '은퇴 기념 파티'라는 의미의 복합 명사로 (D)가 정답이다.

**어휘** sponsor 후원하다 withdraw from ~에서 철수하다 retirement party 은퇴 기념 파티

**119 해석** 카일로 씨는 항상 직정에 지각했기 때문에 그의 상사로부터 질책을 받고 있다.

**해설** 전체적인 의미상 업무은 부사를 선택하는 문제이다. 직정에 항상 지각하기 때문에 상사로부터 질책을 받았다는 의미가 적절하므로 정답은 (A)이다. (C) 현자리, 현명하게 / (D) 착실하게, 꾸준하게

**어휘** consistently 끊임없이, 항상 reprimand 질책하다

**120 해석** 헬렌은 엠포리오 사이 영업 부정으로 근무하는 동안 매출을 거의 20퍼센트 올렸다.

**해설** during은 뒤에 명사가 오며 '~하는 동안'이라는 의미이다. 영업 부정으로 근무하는 동안이라는 의미가 자연스러우므로 정답은 (C)이다.

**어휘** sales manager 영업 부장

**121 해석** 해이티 사이 전디 워는 기계는 신뢰할 수 있을 만큼 무게가 가벼워 유명하다.

**해설** 전체적인 의미상 업무은 명사를 선택하는 문제다. 그 회사이 전디 워는 기계는 신뢰할 수 있을 만큼 가벼운 무게도 유명하다는 의미가 적절하므로 정답은 (A)이다. (B) 결심, 결정 / (C) 의무

**어휘** lawnmower 전디 워는 기계 be renowned for ~으로 유명하다 lightness 가벼움 as much as ~인 만큼 reliability 신뢰할 수 있음, 신뢰성

**122 해석** 새 하역정이 공사가 완성되었기 때문에 그 회사는 선적물을 더 효율적으로 처리할 수 있을 것이다.

**해설** 빈칸 뒤에 〈주어+동사)로 시작 문장이 나온 것으로 보아 반간에는 접 속사가 나와야 한다. 따라서 부사절 접속사인 '~이기 때문에'의 의미 의

---

를 뜻하는 (A)가 적절하다. (B), (D) 뒤에는 명사가 와야 한다.

**어휘** process 처리하다 shipment 수송 수송물 efficiently 효율적으로 construction 건설 공사 loading dock 하역장, 짐 싣는 곳

**123 해석** 두 회사이 자동화는 성능 면에서 겉은 번째 목표로 잡은 고객으로 다르다.

**해설** 빈칸 앞에 형용사를 보여로 취하는 be동사가 있기 때문에 반간에는 형용사가 와야 한다. (B) comparing을 형용사용으로 착각할 수 있는데 comparing은 형용사로 처리되지 않는다. 선택지 중에서 형용사를 보여로 취하는 2 형사 동사에는 appear(to be), become, feel, look, prove(to be), remain(to be), seem(to be), smell, sound, taste, turn out(to be) 등이 있다.

**어휘** automobile 자동차 comparable 비슷한, 비교할 만한 in terms of ~의 측면에서 performance 실적 수행 differ in[from] ~로 다르다 targeted 목표가 된

**124 해석** 차에서 주문하는 식당이 넓은 분석가들은 고객들이 습관 변화 때문에 주말 자세에는 더 늦게 문을 단는 것을 제안했다.

**해설** 동사 suggest는 동명사-ing를 목적어로 취하므로 (A)가 가장 적 절하다. 이와 비슷하게 동명사를 목적어로 취하는 동사에는 enjoy, finish, consider, give up, postpone, discontinue, dislike 등이 있다.

**어휘** drive-through 차에 탄 채로 이용할 수 있는

**125 해석** 도로 서비스 차량은 지속적으로 점검받아야 한다. 그렇지 않으면 극심 한 기상 조건 동안 도로를 작정하게 청소할 수 없는 위험을 겪을 것이 다.

**해설** 빈칸 뒤에 〈주어+동사)를 갖춘 것이 나올기 때문에 접속사가 와야 한 다. 선택지 중에서 접속사로 쓸 수 있는 것은 (D) or else뿐이며, 문맥 상 지속적으로 점검받아야 해야 '그렇지 않을 시'에 위험을 겪을 거라는 의미가 적절하다. (A) ~ 때문에 / (B) ~ 외에, 게다가

**어휘** vehicle 차량 constantly 끊임없이, 지속적으로 run the risk of ~의 위험을 무릅쓰다 properly 제대로, 적절히 extreme 극심한 weather conditions 기상 조건

**126 해석** 경제할 하위를 가진 사람들만이 그 일자리에 지격이 있다.

**해설** 경제할 하위를 가진 '사람들'이 그 일자리에 자격이 있다는 의미가 적절 하다. 대명사 those는 people 대신에 쓰기도 하므로 (A)가 정답이다. 문두에 있는 only는 only의 event나 길이 명사, 대명사, to do, -ing, 전명구, 부사구, 젊절 앞에 위치할 수 있다.

**어휘** degree 하위 be eligible for 자격이 있다 position 위치, 자리

**127 해석** 그 쇼핑몰은 고객들을 더욱 잘 응대하기 위해 24시간 영업하기로 결정 했다.

**해설** 고객을 더 잘 '대접한다는' 의미가 자연스러우므로 정답은 (D)이다. serve는 뒤에 목적어 customer가 와서 자주 쓰이는 것을 알아 둔다. (A) provide는 〈provide+사람+with+사물〉, 〈provide+사물+to+사

---

람〉 형태로 쓰이며 (B) offer는 4형식 동사로서 목적어를 2개 갖는다. (C) 반지하다, 반영하다

**어휘** stay open 영업하다

**128 해석** 알람이 울리는 경우에 모든 직원들은 엘레베이터 사용을 자제하고 지 정된 비상구로 움직여야 한다.

**해설** 〈in the event that+주어+동사), 〈in the event that+주어+동사)이므로 문 제에는 동사가 들어가야 한다. alarm이 단수이므로 주절의 시제가 현재 이기 때문에 반간에 (A) rings가 들어가야 한다.

**어휘** refrain from -ing ~을 삼가다 designated 지정된 emergency exit 비상구 in the event that ~할 경우에는 alarm 알람, 경보

**129 해석** 당신의 구매는 구입일로부터 1년 동안 회사의 제한된 보증 서비스를 보장받을 것이다.

**해설** '구입일로부터'는 의미로 받간 앞의 warranty와도 잘 어울리는 표 현이므로 정답은 (B)이며, 문어에 자주 사용되므로 외워 두면 좋다. (A) 엄장, 팩차 / (D) 소유하는 것

**어휘** purchase 구입, 구매 cover 보장하다 limited 제한된 warranty 품질 보증서

**130 해석** 연 씨는 당신이 회사 신제품의 디자인 결함에 대한 해결책을 낼 수 있을 것이라고 기대한다.

**해설** solution으로 뒤에 전치사 to가 붙어 '~에 대한 해결책'으로 (C)가 정 답이다. a solution to는 solution 뒤에 자주 사용되므로 기억해 두자. 이때 about을 사용하지 않는다는 점에 주의한다.

**어휘** craft 공들여 만들다 flaw 결함 latest 최신의

# PART 6

**[131-134]**

P71

로널드 실바토
182 루이스 스트리트
애클랜드, 오자랜드 30152

소중한 고객님께,

그란니즈 액세서리즈에서 인사드립니다. 저희 매장은 멋진 실을 위한 모든 가정과 공예가의 손으로 만들어진 장신구를 기대할 수 있습니다. 저희 가게의 모든 점원들은 귀하에서 구매에서 최고의 결정을 할 수 있도록 도와드리며 [132] 필수적인 기술들을 가지고 있다고 보장합니다. 훌륭한 제품들과 직원들이 귀하에게 저희 가게로부터 받을 수 있는 유일한 혜택은 아닙니다.

저희는 보증금 정책이 있습니다. [133] 이것은 고객들이 다른 가게에서 더 값비싼 가격에 같은 제품을 찾았을 때 환불을 보장하기 위한 것입니다. 그러나 저희는 귀하에서 그란니즈 액세서리즈보다 더 좋은 가격을 제공하는 [134] 단 하나의 가게도 찾을 수 없을 거라고 확신합니다.

더 많은 정보를 위해서 저희의 웹 사이트를 방문해 주세요. 귀하의 도움을 기대하며 즐거운 쇼핑을 기대합니다.

**어휘** greetings from ~로부터의 인사  accessory 장신구  assist 돕다  household 가정  handcrafted 수제품의  assure 보장하다  excellent 훌륭한  확신하는  guaranteed money policy 보증금 정책  confident 자신만만한, 확신하는

**131 해설** to부장사의 동사변형 자리로, 전체적인 의미상 앞뒤의 동사를 선택하는 문제다. 문맥상 가장과 패션 상품을 '구입할'이라는 의미가 적절하기 때문에 (D)가 정답이다.

**132 해설** 빈칸 뒤에 명사가 있기 때문에 빈칸에 반드시 명사를 수식하는 형용사가 와야 한다. 선택지 중에서 형용사는 (B) necessary뿐이다. (A)는 부사, (C)는 명사, (D)는 타동사 necessitate의 -ing형으로 적절하지 않다. (C) 필수품

**133 (A)** 이것은 고객들이 다른 가게에 더 값싼 가격에 같은 물품을 찾았을 때 환불을 보장하기 위한 것입니다.
(B) 고객들의 환불을 요청할 때 영수증을 가지고 와야 합니다.
(C) 이것은 할인되 제품 혹은 정가가 아닌 제품에는 해당되지 않습니다.
(D) 고객들이 인터넷 상품을 구매할 때 가격을 유지하는 것이 중요합니다.

**해설** 앞에서 guaranteed money back policy가 이에 대한 설명이 와야 한다. 그리고 빈칸 뒤에는 역접을 나타내는 접속부사 However로 시작하며 그란니즈 액세서리즈보다 싼 가격의 제품을 찾을 수 없을 것이라고 했으므로 더 싼 가격의 제품을 찾으면 환불을 보장한다는 (A)가 가장 적절하다.

**어휘** claim 요구하다

**134 해설** 판매상 가격을 제공하는 '단 하나의 가게도 찾을 수 없다'라는 스러므로 (B)가 정답이다. (A) 적절한 / (C) 귀중한 / (D) 작은, 시소한

---

**[135-138]**

우선, 저희의 최고 상품인 VUS 1025를 귀하에게 제공함을 기쁘게 가지게 되어서 기쁩니다. 지금 저희 회사는 수십 년간 해온 출제작과 고객 관리 시스템으로 유명합니다. 이 편지는 귀하에게 구입하신 장비를 잘 잘 [135] 다루기 위해서 사용 받을 수 있을 잘 이해하는 데 도움을 주기 위함입니다.

귀하에게 받으신 제품은 저희 회사가 생산하는 가장 정교하지만 섬세한 기계들 중 하나입니다. 오랫동안 이 기계를 사용하기 위해서 제품을 청소상할 때 표면이 가치 천이 사용을 삼가기를 권해드립니다.

[137] 다음에, 그 제품을 방수가 인 된다는 것을 명심해 주세요. 어떤 종류를 알지 어느 능력이 담겨지지만, 위의 설명사를 따르는 것이 가장 바람직한 사용을 보장해 줄 거라고 자신의 자의 않게 잊을 수 있습니다.

고객들의 필요를 잘 이해하기 위해서 귀하의 의견을 제공해 주세요.

**어휘** valued 귀중한  thorough 철저한  for decades 수십 년간  care for 보살피다, 돌보다  equipment 장비  sophisticated 정교한, 복잡한  confidently 자신 있게  delicate 약한, 섬세한  spillage 엎지름  entirely 완전히  instruction 설명서  feedback 의견  rigorous 엄격한, 혹독한

**135 해설** 문맥상 구입한 장비를 잘 '다루는' 방식을 이해시키기 위해 이 편지를 보냈다는 것이 적절하므로 정답은 (B)이다. (A) 수영하다 / (C) 치루다 / (D) 바꾸다

**136 해설** 빈칸 앞에 전치사 with가 있고 뒤에 명사가 있는 것으로 보아 빈칸은 명사를 수식해 주는 형용사 자리다. 문맥상 표면이 '가친' 천으로 제품을 청소하는 것을 삼가한다는 의미가 적절하므로 정답은 (D)이다. (A) 철저한, 엄격한 / (B) 부드러운 / (C) 바던 같은, 부드러운

**137 해설**
(A) 매일 기계를 닦지 않아도 됩니다.
(B) 귀하가 구매한 제품은 2년어 품질 보증서가 함께 나옵니다.
(C) 표면이 물을 뿌리거나 물에 젖어 스론자를 이용하는 것이 가장 좋습니다.
**(D) 다음이, 그 제품은 방수가 인 된다는 것을 명심해 주세요.**

**해설** 빈칸 뒤에서 제품을 받기를 없게되면 심각한 손상을 입을 수 있다고 했으므로 빈칸에는 방수가 안 되니 조심하라는 내용의 (D)가 적절하다.

**어휘** on a daily basis 매일  keep in mind 명심하다  waterproof 방수의

**138 해설** that 뒤에 완전한 문장이 있으므로 빈칸은 동사의 자리다. 문맥상 설명서를 앞으로 따르는 것이 제품의 사용을 바람직하게 할 수 있다는 것이 적절하므로 미래 시제를 사용해야 한다. 따라서 정답은 (B)이다. (A)는 현재 완료로 과거부터 지금까지 함께 온 일을 나타낼 때 사용한다. (C)는 동사의 과거형으로 지나간 과거에 대해서 나타낼 때 사용한다. (D)는 to부정사로 빈칸에는 동사가 와야 하므로 적절하지 않다.

---

**[139-142]**

최근에, 저희의 회원 서비스분 귀하의 회원권이 다음 달에 [139] 만료될 거라고 알렸습니다. 저희의 연 회원에게만 제공하는 특별한 혜택을 귀하께서 놓치지 않도록 도와 드리기 위해서 이 알림을 보냅니다.

귀하께서 이것씩 회원들을 위한 휴게실 리모델링에 대한 또 하나의 통지를 받으셨기를 바랍니다. [140] 이 수리 때문에 그 장소는 6월 첫째 주에 폐쇄될 것입니다. 이 [141] 몇달에 보상하기 위해서 이 기간 동안 라운지 주와 앰들에게 15퍼센트의 비행기 티켓 할인을 제공할 것입니다.

귀하에게 저희의 회원 서비스에 [142] 등록되기를 원하신다면 가능한 한 빨리 저희에게 알려 주세요. 저희가 내에게 제공하는 놀라운 거래들을 귀하께서 놓치지 않기를 바랍니다!

질문이 있으시다면 고객 관리팀으로 부담 없이 연락 주세요.

**어휘** recently 최근에  notice 통지하다, 공고하다  notification 통지, 알림  exclusively 오로지, 독점적으로  yearly 연간의  previously 이전에  lounge 휴게실  compensate for 보상하다  amazing 놀라운  expire 만료되다  inconvenience 불편

**139 해설** 앞맥은 시제를 선택하는 문제로, expire는 단어 자체가 미래 시점에서 앞어날 일을 뜻하기 때문에 현재 시제인 (C)가 적절하다. (A)는 미래완료 시제로서 어떤 일이 미래의 완료되는 시점을 나타낸다. (B)는 수동태 형으로 회원권이 만료되는 다음 달에 만료된다고 했으므로 적절하지 않다. (D)는 과거 시제로 다음 달에 만료된다는 것과 맞지 않다.

**140**
(A) 휴게실은 소파가 구비되어 있으며 이틀라이 그림으로 장식되어 있습니다.
(B) 멤버들의 출발 전에 휴게실에 가입할 수 있습니다.
**(C) 이 수리 때문에 그 장소는 6월 첫째 주에 폐쇄될 것입니다.**
(D) 대표적인 수리 비용은 1,000달러랍니다.

**해설** 빈칸 뒤에 보상에 대한 내용이 나오고 이 기간 동안 폐쇄될 거라는 기간이 나오므로 특정 기간 동안 폐쇄될 거라는 (C)가 정답이다.

**어휘** renovation 개조

**141 해설** 앞 문장에서 수리 때문에 장소가 잠시 폐쇄될 것이라고 하고 있으므로 휴게실의 리모델링으로 인한 불편을 보상한다는 의미가 자연스럽다. 따라서 (A)가 정답이다. (C) 이점 / (D) 사용

**142 해설** 문맥상 회원 서비스에 등록하는 의미가 적절하고, 전치사 in과 결합해 등록하다'로 쓰이는 동사는 enroll뿐이므로 (B)가 정답이다. (A) 제외하다 / (C) 떠나다 / (D) 건주하다, 여기다

## [143-146]

1월 7일

댄 코디
1825 밸리 스트리트
세인트루이스, 미주리 주 39015

코디 씨에게

이 편지는 귀하께서 보내신 문의에 세부 사항을 확인하기 위해서 보내서졌습니다. 귀하께서 보내신 문의에 개인적인 만남을 위한 귀하의 (B) 요청을 받아들이고 귀한 자료는 케이시 씨에게서 개인적인 시간을 얻어야 합니다. 첫째, 이 모임에 관한 모든 정보는 적어도 모임이 있기 4일 전까지는 보좌관에 이메일 sleiosg@ pmail.com으로 (D) 보내져야 합니다. 또한, 취소할 경우에 귀하께서는 저희가 2일 전에 알 수 있게 미리 알려주셔야 합니다.

케이시 씨는 회사의 연례행사로 바쁠 것이기 때문에 그가 가능한 유일한 시간대는 1월 12일 오전 10시와 1월 21일 오전 11시입니다. 어느 날짜 시간대가 더 편한지 (C) 저희에게 알려 주세요.

무엇이 궁금하시든 케이시 씨에게 직접 연락하는 것은 삼가 주시고, 1-405-291-6281로 언제든 저와 통화할 수 있습니다.

실루 티마거 다림
SGLS 사

**어휘** confirm 확인하다 inform 알리다 spare 여분의, 힘에라다 strictly 엄격히 observe 준수하다 instruction 설명, 지시 사항 regarding ~에 관한 assistant 보조자, 협력자 prior to ~이전에 annual 연례의

**143 해설** 개인적인 미팅 '요청'을 받아들였으나는 내용이므로 (C)가 적절하다. (A) 하신 작업 / (D) 제출, 발표

**144 해설** 제안의 의미를 가진 동사가 나오면 that절에는 '~해야 한다'라는 의미를 가지는 제안의 조동사 (should+동사원형)을 쓰거나 should를 생략하고 동사원형을 써야 한다. 여기에서는 제안의 동사인 insist(주장하다)가 나왔기 때문에 that절에는 동사원형인 go가 와야 한다. 또한, 정보는 보내지는 것이므로 수동태형인 (C)가 적절하다. (A)는 동사의 단수형, (B)는 동사의 과거형, (D)는 명사로서 동사원형의 자리에는 작절하지 않다.

**145** (A) 필요한 정보는 다음 주 내로 귀하에게 주어질 것이다.
(B) 지시 사항들을 읽은 뒤 귀하는 서면으로 확인 편지를 보내야 합니다.
(C) 케이시 씨는 이메일 읽는 것을 좋아하지 않으므로 전화를 알고 계십시오.
**(D) 또한, 취소할 경우에 귀하께서는 저희가 2일 전에 알 수 있게 미리 알려 주셔야 합니다.**

**해설** 빈칸 앞에서 지시 사항 중 첫 번째 내용이 나왔으므로 추가적인 지시 사항이 나와야 한다. 따라서 접속부사 Also로 시작하며 2일 전에 미리 알려줘야 주셔야 한다는 (D)가 정답이다.

**어휘** cancellation 취소 in advance 미리

---

## [146]

**146 해설** 일맞은 형용사를 선택하는 문제로, 앞 문장에 이용 가능한 시간대 두 개를 말해 주고 어느 요일과 시간대가 가장 편한지 물어보는 것이므로 두 개 이상 모두 되는 (A) 지속적인, 한결같은 / (B) 익숙한 / (D) convenient가 적절하다.
(C) 영사된

---

# PART 7

## [147-148]

### 디스틴-메릴 상업 단지

디스틴-메릴 상업 단지 입주자분들께

관리 사무소에서는 **(A)** 재활용의 환경상의 이야에 대한 입주민들의 인식을 높이고 제대로 재활용되지 않는 쓰레기의 양을 줄이기 위해 입주자 이용 중이기 위해 캠페인을 열 예정입니다.

9월 10일부터 재활용에 있어서 가장 큰 개선을 보인 입주자들에게 입주자의 컴 페인 마지막날 특별한 사무용품까지 선물을 드릴 것입니다. 쓰레기 좀 이가 마지막에 간사하는 사무용품의 환경 효과에 대한 일반적인 정보가 가져가 저의 사무소에 있는 전단지에 나와 있습니다. 언제든지 방문해서 가져가시고 궁금한 점은 질문해 주십시오

결과는 로비에 있는 게시판에 공고될 것입니다. 감사합니다.

**148 해설** 조셉 페이커
디스틴-메릴 상업 단지 관리자
1904 미플 로드, 루이스버그 테네시 37012
042-493-5987

**어휘** business park 상업 단지 occupant 입주자 superintendent 입주자 리지, 감독관 week-long 일주일간 raise awareness 인식을 높이 다 recycle 재활용하다 property 제대로, 적절히 treat 처리하다 dispose 처리하다 leaflet 전단 range from A to B (범위가) A부터 B에 이르다 bulletin board 게시판 oversee 감독하다 come by 들르다

**147** 공고문은 왜 만들어졌는가?
(A) 사무용품의 할인을 광고하기 위해
(B) 쓰레기 오염에 대해서 거주자들에게 알리기 위해
(C) 선거 캠페인에 도움을 요청하기 위해
**(D) 새 환경 캠페인에 대한 세부 사용을 알리기 위해**

**해설** 공고문 초반을 보면 단지 내의 환경 캠페인에 대해 알리기 위한 것임을 알 수 있으므로 정답은 (D)이다.

**148** 조셉 베이커는 누구인가?
(A) 환경 단체를 위해 일하는 사람
**(B) 상업 단지를 감독하는 사람**
(C) 루이스버그의 공무원
(D) 상업 단지의 거주자

**해설** 공고문 마지막에 글쓴이가 디스틴-메릴 상업 단지의 관리자라고 쓰여 있으므로 정답은 (B)이다.

---

## [149-150]

| | |
|---|---|
| **앨런 하든** 박람회는 어떻게 되어 가고 있어요? | 오전 10시 29분 |
| **딜런 고든** 오, 그렇지 않아도 전화하려 했어요. | 오전 10시 30분 |
| **앨런 하든** 어떤 일로요? | 오전 10시 31분 |
| **딜런 고든 149** 여기 경쟁업체가 너무 많아요. 일테스 굿맨 씨에게 우리 회사 로고가 **그렇게 하면 우리 부스가 눈에 띌 거예요.** | 오전 10시 35분 |
| **앨런 하든** 일테스 씨는 회의 중이에요. **150** 블레이크 씨가 하도록 할게요. | 오전 10시 36분 |
| **딜런 고든 150** 마케팅 부서의 블레이크 씨요? | 오전 10시 37분 |
| **앨런 하든** 네, 11시가지는 도착할 거예요. 다른 질문이 있으면 저한테 알려 주세요. | 오전 10시 39분 |

**어휘** fair 박람회 competitor 경쟁업체 banner 현수막 stand out 두드러지다, 눈에 띄다 surpass 능가하다

**149** 오전 10시 35분에 고든 씨가 "그렇게 하면 우리 부스가 눈에 띌 거예요"라고 쓸 때 그 의도는 무엇이겠는가?
(A) 부스가 모두 곳에 설치될 수 있게 한다.
(B) 박람회를 성공적으로 후원할 것이다.
**(C) 그글 자리가 눈에 쉽게 띄게 한다.**
(D) 시람들이 예상을 뛰어넘을 것이다.

**해설** stand out은 "눈에 띄다"라는 뜻이다. 박람회에 경쟁업체 부스가 많아 서 자신들의 부스가 눈에 띄기 원한다는 의미로 고든 씨가 한 말임을 알 수 있다. 따라서 정답은 (C)이다.

**150** 누가 현수막을 가져오겠는가?
(A) 하든 씨
(B) 굿맨 씨
(C) 굿맨 씨
**(D) 토레스 씨**

**해설** 굿맨 씨에게 회사 로고가 적힌 현수막을 가져오도록 전해달라고 부탁 하자 굿맨 씨는 지금 회의 중이니 마케팅 부서의 블레이크 씨에게 계 부탁하겠다고 했으므로 정답은 (D)이다.

[151-153]

이베트 젠슨 씨는 1973년 **151** 자신의 첫 번째 옷 가게를 런던의 부모님 집에 있는 매우 우중충하고 허름한 다락방에서 그의의 성공적인 의류 브랜드 허름스를 시작했다. 첫 번째 사업은 성공한 것이어서 한 금 유동 문제로 바느질을. 젠슨 씨는 **152** 자신만의 고유한 바느질로 영국 패션 스타일을 만들기 위해 현 조건으로 독특한 바느질을 시작했다, 비록 첫 사업이 실패했지만 그녀는 더욱 세련된 모습의 허름스 브랜드를 재건하여 참조하여 내는 사업가적 정신을 가졌다. 허름스의 옷에 대한 평판이 입에서 입으로 전해지면서 1980년대에 점점 인기를 얻었다. 그의 런던 패션 디자인이 성공적인 데뷔 후, 허름스는 유럽으로 브랜드를 확장하기 시작했다. **152** 허름스는 동물 친화적인 이조 친환경이나 모피와 섬세한 바느질 곱게 옷인드의 다양 패션 업계의 후에 세계적인 주목을 받았다. 이류 산업에서 높아지는 존재감으로 유명 패션 리더들과 유명 인사들에 의해 회자되었다, 브랜드 지정이 이저 밀라노에 진출하지는 않았지만 도시의 유명한 고급 브랜드들은 신에 스타일을 경쟁하는 것처럼 보인다. 허름스 스타일이 점점 유행하면서 **153** 경쟁사들도 그녀의 스타일을 모방하기 시작했다. 그 러나 허름스는 유럽과 다른 곳에서 계속 인기를 끌면서 경쟁의 모양 문제에 대해 걱정하지 않는 것 같다.

**어휘** rather 상당히　dingy 우중충한　shabby 허름한　attic 다락방　venture 모험적 사업　scrap 조각　fashion 만들다　peculiar 고유의, 독특한　needlework 바느질　ultimately 결국　entrepreneurial 기업가의 refined 세련된　reputation 평판, 명성　meticulous 세심한　stitching 바느질　high-end 고급의　textile 옷감　presence 존재　prominent 유명한　be on guard against ~을 조심하다　vogue 유행　mimic 모방하다　copycat 모방꾼　initial 초기의　be in line with ~와 일치하다　degree 학위　refusal 거절　sophisticated 세련된　diminish 줄이다　employ 이용하다

**151** 젠슨 씨에 대해 암시된 것은 무엇인가?
(A) 첫 창업에서 성공했었다.
**(B) 런던에서 태어났다.**
(C) 그녀의 패션 디자인은 주류 패션과 비슷했다.
(D) 파리에서 학위를 취득했다.

**해설** 런던 패션 위크에서 성공적으로 데뷔한 후 사업을 확장했다고 하므로 (B)가 엄맞다. 첫 사업에서 파산했고, 독특한 자신만의 고유 스타일이 있다고 하며 영국 패션 위크에서 공부했으므로 나머지 선택지는 오답이다.

**152** 이류 브랜드도서 허름스의 특징으로 언급되지 않은 것은 무엇인가?
**(A) 훌륭한 고객 서비스**
(B) 실제 동물 가죽을 사용하지 않음
(C) 정교한 바느질
(D) 질 좋은 옷감

**해설** 동물 친화적인 이조 머리 사용, 섬세한 바느질, 고급 옷감으로 허름스 는 다양 패션 업계의 후에 세계적인 주목을 받았지만, (A)는 나와 있지 않다.

**153** 젠슨 씨의 경쟁사들이 시도하고 있는 것은 무엇인가?
(A) 가격 내리기
(B) 허름스의 평판 깎아내리기
**(C) 허름스의 디자인 모방하기**
(D) 허름스의 사업 전략 이용하기

**해설** 마지막에 허름스 스타일이 유행하면서 경쟁사들이 그녀의 스타일을 모 방하기 시작했다고 언급되어 있으므로 정답은 (C)이다.

[154-155]

**월드와이드 공공 도서관**

72 브라언 드라이브
하튼 미시시피 10473
416-304-5716
모네르 씨께

**154** 이느 귀하께서 3월 2일에 빌리신 3개의 품목이 오행할이 반납 7한이 지나 귀하의 이용 계정이 내일부터 일시적으로 중단될 거라고 도서 계정을 다시 출 섬니다. 귀하의 연체료는 총 7일당(하루 50센트씩)이며 이 책들을 반납해 주시기를 강력히 권고합니다.

아래를 반납해야야 하는 품목입니다.

[프로트아이]
로젤린 그래터 지음
ISBN: 9781453209971

[나민 전사)
니콜라스 에인스우드 지음
ISBN: 9341951203976

[재두의 말]
필립 켄트 지음
ISBN: 9241051203842

**어휘** overdue 기한이 지난　temporarily 일시적으로　suspend 중단하다　late fee 연체료　reactivate 재개하다　materials 자료　hold ~을 보류하다　put … on hold 보류하다

**154** 통지가 보내진 이유는 무엇인가?
(A) 문네드 씨가 상을 탔다는 것을 알리기 위해
(B) 최종적으로 신간 추천서를 알리기 위해
**(C) 문네드 씨에게 연체된 책에 대해 상기시키기 위해**
(D) 도서관 방침의 변화를 공지하기 위해

**해설** 첫 문장에서 반납 기한이 지난 세 개의 품목에 대해 알리기 위해 보낸다 는 통지의 목적이 드러나 있으므로 정답은 (C)이다.

**155** 도서관에 대해 추론할 수 있는 것은 무엇인가?
**(A) 도서관은 참시 동안 문네드 씨의 계정을 정지시킬 것이다.**
(B) 문네드 씨는 도서관에 수배 권의 책을 기부했다.
(C) 문네드 씨는 도서관으로부터 몇몇 자료를 요청했다.
(D) 도서관은 오전 모음을 위한 특별 행사를 개최할 것이다.

**해설** 도서의 반납 기한이 기한으로 지났으므로 이용 계정을 일시적으로 중단할 거라 고 한다. 따라서 (A)가 정답이다. suspend가 put ~ on hold로 표현 되었다.

[156-158]

발신: 글렌 멘데스
수신: 대니엘 길베트
날짜: 3월 26일
제목: 화상 회의 준비

대니엘 씨,

화상 회의가 현재 일정보다 1시간 앞당겨졌어요. **[1]**- 7시는 좀 이른 감이 있 지만 멀리 방무가 없대요. **156** 토론토도 밴쿠버보다 3시간 느리니까요. 그래서 대니엘 씨가 지금 해장으면 하는 건 이 건입니다. **157** 문기별 보고서를 인쇄해서 회 의가 열리는 A-5동이 오 테이블에 둬 주세요. 오디오 장치를 오디오 정비를 확인 하고, 그 옆에 H-5 디스플레이 장치를 갖다 놓으세요. **158** 옆에 준비가 오래된 영사기 디스에 매우 비번 장치를 사용해 왔어요 -**[3]**- 이 모든 질 내일 오전에 다룰 수 있으면 괜찮아요. -**[4]**- 시간에 맞춰 방이 준비만 되면 상관없습니다. 궁금한 게 있으면 언제든 문자 주세요.

글렌 멘데스

**어휘** video conference 화상 회의　print out 출력하다, 인쇄하다　projector 영사기　manage to ~을 가까스로 해내다　be all set 온전히 준비되다　on time 시간에 맞게, 정각에　time difference 시차

**156** 화상 회의 일정은 왜 변경되었는가?
(A) 멘데스 씨가 휴가를 갈 거라서
**(B) 시차가 있기 때문에**
(C) 방이 준비가 되어야 하기 때문에
(D) 몇몇 장비가 없어져서

**해설** 화상 회의가 1시간 앞당겨져서 7시는 좀 이른 감이 있지만 멀리 방도 가 없었고 했다. 토론토는 밴쿠버보다 3시간 느리다는 내용에서 (B)가 정답임을 알 수 있다.

**157** 길베트 씨가 화상 회의를 위해 하지 않을 것은 무엇인가?
(A) 보고서 인쇄하기
**(B) 오디오 정비 확인하기**
(C) 디스플레이 장치 이동시키기
**(D) 오래된 영사기 청소하기**

**해설** 분기별 보고서를 인쇄해 회의실 오디오 정비 확인, H-5 디스플레이 장치 갖다 놓기 등이 언급되었으므로 (A), (B), (C)는 맞다. 오래된 영사기를 청소하라 는 내용은 없으므로 정답은 (D)이다.

**158** [1], [2], [3], [4]로 표시된 부분 중에서 다음 문장이 들어가기에 가장 알맞은 곳 은?
"그러나 다룰 때 조심하세요."
(A) [1]
(B) [2]

(C) [3]
(D) [4]

해설 매우 비싼 장치를 사용해 왔다는 내용 다음에 조심히 다뤄달라는 문장이 와야 자연스럽다. it이 the device를 대신하므로 (C)가 정답이다.

[159-161]

| 수신 | 조나단 말로 |
|---|---|
| 날짜 | 2017년 4월 23일 |
| 시간 | 오후 2:15 |
| 다음 메시지가 있습니다. | |
| 이름 | 셀리 배튼(그리닝 가전의 여자 점원) |
| 전화번호 | 203-893-5248 |
| 메모자 | 회계부의 홀리 |

(159) 부족한 청소 장비를 보충하기 위해 당신이 이전에 문의했던 진공청소기에 대해서 말로렐레에 대해 배튼 씨가 화신하셨습니다. 그녀는 360도 회전하는 진공청소기는 재고가 없으므로 (160) 다시 방문하기 전에 웹 사이트에서 다른 제품을 확인하라고 했습니다. 그리고 다음 달 정오까지 대걸레가 배달될 것이라고 했습니다.

어휘 vacuum cleaner 진공청소기 mop 대걸레 supplement 보충하다 equipment 장비 janitor (건물의) 관리인 restock 재고를 다시 채우다

159 말로 씨는 누구인가?
(A) 회계사
(B) 건물 관리인
(C) 영업자
(D) 전기 기술자

해설 말로 씨가 메시지를 받으면 청소 장비를 보충하기 위해서 필요한 진공청소기에 대한 문의를 했다고 했으므로 건물 관리인이 가장 적절하다. 따라서 (B)가 정답이다.

160 말로 씨가 메시지를 받으면 무슨 일이 일어날 것인가?
(A) 진공청소기를 돌려줄 것이다.
(B) 더 많은 대걸레를 살 것이다.
(C) 웹 사이트를 방문할 것이다.
(D) 그리닝 가전에 전화할 것이다.

해설 360도 회전하는 진공청소기가 없다고 하므로 웹 사이트에서 제품을 검색할 것이다. 따라서 (C)가 정답이다.

161 메시지로부터 추론할 수 있는 것은 무엇인가?
(A) 말로 씨는 전에 가게를 방문했었다.
(B) 말로 씨는 개인적으로 배튼 씨를 안다.
(C) 진공청소기는 최신 모델이다.
(D) 진공청소기는 이번 주에 재배달될 것이다.

해설 another는 또 한 번의라는 의미가 있다. 따라서 전에 말로 씨가 그 가게에 방문했고 다시 한 번 방문을 요청하는 것을 알 수 있으므로 (A)가 정답이다.

[162-165]

| 대니얼 브라운 [오전 11시 24분] |
|---|
| 제시카 리 [오전 11시 25분] |
| 대니얼 브라운 [오전 11시 27분] |
| 폴 피어스 [오전 11시 28분] |
| 대니얼 브라운 [오전 11시 31분] |
| 폴 피어스 [오전 11시 32분] |
| 제시카 리 [오전 11시 34분] |
| 폴 피어스 [오전 11시 37분] |
| 대니얼 브라운 [오전 11시 38분] |
| 제시카 리 [오전 11시 39분] |

**대니얼 브라운 [오전 11시 24분]** (162) 좋은 소식이 있어요! 모니터 선적물이 오늘 오후에 배달될 거래요.

**제시카 리 [오전 11시 25분]** 정말요? 배달이 정말 빨리네요!

**대니얼 브라운 [오전 11시 27분]** 그래게요? 정말 놀라워요. 저는 마감일을 맞추기 위해 우리가 다른 제조업체를 알아봐야 하나 생각했거든요.

**폴 피어스 [오전 11시 28분]** 그럼 이제 뭘 하죠? 정확히 언제 도착한다고 하던가요?

**대니얼 브라운 [오전 11시 31분]** 전화로 통화한 로버트 리스 씨가 트럭이 오후 4시쯤 도착할 거라고 일러줬어요. 그러니 선적물 하차 전에 물품 목록을 재확인할 종분한 시간이 있어요.

**폴 피어스 [오전 11시 32분]** (165) 이번엔 조심해야 할 거예요. (162) (163) 지난번엔 기부드 숫자가 전에 물품 목록과 맞지 않았잖아요.

**제시카 리 [오전 11시 34분]** (164) 전적으로 동의해요. 하지만 누가 확인을 하죠? 저는 오늘 세미나에 참석해야 해요.

**폴 피어스 [오전 11시 37분]** 제가 할게요. 그 다음에 하청업체와 그들이 부주의로 발생한 손실에 대해 통화하려고요.

**대니얼 브라운 [오전 11시 38분]** 거의 그렇죠. 좋아요. 난 가볼게요, 나중에 얘기해요.

**제시카 리 [오전 11시 39분]**

어휘 shipment 선적물, 배송물 inventory 물품 목록 unload (물건 등을) 내리다, 하차시키다 subcontractor 하청업체, 하도급 업자 loss 손실 negligence 부주의 to some degree 어느 정도는

162 브라운 씨는 어떤 회사에서 근무하겠는가?
(A) 컴퓨터 판매 회사
(B) 음식 배달 서비스
(C) 텔레비전 제조업체
(D) 지역 라디오 방송국

해설 오전 11시 24분에 모니터 선적물이 오늘 오후에 배달될 거라는 내용이 나온다. 또 11시 32분에는 기부드가 언급되기 것을 볼 때, 이들은 컴퓨터 판매 회사에서 일하고 있음을 알 수 있으므로 (A)가 정답이다.

163 이전 배송에서 무엇이 문제였는가?
(A) 몇몇 물품이 일정보다 늦게 배송되었다.
(B) 모든 물품이 너무 비쌌다.
(C) 몇몇 물품의 수가 맞지 않았다.
(D) 대부분의 물품이 잘 포장되지 않았다.

해설 지난번엔 기부드 숫자가 물품 목록과 맞지 않았다는 내용에서 정답을 알 수 있다. (C)임을 알 수 있다.

164 누가 물품 확인을 할 것인가?
(A) 브라운 씨
(B) 리 씨
(C) 피어스 씨
(D) 리스 씨

해설 오전 11시 34분에 리 씨가 자기는 세미나에 참석해야 해서 확인을 못한다고 하니까 11시 37분에 피어스 씨가 자신이 하겠다고 말한다. 물품 확인은 피어스 씨가 할 것임을 알 수 있다. 따라서 정답은 (C)이다.

165 오전 11시 34분에 리 씨가 "전적으로 동의해요"라고 쓸 때, 그 의도는 무엇인가?
(A) 어느 정도 피어스 씨에 동의한다.
(B) 물품 목록이 중요하지 않다고 믿는다.
(C) 더 이상 피어스 씨에 동의하지 않는다.
(D) 당연히 조심해야 한다고 생각한다.

해설 I can't agree with you more는 "(더 이상 동의할 수 없을 정도로) 완전히 동의한다"는 의미이다. 11시 32분에 피어스 씨가 "이번엔 조심해야 할 거래요"라고 하셨고, 이에 대한 응답으로 전적으로 동의한다고 했으므로 정답은 (D)이다.

[166-168]

## 제니스 인더스트리

제니스의 영업부와 회계부에서 회사 창립 60주년 기념사 주최를 담당할 것입니다. 제니스 인더스트리 사가 업계에 있은 지 60주년이 되는 12일 금요일에 업무가 끝난 후 (166) 훌륭한 음식 및 모임과 함께 직원들에게 고객 서비스에 대한 특강을 계획하고 있습니다.

강에는 고객 서비스의 F2F 영역의 전문가인 대럴 코너리 씨가 찾을 것입니다. (167A) 코너리 씨는 10년간 호주 전역을 돌며 수많은 영업 사원들과 서비스 선임에 종사하는 사람들에게 강의하고 있습니다. 그는 4년 동안 (167C) 키아치 카폰니게이션즈에서 지사장으로 일한 후, 2004년에 켄트베리 비즈니스 대학에서 석사 학위를 취득하셨습니다. 그의 강의는 많은 사람들에 의해 '실용적'이라는 호평을 받아 있으며 해심에 이르는 자세한 설명과 함께 실제하고 유용한 (167D) 사례 연구에 기초합니다.

강에는 고객의 불만 처리, 고객과 좋은 관계를 유지하기, 효과적인 의사소통 기술에 대한 주제를 다룰 것입니다. 세미나는 금요일 세 번으로 나뉘어 열릴 것입니다. 다음 일정을 참고하세요.

| | |
|---|---|
| 11100 - 12200 | 고객 불만 - 어떻게 처리할 것인가? |
| | 점심 식사 |
| 14400 - 15:15 | (168) 고객의 오랫동안 함께하는 기초 |
| 15:30 - 17:00 | 의사소통 기술의 기초 |

## (좌측 본문)

합병 후에도 저희의 우선순위는 고객입니다. 개인 고객이 저희의 주요 고객들께 서비스를 제공하는 것입니다. 질문이 있으시다면 [171] 1-800-285-8592로 저희 고객 서비스 상담원에게 연락하실 수 있습니다. 또한, 저희의 웹 사이트 www.vcltd.com/qa/merge에서 합병에 대한 더 많은 정보도 저희의 웹 [171] 은행 지점에 방문해서 합병에 대해서 직원에게 물어보셔도 됩니다.

찰스 스탠리
프레스티지 세이빙스 선임 부사장

---

다쎄 모터스 주식회사
124 바자사이드 웨이
센트럴시스코, 캘리포니아 95105
www.dasse.motors.com

**[173-175]**

2월 17일

앤드류 지 마이어스
J.P.A. 주식회사
82 메이플 스트리트
산 호세, 캘리포니아 95131

마이어스 씨께

지난 3년간 J.P.A.와 일한 것은 저희로서는 아주 기쁜 경험이었습니다. -[1]- 하지만, 저희 다쎄 모터스는 더 이상 귀사의 자문 서비스가 필요하지 않게 된 점을 알려드리게 되어 유감입니다. -[2]-

[170] 저희 운영진은 이 침체된 경기에서 커다란 손실을 피하기 위해 새로운 사업 방향으로 나아가기로 결정하였습니다. -[3]- 귀사가 저희에게 제공해 준 전문적인 사업 자문 서비스가 저희가 새로 설정하는 방향에 적합하지 않기 때문에 J.P.A.와의 계약을 해체할 수밖에 없었다는 점을 말씀드려야겠습니다. 이 기회를 빌려 귀사가 저희를 위해 쓴 헌신적인 업무에 감사의 말씀을 드립니다. -[4]-

진심으로 저희는 귀하와 함께 J.P.A.와 좋은 관계를 유지하기를 바랍니다. [174] 세계 경제가 회복되고, 귀사가 저희에게 제공했던 비슷한 서비스가 필요하게 되면, 분명 저희는 J.P.A.를 다시 고려할 것입니다.

로버트 앤더슨
대표 이사, 다쎄 모터스

**어휘** delightful 매우 기쁜 no longer 더 이상 ~하지 않는 advisory 자문의 head in a new direction 새로운 방향으로 향하다 sluggish economy 경기 침체 suitable for ~에 적합한 map out 설계하다 cancel a contract 계약을 해체하다 dedicated 헌신적인 remain on good terms with ~와 좋은 관계를 유지하다 bounce back 반등하다 downturn 하락, 침체 go bankrupt 파산하다

**173** J.P.A. 주식회사는 어떤 회사인가?
(A) 오토바이 제조업체
(B) 도로 건설 회사
(C) 비즈니스 컨설팅 회사
(D) 제약 회사
**해설** 두 번째 단락에서 J.P.A.가 전문적인 사업 자문 서비스를 제공한다는 내용에서 J.P.A. 주식회사는 비즈니스 컨설팅 회사임을 알 수 있다. 따라서 정답은 (C)이다.

**174** 왜 다쎄 모터스는 계약을 해체하길 원하는가?
(A) 세계적인 경기 침체 때문에
(B) 계약 조건이 불공평했기 때문에
(C) 새 자금 방이 필요없기 때문에
(D) 경영상 문제가 있기 때문에

---

**어휘** foundation 설립 catering 음식 공급 get-together 모임, 파티 renowned 명성 있는 F2F 직접 만나서 countless 무수한 attain 획득하다 master's degree 석사 학위 regional director 지사장 separate 분리된 lecture 강의 evaluation 평가 consist of ~로 구성되다 subordinate 하급자, 부하

**166** 공고의 목적은 무엇인가?
(A) 작업 평가가 지연되었음을 알리기 위해
(B) 직원들에게 장기 검진을 알리기 위해
(C) 다가오는 직무 능력 평가일을 알리기 위해
(D) 직원들에게 강의가 있는 행사를 알리기 위해
**해설** 회사 창립 60주년을 기념하며 식사와 함께 직원들에게 고객 서비스에 대한 특강을 연다는 내용의 공고이므로 (D)가 정답이다.

**167** 코너리 씨에 대해 언급되지 않은 것은 무엇인가?
(A) 강의를 하기 위해 전 세계를 여행한다.
(B) 경영 대학원에서 석사를 취득하였다.
(C) 커뮤니케이션 분야에서 일한 경험이 있다.
(D) 그의 강의는 주로 사례 연구로 구성된다.
**해설** 코너리 씨는 10년간 전 세계를 돌아다닌 것이 아니라 호주 전역을 돌아다니며 강의를 했다고 하므로 (A)가 정답이다.

**168** 강의에서 다루는 주제는 무엇인가?
(A) 행동이 불량한 하급자 다루기
(B) 고객과 오래 지속되는 관계 유지하기
(C) 사업 경쟁에서 이기는 전략
(D) 온라인에서 효과적으로 제품을 광고하는 방법
**해설** 일정표에서 두 번째 시간에 하는 강의의 제목을 통해 (B)가 정답임을 알 수 있다.

---

**[169-172]**

11월 17일

프레스티지 세이빙스
182 하이랜드 로드
밀랜드, 뉴저지 19293

고객분들께

저희 은행이 8월 5일 벤저 캐피털스 사와 합병하게 됨을 알리게 되어 기쁩니다.

이 합병으로 저희는 더 안정적 재정과 함께 다양한 은행 서비스 제공을 기대하고 있습니다. 더욱이, 저희는 평소대로 개인 은행 서비스를 계속 진행할 것입니다.

저희는 합병으로 인해 고객의 계좌에 생긴 변경 사항에 대하여 모든 정보를 제공하기 위해서 최선을 다하고 있습니다. 변경 사항은 8월 20일부터 적용될 것입니다. [169] 8월 20일 전에 모든 고객님은 새로운 은행 위치 및 개인 은행 계좌 정보, 저희의 온라인 은행 업무 시스템에 생긴 변경 사항들에 대하여 [172] 은행으로부터 우편으로 서류를 받으실 것입니다.

---

**어휘** merge 합병(하다) stable 안정된 financial 재정의, 금융상의 account 계좌 take effect 효력이 나타나다, 실시되다 priority 우선 사항 representative 대표, 대리인 transfer 양도, 이전 electronically 전자적으로, 컴퓨터로

**169** 고객들은 언제까지 합병에 대한 정보를 받을 것인가?
(A) 합병 직후
(B) 8월 5일
(C) 8월 20일 전
(D) 8월 20일 이후
**해설** 8월 20일 전에 정보가 포함된 서류를 받을 것이라고 언급되어 있으므로 (C)가 있었다.

**170** 다음 중 변경 사항은 무엇인가?
(A) 월급 유지
(B) 지급 양도비
(C) 고객 계좌 번호
(D) 은행 위치
**해설** 은행으로부터 받을 서류에 변경 사항들이 나와 있는데 그중에 새로운 은행 위치가 언급되어 있으므로 (D)가 정답이다.

**171** 합병에 대해서 알 수 있는 방법이 아닌 것은 무엇인가?
(A) 회사 웹 사이트 방문
(B) 현재 은행 지점 방문
(C) 회사에 편지 쓰기
(D) 고객 서비스 부서에 연락하기
**해설** 합병에 대해서 알 수 있는 방법으로 웹 사이트 방문, 지점 방문, 고객 서비스 부서에 연락하기는 언급되어 있지만 편지 쓰기에 대해서는 언급되어 있지 않으므로 (C)가 정답이다.

**172** 어떻게 고객들은 정보 자료를 받을 것인가?
(A) 고객 상담원이 집집마다 방문할 것이다.
(B) 온라인으로 받을 것이다.
(C) 우편을 통해 받을 것이다.
(D) 고객이 요구하지 않으면 받지 않을 것이다.
**해설** 8월 20일 전에 변경 사항들에 대해 은행으로부터 우편을 통해 서류를 받을 것이라고 언급되어 있으므로 (C)가 정답이다.

해설 침체된 경기에서 새로운 사업 방향이 필요했다는 것과 세계 경제가 회복되면 J.P.A.를 다시 고려할 것이라는 내용에서 정답은 (A)이다.

## 175 [1], [2], [3], [4]로 표시된 곳 중에서 다음 문장이 가장 적합한 곳은?

"그 영향이 너무 심해서 저희는 예상 수익과 실제 수익 사이에서 큰 차이를 봤습니다."

(A) [1]
(B) [2]
**(C) [3]**
(D) [4]

해설 침체된 경기가 커다란 손실을 피하기 위해 새로운 사업 방향으로 나아가기로 결정했다는 내용 다음에 '그 침체된 경기가' 영향이 너무 심하다고 말하는 것이 자연스러우므로 정답은 (C)이다. Its impact에서 Its는 sluggish economy를 뜻한다.

---

[176-180]

캐서린 임
9607 매켈런 로드
엘바커키, 뉴메시코 76051

임 씨께,

귀하는 최근 <캘리포니아 매거진>의 정기 구독을 취소하셨으므로 이 편지를 보냅니다. **<176>** 귀하의 고객 만족 설문 조사 작성을 위해 몇 분만 시간을 내어 주셨으면 합니다. 이 설문 조사는 저희가 잘하고, 고객이 원하는 바를 더 이해하는 데 도움이 될 것입니다.

저희 잡지의 구독자이신 귀하에, 귀하의 의견은 저희에게 중요합니다. **<177>** 설문 조사에 응해 주시면, <캘리포니아 매거진>의 축구 티셔츠를 선물로 받으실 겁니다.

**<177>** 저희는 또한 낮은 가격의 정기 구독이나 30퍼센트가 더 할인된 가격으로 정기 구독을 갱신하시기를 권장합니다. 대신에, 모든 새로운 정기 구독자는 전액 무료인 이탈리아 여행권에 응모하실 수 있습니다.

문의하실 내용이 있으시면 연락 주십시오.

**<177>** 앤디 손 올림

## 176 편지의 주된 목적은 무엇입니까?
(A) 임 씨에게 잡지를 소개하기 위해
(B) 임 씨에게 정기 구독 기간 만료를 알리기 위해
**(C) 임 씨에게 설문지를 작성해 달라고 요청하기 위해**
(D) 임 씨에게 정기 구독료를 청구하기 위해

해설 편지에서 최근 잡지의 정기 구독을 취소한 임 씨에게 <캘리포니아 매거진>이 설문 조사를 작성해 달라고 부탁하고 있으므로 정답은 (C)이다.

## 177 앤디 손은 누구인가?
**(A) 판매원**
(B) 잡지 기자
(C) 시장 연구원
(D) 여행사 직원

해설 편지를 보낸 사람인 앤디 손은 정기 구독 갱신에 대해 응모하며 구독 시 잡지 이해에도 연결되고 있다. 또한 고객이 원하는 것을 더 잘 이해할 수 있도록 설문 조사를 요청하고 있으므로 이에 가장 적합한 작업은 (A)이다.

## 178 임 씨가 설문에 응하고 <캘리포니아 매거진>으로부터 받을 물건은 무엇인가?
**(B) 축구 티셔츠**
(C) 이탈리아 여행
(D) 무료 잡지

해설 정기 구독을 취소한 임 씨가 설문 조사를 해 주면 축구 티셔츠를 무료로 준다고 했으므로 정답은 (B)이다. (이는 새로운 정기 구독자들에게 모든 비용이 지불되는 이탈리아 여행에 응모할 수 있게 된다고 언급되었을 뿐이므로 답으로 맞지 않다.

## 179 잡지의 어떤 부분에 임 씨가 가장 흥미롭게 느끼겠는가?
(A) 특집 기사
(B) 행사 일정
**(C) 팁 앤 트릭**
(D) 선율 동향

해설 임 씨가 완성한 설문 조사의 3번에서 중요도 순서로 1위는 팁 앤 트릭이었다. 따라서 임 씨에게 가장 흥미로운 부분은 (C)가 적절하다.

## 180 임 씨는 <캘리포니아 매거진>의 어떤 점이 마음에 들지 않았는가?
(A) 구독료
(B) 사진의 질
(C) 표지 외관
**(D) 여행의 비용 정도**

해설 설문 조사의 7번에서 바꾸면 좋겠다는 것으로 너무 비싼 여행만 소개되는 것보다 좀 더 저렴한 여행도 소개해 줬으면 좋겠다는 점을 지적하였으므로 정답은 (D)가 정답이다.

---

## <캘리포니아 매거진> 고객 만족도 조사

1. 잡지에 대한 전반적인 만족도는 어떠셨습니까?

| | |
|---|---|
| | 매우 만족 |
| | 다소 만족 |
| | 중립 |
| ✓ | 다소 불만족 |
| | 매우 불만족 |

2. 얼마나 자주 저희 잡지를 읽습니까?

| | |
|---|---|
| | 항상 |
| | 자주 |
| ✓ | 때때로 |
| | 드물게 |
| | 전혀 읽지 않는다 |

3. **<179>** 중요한 순서대로 1위를 매기세요.

| 4 | 뉴스 |
|---|---|
| 1 | 팁 앤 트릭 |
| 5 | 행사 일정 |
| 2 | 선율 동향 |
| 3 | 특집 기사 |

4. 다음 항목의 질에 순위를 매기세요.

| 4 | 글 |
|---|---|
| 2 | 배치 |
| 1 | 사진 |
| 3 | 표지 디자인 |

5. 구독을 취소한 이유는 무엇입니까?

| ✓ | 구독료가 너무 비싸다. |
|---|---|
| | 나에게 더 맞는 방향물을 발견했다. |
| | 콘텐츠에 만족하지 않았다. |
| | 가까에서 <캘리포니아 매거진>을 구매하는 것을 선호한다. |

6. <캘리포니아 매거진>에서 즐겨 읽는 것을 말해 주세요.
여행을 즐기기 때문에, 다른 나라에 대한 기사가 매우 흥미로웠다.

7. <캘리포니아 매거진>의 어떤 점이 바뀌길 바라나요?
**<180>** 좀 더 저렴한 여행에 대해서도 소개해 주셨으면 합니다. 실려 있는 여행들 모두 너무 비쌉니다.

8. 구독을 다시 시작하고 싶으시다면:
예 ✓  아니오
'예'라면, 언제 다시 시작하시겠습니까?
9월 1일

어휘 subscription 구독 satisfaction survey 만족도 조사 renew 재개하다 all-expenses-paid trip 경비가 전액 지원되는 여행 numerically 숫자상으로 featured article 특집 기사 layout 배치 publication 출판물 expire 만료되다

---

[181-185]

## [상단 채팅]

**캐슬린 프라사드** — 오후 3시 9분
오빠, 미안한데 나 가족 소풍 못 갈 거 같아요.

**티모시 프라사드** — 오후 3시 11분
무슨 일이야?

**캐슬린 프라사드** — 오후 3시 15분
187 직장 가장 친한 시라가 가족이랑 다른 나라로 이민 간대요. 그래서 저랑 그 애 친구들이랑 송별 파티를 열기로 했고 저 거기 가야 해요.

**티모시 프라사드** — 오후 3시 16분
참 안 됐구나, 좀 미룰 수도 없을까?

**캐슬린 프라사드** — 오후 3시 18분
안돼요. 우리 5월 25일에만 시간이 나요. 우리들 대부분이 아르바이트를 해서요.

**티모시 프라사드** — 오후 3시 20분
좋아, 그럼 가족 여행은 네 여름 방학 때 가는 게 어떻겠니? 나도 선장에 아직 보증금을 지불하지 않았으니까.

**캐슬린 프라사드** — 오후 3시 21분
188 물론 좋죠! 고마워요, 아빠!

---

발신: 티모시 프라사드 <prasad@abcmail.com>
수신: 케빈 딜런 <kdillon@croakvalleycabin.com>
날짜: 5월 21일
제목: 패밀리 룸 예약

딜런 씨께,

187 저송하지만 제 딸이 시간이 되지 않는 관계로, 5월 24일에서 5월 26일 예약을 6월 19일에서 6월 20일로 바꾸고 싶습니다.

귀사에서 이렇게 일찍 예약하는 방을 계속 붙잡아 두시는 것도 너무한 것 같아요. 그래서 189 190 귀사 홈페이지에 있는 계약 조건대로 방에 대한 50%의 보증금을 지불하고 새로 예약에 관해서는 귀사의 데스크에 연락하겠습니다.

티모시 프라사드

**어휘** cabin 선장 deposit due at reservation 예약 시 내는 보증금 balance due 미불액 a bunch of 다수의 farewell party 작별(송별) 파티 You bet 물론(=certainly) make change to ~를 변경하다 booking 예약 put down deposit on ~에 대한 보증금을 내다 terms and conditions 계약 조건

**186** 편지에 언급되지 않은 것은 무엇인가?
(A) 예약한 방의 새로운 세부사항.
(B) 프라사드 가족 3일 동안 산장에 머물 것이다.
(C) 딜런 씨는 일방적 프로모션에 실망했다.
(D) 프라사드 씨의 가족 인원수는 3명이다.

## [186-190]

### 크록 계곡 산장
41 폭스 로드
루이벨레그, CS 461734
(353) 793-3520

티모시 프라사드
317 클링사이드 거리
스톤랜드 웨이, 엑스머
(44) 248-3458

5월 9일
프라사드 씨께

이 편지는 귀하의 예약 사항을 진행하였다는 점을 알려드리기 위한 것입니다.

| 예약 세부 사항 | 결제 세부 사항 |
|---|---|
| 예약 번호: RWYD-5DE3G | 189 총 금액: 800.00달러 |
| 상황: 확인됨 (색상: 파임) | 예약 시 보증금: 0.00달러 |
| 188 체류: 5월 24일~ 5월 26일 (3일) | 미불액: 800.00달러 |
| 188 4명 | |

포트에 머무시는 동안 저희 크록 계곡 산장을 선택해 주셔서 감사합니다. 188 지는 일방적 포트로테를 선택하셨 것이 있으오 kdillon@croakvalleycabin.com으로 이메일을 보내시거나 전화 (353) 793-3523으로 연락 주세요. 189 예약 변경을 원하시면 (353) 793-3525로 저희 예약 데스크에 전화 주시기 바랍니다.

지를에 메우실 진처... 크록 계곡 선장을 감사합니다.

케빈 딜런 산장 주인

---

수신: cs_tripoli@gomail.com
발신: jolene_35@stellavin.com
날짜: 2016년 8월 29일
제목: 사업 문의

안녕하세요?

저는 2016 벨몬슬리 와인 박람회 183 박람회 개막식에서 작지만 총지 않았던 인전사고를 겪었으므로 때문에 자료 박람회를 홍보하기 위해 방문하는 고객증과 유명 인사들이 안전에 대해서 걱정이 되었다. 183 그러한 사고가 다시 일어나는 것을 막기 위해 9월 2일부터 12일까지 서비스를 요청하고 싶었습니다. 182 저희는 다양한 프로그램 두 수용하기 위해 183 37가지의 모든 경호를 요구할 것입니다. 저희는 또한 고객들의 공항 이동을 위한 리무진 5대가 필요한 바랍니다.

업무 관련 세부 사항에 대해 이은하기 위해서 아래서 당신까지 담신 바랍니다.

에스벨라 비아트로 조린 한센

제19회 벨몬슬리 와인 박람회 조직 위원회

**어휘** credibility 진실성, 신뢰성 oriented 지향하는 escort 호위하다 high-profile 세간의 이목을 끄는 A-list 최고의 priority 우선순위 certified 증명된 martial art 무술 undergo 겪다 confidentiality 비밀 adjust 조정하다 specific 구체적인 availability 유용성 inquiry 문의 accommodate 수용하다 requirement 필요 incident 사고 preclude 방지하다 show off 자랑하다 diversify 다각화하다 acquaintance 아는 사람 consecutive 연속적인 bottling company 음료 회사

**181** 트리폴리 시큐리티 서비스에 관해 암시하는 것은 무엇인가?
(A) 다양한 무술 트레이닝을 제공한다.
**(B) 고객에게 경비 요원을 제공한다.**
(C) 국가 기밀 안보에 종사한다.
(D) 새로운 서비스로 다각화하려 하고 있다.

**해설** 광고의 의하면 트리폴리 시큐리티는 경호 서비스 업체이므로 (B)가 정답이다. 무슨을 할 좀 아는 공인된 경호 연맹이 있으며, 특별히 국가 기밀이나 중요 인사의 언급은 없고, 새로운 서비스를 소개한다고 있지도 않다.

**182** 한센 씨가 행사는 어디에서 개최되는가?
(A) 마이애미
**(B) 칼리포니아**
(C) 로스앤젤레스
(D) 트리폴리

**해설** 광고의 의하면 마이애미는 VIP와 프리미엄 서비스만을 이용할 수 있... 며 로스앤젤레스는 VIP서비스만 이용할 수 있다. 한센 씨의 와인 박람회는 캘리포니아에서 열리는 것으로 보는 것이 적절하다. 따라서 (B)가 정답이다.

**183** 한센 씨는 왜 트리폴리 시큐리티의 서비스를 원하는가?
**(A) 더 이상의 안전 문제를 막기 위해**
(B) 행사 예산을 아끼기 위해
(C) 직원들의 더 많은 고객을 유치하기 위해
(D) 방문자들에게 지원하기 위해

**해설** 외인 박람회 조직 위원장이 한센 씨는 개막식에서 안전사고를 겪었으므로 재발을 막기 위해 경호 서비스를 요청하고 있으므로 (A)가 정답이다.

**184** 광고의 5번째 줄 addresses와 의미상 가장 가까운 것은 무엇인가?
(A) 해결하다
(B) 결심하다
**(C) 처리하다**
(D) 맞서다

**해설** address는 태러와 긴급 상황을 '다루다=이'라는 의미로 쓰였다. 선택지 중 (C) deals with와 의미가 가장 가깝다.

**185** 이메일에서 추론할 수 있는 것은 무엇인가?
**(A) 한센 씨는 보안 서비스를 이용해 본 적이 없다.**
(B) 한센 씨는 위원회의 의장을 역임하고 있다.
(C) 한센 씨는 트리폴리 시큐리티에서 일하는 지인을 두고 있다.
(D) 한센 씨는 음료 회사를 소유하고 있다.

**해설** 개막식에서 처음 사고를 겪으면서 경호 서비스를 필요로 하고 있으므로 처음으로 서비스를 이용한다는 것을 알 수 있다. 따라서 정답은 (A)이다. 한센 씨는 본인을 현지 와인 생산자로 소개하고 있으며, 의장 언급과 트리폴리 시큐리티에 지인을 두고 있다는 내용은 확인할 수 없다.

## 화람

**193** 날짜: 2월 23일 화요일
수신: 모든 직원
발신: 제시 헨릭스 총괄 이사
제목: 웹 사이트 문제

지난밤에 고장난 디자인 업체가 우리 회사 홈페이지를 다시 디자인한 이후로 잘 작동들이 이미 홈페이지에 대해 보고하셨다는 사실을 읽고 있습니다. 하지만 페이지 주소가 오작동에 대해 특정 오류가 발생할 수 있다는 것을 당시 디자인 책임자였던 페레즈 씨가 저희 직에게 알려주었습니다. 따라서 이것이 우리가 해킹 당했다는 근거 없는 루머에는 상관없는 것을 여러분께 확실히 컴퓨터드립니다.

**195** 우리 기술 팀이 백엔 새도 불필요해 보이는 쿠키를 요해 살제함으로써 보다 빠르게 인터넷 연결을 제공하기 위한 노력을 하셨는데 역시 잘 되지 않았어요. 따라서 이번 추가키지는 기술적 문제를 해결하기 위해 같은 디자인 회사를 내일 다시 부를 것이고, 저는 우리 회사 홈페이지의 새 디자인이 성공작이고 녹슬지지 않도록 할 것입니다. 업무에 집중하시기 바랍니다.

---

발신: 지말 페레즈 <perez@hcdesign.com>
수신: 벤 나이트 <bknight@hcdesign.com>
날짜: 2월 23일
제목: 무젠 엔지니어 서비스

벤,

방금 무젠 엔지니어의 총괄 이사인 헨릭스 씨로부터 1월 8일 우리가 새로 디자인해 준 홈페이지의 기술적 문제에 관한 전화를 받았어요. 에전 주소를 새 주소로 보내는 과정을 맡은 301 리다이렉션 에러가 발생한 것으로 보여요. 페레즈 씨가 제게 와서 수리해 달라고 했으나, 아시다시피, 저는 연락회의를 위해 내일 아침 일찍 캐나다로 가서 이틀 26일까지는 돌아오지 않아요. 제가 없는 동안에 이 문제를 해결해 주실래요? 그러면 정말 고맙겠어요.

**194** 참고로, 지원이 보증 기간은 3일로 연장되었어요.

미리 감사해요,
지말

---

발신: 벤 나이트 <bknight@hcdesign.com>
수신: 제시 헨릭스 <jhenricks@mugen.engineers.com>
날짜: 2월 24일
제목: 웹 사이트 수리 서비스

헨릭스 씨에게,

1월 8일 디자인에 드린 귀사 홈페이지에 대한 수리 요청에 따라, 제 동료인 페레즈 씨가 오늘 오후 귀사를 방문하셨습니다. 귀사를 만나서 몇 가지 드릴 질문이 있으셨는데 귀하신데 사무실에 안 계시던 듯싶습니다.

제가 서류를 조사해 보고 주소가 바뀔 때 종종 생기는 리다이렉션 오류를 성공적으로 고쳤습니다. 또한 원활한 전환을 위해 모든 추적 스크립트가 제 자리에 있도록 해결하였습니다.

**195** 누군가 필요한 쿠키를 제거한 것으로 보이시지만, 이게 오작동의 주요인으로 보입니다. 귀사의 문제는 심각한 것은 아니지만, 만약을 대비해 복구될 수 있는 백엔 파일을 준비하시길 권고드립니다. **정책이 새로 바뀌어서 추가 요금을 내실 필요는 없습니다.**

궁금하신 점이 있으시면, 페레즈 씨나 제 휴대 전화 973-465-3456으로 연락 주세요.

벤 나이트

---

어휘 general director 총괄 이사 malfunction 오작동, 고장 redesign 새로 디자인하다 error 오류 URL 웹페이지 주소 have nothing to do with ~와 관련이 없다 groundless rumor 근거 없는 루머 hack 해킹하다 attempt 시도 cookie 쿠키, 인터넷 사용자가 브라우저로 보내는 일종의 대이터 묶음 on time 늦지 않게 stay focused on ~에 집중을 유지하다 regarding ~에 대하여 (It) sounded like ~처럼 들렸다(보였다) hinder 방해하다 forward 전달하다 warranty period 보증 서비스 기간 extend 늘리다, 연장하다 as per ~에 따라 examine 조사하다 script 스크립트, 특정 명령에 따라 수행되는 일련의 자동 지침 transition 이행 restore 복구하다 just in case 만약을 대비해 incur (좋지 못한 손실 등을) 초래하다

**191** 화람에 따르면, 어떤 진술이 사실인가?
(A) 배낭 씨가 소문을 퍼뜨렸다.
(B) 헨릭스 씨는 기술 팀에서 일한다.
(C) 무젠 엔지니어는 다른 디자인 업체를 고용할 것이다.
**(D) 해킹명했다고 믿는 사람들이 있다.**

해설 화람에서 우리가 해킹명했다는 근거 없는 루머가 생겼다고 했으므로 해킹을 당했다고 믿는 사람들이 있음을 알 수 있다. 따라서 정답은 (D)이다.

**192** 페레즈 씨에 대해 암시된 것은 무엇인가?
(A) 301 리다이렉션 오류를 일으켰다.
(B) 무젠 엔지니어의 책임자이다.
(C) 처음 홈페이지를 디자인했다.
**(D) 금요일까지 해외에 있을 것이다.**

해설 화람에서 페레즈 씨가 첫 번째 이메일에서 연락 회의를 위해 내일 아침 일찍 캐나다로 가서 이틀 26일까지는 돌아오지 않는다고 했다. 이메일이 작...

---

해설 편지의 예약 세부 사항을 보면, 원래 4명을 위한 방을 예약한 것을 할 수 있다. 이메일에서 가족 모두 가고 싶다고 했으므로 프라사드 씨의 총 6객은 인원수는 4명임을 알 수 있으므로 정답은 (D)이다.

**187** 프라사드 씨는 왜 소개팅을 변경하기를 원하는가?
**(A) 그의 딸이 파티에 참석해야 해서**
(B) 그가 딸이 다른 나라로 이사 가기 때문에
(C) 그가 이미 총액을 지불했기 때문에
(D) 포트로는 고기 만한 지역이 아니기 때문에

해설 이메일에서 딸이 시간이 되지 않는 관계로 예약을 바꾸고 싶다고 했는데 문자 메시지에서 그 이유가 나온다. 친한 친구가 이민을 가는데 가기 전에 송별 파티에 가야 한다고 했으므로 정답은 (A)이다.

**188** 문자 메시지에 오후 3시 2번에 있는 "You bet"과 의미상 가장 가까운 것은?
(A) 농담이라고
**(B) 물론**
(C) 부득이
(D) 따뜻하게

해설 You bet은 '나도 너를 해도 좋아. 그럼 정도로 확실해'라는 의미로 You bet의 다른 표현은 Certainly이다. 따라서 정답은 (B)이다. Certainly는 '틀림없이, 분명히'라는 뜻이지만, 일상생활에서 You bet 대신에 쓰이는 정도로 읽어두어야 한다.

**189** 프라사드 씨는 어떤 번호로 전화를 하게 될 것인가?
(A) (353) 793-3520
(B) (44) 248-3458
(C) (353) 793-3523
**(D) (353) 793-3525**

해설 이메일에서 세부 사항에 콘페런션 예약 디스크에 연락하라는 내용으로 보이 프라사드 씨는 예약 디스크에 연락을 할 것이다. 편지에서 예약 변경을 연락은 (353) 793-3525로 예약 디스크에 연락하라는 내용으로 보이 (D)가 정답이다.

**190** 프라사드 씨는 얼마를 미리 지불하겠는가?
(A) 미화 0달러
(B) 미화 200달러
**(C) 미화 400달러**
(D) 미화 800달러

해설 이메일에서 계약 조건으로 방에 대한 50%이 보증금을 지불할 것이라는 내용으로 보이 그는 50%의 보증금을 지불할 것이다. 이체 편지에 있는 '결제 세부 사항'을 보면 현재 세부 지불에 할 총 금액이 800달러임을 알 수 있다. 800달러에서 50%를 보증금으로 내려면 프라사드 씨는 400달러를 지불하게 될 것이므로 (C)가 정답이다.

**197** 광고에 따르면, 신디의 패션 가게에 정점으로 연급된 것은 무엇인가?

(A) 알맞은 제품 가격
(B) 세준 연체 혜택
(C) 친절한 종업원들
**(D) 정근 용이성**

**해설** 광고에서 점심시간이나 퇴근 후 들르기에 완벽한 위치에 있다는 내용으로 보아 접근 용이한 위치가 정점이라 할 수 있으므로 정답은 (D)이다.

**198** 로스 씨에 대해 암시된 것은 무엇인가?

(A) 그는 월튼에서 20마일 떨어진 곳에 가게를 얻었다.
(B) 그는 퇴근 후 쇼핑하는 걸 좋아한다.
**(C) 그는 버로우스 씨가 쓴 메모를 발견했다.**
(D) 그는 최근 새 매니저로 고용되었다.

**해설** 이메일에서 예전 매니저인 대블 로스 씨가 엄마 메모 가게 해경을 위해 가게 해경할 수 있었다고 했으므로 정답은 (C)이다.

**199** 누가 신디의 패션 가게를 버로우스 씨에게 추천했는가?

(A) 프리슬리 씨
**(B) 햄포서 씨**
(C) 로스 씨
(D) 파뮬리 씨

**해설** 노트에서 가장 친한 친구인 에밀리가 이 가게를 추천했다는 내용이 나오며, 그것만으로 친구의 이름을 완전히 알 수는 없다. 이메일에서 에밀리 햄포서 씨는 지난 수년 동안 저희 가게 단골손님이었다는 내용에서 추천해 준 친구의 이름이 에밀리 햄포서임을 알 수 있으므로 정답은 (B)이다.

**200** 버로우스 씨는 HA-20 귀고리에 대해 할인을 얼마나 받을 수 있는가?

(A) 10퍼센트
(B) 15퍼센트
(C) 20퍼센트
**(D) 30퍼센트**

**해설** 노트에서 버로우스 씨는 HA-20 시리즈라기 가게 문이 닫혀 서지 못했다고 했는데 이메일에서 에밀리 햄포서가 노트에서 언급한 은 귀고리를 구경했다고 했다. 광고에서 은 제품은 30% 할인을 받을 수 있다고 했으므로 정답은 (D)이다.

---

성일은 화원의 작성일인 23일 화요일과 같은 23일임을 알 수 있다. 따라서 26일은 금요일이고, 즉 메체로스 쓰는 금요일까지 해야만 있을 것이므로 정답은 (D)가 정답이다.

**193** 두 번째 이메일에서, 세 번째 단락, 두 번째 줄에 있는 "backup"과 의미상 가장 가까운 것은?

(A) 지지
**(B) 복사본**
(C) 축적
(D) 정체

**해설** 두 번째 이메일에서 만약을 대비해 저장하는 백업 파일을 의미하는 부분에서 backup은 백업(파일)의 의미로 쓰였음을 알 수 있다. 따라서 정답은 (B)이다.

**194** 왜 나이트 씨는 수리를 청구하지 않는가?

(A) 기술적 문제가 구매자의 잘못으로 발생한 것이기 때문에
(B) 뭘 사이트가 새로 디자인될 때 오류가 항상 발생하기 때문에
**(C) 보증 기간 내에 서비스가 제공되었기 때문에**
(D) 무적으로 그렇게 할 권한이 없기 때문에

**해설** 두 번째 이메일에서 새 정책으로 인해 추가 요금을 받지 않는다고 했고 첫 번째 이메일에서 보증 기간이 3급로 연장되었다는 내용이 나온다. 따라서 보증 기간이 연장되어 수리비를 받지 않는 것이므로 (C)가 정답이다.

**195** 누가 홈페이지에 오작동에 대한 책임이 있었는가?

(A) 헤릭스 씨
**(B) 배맛 씨**
(C) 파레이즈 씨
(D) 나이트 씨

**해설** 두 번째 이메일에서 누군가 쿠키를 제거한 것이 오작동 주요 원으로 보인다는 내용이 나온다. 따라서 쿠키를 제거한 사람 때문에 발생한 문제임을 알 수 있다. 화원에서 배것 씨도 불필요하 보이는 쿠키를 식제함으로써 보다 빠른 인터넷 연결을 제공하기 위한 노력을 하였다는 내용에서 쿠키를 삭제한 이가 베갓 씨가 쿠키를 식제했음을 알 수 있다. 따라서 정답은 (B)이다.

---

[196-200]

**신디의 패션 가게**

이사가 목전에 있습니다!

- 최대한 많은 정을 싣지 않고 또 그 정을 가져가는 것을 피하기 위한 행사의 노력입니다!
- 3월 말까지 모든 물품이 있을 때까지입니다!
- 방대한 종류의 패션 주얼리와 액세사리 할인!
  수입은 금귀품은 20%, 은귀품은 30%, 매달 제품은 50% 할인된 가격으로 만나 보세요!
- 점심시간이나 퇴근 후 방문하시기에 완벽한 위치에 있습니다!

---

**프리슬리 씨에게,**

**200** 귀고리(HA-20)를 사러고 가게에 왔는데, 문이 닫혀 있네요. 따라서 26일은 금요일이고, **199** 제 가장 친한 친구인 에밀리가 이 가게를 추천했습니다. 그래서 200일이나 운전하고 온 겁니다. 어떻게 공지 하나 없이 이럴 수 있죠? 이거 읽으시면 연락 주세요.

(241) 456-4576, nburrows@abcmail.com.

낸시 버로우스

---

발신: 신디 프리슬리 〈priestly@cindy_priestly.fashion.com〉
수신: 낸시 버로우스 〈nburrows@abcmail.com〉
날짜: 3월 24일
제목: 진심으로 죄송합니다.

**버로우스 씨에게,**

깊은 사과의 말씀을 드립니다. 저희는 월튼에서 다시 가게를 개장하기 위해 어제 이사했으니, 많은 것들을 준비하는 사노르 나머지 문에 공지를 붙이는 걸 깜박했습니다. 다행히, 저희 예전 매니저인 대블 로스 씨가 엄마 메모 가게를 위해 가기 갔다가 귀하의 메모를 발견했습니다.

**199** 귀하의 친구인 에밀리 햄포서 씨는 지난 수년 동안 저희 가게 단골손님이었습니다. 거의 매일 퇴근 후 들르시곤 했는데, **200** 메모에서 언급하신 은 귀고리를 오늘 오전에 구경하신 것을 기억합니다. 고객 문들에 호응을 계속 주지 않기 위해 3월 말까지 저희는 이사 세일 광고에 적힌 정가 그대로 만들었으니, 어떠한 은 제품 특정 제품에는 변동이 있습니다.

- 물품이, 팬던트, 팔찌로는 10% 할인이고,
- 겹혼반지, 브로치는 15% 할인입니다. 어떤 제품도 만들었던 건에요.

저희 새 가게는 월튼에서 4월 1일에 개장합니다. 언제든 방문하세요! 궁금한 신 점이 있으면, 저희 새 매니저인 브리지 파뮬리 씨께 (910) 876-1467로 연락하시거나 www.cindy_priestly.fashion.com을 방문해 주세요.

신디 프리슬리, 사장

---

**어휘** be upon us ~가 우리의 목전에 있다 last-ditch effort 필사적인 노력 unload (짐을) 내리다 last 지속되다 swing by 잠깐 들르다 a huge selection of 큰 선택의 폭 방대한 종류의 stop in 잠깐 들르다 a pair of earrings 한 쌍의 귀고리 former 이전의 lease termination 임대 계약 해지 as specified in ~에 명시된 대로 inevitable 피할 수 없는 necklace 목걸이 bracelet 팔찌 wedding band 결혼반지

**196** 신디의 패션 가게가 세일 행사를 하는 이유는 무엇인가?

(A) 새 물품을 위한 공간을 만들어야 하기 때문에
**(B) 너무 많은 물건을 옮기고 싶지 않아서**
(C) 건물 임대를 연장하기 어렵기 때문에
(D) 새 매니저를 위한 축하 파티를 열기 때문에

**해설** 광고에서 최대한 많은 정을 싣지 않고 또 정을 가져가는 것을 피하기 위한 필사의 노력이라고 하였으므로 정답은 (B)이다.

# Actual Test 03

## 🎧 Listening Comprehension

**PART 1**

| 1 (C) | 2 (C) | 3 (C) | 4 (C) | 5 (B) | 6 (B) |
|---|---|---|---|---|---|

**PART 2**

| 7 (C) | 8 (B) | 9 (C) | 10 (A) | 11 (C) | 12 (A) | 13 (C) | 14 (A) | 15 (A) | 16 (A) |
|---|---|---|---|---|---|---|---|---|---|
| 17 (C) | 18 (A) | 19 (B) | 20 (B) | 21 (B) | 22 (B) | 23 (A) | 24 (C) | 25 (B) | 26 (B) |
| 27 (A) | 28 (B) | 29 (B) | 30 (A) | 31 (C) | | | | | |

**PART 3**

| 32 (A) | 33 (D) | 34 (C) | 35 (B) | 36 (D) | 37 (C) | 38 (C) | 39 (C) | 40 (D) | 41 (B) |
|---|---|---|---|---|---|---|---|---|---|
| 42 (B) | 43 (D) | 44 (B) | 45 (B) | 46 (A) | 47 (C) | 48 (C) | 49 (A) | 50 (B) | 51 (D) |
| 52 (A) | 53 (D) | 54 (C) | 55 (A) | 56 (D) | 57 (C) | 58 (B) | 59 (A) | 60 (B) | 61 (B) |
| 62 (B) | 63 (A) | 64 (D) | 65 (D) | 66 (A) | 67 (B) | 68 (A) | 69 (C) | 70 (B) | |

**PART 4**

| 71 (B) | 72 (A) | 73 (B) | 74 (C) | 75 (B) | 76 (D) | 77 (B) | 78 (D) | 79 (C) | 80 (C) |
|---|---|---|---|---|---|---|---|---|---|
| 81 (C) | 82 (A) | 83 (C) | 84 (B) | 85 (A) | 86 (C) | 87 (C) | 88 (A) | 89 (C) | 90 (A) |
| 91 (D) | 92 (B) | 93 (C) | 94 (A) | 95 (A) | 96 (B) | 97 (C) | 98 (A) | 99 (D) | 100 (C) |

## 📖 Reading Comprehension

**PART 5**

| 101 (C) | 102 (A) | 103 (C) | 104 (C) | 105 (D) | 106 (C) | 107 (A) | 108 (D) | 109 (B) | 110 (D) |
|---|---|---|---|---|---|---|---|---|---|
| 111 (C) | 112 (B) | 113 (C) | 114 (C) | 115 (D) | 116 (B) | 117 (A) | 118 (D) | 119 (B) | 120 (A) |
| 121 (B) | 122 (C) | 123 (A) | 124 (B) | 125 (D) | 126 (C) | 127 (D) | 128 (D) | 129 (D) | 130 (B) |

**PART 6**

| 131 (B) | 132 (C) | 133 (A) | 134 (C) | 135 (D) | 136 (D) | 137 (D) | 138 (C) | 139 (B) | 140 (A) |
|---|---|---|---|---|---|---|---|---|---|
| 141 (A) | 142 (B) | 143 (B) | 144 (A) | 145 (A) | 146 (D) | | | | |

**PART 7**

| 147 (B) | 148 (C) | 149 (B) | 150 (A) | 151 (A) | 152 (C) | 153 (C) | 154 (A) | 155 (A) | 156 (B) |
|---|---|---|---|---|---|---|---|---|---|
| 157 (D) | 158 (A) | 159 (B) | 160 (C) | 161 (A) | 162 (A) | 163 (C) | 164 (B) | 165 (D) | 166 (A) |
| 167 (A) | 168 (B) | 169 (D) | 170 (D) | 171 (A) | 172 (B) | 173 (D) | 174 (D) | 175 (B) | 176 (C) |
| 177 (A) | 178 (D) | 179 (D) | 180 (A) | 181 (D) | 182 (D) | 183 (B) | 184 (A) | 185 (D) | 186 (C) |
| 187 (B) | 188 (C) | 189 (C) | 190 (B) | 191 (C) | 192 (C) | 193 (C) | 194 (B) | 195 (C) | 196 (C) |
| 197 (B) | 198 (B) | 199 (B) | 200 (C) | | | | | | |

## PART 1

**1** 미W

(A) A man is taking a picture.
(B) A man is sawing a wooden board.
**(C) A man is wearing a safety helmet.**
(D) A man is working on some wires.

(A) 한 남자가 사진을 찍고 있다.
(B) 한 남자가 나무 판을 톱으로 자르고 있다.
**(C) 한 남자가 안전모를 쓰고 있다.**
(D) 한 남자가 전선 작업을 하고 있다.

어휘 saw 톱질하다 work on ~에 대한 작업을 하다 wire 전선

**2** 미M

(A) The road is closed to vehicles.
(B) Some windows are being cleaned.
**(C) The doors of the vehicle are open.**
(D) Some luggage is being unloaded from the bus.

(A) 도로는 폐쇄되어 있다.
(B) 몇몇 창문들이 닦이고 있는 중이다.
**(C) 자동차의 문들이 열려 있다.**
(D) 버스에서 짐이 내려지고 있다.

어휘 vehicle 자동차 luggage 짐 unload 차에서 짐을 내리다

**3** 미W

(A) Some people are seated for a meal.
(B) Chairs have been set up under a pavilion.
**(C) Different containers are placed on the table.**
(D) A waiter is clearing some plates from the table.

(A) 몇몇 사람들이 식사를 하려고 앉아 있다.
(B) 의자들이 임시 구조물 아래 놓여 있다.
**(C) 여러 가지 그릇들이 테이블 위에 있다.**
(D) 웨이터가 탁자에서 접시를 치우고 있다.

어휘 pavilion 임시 구조물 container 용기, 그릇 clear 치우다 plate 접시

**4** 영M

(A) A truck is being towed.
(B) A plane has taken off from a runway.
**(C) An aircraft has been parked.**
(D) People are repairing an airplane.

(A) 트럭이 견인되고 있다.
(B) 비행기가 활주로에서 이륙했다.
**(C) 비행기가 주차되어 있다.**
(D) 사람들이 비행기를 수리하고 있다.

어휘 tow 견인하다 take off 이륙하다 runway 활주로

**5** 미W

(A) Musicians are packing up their instruments.
**(B) People are gathered to watch a performance.**
(C) The audience is standing up to applaud.
(D) Some performers are descending from a stage.

(A) 음악가들이 그들의 악기를 싸고 있다.
**(B) 사람들이 공연을 보기 위해 모여 있다.**
(C) 청중이 박수를 치려고 서 있다.
(D) 몇몇 연주자들이 무대에서 내려오고 있다.

어휘 pack up 짐을 싸다 instrument 악기, 도구 gather 모으다 performance 공연 applaud 박수를 치다 descend 내려가다

**6** 영M

(A) One man is holding a menu.
**(B) Some people are sitting at tables separately.**
(C) Some people are passing by an outdoor café.
(D) Everyone is having a discussion in a large group.

(A) 한 남자가 메뉴판을 들고 있다.
**(B) 몇몇 사람들이 몇 개의 테이블에 따로따로 앉아 있다.**
(C) 몇몇 사람들이 야외 카페를 지나가고 있다.
(D) 모든 사람들이 한 대 모여 토론을 하고 있다.

어휘 separately 따로 떨어져서 pass by ~을 지나쳐 가다

## PART 2

**7** 미M / 미W

Who else is going to the tennis finals?
(A) Yes, they are.
(B) To the gym.
**(C) Scott and Peter are.**

테니스 결승전에 또 누가 갈 건가요?
(A) 네, 그들입니다.
(B) 체육관으로요.
**(C) 스캇이랑 피터요.**

어휘 tennis final 테니스 결승전

**8** 영M / 미W

When did Claire clean out the storage room?
(A) Those cleaners are new.
**(B) After we left.**
(C) At the office supply store.

클레어가 언제 창고를 청소한 가죠?
(A) 저 세제들은 새 거예요.
**(B) 우리가 퇴근한 후에요.**
(C) 사무용품 가게에서요.

어휘 storage room 창고 cleaner 세제

**9** 미W / 미M

What's the round trip fare to Australia?
(A) On vacation.
(B) It doesn't seem to be fair.
**(C) It varies month to month.**

호주까지 왕복 항공료가 얼마인가요?
(A) 휴가로요.
(B) 공정한 거 같지 않네요.
**(C) 매달 바뀝니다.**

어휘 round trip 왕복 fare 요금 fair 공정한 vary 변하다 month to month 다달이

**10** 미M / 영M

When are we supposed to check out the room?
**(A) By eleven thirty.**
(B) Many times.
(C) In Lloyd Hotel.

우리가 언제 방을 체크아웃해야 하나요?
**(A) 11시 30분까지요.**
(B) 여러 번이요.
(C) 로이드 호텔에서요.

어휘 be supposed to ~하기로 되어 있다, ~해야 한다 check out (호텔에서) 도움 지불하고 나가다

**11** 영M / 미M

Are you going to speak at the budget meeting?
(A) We have to stay within budget.
(B) Our speaker was not able to make it.
**(C) Wyatt is going to take my place.**

예산 회의에서 발언을 하실 건가요?
(A) 예산을 초과하진 안 돼요.
(B) 우리 연사가 올 수가 없었어요.
**(C) 와이어트가 저를 대신할 거예요.**

어휘 stay within budget 예산을 초과하지 않다 make it 오다

**12** 미M / 미W

Where can I find a service request form?
**(A) I'll get one for you.**
(B) That is an excellent finding.
(C) I've been served already.

서비스 요청서를 어디서 찾을 수 있죠?
**(A) 제가 하나 갖다 드릴게요.**
(B) 그건 훌륭한 결과예요.
(C) 전 이미 받았어요.

어휘 request form 요청서 finding 결과, 결론 serve 제공하다, (음식을) 차려 주다

**13** 영M / 미W

Do you offer orientation sessions for assembly-line workers?
(A) A production facility.
(B) Safety helmets and goggles.
**(C) Yes, in their first month.**

조립 라인 근로자들을 위한 오리엔테이션 시간을 제공하나요?
(A) 생산 시설이요.
(B) 안전모와 보호 안경요.
**(C) 네, 그들의 첫째 달에요.**

어휘 assembly-line 조립 라인 safety helmet 안전모

**14** The letters on this poster need to be enlarged.
[미W] (A) They look good enough as they are.
[미M] (B) It's been posted since last week.
(C) Yes, but you should write him a letter.

포스터에 있는 글자를 확대해야 됩니다.
(A) 지금 그대로가 좋아 보이는데요.
(B) 지난주부터 공지되어 있었어요.
(C) 네, 하지만 그에게 편지를 쓰셔야 해요.
어휘 letter 글자 ~ enlarge 확대하다 as they are 지금 그대로 post 공지하다

**15** Who is going to water the plants in the lobby?
[미W] (A) You will find the name on the bulletin board.
[영M] (B) I'm not thirsty, thanks.
(C) It's being renovated.

로비에 있는 식물에 누가 물을 줄 건가요?
(A) 게시판에서 이름을 찾으시면 돼요.
(B) 전 목마르지 않아요, 감사해요.
(C) 수리 공사 중이에요.
어휘 water 물을 주다

**16** Why isn't Doyle working on the magazine article?
[미M] (A) I thought he was.
[영M] (B) Next Monday, I think.
(C) Over three pages.

도일이 잡지 기사 일을 왜 하지 않고 있죠?
(A) 전 그가 하고 있는 줄 알았어요.
(B) 다음 주 월요일일 거예요.
(C) 세 페이지 이상요.
어휘 article 기사 work on ~에 노력을 들이다, 애쓰다

**17** Maybe you should apply for the manager position here.
[미W] (A) Who told you that?
[미W] (B) You should bring a copy of your résumé.
(C) That sounds like a good idea.

여기 매니저 직에 지원하시는 게 좋겠어요.
(A) 누가 그것을 말해줬죠?
(B) 이력서 한 부를 가져오세요.
(C) 좋은 생각인 것 같습니다.
어휘 apply for 지원하다 résumé 이력서

**18** How do you know Jessie Kelly?
[영M] (A) We went to the same culinary school.
[미W] (B) Actually, no progress was made.
(C) For over three years.

제시 켈리를 어떻게 아세요?
(A) 같은 요리 학원을 다녔거든요.
(B) 실은, 아무것도 진척된 게 없었어요.
(C) 3년 이상 동안이요.
어휘 culinary school 요리 학원 make progress 진척되다, 진행되다

**19** Can you help me pass this out to all employees?
[미W] (A) Sure, you need to employ a new one.
[미M] (B) It was already distributed the other day.
(C) By 10% this year.

이걸 모든 직원들에게 나눠 주는 거 도와주실래요?
(A) 물론이죠, 새로운 것을 이용해야 합니다.
(B) 며칠 전에 이미 배포했어요.
(C) 올해 10퍼센트요.
어휘 pass ~ out 나눠 주다 employ 쓰다, 이용하다 distribute 배포하다

**20** When will Edwin replace the ink cartridge in this printer?
[미W] (A) About 10 color copies.
[영M] (B) Hasn't he done it yet?
(C) Some papers have been misplaced.

에드윈이 이 프린터의 잉크 카트리지를 언제 교체할 건가요?
(A) 약 10개의 컬러 사본이요.
(B) 그가 아직도 안 했나요?
(C) 서류 일부를 찾지 못했어요.
어휘 replace 교체하다 misplace 제자리에 두지 않아 찾지 못하다

**21** This automobile comes with a five-year warranty, doesn't it?
[영M] (A) It's on the right hand side.
[미M] (B) That's why it is popular with consumers now.
(C) Five years have passed since I started working here.

이 차는 5년간 보증이 됩니다, 그렇죠?
(A) 그것은 오른쪽에 있습니다.
(B) 그래서 요즘 고객들에게 인기가 있죠.
(C) 제가 여기 근무한 지 5년이 흘렀어요.
어휘 automobile 자동차 warranty 보증(서) consumer 소비자

**22** Do you know which client called when I was out?
[미M] (A) I think I'll go out for lunch.
[미W] (B) The man you met with last Monday.
(C) In the conference room.

제가 없을 때 어떤 고객이 전화했는지 아세요?
(A) 전 밖에 나가서 점심을 먹을 거예요.
(B) 지난 월요일에 만나던 그 남자분요.
(C) 회의실 안에서요.
어휘 be out (사무실) 밖에 있는

**23** I can't reach that file folder on the top shelf.
[영M] (A) Use the ladder over there.
[미W] (B) Yes, all the paperwork is complete.
(C) The office is always messy.

맨 위 선반에 있는 파일 폴더에 손이 닿지 않아요.
(A) 저기 있는 사다리를 이용하세요.
(B) 네, 모든 서류 작업은 끝났어요.
(C) 사무실은 항상 지저분한데요.
어휘 messy 지저분한

**24** Why are you taking an online distance learning course?
[미W] (A) Five courses in total.
[미M] (B) The classroom is on the second floor.
(C) It'll help me get promoted.

온라인 원격 교육 과정을 왜 듣는 건가요?
(A) 총 다섯 개의 과정이요.
(B) 교실은 2층에 있어요.
(C) 제가 승진하는 데 도움이 될 거예요.
어휘 distance learning 원격 교육 in total 총, 통틀어 get promoted 승진하다

**25** Should I make the reservation at the Chinese restaurant or the Japanese one?
[미W] (A) I booked my flight yesterday.
[영M] (B) I don't have a preference.
(C) Call the manager for directions.

제가 중식당을 예약해야 할까요, 일식당을 예약해야 할까요?
(A) 어제 비행편을 예약했어요.
(B) 특별히 선호하는 게 없어요.
(C) 길 안내를 위해 매니저에게 전화하세요.
어휘 preference 선호, 기호 directions 길 안내

**26** You have time to organize the reception, don't you?
[영M] (A) The reception was a great success.
[미M] (B) Not if I'm assigned one more project this week.
(C) Sorry, I missed your call.

환영 행사를 맡을 시간이 되시죠, 그렇죠?
(A) 환영회는 아주 성공적이었어요.
(B) 이번 주에 프로젝트 하나를 더 맡으면 못할 거예요.
(C) 죄송해요, 당신 전화를 못 받았어요.
어휘 assign 배정하다

**27** You were informed of Amy's promotion to senior researcher, weren't you?
[미M] (A) Yes, she really deserved it.
[미W] (B) I believe Ms. Lawrence is.
(C) The corporate headquarters.

에이미가 선임 연구원으로 승진했단 소식을 들으셨죠, 그렇죠?
(A) 네, 그녀는 정말 그럴 만해요.
(B) 로렌스 씨라고 생각해요.
(C) 회사 본사요.
어휘 inform 알리다 promotion 승진 senior researcher 선임 연구원 headquarters 본사

# PART 3

**28**

[영M] My movie review will be published in the June issue of the magazine.

[영M] (A) An assistant editor is being hired.
(B) I'll certainly look for it.
(C) It is currently out of stock.

제 영화평이 그 잡지 6월호에 실릴 거예요.
(A) 부편집자가 채용될 거예요.
(B) 제가 꼭 찾아볼게요.
(C) 현재 품절되었어요.

어휘 movie review 영화평 issue 잡지(간행물)의 호 out of stock 품절 되어, 매진되어

**29** Where should we take the investors for dinner?

[미W] (A) For vegetarians.
[영M] **(B) We went to a seafood restaurant last time.**
(C) The meeting went very well.

저녁식사로 투자자들을 어디로 모셔야 할까요?
(A) 채식주의자들을 위해서요.
(B) **해산물 레스토랑은 지난번에 갔었어요.**
(C) 미팅은 매우 잘 진행됐어요.

어휘 investor 투자자 vegetarian 채식주의자 go well 잘 진행되다

**30** Could you please move your truck forward a bit so the workers can load the equipment?

[미W] **(A) Sure, just let me get my key.**
[영M] (B) No problem, I'll turn the volume down.
(C) I've got too many.

인부들이 장비를 실을 수 있도록 트럭을 조금 더 앞쪽으로 이동해 주시겠어요?
(A) **물론이죠, 제가 키를 가져올게요.**
(B) 그럼요, 볼륨을 줄일게요.
(C) 너무 많이 가지고 있어요.

어휘 equipment 장비 turn down (볼륨을) 줄이다

**31** Please make a right turn at the next intersection.

[미W] (A) The section chief will figure it out.
[영M] (B) You should turn it in by 2:00 today.
**(C) It's a shortcut, right?**

다음 교차로에서 우회전하세요.
(A) 부서장이 알아낼 거예요.
(B) 오늘 2시까지 그걸 제출하셔야 해요.
(C) **그게 지름길이죠, 그렇죠?**

어휘 make a right turn 우회전하다 intersection 교차로 figure out 알아내다 turn in 제출하다 shortcut 지름길

P103

**Questions 32-34 refer to the following conversation.** [미W] [영M]

W Hello, **32** do you have the equipment to transfer video tapes to DVD? I have a number of tapes from family holidays that I would like to watch on my DVD player.

M We do, but there can be a problem with the quality of old video tapes. **33** Sometimes the sound is distorted. I'm not sure that you will be satisfied with the result if you transfer the footage.

W Oh, I see. **34** Perhaps I will just buy a new video player. Do you know anyone who still sells them?

여 안녕하세요, 비디오테이프를 DVD로 옮기는 장치가 있나요? 가족 휴가 때 찍은 많은 테이프들이 있는데, 제 DVD 플레이어에서 보고 싶거든요.

남 있기 하지만 이전 비디오테이프의 품질에 문제가 있을 수도 있어요. 가끔씩 소리가 일그러져 있어요. 영상을 전환한다면 그 결과에 만족하실지 모르겠 네요.

여 아, 그렇군요. 그냥 새로운 비디오 플레이어를 사야 할지도 모르겠어요. 아 직 그걸 판매하는 분을 알고 계세요?

어휘 transfer (정보나 파일 등의 기록 방법을 달리하여) 복사하다, 전환하다 footage 영상; 장면, 화면 distorted 비뚤어진 일그러진 delete 삭제하다 expire 만료되다 instruction manual 사용 설명서 out of date 구식인 뒤떨어진

**32** Why is the woman at the shop?
**(A) To get video footage transferred**
(B) To buy a DVD player
(C) To take a family video
(D) To purchase an instruction manual

여자가 상점에 있는 이유는 무엇인가?
(A) **비디오 영상을 전환하려고**
(B) DVD 플레이어를 사려고
(C) 가족 비디오를 찍으려고
(D) 사용 설명서를 구입하려고

**33** What problem does the man mention?
(A) The tape will be deleted.
(B) The warranty has expired.
(C) The video player is out of date.
**(D) The sound can be unclear.**

남자가 언급하는 문제는 무엇인가?
(A) 테이프가 삭제될 것이다.
(B) 보증서가 만료되었다.
(C) 비디오 플레이어가 오래되었다.
(D) **소리가 분명하지 않을 수도 있다.**

패러프레이징 distorted → unclear

**34** What will the woman most likely do next?
(A) Purchase more video tapes
(B) Repair some items
**(C) Search for new hardware**
(D) Borrow some video equipment

여자가 다음에 하게 될 일은 무엇인가?
(A) 더 많은 비디오테이프 구입
(B) 물건 수리
(C) **새로운 기기 찾기**
(D) 비디오 장비 대여

패러프레이징 buy a new video player → Search for new hardware

**Questions 35-37 refer to the following conversation.** [미W] [영M]

W Excuse me, ma'am, do you have tickets left for the show on Saturday night?

M Yes, ma'am. **35** We have plenty of tickets available for the 6 o'clock and 7.30 shows. Which one do you prefer?

W Well, my coworkers and I can make the earlier time if we hurry, but I think it will be too rushed. There's 20 of us and we'll need to have dinner. Better make it the later time.

M All right then. **36** **37** You need 20 tickets for 7.30. Since there are more than 15 people in your group, **37** you can pay the group rate, $20 per person which is 30% off the regular price.

여 실례지만, 토요일 밤에 하는 공연 표가 남아 있나요?

남 네, 있습니다. 6시와 7시 30분 공연 표가 많이 있습니다. 어떤 걸로 드릴까요?

여 동료들과 제가 서두르면 더 빨리 하는 경우는 있지만 너무 서두르는 것 같 아서요. 저희가 20명인데 저녁도 먹어야 해서요. 나중의 표를 사는 게 낫지 싶어요.

남 알겠습니다. 그러면 7시 30분 걸로 20장이 필요하시네요. 15명 이상이기 때문에 단체 요금이 적용되니, 정상 가격에서 30퍼센트 할인된 가격으로 1 인당 20달러 내시면 됩니다.

어휘 plenty of 많은 rushed 서두른, 성급한 group rate 단체 요금

**35** Who most likely is the man?
(A) A show organizer
**(B) A ticket office clerk**
(C) A musician
(D) A waiter

Actual Test 03 058 • 059

M Hi, ㊶ I'm wondering if there's a rental car available for a week. My car is at the repair shop right now.

W You came to the right place! What kind of car are you looking for? A compact car or something larger?

M I have to pick up a group of five clients from Chicago at the airport tomorrow and show them around our factories. ㊷ I don't care that much about the fuel efficiency as long as it is something big enough to seat more than 5 passengers. I was looking at the minivans you have in the parking lot. Do you have any of those available?

W Of course we do. If you give me a minute, ㊸ I'll have our representative show you what we have.

남 안녕하세요, 일주일 동안 렌탈할 수 있는 차가 있는지 궁금합니다. 제 차가 지금 수리 중이거든요.

여 제대로 오셨습니다! 어떤 차를을 찾고 계세요? 경차요, 아니면 좀 더 큰 거요?

남 내일 공항에서 시카고에서 오시는 5명의 단체 손님을 태워서 우리 공장들을 견학시켜 드려야 해요. 5명 이상이 탈 수 있다면 연비는 별 문제가 안 돼요. 주차장에 전시된 미니밴을 봤어요. 그중에서 지원에게 자료 직원에게 자를 보여 드리라고 할게요.

여 물론입니다. 잠깐 시간을 주시면 제가 자료 직원에게 차를 보여 드리라고 할게요.

어휘 rental car 렌터카 repair shop 수리점 compact car 경차 show around 돌리보게 하다 care about 신경 쓰다 fuel efficiency 연료의 효율성(연비) seat 앉히다 representative 직원 transmission 변속 기어

**41** Where most likely are the speakers?
(A) At a car repair shop
(B) At a car rental store
(C) At an airport
(D) At a factory
화자들은 어디에 있는가?
(A) 자동차 수리점
(B) 렌터카 영업점
(C) 공항
(D) 공장

**42** What feature is the man looking for?
(A) Fuel efficiency
(B) Comfortable space
(C) Automatic transmission
(D) GPS navigation
남자는 어떤 특징을 찾고 있는가?
(A) 연비
(B) 편안한 공간

---

남자는 누구인가?
(A) 공연 기획자
(B) 매표소 직원
(C) 음악가
(D) 케이터

**36** What time does the woman buy tickets for?
(A) 5:00 P.M.
(B) 5:40 P.M.
(C) 6:00 P.M.
(D) 7:30 P.M.
여자는 몇 시 표를 사는가?
(A) 오후 5시
(B) 오후 5시 40분
(C) 오후 6시
(D) 오후 7시 반

**37** How much does the woman need to pay for the tickets?
(A) $200
(B) $300
(C) $400
(D) $500
여자는 표를 사기 위해 얼마를 지불해야 하는가?
(A) 200달러
(B) 300달러
(C) 400달러
(D) 500달러

M ㊳ Hi, Professor Kelly. Did you see the course schedule for next semester? I need your confirmation before I post it online.

W Oh, yes. In fact, I was looking at it right now. Hmm.... I see these two classes are scheduled back-to-back.

M Yes, is there any problem with that?

W Well, I teach the History and English class in the Laskin Building and History and Modern Languages in Braun Hall. ㊴ This means that I have only 10 minutes to wrap up one class, walk about 100 meters to reach another building, and then get ready for another class. All within just 10 minutes!

M Ah, that's a good point. ㊴ No one can do that. ㊵ How about I push back your History and Modern Languages class from 11 A.M. to 1 P.M.?

남 안녕하세요, 켈리 교수님. 다음 학기의 수업 스케줄은 보셨나요? 온라인에 올리기 전에 확인이 필요해서요.

여 네, 실은 지금 보고 있었어요. 흠... 이 두 수업이 연속으로 스케줄이 잡혀 있네요.

남 네, 문제라도 있나요?

여 음, 저는 역사와 영어 수업은 라스킨 빌딩에서 하고 역사와 현대 언어를 브라운홀에서 해요. 그 말은 제가 단 10분 동안 한 수업을 마무리하고, 100미터를 걸어서 다른 건물에 도착한 다음 또 하나의 수업을 준비해야 한다는 뜻이에요. 전부를 단 10분 내에요!

남 아, 좋은 지적이네요. 누구도 그렇게는 할 수가 없죠. 제가 교수님의 역사와 현대 언어 수업을 오전 11시에서 오후 1시로 미루면 어떨까요?

어휘 course schedule 강좌 스케줄 semester 학기 confirmation 확인 back-to-back 연속해서 wrap up 마무리하다 within ~ 이내에 push back (일정을) 미루다, 늦추다 task 주어진 일, 업무 workload 업무량

**38** Where do the speakers mostly like work?
(A) At a fitness center
(B) At a library
(C) At a university
(D) At a travel agency
화자들은 어디서 일할 것 같은가?
(A) 피트니스 센터
(B) 도서관
(C) 대학교
(D) 여행사

**39** What does the woman imply when she says, "All within just 10 minutes"?
(A) She needs to hire an assistant.
(B) She tries to exercise regularly.
(C) She thinks the task is impossible.
(D) She is interested in the man's opinion.
여자가 "전부를 단 10분 이내에"라고 말한 의도는 무엇인가?
(A) 그녀는 조수를 고용해야 한다.
(B) 그녀는 규칙적으로 운동하려고 한다.
(C) 그녀는 그 일이 불가능하다고 생각한다.
(D) 그녀는 남자의 의견에 관심이 있다.

**40** What does the man offer to do?
(A) Reduce her workload
(B) Rearrange an office
(C) Employ more staff
(D) Revise the schedule
남자는 무엇을 해주겠다고 하는가?
(A) 여자의 업무량을 줄이는 것
(B) 사무실을 재정리하는 것
(C) 직원을 더 고용하는 것
(D) 스케줄을 수정하는 것

Questions 47-49 refer to the following conversation. 미W 미M

W Wow, Ronald. Look at all these coins! There are so many and from a lot of countries!

M 47 I have been collecting coins since I was a child. When I was young, 48 my father would give me coins left over from his business trips. They have fascinated me ever since. Then when I became an adult, I collected them from my own trips abroad. I will continue with this hobby as long as I can.

W A childhood love has turned into a lifelong passion. Wonderful!

M 49 I also have collected rare coins. They are in another case. Would you like to see them?

여 와, 로날드. 이 동전들 좀 봬. 정말 많은 나라의 동전이네!

남 47 어렸을 때부터 계속 모았어. 48 어렸을 때 아버지께서 출장 다녀오시면 주시고 했어. 그때부터 오직 동전이 매력에 빠졌지. 어른이 되었을 땐 내가 여행을 다니면 모았어. 할 수 있는 한 취미로 이어 가려고 해.

여 어릴 때 좋아하던 게 평생 좋아하는 취미가 되었구나. 멋지다!

남 49 희귀한 동전도 모았어. 다른 케이스에 있는데 좀 볼래?

어휘 collect 모으다  fascinate 마음을 사로잡다  childhood 어린 시절  lifetime 평생  passion 열정 열중하다  취미 활동  rare 희귀한

47  What are the speakers talking about?
(A) The countries the man has been to
(B) The man's childhood
(C) The man's longtime interest
(D) The man's family traditions

화자들은 무엇에 대해 이야기하는가?
(A) 남자가 가 본 나라
(B) 남자의 어린 시절
(C) 남자의 평생 흥미
(D) 남자의 가족 전통

48  From whom did the man get the coins in his childhood?
(A) From his friend
(B) From his teacher
(C) From his parent
(D) From his neighbor

남자는 어릴 시절에 동전을 누구로부터 얻게 되었나?
(A) 친구로부터
(B) 선생님으로부터
(C) 부모로부터
(D) 이웃으로부터

---

(C) 자동 변속 기어
(D) 내비게이션

43  What will the woman most likely do next?
(A) Show the man another model
(B) Have a car inspected
(C) Take the man to the parking lot
(D) Ask a colleague to help the man

여자가 다음에 할 일은 무엇인가?
(A) 남자에게 다른 모델 보여 주기
(B) 차를 점검받기
(C) 남자를 주차장으로 데려 가기
(D) 동료에게 남자를 도와주라고 요청하기

---

Questions 44-46 refer to the following conversation with three speakers. 영M 미W 영W

M Hi. Please come in. So, 44 how are you two doing with the new customer database? Have you finished transferring all the paper files to electronic ones?

W1 Well, most of the information of our existing customers has been entered into the new system that I've created. And Ms. Barret is working on our online ordering system right now.

W2 Yes. 45 I'm in the middle of upgrading the online ordering system so that contact information is automatically linked to purchase history.

M That's very good. But the electronic database should be made available by the end of this week. 46 Why don't you have some interns assist you with the upgrade?

W2 Okay. That's a good idea.

남 안녕하세요. 들어오십시오. 두 분이 하고 있는 새로운 고객 데이터베이스는 어떻게 되고 있나요? 종이 파일을 전자 파일로 옮기는 것은 다 끝났나요?

여1 음, 대부분의 기존 고객 정보는 제가 만든 새 시스템에 입력되었습니다. 그리고 베렛 씨가 지금 온라인 주문 시스템을 작업하고 있어요.

여2 네. 저는 온라인 주문 시스템을 업그레이드해서 연락 정보와 구매 내역이 자동으로 연결되도록 하는 중입니다.

남 매우 좋습니다. 그런데 그 전자 데이터베이스는 이번 주말까지는 이용이 가능하도록 해야 됩니다. 인턴들이 그 업그레이드를 돕도록 시키는 게 어떨까요?

여2 네. 좋은 생각입니다.

어휘 transfer ~을 ~로 옮기다  existing 기존의  automatically 자동적으로  link 연결하다  purchase history 구매 내역  migrate 이동시키다  deal with 처리하다

44  What are the speakers mostly discussing?
(A) Improving communication skills
(B) Migrating information to a database
(C) Dealing with customer complaints
(D) Transferring to another department

화자들은 무엇에 대해 이야기하는가?
(A) 의사소통 기술을 향상시키는 것
(B) 정보를 데이터베이스로 옮기는 것
(C) 고객 불만을 처리하는 것
(D) 다른 부서로 이전하는 것

패러프레이징  transferring → Migrating

45  What is Ms. Barret currently working on?
(A) A construction project
(B) A system upgrade
(C) A business presentation
(D) A product test

베렛 씨는 현재 어떤 작업을 하고 있는가?
(A) 공사 프로젝트
(B) 시스템 업그레이드
(C) 사업상의 발표
(D) 상품 테스트

46  What does the man suggest?
(A) Getting some assistance
(B) Speaking to a supplier
(C) Closing a business early
(D) Working extra hours

남자는 무엇을 제안하는가?
(A) 도움을 받는 것
(B) 공급업체와 이야기하는 것
(C) 업체를 일찍 닫는 것
(D) 추가 근무를 하는 것

**49** What does the man suggest the woman do?
(A) Look at some rare items
(B) Help him collect coins
(C) Tell him about her hobby
(D) Go on a trip with him
남자가 여자에게 제안하는 것은 무엇인가?
(A) 희귀한 물건 보기
(B) 동전 수집 돕기
(C) 여자의 취미에 관해 얘기하기
(D) 그와 여행 가기
패러프레이징 rare coins → some rare items

Questions 50-52 refer to the following conversation. 미W 영M
W Oh, not again! **50** This is the second time the program has erased some of my work. Why does the computer keep deleting my files? **50** This new software must have a bug in it.
M Sorry to hear that, Kaetlyn. But I'm using the program just fine. **51** Maybe you're saving your work in the wrong location. **52** Try searching for your file by name.
W Could that be it? **52** Would you please show me how I can do that? You know computers better than me. Or should I get a computer guy to show me? I've got to get this out by 5 today.
M I'm not expert but I can take a look. If nothing else, you can explain the situation to the team manager.

여 아, 또 그래네 프로그램이 제 작업을 지운 게 두 번째예요. 왜 컴퓨터가 계속 제 파일을 지우는 걸까요? 새 소프트웨어에 오류가 있는 게 분명해요.
남 안됐군요, 케이틀린. 하지만 저는 잘도 쓰는데 괜찮아요. 아마 당신이 파일 저장을 잘못된 곳에 한 게 아닐까요. 이름으로 파일을 찾아보세요.
여 그게 가능해요? 어떻게 하는지 보여 주시겠어요? 당신이 저보다 컴퓨터를 더 잘 아니까요. 아니면 제게 컴퓨터 기사를 불러야 할까요? 오늘 5시까지는 해결해야 해요.
남 제가 전문가는 아니지만 볼 수 있어요. 이번이 아니면 당신 팀장님에게 이 상황을 설명하면 돼요.

어휘 erase 지우다  bug 오류  get out 해결하다  incorrectly 잘못되게 setting 설정

**50** What is the woman's problem?
(A) An important document is missing.
(B) Some of her files have been deleted.
(C) A proposal has been rejected.
(D) A project is behind schedule.
여자의 문제는 무엇인가?
(A) 중요한 서류가 없어졌다.
(B) 몇몇 파일이 지워졌다.
(C) 제안서가 거절되었다.
(D) 프로젝트가 예정보다 늦어졌다.
패러프레이징  has erased → have been deleted

**51** According to the man, what may be the cause of the problem?
(A) The woman got a virus on the computer.
(B) The woman downloaded a new program.
(C) The woman didn't upgrade her computer.
(D) The woman may be saving her files incorrectly.
남자에 따르면 문제의 원인은 무엇인가?
(A) 여자의 컴퓨터가 바이러스에 걸렸다.
(B) 여자는 새 프로그램을 다운로드했다.
(C) 여자는 컴퓨터를 업그레이드하지 않았다.
(D) 여자가 파일을 잘못 저장했을 수도 있다.
패러프레이징  in the wrong location → incorrectly

**52** What does the woman ask the man to do?
(A) Help her locate her files
(B) Call a computer technician
(C) Look for a new program
(D) Check her software settings
여자가 남자에게 요청하는 것은 무엇인가?
(A) 파일 찾는 것 돕기
(B) 컴퓨터 기술자에게 전화하기
(C) 새 프로그램 찾기
(D) 소프트웨어 설정 확인하기

Questions 53-55 refer to the following conversation. 미W 미M
W Hey, Sean. What are you doing? Are those the restaurant comment cards?
M Yes. You know **53** I've been meaning to go through them for a while, and I'm doing it now.
W That's good. Did you find anything interesting?
M Yes, there are actually a lot of positive reviews. And a lot of customers suggested that we stay open late during weekends and holidays.
W Yeah, I agree with that. **54** Most of the other restaurants in the area have recently extended their hours. So I think we should try the same.
M Okay, **55** I'll speak to Mr. Lohan about the idea tomorrow morning. If he approves it, we can offer longer hours to our customers starting this Saturday.

여 연결하세요, 선 뭐하고 있어요? 그거 레스토랑 의견 카드인가요?
남 맞아요, 한 동안 살펴보려고 했었는데 이제야 보고 있어요.
여 좋네요. 흥미로운 거라도 찾으셨어요?
남 네, 실은 긍정적인 후기들이 많이 있어요. 그리고 많은 고객들이 제안하기를 주말이나 휴일에는 늦게까지 문을 열어 달라고 해요.
여 네, 저도 동의합니다. 이 주변의 다른 대부분의 레스토랑들도 최근에 영업시간을 연장했거든요. 그래서 우리도 같은 것을 시도해봐야 한다고 생각해요.
남 알겠어요, 내일 아침에 로핸 씨에게 이 아이디어를 얘기해 볼게요. 만약 그가 찬성한다면, 우리는 이번 주 토요일부터 고객들에게 연장된 영업시간을 제공할 수 있어요

어휘 comment card (고객) 의견 카드  go through 살펴보다  extend 연장하다  approve 찬성하다, 승인하다  post card 엽서  hours 영업시간을 연장하다  excuse 변명  expand 확장하다  product line 생산(제품) 라인  budget 예산

**53** What is the man doing?
(A) He is writing a news article.
(B) He is collecting some post cards.
(C) He is making a reservation.
(D) He is reading customer feedback.
남자는 무엇을 하는 중인가?
(A) 신문 기사를 쓰는 중이다.
(B) 엽서를 모으는 중이다.
(C) 예약을 하는 중이다.
(D) 고객 피드백을 읽는 중이다.

**54** Why does the woman say, "we should try the same"?
(A) To change a plan
(B) To make an excuse
(C) To agree with a suggestion
(D) To request some help
여자는 왜 "우리도 같은 것을 시도해봐야 한다"고 말하는가?
(A) 계획을 바꾸려고
(B) 해명을 하려고
(C) 제안에 동의하려고
(D) 도움을 요청하려고

**55** What will the man do tomorrow morning?
(A) Discuss an idea
(B) Expand a product line
(C) Hold a special event
(D) Revise a budget plan
남자는 내일 아침에 무엇을 할 것인가?
(A) 아이디어에 대해 논의한다.
(B) 생산 설비를 확장한다.
(C) 특별 행사를 연다.
(D) 예산 계획을 수정한다.

**59** Where most likely do the speakers work?
(A) At a factory
(B) At a repair shop
(C) At a hardware store
(D) At a delivery service

화자들은 어디에서 근무하는가?
(A) 공장
(B) 수리점
(C) 철물점
(D) 배송사

**60** What caused the delay of the shipment?
(A) An overdue payment
(B) A technical problem
(C) An incomplete form
(D) A change in work schedule

배달이 지연된 이유는 무엇인가?
(A) 연체된 지불
(B) 기술적 문제
(C) 불완전한 양식
(D) 근무 일정 변화

**61** What will the man probably do next?
(A) Buy new machines
(B) Talk to a coworker
(C) Check a delivery
(D) Search for a repairman

남자가 다음에 할 일은 무엇인가?
(A) 새 기계 구입하기
(B) 동료에게 얘기하기
(C) 배송 확인하기
(D) 수리 기사 찾기

Questions 59-61 refer to the following conversation. 미W 미M

W  I'm wondering if the latest shipment of training shoes has gone out to the stores yet. You mentioned there was a delay so I want to make sure it doesn't affect our delivery schedule too much.

M  What happened was 60 a machine on the production floor broke down last week, but I had it repaired over the weekend and it's up and running again. Our stores should have everything just a couple of days later than they originally requested.

W  That's a relief! It's about time that we have our machinery checked up on a regular basis to prevent this from happening again.

M  Good idea. 61 I'll have Sharon look for someone to periodically repair and maintain our equipment.

여  최근 배송된 우리 운동화가 매장에 도착했는지 궁금하네요. 지난번에 지연이 있었다고 하셨어서 배송 일정에 크게 차질이 없도록 분명히 하려고요.

남  지난주에 생산 부서에 기계가 고장이 났지만 제가 주말 동안 수리를 해서 지금은 다시 작동을 합니다. 우리 매장에서는 원래 요청했던 날짜보다 불과 이틀 정도 늦게 물건을 받을 겁니다.

여  다행이군요! 그런 일이 다시 발생하지 않도록 기계를 정기적으로 점검해야 할 때였네요.

남  좋은 생각입니다. 샤론에게 우리 장비를 정기적으로 수리하고 유지 관리할 사람을 알아보라고 할게요.

어휘  shipment 배송  up and running 작동하는  originally 원래  relief 안도  on a regular basis 정기적으로  periodically 정기적으로  incomplete 불완전한

---

Questions 56-58 refer to the following conversation. 영M 미W

M  Hello, Catori. How's everything been? 56 I just dropped by to see how the new sprinkler system is working here in your yard.

W  Oh, it works fantastic. It is very convenient to have the lawn and all my flowers automatically watered even in the early dawn. And as we don't get much rain nowadays, it is important to have it watered on a regular basis.

M  Right. 57 It's easier than doing it by hand and even cuts down on your utility bill. I told you it was worth the money.

W  True. Now I am planning to install another one there inside my greenhouse. 58 Some more plants will grow there before the end of this year and it's crucial to water them well.

남  안녕하세요, 카토리 씨. 잘 지내셨어요? 새로운 스프링클러가 여기 마당에서 어떻게 작동하는지 알아보기 위해 잠깐 들렀어요.

여  아, 정말 잘됐요. 심지어 새벽에도 잔디와 꽃에 물 주기가 2주 편리해요. 요즘은 비가 별로 안 오기 때문에 정기적으로 물을 주는 게 중요하잖아요.

남  맞아요. 손으로 하는 것보다 쉽고 게다가 공과금도 절약해 줘요. 도움 들인만 한 가치가 충분히 있다고 말씀드렸잖아요.

여  그렇습니다. 이제 제 비닐하우스에도 하나 설치할 계획이에요. 올 연말 전에 식물을 더 심을 건데 물을 잘 주는 게 관건이죠.

어휘  have ~ watered ~에 물을 주다  on a regular basis 정기적으로  cut down on 줄이다  utility bill 공공요금  greenhouse 온실  crucial 매우 중요한  cut down (가격을) 내리다  harvest yield 수확량

**56** Where are the speakers?
(A) In a greenhouse
(B) At a café
(C) At a flower shop
(D) In a garden

화자들은 어디에 있는가?
(A) 온실
(B) 카페
(C) 꽃가게
(D) 정원

**57** What advantage is mentioned about the new equipment?
(A) It comes with a manual.
(B) It can be installed easily.
(C) It costs less on utilities.
(D) It has come down in price.

---

새로운 장비에 관해 어떤 장점이 언급되는가?
(A) 사용 설명서가 딸려 나온다.
(B) 쉽게 설치할 수 있다.
(C) 공과금이 절약된다.
(D) 가격이 내렸다.

매뉴프레이징  cuts down on your utility bill → costs less on utilities

**58** According to the woman, what will happen later this year?
(A) Harvest yields will remain the same as last year.
(B) She will grow new plants indoors.
(C) The weather in the area will improve.
(D) The installation fee will increase.

여자에 따르면, 올 연말에 일어날 일은 무엇인가?
(A) 수확량이 지난해와 똑같을 것이다.
(B) 실내에 새로운 식물을 심을 것이다.
(C) 그 지역 날씨가 좋아질 것이다.
(D) 설치비가 인상될 것이다.

| Company | Location |
|---|---|
| Avon Brochure | Dallas |
| Elddis | Houston |
| Wave Design | New Orleans |
| Vista Print | Phoenix |

W: Jeff, I'm really looking forward to [62] the annual marathon our company is hosting. It'll be great publicity for us!

M: Oh, speaking of which, have you reviewed the list of brochure design companies? We have to select one now to get all the promotional materials done in time.

W: You're right. I'm actually considering this firm. Designers at Elddis are great people to work with. As you know, they did an excellent job last year. [63] But my only concern is our budget. It has been cut by 20% so maybe we can't afford Elddis now.

M: I know. [64] Why don't we go for the one that's located in Phoenix? It is very close to us so we'll be able to save some money on delivery.

| 회사 | 위치 |
|---|---|
| 애이본 브로셔 | 댈러스 |
| 엘디스 | 휴스턴 |
| 웨이브 디자인 | 뉴올리언스 |
| 비스타 프린트 | 피닉스 |

**62** What type of event is the company organizing?
(A) A fundraiser
**(B) A sporting event**
(C) A seasonal sale
(D) A musical performance

이 회사는 어떤 종류의 행사를 준비하고 있는가?
(A) 기금모금 행사
**(B) 스포츠 행사**
(C) 계절 세일
(D) 음악 공연

**63** What is the woman concerned about?
**(A) A reduced budget**
(B) A scheduling conflict
(C) A shortage of employees
(D) A late delivery

여자는 무엇에 대하여 염려하는가?
**(A) 줄어든 예산**
(B) 겹친 일정
(C) 직원 부족
(D) 늦은 배송

**64** Look at the graphic. Which company will probably be hired?
(A) Avon Brochure
(B) Elddis
(C) Wave Design
**(D) Vista Print**

시각 자료를 보시오. 어떤 회사가 고용될 것인가?
(A) 애이본 브로셔
(B) 엘디스
(C) 웨이브 디자인
**(D) 비스타 프린트**

여: 제프, 전 우리 회사가 개최하는 연례 마라톤 경주가 정말 기대 돼요. 우리에게 좋은 홍보가 될 거예요!

남: 그 얘기 나와서 말인데요, 브로셔 디자인 회사 명단은 살펴보셨어요? 제 때에 모든 홍보물을 다 끝내려면 이제 한 곳을 선택해야만 해요.

여: 맞아요, 전 사실 이 회사를 고려하고 있어요. 엘디스의 디자이너들은 함께 일하기 정말 좋은 사람들이죠. 아시다시피, 작년에도 일을 훌륭하게 해 냈어요. 하지만 제 유일한 걱정은 우리 예산이에요. 20%가 깎여서 이젠 엘디스를 할 만한 여유가 없을 거예요.

남: 맞죠. 저희 피닉스에 있는 업체로 해 볼까요? 우리랑 무척 가까워서 배송에서 돈을 좀 절약할 수 있을 거예요.

**어휘** publicity 홍보 brochure 브로셔 promotional materials 홍보물 do an excellent job 일을 훌륭하게 하다 scheduling conflict 겹치는 일정 shortage 부족

---

| Argos Bedding | | |
|---|---|---|
| | | Order No. 8901 |
| Item | Quantity | Total Price |
| Blanket | 1 | $15 |
| Pillow | 1 | $50 |
| Pillowcase | 4 | $12 |
| Curtain | 2 | $80 |

W: Hi. How may I help you, sir?

M: Hello. I ordered several items from your online store last week. But when I received the delivery, [65] there was one item missing from the package. Because [66] I lost one of my bed pillows during the move, I ordered a replacement. But it did not arrive with the other items.

W: Sorry about that. Let me find out why that happened. Did you bring your shipping invoice?

M: Yes, here it is.

W: Ah... here's what happened. Because the manufacturer has discontinued that particular latex pillow, we just sent the rest of the order to you. I'm very sorry about that. [67] I'll give you a refund for the pillow and this gift certificate as a token of my apology.

M: Oh, thank you, I'd appreciate that.

| 아교스 침구 | | |
|---|---|---|
| | | 주문번호 8901 |
| 상품 | 수량 | 총 금액 |
| 담요 | 1 | 15달러 |
| 베개 | 1 | 50달러 |
| 베개커버 | 4 | 12달러 |
| 커튼 | 2 | 80달러 |

여: 안녕하세요. 어떻게 도와 드릴까요?

남: 안녕하세요. 제가 지난주에 온라인 상점에서 물건 및 개를 주문했습니다. 그런데 배달을 받아보니 물건 하나가 소포에 없더군요. 제가 이사 중에 침대 베개 하나를 잃어버려서 교체품을 주문한 기셨습니다. 그런데 다른 상품들과 함께 도착하지 않았어요.

여: 죄송합니다. 왜 그런 일이 있었는지 알아볼게요. 배달 송장은 가져오셨나요?

남: 네, 여기 있어요.

여: 아, 이렇게 된 것이네요. 생산자가 그 라텍스 베개를 생산 중단했기 때문에 나머지 주문만 보내던 겁니다. 정말 죄송합니다. 베개 비용은 환불을 해 드리고 사과의 의미로 이 상품권도 드리겠습니다.

남: 오, 감사합니다.

**어휘** pillow 베개 replacement 교체품 find out 알아보다 shipping 배송 invoice 배달 송장 discontinue (생산을) 생산 중단하다 gift certificate 상품권 as a token of ~의 의미로 misplace 두지 않이 찾지 못하다

**65** What is the man's problem?
(A) He cannot order an item online.
(B) He does not like what he purchased.
(C) He did not bring an original receipt.
**(D) He received an incomplete order.**

남자의 문제는 무엇인가?
(A) 온라인으로 물건을 주문할 수 없다.
(B) 구입한 물건이 마음에 들지 않는다.
(C) 영수증 원본을 가져오지 않았다.
**(D) 완전한 주문품을 받지 못했다.**

**66** According to the man, what happened during the move?
**(A) An item was misplaced.**
(B) Some movers arrived late.
(C) A truck broke down.
(D) Some furniture was damaged.

남자에 따르면, 이사 중에 어떤 일이 있었는가?
**(A) 물건이 분실됐다.**
(B) 이사 직원들이 늦게 도착했다.
(C) 트럭이 고장 났다.
(D) 가구가 손상됐다.

**패러프레이징** lost → was misplaced

**67** Look at the graphic. How much money will the man be refunded?
(A) $15
**(B) $50**
(C) $12
(D) $80

시각 자료를 보시오. 남자는 얼마의 금액을 환불받을 것인가?
(A) 15달러
**(B) 50달러**
(C) 12달러
(D) 80달러

---

Questions 68-70 refer to the following conversation and schedule.
영M 미W

| Schedule | |
|---|---|
| Stage 1 | Suites |
| Stage 2 | Ballroom |
| Stage 3 | Pools |
| Stage 4 | Building Exterior |

M Alice, **68** how's the hotel renovation project going?

W **69** It's going very well. I was a little concerned because the hotel was very old. However, there haven't been any unexpected challenges so far. **68** We're a little ahead of schedule.

M I'm happy to hear that. The client wants to reopen the facilities for the tourist season, which begins in June. Can you meet the deadline?

W Let me check the timeline. We refurbished all the suites last week. And **70** we're about to start working on the grand ballroom now. So, yes, I think all the work should be completed by the end of May.

M Perfect! Could you send a copy of the renovation timeline to the client?

| 스케줄 | |
|---|---|
| 1단계 | 스위트룸 |
| 2단계 | 연회장 |
| 3단계 | 수영장 |
| 4단계 | 건물 외관 |

남 앨리스, 호텔 보수 프로젝트는 어떻게 진행되고 있나요?

여 아주 잘 진행되고 있어요. 호텔이 아주 오래돼서 조금 걱정을 했었거든요. 그런데 지금까지 예상치 못한 어려운 점은 없었어요. 일정보다 조금 앞서 있어요.

남 그렇다니 다행이네요. 고객이 여행 시즌을 맞이해 시설을 재개장하기를 원하거든요. 마감일을 맞출 수 있을까요?

여 일정을 체크해 볼게요. 지난주에 모든 스위트룸을 재단장했어요. 그리고 이제 대연회장의 작업을 시작하려고 해요. 그래서 네, 5월 말까지는 모든 작업이 완료될 거예요.

남 완벽해요. 보수 공사 일정을 고객에게 한 부 보내줄 수 있을까요?

**68** What kind of company does the woman most likely work for?
**(A) An architectural firm**
(B) A hotel
(C) An apparel company
(D) A graphic design company

여자는 어떤 종류의 회사에서 일할 것 같은가?
**(A) 건축 회사**
(B) 호텔
(C) 의류 회사
(D) 그래픽 디자인 회사

**69** What does the woman say about the ongoing project?
(A) She is dealing with some challenges.
(B) A client is very demanding.
**(C) It is on the right track.**
(D) A status report has been completed.

여자는 진행 중인 프로젝트에 대해 뭐라고 말하는가?
(A) 몇몇 문제들을 처리하고 있다.
(B) 고객이 매우 까다롭다.
**(C) 잘 진행되고 있다.**
(D) 상태 보고서가 완료되었다.

**70** Look at the graphic. What stage of the project will begin now?
(A) Stage 1
**(B) Stage 2**
(C) Stage 3
(D) Stage 4

시각 자료를 보시오. 프로젝트의 어떤 단계가 이제 시작될 것인가?
(A) 1단계
**(B) 2단계**
(C) 3단계
(D) 4단계

**어휘** ahead of schedule 일정보다 앞선 refurbish 재단장하다 be about to 막 ~을 하려고 하다 grand ballroom 대연회장 apparel 의류 ongoing 진행 중인 demanding 까다로운 on the right track 올바른 방향으로 나아가는 status 상태

# PART 4

Questions 71-73 refer to the following announcement. 미M

Good afternoon, passengers. ⑦ This is your captain speaking. You're now on board Flight 7D9 with service from Hong Kong to Dusseldorf. We're expecting to take off 20 minutes later than the scheduled time ⑦ in order to allow some passengers from a connecting flight to board the plane. ⑦ But this delay will not affect our anticipated arrival time since weather conditions are favorable. We're still expecting to arrive in Dusseldorf at 6 A.M. local time. Thank you for your patience.

좋은 오후입니다. 승객 여러분. 저는 기장입니다. 현재 홍콩에서 뒤셀도르프로 가는 7D9 항공기에 탑승하고 계십니다. 연결 항공기의 승객들이 탑승해야 하므로 우리는 예정된 시간보다 20분 늦게 이륙할 것으로 예상됩니다. 그러나 날씨가 좋기 때문에 이 지연이 예정된 도착 시간에는 영향을 주지 않을 것입니다. 우리는 여전히 뒤셀도르프에 현지 시간 오전 6시에 도착할 것으로 예정입니다. 인내심에 감사드립니다.

어휘 captain (비행기) 기장 on board 탑승한, 탑승 중인 connecting flight 연결 항공편 anticipated 예상된, 예정된 affect 영향을 미치다 favorable (날씨가) 좋은 local time 현지 시간 overbook 초과 예약하다 on time 제때에 runway 활주로 load (짐을) 싣다

71 Where most likely are the listeners?
(A) In a waiting room
**(B) On a plane**
(C) In a train station
(D) On a bus

청자들은 어디에 있을 것 같은가?
(A) 대기실
**(B) 비행기**
(C) 기차역
(D) 버스

72 What is the cause of the delay?
**(A) Some passengers have not arrived.**
(B) Some luggage is being loaded.
(C) A runway has been blocked.
(D) A flight has been overbooked.

지연의 원인은 무엇인가?
**(A) 일부 승객이 도착하지 않았다.**
(B) 짐이 실어지고 있다.
(C) 활주로가 막혀 있다.
(D) 항공기가 초과 예약되었다.

73 What does the speaker say will happen?
(A) The weather will change.
**(B) The plane will arrive on time.**
(C) Some seats will become available.
(D) Some food will be provided.

화자는 무슨 일이 있을 것이라고 하는가?
(A) 날씨가 변할 것이다.
**(B) 비행기가 제때에 도착할 것이다.**
(C) 몇몇 좌석이 이용 가능해질 것이다.
(D) 약간의 음식이 제공될 것이다.

---

Questions 74-76 refer to the following talk. 영W

Hello and welcome to our newly opened Henz Department Store. ⑦ I am delighted that you are now members of our sales team. ⑦ This morning you will take a couple of training sessions before we open the doors to the public. We are expecting a lot of people and for our first day of trading, we are offering a welcome gift to our customers. ⑦ Customers who visit the store will receive a free gift. They can choose between a pair of gloves and a woolly hat. This will promote our winter collection.

안녕하세요. 새로 개장한 헨즈 백화점에 오신 것을 환영합니다. 여러분이 지금 우리 영업팀의 멤버라는 것이 아주 기쁩니다. 일반 고객들에게 문을 열기 전 오늘 아침 여러분은 두어 개의 교육을 받게 될 것입니다. 우리는 많은 사람들이 올 것을 기대하고 있으며, 영업 첫날을 위해 고객들에게 환영 선물을 제공할 것입니다. 매장을 방문한 고객들은 무료 선물을 받게 됩니다. 그들은 한 켤레의 장갑과 털실로 짠 모자 중에서 하나를 선택할 수 있습니다. 이것으로 우리의 겨울 컬렉션을 홍보할 것입니다.

어휘 training session 교육 trading 거래, 영업 woolly 털실로 만든[짠] promote 홍보하다 store detective 백화점[상점] 경비원 complimentary 무료의 try on 입어보다

74 Who most likely is the speaker addressing?
(A) Reception staff
(B) Food suppliers
**(C) Sales people**
(D) Store detectives

화자는 누구에게 말하는 것 같은가?
(A) 접수처 직원
(B) 음식 공급업자
**(C) 영업 사원**
(D) 상점 경비원

75 What will the listeners do this morning?
(A) Take inventory
**(B) Receive training**
(C) Visit a new store
(D) Watch a video

청자들이 오늘 아침에 할 일은 무엇인가?
(A) 재고 목록 만들기
**(B) 교육받기**
(C) 새로운 매장 방문하기
(D) 비디오 관람하기

패러프레이징 take a couple of training sessions → Receive training

76 What will be provided for customers?
(A) A facility tour
(B) A free shuttle bus
(C) A discount coupon
**(D) A welcome gift**

고객들에게 무엇이 제공될 것인가?
(A) 시설 견학
(B) 무료 셔틀 버스
(C) 할인 쿠폰
**(D) 환영 선물**

패러프레이징 a free gift → A welcome gift

---

Questions 77-79 refer to the following telephone message. 호M

Good afternoon, Mr. Turner. This is Alex Choudhary from Bitson Research Lab. We'd like to thank you for interviewing with us the other day. ⑦ I am calling to inform you that unfortunately, the position has been filled by another candidate at this time. However, your qualifications and positive attitude impressed us very much. ⑦ As the company expands, we expect to be recruiting more staff in the near future, so ⑦ with your permission, we would like to keep your résumé on our eligible list until something more suited to your talents comes up. Thank you again and have a good day.

안녕하세요, 터너 씨. 저는 빗슨 리서치 랩의 알렉스 초드헤리입니다. 며칠 전 면접에 참석해 주셔서 정말 감사합니다. 안타깝게도 지원하신 직책은 이번에 다른 지원자로 충원되었음을 알려 드리고자 전화 드립니다. 하지만 귀하의 자질과 긍정적인 태도는 저희에게 정말 큰 인상을 남겼습니다. 회사가 확장됨에 따라, 저희는 가까운 시일 내에 더 많은 직원들을 채용할 것으로 예상하도록 허락하신다면, 귀하의 재능에 더 적합한 직책이 나올 때까지 귀하의 이력서를 채용 후보 명단에 올려 두고 싶습니다. 다시 한 번 감사드리며 좋은 하루 되세요.

어휘 candidate 후보자, 지원자 qualification 자질, 자격 recruit 채용하다 eligible list 채용 후보자 명단 suit 적합하다 assignment 업무 diversify 다각화하다, 다변화하다 funding 자금 keep ~ on file ~을 파일로 보관하다

**77** Why is the speaker calling?
(A) To offer a position
**(B) To explain a decision**
(C) To request a document
(D) To schedule an interview

화자가 전화하는 이유는 무엇인가?
(A) 일자리를 제안하려고
**(B) 결정에 대해 설명하려고**
(C) 서류를 요청하려고
(D) 인터뷰 일정을 잡으려고

**78** What does the speaker expect will happen soon?
(A) Assignments will be diversified.
(B) Funding will be increased.
(C) A contract will be renewed.
**(D) Other positions will be available.**

화자는 곧 무엇이 일어나기를 예상하는가?
(A) 업무가 다양해질 것이다.
(B) 자금 지원이 늘어날 것이다.
(C) 계약이 갱신될 것이다.
**(D) 다른 직책이 가능할 것이다.**

**79** What does the speaker offer to do?
(A) Revise some regulations
(B) Examine a budget
**(C) Keep a document on file**
(D) Provide a reference

화자가 제의하는 것은 무엇인가?
(A) 몇 가지 규정 수정하기
(B) 예산 검토하기
**(C) 서류를 파일로 보관하기**
(D) 추천서 제공하기

**패러프레이징** keep your résumé in our eligible list → Keep a document on file

**80** What happened this morning?
(A) A commercial building was sold.
(B) A new policy was announced.
**(C) A public facility was reopened.**
(D) A sports season began.

오늘 아침에 일어난 일은 무엇인가?
(A) 상업 건물이 팔렸다.
(B) 새로운 정책이 발표됐다.
**(C) 공공 시설물이 재개장했다.**
(D) 스포츠 시즌이 시작됐다.

**81** What is mentioned about the center?
(A) The opening date has been delayed.
(B) Parking is limited.
**(C) Some areas are available for rent.**
(D) A baseball game will be held.

**어휘** intensive 집중적인    unveil 발표하다    expand 확장하다    fitness 건강
accessible 접근이 가능한    take place 열리다    commercial 상업적인
resident 거주자    free of charge 무료로    take a look at 한 번 보다

---

Questions 80-82 refer to the following news report. 미W

And now for local news. ⑩ After 18 months of intensive work, the city of South Montana finally unveiled its new and improved Community Center this morning. The facility now features an expanded fitness center, meeting rooms, and a larger parking lot. In addition, wireless Internet is now accessible throughout the building. Most of all, a brand new gymnasium has been added featuring a basketball court, volleyball court, and even a swimming pool. ⑪ It is even available to rent out for a small fee for various activities such as birthday parties. A re-opening ceremony is scheduled to take place on Saturday at 1 o'clock. ⑫ Those who want to know more details about upcoming events at the Community Center can visit its website or call the Center. Coming up next, Grace's Trends in the housing market.

다음은 지역 소식입니다. 18개월간의 집중적인 작업 끝에 사우스 몬태나 시는 마침내 오늘 아침 새롭고 더 좋아진 시민 문화 회관을 공개했습니다. 그 건물은 이제 확장된 건강 센터, 모임 공간, 주차장을 갖추고 있습니다. 게다가 건물 전체에서 무선 인터넷 접속이 가능합니다. 무엇보다, 새로운 체육관은 농구 코트, 배구 코트, 심지어 수영장까지 갖추었습니다. 심지어 생일 파티와 같은 다양한 활동을 위해 적은 요금을 내고 대여가 가능합니다. 토요일 오후 1시에 재개장식이 이뤄질 예정입니다. 커뮤니티 센터에서 앞으로 하게 될 행사의 관해 더 알고 싶다면 웹 사이트를 방문하시거나 센터로 전화 주세요. 다음 소식은 그레이스의 주택 시장 동향입니다.

---

**82** What are listeners advised to do for more information?
**(A) Look online**
(B) Visit City Hall
(C) Call the station
(D) Check the newspaper

청자들이 더 많은 정보를 얻으려면 무엇을 하길 권고받는가?
**(A) 온라인으로 보기**
(B) 시청 방문하기
(C) 방송국에 전화하기
(D) 신문에서 확인하기

**패러프레이징** visit its website → Look online

---

Questions 83-85 refer to the following excerpt from a meeting. 호M

Okay, now, I'd like to make an announcement about our company's Go Green projects. The management has decided to join the nationwide efforts to save the environment. ⑬ What we can do here at ICA Marketplace is to stop using plastic bags any more. So starting next Monday, ICA cashiers are asked to stop providing customers with plastic bags. Well, I understand your concerns. ⑭ We've tried this before without great results because many customers found it inconvenient and complained. However, this time ⑮ we're going to offer customers store credits as a form of motivation. We'll give it a try for the first two months and see how it goes.

좋습니다. 이제 우리 회사의 친환경 프로젝트에 대해 발표하겠습니다. 경영진은 환경을 살리기 위한 국가적인 노력에 동참하기로 결정하였습니다. 이곳 ICA 마켓에서 할 수 있는 것은 비닐봉지를 더 이상 사용하지 않는 것입니다. 그래서 다음 주 월요일부터 ICA 계산원들은 고객들에게 비닐봉지 제공하는 것을 중단해 주셔야 합니다. 네, 여러분의 염려를 이해합니다. 우리는 지난번에 이것을 시도 했었는데 많은 고객들이 불편하게 생각하고 불평을 해서 좋은 결과를 내지 못했죠. 그러나 이번에는 고객들에게 동기 부여로서 현금 포인트를 제공할 것입니다. 첫 두 달 동안 시도해 보고 진행 상황을 보도록 하겠습니다.

**어휘** Go Green project 환경을 지키기 위한 프로젝트    management 경영
진    nationwide 국가적인 전국의    plastic bag 비닐봉지    store credit
(가게에서 쓸 수 있는) 현금 포인트    motivation 동기    consumption 소비
implement 시행하다    initiative 계획

**83**
According to the speaker, what is the company trying to do?
(A) Reduce water consumption
(B) Save electricity
(C) **Stop the use of plastic bags**
(D) Implement carpooling

화자에 따르면, 회사는 무엇을 시도하려고 하는가?
(A) 물 사용을 줄이는 것
(B) 전기를 아끼는 것
(C) **비닐봉지의 사용을 중지하는 것**
(D) 카풀을 시행하는 것

**84**
What does the speaker mean when he says, "I understand your concerns"?
(A) He predicts that an initiative will fail.
(B) **He knows why listeners have doubts.**
(C) He does not like a suggested idea.
(D) He understands the details of a plan.

화자가 "여러분의 염려를 이해합니다"라고 말한 의미는 무엇인가?
(A) 계획이 실패할 것으로 예측한다.
(B) **청자들이 의심을 갖는 이유를 안다.**
(C) 제안된 아이디어를 좋아하지 않는다.
(D) 계획의 세부 사항을 이해한다.

**85**
What will the ICA customers receive for the next two months?
(A) **Store credits**
(B) Meal vouchers
(C) Free delivery
(D) Paper bags

ICA 고객들은 앞으로 두 달 동안 무엇을 받게 되는가?
(A) **현금 포인트**
(B) 식사 쿠폰
(C) 무료 배송
(D) 종이봉투

---

Questions 86-88 refer to the following excerpt from a meeting. 영W

Good morning, everyone. ⑧⑥ We'll be reviewing the results of the product survey for our new microwave oven, the RX700. As you know, a lot of new capabilities are included in this model and ⑧⑦ our customers seem to like the convection feature best. According to some of the customer reviews, baking and roasting can be done in convection mode, which you wouldn't want to do in a regular microwave. Now the user's manual needs to be revised so that it includes the added features.

좋은 아침이에요. 우리 신상품 전자레인지인 RX700에 대한 상품 설문조사의 결과를 검토해 보겠습니다. 아시다시피, 많은 새로운 기능이 이 모델에 포함되었는데 우리 고객들은 컨벡션 기능을 가장 좋아하는 것 같습니다. 일부 고객 후기에 따르면, 컨벡션 모드에서는 베이킹과 로스팅도 할 수 있다고 하는데, 일반 전자레인지에서는 하지 않을 것입니다. 이제 추가된 기능들을 포함하도록 사용 설명서가 수정되어야 합니다.

어휘 product survey 상품 설문조사  microwave oven 전자레인지  convection 기능 (오븐 등의) 컨벡션 기능  capability 기능  competitor 경쟁사  preprogram 사전에 프로그램을 설정하다  criticize 비평하다  publicize 홍보하다

**86**
What is the main purpose of the meeting?
(A) To select a new supplier
(B) To analyze a competitor's product
(C) **To go over survey results**
(D) To publish a magazine

회의의 주 목적은 무엇인가?
(A) 새로운 공급업체를 선정하려고
(B) 경쟁사의 제품을 분석하려고
(C) **설문 결과를 검토하려고**
(D) 잡지를 출판하려고

패러프레이징 reviewing the results of the product survey
→ go over survey results

**87**
What feature of the product is the most popular?
(A) A cooking time sensor
(B) A preprogrammed keypad
(C) **A convection feature**
(D) A multiple cooking mode

상품의 어떤 기능이 가장 인기 있는가?
(A) 요리시간 감지 센서
(B) 사전 설정 키패드
(C) **컨벡션 기능**
(D) 다중 요리 모드

**88**
Why does the speaker say, "which you wouldn't want to do in a regular microwave"?
(A) **To give a comparison**
(B) To criticize a competitor
(C) To make a suggestion
(D) To publicize a product

화자는 왜 "일반 전자레인지에서는 하지 않는 것이죠"라고 말하는가?
(A) **비교를 하려고**
(B) 경쟁사를 비판하려고
(C) 제안을 하려고
(D) 상품을 홍보하려고

---

Questions 89-91 refer to the following advertisement. 영M

What is your number one New Year's resolution? Isn't it getting in shape? ⑧⑨ If so, come to the Amaru Sports Center, which is located in O'Fallon Sports Park. We're offering special deals right now. ⑨⑩ If you become a member during the month of December, you'll get a 30% discount on any membership you choose. That's not all. ⑪ Our sports equipment store is having the biggest sale of the year from December 1 to 31. Everything, from treadmills to exercise DVDs, will be on sale. Don't miss out on this opportunity! Come to the Amaru Sports Center in O'Fallon Sports Park.

당신의 첫 번째 새해 결심은 무엇인가요? 건강한 몸을 만드는 것 아닌가요? 만약 그렇다면, 오팰론 스포츠 공원에 있는 아마루 스포츠 센터로 오세요. 저희는 지금 특가 혜택을 제공하고 있습니다. 12월 중에 회원이 되시면, 어떤 회원권을 선택하든지 30%의 할인을 받을 수 있습니다. 그게 다가 아니죠. 우리 스포츠 장비 상점에서는 12월 1일부터 31일까지 일 년 중 가장 큰 세일을 합니다. 러닝머신부터 운동 DVD까지 모두 할인됩니다. 이 기회를 놓치지 마세요. 오팰론 스포츠 공원에 있는 아마루 스포츠 센터로 오세요.

어휘 New Year's resolution 새해 결심  get in shape 건강한 몸 상태를 만들다  treadmill 러닝머신  dietary supplement 건강 보조 식품

**89**
Why does the speaker say, "Isn't it getting in shape"?
(A) To introduce a famous athlete
(B) To advertise dietary supplements
(C) **To motivate listeners to exercise**
(D) To satisfy consumer tastes

화자는 왜 "건강한 몸을 만드는 것이 아닌가요?"라고 말하는가?
(A) 유명 선수를 소개하려고
(B) 건강 보조 식품을 홍보하려고
(C) **청자들이 운동을 하도록 하려고**
(D) 고객의 취향을 만족시키려고

Questions 95-97 refer to the following announcement and graph. (호M)

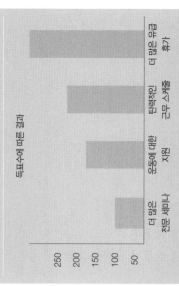

Results by the number of votes

Thank you for attending **95** today's staff meeting. In order to improve employee satisfaction, **96** we conducted a survey last month. Its main purpose was to find out what the company should do to improve happiness in the workplace. I'd like to talk about the results now. As you can see, our employees' number one desire is having more paid vacation time, which unfortunately we cannot afford just yet. **97** However, we are able to act on the second most popular suggestion. In fact, each department will have a meeting to discuss details about it.

오늘의 직원 회의에 참석해 주셔서 감사합니다. 직원 만족을 향상시키기 위해서 우리는 지난달에 설문조사를 했습니다. 주된 목적은 직장에서의 행복감을 높이기 위해 회사가 무엇을 하면 될지 파악하기 위해서였습니다. 이제 결과에 대해 얘기하겠습니다. 보시다시피, 우리 직원들이 가장 원하는 것은 유급 휴가를 더 갖는 것이었지만, 안타깝게도 회사로서는 아직 감당할 수가 없습니다. 그러나 우리는 두 번째로 가장 많았던 제안 사항은 실행할 수 있습니다. 그래서 이것에 대한 세부 사항을 논의하기 위해 각 부서별로 회의를 갖도록 하겠습니다.

---

**90** According to the advertisement, what will happen during December?

(A) Special offers will be available.
(B) More classes will be added.
(C) Business hours will change.
(D) More instructors will be hired.

광고에 따르면, 12월에 어떤 일이 있을 것인가?

(A) **특별 혜택이 가능해질 것이다.**
(B) 더 많은 수업이 추가될 것이다.
(C) 영업 시간이 변경될 것이다.
(D) 더 많은 강사들이 고용될 것이다.

**91** What additional event is being mentioned?

(A) A competition
(B) A demonstration
(C) A concert
(D) A sale

어떤 추가적인 행사가 언급되고 있는가?

(A) 대회
(B) 시연회
(C) 콘서트
(D) **세일**

---

Questions 92-94 refer to the following speech. (미W)

Good afternoon. **92** As the editor-in-chief of Sporting Today magazine, I don't often have the chance to meet the sales team. Today's meeting is an opportunity for me to do so. **93** I am overjoyed with the revenue generated by the sales department, despite the current economic uncertainty for an industry such as ours. **94** Many of our competitors in the business have been forced into bankruptcy. However, you have managed to capitalize on this and increase quarterly profits by over 20 percent. This is a result of your hard work and perseverance. Now please accept my good wishes and enjoy your dinner.

안녕하세요. 스포팅 투데이 잡지의 편집장으로서 저는 영업팀을 만날 기회가 자주 있지 않습니다. 오늘 회의는 제게 그러한 기회입니다. 저는 저희와 같이 이런 업계에 대한 현재의 경제적 불확실성에도 불구하고 영업 부서가 창출한 수익에 매우 기쁩니다. 이 분야 우리의 많은 경쟁업체들이 부도를 맞았습니다. 하지만 여러분은 은 올해도 이를 기회로 삼아 분기 수익을 20퍼센트 이상 증가시켰습니다. 이는 여러분의 노고와 인내의 결과입니다. 이제 저의 축하를 받아주시고 저녁 식사를 즐기세요.

**어휘** editor-in-chief 편집장  overjoy 매우 기쁘게 하다  revenue 수익  generate 창출하다  uncertainty 불확실성  bankruptcy 부도  manage to 용케 ~하다  capitalize on ~을 기회로 삼다  perseverance 인내

---

**92** Who most likely is the speaker?

(A) A company president
(B) **A publishing director**
(C) A financial manager
(D) A sales representative

화자는 누구이겠는가?

(A) 회사 사장
(B) **출판 책임자**
(C) 금융 매니저
(D) 영업 직원

**93** What is the main purpose of the speech?

(A) To schedule future editorials
(B) To announce company layoffs
(C) **To congratulate the employees**
(D) To say farewell to colleagues

연설의 주된 목적은 무엇인가?

(A) 앞으로의 사설 일정을 잡으려고
(B) 회사의 해고를 발표하려고
(C) **직원들을 축하하려고**
(D) 동료들에게 작별을 고하려고

**94** What does the speaker say is happening in the industry?

(A) **Publications are closing down.**
(B) Employment opportunities are increasing.
(C) Financial aid is being offered.
(D) Conferences are being held.

화자는 이 업계에서 어떤 일이 일어난다고 하는가?

(A) **출판사들이 폐업하고 있다.**
(B) 고용 기회가 늘어나고 있다.
(C) 재정 지원이 제공되고 있다.
(D) 회의가 개최되고 있다.

**패러프레이징** have been forced into bankruptcy → are closing down

**어휘** good wishes 호의  editorial 편집의, 사설  say farewell to ~에게 작별인사를 하다  financial aid 재정 지원  layoff 해고  financial aid 재정 지원

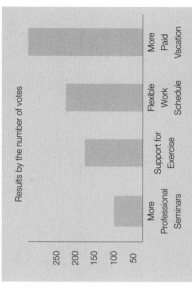

득표에 따른 결과

**95** Who is the speaker addressing?
(A) Office workers
(B) University professors
(C) Small business owners
(D) City officials

화자는 누구에게 말하는가?
**(A) 사무실 직원들**
(B) 대학 교수들
(C) 소규모 자영업자들
(D) 시 공무원들

**96** According to the speaker, what happened last month?
(A) A company outing was held.
**(B) A survey was given to employees.**
(C) A new board member was appointed.
(D) A revised policy was introduced.

화자에 따르면, 지난달에 무슨 일이 있었는가?
(A) 회사 야유회가 열렸다.
**(B) 직원들에게 설문조사가 주어졌다.**
(C) 새로운 임원이 임명되었다.
(D) 수정된 정책이 소개되었다.

**97** Look at the graphic. Which suggestion will be accepted by the company?
(A) More professional seminars
(B) Support for exercise
**(C) Flexible work schedule**
(D) More paid vacation

시각 자료를 보시오, 어떤 제안이 회사에 의해 수락될 것인가?
(A) 더 많은 전문 세미나
(B) 운동에 대한 지원
**(C) 탄력적인 근무 스케줄**
(D) 더 많은 유급 휴가

---

Questions 98-100 refer to the following telephone message and expense report. 영W

| Expense Report | | |
| --- | --- | --- |
| DATE | DESCRIPTION | AMOUNT |
| November 8 | Air fare | $1000 |
| November 9 | Restaurant | $45 |
| November 10 | Accommodation | $220 |
| November 12 | Car Rental | $300 |

99 This is Jennifer calling from accounting. I've received the expense report you submitted for your recent business trip to Tokyo. It looks fine except that one of the receipts included with your report doesn't seem to be the original. 98,100 The expense of $220 on the 10th needs to be confirmed by the original receipt. I'll take care of your reimbursement request as soon as I have all the necessary documents. Please give me a call at extension 5 if you have any questions.

| 비용 보고서 | | |
| --- | --- | --- |
| 날짜 | 내용 | 비용 |
| 11월 8일 | 항공료 | 1000달러 |
| 11월 9일 | 레스토랑 | 45달러 |
| 11월 10일 | 숙소 | 220달러 |
| 11월 12일 | 자동차 렌털 | 300달러 |

회계부서의 제니퍼입니다. 최근 도쿄 출장 관련해서 제출하신 비용 보고서를 받았습니다. 다 좋으나 보고서와 함께 첨부하신 영수증 중 하나가 원본 보고서를 받았습니다. 다 좋으나 220달러로 된 비용이 원본 영수증으로 확인되어야 합니다. 필요한 서류가 다 오면 바로 요청하신 환급 건을 처리해 드리겠습니다. 질문 있으시면 내선 번호 5번으로 전화 주세요.

**98** What is the purpose of the message?
**(A) To request an original document**
(B) To respond to an inquiry
(C) To accept a business proposition
(D) To reschedule a meeting

메시지의 목적은 무엇인가?
**(A) 원본 서류를 요청하려고**
(B) 문의에 답하려고
(C) 사업상 제안을 수락하려고
(D) 회의의 일정을 바꾸려고

패러프레이징 the original receipt → an original document

**99** Which department does the speaker probably work in?
(A) Sales
(B) Shipping
(C) Advertising
**(D) Accounting**

화자는 어떤 부서에서 일할 것 같은가?
(A) 영업
(B) 배송
(C) 광고
**(D) 회계**

**100** Look at the graphic. Which expense needs to be confirmed?
(A) Air fare
(B) Restaurant
**(C) Accommodation**
(D) Car rental

시각 자료를 보시오, 어떤 비용이 확인되어야 하는가?
(A) 항공료
(B) 레스토랑
**(C) 숙소**
(D) 자동차 렌털

# PART 5

P110

**101** 해석 조사 위원회는 8월 1일부터 데이비스 씨가 총장으로 그녀의 임기를 시작한다는 것을 발표하며 만족해 하고 있다.
해설 문장에 동사가 없기 때문에 빈칸은 동사 자리이다. '8월 1일부터라는 표현이 있기 때문에 미래 시제인 (C) will be starting이 적절하다.
어휘 investigation 조사 committee 위원회 effective 시행되는, 발효되는 start one's term 임기를 시작하다 chancellor 수상, 총장

**102** 해석 그 기술자가 컴퓨터 시스템의 고장을 발견할 때쯤에는 많은 파일들이 사라진 상태였다.
해설 (by the time+주어+동사) 구문에서 동사의 시제가 과거이면 주절에는 과거완료 시제가 와야 하고, 동사의 시제가 현재나 미래이면 주절에는 미래완료 시제가 와야 하므로 정답은 (A)이다. (by the time+주어+동사) 구문의 시제를 묻는 문제는 주절에 자주 출제되므로 하나의 공식처럼 외우고 있는 것이 좋다.
어휘 technician 기술자, 기사 disappear 사라지다 failure 고장

**103** 해석 그가 동료들로부터 공로상을 받을 수 있었던 것은 화학 분야에 대한 그의 20년간의 한신 덕분이다.
해설 빈칸 뒤에 목적어가 두 개가 있으므로 선택지 중에서 4형식 동사를 찾아야 한다. win은 자·타동사 둘 다 가능하며 사람이 주어일 때 4형식 동사로 쓰여 '~에게 ~을 얻을 수 있게 하다'라는 의미로 정답은 (C)이다. 문장은 ~ that 강조 구문으로 his 20 years of contributions in the field of chemistry를 강조하고 있다.
어휘 contribution 기여 chemistry 화학 win an award 상을 타다 colleague 동료 lifetime achievement award 공로상

**104** 해석 그 조사는 디지털 기술의 발전에도 불구하고 청중들은 여전히 주로 라디오 방송을 통해서 새로운 방송을 처음 듣는다는 것을 보여 줬다.
해설 빈칸 뒤의 전치사 through radio broadcasts를 수식할 수 있는 품사는 부사뿐이다. predominantly는 '주로'라는 뜻으로 청중들은 새로운 방송을 주로 라디오 방송을 통해서 처음 듣는다는 의미로 자연스러우므로 정답은 (C)이다. (D) 우세한, 무엇한
어휘 survey 조사 indicate 나타내다 broadcast 방송

**105** 해석 카테리스 사의 엔진 부품은 엄격한 검사 절차를 받았다.
해설 선택지가 모두 형용사이므로 일맞은 형용사를 선택하는 문제이다. 문제 상 엔진 부품들이 '엄격한' 검사 절차를 거쳤다는 의미가 적절하므로 정답은 (D)이다. (A) (~을 주지 않은 / (B) 관리의 / (C) 기초의 /~한
어휘 parts 부품 put through 받다, 경험하다 stringent 엄격한 inspection procedure 검사 절차

**106** 해석 지역 사회봉사에 지원하는 모든 학생들은 기능한 한 빨리 지원해야 한다.
해설 관계대명사 who 뒤에 is가 오는 것으로 볼 때 빈칸에는 단수 취급을 하는 형용사가 와야 한다. all, few, both는 뒤에 복수 명사가 오기 때...

**107** 해석 4월 30일까지 아니스트 씨에 사는 티켓 판매로 전례 없는 수익을 기록했고 심지어 이후로는 더 기록했다.
해설 비교급 more를 강조하기 위해서 비교급 강조의 표현이 필요한데 비교급 강조의 표현으로는 (A)이다. very는 주로 형용사나 부사를, a lot 등 비교급 강조 부사는 비교급을 강조한다.
어휘 unprecedented 전례 없는 revenue 수익 period ending 마감 ticket sales 티켓 판매

**108** 해석 우리의 주요 개발자는 그 분야에서의 수년간의 경험뿐만 아니라 소프트웨어 건축을 설계하는 지식을 가지고 있다.
해설 have knowledge of의 표현을 묻는 문제로 (A) ability to do가 뒤에 와서 '~하기 위한 능력'으로 사용된다. (C) 수강가
어휘 chief 주된 developer 개발자 have knowledge of ~을 알다 extensive 광범위한 architecture 건축 years of experience 수년간의 경험

**109** 해석 안전하고 믿을 수 있는 인터넷 서비스를 보장하기 위해 피어버넷 사는 안전 시스템으로 가능한 모든 예방 조치를 취한다.
해설 반칸에 가장 일맞은 명사는 (B)로, '대비책을 강구하다, 예방 조치를 취하다'는 뜻으로 이와 비슷한 표현으로 take precaution을 알아 두어야 한다. 이와 비슷한 표현으로는 take measures(steps, action) 등이 있다. (D) 입장
어휘 ensure 보장하다 reliable 신뢰할 수 있는 security 안전

**110** 해석 주벤타 사이 포부는 세 지역으로 확장을 통해 아시아에서 최고의 소매업자 중 하나가 되는 것이다.
해설 그 회사의 주요한 목표는 최고의 소매업자 중 하나의 '위치'를 달성하는 것이라는 의미가 적절하므로 정답은 (D)이다. 빈칸 앞에 attain과 잘 어울리는 동사를 생각하면 쉽게 정답을 유추할 수 있다.
어휘 ambition 야망, 포부 attain 이루다, 획득하다 position 위치, 지위 retailer 소매업자, 소매점 expansion 확장 territory 지역, 영역

**111** 해석 캠브 모터스의 엘리슨 씨는 상호 결과를 가져올 것이라는 투자 결과를 가져올 것으로 ~했다.
해설 '상호 간에' 이익이 되는 사업 관계라는 의미가 주요 자연스러우므로 (C)가 정답이다. (B) respectively는 주로 문장 끝에 위치해서 '제각기, 각각을 의미한다. (A) 정확하게, 꼼꼼하게 / (B) 각각 / (D) 정성되
어휘 enter into ~에 착수하다 joint 공동의, 합동의 result in 그 결과 ~가 되다 beneficial 유익한, 이로운 venture 벤처 (사업)

**112** 해석 그 지역의 자격을 갖춘 모든 간호사들은 간호사 윤리와 행동별 준수할 것을 요청받았다.

**113** 해석 그 식당이 처음 문을 열었을 때 모든 간판들을 주황색과 검정색으로 칠해져 있었지만 지금 그 표지들은 더 세련된 모습이 되었다.
해설 모든 간판들이 주황색과 검정색으로 칠해져 있었다는 의미가 적절하므로 정답은 (C)이다. (A) transfer는 '옮기다'라는 뜻 외에 '전화, 전근, 전임하다'라는 뜻으로 쓰이며, (B) alternate는 '번갈아 일어나다', 교대하다'라는 뜻으로.
어휘 have gone for ~ 상태로 되다 modern look 세련된 모습

**114** 해석 자동차 관세에 대해 토론하는 동안 로버트슨 상원 의원은 솔직했고 요점을 막 집어냈다.
해설 to the point는 '적절하게, 딱 들어맞는, 간단명료하'이라는 뜻이므로 정답은 (C)이다. 문에 (핵심을 찌르는) 숙어이므로 알아 두자.
어휘 senator 상원 의원 straightforward 간단한, 솔직한 debate 토론, 논쟁 tariff 관세

**115** 해석 높은 수준의 고객 만족을 유지하면서 하도급 업체에게 고객 서비스를 맡기는 것은 우리가 지출을 감소할 수 있도록 해준다.
해설 5형식 동사는 목적어 다음에 to부정사로 목적어의 행위를 표현한다. 이번 동사는 목적어 주로 예상, 요청, 허락, 지시, 권유 등의 의미를 가진다. enable도 5형식 동사로서 (enable+A+to부정사)로 'A가 ~할 수 있게 하다'라는 의미이다. 문에서 하청 업체에게 일을 주는 것이 우리의 지출을 감소시킬 수 있다는 의미가 적절하므로 정답은 (D)이다. (B) 억제하다, 금하다
어휘 subcontract 하도급을 주다 outside agency 외부 대행사 high level of 높은 수준의 customer satisfaction 고객 만족 expenditure 지출

**116** 해석 결혼 티워에게서 차로 10분 거리에 식료품 소핑몰, 극장, 여러 식당들이 모두 있다.
어휘 grocery store 식료품점 within a ten-minute drive 차로 10분 이내의 거리에

**117** 해석 within은 '~ 이내에라는 뜻으로 범위의 전치사로서 뒤에 기간, 장소, 거리, 예산의 의미를 가진 명사가 나오므로 (B)가 정답이다. (A) onto는 '~ 위에'라는 의미로 get onto a horse의 '말에 올라타다' 등으로 쓰이며, (C) so that으로 뒤에 (주어+동사)가 나와 '~하기 위해서'라는 의미로 사용된다. (D) much as는 '현금 비교 표현 much as ~~만큼 많이'이의 형태로 사용된다.

require는 5형식 동사로 〈require+목적어+to부정사〉 형식으로 사용되며, 수동태가 되는 경우 〈be required+to부정사(행)〉로 함께 사용된다. 따라서 (B)가 정답이다. (be required to~동사원형) 등으로 쓰여 '~하도록 요구되다'라는 의미 전달. (be asked/invited, allowed, required, encouraged, instructed)+to+동사원형 등도 자주 사용되므로 함께 알아 두자. 빈칸 앞에 required가 있기 때문에 동사원형 (A), (C)는 올 수 없다.
어휘 province 지역 be required to ~해야 한다 adhere to+명사 ~을 준수하다 ethics 윤리 standards 규범

그 식당이 기꺼이 ~하고자 volunteer 자원봉사하다 local community service 지역 사회봉사

문제에 복수 동사가 와야 한다. 이와 비슷하게 뒤에 복수 명사를 취하는 표현에는 a number of, a variety of, several 등이 있다. any가 긍정문에 쓰일 때는 '모든 ~'라는 의미를 나타내므로 정답은 (C)이다.
어휘 be willing to 기꺼이 ~하다

**129** 해석 최근 보고서들은 국가 통화 가치가 경기 침체기 동안 급격히 떨어졌다는 것을 나타낸다.

해설 문맥상 적절한 명사를 고르는 문제로 국가 통화의 '가치'가 급격히 떨어졌다는 의미가 자연스러우므로 (D)가 정답이다. 급격히 떨어지는 stock으로 가치 있는 물건(주가), a good value for money(금전적으로 가치 있는 물건)등의 표현도 알아 두자. (C) 교통 요금

어휘 latest 최근의 indicate 나타내다 currency 통화 dramatically 급격히 economic slump 경기 침체

**130** 해석 25개사 이상에서 구독자들을 가지고 있는 〈스마트 머신〉이 선도적인 과학 기술 출판물 중 하나이다.

해설 빈칸에 25개사 이상에게 '구독자'들을 갖춘 〈스마트 머신〉은 선도적인 출판물이라는 의미가 적절하므로 (B)가 정답이다. 문장의 publications를 통해서 (B) subscribers를 유추할 수 있다. (A) 구경꾼, 관객 / (C) 참가자 / (D) 증인, 목격자

어휘 subscriber 구독자 leading 선도적인 publication 출판물

---

해설 빈칸 뒤의 for reimbursement를 통해서 담당 유형을 수 있다. 상환이라는 뜻은 되돌려 받는다는 의미인데, 출장 중에 썼던 돈을 상환받기 위해서 '영수증을 제출하라는 의미가 적절하므로 (A)가 정답이다. (B) 방향 지시 / (C) 여행 / (D) 절차

어휘 hand in 제출하다 reimbursement 상환 itemized 항목별로 구분된 transaction 거래 business trip 출장

어휘 crucial 중대한, 결정적인 mining 광업 be located in ~에 위치하다 region 지역 Department of Commerce 상무부 province 지방

**118** 해석 인사 담당자는 사람에 있는 세 지사에 보낼 경험 많고 지원이 우수한 직원을 찾고 있다.

해설 motivate는 감정 유발 타동사로 사람을 수식할 때는 motivated(동기를 부여받은), 사물을 수식할 때는 motivating(동기를 부여하는)의 뜻으로 쓰이며, 빈칸 뒤에 사물 명사 employee가 있으므로 (D)가 와야 한다.

어휘 seek ~을 찾다 experienced 경험 많은 qualified 자격을 갖춘 team-oriented 팀워크 지향적인

**123** 해석 회계 부서는 우리 영업 사원들로부터 모든 모든 영수증을 처리한다.

해설 명사(the receipts)가 나오고 빈칸 뒤에 동사(have been collected)가 나왔으므로 관계대명사 주어 역할을 할 수 있다. 이때 the receipts가 선행사이므로 관계대명사 that이 적절하다. 따라서 (A)가 정답이다. 참고로 관계대명사 what은 선행사를 포함하고 있으므로 앞에 선행사가 필요하지 않다.

어휘 accounting department 회계 부서 process 처리하다

**119** 해석 〈크로니클〉 지는 클라인 뒤의 명사는 슬로건 출판사에 의해 매월 발간되는 시사 잡지이다.

해설 빈칸이 포함되어 있는 콤마 뒤의 명사는 슬로건 뒤의 출판사에 대한 설명이다. 문맥상 슬로건 출판사는 클라인 마다의 그룹이 지원사라고 보는 것이 자연스러우므로 정답은 (B)이다. (A) 부호, 부서 / (C) 분리, 분할 / (D) 선발, 선택

어휘 be issued 발간되다 publisher 출판사 division 분할, 분과

**124** 해석 불행하게도 우리 축구팀은 결승전 진출은 말할 것도 없이 단 한 번도 승리하지 못했다.

해설 빈칸 뒤에는 〈주어+동사〉를 갖춘 문장이 아니라 명사구까가 존재하므로 빈칸에는 전치사가 와야 한다. 문맥상 결승전 진출은 말할 것도 없이라는 의미가 적절하므로 (B)가 정답이다. (A) 그럼에도 불구하고 / (C) ~의 경우에 대비하여 / (D) ~와 반대로

어휘 advance 진보, 진출 post 〈스코어를〉기록하다 single 단 하나의

**120** 해석 우리 회사는 현재 기술적인 문제를 겪고 있기 때문에 회사 인터넷 연결이 중단되었다.

어휘 technical 기술적인 interruption 중단

**125** 해석 우리 식당은 낮은 서비스 수수료 때문에 1달러 이하의 구매에 대해 신용 카드를 더 이상 받지 않을 것이다.

해설 빈칸 뒤에 credit cards가 있는 것으로 볼 때 카드를 '받지' 않는다는 의미로 유추할 수 있으므로 (D)가 가장 적절하다. (A) 수리하다, 개조하다 / (B) 만들다, 배출다

어휘 accept 받아 주다 service fee 서비스 수수료

**121** 해설 because절의 동사는 is로 현재 시제이다. 선택지 중에 현재 시제일 때 쓸 수 있는 부사는 (A) currently뿐이다. 이와 비슷하게 현재 시제일 때 쓸 수 있는 부사로 usually, normally, regularly, frequently, often, always, generally, typically 등이 있다. lately, recently, already 는 과거나 완료 시제 부사로 쓰이며, soon, shortly는 미래 시제에 부사로 쓰이며 (B) 최근에 / (C) 일반적으로 / (D) 보통

어휘 technical 기술적인 interruption 중단

**126** 해석 주최자의 천선의 노력에도 불구하고, 측면에서 보였을 때 무대의 몇몇 부분들이 카드 뒤에 가려져 있었다.

해설 behind는 ~의 뒤에, 배후에라는 뜻으로, 문맥상 무대의 일부가 카드 뒤에 '있다'는 의미가 적절하므로 (C)가 정답이다. (B) within으로 범위의 전치사로서 뒤에 기간, 장소, 거리, 예산의 의미를 가진 명사가 나온다.

어휘 side 옆면, 측면 organizer 주최자

**122** 해설 문맥상 그 지방 '전체에' 걸친 해당 산업들이 이 지역들에 위치해 있기 때문에 그 지방 '전체에' 걸친 접속을 원했다는 의미가 적절하고, throughout은 '~ 전체에 걸쳐'라는 의미가 적절하므로 (C)가 정답이다. 특히 광역이나 넓명 같은 해당 산업들이 이 지역에 위치해 있기 때문에 그 지방 '전체에' 걸친 변화를 원했다. 문맥상 그 지방 '전체에' 걸쳐 들어간 경우 '구석구석'이라는 뜻으로 쓰이므로 (C)가 정답이다. (A) 어디에나 / (B) 게다가 / (D) 아는 정도, 약간

**127** 해석 범죄율을 줄이는 그 지역으로 기업들이 이주하도록 설득함으로써 시장은 시 위원회와 지역 상인과 함께 해온 지역을 많이 구했다.

어휘 persuade 설득하다 committee 위원회 merchant 상인 restore 복구하다 waterfront district 해안 지역 mayor 시장

**128** 해석 고객 만족감을 향상시키고 새로운 고객을 유치하기 위해 캐롤라이나 사의 웹 사이트는 상당한 변화를 겪을 것이다.

해설 고객을 많기 위해 회사의 웹 사이트를 '많이 변화시킨다'는 의미가 적절하므로 (D)가 정답이다. (B) 성숙한, 발달된 / (C) 소모품의

어휘 undergo (변화를) 겪다, 경험하다 substantial 상당한

# PART 6

[131-134]

설립자인 존슨 씨가 성공한 젊은 기업가로서 그의 초기 경험들을 연설하기 위해 초대를 받아들였다는 것을 알리게 되어 지원스럽습니다.

지원하는 모든 사람들이 이 행사에 참석하기를 적극 권장합니다. 존슨 씨는 출처 평가받는 한 사람(?)로 휴대용 전자기기 산업에 혁신을 일으켰고 그 여러분은 그의 연설을 개인적인 경험뿐만 아니라 사업가가 되기 위해서 그가 가장 필수적이라고 여기는 기술들을 포함할 것입니다.

그 행사는 존슨 씨의 연설로 시작될 것입니다. 그 연설 이후에 회의에 초대받은 다른 선임들이 많은 대표자들이 각각의 산업에 관해 참석자들의 질문을 할 수 있게 답을 할 것입니다. 참석자들은 다음 신청서를 작성해 주시고, 행사에 대해 질문이 있으시다면 1-285-462-2621로 저에게 알려 주세요.

**어휘** founder 설립자 give a speech 연설하다 entrepreneur 사업가 encourage 격려하다, 권장하다 well-regarded 출처 평가받는 innovate 혁신하다 portable 가지고 다닐 수 있는, 휴대용의 device 장치 following 이후에 session 시간, 기간 attendant 참석자 regarding ~에 관한 beverage 음료 application form 신청서

**131 해설** 문맥상 자신들의 초대를 연설을 하러 온다는 의미가 되므로 정답은 (B)이다.

**132 해설** 관계대명사 문제이다. 빈칸 앞에 사람(businessman)이 있으므로 정답은 (C) who이다.

**133 (A)** 그의 연설은 그의 개인적인 경험과 사업가가 되기 위해서 필요한 기술들을 포함할 것입니다.
(B) 참여적인 생각은 기술적, 경제적 발전을 불러오기 위해서 필수적입니다.
(C) 사업을 하는 것은 전문 기술을 포함한 다른 사람들에게 인정을 받는 첫 단계입니다.
(D) 그가 자원의 제안을 거절했다는 것은 유감이지만 저희는 다른 후보를 찾을 것입니다.

**해설** 빈칸 앞에서 연설을 하는 사람이 존슨 씨에 대한 내용이 나오므로 빈칸 이후 그의 연설에 관련된 내용이 오는 것이 적절하다. 따라서 (A)가 정답이다.

**어휘** recognition 인정

**134 해설** 빈칸 앞에 many가 있기 때문에 반칸에는 복수 명사가 나와야 한다. 선택지 중에서 복수 명사는 representatives뿐이므로 (C)가 정답이다. (A)는 동사, (B)는 부사, (D)는 동사의 -ing형으로 복수 명사 자리에는 적절하지 않다. (A) 대표하다 / (B) 대표하여

---

[135-138]

수신: 케빈 손
발신: 잭 콜린턴
날짜: 6월 11일
제목: 초청 연사

이것은 연 2회 행사에 관한 긴급 이메일입니다. 현재 초청 연사였던 스티브 스탐코스 씨는 그의 심각한 질병 때문에 더 이상 참석이 어렵습니다. 새로운 전단지를 인쇄하기 위해서 초청 연사는 행사 전 적어도 3일 전에 정해져야 하기 때문에 대체 연사를 대체 찾아야 합니다.

새로운 초청 연사를 뽑기 위해서 그 연사가 자료 분야에서 잘 알려진 인물이어야 한다는 점을 명심해야 합니다. 그 사람의 자료 회사에 어떤 방법으로든 연관되어 있어야 합니다.

제가 한 후보자를 생각하고 있습니다. 페리스 프린츠 씨의 설립자인 휴 페리가 그 일에 가장 적절한 후보자라고 생각합니다. 그도 자료 산업에 연관되어 있지 않으신다면, 그 일에 가장 잘 갖추어진 지식을 찾아주시며 신종 회사와의 긴급 프로젝트를 하나에 귀하가 느낄 점을 지원에 답장해 주세요.

이것으로 긴급한 문제이기 때문에 빨리 답변해 주시를 기다리겠습니다. 귀하께서 페리 씨를 새로운 연사로 원하지 않으신다면, 그 일에 가장 잘 갖추어진 지식을 찾아주시며 신종 회사와의 긴급 프로젝트를 하나에 귀하가 느낄 점을 연사로서 페리 씨에 대해 귀하가 느낀 점을 지원에 답장해 주세요.

잭

**어휘** guest speaker 초청 연사 urgent 긴급한 biannual 연 2회의 initial 처음의 severe 심각한 medical condition 질병 전단지 replacement 교체, 대체 flyer 전단지 keep in mind 명심하다 figure 인물 be related to ~와 관계가 있다 candidate 후보자, 지원자 participate in 참여하다, 참여하다

**135 해설** 전체적인 의미상 앞맞은 p.p.형의 동사를 선택하는 문제이다. 문맥상 행사 전 적어도 3일 전까지 초청 연사가 정해져야 한다는 의미인 (D)가 적절하며, (A) 수여하다 / (B) 바꾸다, 변형시키다 / (C) 치우다, 깨끗이 하다

**136 해설** 위 문제는 to부정사의 부사적 용법을 물어보는 문제이다. 〈in order to+동사원형〉은 '~하기 위해서'의 의미로 (to+동사원형)의 형태인 (D)가 정답이다.

**137 (A)** 손님들은 연설 중 조용히 있어야 할 것을 기억해야 합니다.
(B) 초청 연사에게 무료 차비를 제공할 것입니다.
(C) 스탐코스 씨는 연락처를 포함한 그의 개인 정보를 제출해야 합니다.
(D) 페리스 씨는 연락처를 포함한 그의 개인 정보를 제출해야 합니다.

**해설** 빈칸 앞에서 초청 연사가 정해질 조건에 대한 내용이 나오므로 다음으로 반칸 앞에서 초청 연사가 정해질 어떤 방법으로든 연관되어 있어야 합니다.

Moreover로 시작하며 회사와 관련이 있어야 한다는 또 다른 조건을 나타내는 (D)가 가장 적절하다.

**어휘** complementary 무료의

**138 해설** 문맥상 그는 매우 좋은 지식을 갖추었다는 의미가 적절하다. 따라서 '매우'라는 뜻을 가진 (C) extremely가 적절하다. (A) 자신 있게 / (B) 현명하게 / (D) 주로, 대부분

---

[139-142]

# GBI 사 근로자의 거리 시위

GBI 사의 많은 직원들이 애플랜티 보로드의 본사에 있는 오스가 사의 건물 입구를 막는 시간이 있었습니다. 그 시위는 GBI 사의 사업 파트너 회사의 부도덕한 사업 전략 때문에 시작되었습니다. 사업 파트너인 오스가 사가 GBI 사의 가장 유망한 제품에 부품 1개의 개발 공급하는 거래를 취소했기 때문에 발생했습니다.

이 일로 인해서 GBI 사는 공식적으로 3백만 달러의 손실을 보았다고 밝혀졌지만, 몇몇 전문가들은 이미도 3백만 달러 이상이 되는 영의 손실이 큰 수익의 손실을 그 회사가 보았다고 주장하고 있습니다.

사원자들이 큰 소동 없이 수수했지라도 오스가 사가 그 거래를 기꺼이 재고하지 않을 것이기 때문에 경찰청이 그 갈등을 해결하는 데 어려움을 겪고 있습니다.

**어휘** protest 항의, 시위 incident 사건, 일 block 막다, 차단하다 conflict 갈등 arise 발생하다 supply 공급하다 officially 공식적으로 reveal 드러내다, 밝히다 incident 사고 expert 전문가 probably 이마도 significantly 상당히 revenue 수익 withdraw 취수하다, 물러나다 reconsider 재고하다

**139 (A)** 이 사건의 이유는 지금까지 알려지지 않았습니다.
(B) 그 시위는 GBI 사의 사업 파트너 회사의 부도덕한 사업 전략 때문에 시작되었습니다.
(C) 직원들은 그들이 한 것에 대해 책임을 질이 있었습니다.
(D) 오믹스 타워의 보수 공사는 다음 주 화요일에 시작될 것입니다.

**해설** 반칸 앞은 직원들이 입구를 가로막은 시간에 대한 내용이고 뒤는 왜 갈등이 일어났는지에 대한 내용이 나와 합니다. 부도덕한 사업 전략 때문에 시작되었다는 (B)가 정답이다.

**어휘** immoral 비도덕적인 strategy 전략

**140 해설** 문맥상 오스가 사가 거래를 '취소해서' 갈등이 생겼다는 의미가 적절하므로 (A)가 정답이다. (B) ~을 만들다 / (C) 참가하다 / (D) 준비하다

**141 해설** 문맥상 많은 양의 수익이 적절하며, 앞을 나타낼 때는 (an amount of+명사)(양이 많은가 적절하므로 (A)가 정답이다. (B)는 "~의 수"를 나타낼 때 (the number of+복수 명사+단수 동사)로 써야 와야 한다. (C)는 a collection of songs(많은 모음집)에 ~의 모음처럼 ~의 모음 모음을 나타낸다.

**142 해설** 반칸 앞에 이미 해체완료 동사가 있으므로 반칸에는 p.p.형이나 -ing형만이 가능하다. 문맥상 보도된다는 의미가 적절하므로 p.p.형인 (B)가 정답이다. it has been reported는 '~로 알려졌다는 뜻으로 쓰이는 표현이므로 알이 두다.

# PART 7

## [143-146]

수신: 조 장
발신: 마이크 해밀리
날짜: 8월 12일
제목: 프로젝트 모임 조직과 관련하여

이 메모는 이사회가 그 프로젝트팀에게 당신의 제안을 **[143]** 승인했다고 알리기 위해 보내졌습니다.

이사회가 귀하의 계획에 만족하셨을지라도, 세부 사항들을 요구했습니다. 가장 중요한 것은 모든 종류의 훈련 요구 자각의 조직 구성원의 **[144]** 책무들이 명시돼야 합니다. 또한, 각 구성원들은 직무에 대한 그룹의 능력을 평가하기 위해서 연결을 받아야 합니다.

이사회는 이 프로젝트에 대한 귀하의 **[145]** 기여를 인정하고 있습니다. 또한 보기 위해서 이번 프로젝트 결과를 보기를 기대하고 있습니다. 그 프로젝트 기대나 기대대로 회사 수익의 20퍼센트를 가져올 거라고 기대하는 프로젝트를 리더로서 귀하의 역할을 강조했습니다.

당신의 팀과 팀원의 역할에 관한 더 넓은 세부 사항이 적힌 문서를 제출해 주세요. 이사회는 귀하에게 항문을 열 밖에 또한 회사의 미래를 위한 노력에 감사 드립니다.

마이크 해밀리
이사회 보좌관

**어휘** organization 조직, 단체, 기구  notify 통지하다, 알리다  board 이사회, 위원회  proposal 제안  specifics 세부 사항  indicate 명시하다, 나타내다  confusion 혼란  recognize 인정하다, 알아보다  outcome 결과  revenue 수익  quarter 4분의 1  emphasize 강조하다

**143** 해설  문맥상 이사회가 귀하의 계획을 승인했다는 의미가 적절하므로 (B)가 정답이다. (A) 가정하다 / (C) 완성하다 / (D) 마무리 짓다, 완성하다

**144** 해설  문맥상 훈련을 맡기 위해 각각의 구성원들의 '책무'가 명시돼야 한다가 지연스러우므로 (A)가 정답이다. (B) 모사, 대표 / (C) 관계 / (D) 지식

**145** (A) 또한, 각 구성원들은 직무에 대한 그룹의 능력을 평가하기 위해서 연결을 받아야 합니다.
(B) 귀하는 서류 혹은 서식을 제출하지 않아도 됩니다.
(C) 귀하의 팀은 가능한 한 빨리 누가 프로젝트 리더인지 결정해야 합니다.
(D) 귀하가 요청하신 대로, 이 프로젝트는 회사와 관련되지 않을 것입니다.

**해설**  빈칸 앞에서 이사회가 세부 사항을 요구했다고 했으며 세부 사항을 첫 번째로 책무들이 명시돼야 있어야 한다고 했다. 빈칸에는 추가적인 세 부 사항이 오는 것이 적절하므로 Also로 시작하며 연결을 받아야 한다는 (A)가 적절하다.

**어휘** task 과제, 과제

**146** 해설  빈칸 앞에 소유격이 있기 때문에 빈칸은 소유격 뒤에 올 수 있는 명사 자리이다. 또한, 문맥상 프로젝트에 대한 귀하의 '기여'가 지연스러우므로 (D)가 정답이다. (A)는 동사의 단수형으로 '기여하다, 기증하다'라는 의미이며, (B)는 복수 주어인 경우에 쓰이는 동사이다. (C)도 명사이지만 '기증자' '기여자'이므로 문맥상 적절하지 않다

## [147-148]

수신: 마리코 이노우에
발신: 토마스 강
날짜: 11월 19일
제목: 연 2회 보너스

이노우에 씨께

**[147]** 연 2회 보너스가 결정되기 전에 직원 평가서를 제출하셔야 합니다. 다음 주 화요일에 있을 연차 회의 전에 모든 정산서 마치고자 합니다. **[148]** 필요한 모든 문서를 작성하시고, 서명하신 원본을 가능한 한 빨리 저에게 제출해 주세요. 모든 평가 자료나 복사본을 보관하시는 것도 잊지 마십시오.

토마스 강
선임 회계사

**어휘** biannual 연 2회의  documentation (문서로 하는) 기록  original 원본  minutes 회의록  permission 허가

**147** 이메일의 목적은 무엇인가?
(A) 받은 편지에 대해 당정하기 위해
(B) 평가 서류을 요구하기 위해
(C) 독사한 문서를 요청하기 위해
(D) 이력서를 보내기 위해

**해설**  연 2회 보너스를 활정하기 위해 필요한 직원 평가서를 제출해 달라는 요청을 하고 있다. 따라서 정답은 (B)이다.

**148** 토마스 강이 마리코 이노우에에게 무엇을 부탁하는가?
(A) 모든 영수증에 서명하기
(B) 회의록 복사하기
(C) 업무 성과 평가하기
(D) 보너스에 대한 허가 얻기

**해설**  직원 평가서 제출을 위한 모든 문서를 작성하라는 것은 업무 성과를 작성하라는 의미이다. 따라서 정답은 (C)이다.

## [149-150]

| | |
|---|---|
| 캐빈 마피 | 오후 3시 51분 |
| 줄리아나 씨, 이번 세미나가 제 생각보다 길어지네요. 도움이 필요해요. | |
| 줄리아나 해리스 | 오후 3시 52분 |
| 네, 제가 무엇을 해 줄 수 있을까요? | |
| 캐빈 마피 | 오후 3시 54분 |
| **[149]** 제 고객을 만나서 우리가 제공하는 금융 서비스에 대한 간단한 상담을 해 주세요. | |
| 줄리아나 해리스 | 오후 3시 55분 |
| 고객 이름이 뭐죠? **[150]** 다른 건 없나요? | |
| 캐빈 마피 | 오후 3시 56분 |
| 그게 다예요. 이름은 루이스 해밀턴이고요. 자세한 정보는 제 책상 위에 있어요. | |
| 줄리아나 해리스 | 오후 4시 06분 |
| 아, 그 고객이 오늘 계좌를 만들었군요 | |
| 캐빈 마피 | 오후 4시 07분 |
| 네. 궁금한 게 있으면, 언제든 문자 주시고요. | |

**어휘** give a consulting on ~에 대한 상담을 하다  that's it 그게 다예요  open a (bank) account (은행) 계좌를 만들다

**149** 해리스 씨는 어떤 회사에서 근무하겠는가?
(A) 서점
(B) 은행
(C) 박물관
(D) 병원

**해설**  오후 3시 54분에 마피 씨가 자신의 고객을 만나서 금융 서비스에 대한 간단한 상담을 해달라고 하다. 또, 오후 4시 06분에 해리스 씨가 고객이 계좌를 만드는 것을 언급한 내용을 보면, 이들은 은행에서 일하고 있음을 알 수 있다. 따라서 정답은 (B)이다.

**150** 오후 3시 56분에, 마피 씨가 "그게 다예요"라고 쓸 때 그 의도는 무엇이겠는가?
(A) 해리스 씨에게 다른 건 더 부탁하지 않겠다.
(B) 세미나가 임박 끝날 것이라고 예상한다.
(C) 해리스 씨가 회사에서 비빠다는 것을 안다.
(D) 가능한 한 빨리 자기의 고객을 만나겠다.

**해설**  That's it은 여러 뜻이 있으나 "그게 다야"라는 뜻이 있다. 처음 마피 씨가 도움이 필요하다고 했고, 오후 3시 55분 해리스 씨의 "다른 건 없나요"라는 물음에 대해 그게 다라는 말을 한 것이므로, 다른 건 더 부탁하지 않겠다는 (A)가 정답이다.

[151-152]

## 도쿄 자동차

1963년에 설립된 자동차 회사인 도쿄 자동차는 창립 50주년을 기념합니다!

152a 연례 도쿄 자동차 다이너비 151 박람회는 최신 자동차 드루를 소개하기 위한 행사입니다. 항 장치, 브레이크, 주행 기술과 관련된 튜닝 도구를 소개할 수 있습니다. 152b 모든 장비들은 특별 보급 가격으로 구매하실 수 있습니다. 박람회는 도쿄 자동차와 국가 기술 협회가 공동으로 진행하는 합당 이벤트입니다.

엑스포는 기초 전화작이고 편입하며, HY전승 옵션을 소개할 수 있는 유수한 행사가 될 것입니다. 또한 어느 도쿄 자동차 지점에서는 상품과 교통이 가능한 152c 1만 달러 상품권을 받으실 수 있는 혜택 자동차 대화에도 참가하실 수 있습니다.

날짜: 8월 30일
시간: 오전 9시에서 오후 5시까지
장소: 도쿄 자동차 센트럴시스코 지사

이 박람회는 제조 및 공학 행사이며, 주요 자동차 및 비즈니스 리더들과 기술 전문가를, F&A 전문가, 컨설턴트들이 참석합니다.

온라인으로 티켓을 예약하여 30달러 할인을 받으세요! 예약은 www. tokyovehicle.com으로 방문하세요.

**어휘** automotive 자동차의 showcase 전시하다 component 구성 요소 tuning 조율 suspension 서스펜션(차체의 무게를 받쳐 주는 장치) steering 조향 장치 introductory price 보급 가격 jointly 공동으로 gift certificate 상품권 redeemable 교환할 수 있는

### 151 어떤 행사가 공지되고 있는가?
(A) **자동차 장비 산업 박람회**
(B) 자동차 대리점 개장식
(C) 유명 레이서의 전시회
(D) 운전면허 시험 경자 등록

**해설** 지문 첫 단 첫 번째 줄에서 한 자동차 회사가 자동차 장비 박람회를 갖는다는 사람을 알 수 있으므로 정답은 (A)이다.

### 152 행사에 대해 언급되지 않은 것은 무엇인가?
(A) 1년에 한 번씩 개최된다.
(B) 판매하는 물건이 있을 것이다.
(C) **온라인 티켓은 30달러이다.**
(D) 상품이 수여된다.

**해설** 온라인으로 티켓을 예약하면 30달러를 절약할 수 있다고만 했을 뿐 티켓의 정확한 가격은 명시되어 있지 않으므로 정답은 (C)이다. 1년에 한 번 하는 연례(annual) 행사이므로 (A)는 정답이 될 수 없고, 모든 장비는 특가로 구입할 수 있으므로 (B) 역시 오답이며, 하차 자동차 대회에 참가하면 상품 교환권을 받을 수 있는 응모 기회가 있다고 했으므로 (D)도 제외된다.

[153-154]

## 특별 패키지
애리조나 피트니스 클럽

애리조나 피트니스 회원권에 여러분의 인생에 혜택을 제공합니다. 여러분의 목표 희망과 꿈을 위한 것입니다. 그것은 여러분의 건강입니다. 저희 헬스클럽에서의 시간이 나머지 23시간에 긍정적인 영향을 미칠 수 있다고 생각합니다.

153a 저희는 미국 전역에 편리한 곳에 위치한 600개 헬스클럽을 하루 24시간 운영합니다. 또한, 애리조나 피트니스 클럽은 영국, 남아프리카, 현지, 캐나다 등 30개 국가에서 찾으실 수 있어요. 저희는 아직도 성장하는 중입니다. 여러분에게 맞는 수업과 운동을 선택하실 수 있을 뿐만 아니라 여러분이 예산에 맞는 지불 방식 또한 선택하실 수 있습니다.

153b 30퍼센트 할인된 가격으로 오늘 가입하세요! 154 애리조나 헬스클럽은 현재 8월 30일까지 신규 회원들에게 특별 가격으로 모십니다! 153c 1-848-948-0082로 전화 주십시오

자회의 혜택과 운동 시설에 대한 자세한 내용을 알고 싶으시면 웹 사이트 www. azfitness.com을 방문하시거나

**어휘** benefit ~에게 이익이 되다, 득이 되다 facility 시설 flexible 응동성 있는

### 153 광고에서 제공되지 않은 정보는 무엇인가?
(A) 미래에 있는 지점의 수
(B) **멤버십 가격**
(C) 신입 회원을 위한 할인
(D) 헬스클럽의 대표 전화번호

**해설** 멤버십의 할인율이 30퍼센트라는 말만 나왔을 뿐 멤버십의 가격은 언급되지 않았으므로 정답은 (B)이다.

### 154 8월 30일 이후에는 어떤 일이 일어날 것인가?
(A) **신규 회원은 전액을 지불할 것이다.**
(B) 단독적인 지급 방식을 더 이상 사용할 수 없다.
(C) 회원들이 30퍼센트를 절감할 것이다.
(D) 헬스클럽이 미국에서 사업을 확장할 것이다.

**해설** 신규 회원들에게 특별 가격을 지원하는 것은 8월 30일까지라고 하므로 8월 30일 이후의 신규 회원들은 전액을 지불해야 할 것이다. 따라서 정답은 (A)이다.

[155-157]

미켈 후프먼
2760 남쪽 스트리트
세크러멘트, 캘리포니아 79028
고객님들께

155 힐리어드 비디오는 귀하의 구매에 감사를 표합니다. 최신 DV-576 플레이어에 만족하셨길 바랍니다. 감사의 의원으로 인쳅니다 이의 주연된 최신 영화 (슈퍼 레이스) 무료 DVD를 드립니다.

156 고객님의 구매에는 3년간 무료 세정이 포함되어 있습니다. 6개월마다 한번씩 전문적으로 DVD를 청소하면 수년간 제대로 작동될 것입니다. 구입 영수증 원본을 들고 가까운 지점을 방문하면 무료 서비스를 받으실 수 있습니다.

다시 한 번 구매에 감사드립니다. 157 질문 또는 문제가 있으시면 기술 지원 담당자 노먼 미즈리 씨에게 1-847-928-9383으로 연락 주십시오

램프서 다먼
영부문 부장

**어휘** token 표시, 기념물 gratitude 감사 complimentary 무료의 star 주연을 없다 professionally 전문적으로 ensure 보장하다 function 작동하다

### 155 편지의 목적은 무엇인가?
(A) **감사를 표하기 위해**
(B) DVD플레이어를 광고하기 위해
(C) 정책 변경에 대해 알리기 위해
(D) 고객에게 특별한 가격을 알리기 위해

**해설** DVD플레이어를 구매해 준 것에 감사의 표시로 무료 DVD를 주는 내용으로 보이 (A)가 적절하다.

### 156 힐리어드 비디오가 무료로 제공하는 것은 무엇인가?
(A) 영화 티켓
(B) **서비스 플랜**
(C) DVD플레이어
(D) 상품 배달

**해설** 3년간의 무료 DVD플레이어 세정이 포함되어 가까운 지점에서 무료 서비스를 받을 수 있다는 것으로 보아 (B)가 알맞다.

### 157 노먼 미즈리는 누구인가?
(A) 영화배우
(B) 매니저
(C) 영업부 부장
(D) **기술자**

**해설** 문의할 내용은 기술 지원 공급자 노먼 미즈리에게 연락하라고 한 것으로 보아 (D)가 적절하다.

**공동 연구 협약**

2017년 7월 22일 서명

계약 당사자:

셰이저빌리 제작사(491 오스나브룩 로드, 그랜드 폭스, 브리티시 컬럼비아)와 웰라 먼 대학교의 펄프 제지 선임 대학(93 그드노블 경 로드, 프레이저 밸리, 브리티시 컬럼비아)

이 계약은 셰이저빌리 제작사와 웰라먼 대학의 펄프 제지 선임 대학 간에 2017년 7월 22일 맺어졌다. R&D 공동 연구 계약에 관한 조건은 다음과 같다.

1. 상기 두 당사자들은 R&D 프로젝트에 펄프 제지 산업을 구축하는 계약 체결을 개발하는 데 있다.

2. **159** 협약은 향후 3년 또는 계약 당사자들이 상호 동의하에 그 이후의 기간 내에 유효하다.

3. **158** 1십만 달러의 초기 투자는 셰이저빌리 제작사에 의해 지급되며, 투자 협약의 철회는 함병적 조치로 처리된다. 요구되는 추가 자금은 셰이저빌리 제작사에 의해 지급되는 것으로 처리된다.

4. **159** 판매에 의한 미래 수익 문배는 세 제품이 개시된 후 처음 3년 동안 벤 큐버 시 정부가 3퍼센트, 펄프 제지 선임 대학이 27퍼센트 **160** 셰이저빌리 제작사가 70퍼센트이다.

5. 프로젝트 기간 동안 취득되는 **159** 모든 관련 정보나 기술적인 발견을 기밀로 한다. 계약 조건 위반 시 관련 당사자들이 각 관련 당사자들의 손해를 보상하는 데 책임을 지며, 프로젝트는 폐지된다.

서명:

셰이저빌리 제작사            펄프 제지 선임 대학

**어휘** collaboration 공동 작업 agreement 협정 party 당사자 term 조건 consent 동의하다 cooperative 협력적인 facilitate 용이하게 하다 duration 지속 기간 mutual 상호 간의 consensus 협의 initial 처음의 funding 자금 withdrawal 철회, 인출 measure 조치 division 분배 launch 개시, 착수 relevant 관련 있는 confidential 기밀의 violation 위반 annulment 취소, 폐지 compensate 보상하다 relevant 관련된 signature 서명 steering committee 운영 위원회 sole 단독의

**158** 첫 투자는 어느 쪽에서 담당하는가?

(A) 벤쿠버 시 정부
(B) 셰이저빌리 제작사
(C) 웰라먼 대학교
(D) 운영 위원회의 기부

**해설** 계약 조건 3번에 첫 1십만 달러의 투자는 벤쿠버 시 정부가 한다고 언급되어 있다. 따라서 정답은 (A)가 정답이다.

**159** 협약에 의도되지 않은 것은 무엇인가?

(A) 기술 정보의 처리
(B) **법정 대리인**
(C) 향후 수익의 분배

**해설** 협약에서 법정 대리인에 대해서는 언급되어 있지 않으므로 (B)가 정답이다.

**160** 셰이저빌리 제지에 대해 알 수 있는 것은 무엇인가?

(A) 그 회사의 특허는 가장 적을 것이다.
(B) 20년 동안 사업을 해 왔다.
(C) **판매 수익의 대부분을 가질 것이다.**
(D) 정보 사용에 유일한 권리를 가진다.

**해설** 4번 항목에 셰이저빌리 제작사가 판매 수익의 70퍼센트를 가진다고 나와 있으므로 (C)가 정답이다. (A)와 (B)는 협약 내용으로는 추론할 수 없으며, 5번 항목에 모든 관련 정보나 기술적인 발견을 기밀로 한다고 하므로 (D)는 알맞지 않다.

---

수신: 에이드 잭슨
발신자: 키임 매케인
날짜: 1월 27일
제목: C-2B 메일 송장

에이드 씨,

**162** 관리부에 앰버 로즈 씨로부터 방금 이메일을 받았어요. -[1]- 그녀가 제 게 좀 더 시간을 달라고 요청하더군요. -[2]- N.I. 테크 케미컬에서 주문한 C-2B 메일의 견적 가격에서 일치하지 않는 부분을 발견했어요. -[3]- **161** 그녀의 새 조수인 벨라 스완 씨가 실수로 작년 가격표를 첨부한 것으로 드러났어요. 이번 건은 긴급 건이라서, 관리부 모두 씨가 다시 써고 있습니다. -[4]- 그들이 그 작업을 다행해, 회계부에 페이지가 나가로 한번 송장을 확인 함 것입니다.

키임 매케인
마케팅팀

**어휘** invoice 송장 quote 견적을 내다 discrepancy 불일치 urgent 긴급한 Administration (Department) 관리부 refer to ~을 참고하다 by mistake 실수로 Accounting (Department) 회계 부서

**161** 이메일의 목적은 무엇인가?

(A) 늦어지는 이유를 설명하려고
(B) 새 제품 출시를 발표하려고
(C) 송장 작성에 도움을 요청하려고
(D) 메일 재료를 주문하려고

**해설** 관리부의 앰버 로즈 씨가 이메일에서 좀 더 시간을 달라고 요청했으며, 그 이유로 벨라 스완 씨가 실수로 작년 가격표를 참고했다 서, 그 때문에 늦어진다고 설명하고 있다. 따라서 정답은 (A)이다.

**162** 무슨 부서에서 오류가 발생하였나?

(A) **관리부**
(B) 인사부
(C) 회계부
(D) 마케팅부

**해설** 관리부에서 앰버 로즈 씨에 새 조수인 벨라 스완 씨로부터 실수가 비롯된 것이므로, 관리부에서 오류가 발생하였음을 알 수 있다. 따라서 정답은 (A)이다.

**163** [1], [2], [3], [4]로 표시된 곳 중에서 다음 문장이 가장 적합한 것은?

"가격이 이럴 조에서 나온 가격표와 맞지 않았어요."

(A) [1]
(B) [2]
(C) **[3]**
(D) [4]

**해설** "C-2B 메일의 견적 가격에서 일치하지 않는 부분을 발견했다"는 내용 다음에 이럴 조에 나온 가격표와 맞지 않다는 내용이 와야 자연스럽다. They're the prices를 대신하므로, 정답은 (C)이다.

---

8월 1일

**모잉 푸드가 새로운 이첨 시리얼을 소개합니다!**

바쁜 하루의 요구에 지면한 요즘. 어떤 분들은 이침 분들을 선택할 때 영양보다는 편의를 선택합니다. 그분들에게 새로운 선택을 제공하기 위해, 모잉 푸드는 한 끼에 150칼로리 미만의 편리한 식사 방법인 슈거 크리스프 시리얼을 소개 합니다.

**164** 물로리대에 본사를 둔 이 회사는 새로 나온 이침 식사용 시리얼을 전국에 유통한다고 홍보를 인넌에 발표하였습니다. **164** 새로운 시리얼 제품은 8월 3일부터 전국 판매 상점에 선반에 놓일 것입니다. 전국 유통을 하루 앞두고 주요 TV방송국과 라디오 방송국이 광고가 시가고요 로스엔젤레스에서의 홍보 행사에 광고를 내 보낼 것입니다.

**165** 판매 첫날에는 참석자 신문에 신문의 리스페이지스에서의 주요 행사를 다. 보일 것입니다.

이 제품은 회사에서 지난 2년 동안 다섯 번째로 출시되는 라인입니다. 이 기간 에 추가된 **167** 새로운 시리얼 제품 라인으로 옥수수 크로와 크리스피, 파이버 웬 저스를 반쿠나가 출시되었습니다. **165** 이 회사는 판매 반등구로 새로운 제품으로 보완하기 위해 노력해 왔습니다. 슈거 크리스프는 전통적으로 매출이 높았던 전략 시장인 시가고로 로스엔젤레스에서 주요 유통될 것입니다.

**어휘** serving (음식의) 1인분 distribution 유통 문배 mark 나타내다 supplement 보충하다 established 인정받는 tackle (문제를) 다루다 traditionally 전통적으로 unexplored 아직 탐구되지 않은 potential 잠 재적 rebrand 브랜드 이미지를 새롭게 하다

**164** 새 시리얼은 전국적으로 언제 살 수 있는가?

(A) 8월 1일
(B) **8월 3일**
(C) 8월 4일
(D) 8월 5일

**해설** 두 번째 문단에서 새로운 시리얼이 전국 상점에 놓이기 시작하는 날짜 는 8월 3일이라고 한다. 따라서 정답은 (B)이다.

[172-175]

## 롯센느 뉴스  3월 15일

3월 2일 기자 회견에서 M.E.S. 투자 회사의 시장이 리암 둘린 씨가 롯센느로부터 불과과 10km 떨어진 오클랜드 시에 스카이랜드 월드 놀이공원의 건설 착수를 발표했다. 둘린 씨는 시 주민으로부터 많은 사업 투자자들을 유치함으로써 이 거대한 프로젝트가 지역 경제를 발전시킬 것이라는 높은 기대감을 드러냈다. -[1]-

**175** 거대해지는 시가 주변 지역을 잠식하는 우려의 목소리가 나온다. -[2]- **172 173** 한 조사에 따르면 주변 지역 대다수의 시민들은 이를 긍정적인 조심으로 본다. **173** "많은 관광객들이 올 테호, 그리고 장기적으로 이 전체 지역이 이득을 볼 것니다. '라고 록센느 시민 루이스 클라인 씨는 말한다. -[3]- 놀이공원의 영웅을 위한 큰 전망자이고, 놀이 공원자이고, 근처 사업에나 이벤트는 많은 시민들에게 증가움을 제공한다. **172 173** 전문가들도 현지 관광산업에 활기를 북돋우 거라는 점에 동의한다. -[4]- ... 또한, 수익은 입장료, 주차료, 기념품과 식음료 판매에서 오지만, 많은 지역 신문에 광고가 개재될 것이며, 이 대부분의 신문들로 시 주변 지역에 본사를 둔 회사들로부터 출판된다.

**어휘** press conference 기자 회견  massive 거대한  regional economy 지역 경제  attract 끌어 모으다  encroach on ~을 잠식하다  the majority of 대다수의  neighboring area 주변 지역  in the long term 장기적으로  theme park 테마공원 놀이공원  attraction (관광) 명소  ride 놀이 기구  invigorate 기운 나게 하다  revenue 수익  souvenir 기념품  advertising 광고  surrounding 인근의, 주위의  sustain 지속시키다  boost 신장시키다  stimulate 활성화하게 하다

---

**어휘** office equipment 사무실 장비  belong to ~에 속하다, 귀속되다  decision-making 의사 결정  replace 교체하다  photocopier 복사기  memorandum 같은 조직 내에서 구성원들끼리 소통하는 문서, 회람  financial records 재무 기록  quarterly expenses report 분기별 지출 보고서

---

**165** 인쇄 광고는 어느 곳에서 나올 예정인가?
(A) 로스앤젤레스
(B) 시카고
(C) 블로리다
(D) 라스베이거스
**해설** 인쇄 광고는 잡지와 신문이며 이 광고들은 라스베이거스에서 나올 것이라고 한다. 따라서 정답은 (D)이다.

**166** 새로운 시리얼을 개발하는 이유는 무엇인가?
(A) 기존 제품의 판매의 하락
(B) 국내 시장의 치열한 경쟁
(C) 새로운 전략 시장에의 미개척된 가능성
(D) 회사의 이미지 재고를 위해 새 베스트셀러 찾는 것
**해설** 판매 감소를 막기 위해 새로운 제품을 개발하여 보완한다고 하므로 (A)가 가장 적절하다.

**167** 과거 24개월 동안 출시되지 않은 시리얼은 무엇인가?
(A) 네도 엔 하니
(B) 옥수수 체스
(C) 크로이 크리스피
(D) 저스트 번치스
**해설** 2년간 옥수수 체스와 크로이 크리스피, 페이버 엔 저스트 번치스가 출시되었고 이제 네도 엔 하니가 추가될 것이다. 따라서 정답은 (A)이다.

**168** 노엘 씨는 어느 부서 소속이겠는가?
(A) 마케팅
(B) 영업
(C) 고객 서비스
(D) 회계
**해설** ... 정답은 (D)이다.

**169** 오전 10시 22분에 조던 씨가 "이해가 잘 안 가는데요"라고 쓸 때, 그 의도는 무엇이겠는가?
(A) 노엘 씨가 너무 빨리 걸어서 따라잡기 힘들다고 생각한다.
(B) 정보에 대한 새로운 사용을 알아낼 수 없다.
(C) 노엘 씨가 회사 방침을 따를 거라고 예상한다.
(D) 무슨 정보가 필요하다는 건지 이해할 수 없다.
**해설** I'm not following you는 '당신의 말을 이해할 수 없다'의 뜻이다. 오전 10시 22분에 조던 씨는 I'm not following you라고 하고 그 다음에 바로 '정확히 무슨 정보요'라고 하였으므로, 그녀는 정확히 무슨 보가 필요한지에 관한 것임을 알 수 있다. 따라서 정답은 (D)이다.

**170** 정보는 언제 수집되기 시작하겠는가?
(A) 월요일
(B) 화요일
(C) 목요일
(D) 금요일
**해설** I'm not following you는 '당신의 말을 이해할 수 없다'의 뜻이다. 오전 10시 22분에 조던 씨는 I'm not following you라고 하고 그 다음에 바로 '정확히 무슨 정보요'라고 하였으므로, 그녀는 정확히 무슨 보가 필요한지에 관한 것임을 알 수 있다. 따라서 정답은 (D)이다.

**171** 노엘 씨에게 어떤 장비가 교체되어야 하는지 왜 정보가 필요한가?
(A) 어떤 장비가 교체되어야 하는지 알기 위해
(B) 특별 세금 혜택을 누리기 위해
(C) 예산을 다음 분기로 이월시키기 위해
(D) 분기별 지출 보고서와 비교하기 위해
**해설** 조던 씨가 의사 결정을 위해 필요한 정보에 관한 정보라고 대답했고, 이어서 노엘 씨가 그 장비가 수명이나 상태에 관한 정보라고 등을 교체할 수 있다고 말한다. 따라서 어떤 장비가 교체되어야 하는지 알기 위해 정보가 필요하다는 것을 정답은 (A)이다.

---

[168-171]

| | | |
|---|---|---|
| 브라이언 레벨 [오전 10시 18분] | | 우리 부서가 회사에 귀속되는 모든 사무실 장비를 체크할 거라는 사실 알고 있소? |
| 니콜 조던 [오전 10시 19분] | | 무슨 일로요? |
| 티미 노엘 [오전 10시 21분] | **171** 그 얘기 들었어요. 월요일에 널리 케인 씨가 의사 결정 과정을 위한 정보를 우리가 수집한게 될 거라고 말해 줬어요. |
| 니콜 조던 [오전 10시 22분] | 이해가 잘 안 가는데요. 정확히 무슨 정보요? |
| 브라이언 레벨 [오전 10시 23분] | 각 장비들이 수명이나 상태 같은 거 말하는 거죠. |
| 티미 노엘 [오전 10시 24분] | 그래야 4년 이상 사용한 컴퓨터 복사기들을 교체할 수 있거든요. |
| 니콜 조던 [오전 10시 26분] | 근데, 저는 이거 그에 관한 회람을 못 받았는데요. |
| 티미 노엘 [오전 10시 28분] | **170** 이번 주 목요일에 받을 거예요. 그래야 바로 다음 날 시작할 수 있거든요. 이 다음 날 금요일에 한 정보예요. |
| 니콜 조던 [오전 10시 29분] | **168** 어쨌든 보고서를 보고서와 비교하려고요? |
| 브라이언 레벨 [오전 10시 30분] | 바로 그거죠. 그러니 같이 준비합시다. |

---

**172** 기자는 무엇을 다루고 있는가?
(A) 투자 회사의 비즈니스 프로젝트
**(B) 놀이공원이 주변 지역에 미치는 영향**
(C) 럼지가 선정한 관광 명소
(D) 엔터테인먼트 산업의 중앙상서
**해설** 전반적인 내용은 오클랜드 시에 들어설 놀이공원이 지역 경제 활성화 등 주변 지역에 미치는 긍정적인 영향을 다루고 있다. 따라서 정답은 (B)이다.

**173** 지역 주민들은 왜 프로젝트를 받아들이는가?
(A) 투자 회사의 신뢰를 받아서
(B) 환경을 지속하기 위한 것이다.
(C) 지역 무역 경제에 살림을 도울 것이다.
**(D) 지역 경제를 신장시킬 것으로 기대된다.**
**해설** 주변 지역 대다수의 시민들은 이를 긍정적인 조심으로 본다는 내용과 많은 관광객으로 인해 지역 전체가 이득을 볼 것이라는 시민의 인터뷰 내용을 통해 정답은 (D)임을 알 수 있다.

**174** 스카이랜드 월드 놀이공원의 수입 원천이 아닌 것은 무엇인가?
(A) 입장료
(B) 주차료
(C) 기념품 판매
**(D) 광고비**
**해설** ...

해설 입장료, 주차료, 기념품과 식음료 판매를 통해 수익을 얻는다는 내용이 나오지만 많은 지역 신문의 광고를 통한 것이 대부분이 대부분의 수입 원천이 될 것이다. 따라서 (D)가 정답이다.

**175** [1], [2], [3], [4]로 표시된 곳 중에서 다음 문장이 들어갈 가장 적절한 곳은?

"그럼에도 불구하고 높이명원이 주변 지역 경제를 활발하게 할 것이라는 것에 의심의 여지가 없다."

(A) [1]
**(B) [2]**
(C) [3]
(D) [4]

해설 두 번째 문단에서 거대해지는 시가 주변 지역을 잠식하지도 모른다는 부정적인 내용이 나오는데 바로 이어서 경제를 활발하게 이를 긍정적인 조짐으로 본다고 했다. 따라서 이 사이에 그럼에도 불구하고 주변 지역 경제를 활발하게 할 것이라는 내용이 와야 자연스럽다. 따라서 (B)가 정답이다.

[176-180]

고객님들께

토론토 시내에서 ⓐ 퓨전 도미니카 요리를 전문으로 하는 라 시에스타가 취급 1988년에 산토 도밍고 요리 하급을 졸업하고 스페인의 평가 부문 비도 하고에서 요리 공부를 더 하였습니다. 그의 경력은 고향 산토 도밍고의 작은 식당에서 시작되었습니다. 그곳에서 그만의 독특한 요리법을 개선시켰으며 그 요리법은 매우 인기가 있어서 사매는 그를 공식 요리사로 임명하였습니다. 그는 불과 한 달 전에 캐나다로 이민을 와서 도미니카 요리가 이국적이고 이국적인 맛을 가지었습니다.

ⓐ 저희 새 주방장을 축하하기 위해서 라 시에스타는 ⓐ 특별 요리를 제공하고 모든 요리를 10퍼센트 할인해 드립니다. 저희는 또한 이러치 세프가 직접한 고 있으며 주방장의 주방정으로 맞이했습니다. 마누엘 이러치 씨는 오일은 매우 낮은 가격인 10.99달러에 판매합니다. 고객들은 포함 ⓐ 축하 특집에 참여하실 수 있으니, 당첨되시면 20달러의 할인 쿠폰과 이러 차 세프가 제공하는 개인 만찬 요리를 즐기실 수 있습니다.

이러치 세프가 개발한 새 메뉴에 대해 알아보시려면 www.ollasiesta.com으로 방문하시거나 ⓐ 고객 서비스부 켈리 카렌즈키 (Kalenzky kelly_kal@ollasiesta.com)로 마케팅 매니저 켈리 카렌즈키 하우 (bh7809@ollasiesta.com)

라 시에스타

---

발신: ⓐ kal@ollasiesta.com
날짜: 2017년 8월 31일

제목: 새 메뉴에 대한 의견

안녕하세요?

저는 최근 토론토 중심가에서 독특하 요리를 제공하는 귀하의 고급 식당에서 식사하였습니다. 저는 식사를 맛있게 했지만 식당의 개선을 위해 몇 가지 언급하겠습니다.

저는 이러차 세프가 제공한 뜨겁고 매운 새로운 요리 때문에 약간 충격을 받았습니다. 저에게 있어서 라 시에스타는 모든 사람이 즐기는 다소 완화되고 반찬이 많지 않은 요리를 내놓는 격식을 차리지 않은 식당이었습니다. 그러나 저는 가 맛었던 대부분의 요리는 너무 매워서 굽힐없이 물을 마시면서 먹지 못했습니다. 이러차 세프가 고향에서 습득한 오랜 경력을 없애는 것은 어렵지 만 저는 매운 정도를 줄이기 위해서 약간 ⓐ 변경을 가하는 것이 라 시에스타에 필요하고고 생각합니다.

넘판내 저는 귀하의 식당에서 식사하는 것을 무척 즐기고 앞으로 몇 년간 계속 기고 싶습니다. 새 요리사의 열정이 저의 저제을 앞으로 지켜줄 주기를 바랍니다.

감사합니다.

**176** 공고문의 목적은 무엇인가?

(A) 토론토의 인기 있는 식당을 소개하기 위해
(B) 도미니카의 가장 요리에 대한 팀을 제공하기 위해
**(C) 새 요리사를 환영하는 특별 행사를 알리기 위해**
(D) 새 식당의 개업을 축하하기 위해

해설 공고문의 첫 번째 문장에 새 주방장을 맞이하며 그에 대해 이야기하고 있다. 또 이를 기념하기 위해 할인이나 축하 복권 행사를 열고 있다. 따라서 정답은 (C)이다.

**177** 라 시에스타가 전문으로 하는 것은 무엇인가?

**(A) 도미니카 요리**
(B) 스페인의 음식과 와인
(C) 정통 도미니카 요리
(D) 유기농 요리

해설 공고문에서 라 시에스타는 퓨전 도미니카 요리를 전문으로 한다고 언급되어 있다. 따라서 정답은 (A)이다.

**178** 이메일은 누구에게 보내는 것인가?

(A) 토론토의 미식가
**(B) 라 시에스타의 직원**
(C) 식당 고문
(D) 음식 비평가

해설 이메일은 최근에 라 시에스타에서 식사했던 손님이 식당에 대해 비평하는 내용이다. 공고에 나온 연락처 중 고객 서비스팀에서 일하는 켈리 가 렌즈키의 이메일 주소가 수신인에 있으므로 (B)가 정답이다.

**179** 다음 중 기념 행사의 일부가 아닌 것은 무엇인가?

(A) 낮은 가격의 와인
(B) 복권
(C) 몇몇 요리의 할인
**(D) 무료 디저트**

해설 와인을 낮은 가격에 판매하고 일부 요리를 10퍼센트 할인해 주며, 축 하 복권 행사에 참여할 수 있다고 하지만 무료 디저트에 대한 언급은 없다. 따라서 정답은 (D)이다.

**180** 이메일의 두 번째 단락, 6번째 줄의 modification과 의미상 가장 가까운 것 은 무엇인가?

**(A) 수정**
(B) 제거
(C) 혼합
(D) 희망

해설 modification는 '변경, 수정'의 의미로 (A) adjustments가 정답이다.

[181-185]

어휘 utmost 최고의 cuisine 요리 executive 중역의 culinary 요리의 further 발전시키다 cookery 요리 designate 임명하다 immigrate 이 민을 오다 zesty 자극을 주는 remarkably 매우 congratulatory 축하 의 raffle 복권 translate 바꾸다 casual 격식을 차리지 않은 classy 그럼의 세련미 modified 완화된 get rid of ~을 제거하다 take … into consideration ~을 고려하다 authentic 진짜의 gourmet 미식가

---

테사 가전

**183** 일부 제품 40퍼센트 가격 인하! 크리스마스 주간!!

초고용량 냉장고 - 40퍼센트 할인
오븐이 딸린 전기 레인지 - 40퍼센트 할인
스테인리스 스틸 전자레인지 - 40퍼센트 할인
65인치 스마트 TV - 40퍼센트 할인
그리고 더 많은 제품 할인이 있습니다.

한정 기간 동안 모든 고객에게 특별 가격을 제공합니다. 높은 품질의 가전제품 을 40퍼센트 할인되 가격에 가져보세요? **181-ⓐ** 최저 가격 보장입니다! 이 놀라운 할인은 12월 21일부터 12월 27일까지입니다. 댈러스 근로 쇼핑센터의 유지 영 업시간인 12월 21일부터, 매일 오전 8시에서 오후 9시까지 저희 고객에 영업합니다.

누구도 따를 수 없는 서비스

**181-ⓑ 185** 댈러스-포트 워스 지역 내에서 대부분의 주문*이 무료 배송
**181-ⓒ** 월요일부터 토요일까지 24시간 내내 주문 및 고객 지원
- 모든 교환 제품에 대해 60일 환불 보장
- 무료 배송 지역에서는 제품 설치도 도와 드립니다**
- 포괄적인 매장 내 서비스 및 보증**

**182** *추가 재고가 있는 조건입니다.

*전문적인 설치가 포함됩니다**

수신: d_perez@teschappliance.com
발신: hansen8678@uxuraconstr.com
날짜: 12월 22일 17:05

패러디스 씨께

덕슈라 건설 회사를 대표하여 이메일을 보냅니다. 저희는 현재 100가구인 아파트의 공사를 거의 마쳤습니다. 각 가구에는 기본적인 가전제품(냉장고, 세탁기, 건조기, 전자레인지)을 갖출 것입니다. 몇몇 제 동료들이 귀하의 매장을 매우 추천하였고 지금 진행하는 할인으로 제가 확실히 많은 돈을 절약할 수 있을 것 같습니다.

저는 화씨와 귀하로부터 모든 필요한 정보를 구입하는 데 관심이 있지만, 저희 현재 공사 일정에 따라 1월 15일 이후에 가전제품 설치 준비가 될 것 같습니다. 제 예상 주문량을 감안할 때 그 날짜까지 할인 날짜를 연장하실 수 있는지 여쭤고 싶습니다. 연장이 가능하다면 그 날짜에 맞춰 설치 서비스도 알려 주시오.

소식 기다리겠습니다.

엘리자 한센
덕슈라 건설

어휘 appliance (가정용) 기기 electric range 전기 레인지 incredible 믿을 수 없는 round the clock 24시간 내내 installation 설치 comprehensive 포괄적인 on behalf of ~을 대신하여 be equipped with ~을 갖추고 있다 prospective 유망한

181 테슈라 가전은 어떤 서비스를 제공하는가?

(A) 주 7일 고객 서비스
(B) 무료 제품 서비스의 보증
**(C) 댈러스-포트 워스 지역에서 최저 가격**
(D) 모든 주문 무료 배송

해설 광고에 의하면 최저 가격이 거의 보장된다고 하는데, 테슈라 가전은 댈러스 근 로 쇼핑센터에 있고, 댈러스-포트 워스 지역 내에서 대부분의 주문의 무료 일일 배송하고 제품 설치도 도울 수 있다고 하는 것으로 보이 멀 러스-포트 워스 지역에서 최저 가격을 보장하는 것으로 볼 내릴 수 있다. 따라서 정답은 (C)이다.

182 광고에 의하면, 일일 배송이 안 되는 경우는 무엇인가?

(A) 전화로 주문을 했다.
(B) 토요일에 주문되었다.
(C) 해외로 배송하여야 한다.
**(D) 창고에 재고가 떨어졌다.**

해설 광고의 서비스 내용에 부분을 보면 댈러스-포트 워스 지역 내에서 대부분의 주문이 무료 일일 배송이지만 별표(*)로 표시되어 있고 그 밑에 재고 상태에 따라 안 될 수도 있음을 알리고 있다. 따라서 정답은 (D)이다.

183 크리스마스 주간 이후에 무슨 일이 있을 것인가?

(A) 모든 주문이 배송될 것이다.
**(B) 할인이 끝날 것이다.**

(C) 건설 공사가 시작될 것이다.
(D) 회의가 열릴 것이다.

해설 할인 기간은 12월 21일부터 12월 27일까지이므로 이 기간이 지나면 제품 할인이 끝난다는 것을 알 수 있다. 따라서 정답은 (B)이다.

184 한센 씨가 패러디스 씨에게 이메일을 쓰는 이유는 무엇인가?

**(A) 특별히 고려해 달라고 요청하기 위해**
(B) 배송 지연에 대해 항의하기 위해
(C) 기술 지원을 요청하기 위해
(D) 몇몇 가전제품의 주문을 취소하기 위해

해설 한센 씨는 공사 일정상 할인 행사가 끝난 후에야 가전제품을 아파트에 설치할 수 있으므로 할인 날짜를 조금 연장해 달라는 요청을 하고 있 다. 따라서 정답은 (A)이다.

185 덕슈라 건설 회사에 대해 암시된 것은 무엇인가?

(A) 재정적 어려움에 처해 있다.
(B) 본사는 댈러스에 있다.
**(C) 공사 일정이 변경되었다.**
(D) 새 아파트가 댈러스-포트 워스 지역 내에 있다.

해설 이메일 마지막에서 설치 서비스가 필요 없다는 사실을 알려주고 있다. 준디고 했으니 이를 통해 공사 중인 아파트가 무료 배송 지역 내에 있음을 알 수 있다. 따라서 정답은 (D)이다.

---

http://www.sttech.com/product

[186-190]

| | | ST 테크 | | |
|---|---|---|---|---|
| | | 당신의 눈을 통해 상상을 보는 기술 | | |
| 메인 화면 | **제품** | 저장소 | 평가 | 연락처 |

**YL-100S 모델**

(C) 다음으로 된에 다양한 기능이 든에이 이외 활동을 위한 일련의 방수 기능 모델이 4월에 출시될 것입니다.

(18) ST 테크 센서는 생리적으로 당신의 눈의 움직임을 측정합니다.

(E) 가속도계 시스템은 진동식는 동일 기술을 기록합니다.

(F) 자이로스코프 기술이 적용되어 당신의 위치를 찾고 다음 경로를 계획하도록 도와주는 내비게이션 시스템 상의 기준 방향을 제공합니다.

(G) 자료 최신 이어폰에는 당신이 일어나는 순간부터 잠자리에 드는 순간까지 일 생의 동료처럼 당신과 함께 세상을 볼 것입니다.

---

http://www.sttech.com/review

| | | ST 테크 | | |
|---|---|---|---|---|
| | | 당신의 눈을 통해 상상을 보는 기술 | | |
| 메인 화면 | 제품 | 저장소 | **리뷰** | 연락처 |

이름: 오스틴 골드
모델: YL-100S
시리얼 번호: GL205483A
구매 날짜: 1월 10일
의견:

YL-100S를 구매하고 굉장히 만족합니다. 제가 매일 차로 출퇴근을 해야 하는데, 때때로 조석 근무를 하면 정말 (18) 녹초기 됩니다. 매일 전 일이 산더미처럼 많아요. (19) 퇴근 후 운전하며 오다가 너무 졸려서 눈이 감기기 시작했는데, 그때 제 운전 친구가 저를 깨웠고 저는 차 사고를 면할 수 있었으니다. (189) 이 녀석 덕에 저는 더 편안히 안전하게 운전할 수 있어요.

---

(186) 웨어러블 산업은 우리가 입지 않는 것과 기술 사이의 격차를 메우려고 있 다. 우리 몸에 착용할 수 있는 활동 추적기나 스마트 시계 같은 스마트 전자기기 등도 액세서리로 출범했지만, 지금은 우리 건강을 측정하고 옷의 천 형태 또는 상자에 우리 피부에 붙이는 패치에 내장되는 장치가 되어 꽃 피우고 있는 것이다.

스마트 직물
GPS 기술이 내장된 스마트 시계는 우리의 움직임이나 걸음 수 같은 정보를 추적하고 우리가 소모하는 칼로리에 대해 개속 알려준다.

테크 직물
테크 직물 혹은 직물 기술은 우리 몸의 생리 정보로뿐 아니라 날씨와 자외선 비율에 대해서도 측정한다. 스마트 옷은 스마트폰을 열고 명령을 디지털로 교체할 것으로 예상된다.

VR 안경
(189) 스마트 안경은 평범히 인경처럼 착용되지만, 내장된 바이오 센스 기술은 안 전상 목적으로 우리 눈의 변화를 감지한다. 운전 중 졸음이 오는 운전자에게 경고를 들린다.

스마트 패치
(187) 스마트 패치는 심장의 호흡수가 높은 수준의 스트레스 상태를 나타날 때 이를 진정시키기 위해 고안되었으며, 스트레스 반응이 감지될 때, 호흡을 심장의 회복 리듬으로 이끌기 위해 진동하기 시작한다.

어휘 wearable (technology) 옷에 착용하는 기술 fill a gap 차이를 메우다 activity tracker 활동량을 추적하는 장치 blossom into ~로 꽃피우다 fabric 직물, 천 patch 패치, 부분 built-in 내장된 keep us posted on ~에 대해 계속 알려주다 biometric data 생체 정보 ultraviolet rating 자외선 비율 business card 명함 embedded 내장된 nod off 깜박 졸다 behind the wheel 운전 중인 initiate 개시하다, 착수하다 calming 진정시키는 운동 exercise 진정시키는 운동 elevated levels of stress 높은 수준의 스트 레스 vibrate 진동하다 restorative rhythm 회복 리듬 versatile 다용 도의 frame 틀, (안경테) outdoor activity 야외 활동 waterproof 방수 physiological 생리적인 fashion 방식 accelerometer 가속도계 acceleration 가속 gyroscope 자이로스코프(왼제는 방향 기준 평 reference direction 기준 방향 state-of-the-art 최신의 lifelong companion 일생의 동반자 drive to and from work 차로 출퇴근하다 work overtime 초과 근무하다 be up to

**어휘** fitting (장비, 가구의 직원) 부품 nationwide 전국적인 valid 유효한 at the time of purchase 구매 시에 custom clearance item 통관 수속 물품 be combined with ~와 결합되다 associate discount 제휴 할인 reproduction 복제, 복사 shipping 배송 handling 처리, 취급 issue a coupon 쿠폰을 발행하다 price list 가격표 fit one's needs ~의 필요에 맞다, 적합하다 file cabinet 문서 보관함 multi function 복사기 photocopy machine 복사기

**[191-195]**

30% 할인

105 400달러 이하 하나의 정규 물품! 온라인 쇼핑에만 유효하지 않습니다.

**넥소바 사무실 가구류 및 부품**
104 전국 모든 넥소바 상점에서 쇼핑하세요

쿠폰은 구매 시 제시되어야 합니다. 통관 수속 물품에는 유효하지 않습니다. 다른 쿠폰이나 제휴 할인과 결합 사용하지 못함 수 있습니다. 구입 물건장 하나의 쿠폰만 적용됩니다. 복제 불가합니다. 배송, 처리, 세금 등이 포함되지 않습니다. 11월 30일까지 오직 미국 내 상점에서만 유효합니다.

수신: inquiry@nexovaoffice.com/boston
발신: 코비 바버롤리 <kbarbiroli@horah.com>
날짜: 9월 28일
제목: 30퍼센트 할인 쿠폰
담당자 분께,

제가 로스엔젤러스의 한 넥소바 상점에서 발행한 30퍼센트 할인 쿠폰을 가지고 있는데요, 102 우리 회사가 여기 보스턴으로 이사를 한 관계로 구매의 상점에서 사용하고 싶습니다.

쿠폰에는 102 "400달러 이하 하나의 정규 물품"이라고 적혀 있는데, 103 제가 적용 가능한 어떤 물품을 가지고 있고 가격은 어떻게 되는지 모릅니다. 101 저는 종이를 인쇄할 수 있는 사무실 기계 구입에 관심이 있습니다. 그 기능만 있다면, 일할 때 딱히 중요한 건 없어요. 제가 보스턴으로 이사를 한 관계로 보완의 기계표를 보내주실 수 있나요?

코비 바버롤리

**넥소바 사무실 가구류 및 부품**
귀하의 사무용도에 맞는 최고급 제품들을 판매합니다.

| 품목 | 가격 |
| --- | --- |
| - 문서 보관함 | 200달러 |
| - 테이블 | 300달러 |
| - 컴퓨터 | 1,100달러 |
| - 에어컨 | 700달러 |
| 105 - 독립기능 프린터 | 300달러 |
| - 전화기 | 150달러 |
| 105 - 복사기 | 5,500달러 |

가격표 – 12월 15일까지 유효

---

one's ears in work 일이 산더미처럼 많다 (eyes) fall shut (눈이) 감기다 tech-savvy 기술을 잘 다루는

**186** 정보지는 누구를 위한 것이겠는가?
(A) 건설 인부
(B) 패션 디자이너
**(C) 최신 기술 소비자**
(D) 프로 운동선수

해설 정보지는 웨어러블 선원은 우리가 입는 것과 입지 않는 기술 사이의 격차를 매우고 있다는 내용으로 전반적으로 새로운 웨어러블 기술에 대한 것이다. 따라서 정답은 (C)이다.

**187** 정보지에 따르면 누가 스마트 패치에 가장 관심을 보이겠는가?
(A) 우산을 항상 잃어버리는 사람들
(B) 패션 동향을 알고 싶어 하는 사람들
**(C) 쉽게 스트레스를 받는 사람들**
(D) 매일 수영하는 걸 즐기는 사람들

해설 정보지에서 스마트 패치는 이를 나타낼 때 이를 진정시키기 위해 고안되었다고 했으므로, 쉽게 스트레스를 받는 사람이 이 제품에 관심을 가질 것이다. 따라서 정답은 (C)이다.

**188** 온라인 평가에서 첫 번째 단락 두 번째 줄의 exhausted와 의미상 가장 가까운 것은 무엇인가?
(A) 매우 기쁜
(B) 건망증이 있는
**(C) 매우 피곤한**
(D) 스마트 패치

해설 exhausted의 뜻은 '매우 피곤한(very tired)'이므로 정답은 (C)이다.

**189** 글드 씨가 쓴 온라인 평가에서 어떤 제품을 언급하는가?
(A) 스마트 시계
(B) 테크 직물
**(C) VR 인경**
(D) 스마트 패치

해설 글드 씨가 쓴 온라인 평가에서 YL-100S 덕에 더 편하고 안전하게 운전할 수 있다는 내용이 나온다. 정보지에서 VR 인경 중 졸음이 오는 운전자에게 경고를 한다고 하였으므로, 글드 씨가 구매한 YL-100S는 정보지에서 VR 인경 항목에 해당됨을 알 수 있다. 따라서 정답은 (C)이다.

**190** YL-100S의 어떤 특징이 글드 씨가 차 사고를 피할 수 있도록 도왔는가?
(A) 다용도 틀
**(B) ST 테크 센서**
(C) 기술도계 시스템
(D) 자이로스코프 기술

해설 글드 씨가 쓴 온라인 평가에서 운전 중 너무 졸려 눈이 감기기 시작했다는 내용이 나온다. 이제 YL-100S의 특징이 나와 있는 웹 페이지를 보면, "ST 테크 센서는 생리적으로 눈의 움직임을 측정한다고 했으

---

**191** 30퍼센트 할인 쿠폰에 대해 무엇이 사실인가?
(A) 통관 수속 물품에 유효하다.
(B) 다른 쿠폰과 함께 사용 가능하다.
**(C) 배송비는 제외한다.**
(D) 연말까지 사용 가능하다.

해설 쿠폰 하단의 설명을 보면, "통관 수속 물품에는 배송, 처리, 세금 등이 포함되지 않습니다"라고 했으므로, 배송비는 제외된다는 (C)가 정답이다. 통관 수속 물품에는 유효하지 않다고 했으므로 (A)는 틀렸고, 다른 쿠폰이나 제휴 할인과 중복 사용되지 못할 수 있다고 하였으므로 (B)도 틀렸으며, 11월 30일까지만 사용 가능하다고 하였으므로 (D)도 틀렸다.

**192** 바버롤리 씨는 어떤 사업을 하고 있겠는가?
(A) 요식업
(B) 운송업
**(C) 출판업**
(D) 항공우주

해설 이메일을 보면, "저는 종이를 인쇄할 수 있는 사무실 기계 구입에 관심이 있습니다. 그 기능만 있다면, 일할 때 딱히 중요한 건 없어요"라고 하였으므로 종이 인쇄가 업무의 주를 이루는 사업을 출판업이라고 볼 수 있다. 따라서 정답은 (C)이다.

**193** 이메일에서 두 번째 단락 네 번째 줄의 matters와 의미상 가장 가까운 것은 무엇인가?
(A) 사라지다
(B) 감소하다
**(C) 중요하다**
(D) 번제되다

해설 matters는 동사로 '중요하다'라는 뜻이므로 정답은 (C)이다.

**194** 넥소바 사무실 가구류 및 부품에 대해 암시된 것은 무엇인가?
(A) 세계적으로 유명한 부품을 발행한다.
**(B) 보스턴에 지사가 있다.**
(C) 최근에 설립되었다.
(D) 최고의 기술을 제공한다.

해설 쿠폰에서 "전국 모든 넥소바 상점에서 쇼핑하세요"라는 문구가 있고 이 메일에서 "우리 회사가 여기 보스턴으로 이사를 한 관계로 귀하의 상점에서 사용하고 싶습니다"라는 내용을 보면, 넥소바는 보스턴에도 상점이 있음을 알 수 있다. 따라서 정답은 (B)이다. 가장 가구류 판매점이므로 (A)는 틀렸고, 미국 내 상점에서만 유효하다고 쿠폰에 적혀 있으므로 (C)도 틀렸고, (D)는 알 수 없는 선택지이

**195** 바버롤리 씨는 어떤 물품을 구매하겠는가?

(A) 문서 보관함
(B) 컴퓨터
**(C) 독립기능 프린터**
(D) 복사기

해설 이메일에서 바버롤리 씨는 종이를 인쇄할 수 있는 사무기기에 관심이 있고 구독을 사용하기를 원한다. 구독은 400달러 이하의 제품에 대해서만 사용 가능하므로 가격에서 종이를 인쇄할 수 있고 400달러 이하인 (C) 독립기능 프린터가 정답이다.

[196-200]

🍽 **사와디 레스토랑**

정통 태국 레스토랑

저희는 편안한 분위기와 함께 태국 음식의 가장 신선한 맛을 취급합니다. **197** 저희의 숙련된 태국 원주민 주방장은 세련된 미식가들의 미각을 충족시켜 줄 것입니다!

**196** 포장이 가능합니다!

🍽 점심: 월요일 ~ 금요일 오전 11시에서 오후 2시까지
🍽 저녁: 화요일 ~ 토요일 오후 5시에서 오후 10시까지
일요일에 월요일만 오후 5시에서 오후 9시까지

칠리소스 치킨, 튀긴 생선 케어, 명품 소스 치킨 윙, 마른 버섯 거래 등 마드지 말하세요, 더 있습니다!

1900 베르노 로드
포우드, 스토벨레 지역
6426-3621
센트럴에 애버뉴 건너편

발신: 에드워드 호머
수신: 웨이트로 대매
날짜: 7월 17일
제목: 견학 일정 및 저녁 식사

안녕하세요, 대매 씨.

전화상으로 얘기했듯이, 대매 씨가 **199** 우리 공장 견학을 온다고 저희 사장님이 로베트 스톤 씨께 알려주셨습니다. 견학은 오전 8시에 시작할 예정이고 점심 휴식 시간은 오후 12시입니다. 견학은 1시간 휴식 후 계속 이어져 오후 6시에 끝날 것입니다.

**199** 태국 음식을 좋아한다고 들었는데요, 제가 스토벨레에 괜찮은 레스토랑을 아는데, 공장에서도 5미터밖에 안 떨어져 있습니다. 저는 거기 단골손님이고 **200** 저는 내게 씨와 같은 음식 주방장이 천차가 있었는데 오랫동안 주방장 주방장을 주문할 음식을 주문할 것입니다.

에드워드 호머

---

**196** 사와디 레스토랑에 대해 사실인 것은 무엇인가?

(A) 중국 요리 전문이다.
(B) 주말에는 휴업한다.
**(C) 포장 서비스를 제공한다.**
(D) 많은 분점이 있다.

해설 광고에서 "포장 가능합니다"라고 했으므로 정답은 (C)이다. (A)는 태국 요리 레스토랑이고, (B)는 토요일, 일요일에도 영업을 하므로 오답이다.

**197** 천차 씨에 대해 암시된 것은 무엇인가?

(A) 공장을 견학했다.
**(B) 태국 출신이다.**
(C) 호머 씨와 상사이다.
(D) 광고를 냈다.

해설 이메일과 광고의 연계 문제이다. 이메일에서 "주방장이 천차이 씨도 오랫동안 일이었지만"이라는 내용으로 보아 천차이 씨는 주방장임을 알 수 있다. 광고에서 "저희 숙련된 태국 원주민 주방장"이라는 표현에서 그가 태국인임을 알 수 있다. 따라서 정답은 (B)이다.

---

🍽 **사와디 레스토랑**

시간을 내서 이 의견서를 작성해 주세요. 여러분의 의견으로 저희가 무엇을 잘하고 있고 또 무엇에 더 분발해야 할지 배우겠습니다!

몇 분 방문하셨나요? 2명　　날짜: 7월 20일

언제 방문하셨나요? ☐ 아침 ☐ 점심 ☑ 저녁

| | 매우 좋음 | 좋음 | 괜찮음 | 나쁨 |
|---|---|---|---|---|
| **198** 음식 품질: | ☑ 매우 좋음 | ☐ 좋음 | ☐ 괜찮음 | ☐ 나쁨 |
| **198** 음식량: | ☐ 매우 좋음 | ☑ 좋음 | ☐ 괜찮음 | ☐ 나쁨 |
| 주문 난이도: | ☑ 매우 좋음 | ☐ 좋음 | ☐ 괜찮음 | ☐ 나쁨 |
| 서비스: | ☐ 매우 좋음 | ☑ 좋음 | ☐ 괜찮음 | ☐ 나쁨 |
| 청결함: | ☑ 매우 좋음 | ☐ 좋음 | ☐ 괜찮음 | ☐ 나쁨 |
| 전반적 가치: | ☐ 매우 좋음 | ☑ 좋음 | ☐ 괜찮음 | ☐ 나쁨 |

나이: ☐ 18세 이하　☐ 19-35　☑ 36 - 60　☐ 60 이상

웨이터 이름: 제이 콘스

무엇을 주문하셨나요? **200** 명품 소스 치킨 윙 & 태국 누수 많이

의견 **198 199** 제 비즈니스 파트너인 에드워드 씨가 추천해서 같이 왔습니다. 하루 종일 견학을 해서 정말 무척 배가 고팠는데 1인분 양이 좀 적었습니다. 물론 맛은 정말 좋았다고 생각하지만, 그 부분에 좀 신경 쓰시면 될 것 같습니다.

저희를 어떻게 알게 되셨나요?
☐ 신문　☐ TV　☐ 라디오　☑ 친구　☐ 기타: _____

---

어휘 **authentic** 진짜의, 정통의　**feature** 특징으로 하다　**combined with** ~와 결합된　**relaxing atmosphere** 편한 분위기　**experienced** 숙련된　**taste bud** (혀의) 미뢰　**sophisticated** 세련된　**gourmet** 미식가　**take-out** (식당 안에서 먹지 않고) 가지고 가는 포장　**wrap up** ~을 끝내다, 마무리 짓다　**regular customer** 단골손님　**server** 웨이터, 웨이트리스　**portion** 1인당 음식의 양　**serving** 1인분 음식　**cuisine** 요리

---

**198** 의견서에 따르면 사와디 레스토랑에서 무엇이 개선되어야 하는가?

(A) 음식 품질
**(B) 음식량**
(C) 주문 난이도
(D) 청결함

해설 의견서에서 '나쁨'에 표시한 것은 음식량이다. 따라서 정답은 (B)이다.

**199** 의견서를 작성한 사람은 누구이겠는가?

(A) 호머 씨
**(B) 대매 씨**
(C) 스톤 씨
(D) 존스 씨

해설 대매 씨에게 보낸 이메일에서 '태국 음식을 좋아한다고 들었는데요, 제가 스토벨레에 괜찮은 레스토랑을 아는데'라는 내용이 나온다. 의견서가 비즈니스 파트너인 에드워드 씨가 추천해서 같이 왔습니다'라는 내용으로 보아 대매 씨는 레스토랑을 추천한 호머 씨와 같이 와서 식사를 하고 의견서를 작성한 것임을 알 수 있다. 따라서 정답은 (B)이다.

**200** 사와디 레스토랑에서 호머 씨는 무엇을 식사하였겠는가?

(A) 칠리소스 치킨
(B) 튀긴 생선 케어
**(C) 명품 소스 치킨 윙**
(D) 마른 버섯 거래

해설 호머 씨가 쓴 이메일에서 대매 씨와 같은 음식을 주문할 것이라는 내용이 나온다. 따라서 호머 씨는 대매 씨와 같은 음식을 주문했을 것이다. 의견서를 작성한 사람은 대매 씨이고, 대매 씨가 주문한 음식을 의견서에서 보면 '명품 소스 치킨 윙 & 태국 누수 많이'임을 알 수 있으므로 (C)가 정답이다.

# Actual Test 04

## 🎧 Listening Comprehension

본책 P140

**PART 1**

| | | | | | |
|---|---|---|---|---|---|
| 1 (B) | 2 (C) | 3 (C) | 4 (A) | 5 (B) | 6 (B) |

**PART 2**

| | | | | | | | | | |
|---|---|---|---|---|---|---|---|---|---|
| 7 (B) | 8 (A) | 9 (C) | 10 (B) | 11 (B) | 12 (B) | 13 (C) | 14 (B) | 15 (C) | 16 (C) |
| 17 (C) | 18 (A) | 19 (B) | 20 (C) | 21 (B) | 22 (B) | 23 (B) | 24 (B) | 25 (A) | 26 (B) |
| 27 (C) | 28 (B) | 29 (A) | 30 (B) | 31 (B) | | | | | |

**PART 3**

| | | | | | | | | | |
|---|---|---|---|---|---|---|---|---|---|
| 32 (B) | 33 (D) | 34 (B) | 35 (B) | 36 (C) | 37 (B) | 38 (B) | 39 (A) | 40 (A) | 41 (B) |
| 42 (A) | 43 (D) | 44 (D) | 45 (B) | 46 (C) | 47 (B) | 48 (C) | 49 (A) | 50 (B) | 51 (B) |
| 52 (A) | 53 (D) | 54 (B) | 55 (C) | 56 (B) | 57 (D) | 58 (A) | 59 (C) | 60 (A) | 61 (B) |
| 62 (C) | 63 (C) | 64 (B) | 65 (C) | 66 (A) | 67 (C) | 68 (A) | 69 (B) | 70 (C) | |

**PART 4**

| | | | | | | | | | |
|---|---|---|---|---|---|---|---|---|---|
| 71 (B) | 72 (C) | 73 (C) | 74 (D) | 75 (C) | 76 (A) | 77 (B) | 78 (A) | 79 (B) | 80 (B) |
| 81 (D) | 82 (A) | 83 (A) | 84 (C) | 85 (B) | 86 (A) | 87 (D) | 88 (C) | 89 (D) | 90 (C) |
| 91 (B) | 92 (B) | 93 (D) | 94 (B) | 95 (B) | 96 (B) | 97 (D) | 98 (D) | 99 (B) | 100 (C) |

## 📖 Reading Comprehension

본책 P152

**PART 5**

| | | | | | | | | | |
|---|---|---|---|---|---|---|---|---|---|
| 101 (D) | 102 (A) | 103 (A) | 104 (D) | 105 (D) | 106 (D) | 107 (C) | 108 (C) | 109 (A) | 110 (B) |
| 111 (C) | 112 (C) | 113 (C) | 114 (C) | 115 (C) | 116 (D) | 117 (B) | 118 (D) | 119 (C) | 120 (B) |
| 121 (A) | 122 (C) | 123 (C) | 124 (A) | 125 (B) | 126 (C) | 127 (A) | 128 (A) | 129 (A) | 130 (A) |

**PART 6**

| | | | | | | | | | |
|---|---|---|---|---|---|---|---|---|---|
| 131 (C) | 132 (A) | 133 (B) | 134 (A) | 135 (A) | 136 (A) | 137 (B) | 138 (B) | 139 (D) | 140 (C) |
| 141 (C) | 142 (A) | 143 (A) | 144 (D) | 145 (C) | 146 (D) | | | | |

**PART 7**

| | | | | | | | | | |
|---|---|---|---|---|---|---|---|---|---|
| 147 (A) | 148 (C) | 149 (D) | 150 (A) | 151 (C) | 152 (B) | 153 (D) | 154 (D) | 155 (B) | 156 (B) |
| 157 (A) | 158 (A) | 159 (B) | 160 (D) | 161 (B) | 162 (C) | 163 (B) | 164 (A) | 165 (B) | 166 (D) |
| 167 (C) | 168 (B) | 169 (C) | 170 (B) | 171 (A) | 172 (A) | 173 (C) | 174 (B) | 175 (D) | 176 (D) |
| 177 (C) | 178 (B) | 179 (D) | 180 (A) | 181 (B) | 182 (D) | 183 (C) | 184 (B) | 185 (A) | 186 (A) |
| 187 (A) | 188 (C) | 189 (C) | 190 (B) | 191 (B) | 192 (A) | 193 (C) | 194 (C) | 195 (C) | 196 (B) |
| 197 (D) | 198 (D) | 199 (C) | 200 (C) | | | | | | |

## PART 1

P140

**1**
[미W] (A) She is walking into the store.
**(B) She is reaching for an upper shelf.**
(C) She is pointing at an exit sign.
(D) She is setting a box of merchandise on the shelf.

(A) 여자가 가게 안으로 걸어가고 있다.
**(B) 여자가 위의 선반으로 손을 뻗고 있다.**
(C) 여자가 비상구 표지판을 가리키고 있다.
(D) 여자가 선반에 물건 상자를 놓고 있다.

**어휘** reach for 손을 뻗다  upper 위의  shelf 선반  point at ~를 가리키다  exit 비상구  merchandise 물건, 상품

**2**
[영M] (A) The man is putting up a shelf.
(B) The man is folding an umbrella.
**(C) The man is pushing a cart.**
(D) The man is paying for an item.

(A) 남자가 선반을 달고 있다.
(B) 남자가 우산을 접고 있다.
**(C) 남자가 수레를 밀고 있다.**
(D) 남자가 물건 값을 지불하고 있다.

**어휘** put ~ up (건물 등을) 세우다, 짓다  fold 접다  item 물품

**3**
[미W] (A) The roof of the house is flat.
(B) An electrical pole is being set up.
**(C) Bricks are piled up in several rows.**
(D) A gravel path leads to the door.

(A) 집 지붕이 편평하다.
(B) 전봇대가 세워지고 있다.
**(C) 벽돌이 여러 줄로 쌓여 있다.**
(D) 자갈길이 문으로 이어져 있다.

**어휘** flat 편평한  electrical pole 전봇대  brick 벽돌  pile up 쌓다  gravel 자갈  lead to ~로 연결되다

**4**
[미M] (A) The shelves are stocked with books.
(B) Books are being loaded on a cart.
(C) A librarian is arranging some books.
(D) A ladder is leaning against the wall.

**(A) 책장은 책으로 가득 차 있다.**
(B) 책이 카트에 실리는 중이다.
(C) 사서가 몇몇 책을 정리하고 있다.
(D) 사다리는 벽에 기대어 있다.

**어휘** be stocked with ~로 가득 차다  load 싣다  librarian 사서  lean against 기대다

**5**
[미W] (A) Some boats are floating close to a dock.
**(B) Railings border a body of water.**
(C) Bicycles are parked on a bike rack.
(D) Some people are marching down the street.

(A) 보트들이 부두 가까이에 떠 있다.
**(B) 난간이 수역의 경계를 이루고 있다.**
(C) 자전거들이 자전거 보관대에 주차되어 있다.
(D) 몇몇 사람들이 거리 행진을 하고 있다.

**어휘** float 뜨다  dock 부두  railing 난간  border 가장자리를 이루다  a body of water (바다나 호수 등의) 수역  rack 걸이, 선반  march 행진하다  down the street 거리 행진을 따라서

**6**
[영M] (A) The exterior of the building is being refurbished.
**(B) Some hoses have been extended from a vehicle.**
(C) The car is being sprayed with water.
(D) Some workers are standing near the entrance.

(A) 건물의 외면이 재단장되고 있다.
**(B) 호스가 차량에서부터 늘어뜨려져 있다.**
(C) 차에 물이 뿌려지고 있다.
(D) 일하는 사람들이 출입구 근처에 서 있다.

**어휘** exterior 외면  refurbish 재단장하다  extend 연장하다  spray 뿌리다  entrance 출입구

## PART 2

P144

**7**
[미M] Where is the entrance to the museum?
(A) Yes, some of each.
**(B) To the left of the staircase.**
(C) It was a good film.

미술관으로 들어가는 문이 어디죠?
(A) 네, 각각 조금씩요.
**(B) 계단 왼쪽이에요.**
(C) 재미있는 영화였어요.

**어휘** staircase (건물 내부의) 계단

**8**
[영M] Why was the flight from Toronto delayed?
**(A) Because of the weather.**
(B) No, it's a direct flight.
(C) She lives there.

토론토에서 오는 항공편이 왜 지연되었죠?
**(A) 날씨 때문이요.**
(B) 아니요, 그건 직항편이에요.
(C) 그녀는 그곳에 살아요.

**어휘** direct flight 직항 항공편

**9**
[미W] I liked the candidate we interviewed this morning.
(A) A copy of your résumé.
(B) Let's do it tomorrow.
**(C) Yes. She's my favorite, too.**

저는 우리가 오늘 아침에 면접 본 지원자가 좋았어요.
(A) 당신의 이력서 한 부요.
(B) 그건 내일 합시다.
**(C) 네, 저도 그녀가 제일 좋았어요.**

**어휘** candidate 지원자  favorite 가장 좋아하는 것/사람

**10**
[미W] Who will notify the new employees of the schedule changes?
(A) The meeting was rescheduled.
**(B) The department manager.**
(C) I don't have change.

누가 신입사원들에게 스케줄 변경에 대해 알릴 건가요?
(A) 그 회의는 일정이 바뀌었어요.
**(B) 부서장이요.**
(C) 저는 잔돈이 없어요.

**어휘** change 변경 사항, 잔돈

**11**
[영M] When is Mr. O'pry sending the bid?
(A) He really loved it.
**(B) As soon as it's completed.**
(C) It depends on how much you spent.

오프리 씨가 언제 입찰가를 보낼 예정인가요?
(A) 그는 정말 그걸 좋아했어요.
**(B) 완료되는 대로요.**
(C) 당신이 얼마를 썼느냐에 따라 달라요.

**어휘** bid 가격 입찰  depend on ~에 따라 다르다

**12**
[미M] Is the meeting about rent or sale?
(A) It is scheduled a week ago.
**(B) Neither. It's about relocation.**
(C) It'll be in the convention hall.

회의는 임대에 관한 것인가요, 판매에 관한 것인가요?
(A) 1주일 전에 예정되어 있었어요.
**(B) 둘 다 아니에요. 이전에 관한 거예요.**
(C) 컨벤션 홀에서 할겁니다.

**어휘** rent 임대  relocation 이전, 재배치

**13**
[영M] Which train should I take?
[미W] (A) It is a southbound bus.
(B) The passengers will get off at the next station.
**(C) The one on track number five.**

제가 어느 기차를 타야 하죠?
(A) 이건 남쪽으로 가는 버스예요.
(B) 승객들이 다음 역에서 내릴 거예요.
(C) 5번 트랙에 있는 거예요.
어휘 southbound 남쪽 방향의 get off 내리다 station 역, 정거장

**14** Why didn't you come to the grand opening on Monday?
미W (A) No, let's meet on Tuesday.
미M (B) Sorry, I had another engagement.
(C) We didn't know each other at that time.
월요일 개장 때 왜 안 왔어요?
(A) 아니요, 화요일에 만납시다.
(B) 죄송해요, 다른 약속이 있어서요.
(C) 그때는 우리가 서로 몰랐어요.
어휘 grand opening 개장, 개업 engagement 약속

**15** Our newest novel is being published next month.
미W (A) Yes, she's planning to.
영M (B) On the left side.
(C) I think it will sell well.
새 소설이 다음 달에 출간됩니다.
(A) 네, 그녀가 그럴 계획이랍니다.
(B) 왼쪽이요.
(C) 제 생각에는 잘 팔릴 거예요.
어휘 novel 소설 publish 출간하다

**16** How do I cancel my subscription to the monthly magazine?
미W (A) Sorry, I already did it.
영M (B) You can renew your subscription anytime.
(C) I'll give you a number.
월간지 정기 구독을 취소하려면 어떻게 해야 할까요?
(A) 죄송해요, 이미 했어요.
(B) 언제든 정기 구독을 갱신할 수 있어요.
(C) 전화번호 알려 드릴게요.
어휘 subscription to ~의 구독 monthly 월간의 renew 갱신하다

**17** Can you work on the case or should I look for a replacement?
미W (A) I work out regularly.
미W (B) I didn't know which one to choose.
(C) I think I can do it.
이 건 맡으실 수 있어요, 아니면 대신할 사람을 찾아볼까요?
(A) 전 규칙적으로 운동을 해요.
(B) 어떤 것을 골라야 할지 몰랐어요.
(C) 제가 할 수 있을 것 같아요.
어휘 replacement 대체할 사람 work out 운동하다 regularly 규칙적으로

**18** You're working the night shift tomorrow, aren't you?
영M (A) I do so every Tuesday.
미W (B) Because it opens early.
(C) They're on my desk.
당신은 내일 야간 근무를 해요, 그렇지 않나요?
(A) 전 매주 화요일마다 합니다.
(B) 일찍 문을 열기 때문에요.
(C) 그것들은 제 책상 위에 있어요.
어휘 night shift 야간 근무

**19** That's the new computer you bought, isn't it?
미W (A) Of course, you can.
미W (B) Yes, it arrived yesterday.
미M (C) No, I didn't have time to watch the news.
저게 당신이 산 새 컴퓨터인가요?
(A) 물론이죠, 하실 수 있어요.
(B) 네, 어제 왔어요.
(C) 아니요, 뉴스를 볼 시간이 없었어요.
어휘 arrive 도착하다

**20** I can't come up with anything better.
미W (A) Yes, I can come.
미W (B) He made the problem worse.
영M (C) We'll have to go with this one then.
더 좋은 게 생각나지 않네요.
(A) 네, 저는 갈 수 있어요.
(B) 그는 문제를 더 악화시켰어요.
(C) 그럼 이것으로 가야겠네요.
어휘 come up with 떠오르다

**21** How many birthday cards do you want us to buy?
영M (A) To the address on this present.
미W (B) Let's do around fifty.
(C) That's a little much.
생일 카드 몇 개 살까요?
(A) 이 선물에 나와 있는 주소로요.
(B) 50개 정도요.
(C) 양이 좀 많아요.
어휘 address 주소

**22** Have you read the text message from Minho Lee?
미M (A) It is the answering machine I ordered last week.
미W (B) There is a problem with my cell phone.
(C) No, it's already been activated.
이민호에게서 받은 문자 읽어 봤어요?
(A) 이게 지난주에 제가 주문한 자동 응답기입니다.
(B) 제 휴대폰에 문제가 있어요.
(C) 아니요, 벌써 작동되고 있어요.
어휘 text message 문자 answering machine 자동 응답기 activate 작동하다

**23** Who's going to take the lead when Ms. Knight retires?
영M (A) She's going to go to Dublin after retiring.
미W (B) It hasn't been revealed yet.
(C) I'm very close to Ed McGuire.
나이트 씨가 퇴직하면 누가 책임자가 될까요?
(A) 그녀는 퇴직 후에 더블린에 갈 거예요.
(B) 아직 발표되지 않았어요.
(C) 전 에드 맥과이어와 아주 친해요.
어휘 take the lead 선두에 서다, 지도적 위치를 차지하다 retire 퇴직하다 reveal 밝히다

**24** We're supposed to submit our product design by the end of the day, aren't we?
미M (A) Submit it to Mr. Hanson.
미W (B) Actually, it's due next Wednesday.
(C) No, it doesn't look attractive.
오늘까지 제품 디자인을 제출하도록 되어 있죠, 그렇지 않나요?
(A) 핸슨 씨에게 그것을 제출하세요.
(B) 사실 다음 주 수요일까지예요.
(C) 아니요, 그건 멋지지 않네요.
어휘 due 마감인 attractive 매력적인 멋진

**25** Who's in charge of the Stevens project?
미W (A) I'm handling that.
영M (B) By a well-known author.
(C) Yes, that's right.
누가 스티븐스 프로젝트의 책임을 맡고 있죠?
(A) 제가 그걸 맡고 있어요.
(B) 유명한 작가에 의해서요.
(C) 네, 그게 맞습니다.
어휘 be in charge of ~의 책임을 맡다 handle 맡다, 처리하다 well-known 유명한

**26** Hasn't the catering service sent us a price list yet?
영M (A) They serve some quality food.
미M (B) It's on the desk in your office.
(C) By overnight delivery.
아직 출장 요리 업체가 가격 목록표를 안 보냈나요?
(A) 그들은 양질의 음식을 제공합니다.
(B) 당신 사무실 책상 위에 있어요.
(C) 익일 배송으로요.
어휘 catering 출장 요리업 quality 양질의

**27** I'm sorry, but we have to reschedule tomorrow's meeting.
미M (A) I'm afraid she's not in.
미W (B) At 9 in the morning.

# PART 3

P145

Questions 32-34 refer to the following conversation. 미W 영M

W I don't know if I can return from downtown in time for my interview. It'll take me at least two hours to get back. I guess I could go downtown myself. I have a few errands to run there. Could I make the trip for you?

M Oh, that would be wonderful. ㉝㉝ I just need to drop this off at school. Won't that be too much trouble?

W No problem. ㉞ I'll make sure to do it. Good luck on your interview.

여 면접 시간에 맞춰 시내에서 돌아올 수 있을지 모르겠어요. 오는 데 적어도 2시간은 걸릴 텐데요. 제가 시내에 가면 돼요. 거기서 할 일이 좀 있어요. 제가 대신 갈까요?

남 그러면 너무 좋죠. ㉝㉝ 학교에 이걸 갖다 줘야 하거든요. 너무 번거롭지 않으실까요?

여 괜찮아요. ㉞ 꼭 할게요. 면접 잘 보세요.

어휘 downtown 시내　in time ~에 시간 맞춰　run an errand 심부름을 하다　trip 이동, 오고 감　drop off 갖다 주다　pick up 찾아가다　head 향하다

**32** Why is the woman concerned?
(A) She is out of town.
(B) She has something to do first.
(C) She is not ready for her interview.
(D) She has to pick up something from school.
여자가 걱정하는 이유는 무엇인가?
(A) 그 도시를 떠나 있다.
(B) 먼저 처리해야 할 일이 있다.
(C) 면접 볼 준비가 안 되어 있다.
(D) 학교에서 찾아올 게 있다.

**33** What does the woman ask the man to do?
(A) Pick up a friend
(B) Give her a ride
(C) Attend an interview
(D) Go to a school
여자가 남자에게 요청하는 것은 무엇인가?
(A) 친구 데리러 가기
(B) 차 태워 주기
(C) 면접 참여하기
(D) 학교에 가기

**34** What will the man probably do next?
(A) Head to the subway station
(B) Deliver something
(C) Go to an interview
(D) Run to the school
남자가 다음에 할 일은 무엇인가?
(A) 지하철역으로 가기
(B) 물건 갖다 주기
(C) 면접에 가기
(D) 학교로 뛰어 가기

Questions 35-37 refer to the following conversation with three speakers. 미M 미W 영W

M ㉟ Our weekly newspaper will have a feature story on local bakeshops next week. Who's interested in this assignment?

W1 Actually, I am. ㊱ There's an award-winning bakery on Park Avenue, and I've always wanted to write about it.

M Oh, I've heard of that place. ㊱ The owner of the bakery is the winner of last year's baking world cup. Do you think you can set up an interview with him?

W1 Yes, I think so. ㊲ Hey, Christine. Do you have time to come along with me? I'd like you to shoot photos during the interview.

W2 Sure thing. I'm a huge fan of their baguettes anyway.

W1 Perfect. Can you meet me later this afternoon to discuss details about the interview?

남 ㉟ 우리 주간 신문에서 다음 주에 지역 빵집에 대한 특집 기사를 낼 거예요. 누구 관심 있는 사람 있어요?

여1 실은 제가 관심 있어요. ㊱ 파크 애비뉴에 상을 받은 빵집이 있는데 항상 그 곳에 대한 기사를 쓰고 싶었어요.

남 그곳에 대해서 들어 봤어요. ㊱ 그 빵집 주인이 지난해 베이킹 월드컵 우승자예요. 그 사람과 인터뷰 일정을 잡을 수 있겠어요?

여1 네, 할 수 있어요. ㊲ 크리스틴, 저랑 같이 갈 시간 되세요? 인터뷰 동안 사진을 찍어 줬으면 하는데요.

여2 당연하죠. 안 그래도 거기 바게트를 무척 좋아하거든요.

여1 잘됐네요. 이따 오후에 만나서 인터뷰에 대한 세부 사항을 논의할 수 있겠어요?

어휘 feature story 특집 기사　assignment 임무, 업무　award-winning 상을 받은, 수상 경력이 있는　set up ~을 잡다　come along with ~와 함께 가다　pastime 취미

**35** What are the speakers talking about?
(A) A popular pastime
(B) A new assignment
(C) An upcoming competition
(D) A nearby restaurant
화자들은 무엇에 대해 말하고 있는가?

---

(C) How about Thursday?
죄송하지만 내일 회의의 일정을 바꿔야겠어요.
(A) 그녀는 안 계세요.
(B) 아침 9시예요.
(C) 목요일은 어때요?
어휘 reschedule 일정을 바꾸다

**28** Could you help me find the key to the supply room?
영M (A) The office is upstairs.
미M (B) Where did you have it last?
(C) A box of office supplies.
창고 열쇠 찾는 것을 좀 도와주실래요?
(A) 그 사무실은 위층입니다.
(B) 마지막으로 어디서 썼나요?
(C) 사무용품 한 박스요.
어휘 supply room 물품실, 창고

**29** Shall we brainstorm ideas for this year's awards banquet?
미W (A) Okay, do you have any good suggestions?
미M (B) I had a lot of fun.
(C) Most of them like the idea.
올해의 시상식에 대한 아이디어를 생각해 볼까요?
(A) 좋아요, 좋은 제안이라도 있으세요?
(B) 재미있었습니다.
(C) 대부분은 그 아이디어를 좋아해요.
어휘 brainstorm 아이디어를 떠올리다　awards banquet 시상식

**30** How often do you go to the movies?
미W (A) It was released yesterday.
영M (B) I haven't had a chance to lately.
(C) Joshua Chang is a great actor.
얼마나 자주 영화 보러 가세요?
(A) 그건 어제 개봉했어요.
(B) 최근에는 그럴 기회가 없었어요.
(C) 조슈아 챙은 훌륭한 배우예요.
어휘 go to the movies 영화 보러 가다　release 개봉하다; 출시하다　chance 기회

**31** I thought you were interested in the sales position.
영M (A) Yes, I saw him.
미M (B) They told me I had to travel a lot.
(C) Those are mine.
전 당신이 그 판매직에 관심이 있는 줄 알았어요.
(A) 네, 그를 만났어요.
(B) 출장이 많다고 하더라고요.
(C) 그것들은 제 건데요.
어휘 sales position 판매직

패러프레이징 shoot photos → Take photographs

(A) 인기 있는 취미 생활
(B) 새로운 업무
(C) 다가오는 대회
(D) 근처의 식당

**36** What is mentioned about a bakery?
(A) It has recently opened.
(B) It offers many kinds of bread.
(C) It has won a competition.
(D) It is conveniently located.
빵집에 대해 무엇이 언급되었는가?
(A) 최근에 문을 열었다.
(B) 많은 종류의 빵을 제공한다.
(C) 대회에서 우승했다.
(D) 편리한 곳에 위치해 있다.
패러프레이징 an award-winning bakery → has won a competition

**37** What is Christine asked to do?
(A) Set up an interview
(B) Write an article
(C) Taste some food
(D) Take photographs
크리스틴은 무엇을 해달라고 요청받는가?
(A) 인터뷰를 잡아줄 것
(B) 기사를 쓸 것
(C) 음식을 맛볼 것
(D) 사진을 찍을 것
패러프레이징 shoot photos → Take photographs

Questions 38-40 refer to the following conversation. 영M 미W

M Patricia. 38 What usually takes place at these Monday meetings?
W We mainly discuss last week's sales. Sometimes we brainstorm for new marketing strategies. Routine stuff, you know.
M Okay. 40 Where is the meeting room exactly?
W 40 Just follow me. We're about to start soon. 39 I think the focus today will be on our home décor items. That's been a focus of ours lately.

남 패트리샤, 이러한 월요일 회의에서는 주로 무슨 일을 하죠?
여 주로 지난주 판매에 대해 논의해요. 때로 새로운 마케팅 전략을 고안하기도 하고요, 늘 하던 일이죠 뭐.
남 좋아요, 회의실은 정확히 어디죠?
여 따라오세요, 곧 시작하려고 했거든요. 오늘 회의의 핵심은 가정용 장식 물품일 거예요. 최근에 계속 저희의 이슈였죠.

---

어휘 take place 발생하다 brainstorm 의견이나 계획을 개진하고 나누다 routine 판에 박힌 일상 décor 건물의 실내 장식 make an observation 의견을 말하다 layout 배치도

**38** What are the speakers mainly discussing?
(A) New marketing strategies
(B) A weekly meeting
(C) An employee schedule
(D) The office environment
화자들이 주로 이야기하는 것은 무엇인가?
(A) 새로운 마케팅 전략
(B) 주간 회의
(C) 직원 스케줄
(D) 사무실 환경

**39** What type of company do the speakers work for?
(A) An interior design firm
(B) An architecture company
(C) A home appliances store
(D) An advertising agency
화자들이 일하는 회사는 어디인가?
(A) 인테리어 디자인 회사
(B) 건축 사무소
(C) 가정용 전기제품 매장
(D) 광고 대행사

**40** What does the woman offer to do for the man?
(A) Show him to a room
(B) Make observations for him
(C) Draw a layout
(D) Help him with a project
여자는 남자에게 무엇을 해 주겠다고 제안하는가?
(A) 회의실을 보여 주기
(B) 대신 의견을 말하기
(C) 배치도 그리기
(D) 프로젝트를 돕기

---

Questions 41-43 refer to the following conversation. 미M 미W

M Good morning. This is Greg Miller at Townsend Securities. How can I help you?
W Hello, this is Nitasha Lark. 41 I have an appointment with you this evening at seven to discuss signing into a mutual fund. I'm wondering what kind of documents I should bring with me.
M Oh yes, 42 you have to bring your ID card, bank statements documenting your annual income, and records of your expenses.
W I see. Alright then, 43 I'll be there about ten minutes in advance to review your brochures of the different funds. See you then.

남 안녕하세요. 타운센드 증권의 그레그 밀러입니다. 무엇을 도와 드릴까요?
여 안녕하세요. 저는 니타샤 락입니다. 오늘 저녁 7시에 뮤추얼 펀드 신청하는 거 의논하려고 약속했었는데요. 제가 어떤 서류를 가져가야 하나요?
남 네, 신분증, 연 소득이 나와 있는 은행 입출금 내역서, 지출 기록을 가져 오셔야 합니다.
여 알겠습니다. 그럼 저는 10분 먼저 가서 다른 펀드에 관한 안내 책자를 보고 있을게요. 그때 봬요.

어휘 security 증권 bank statement 입출금 내역서 document 기록하다 savings account 저축 계좌 reference letter 추천서 duplicate 복사하다 agreement 계약서

**41** Why is the woman meeting the man?
(A) To open a savings account
(B) To invest in a mutual fund
(C) To discuss a job opportunity
(D) To seek financial support
여자는 왜 남자를 만나는가?
(A) 예금 계좌를 개설하려고
(B) 뮤추얼 펀드에 투자하려고
(C) 일자리에 대해 얘기하려고
(D) 재정적인 도움을 구하려고

**42** What is the woman asked to bring?
(A) A piece of identification
(B) A reference letter
(C) A copy of a contract
(D) An application form
여자는 무엇을 가져오라는 요청을 받는가?
(A) 신분증
(B) 추천서
(C) 계약서 사본
(D) 지원 양식
패러프레이징 your ID card → A piece of identification

**43** What does the woman say she will do?
(A) Duplicate an agreement
(B) Request documentation
(C) Pay for a purchase
**(D) Review some information**

여자는 무엇을 할 것이라고 말하는가?
(A) 계약서 복사하기
(B) 서류 요청하기
(C) 구매료 도 지불하기
**(D) 정보 검토하기**

패러프레이징 review your brochures → Review some information

**Questions 44-46 refer to the following conversation.** 영M 미W

M ④④ Has the schedule been finalized for your business trip to Europe?
W Yes, I just got it from my secretary. I'll be in London until the ninth and then spend two days in Paris. After that, I go to ④⑤ Madrid for another three days, and then head home. The whole trip will take about two weeks.
M Wow. That's a pretty tight schedule. ④⑥ You should get some rest before you leave. You might feel worn out on such a long journey.
W Well, I wish I could, but I have to finish the materials for the conference before I leave.

남 유럽 출장 일정이 확정됐어요?
여 네. 비서한테 막 받았어요. 9일까지 런던에 있고 후에 파리에서 이틀 있을 거예요. 그런 다음 마드리드로 가서 3일 머물고 돌아올 거예요. 전체 여행이 2주 정도 걸리겠네요.
남 와. 정말 빡빡한 일정이네요. 떠나기 전에 좀 쉬세요. 그렇게 길게 다니면 지칠 것 같은데요.
여 저도 그러고 싶지만 출발 전까지 회의 자료를 끝내야 해요.

어휘 finalize 마무리 짓다  head 향하다  tight 빡빡한  worn out 매우 지친  call off 취소하다

**44** What are the speakers discussing?
(A) How to meet a deadline
(B) How to get some rest
(C) The man's vacation plan
**(D) The woman's business itinerary**

화자들이 이야기하는 것은 무엇인가?
(A) 어떻게 마감을 맞출지
(B) 어떻게 휴식을 취할지
(C) 남자의 휴가 계획
**(D) 여자의 출장 일정**

**45** How long will the woman stay in Madrid?
(A) For two days
**(B) For three days**
(C) For nine days
(D) For two weeks

여자는 마드리드에 얼마나 있을 것인가?
(A) 2일 동안
**(B) 3일 동안**
(C) 9일 동안
(D) 2주 동안

**46** What does the man suggest?
(A) Leaving as soon as possible
(B) Working on the conference materials
**(C) Getting some relaxation**
(D) Calling off the business trip

남자가 제안하는 것은 무엇인가?
(A) 가능한 한 빨리 떠나는 것
(B) 회의 자료를 작업하는 것
**(C) 휴식을 취하는 것**
(D) 출장을 취소하는 것

패러프레이징 get some rest → Getting some relaxation

**Questions 47-49 refer to the following conversation.** 미W 미M

W Mitch, our rooftop garden has just been redecorated. So I'm thinking that ④⑦ ④⑧ we should move the retirement party outside.
M Well, we're going to play a video clip for Ms. Wang after her speech. I don't think we'll be able to do that outside because of technical difficulties.
W That's a good point. The garden looks gorgeous though.
M ④⑨ Why don't we have an after party in the garden? That way, we can just enjoy the nice weather and mingle freely. It doesn't have to be anything formal and we don't have to set up all the tables and chairs, either.
W Yeah, that sounds like a good idea.

여 미치, 우리 옥상 정원이 막 새 단장이 되었어요. 그래서 전 은퇴 파티를 이외로 옮겨가 하는 게 좋을 것 같아요.
남 음. 왕 씨에게 연설 후에 우리가 그를 위해 동영상을 틀 거잖아요. 기술적인 어려움 때문에 이외에서는 그걸 할 수가 없을 거예요.
여 좋은 지적이네요. 그렇지만 정원이 정말 아름다워요.
남 애프터 파티를 정원에서 여는 것은 어때요? 그렇게 하면 좋은 날씨를 좀 기분 좋게 즐기고 여유롭게 섞일 수 있잖아요. 격식을 갖출 필요가 없고 테이블과 의자도 준비하지 않아도 되고요.
여 네, 좋은 생각인 것 같아요.

어휘 rooftop 옥상  redecorate 새 단장하다  video clip 동영상 파일  technical difficulties 기술적인 어려움  gorgeous 이름다운  mingle 어울리다  preparation time 준비 시간  gardening 정원 손질

**47** What event are the speakers discussing?
(A) An award ceremony
**(B) A retirement party**
(C) A welcome reception
(D) A grand opening

화자들은 어떤 행사에 대해 이야기하는가?
(A) 시상식
**(B) 은퇴 파티**
(C) 환영 파티
(D) 개점 행사

**48** What does the woman mean when she says, "The garden looks gorgeous though"?
(A) She would like more preparation time.
(B) She enjoys outdoor activities.
**(C) She wants to have the event outdoors.**
(D) She is talented at art and design.

여자가 "그렇지만 정원이 정말 아름다워요"라고 말한 의도는 무엇인가?
(A) 여자는 더 많은 준비 시간이 있었으면 한다.
(B) 여자는 야외 활동을 즐긴다.
**(C) 여자는 행사를 야외에서 하기를 원한다.**
(D) 여자는 미술과 디자인에 재능이 있다.

**49** What does the man suggest?
**(A) Moving to a different location for another party**
(B) Offering a variety of entertainment
(C) Hiring additional workers to do the gardening
(D) Installing some equipment outside

남자는 무엇을 제안하는가?
**(A) 또 하나의 파티를 위해 자리를 이동하는 것**
(B) 다양한 종류의 즐길 거리를 제공하는 것
(C) 정원 작업을 위해 일꾼을 더 고용하는 것
(D) 야외에 기기를 설치하는 것

Questions 50-52 refer to the following conversation. 영M 미W

M  Ms. Lauder has asked me to make 100 copies of these documents before the afternoon meeting. But ⑤⓪ none of the copy machines on this floor are working.

W  How about the copy machines on other floors?

M  The only ones that can make copies in bulk are on this floor and the third floor, but the machine on the third floor is busy with the marketing team's documents.

W  Lunch time will be over in about half an hour. ⑤② Why don't you try the copy store down the street from our building? They don't charge much, and they are known to be quick.

남  로더 씨가 오후 회의 전에 이 서류를 100장 복사하라고 하셨어요. 그런데 ⑤⓪ 이 층에 있는 복사기가 되는 게 하나도 없네요.

여  다른 층에 있는 복사기는 어때요?

남  대량 복사를 할 수 있는 복사기가 이 층과 3층에 있긴 하지만 3층 복사기는 마케팅 팀 서류 복사로 인해 사용 중이에요.

여  30분 후면 점심시간이 끝날 거예요. ⑤② 우리 건물에서 나가 길 따라 있는 복사 점에 가 보시는 건 어때요? 비용도 많이 들지 않고 복사를 빨리 하는 걸로 유명하대요.

어휘  in bulk 대량의  charge 비용을 부과하다  fill in for ~를 대신하다  misplace 제자리에 두지 않다 잘못 둔 곳을 잊다

**50**  What is the man's problem?
(A) He is busy with the marketing team's work.
(B) No copy machine is available.
(C) He has misplaced some documents.
(D) A lunch break is almost over.

남자의 문제는 무엇인가?
(A) 그는 마케팅 팀의 일로 바쁘다.
(B) 쓸 수 있는 복사기가 없다.
(C) 그는 서류를 잃어버렸다.
(D) 점심시간이 거의 끝나간다.

**51**  What does the woman imply when she says, "Lunch time will be over in about half an hour"?
(A) The man has to fix the copy machine.
(B) The man doesn't have much time left.
(C) The meeting will end in about half an hour.
(D) The man doesn't have time to attend the meeting.

여자가 "30분 후면 점심시간이 끝날 거예요"라고 말한 의도는 무엇인가?
(A) 남자는 복사기를 수리해야 한다.
(B) 남자는 시간이 별로 남지 않았다.
(C) 회의가 약 30분 후에 끝날 것이다.
(D) 남자는 회의에 참석할 시간이 없다.

**52**  What does the woman recommend to the man?
(A) Go to a print shop
(B) Bring some supplies
(C) Find out the hours of operation
(D) Call the third-floor staff

여자가 남자에게 권하는 것은 무엇인가?
(A) 복사점에 가기
(B) 비품 가져오기
(C) 운영 시간 알아보기
(D) 3층 직원에게 전화하기

패러프레이징  try the copy store → Go to a print shop

Questions 53-55 refer to the following conversation. 미W 미M

W  ⑤③ I'd like to buy two tickets for *Scandal* at 8:00.

M  Well, look at the screen and tell me what two seats you would like.

W  Hmm. The middle seats are almost sold out. It's either second row from the front or the sixth row from the back. ⑤④ What do you suggest?

M  The theater is not that large, so it won't be a problem to be sitting near the back. Plus, you could be near the middle whereas the second row are aisle seats. ⑤⑤ I would suggest the back ones. Would you like those two seats?

여  8시 〈스캔들〉 2장 주세요.

남  화면 보시고 원하는 자리 말씀해 주세요.

여  흠. 중간 자리는 거의 없고 앞쪽 두 번째 줄이나 뒤쪽 여섯 번째 줄에서 골라야겠어요. 추천하실 자리 있나요?

남  극장이 크지 않아서 뒤쪽에 앉으셔도 문제는 없을 겁니다. 게다가 중간 정도에 앉으실 수 있지만, 두 번째 줄은 통로 좌석이기도요. 뒤쪽 좌석을 권해 드립니다. 이 자리 2장으로 할까요?

어휘  sold out 매진된  row 줄  whereas 반면  selection 선택  in advance 미리

**53**  Where are the speakers?
(A) At an outdoor concert
(B) In a train station
(C) In an airport
(D) At a box office

화자들은 어디에 있는가?
(A) 야외 콘서트
(B) 기차역
(C) 공항
(D) 극장 매표소

**54**  What does the woman ask about?
(A) Available snacks
(B) Seat selection
(C) Ticket prices
(D) The ending time of the movie

여자가 남자에게 권하는 것은 무엇인가?
(A) 구입할 수 있는 간식
(B) 좌석 선택
(C) 표의 가격
(D) 영화가 끝나는 시간

**55**  What does the man suggest the woman do?
(A) Exchange tickets before the show
(B) Purchase tickets in advance
(C) Take the seats near the back
(D) Return at a later time

남자가 여자에게 제안하는 것은 무엇인가?
(A) 영화 시작하기 전에 표 교환하기
(B) 미리 티켓 구입하기
(C) 뒤쪽 좌석 선택하기
(D) 나중에 다시 오기

## Questions 56-58 refer to the following conversation. (영M) (미W) (호M)

**M1** Hi, Megan and Bill. ⑤ I just heard about an annual evaluation of employee performance throughout the year. Isn't it mandatory for all employees?

**W** Yes, that is correct.

**M2** Yeah, I had my first performance reviewed with Mr. Stanton about a week ago. Why do you ask?

**M1** Well, I've been working here for almost a year now but nobody told me about the employee evaluation yet. I'm not sure what to do.

**W** You should've already been told by your immediate supervisor, but ⑱ Ms. Barry has been away on business.

**M2** Yeah, she's been very busy. It's possible that she forgot.

**W** ⑱ I think you should ask her about it when she gets back from her trip.

남1 안녕하세요, 메간 그리고 빌. 제가 방금 일 년 동안의 직원 업무 평가하는 것에 대해서 들었는데요. 모든 직원들에게 필수적인 것 아닌가요?

여 네, 맞아요.

남2 네, 그러기 계속 생각이 안 해요. 그렇죠? 하지만 직어도 당신은 그것이 회사의 수 음을 위해 좋았다고 보고할 수 있을 거예요.

여 음, 제가 이곳에서 일한 지 거의 일 년이 다 됐는데 아직 아무도 저한테 직원 평가에 대한 애기를 안 해서요. 어떻게 해야 할지 잘 모르겠어요.

남2 당신의 직속 상사로부터 평가가 이미 들었어야 하지만, 배리 씨가 출장 가서 없었군요.

남1 네, 그녀가 계속 많이 바빴죠. 깜빡 잊었을 가능성이 있어요.

여 제 생각에는 그녀가 출장에서 돌아오면 당신이 그녀에게 물어봐야 할 듯 해요.

**어휘** evaluation 평가 employee performance 직원 업무 mandatory 필수인 immediate supervisor 직속 상사 permission 허락 verify 확인하다

### 56 What are the speakers mainly discussing?

(A) A progress report
(B) An employee evaluation
(C) A business trip
(D) An annual budget

화자들은 무엇에 관해 이야기하는가?
(A) 중간 경과 보고서
**(B) 직원 평가**
(C) 출장
(D) 연간 예산

### 57 Why does the woman say, "Ms. Barry has been away on business"?

(A) To give the man permission
(B) To report a change in schedule
(C) To verify some information
**(D) To offer a possible reason**

여자는 왜 "배리 씨가 출장 가서 없었군요"라고 말하는가?
(A) 남자에게 허가를 해주려고
(B) 스케줄 변경을 알리려고
(C) 정보가 맞는지 확인하려고
**(D) 납득할 만한 이유를 제공하려고**

### 58 What does the woman suggest the man do?

**(A) Talk to his supervisor**
(B) Go on a business trip
(C) Train his employees
(D) Evaluate some employees' performance

여자는 남자에게 무엇을 하라고 제안하는가?
**(A) 상사와 이야기하기**
(B) 출장 가기
(C) 직원 교육 시키기
(D) 직원 업무 평가하기

### 59 What is the man about to do?

(A) Analyze company earnings
(B) Combine two companies
**(C) Give a presentation**
(D) Interview potential employees

남자가 하려는 것은 무엇인가?
(A) 회사 수익 분석
(B) 두 회사 합병
**(C) 발표**
(D) 채용 후보자들 면접

### 60 Who will the man meet with?

**(A) Company leaders**
(B) Book publishers
(C) Rival executives
(D) Industry analysts

남자는 누구를 만날 것인가?
**(A) 회사 간부들**
(B) 출판업자들
(C) 경쟁 회사 간부들
(D) 선업 분석가들

**패러프레이징** the regional heads → Company leaders

## Questions 59-61 refer to the following conversation. (미W) (미M)

**W** ⑤ Are you ready for your presentation? ⑳ All the regional heads will be there.

**M** Well, it's a lot of pressure but I'm just going to lay things out as they are. The picture is mixed ⑴ after all the merging and reorganizing last month.

**W** Some of the changes have been huge, haven't they? But at least you can report that it's been great for company earnings.

**M** Thankfully, it was better than what some analysts predicted in the media.

여 프레젠테이션 준비됐어요? 모든 지부장들이 거기에 참석할 거예요.

남 글쎄, 스트레스가 많지만 있는 그대로 잘 정리해서 보여 주려고 해요. 지난 달에 회사들이 합병하고 구조 조정한 후에 좀 복잡해졌어요.

여 몇 가지 변화가 엄청났죠, 그렇죠? 하지만 적어도 당신은 그것이 회사의 수 음을 위해 좋았다고 보고할 수 있을 거예요.

남 다행스럽게도 언론에서 분석가들이 예상했던 것보다 좋았어요.

**어휘** lay out 제시하다, 펼치다  merge 합병하다  earnings 소득, 수입  potential 잠재적인  aggressive 공격적인  diversified 다양한

### 61 What caused an increase in profits?

(A) Aggressive advertising
**(B) Rearranging the company**
(C) A diversified product line
(D) Workshops for employees

이윤의 증가 원인은 무엇인가?
(A) 공격적인 광고
**(B) 회사 재정비**
(C) 다양한 생산 라인
(D) 직원들을 위한 워크숍

**패러프레이징** all the merging and reorganizing → Rearranging

어휘 vary 다양하다 depending on ~에 따라서 penalty 벌금, 위약금
multiple connection 다중 접속 capability 능력 selection (상품의) 종류

**65** What feature of the plan is the woman looking for?
(A) Free online games
(B) Cancellation without a penalty
(C) Internet access on the move
(D) Multiple connection capability

여자는 가입제의 어떤 점을 찾고 있는가?
(A) 무료 온라인 게임
(B) 위약금 없는 취소
(C) 이동 중 인터넷 접속
(D) 다중 접속 기능

패러프레이징 on the go → on the move

**66** What does the man say about the plans?
(A) Prices vary according to the speed.
(B) His store offers the largest selection.
(C) No plan meets the woman's needs.
(D) Information can be viewed online.

남자가 가입제에 대해 뭐라고 얘기하는가?
(A) 가격은 속도에 따라 다양하다.
(B) 그의 상점이 가장 다양한 상품을 제공한다.
(C) 여자의 요구를 충족시키는 가입제가 없다.
(D) 정보는 온라인에서 볼 수 있다.

**67** Look at the graphic. How much has the woman agreed to pay?
(A) $70
(B) $80
(C) $100
(D) $150

시각 자료를 보시오. 여자는 얼마를 내기로 동의했는가?
(A) 70달러
(B) 80달러
(C) 100달러
(D) 150달러

Questions 68-70 refer to the following conversation and phone directory. 미W 영M

| Extension Number | |
| --- | --- |
| Information Desk | 120 |
| Printing Station | 130 |
| Lost and Found | 140 |
| Facilities | 150 |

(D) The types of ornaments

여자가 요구하는 것은 무엇인가?
(A) 가격에 대한 합의
(B) 남자의 이메일 주소
(C) 건물의 지도
(D) 장식의 종류

Questions 65-67 refer to the following conversation and chart. 미W 미M

| Choose the speed that suits your needs | | | |
| --- | --- | --- | --- |
| 15 Megabytes | 25 Megabytes | 50 Megabytes | 100 Megabytes |
| $70 | $80 | $100 | $150 |

W Hello, I'd like to sign up for a wireless Internet plan. 65 If I can access high-speed Internet when I'm on the go, it would be perfect.

M Yes, we certainly have what you're looking for. Take a look at this chart. It shows the mobile Internet services that we offer. As you can see, 66 prices vary depending on the speed.

W I see. 67 It should be faster than 25 megabytes but I don't need the highest speed.

M Okay, then this plan would be the best for you. Would you like to sign the contract now?

W Yes. Let's do that.

| 당신에게 맞는 속도를 고르세요. | | | |
| --- | --- | --- | --- |
| 15 메가바이트 | 25 메가바이트 | 50 메가바이트 | 100 메가바이트 |
| 70달러 | 80달러 | 100달러 | 150달러 |

여 안녕하세요, 저는 무선 인터넷을 신청하려고 하는데요, 이동 중에도 초고속 인터넷에 접속할 수 있다면 것이 가장 좋을 것 같아요.

남 네, 당연히 찾으시는 것이 있습니다. 이 차트를 한번 보세요. 저희가 제공하는 모바일 인터넷 서비스가 나와 있습니다. 보시다시피, 가격은 속도에 따라 다양합니다.

여 그렇군요. 25메가바이트보다는 빨라야 하지만 가장 빠른 속도는 많이 없어요.

남 좋습니다, 그러면 이 가입제가 가장 좋을 것 같네요. 지금 계약서에 서명하시겠습니까?

여 네, 그렇게 하죠.

어휘 plan (인터넷, 보험 등의) 가입제 access 접속하다 on the go 이동 중

---

Questions 62-64 refer to the following conversation. 영M 미W

M Hello. I'm calling from the Seoul Arts Center. 62 We called earlier about our upcoming Award Show decorations.

W Right. I remember you wanted a couple of large floor-standing arrangements.

M Yes, and 63 how much if you also add a couple of smaller ones for the entrance?

W That depends on the type of flower and any ornaments you want to add. 64 If you give me your e-mail address, I can send you some suggestions and an estimate.

어휘 decoration 장식 floor-standing 바닥 직립형 arrangement 배치, 배열 꽃꽂이 ornament 장식 estimate 견적

**62** Why is the man making a call?
(A) He wants decorations.
(B) He needs tickets to the concert.
(C) He needs a space for a show.
(D) He wants seating arrangements.

남자가 전화를 거는 이유는 무엇인가?
(A) 장식을 원한다.
(B) 콘서트 티켓이 필요하다.
(C) 쇼를 하는 공간이 필요하다.
(D) 좌석 배치가 필요하다.

**63** What does the man want to know?
(A) The time of the show
(B) The size of the center
(C) The cost of the arrangements
(D) The number of samples

남자가 알기 원하는 것은 무엇인가?
(A) 쇼의 시간
(B) 센터의 규모
(C) 꽃꽂이 비용
(D) 샘플의 수

**64** What does the woman request?
(A) An arrangement over the price
(B) The man's e-mail address
(C) A map of the facility

# PART 4

Questions 71-73 refer to the following recorded message. (영W)

This message is for Mr. Hendricks. Apolo has received your application 72 for the open position in the advertising department. 71 We want to encourage you to complete your application form as soon as possible. Apolo cannot make a decision until your file is complete. Information on how to complete the process can be found on our website at www.apolo.com in order to complete your application. You can call the human resources department at 1-800-200-1309 in order to complete your application. Thank you, and have a nice day.

핸드릭스 씨께 전하는 메시지입니다. 아폴로 사는 광고팀 구인에 지원하신 귀하의 지원서를 받았습니다. 저희는 귀하께서 가능한 한 빨리 지원서를 마무리하라고 말씀드리고자 합니다. 아폴로 사는 사원기 다 준비될 때까지 결정을 할 수가 없습니다. 절차에 관한 내용은 저희 홈페이지 www.apolo.com에서 보실 수 있고 지원서를 완료하기 위해서 인사부 1-800-200-1309로 전화 주시면 됩니다. 감사합니다. 좋은 하루 되세요.

어휘 encourage 격려하다, 지원하다 process 절차 human resources department 인사부 inform 알려 주다 remind 상기시키다 relevant 관련 있는

**71** What is this message about?
(A) Informing an applicant of a decision
**(B) Encouraging an applicant to finish his form**
(C) Reminding an applicant about the application deadline
(D) Advertising a company's products

메시지는 무엇에 관한 것인가?
(A) 지원자에게 결정 사항을 알림
**(B) 지원자가 서류 작성을 완료하도록 독려하기**
(C) 지원자에게 지원 마감일을 상기시키기
(D) 회사 제품 광고

패러프레이징 encourage you to complete your application form
→ Encouraging an applicant to finish his form

**72** In what department did Mr. Hendricks apply?
(A) Web Design
(B) General Affairs
**(C) Advertising**
(D) Human resources

핸드릭스 씨가 지원한 부서는 어디인가?
(A) 웹 디자인
(B) 총무
**(C) 광고**
(D) 인사

---

**68** Where most likely is the conversation taking place?
**(A) At an information desk**
(B) At a printing shop
(C) In a rest room
(D) In a hotel lobby

대화는 어디서 일어나고 있는가?
**(A) 안내 데스크**
(B) 인쇄소
(C) 화장실
(D) 호텔 로비

**69** What is the man's problem?
(A) He cannot use a library card.
**(B) He has misplaced something.**
(C) He is lost at the library.
(D) He did not bring an ID card.

남자의 문제는 무엇인가?
(A) 도서관 카드를 이용할 수 없다.
**(B) 뭔가를 잃어버렸다.**
(C) 도서관에서 길을 잃었다.
(D) 신분증을 가져오지 않았다.

패러프레이징 lost my wallet → has misplaced something

**70** Look at the graphic. Which extension number will the woman dial?
(A) 120
(B) 130
**(C) 140**
(D) 150

시각 자료를 보시오. 여자는 어떤 내선 번호로 전화를 걸 것인가?
(A) 120
(B) 130
**(C) 140**
(D) 150

---

W 68 Welcome to the information desk. How can I help you?
M Hi. I think 69 I lost my wallet here at the library. Could you tell me what I need to do?
W Oh, perhaps I can help you find it. Do you remember where you had it last?
M Yes, I certainly had it when I bought one of those library copy cards about 2 hours ago. I've already checked every possible place, like the printing stations and men's rooms, but I couldn't find it.
W Well, 70 you haven't checked with the lost and found department, have you?
M No, I haven't.
W Usually, lost items are turned in to the lost and found. 70 Let me give them a call and see if they have it. Is there anything in your wallet that you can identify?
M Yes, my driver's license is in it and my name is Scott Johnson.
W Okay, Mr. Johnson. Please wait for a second.

| | 내선 번호 |
|---|---|
| 안내 데스크 | 120 |
| 복사실 | 130 |
| 분실물 보관소 | 140 |
| 시설 관리실 | 150 |

여 안내 데스크입니다. 무엇을 도와 드릴까요?
남 안녕하세요. 제가 이 도서관에서 지갑을 잃어버린 것 같아요. 어떻게 해야 할지 좀 알려 주시겠어요?
여 오, 제가 찾는 것을 도와 드릴게요. 마지막에 어디서 갖고 있었는지 기억나세요?
남 네, 제가 한 2시간 전에 도서관 복사 카드를 살 때 분명히 갖고 있었어요. 복사실이나 남자 화장실처럼 이미 있을 만한 곳은 확인을 했습니다. 그런데 찾을 수가 없어요.
여 음 분실물 보관 부서는 확인을 안 해 보셨죠, 그렇죠?
남 아니요, 안 했어요.
여 보통 잃어버린 물건들은 분실물 보관소로 가거든요. 제가 전화를 해서 거기 있는지 알아볼게요. 지갑 안에 본인 것이라는 걸 확인해 줄 수 있는 물건이 있나요?
남 네, 제 자동차 운전면허증이 지갑 안에 있고 제 이름은 스캇 존슨이에요.
여 네, 존슨 씨. 잠시만 기다리세요.

어휘 copy card 복사 카드 printing station 복사실 lost and found 분실물 보관소 identify (신원을) 확인하다 misplace 제자리에 두지 않아 둔 곳을 잊다

# 73 How can Mr. Hendricks find the information needed?
(A) By requesting an interview
(B) By visiting the company
**(C) By calling the relevant department**
(D) By sending an e-mail to the human resources department

핸드릭스 씨가 필요한 정보를 어떻게 찾을 수 있는가?
(A) 면접을 요청한다.
(B) 회사를 방문한다.
(C) **관련 부서에 전화한다.**
(D) 인사부로 이메일을 보낸다.

**패러프레이징** call the human resources department → calling the relevant department

## Questions 74-76 refer to the following news report. 호M

This is Gary Thomson reporting for Channel 8 News. I'm standing in the River Yacht Club, right outside Dashi, **74** a fine-dining Japanese restaurant. This is the first authentic Japanese restaurant in the city, but the head chef Hayato is already very well-known worldwide. To celebrate its grand opening this evening, **75** the restaurant is offering a complimentary drink to each customer. But only the first 100 customers will be able to enjoy this traditional Japanese cocktail. **76** As a standalone restaurant inside the yacht club, **76** nearly every seat offers waterfront views. Even if you miss the free drink, Dashi is worth a visit.

채널8 뉴스의 게리 톰슨입니다. 저는 지금 클럽 요트 리버 안에 있는 고급 일본 레스토랑인 다시 바로 앞에 서 있습니다. 우리 도시에서는 첫 번째 정통 일식 레스토랑이지만, 주방장인 하야토는 이미 전 세계적으로 매우 유명합니다. 오늘 저녁 오프닝을 축하하기 위해서 각 손님에게 무료 음료를 제공합니다. 그러나 첫 100명의 손님만이 전통 일본 칵테일을 즐길 수 있을 것입니다. 요트 클럽 안에 단독으로 있는 레스토랑으로서, 거의 모든 좌석에서 바다를 볼 수 있습니다. 무료 음료를 놓치더라도, 다시는 방문해 볼 가치가 있습니다.

**어휘** fine-dining 고급 요리 authentic 진짜의, 정통의 complimentary 무료의 standalone 독립제, 단독으로 있는 waterfront 물가의 characteristic 특징 warn 경고하다 option (배우에 있는) 항목

## 74 What type of business is being discussed?
(A) A cocktail bar
(B) A coffee shop
(C) An art gallery
**(D) A restaurant**

어떤 종류의 업체에 대해 이야기하는가?
(A) 칵테일바
(B) 커피숍
(C) 미술관
**(D) 레스토랑**

## 75 What will some customers receive this evening?
(A) Traditional desserts
(B) Free recipe books
**(C) Complimentary drinks**
(D) Discount coupons

일부 손님들은 오늘 저녁에 무엇을 받을 것인가?
(A) 전통적인 디저트
(B) 무료 요리책
**(C) 무료 음료**
(D) 할인 쿠폰

## 76 Why does the speaker say, "As a standalone restaurant inside the yacht club"?
**(A) To emphasize a key characteristic**
(B) To warn listeners of danger
(C) To propose a new dinner option
(D) To offer directions to a business

화자는 왜 "요트 클럽에 단독으로 있는 레스토랑으로서"라고 말하는가?
**(A) 핵심적인 특징을 강조하려고**
(B) 청자들에게 위험을 경고하려고
(C) 새로운 저녁 메뉴를 제안하려고
(D) 업체까지 가는 길을 알려주려고

## Questions 77-79 refer to the following announcement. 미W

Attention shoppers! **77** Most of our retailers are clearing out their winter products to make space for their spring items. This is a great opportunity for you to take advantage of their clearance sales. Eastland Mall will be full of bargains as stores hold their winter sales **78** during the week of March 20th to 26th. There will be prices slashed on many seasonal items of clothing and shoes. Special holiday hours for the mall are from 9 A.M. to 10 P.M. **79** Pick up a list of participating stores at the information desk or mall entrances.

쇼핑하시는 고객님들 주목해 주세요! 저희 소매점들 대부분은 봄 제품을 위한 공간을 확보하기 위해 겨울 제품을 처분하고 있습니다. 창고 정리 세일을 활용하실 좋은 기회입니다. 상점들이 3월 20일에서 26일 한 주 동안 겨울 세일을 하고 있기 때문에 이스트랜드 몰이 할인 물품이 가득할 것입니다. 계절 상품인 의류와 신발에 대해 할인된 물건 많이 있습니다. 이스트랜드 몰의 특별 행사 시간은 오전 9시에서 오후 10시까지입니다. 인내 데스크나 쇼핑몰 입구에서 참여 행사 할인 참여 상점 리스트를 받으세요.

**어휘** retailer 소매업자 take advantage of ~을 이용하다 clearance sale 창고 정리 세일 bargain 싸게 사는 물건 slash 대폭 줄이다 seasonal 계

---

절적인 participate 참여하다 go out of business 폐업하다 unload 처분하다 on the rise 상승 중인

## 77 Why is the sale being held?
(A) The mall is going out of business.
**(B) Stores are unloading last season's products.**
(C) The economy is on the rise.
(D) It is to celebrate the start of spring.

할인을 하는 이유는 무엇인가?
(A) 쇼핑몰은 폐업할 계획이다.
**(B) 상점들이 지난 계절의 제품을 처분한다.**
(C) 경기가 좋아지고 있다.
(D) 봄의 시작을 기념한다.

**패러프레이징** clearing out their winter products → unloading last season's products

## 78 When does the March sale begin?
**(A) On the 20th**
(B) On the 21st
(C) On the 23rd
(D) On the 26th

3월 세일은 언제 시작하는가?
**(A) 20일**
(B) 21일
(C) 23일
(D) 26일

## 79 Where can people get information about the sale?
(A) In a clothing store
**(B) At the information booth**
(C) At the center of the mall
(D) On a notice board

사람들은 세일 정보를 어디에서 얻을 수 있는가?
(A) 의류 매장
**(B) 안내 부스**
(C) 쇼핑몰 중앙
(D) 게시판

무엇이 공지되고 있는가?

**(A) 거리 폐쇄**
(B) 기상 재해
(C) 건설 현장 청소
(D) 차량의 중대한 고장

패러프레이징　will be closed → shutting down

---

**84** What has caused the problem?

(A) An overflow of water tank
(B) Road repairs
**(C) A burst sewage pipe**
(D) A detour route

무엇 때문에 문제가 발생했는가?

(A) 물탱크 범람
(B) 도로 보수 공사
**(C) 파열된 하수관**
(D) 우회로

패러프레이징　A break in a major sewage pipe → A burst sewage pipe

---

**85** Who will be most affected by the incident?

(A) News reporters
**(B) Local residents**
(C) Construction workers
(D) City officials

이 사건으로 누가 가장 영향을 받을 것인가?

(A) 뉴스 기자들
**(B) 지역 주민들**
(C) 건설 인부들
(D) 시 공무원들

---

Questions 83-85 refer to the following news report.　[영M]

**⑧** The residential area on Three Rivers Drive, between 8th and Euclid Streets, will be closed until further notice. **⑧** A break in a major sewage pipe has flooded much of the area. Motorists headed to that area are requested to use Baltic Avenue. Local engineers are currently attempting to pump out the excess water, but it will not be known how much essential damage has been done until this operation is completed. **⑧** Homes along Three Rivers Drive will remain evacuated until the problem has been resolved.

8번 가와 유클리드 가 사이에 있는 쓰리 리버스 드라이브 일대 주거지는 추가 공지가 있을 때까지 폐쇄됩니다. 주요 하수관의 파손으로 일대가 범람했습니다. 이 지 역으로 운전하시는 자동차 운전자들은 발틱 가를 이용하시길 바랍니다. 지역 엔지니어들이 현재 넘치는 물을 퍼내려고 시도하고 있습니다만, 얼마나 많은 중대한 피해가 있는지 이 공사가 끝나야 알 수 있을 듯 합니다. 쓰리 리버스 드 라이브 주변의 주택들은 문제가 해결될 때까지 모두 비워야 됩니다.

어휘　residential 주거의　sewage 하수, 오물　attempt to 시도하다　excess 초과량　evacuate 비우다　resolve 해결하다　malfunction 고장　overflow 범람, 넘침　burst 터지다, 파손시키다 (과거 및 과거분사 동일)　landscaper 조경업자, 정원사

---

**83** What is being announced?

**(A) A street shutting down**
(B) A weather disaster
(C) A construction cleaning
(D) A major malfunction of the vehicle

---

Questions 80-82 refer to the following announcement.　[영W]

Good evening and welcome to the Clark County School District's annual employee awards dinner. **⑧** We're happy to be holding it here again at the Kim's Restaurant in the Grand Hotel. This evening, in addition to thanking all of our employees for their hard work, we would like to especially honor our cafeteria director Michael Clare. **⑧** Mr. Clare and his staff have created an award-winning meal program for our students, which is a model for all other districts. Thanks to their hard work, our school district lunches are ranked the healthiest in the state. Now to begin the evening, let's all enjoy the wonderful dinner here at Kim's before proceeding with the ceremonies. After that, **⑧** we will have an address by Principal Wallace followed by live music and dancing.

안녕하세요, 클락 카운티 학군의 연례 직원 수상 만찬에 오신 걸 환영합니다. 그 랜드 호텔의 킴스 레스토랑에서 다시 개최하게 되어 기쁩니다. 오늘 저녁, 우리 직원들의 노고에 대해 감사를 표할 뿐만 아니라 그의 직원들은 다른 학 군에게 사이에서 영예를 돌리고 싶습니다. 클레어 씨와 그의 직원들은 우리 학 생들이 되는 식단 프로그램으로 수상을 했습니다. 그 분들이 애쓰신 덕 분에 우리 학군의 점심 메뉴는 건강한 식단으로 평판되었습니다. 이제 저녁 시작하면서 식사을 진행하기 전에 여기 킴스에서 맛있는 저녁을 즐기시 길 바랍니다. 그러고 나서 월레스 교장 선생님의 연설을 들으시고 라이브 무직과 댄스의 시간도 갖겠습니다.

어휘　school district 학군　annual 연례의　honor 영예를 주다　hold 개최하다　address 연설　principal 교장　cafeteria 구내식당　proceed 진행하다　followed by 뒤이어　make a speech 연설하다

---

**80** Where most likely is the speaker?

(A) At a convention center
**(B) At a hotel restaurant**
(C) At an auditorium
(D) At a school's cafeteria

화자는 어디에 있는가?

(A) 컨벤션 센터
**(B) 호텔 식당**
(C) 강당
(D) 학교 식당

---

**81** What is mentioned about Michael Clare?

(A) He runs a small business.
(B) He has organized an awards ceremony.
(C) He was elected the best chef in the state.
**(D) He has improved school lunch programs.**

마이클 클레어에 관해 언급한 것은 무엇인가?

(A) 작은 사업체를 운영한다.
(B) 시상식을 기획했다.
(C) 주에서 가장 훌륭한 요리사로 뽑혔다.
**(D) 학교 급식 프로그램을 향상시켰다.**

---

**82** What will happen after dinner?

**(A) Ms. Wallace will make a speech.**
(B) An election will take place.
(C) Some of the employees will play music.
(D) The principal will give his name and address.

저녁 식사 후 있을 일은 무엇인가?

**(A) 월레스 씨가 연설을 할 것이다.**
(B) 선거가 행해질 것이다.
(C) 일부 직원들이 악기를 연주할 것이다.
(D) 교장이 이름과 주소를 알려 줄 것이다.

패러프레이징　have an address → make a speech

Questions 86-88 refer to the following excerpt from a meeting.

(호M)

I've called this department head meeting **86** to discuss the budget. Our new electric car was expected to be launched next month, but the release date has been postponed again. **87** Due to a series of delays, we will be facing a cash-flow crunch until the product launch, which is unfortunately still unclear. **88** Our finances will be tied up, so from now on, we need to cut down expenses as much as possible. I'd like each department head to come up with a cost reduction plan that can be implemented in your department. After that, **88** I'll be working with you individually to review your departmental budgets.

예산에 대한 이야기를 하려고 부서장 회의를 소집했습니다. 우리 신형 전기차가 다음 달에 출시될 계획이었으나 출시 날짜가 또 미뤄졌습니다. 일련의 지연 때문에 제품 출시 시까지 자금난을 겪게 될 것 같은데, 불행히도 출시일도 아직 확실하지 않습니다. 자금이 매우 부족할 테니 이제부터는 가능한 한 많은 비용을 절감해야 합니다. 각 부서장은 해당 부서에서 실행할 수 있는 지금 절감 계획을 생각해 보십시오. 그 후에 제가 여러분과 개인적으로 만나 부서 예산에 대해 검토하겠습니다.

어휘 electric car 전기차 release date 출시 날짜 a series of 연속된 cash-flow crunch 자금난 be tied up 묶이다, 부족하다 cut down 줄이다 come up with 내놓다 implement 실행하다 additional 추가의 government grant 정부 보조금

**86** What is the topic of the meeting?
회의의 주제는 무엇인가?
(A) Reducing expenses
(B) Promoting a new vehicle
(C) Reorganizing a company
(D) Implementing a new policy
(A) 경비를 줄이는 것
(B) 신차를 홍보하는 것
(C) 회사를 개편하는 것
(D) 새로운 정책을 실행하는 것

**87** What does the speaker imply when he says, "which is unfortunately still unclear"?
화자가 "불행히도 출시일도 여전히 확실하지 않습니다"라고 말한 의미는 무엇인가?
(A) He hopes to get additional funding.
(B) He does not know when he will retire.
(C) He thinks a new product will not sell well.
(D) **He is unsure when a product will be released.**
(A) 추가 지금을 얻고 싶다.
(B) 언제 은퇴할지 모른다.

(C) 신상품이 잘 안 팔릴 것으로 생각한다.
(D) **상품이 언제 출시될지 확실하지 않다.**

**88** What does the speaker say he will do?
(A) Apply for a government grant
(B) Hold a press conference
(C) **Meet with employees individually**
(D) Consider a corporate merger
화자는 무엇을 할 것이라고 하는가?
(A) 정부 보조금 신청하기
(B) 기자 회견 열기
(C) **직원들을 한 명씩 만나기**
(D) 기업 합병 고려하기
패러프레이징 working with you individually → Meet with employees individually

Questions 89-91 refer to the following excerpt from a meeting.
(미M)

Before we wrap up the meeting, there is one more thing I'd like to tell you about. **89** **90** As of the first day of next month, a new company-wide payroll system will go into effect and it will change the way you get paid. Instead of the usual biweekly paycheck you would have received on **90** May 30th, all employees are now going to be paid once at the start of the month. We changed the system because the accounting department has been having a hard time calculating the paycheck of each employee since we started hiring part-time workers. Too many of them come and go in a short period of time. **91** For more details on the system, I instructed the managers of each department to pass around a memo. I hope you all can smoothly adjust to the new system.

회의를 끝내기 전에 여러분께 말씀드릴 게 하나 더 있습니다. 다음 달 1일부터 새로운 회사 급여 지급 체계가 발효되며, 지금까지 급여를 지급받던 방식이 변경됩니다. 5월 30일에 받게 될 보통 격주 지급의 급여 대신 모든 직원들은 이제 매 월 초에 한 번 받게 됩니다. 파트타임 직원들을 고용하기 된 이후 회계팀이 모든 직원의 급여를 계산하는 데 어려움이 많아서 방식을 바꾸게 되었습니다. 많은 시간제 근무자들을 단기간에 입사하고 퇴사합니다. 이 방식에 관해 자세한 사항에 대해서는 제가 각 부서장에게 회람을 돌리라고 지시했습니다. 새로운 방식에 잘 적응하셨으면 합니다.

어휘 wrap up 마무리 짓다 as of ~로부터 company-wide 회사 전반 의 payroll 급여 총부 go into effect 효력이 발생하다 biweekly 격주의 paycheck 급여 calculate 계산하다 instruct 지시하다 pass around 돌려보다 adjust to ~에 적응하다 pay raise 급여 인상

**89** What is the main purpose of the talk?
(A) To request feedback on revised regulations
(B) To describe plans for a pay raise
(C) To explain new work shifts
(D) **To announce a new pay schedule**
발표의 주된 목적은 무엇인가?
(A) 수정된 규정에 관한 피드백 요청
(B) 급여 인상안 설명
(C) 새로운 근무조 설명
(D) **새로운 급여 일정 발표**

**90** When will the change take effect?
(A) May 1st
(B) May 30th
(C) **June 1st**
(D) June 25th
변경안은 언제부터 효력이 있는가?
(A) 5월 1일
(B) 5월 30일
(C) **6월 1일**
(D) 6월 25일

**91** How can listeners get more information?
(A) By speaking to their manager
(B) **By reading a memo**
(C) By visiting a website
(D) By checking their bank statements
청자들이 더 많은 정보를 얻으려면 어떻게 해야 하는가?
(A) 담장에게 이야기하기
(B) **회람 읽기**
(C) 웹 사이트 방문하기
(D) 은행 내역 확인하기

Questions 95-97 refer to the following announcement and chart.

[호]M

| Jelly Doughnut Shop | |
|---|---|
| Free Gift | Location |
| Sport Bottle | Bowles |
| Eco Bag | Rivers Mall |
| Key Holder | Lindbergh |
| Coffee Mug | Florissant |

Attention, customers! **95** Jelly Doughnut Shop is celebrating its 20th anniversary this weekend. To express our appreciation, we're offering free giveaways at our four locations. **96** Here at this branch, you'll get a reusable eco bag with your purchase. Our other locations are giving away different promotional items right now, so **97** please check our leaflet or find information on our website at www. jellydoughnut.com. Thank you.

| 젤리 도넛숍 | |
|---|---|
| 무료 선물 | 지점 |
| 운동용 물병 | 보울스 |
| 에코백 | 리버스 몰 |
| 열쇠 고리 | 린드버그 |
| 커피잔 | 플로리선트 |

고객님 주목해 주세요! 이번 주말에 젤리 도넛숍이 20주년을 맞게 됩니다. 감사를 표하기 위해 저희 4개의 지점에서 무료 사은품을 받을 수 있습니다. 여기 이 지점에서는 구매하실 때 재사용할 수 있는 에코백을 받을 수 있습니다. 다른 지점에서는 지금 다른 홍보 물품을 드리고 있으니 저희 전단지를 확인하시거나 저희 웹 사이트 www.jellydoughnut.com에서 더 많은 정보를 확인하세요. 감사합니다.

**어휘** appreciation 감사 giveaway 사은품, 증정품 location 지점 reusable 재사용 가능한 promotional item 홍보용 물건 leaflet 전단지 acquaintance 지인

95 What is Jelly Doughnut Shop celebrating?
(A) A grand opening
**(B) An anniversary**
(C) A profitable year
(D) A local festival

젤리 도넛숍은 무엇을 축하하는가?
(A) 개점

---

Questions 92-94 refer to the following telephone message and floor plan. [영]W

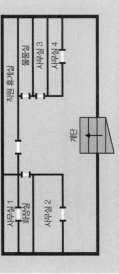

Hi, Sergio. It's Ella. I'm calling about our meeting scheduled for this afternoon. **92** I asked you to come by my office by 3, but I just realized that I need to leave the office in an hour to attend the regional managers' meeting. I won't be back until 7 tonight, so **93** please just drop off your proposal at my office. And remember, my new office is in the west building. To get here, take the stairs to the second floor and walk toward the employee lounge. **94** My office is the first one on your left. If you see the rest room, you've gone too far.

인녕하세요, 세르지오. 엘라입니다. 오늘 오후에 예정된 미팅 때문에 전화했어요. 3시까지 제 사무실로 와 달라고 했는데, 지부장 회의에 참석하기 위해 제가 한 시간 후에 나가야 한다는 게 생각났어요. 저녁 7시가 되어야 돌아오니까 당신의 제안서를 제 사무실에 그냥 갖다 놓아 주세요. 기억하세요, 제 새로운 사무실은 서쪽 별관에 있어요. 여기 오려면, 계단을 타고 2층으로 와서 직원 휴게실 쪽으로 걸어오세요. 제 사무실은 왼쪽 첫 번째 것이에요. 화장실이 보이면, 너무 많이 간 겁니다.

**어휘** come by 들르다 realize 깨닫다 drop off 가져다주다

92 What is the purpose of the message?
(A) To discuss a proposal
**(B) To cancel an appointment**
(C) To provide a reminder
(D) To request a floor plan

메시지의 목적은 무엇인가?
(A) 제안서에 대해 논의하려고
**(B) 약속을 취소하려고**
(C) 일정을 상기시켜 주려고
(D) 건물 도면을 요청하려고

93 What is the listener asked to do?
(A) Move to another building
(B) Leave the office early
(C) Meet the deadline
**(D) Deliver the document**

청자는 무엇을 하라는 요청을 받는가?
(A) 다른 건물로 이사할 것
(B) 일찍 퇴근할 것
(C) 마감을 맞출 것
**(D) 서류를 가져올 것**

**패러프레이징** drop off your proposal → Deliver the document

94 Look at the graphic. Which office belongs to the speaker?
(A) Office 1
**(B) Office 2**
(C) Office 3
(D) Office 4

시각 자료를 보시오. 어떤 사무실이 화자의 것인가?
(A) 사무실 1
**(B) 사무실 2**
(C) 사무실 3
(D) 사무실 4

**(B) 기념일**
(C) 수익성 높은 해
(D) 지역 축제

**96** Look at the graphic. At which doughnut shop is the announcement being made?
(A) Bowles
**(B) Rivers Mall**
(C) Lindbergh
(D) Florissant

시각 자료를 보시오. 어떤 도넛숍에서 이 공지가 이뤄지고 있는가?
(A) 보울스
**(B) 리버스 몰**
(C) 린드버그
(D) 플로리산트

**97** How can listeners learn more about the promotion?
(A) By writing a customer review
(B) By asking an acquaintance
(C) By visiting a nearby store
**(D) By checking an advertisement**

화자들은 어떻게 이 행사에 대해서 더 알 수 있는가?
(A) 고객 후기를 작성해서
(B) 지인에게 물어봐서
(C) 근처 상점을 방문해서
**(D) 광고지를 확인해서**

**패러프레이징** check our leaflet → checking an advertisement

Questions 98-100 refer to the following telephone message and schedule.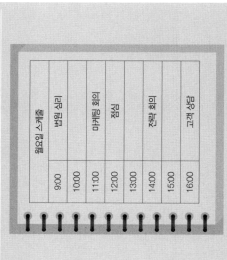

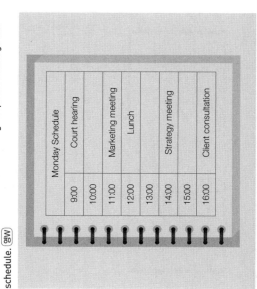

| Monday Schedule | |
| --- | --- |
| 9:00 | |
| 10:00 | Court hearing |
| 11:00 | Marketing meeting |
| 12:00 | |
| 13:00 | Lunch |
| 14:00 | Strategy meeting |
| 15:00 | |
| 16:00 | Client consultation |

Hi, Mark. It's Abigail. I'm glad to hear that ⑨⑧ we're finally hiring two more lawyers next month. We've been short-staffed for quite a while. Well, ⑨⑨ I'd like to talk to you about the hiring process before we begin interviewing candidates. I was wondering if you are available this afternoon. I'm looking at my schedule right now. I'm free after a court hearing at 9, and you and I are both attending the strategy meeting. So ⑩⑩ why don't we meet an hour before the meeting starts? Please let me know if that works for you. Thank you.

| 월요일 스케줄 | |
| --- | --- |
| 9:00 | 법원 심리 |
| 10:00 | |
| 11:00 | 마케팅 회의 |
| 12:00 | 점심 |
| 13:00 | |
| 14:00 | 전략 회의 |
| 15:00 | |
| 16:00 | 고객 상담 |

안녕하세요, 마크. 아비게일이에요. 우리가 드디어 다음 달에 두 명의 변호사를 더 고용한다는 얘기를 들으니 기쁘네요. 꽤 오랫동안 사람이 부족했으니까요. 자, 우리가 지원자들을 면접하기 전에 당신과 고용 절차에 대한 이야기를 나누고 싶어요. 오늘 오후에 시간이 되는지 궁금합니다. 지금 제 스케줄을 보고 있는데요, 저는 9시 법원 심리 이후에 시간이 되고, 우리 둘 다 전략 회의에 참석하네요. 그럼 회의 시작 한 시간 전에 만나는 게 어떨까요? 당신도 괜찮은지 저에게 알려주세요. 감사합니다.

**어휘** short-staffed 직원이 부족한 일손이 딸리는 hiring process 고용 절차 court hearing 법원 심리

**98** Where most likely does the speaker work?
(A) At an employment agency
(B) At an accounting firm
(C) At a financial institute
**(D) At a law firm**

화자는 어디서 일할 것 같은가?
(A) 직업소개소
(B) 회계 사무실
(C) 금융 기관
**(D) 법률 회사**

**99** Why does the speaker want to meet the listener?
(A) To handle a client complaint
**(B) To discuss a hiring process**
(C) To explain an increase in rent
(D) To get a project budget approved

왜 화자는 청자를 만나고 싶어 하는가?
(A) 고객 불만을 처리하려고
**(B) 고용 절차에 대해 논의하려고**
(C) 임대료 증가에 대해 설명하려고
(D) 프로젝트 예산을 승인받으려고

**100** Look at the graphic. What time does the speaker want to meet with the listener?
(A) At 9:00 A.M.
(B) At 10:00 A.M.
**(C) At 1:00 P.M.**
(D) At 3:00 P.M.

시각 자료를 보시오. 화자는 몇 시에 청자를 만나고 싶어 하는가?
(A) 오전 9시에
(B) 오전 10시에
**(C) 오후 1시에**
(D) 오후 3시에

# PART 5

P152

**101**
해석　랜들 씨는 공장용 오븐을 사용했던 경험은 있지만 성용을 냉각 기술자로 훈련받지 않았다고 설명했다.
해설　be trained as(~로서 훈련받다)에서 as 다음에는 항상 성용 사람이 온다. 선택지 중에서 사람을 나타내는 것은 technician뿐이므로 (D)가 정답이다. 빈칸 앞에 〈형용사+명사〉가 있기 때문에 형용사인 (B) technical은 올 수 없다. (A) 세부적인 내용 / (C) 기술
어휘　commercial 상업용의　refrigeration 냉각, 냉장　technician 기술자　industrial 공업용의

**102**
해석　모든 부적절한 거래들은 제정 선임과 관련한 감독 위원회에 전달될 것이다.
해설　금융 업무와 관련된 모든 것이 감독 위원회에 보내진다는 의미로 보낸을 '부적절한' 거래라는 의미가 자연스러우므로 (A)가 정답이다. 빈칸 뒤의 부사를 수식할 수 있는 anxious는 사람이 의자로 관련된 것으로 사람에게만 쓰이고, 참고로 any가 긍정문에 쓰일 때는 모든'이라는 의미이다. (C) 열중되 시키다
어휘　improper 부적절한　transaction 거래　forward 보내다　monitoring committee 감독 위원회　supervise 감독하다　finance 재정, 재무

**103**
해석　수석 담당자의 카스텔리 씨는 회사 관리자의 능력을 감독하는 데 시간을 보냈다.
해설　문맥상 회사 매니저들의 능력을 향상시키기 위해 지도력을 제공한다는 의미가 적절하므로 (A)가 정답이다. provide는 보통 〈provide+사람 +with+사물〉, 〈provide+사물+to+사람〉으로 쓰인다. (B) 승인하다
어휘　senior director 수석 담당자　ability 능력, 재능　manager 관리자

**104**
해석　기로벨스 씨는 주말 내내 내년 예산에 제안된 변화들을 검토하는 데 시간을 보냈다.
해설　be동사+~ing 있는 경우 앞에 p.p.가 혼자라면 항상 명사 앞에서 수식을 해 주지만 p.p.가 길어지면 뒤에서 수식한다; propose는 타동사로서 뒤에 목적어를 갖기 때문에 (A), (B), (C)는 답이 될 수 없고 (D)가 정답이다. 문맥상 '제안된' 변화라는 의미이며 원래 문장은 the changes (which were) proposed for next year's budget이다.
어휘　spend ~ing ~하며 보내다　whole 전체의

**105**
해석　운전하는 경우 우편 서비스에 대한 주소 양식의 변화는 때때로 작성되어 다른 기관들에 우편 발송되어야 한다.
해설　문맥상 운전하는 경우 주소 서비스에 대한 주소 양식에 변화는 '막대마로' 작성되어야 한다는 의미가 적절하므로 (D)가 정답이다. 빈칸 뒤의 different agencies를 통해 정답을 쉽게 유추할 수 있다. (A) 다양한 게 / (B) 공통으로 / (C) 부분적으로
어휘　postal service 우편 서비스　fill out 작성하다　agency 대리점, 기관

**106**
해석　벨라 박사는 사춘기 청소년들 행동에 관한 폭넓은 실험 경험이 있는 유명한 심리학자이다.

**107**
해석　그 두 외장의 많은 부분은 도장자이지만 개조 업체는 2주 전에 테라스를 설치했다.
해설　개조 업체가 테라스를 설치했다는 의미가 적절하므로 (C)가 정답이다.
어휘　exterior 외부, 외면　original 원래의　renovation 개조

**108**
해석　연구원들은 플라스틱으로만 만들어진 전자 화면 표시 장치를 만드는 데 더 가까이 가도록 돌파구를 찾아나섰다.
해설　빈칸 뒤의 부사구를 수식할 수 있는 품사는 부사에만 있으므로 (C)가 가장 적절하다. '전적으로, 온통'이라는 뜻으로 전자 화면 표시 장치를 플라스틱으로만 만들어진 것으로 사람에게만 쓰이는 것을 만든다는 의미이다.
어휘　come up with 찾아내다　breakthrough 돌파구　electronic 전자의　display 전시, 디스플레이　make out of ~로 만들다

**109**
해석　우리 회사가 성공할 수 있었던 요인 중 하나는 에러이 일일이 제품을 직접 테스트하는 것을 좋아한다는 것이다.
해설　빈칸에 부사가 들어가야 하므로 강조의 용법으로 쓰인 재귀대명사 (A) himself가 와야, 재귀대명사는 재귀적 용법과 강조적 용법으로 쓰이는데, 재귀사나 전치사가 있는 것이 특징이다. 강조의 용법으로 주로 목적어 뒤에, 주체를 다시 한 번 더 써서 동작의 행위자를 강조한다. 재귀의 용법이라 달리 강조의 용법의 재귀대명사는 부사로 취급되기 때문에 생략해도 문장이 성립된다.
어휘　personally 직접

**110**
해석　올해 비가 많이 왔기 때문에 농부들은 수확기가 최소 3주일간 더 계속될 거라고 기대하고 있다.
해설　for는 기간을 나타내는 전치사로서 뒤에는 구체적인 기간과 길어가 오며, '일주일간'이 수확을 계속할 수 있을 것이라는 의미가 자연스러우므로 (B)가 정답이다. 기간을 나타내는 전치사에는 in, during within, for, over, throughout 등이 있다.
어휘　plentiful 풍부한　rainfall 비　anticipate 예상하다, 기대하다　harvest season 수확 철

**111**
해석　반드시 건설의 최고 경영자는 지역 경제 개발의 토론회에 참석하도록 조래받았다.
해설　문맥상 토론회에 '참석하는' 의미가 적절하므로 (C)가 정답이다. (B) 포함하다 / (D) 일어나다, 발생하다
어휘　CEO 최고 경영자　regional 지역의　symposium 토론회

**112**
해석　엘리엇스 사의 대표 이사가 롱 라디오는 부동산에 투자함으로써 그의 경력을 시작했다.
해설　정답은 (C)로, by -ing는 ~함으로써의 의미로 토익에 자주 나오므로 알아 두자.
어휘　career 경력　invest in ~에 투자하다　real estate 부동산

**113**
해석　M & G 사의 특별 상여금은 회사의 두 부서 간에 균등하게 배분될 것이다.
해설　among은 셋 주로 이상, between은 두 사이이다. 문맥상 회사의 두 부서 간에 고르게 분배될 것이므로 (C) among의 의미로 적절하다. 빈칸 뒤에 명수만 방향을 나타내는 의미로 사용된다. (A) 힘, 영향력 / (B) 법적 규제, 통제 / (D) 이쪽면으로
어휘　bonus 상여금　be distributed 배분되다　evenly 균등하게　department 부서

**114**
해석　그 회사의 노사는 다음 해에 받을 급여와 혜택에 대한 협상으로 바빴다.
해설　다음 해에 받아야 할 급여와 '혜택'에 대한 협상으로 바쁘다는 의미가 적절하므로 (C)가 정답이다. benefit은 복수형으로 사용되는 경우 '혜택을 뜻으로 사용된다. (A) 힘, 영향력 / (B) 법적 규제, 통제 / (D) 이쪽면에
어휘　union and management 노사　be engaged in ~로 바쁘다　negotiation 협상　pay 급여　benefits 혜택

**115**
해석　당신은 8월 12일까지 거처를 찾아야 하며, 그럴 당신은 우리 통신망에 대한 업무를 시작할 것이다.
해설　관계대명사 앞에 콤마(,)를 두는 것은 관계대명사의 계속적 용법이며 앞 명사에 대해 추가 설명을 하는 경우이므로 콤마 이전까지를 먼저 해석해야 한다. at the time은 '그 당시에, 그 시점에'라는 의미이고, 관계대명사의 계속적 용법으로 쓰여 〈at which time+주어+동사〉로 바꿔쓸 수 있다. 따라서 정답은 (C)이다. 이와 비슷하게 (by the time+주어+동사)가 〈by which time+주어+동사)로 바꿔 사용된다.
어휘　somewhere 어딘가에　communications network 통신망

**116**
해석　FTR 익스프레스 사는 나쁜 날씨에도 불구하고 배달 일정을 맞출 거라고 고객들에게 보장했다.
해설　문맥상 동사가 없기 때문에 동사가 들어가야 한다. 선택지 중에서 동사는 (A), (D)이며, (A)는 동사원형으로 3인칭 단수인 주어가 나올 수 없고, 의미상 미래 시제가 적절하므로 (D)가 정답이다. assure는 〈assure+사람+that)절, 〈assure+사람+of+사물)의 형식으로 쓸 수 있다. 이와 비슷한 동사로 tell, remind, advise, inform, notify 등이 있다.
어휘　assure 장담하다　client 고객　delivery schedule 배달 일정

**117**
해석　깨끗한 근무 환경이 우리 고객들과의 좋은 관계를 보장하는 데 책임이 있는 루니가 우리의 리자인트를 지배인이다.
해설　문맥상 '깨끗한' 근무 환경을 만드는 책임이 있는 의미가 의미가 자연스러우므로 (D)가 정답이다. be 동사가 있으며 ~는 동사만으로 쓸 수 있다. 이것이 입술사 as와 수동태로 Responsible을 쓸 때 문장은 As he is responsible for ~이다. 명사 Responsible은 be동사로 바뀌고 being으로 바뀐 후 생략되고, Responsible for가 남아서 being을 보어 형용사로 머리에 문장 첫 머리에 등장하기 위해 나오는 형용사이다.

개 되어, 우리가 보통 본사구역이 생산 향해라고 말하는 표현이 되었다.

(A) 성상한 / (C) 부서지기 쉬운 / (D) 자신감 있는

어휘 ensure 확실히 하다 / working environment 근무 환경 / resident 투숙객

118 해석 최근의 쓰나미에도 불구하고 그 지역 사람들은 놀랍도록 긍정적이고 침착하다.

해설 뒤에 명사가 나왔기 때문에 반대에는 전치사가 들어가야 한다. prior to(~전에)와 in spite of(~에도 불구하고) 중에서 문맥상 최근에 닥쳤던 쓰나미에도 '불구하고' 그 지역 사람들은 긍정적이라는 의미가 작절하므로 (D)가 정답이다. (A) however는 부사, (C) yet은 접속사 또는 부사로 쓰인다.

어휘 surprisingly 놀랍게도 calm 침착한 positive 긍정적인

119 해석 배열리가 일하러 나가기 직전에 그의 부인이 그의 전화기를 가져갔 을 상기시켰다.

해설 문맥상 '출근을 하려 할 때라는 의미가 작절하므로 출발하다라는 뜻을 가진 (C) off가 정답이다. (A) nearly는 almost와 같은 뜻으로 '거의, 전향' 등이 뜻이다.

어휘 remind 상기시키다

120 해석 최고 경영자가 내일 기자 회견을 여는 경우 장기 휴회는 다음 달까지 연기될 것이다.

해설 문맥상 내일 기자 회견을 여는 경우에 장기 휴회는 다음 달까지 '연기될' 것이라는 의미가 작절하므로 (B)가 정답이다. (D) 계획하다, 예상하다

어휘 regularly 정기적으로 in the event that+주어+동사 ~의 경우에는 hold a press conference 기자 회견을 열다

121 해석 당신이 우리의 다양한 디자인들 중 한 영으로부터 물건을 고른다면 그 물품들은 빠른 우편을 통해 보내질 것이다.

해설 문맥상 다양한 디자인들 중 한 영으로부터 물건을 고른다는 의미가 작절하므로 (A)가 정답이다.

어휘 ship 배송하다 express mail 속달 우편

122 해석 우리는 대학교 근처에 새로 생긴 우리의 새 식당이 3월 31일까지 문을 열어서 학생들이 봄 학기를 시작할 때 우리가 개장하길 수 있기를 바랍니다.

해설 by, until은 '~까지'의 의미로 by는 순간적인 완료 시점을 나타내며, until은 계속되는 상태의 완료 시점을 나타낸다. 예를 들어, the store will be closed by 10 o'clock(그 상점은 10까지 문을 닫을 것이다)에서 by는 현재에 열어나 10시가 되어서 순간적으로 일어날 일이다. The store will be open until 10 o'clock(그 상점은 10시까지 문을 열 것이다)에서 until은 지금부터 10시까지 지속적으로 열어 있을 일이다. 문제에서는 3월 31일이 되어서야 문을 여는 의미가 그때까지 문을 열고 있다는 의미가 아니므로 by가 일이다. 참고로 until은 동사 last, stay, continue 등과 자주 사용된다.

어휘 grand opening 개장, 개점 semester 학기

# PART 6

**P155**

## [131-134]

붐은 소통의 시간입니다! 산타페 바이센테니얼 파크는 파크는 오랜 공사 후에 이제 막 개장했습니다. 공사 기간 동안 거주민들의 인내에 감사하기 위해서 산타페어 가 주민들에게 20퍼센트 입장료 할인 제공하기로 결정했습니다. 다시 말해서, 모 든 산타페 거주민들은 할인을 131 받을 수 있습니다.

할인된 가격은 얻기 위해 다른 어떤 요구 사항도 없습니다. 이 편지와 함께 제공된 사서에 경험 있는 물품을 통 표소에서 자동으로 요구 사항을 132 거주민들은 매 표소에서 자동으로 할인 티켓을 받을 것입니다. 처음 두 달 동안인 도시에 성장 히 많은 방문객들이 예상됩니다만 저의 거주민들에게 점 거주민들에게 할인을 예상하는 지 133 거주민들은 매 표소에서 자동으로 할인 티켓을 받을 것입니다. 매표소는 단 지 6개를이어서 공원 134 덩망 드리겠지. 결국 수 있다는 것을 저렇게 예 상하고 있습니다.

공원이나 할인기에 대해서 질문이 있으시다면 www.santafeparks.gov로 저희 에게 이메일을 보내 주세요. 모든 문의에 가능한 한 빨리 이메일을 받기 때문에 단 지 자료기 하루에 2,000개 이상의 이메일 이상의 문의에 안내 문의를 요청합니다.

**어휘** bicentennial 200년간 계속되는 lengthy 긴 construction 건설, 공사 appreciation 감사 resident 거주민 patience 인내 admission 입장 in other words 다시 말해서 be eligible for 자격이 있다 discount 할인 requirement 필요, 요건 entrance 입장 ticket booth 매표소 inquiry 문의

**131** 문맥상 거주민들이 함인에 '자격을 갖추었다'는 의미가 적절하므로 (C)가 정답이다. (A) 선호되는 / (B) 대체 가능한 / (D) 선택적인

**132 (A) 거주민들은 매표소에서 자동으로 할인 티켓을 받을 것입니다.**
(B) 할인은 기부를 한 사람들에게만 적용될 것입니다.
(C) 20세 이상 거주민들은 신분증을 제시해야 합니다.
(D) 매주 일요일마다 공원에서 특별 공연이 있을 것입니다.
**해설** 거주민들은 모두 할인을 받을 수 있다는 내용이 나오고 바로 앞에서는 어떠한 요구 사항도 없다고 했다. 따라서 빈칸에는 할인 티켓을 받는 방법에 대한 내용이 나와야 한다. 매표소에서 자동으로 할인 티켓을 받 을 수 있다는 (A)가 정답이다.

**어휘** automatically 자동으로

**133 해설** 빈칸은 that절의 동사 자리이다. 매표소가 6개밖에 없어서 40분 정도 결릴 수도 있다고 예상된다고 했으므로 미래로 불확실성을 추 측을 나타내는 (B) may take가 적절하다. (A)는 과거이므로 시제, (C)는 과거나 미래 시제를 나타내지 못하므로 적절하지 않다. (D)는 동사의 -ing형으로 동사가 아니다.

**134 해설** 문맥상 문의에 가능한 빨리 '응답한다'는 의미의 (A)가 적절하다. (B) 발표하다 / (C) 동지하다 / (D) 대답하다

## [135-138]

수신: 제이콥 제리오
발신: 마틴 제로니모
제목: 디자인 부서 이동에 관련하여

귀하께서 1주일 전에 통지받으셨듯이, 디자인 부서는 현 건물 옆에 있는 새로 지어진 건물로 135 이동할 것입니다. 배정된 새 공간은 카다 TV와 세 컴 퓨터를 특별히 포함합니다.

이 135 이동은 6월 1일에 있을 예정입니다. 전문적인 운송 회사가 모두 무거운 가구와 장비를 옮길 것입니다만 개인적인 소지품을 챙기기를 기대합니다. 모든 작은 물품들은 이동이 있기 이틀 전에 깨끗이 치워져야 합니다. 바로 새로운 공간이 기존보다 작을지라도 그곳에는 디자인 부서가 처할 수 있는 많은 혜택이 있습니다. 137 예를 들어, 새 사무실은 광고부나 더 효율적으로 작업할 수 있도록 또는 광고 부서 옆에 위치해 있습니다. 계단이 새로운 사무실이 세 에어컨 시스템을 갖추고 있습니다. 138 이것은 우리의 작업들에게 더 좋은 업무 환경을 제공해 줄 것입니다.

**어휘** notify 알리다 current 현재의 assign 배정하다, 배치하다 feature 특 별히 포함하다 take place 일어나다 prior to ~이전에 belongings 소유물 transport 소송하다, 이동시키다 efficiently 효율적으로 original 원래의 brand new 새로운

**135 해설** 문맥상 디자인 부서가 새로 지어진 건물로 이동할 것이라는 미래의 의미를 가지고 있으므로 미래 시제 동사인 (A)가 와야 한다. (B)는 강조 동사 did가 쓰인 과거 시제이다. (C)는 지금 진행되는 일이 미래에 완 료됨을 나타낸다. (D)는 과거 동사이므로 적절하지 않다.

**136 해설** 문맥상 부서의 '이동'은 6월 1일에 예정되어 있다는 것이 적절하므로 (A)가 정답이다. (B) 변화, 변신 / (C) 준비 / (D) 지원, 응용

**137 해설** 위 문제는 해석이 필요한 문제이다. 빈칸 앞 문장에 많은 혜택이 있을 거 라고 했으며 빈칸 뒤의 문장들이 혜택의 세부 내용이므로 받건대의 (B) For example이 적절하다. (C)는 부사절 접속사로 뒤에 〈주어+동사〉 를 갖춘 절이 나와야 한다. (A) 따라서 / (D) 게다가

**138 (A)** 우리는 직원들이 변화를 좋아하지 않을까 걱정하고 있습니다.
**(B) 이것은 우리의 작업들에게 더 좋은 업무 환경을 제공해 줄 것입니다.**
(C) 광고부는 에어컨 시스템 설치를 책임져 있습니다.
(D) 새로운 에어컨 시스템의 예상되는 가격은 200달러입니다.
**해설** 빈칸 앞에 에어컨 시스템을 갖추고 있다고 했으므로 앞으로 받건대에 에어컨 이 있어서 좋은 점에 대한 내용이 와야 한다. 따라서 더 좋은 업무 환경 을 제공할 것이라는 (B)가 정답이다.

**어휘** working environment 업무 환경

## [139-142]

### 편 씨에게

귀하께서 최근에 저희로부터 구입하신 제품이 기능을 제대로 발휘하지 못한다는 것을 듣게 되어 유감입니다. 이 하나의 제품에 대한 139 불만이 저희 회사에 대 한 귀하의 생각에 영향을 시으로도 미치지 않기를 바랍니다. 저희는 이 문 제를 가능한 한 빨리 처리해서 귀하를 인심시키기를 원합니다.

귀하께서 해주셔야 할 일은 이 편지와 함께 제공된 사서에 경험 있는 물품을 동 봉해서 저희 고객 관리 부서에 보내는 것입니다. 귀하는 140 환불이나 교체를 요청할 수 있습니다.

저희 회사는 고객들이 기대를 만족시키고 그들에게 가능한 최상의 서비스를 제 공하는 데 141 전념한다는 점을 믿으실 수 있습니다. 142 경험이 있는 제품에 대해 진심으로 사과드립니다.

질문이나 요청 사항이 더 있으시다면 망설임 없이 저희 고객 관리 부서 1-825-288-2836으로 연락 주세요.

**어휘** recently 최근에 purchase 구입하다 malfunction (기능이) 제대로 작동하지 않다 in any way 어떤 식으로든 assure 보증하다, 정담 하다 enclose 동봉하다 defective 결함 있는 expectation 기대 dissatisfaction 불만

**139 해설** 문맥상 구입한 제품이 기능이 제대로 작동하지 않아 생긴 '불만'이 회사 에 대한 이미지에 영향을 미치지 않았으면 좋겠다는 내용이므로 '불만'이 란 뜻의 (D)가 적절하다. (A) 불리한 점 약점 / (B) 기쁨, 즐거움 / (C) 시 도

**140 해설** 연관된 표현이 항상 같이 다녀는 접속사가 상관접속사이며, 토익에서는 상관접속사가 자주 나오므로 알아 두자. 여기서는 either A or B/A 또 는 B 둘 중 하나가 쓰였으므로 정답은 (C)이다.

**141 해설** 문맥상 회사는 고객들이 기대를 충족시키기 위해 '전념한다'가 자연스 러우므로 (C)가 정답이다. be dedicated to는 '~에 전념하다'라는 의 미이며 이때 to는 전치사이다. (A) 결정하다 / (B) 받아쓰게 하다, 지시 하다 / (D) 나누다

**142 (A) 경험이 있는 제품에 대해 진심으로 사과드립니다.**
(B) 화불이 되지 않는다는 것을 유념해 주십시오.
(C) 저희 제품을 구매해 주셔서 감사합니다.
(D) 귀하의 명함에는 지원은 인정합니다.
**해설** 문맥상 바로 앞에 나오는 문장으로 정답을 고르기 어려운 문제이다. 글 전체 내용을 파악해야 하는데 전체적으로 결함이 있는 제품에 대해서 어떻 게 해결 하는지 알려 주고 있으므로 사과의 말을 전하는 (A)가 적절한 다.

**어휘** continuous 지속적인

[147-148]

**3월의 무료 영화 축제**

[147] 저녁 8시에 영화가 시작된 후, 더 이상 극장에 들어오실 수 없습니다. 모든 참석자는 영화 시작 전에 극장에 있어야 합니다. [148] 30포인트를 얻으시려면 보통 2시간 동안 상영되는 영화를 끝날 때까지 있으셔야 합니다. 이번 달에 보실 수 있는 영화는 다음과 같습니다.

| 일 | 월 | 화 | 수 | 목 | 금 | 토 |
|---|---|---|---|---|---|---|
| | | | | | 1 | 2 |
| 3 | 4 | 5 임거나 잃거나 | 6 | 7 골든 티켓 눔바번 | 8 | 9 |
| 10 | 11 | 12 7인의 기사 | 13 | 14 제2차 세계 대전 | 15 | 16 |
| 17 | 18 | 19 이웃 랜드 | 20 | 21 | 22 | 23 |
| 24 | 25 | 26 프레스트 하우스 | 27 | 28 | 29 흥일밤의 파수꾼 | 30 |
| 31 | | | | [148] 현충일 | | |

[148] ● 국경일 휴무

**어휘** no longer 더 이상 ~ 않다  attendant 안내원, 참석자  normally 보통  national holiday 국경일

**147** 영화를 보는 사람들은 언제 포인트를 받는가?

(A) 10시경
(B) 9시 직후
(C) 8시 정각
(D) 6시경

**해설** 30포인트를 얻기 위해서는 영화가 끝날 때까지 있어야 하는데, 영화는 2시간 동안 상영된다고 한다. 영화가 시작하는 시간은 저녁 8시라고 했으므로, 8시에서 2시간이 지난 10시에 포인트를 받는 시간이다. 따라서 (A)가 정답이다.

**148** 영화편이 문을 닫는 날은 언제인가?

(A) 3월 5일
(B) 3월 12일
(C) **3월 21일**
(D) 3월 26일

**해설** 영화편이 문을 닫는 날은 "우리와 거의 10년 일하면서, 편집장으로 오랫동안 흥미 있었던 채플린 씨는 내일에는 (A)가 정답일 듯 알 수 있다.

---

[143-146]

수신: 존 이담스
발신: 케이트 쿠친스키
날짜: 12월 2일
제목: 세금 상환

이담스 씨께

당신의 세금 상환 과정에서 작은 문제가 발생했다는 것을 알리기 위해 이 메일을 보냅니다. 정부 [143] 정책이 지난 이후로 바뀌는 바람에 저희는 당신에 몇 가지 수정을 해야 했습니다.

따님에 대한 등록금은 가족 문제이기 때문에 당신이 그것을 개인적인 지출로 표시한 점을 이해합니다. 그러나 올해부터 만 달러 이상의 개인적인 지출로 세금 상환이 인정되지 않습니다. 개인적인 지출로 등록금을 표시하는 [144] 대신에 교육적 지출로 표시하셔야 합니다.

또한, 당신이 [145] 완전한 세금 상환을 받기 위해 회사의 법인 카드로 사용된 지출 내역서를 제출하기를 권해 드립니다. [146] 회사에 대한 지출은 또한 세금 상황으로 간주될 수 있습니다.

제가 요청했던 정보를 가능한 한 빨리 저희에게 답해 주세요.

감사합니다.

케이트 쿠친스키

**어휘** reimbursement 상환  process 과정  adjustment 수정  minor 작은  tuition (대학) 등록금  statement 성명서, 내역서  indicate 나타내다, 표시하다  be eligible for ~의 자격이 있다

**143** 문맥상 정부 '정책'이 바뀌었기 때문에 문서에 수정을 해야 한다가 직접 하므로 정답은 (A)가 정답이다. (B) 장치 / (C) 재산, 소유물 / (D) 전자사

**144** 빈칸 뒤에 동명사가 왔으므로 받기에는 '대신에' 전치사가 와야 한다. 문맥상 개인적인 지출로 표시하는 '대신에' 교육적으로 표시하라는 내용의 (주어+동사)가 나오므로 (D)가 적절하다; (A)는 부사절 접속사로 뒤에 ~하지 않는다면이라는 뜻이다.

**145** 문맥상 '완전한' 세금 상환을 받기 위해서 내역서를 제출하기를 권한다는 것이 적절하므로 (C)가 정답이다. (A) 가득 찬 / (B) 최종적인 마지막의 / (D) 좋은; 봄날

**146** (A) 저희는 귀하가 세금 상환을 받을 수 있을지 확신하지 않습니다.
(B) 저희는 귀하가 세금 상환 비율에 대한 내역서를 제출하라고 했으므로 회사에 근무하는 모든 사람들은 신용 카드를 받을 자격이 있습니다.
(C) 귀하의 회사에 근무하는 있는 모든 사람들은 신용 카드를 받을 자격이 있습니다.
(D) **회사 문제에 대한 지출도 또한 세금 상황으로 간주될 수 있습니다.**

**해설** 빈칸에서 회사 신용 카드로 지출한 비용에 대한 내역서를 제출하라고 했으므로 회사와 관련된 지출에 대한 내용이 와야 한다. 회사 지출 역시 세금 상황이 된다는 (D)가 정답이다.

---

[149-150]

**리베카 훌리** 브라이언, 올리비아 씨 송별 파티에 오죠?

**브라이언 캐스트로** 올리비아 씨 곧 떠날 거군요. 오후 6시 거 같은데요. 7시에 시작하는 거 맞죠?

**리베카 훌리** 네, 아직도 세미나 중인가요?

**브라이언 캐스트로** [149] 인턴강제도, 한 두 시간 더 소요될 거 같은데요. 이따 못 갈 거 같아요.

**리베카 훌리** 왜 이래요. 그러기 우리 회사에 얼마나 근무하면서 송별 파티에는 못 갈 런데요?

**브라이언 캐스트로** 알아요, 전화해서 행복하게 은퇴하시길 바란다고 함께 봐요.

**리베카 훌리** 꼭 그랬으면 해요. 다음에 봐요.

**어휘** farewell party 송별 파티  make it 시간에 맞게 특정 장소에 도착하다  oversee 감독하다  make a great contribution to ~에 큰 공헌을 하다  retirement 은퇴, 퇴직  chief editor 편집장

**149** 오후 6시 48분에, 캐스트로 씨가 "이따 못 갈 거 같습니다"라고 쓸 때, 그 의도는 무엇인가?

(A) 곧 세미나를 위한 파티를 열기 힘들다고 생각한다.
(B) 곧 씨가 정말로 공헌을 했는지에 대해 동의하지 않는다.
(C) 오후 7시까지 계속되는 세미나에는 참석하지 않겠다.
(D) **파티에 참석할 수 없을 거라고 생각한다.**

**해설** make it은 '상황이 힘들어도 늦지 않게 특정 장소에 도착하다'는 뜻이다. 오후 6시 48분에 캐스트로 씨가 "불행하도, (세미나가) 한 두 시간 더 소요될 거 같아요"라고 했으므로, 송별 파티에는 못 갈 것이라는 의미로 한 말임을 알 수 있다. 따라서 (D)가 정답이다.

**150** 훌리 씨는 어떤 회사에서 근무하겠는가?

(A) **출판업체**
(B) 은행
(C) 식료품점
(D) 영화관

**해설** 오후 6시 50분에 훌리 씨가 쓴 "우리와 거의 10년 일하면서, 편집장으로 오랫동안 흥미나 많은 채플을 냈다으로"라는 내용에서 (A)가 정답일 알 수 있다.

---

**해설** 마지막에 국경일은 휴무라고 하며, 일정에서는 3월 21일이 현충일이므로 (C)가 정답이다.

[151-152]

## 세계 전통 의상 박물관

**151** 300벌 이상의 의상이 진열된 세계 전통 의상 박물관은 세계에서 가장 유명한 의상 박물관들 중 하나입니다. 박물관은 세계 의상 서울에 있고, 특히 16세기와 17세기에 초점을 둡니다. 박물관은 파리 경위 가족이 소장하고 있던 귀족 복장을 포함하여 세계에 뛰어난 많은 패션 샘플을 전시합니다. 박물관은 활요일을 제외하고 매일 엽니다. **152** 표는 성인은 각각 10달러, 65세 이상의 노인은 7달러, 아이들은 각각 5달러입니다.

**어휘** display 보여 주다  costume 의상, 복장  particular 특정한  exceptional 뛰어난  aristocratic 귀족의  garment 의복  attraction 의역  ethnic 민족 전통의  classic 고전의  cosmetic 화장품  antique 골동품의  attire 의상  antique 골동품인

**151** 세계 전통 의상 박물관의 주요 볼거리는 무엇인가?
(A) 일류 보석
(B) 전통 화장품
**(C) 민족 전통의 의상**
(D) 골동품 가구

**해설** 세계 전통 의상 박물관은 세계에서 가장 유명한 의상 박물관 중 하나로, 세계각국의 많은 패션 샘플을 전시한다고 한다. 따라서 (C)가 정답이다.

**152** 82세의 사람은 얼마나 요금을 지불해야 하는가?
(A) 5달러
**(B) 7달러**
(C) 10달러
(D) 11달러

**해설** 마지막 문장에 표의 가격이 나와 있다. 성인은 10달러, 65세 이상의 노인은 7달러, 아이는 5달러라고 했으므로 정답은 (B)이다.

[153-154]

## **153** 직원들을 위한 세미나

고용 전문가들에 의하면, 직장인들이 약 25퍼센트가 어떻게든 교대 근무에 사련된다고 합니다. 만약 개인이 교대 업무를 적절하게 관리할 수 없다면 **154** 소화 문제로 고통 받고, 수면 방해를 겪으며, 사고 발생률이 더 높기 쉽다는 연구가 있습니다.

이 세미나에서는 교대 근무 일정에서 발생하는 문제들을 극복하기 위해 신체적, 사회적으로 작용시킬 몇 가지 기조치을 팀이나 전략들을 설명할 것입니다. 세미나 동안, 수면의 문제나 단계, 생체 시계와 생물학적 주기 리듬의 역할, 건강과 안전을 향상시키기, 피로감 줄이기에 관한 정보가 주어질 것입니다.

수용도: 110달러
일정: 다음은 일정 개요이며, 이는 변경될 수 있고 등록 날짜에 따릅니다.
장소: 미라지 빌딩
날짜: 2017년 2월 17일
시간: 아침 9시 30부터 오후 4시까지

더 많은 정보나 강연 등록은 무료 전화 1-871-758-6571로 전화하세요. 이메일 personnel@creativepersonnel.com으로 연락하실 수 있습니다.

**어휘** employment 고용  expert 전문가  be involved with ~에 관련되다  shift work 교대 근무  one way or another 어떻게 해서든  individual 개인  properly 올바로  be prone to ~하기 쉽다  digestive 소화의  disruptive 지장을 주는  adapt 적용시키다  arise from ~로부터 발생하다  biological clock 생체 시계  circadian 생물학적 주기  fatigue 피로  outline 개요  overcome 극복하다  enrollment 등록  toll free 수신자 부담  side-effect 부작용  frequency 빈도  insomnia 불면증

**153** 2017년 2월 17일에 무슨 행사가 개최되는가?
(A) 건강 검진
(B) 공연
(C) 회의
**(D) 강연**

**해설** 제목에서 직원들을 위한 세미나라고 명시하고 있다. 세미나는 교대 근무 일정에서 발생하는 문제들을 극복하기 위한 팀이나 전략을 설명한다고 하였으므로 정답은 (D)이다.

**154** 메모에서 교대 근무의 부작용으로 언급된 것은 무엇인가?
(A) 운동 욕구를 느끼지 못하는 것
(B) 직업을 자주 바꾸는 것
(C) 우울해지는 것
**(D) 불면증**

**해설** 첫 번째 단락의 마지막에 수면 방해를 언급하고 있으므로 정답은 불면증인 (D)이다.

[155-157]

수신: 회사 전 직원
발신: 구내식당 매니저
날짜: 8월 27일 금요일
제목: 주말 시간과 메뉴 품목

무드 코트에 악간의 어려움 때문에 식당은 주말 동안 11시 30분부터 13시 까지만 운영할 것입니다. **155** 모든 쓰레기를 처리하고, 쟁반을 반드시 정리해 주시면 감사하겠습니다.

**156** 스프와 샐러드바에서는 6.98달러에 판매합니다.
**157** 소금과 화학조미료는 별표로 표시된 음식에는 사용되지 않습니다.

다음은 이번 주말에 가능한 점심 메뉴입니다.

|  | 스프 | 아이스크림 | 샐러드 | 메인 요리 |
|---|---|---|---|---|
| 토요일 | 3.99달러 | 3.99달러 | 4.99달러 | 5.99달러 |
|  | *옥수수 | 딸기 | **157** *하우스 | 피자 |
|  | 소고기 | 바닐라 | 치킨 | 라자냐 |
| 일요일 | 3.99달러 | 초콜릿 | 치즈 | *아채 조반 |
|  | *채소 | 녹차 | *과일 | 수불라기 |
|  | **156** *브로콜리 |  |  |  |

**어휘** keep in mind 염두하다  resume 재개하다  dispose ~을 처리하다  chemical seasoning 화학조미료  asterisk 별표

**155** 구내식당 매니저가 고객들에게 요청한 것은 무엇인가?
(A) 원하는 메뉴를 빨리 결정하기
**(B) 식사 후 치우기**
(C) 주말 동안 무드 코드 이용하기
(D) 다음 주 메뉴를 제안하기

**해설** 주목할 내용 중 첫 번째 쓰레기를 치우고 쟁반을 돌려 달라고 했으므로 정답은 (B)이다.

**156** 일요일에 스페셜 콤보로 먹을 수 있는 것은 무엇인가?
(A) 옥수수 스프와 바닐라 아이스크림
**(B) 브로콜리 스프와 치즈 샐러드**
(C) 녹차 아이스크림과 아채 초반
(D) 과일 샐러드와 수불라기

**해설** 6.98달러로 스프와 샐러드 세트를 이용할 수 있다고 하였고, 일요일에는 이채 스프와 브로콜리 스프, 치즈 샐러드와 과일 샐러드가 제공되므로 정답은 (B)이다.

**157** 나트륨을 많이 포함하지 않는 음식은 무엇인가?
**(A) 하우스 샐러드**
(B) 녹차 아이스크림
(C) 치킨 샐러드
(D) 라자냐

해설 화학조미료와 소금이 첨가되지 않은 메뉴에 별표로 표시를 했고, 선택지 중에서는 하우스 샐러드에만 별표가 있으므로 정답은 (A)이다.

[158-160]

회사가 안정된 속도로 잘 발전되어 왔고, 특히 기술적인 분야를 바탕해 많은 분야에서 입지를 강화하는 것으로 국가 경제를 도왔다는 사실에 우리는 자부심을 갖고 있습니다. 과거 20년 동안 환경친화적인 업계의 선두적인 회사였으며, 쓰레기를 효율적으로 줄이는 것뿐만 아니라 오염 수준을 감소시키기 위해 모든 분야에 첨단 소각로를 운영한 지원들을 고용했습니다. [158] 우리 시설의 앞 다음 세대를 위하여 우리는 환경과 관련된 프로젝트에 더 투자하기로 했습니다. 1992년 이래로 지금까지 우리 조직이 이루어진 구조적 변화의 개요입니다.

| 연도 | 직원 수 | 공장 부지 | 연간 생산량 (백만 달러) | 근무자 당 연간 생산량 (달러) |
|---|---|---|---|---|
| 1992 | 72 | 3 | 1.4 | 9,747 |
| 1997 | 101 | 5 | 2.5 | 11,918 |
| 2002 | 143 | 6 | 2.7 | 13,334 |
| 2007 | 219 | 9 | 3.8 | 15,047 |
| 2012 | 278 | 11 | 4.5 | 16,719 |
| 2017 | 315 | 15 | 5.7 | 18,052 |

어휘 take pride in ~을 자랑하다 steady 안정된 field 분야 leading 대표하는 eco-friendly 환경친화적인 high-tech 첨단 기술의 incinerator 소각로 for the sake of ~을 위해서 overview 개요, 개관 structural 구조적인 growth potential 성장 가능성

158 회사가 설립된 지 얼마나 되었는가?
(A) 26년
(B) 24년
(C) 20년
(D) 15년

해설 회사는 1992년에 설립되었고 아래 표로 보아 연혁이 2017년에나가 될 나므로 2017-1992+1=26(년)으로 계산될 수 있다. 따라서 (A)가 정답이다.

159 위의 표와 함께 언급되어 있는 내용은 무엇인가?
(A) 공장의 크기는 경제적 문제 때문에 축소되어 왔다.
(B) 직원들의 수는 꾸준하게 증가되어 왔다.
(C) 회사의 직원 수를 상당히 감소시켰다.
(D) 연간 생산량은 2002년에 상당히 감소했다.

해설 표를 보면 직원 수가 꾸준히 증가되고 있는 것을 볼 수 있으므로 정답은 (B)이다. 2002년 연간 생산량이 상당히 감소했다고 볼 수 없다.

160 회사에 대해 서술된 것은 무엇인가?
(A) 큰 성장 잠재력의 한계에 도달할 것이다.
(B) 공장 시설들의 크기를 늘릴 것이다.
(C) 다른 회사와 합칠 것이다.
(D) 환경적 프로젝트들에 더 투자할 것이다.

해설 사회와 다음 세대를 위해 환경과 관련된 프로젝트에 더 투자를 할 것이라고 하므로 정답은 (D)이다.

[161-163]

회람

수신: 물류 부서 전 직원
발신: 제이 존스
날짜: 8월 9일
제목: 전산 시스템 점검

우리 부서 전산 시스템에 대한 간단한 점검이 8월 11일 화요일에 있을 예정입니다. -[1]-. 이번 달에 근무 시 인터넷이 느리다는 기술적 문제들이 많이 보고되고 있는데, -[1]- 많은 부서 직원들이 동시에 인터넷 클라이언트 오류를 겪었다는 점에서 이는 흔하지 않은 일입니다. -[2]- 우리는 이것이 멘지 데이터 및 장시간 공유하고 다중 클라이언트 사이에서 작업을 분산하는 메인 서버와 다소 관련되지 있다고 추정하고 있습니다. [162] 컴퓨터가 자동으로 연결이 끊기기 전에 작업 중인 모든 데이터를 저장하도록 컴퓨터 화면에 메시지 창이 뜰 것입니다. -[3]- 점검 후에는 메인 서버가 다시 시작될 것입니다. -[4]- 시작 전후로 한 번의 짧은 서비스 중단이 있을지도 모른다는 점을 숙지하기 바랍니다. 보수는 두세 시간 소요될 예정이며, 완료 시 업무를 재개하시면 됩니다.

어휘 logistics department 물류 부서 computerized system 전산 시스템 inspection 점검 regarding ~에 관한 lagging 느린 unusual 특이한 relate to ~와 관련 있다 distribute 분배하다 pop up ~가 갑자기 떠오르다 brief 짧은 maintenance 보수 resume 재개하다, 다시 시작하다 negligent 부주의한 power outrage 정전

161 기술적 문제로 원인으로 무엇이 서술되었는가?
(A) 부주의한 보수
(B) 메인 서버 에러
(C) 부정적한 인터넷 공급업체
(D) 예상치 못한 정전

해설 "우리는 이것이 데이터 및 지원을 공유하고 다중 클라이언트 사이에서 작업을 분산하는 메인 서버와 다소 관련되지 않았나 추정하고 다"는 내용에서 정답은 (B)임을 알 수 있다.

162 직원들은 무엇을 하라는 충고를 받았는가?
(A) 서버 하나를 보수하라고
(B) 새 개인 컴퓨터를 고객에게 팔라고
(C) 연결이 끊기기 전에 필요한 데이터를 저장하라고
(D) 에러를 피하기 위해 업무를 분배하라고

해설 컴퓨터가 자동으로 연결이 끊기기 전에 작업 중인 모든 데이터를 저장하도록 하라는 메시지가 나온다는 내용으로 볼 때, 정답은 (C)이다.

163 [1], [2], [3], [4]로 표시된 곳 중에서 다음 문장이 가장 적합한 곳은?
"따라서, 어떤 개인 컴퓨터가 이러한 오류를 발생시킬 확률은 매우 낮습니다."
(A) [1]
(B) [2]
(C) [3]
(D) [4]

해설 많은 부서 직원들이 동시에 인터넷 클라이언트 에러를 겪었다는 내용 다음에 어떤 특정 개인 컴퓨터로 인해 발생한 오류는 아니라는 문장이 와야 자연스럽다. 따라서 정답은 (B)이다.

[164-167]

바나 밀크

7월 13일

더글러스 리스
B21 웨스트 위컴
브롬리, 런던
리스 씨에게,

자료 상품에 관해 문의해 주셔서 감사드립니다. [164] 귀하에게 가까이 탈지유, 전유, 균질 우유. 버터 우유 등의 여러 유제품이 수입 주로 판매합니다. [165] 저희 제품은 우리병(260ml, 500ml, 1000ml, 1800ml), 종이팩(200ml, 500ml, 1500ml), 병(3000ml)를 보유하고 있습니다. 저희는 다양한 종류의 포장으로 슬러지 치즈와 크림치즈를 공급할 수 있을 뿐만 아니라, [166] 클레인 요거트나 유기농 과일로 만든 요거트를 생산하고 수출하기도 합니다. [167] 우리에 하나니 수입 주문서가 포장됨이 있을 것입니다. 저희 저희 상품을 받으시려면 주문서를 작성하셔서 보내 주세요. 질문이 있으시면 언제든지 물어 보시고 추가 정보는 웹 www.vinamilk.com을 방문하십시오. 단신을 바랍니다.

토마스 브렝 올림
바나 밀크 판매부 부장

어휘 skim milk 탈지유 whole milk 전유 homogenized milk 균질 우유 carton 상자 unit bulk 대량의 packaging 포장 export 수출하다 organic 유기농의 packet 꾸러미 express mail 속달 우편 import 수입하다 component (구성) 요소

164 편지의 목적은 무엇인가?
(A) 잠재 고객에게 상품의 기본 정보를 주기 위해
(B) 주문의 배송을 확인하기 위해
(C) 회사에 그룹이 받아들 꾸러미에 대해 알리기 위해
(D) 몇몇 수치에 대해 질문하기 위해

해설 회사에서 취급하는 제품을 무엇이든 제공하면 기쁘겠다 하므로 잠재 고객인 더글러스 리스 씨에게 상품의 개략적인 정보를 주기 위함이다. 따라서 정답은 (A)이다.

**165** 편지에 의하면 바나나 밀크 제품에서 제조되지 않는 것은 무엇인가?

(A) 버터 우유
(B) 치즈 가루
(C) 균질 우유
(D) 요구르트

**해설** 초반에 균질 우유와 버터 우유가 나오고, 중반에 요구르트를 생산해서 수출한다고 했으므로 언급되지 않은 (B)가 정답이다.

**166** 바나나 밀크에 관하여 추론할 수 있는 것은 무엇인가?

(A) 모든 성분은 해외에서 수입된다.
(B) 매장에서 10종류 이상의 자연 식품이 판매된다.
(C) 요구르트에는 어떠한 화학 성분도 들어가 있지 않다.
(D) 보통 우편으로 상품을 배달한다.

**해설** 바나나 밀크에서 꾸러미 하나가 속달로 보내질 것이라고 했으므로 (D)가 가장 적절하다. 본문에서 요구르트는 유기농 과일로 만들었다고 되어 있지만 화학 성분이 들어 있지는지는 알 수 없다.

**167** 주문은 어떻게 해야 하는가?

(A) 회사의 판매 부장에게 전화한다.
(B) 설문 조사를 작성해서 보낸다.
(C) 우편 발송된 서류를 작성하고 다시 돌려보낸다.
(D) 부장에 개인적으로 연락한다.

**해설** 주문서와 전단지를 같이 보낸다고 했으며, 제품을 받으려면 주문서를 작성해서 회신하라고 하므로 정답은 (C)이다.

[168-171]

| | |
|---|---|
| 이단 제리미 [오전 9시 21분] | 안녕하세요, 들어 보요. **168** **169** 월드 브리 즈반에서의 숙박 시장이 지난 5년간 연 20 파센트의 성장을 했기 때문에 우리는 공격적인 마케팅 전략을 실행해야 합니다. |
| 애나 대빈 [오전 9시 22분] | 거기 새 체인점 개장에 관하 건가요? |
| 이단 제리미 [오전 9시 23분] | 네, 맞아요. 의견 있나요? |
| 로건 킴 [오전 9시 26분] | 저는 좀 천천히 가야 한다고 생각해요 |
| 이단 제리미 [오전 9시 27분] | 그게 무슨 말이에요? |
| 로건 킴 [오전 9시 30분] | 투자는 양날의 검이에요, 특히 숙박 시장이 분명 하고, 경쟁적이 방성에서 이미 구축된 월드 브리 즈반에서는요. **170** 위험은 크고 수익은 낮 조 |
| 애나 대빈 [오전 9시 31분] | 무슨 말을 하려는지 알 거 같아요. 그럼 킴 씨의 제안은 뭔가요? |
| 로건 킴 [오전 9시 33분] | 제한된 예산으로 마케팅 활동에 많은 돈을 투자하는 대신에 **168** "우리는 호텔보다 싸 다"는 것과 같은 간단한 메시지에 초점을 맞 춰야 한다고 봅니다. |
| 애나 대빈 [오전 9시 34분] | **171** 여기에 대해서 지도 로건 씨와 의견이 같이요. |
| 이단 제리미 [오전 9시 35분] | 좋아요, 주간 회의에서 이에 대해 자세히 논 의해 봅시다. |

**어휘** accommodation 숙박(시설) at an annual rate of 연 ~의 비율로 implement 시행하다 이행하다 refer to ~을 의미하다 slow down 속 천히 가다 double-edged sword 양날의 검 defined 분명한 get at ~을 의미하다(=mean) limited budget 제한된 예산 lodging 숙박 hostel 호스텔, 숙소 lodging 숙소

**168** 제로미 씨는 어떤 사업에서 일하고 있겠는가?

(A) 레스토랑
(B) 호스텔
(C) 종합 병원
(D) 렌터카

**해설** 오전 9시 21분에 제로미 씨가 숙박 시장을 언급하고, 오전 9시 33분 에 킴 씨가 "우리는 호텔보다 싸다" 등의 표현을 보면, 정답이 될 수 있 는 사업은 호스텔밖에 없다. 따라서 정답은 (B)이다.

**169** 제로미 씨는 왜 공격적인 마케팅 전략을 제시했었는가?

(A) 시장에 경쟁자들이 없다.
(B) 항상 높은 수익을 보장한다.
(C) 숙박 시장이 구준히 성장하였다.
(D) 그도 회사가 확장되기를 원한다.

**해설** 오전 9시 21분에 제로미 씨 숙박 시장이 지난 5년간 연 20파센트의 성장을 했기 때문에 우리는 공격적인 마케팅 전 략을 실행해야 한다"라는 내용을 보면 정답은 (C)임을 알 수 있다.

**170** 오전 9시 26분에, 킴 씨가 저는 좀 천천히 가야 한다고 생각해요"라고 쓸 때, 그 이유는 무엇인가?

(B) 공격적 전략이 좋지 않다고 생각한다.
(A) 로튼 종 제로미 씨가 전천히 태도를 치기 원한다.
(C) 마케팅 기획은 매우 중요하다고 예상한다.
(D) 화요일 준비하는 대에는 많은 시간이 걸림을 안다.

**해설** slow down은 기본적으로는 '전천히 가다'는 뜻이지만, '좀 일 염두 하지' 죽은 앞 그대로 '시험 등에서 좀 천천히 가자'는 뜻이 있다. 김 씨가 이 말을 한 후에 대빈 씨가 그 이음을 물었고, 오전 9시 30분에 투자는 양날의 검이라면서 위험은 크고 수익은 낮다고 했다. 따라서 공 격적 전략이 좋지 않다고 한 말임을 알 수 있으므로 (B)가 정답이다.

**171** 대빈 씨에 대해 알 수 있는 것은 무엇인가?

(A) 월드 브리즈번에서 산다.
(B) 매니저가 될 것이다.
(C) 킴 씨의 의견에 동의한다.
(D) 주간 회의를 열 것이다.

**해설** 오전 9시 34분에 대빈 씨가 "여기에 대해서 지도 로건 씨와 의견이 같아요"라는 표현에서 정답은 (C)임을 알 수 있다.

[172-175]

## 익스트림 스포츠 월드

- 6월 1일 -

급류를 타는 것은 오직 대자연과 직접 접함으로써 만들어지는 모험 이다. 거품 덩어리를 기포지대까지 흐르는 물살은 이상의 극한 스포츠를 좋아하는 사람들을 매료시킨다. -[1]- 전율, 래프팅은 고무보트를 타고 강을 따라 내려 가는 흥미로운 스포츠인 것이다.

래프팅이 개인에게 신나는 경험일 수도 있으니, 그것은 극한 스포츠 도 간주되 고 매우 위험하며 심지어 치명적일 수도 있다. 그 이유로 활동이 요구되기도 한 다. -[2]- **173** "혼자 래프팅을 하러 가는 것은 매우 위험합니다. 특히 강에 대 한 충분한 지식 없이 말이죠."라고 모알도 네이처 여행사의 래프팅 가이드인 노 아 솔리는 말한다. "강에서 많은 사고가 발생하는데, 주로 충분하지 않은 연구와 준비 부족으로 인한 것입니다."

**172** 사고를 예방하기 위해 협회는 구명조끼를 착용하는 것은 의무이다. -[3]- **174** 또한 참가자들의 높은 수준의 신체 지구력이 필요하기 때문에 나이 제한은 래프팅이 넘어요에 따라 결정된다. 이울러, **175** 래프팅을 시도하는 사람들은 여 분의 맞춧하고 마은 웃음 가져가는 것이 좋다. -[4]-

**어휘** rapids 급류 spine-tingling 등골이 오싹한, 스릴 넘치는 encounter (예 상치 밖의) 만남, 접촉 Mother Nature 대자연 a mass of bubbles 거품 (기포) 덩어리 fascinate 매료시키다 extreme (outdoor) sports (야 외의) 극한 스포츠 raft 뗏목, 고무보트 exhilarating 매우 신나는 fatal 치명적인, 매우 위험한 co-operation 협력, 협동 on one's own 혼

자 extensive knowlege 해박한(광범위한) 지식 insufficient 불충분한 구매조기 compulsory 강제적인 강제적인 필수의 restriction 제한 physical stamina 신체 지구력 participant 참가자

**172** 기사의 목적은 무엇인가?
(B) 대회에 대한 필요한 정보를 제공하려고
(C) 외국 여행사를 추천하기 위해서
(D) 레포팅 가이드 제공 공고를 발표하려고
해설 "사고를 예방하기 위해 헬멧과 구조가를 착용하는 것은 의무이다"라는 내용과 같이 레포팅을 할 때 알아야 할 몇 가지 정보를 주고 있는 기사이다. 따라서 정답은 (A)이다.

**173** 슬티 씨에 따르면, 레포팅에서 무엇이 위험한가?
(A) 스릴 넘치는 모험을 위해 다이빙하는 것
(B) 기종 넘어리를 가로지르며 수영하는 것
(C) 충분한 지식 없이 혼자 레포팅하는 것
(D) 신나는 코스를 따라 레포팅하는 것
해설 "혼자 레포팅을 하러 가는 것은 매우 위험합니다, 특히 강에 대한 충분한 지식 없이 많이요"라는 슬티 씨의 인터뷰 내용을 보면, 정답은 (C)이 음을 알 수 있다.

**174** 난이도에 따라서 무엇이 결정되는가?
(A) 헬멧 크기
(B) 나이 제한
(C) 구명조기 무게
(D) 레포팅 가이드의 수
해설 "나이 제한은 레포팅의 난이도에 따라 결정된다"는 내용에서 정답은 (B)임을 알 수 있다.

**175** [1], [2], [3], [4]로 표시된 곳 중에서 다음 문장이 가장 적절한 곳은?
"그렇지 않으면, 나중에 껏은 못 때문에 불편해질 수 있다."
(A) [1]
(B) [2]
(C) [3]
(D) [4]
해설 "레포팅을 시도하는 사람들은 얇은 다음에 그렇지 않으면 나중에 옷이 젖어 불편할 수 있다"라는 내용 다음에 자연스러운 것이다. 따라서 정답은 (D)이다.

---

[176-180]

**경비 지출 명세표**

이름: 제이크 포드
종료 기간: 2017년 5월 8일

176 번째 비용
176 호텔/숙박: 900달러
식사: 200달러
세금: 110달러
이동(항공): 900달러
180A 개인 교통: ____ 마일 ____ 달러
기타(항목별로): 24시간 자동차 렌트 72달러, 택시 요금 40달러
총 비용: 2,222달러

모든 비용은 회사의 규정에 의거하며, 저는 위해 진술된 모든 정보가 진실임을 확인합니다. 영수증이 첨부되었습니다.
제이크 포드

수신 제이크 포드
발신: 회게부 조서 스툴
제목: 경비 지출 명세표

회사의 정책에 의거하여, 당신의 명세표는 회사의 지침에 얼마나 도를 넘었는지 명백하게 의거해 줍니다. 177 177 배상을 위한 총 비용은 1차에 250달러로 제한되어 있지만 숙박비에 쓴 총 비용이 제한 금액보다 150달러 더 많습니다.
180A 회의가 있었고, 회사에서 당신에게 보내는 결정이 늦었던 사실 때문에 숙박 이 요금을 예측할 수 없었기에 회사에 선택의 폭이 넓지 않았다는 것을 이 해합니다. 그럼에도 당신을 부구하고, 전체 비용을 배상받기를 바란다면 당신은 177 이 지역에 동봉되어 있는 '8응 경비 기준 초과 지출대까지 이 서류를 제출하기 바랍니다. 비용 상환받기 위해서 다음 주 금요일까지 이 서류를 제출하기 바랍니다.
조서 스툴

어휘 expense account (업무 비용 계정, 경비 지출 내역서 statement 내역서 reimbursable 변제할 수 있는 incur (비용을) 발생시키다 lodging 숙소 itemize 항목별로 적다 in accordance with ~에 따라서 assure 확인하다 overstep 도를 넘다 compensation 보상 a wide range of 넓은 영역의 arouse suspicion 의심을 불러일으키다 approval 승인 exceed 초과하다 accommodation 숙소 paycheck 급료 deduction 공제 supplementary 추가의, 보충의

**176** 내역서는 왜 제출되었는가?
(A) 호텔을 예약하기 위해
(B) 출장 승인을 얻기 위해
(C) 지출 금액에 관해 의심을 불러일으키기 위해
(D) 출장 비용을 상환받기 위해
해설 내역서에는 출장으로 인한 발생 변제 비용에 대해 정리되어 있으므로 출장비를 상환받기 위해 제출되었음을 알 수 있다. 따라서 정답은 (D)이다.

**177** 회사의 기준 제한액에서 초과 지출된 것은 무엇인가?
(A) 식대
(B) 교통비
(C) 숙소
(D) 주차
해설 메모에서 하룻밤에 250달러가 배상될 수 있는데 150달러가 초과되었다고 하므로 정답은 숙박을 나타내는 (C)이다.

**178** 포드 씨는 호텔에서 며칠 숙박했는가?
(A) 2박
(B) 3박
(C) 4박
(D) 5박
해설 명세표에는 900달러가 숙박 요금으로 지출되었고, 메모에서는 하룻 밤에 250달러씩 보상될 수 있는데 150달러를 초과했다고 했으므로 공사이 성립된다. 따라서 호텔에서 3박을 한 것임을 알 수 있으므로 (B)가 정답이다.

**179** 메모에 공제된 것은 무엇인가?
(A) 몇몇 출장 경비 영수증들
(B) 직원의 급료
(C) 급여에서 공제된 것을 나타내는 양식
(D) 추가 비용을 위한 양식
해설 메모에서 하룻 비용 초과 상환서를 동봉하니 비용을 상환받기 위해서는 작성해서 제출해야 한다고 한다. 따라서 비용을 받기 위한 양식 이 동봉되었으므로 정답은 (D)이다.

**180** 포드 씨의 출장에 관하여 무엇을 알 수 있는가?
(A) 회의에 참석했다.
(B) 자기 소유의 차를 운전했다.
(C) 하루된 것보다 더 많은 돈을 출장 가 있었다.
(D) 한 곳 이상의 호텔에서 머물렀다.
해설 메모를 통해 포드 씨가 회의에 참석하기 위해 출장을 갔음을 알 수 있 다. 따라서 정답은 (A)이다. 명세표의 개인 차량에 표시(되지 않았으므로 (B)는 옳지 않으며, 숙박 비용이 초과된 것은 1박에 300달러인 곳에 서 머물렀기 때문이지 더 많은 날을 숙박했기 때문으로 볼 수 없으므로 (C)도 옳지 않다.

## [181-185]

월드 항공
연간 실적(초안)

**183** 임프레드 슬라바
2017년 10월 21일

### 영업

월드 항공은 이번 연도 초기에는 시장에 매우 좋았지만, 전체 항공 산업에 힘든 한 해가 되었던 몇 주일이 있었습니다. 0시에와 북미의 관광객이 적어졌기 때문에 그 지역들을 운행하는 승객이 수가 감소했습니다. 또한, 유럽 경제가 거고 있는 어려움에 업계가 부정적으로 영향을 받았습니다. 그러나 월드 항공은 유럽에서 가장 큰 회사이기 때문에 0시에의 경기가 회복되면 선두를 유지하고 수익의 거의 수도 있습니다.

### 새로운 노선

**182** 대부분의 기존 항로들에 관한 높은 수요로 화물 배송부는 올해에 엄청난 성과를 달성할 수 있었습니다. 여기에 새로운 화물 배송 노선이 이익이 되는 것으로 나타났습니다. 이 결과로 화물 배송부가 회사의 전체 실적을 급증시키는 데 도움이 되었습니다.

### 인사

인터킨게이트 재정적 상황으로 인해 130명의 직원들을 해고해야 했습니다. 매우 어려운 결정이었지만, 회사의 생존이 더 큰 이익이 달린 문제였습니다. 추가적으로 777 기종 두 대는 낙후되어 폐기되었습니다.

수신: 클리 연간 실적
발신: 임프레드 슬라바
용건: 연간 실적

안녕하세요, 임프레드. 당신이 보고서 초안을 읽었고 **183** 당신이 다음 달 이사회에서 발표를 마무리할 때 도움이 될지도 모르는 약간의 조언을 드리려 해요. *세부 사항: 발표를 길게 하는 한 가지 방법으로 수치와 통계를 사용하는 것입니다. **185-A** **185-B** 캔버의 월별, 분기별 여객기의 수들 제공할 수 있고, 에라 가는 화물의 수치를 제공할 수 있습니다. 이 수치들을 추가하면 보고서가 더 유용해질 겁니다.

*재정: 어느 누구도 나쁜 소식을 듣는 것을 좋아하지는 않지만, 단순히 듣기 않은 한 해를 보냈다고 말하는 것 외엔 문제를 집어넣지는 못 합니다. 수치를 좀 추가하고, 우리가 진정 어떤 상황에 있는지 보여 주기 위해 우리의 예상과 비교하세요. 그 외에 **185-D** 실적과 직원들에게 제공하는 고용 계약 세부를 노의해야 합니다. 우리의 상황이 얼마나 나쁜가요?

**어휘** annual result 연간 실적   draft 초안   promising 유망한   factor 요인   tough 힘든   negatively 부정적으로   gain in 많아지다   profitability 수익성   route 경로, 노선   lucrative 이익이 되는   cargo 화물   quarterly 분 lay off 해고하다   incredibly 매우   finalize 마무리 짓다   freight 화물   informative 유용한   passenger line 여객기   point out 지적하다   projection 예상 추정   substantial 실속이 있는   severance 고용 계약 해지   resolve 해결하다   relocate 이전시키다   team up with ~와 협동하다   lessen 줄이는 중이다

---

## [186-190]

✂ 몬트레 주간 뉴스 ✂
10월 23일

인터넷은 자신의 비즈니스를 알리는 데 가장 효율적인 방법이다. 홈페이지가 회사의 신뢰성과 자질을 보여준다고 알려져 있지만, 모든 종류의 사업주들에게 유일한 것은 아니다. **186** 메트릭스 기업이 홈페이지를 만드는 데 드는 돈을 낭비한다고 한다. 60 퍼센트 이상의 사업주는 홈페이지를 홍보하거나 사업 관련 문제들을 다루기 위해 서 홈페이지를 적극적으로 운영에 오지 않은 것으로 드러났다.

다른 한편으로, 블로그는 매개체이고 신선한 콘텐츠를 보유하고 있어 사업들에게 비즈니스에 관심이나 흥미들을 갖게 하는 좋은 방법이다. **187** 블로그는 소규모 사업주들이 웹 사이트를 가질 수 있는 시고 쉽게 대안이 될 수 있다. "당신은 이 단계에서도 업데이트할 수 있고, 사람들은 언제든 소통하고 맞장을 담을 수 있습니다."라고 메트릭스 그래픽 디자이너이자 대표인 유 류후 씨는 말한다. **188** 메트릭스 기업의 지원팀원에서 대표로 레베카가 다만 씨는 10월 29일 몬트레 시 리크로 시민문화회관 C-5 건물에서 사업주가 무료 블로그를 사용하는 방법 에 대해 강의한다.

소미 레이놀드, 전속 기자

발신: 0베게일 도일
수신: inquiry@lacronecc.org
날짜: 10월 24일
제목: 발표회 일정
담당자 문제

몬트레 주간 뉴스를 보다가, 블로그에 관한 기사에 매우 흥미를 느꼈습니다. 저 는 독소나 애버뉴에서 작은 제과점을 운영하고 있고요, **189** 제과점을 위해 홈페 이지를 개설할 여력은 없었습니다. 하지만 항상 제 사업을 홍보하기 위해서 인터 넷을 사용하면 좋겠다는 생각은 있었습니다. **188** 문제는 도래 시간이지요, 이런 이유로 발표회가 저 같은 사람에게는 매우 유익할 것 같다는 생각이 듭니다. 회사의 인사에 관한 보고에서 회사에서 재정적으로 어려워 130명의 직원이 연봉 하겠다고 했다고 하므로 (B)가 정답이다.

**190** 메트릭스 기업의 지원팀원에서 대표로 어려 130명의 직 원을 해고해야 하므로 (B)가 정답이다.

0베게일 도일

---

리크로 시민문화회관
**190** 발표회: 인터넷과 블로그 활용

| | |
|---|---|
| 오전 1000 – 오전 1030 | 등록 |
| 오전 1030 – 오전 1100 | 시민문화회관장의 마이클 딜런 씨의 젊은 인사말 |
| 오전 1100 – 오후 1200 | 인터넷 활용 |
| 오후 1200 – 오후 1:00 | 시민문화회관 식당에서 점심 식사 |
| 오후 1:00 – 오후 2:30 | **188** 권리의 사업을 위한 블로그 |

궁금하신 점이 있으면 642-3544로 전화 주시거나 inquiry@lacronecc.org로 0이메일 주세요.

---

**181** 월드 항공은 언제 다시 좋은 업무 성과를 보여 줄 것으로 기대되는가?

(A) 0시에 지역 시장이 전망할 때
**(B) 경제가 회복할 때**
(C) 새로운 여객기 노선을 획득할 때
(D) 과거의 문제들을 해결한 후에

**해설** 보고서의 영업 부분에 유럽의 재정적인 어려움의 영향을 받고 있지만 유럽에서 경기가 회복되면 나아질 것으로 전망하고 있다. 따라서 정답은 (B)다. 새로운 화물 배송 노선이 수익성이 좋다고 하므로 (C)는 알맞 지 않다.

**182** 어느 부서에서 회사가 재정적 이득을 보도록 돕는 역할을 했는가?

(A) 마케팅부
(B) 정비부
(C) 회계부
**(D) 배송부**

**해설** 보고서에서 화물 배송 부서의 수요가 높아 큰 업무 성과를 보냈다고 하 므로 정답은 (D)이다.

**183** 슬라바 씨는 언제 발표를 할 것인가?

(A) 9월
(B) 10월
**(C) 11월**
(D) 12월

**해설** 이메일을 통해 슬라바 씨가 다음 달에 있는 이사회에 발표를 위해 보 고서를 준비했었음을 알 수 있다. 보고서 초안 작성일이 10월이므로 11 월에 발표를 한다는 것을 알 수 있으므로 정답은 (C)이다.

**184** 회사의 재정적 상황으로 인해 다음 달에 있는 어떤 영향을 미쳤는가?

(A) 7777기종이 직원들은 영향을 받지 않았다.
**(B) 130명이 일자리를 잃었다.**
(C) 월드 항공이 운영을 줄였다.
(D) 몇몇 직원들이 다른 부서로 이동했다.

**해설** 회사의 인사에 관한 보고에서 회사에서 재정적으로 어려워 130명의 직 원을 해고해야 했다고 하므로 (B)가 정답이다.

**185** 임프레드에게 하는 클린의 충고에 포함되지 않은 것은 무엇인가?

**(A) 예기가에서 월별, 분기별 여객기의 수에 관해 묻기**
(B) 업무의 양을 줄이기 위해 직원들과 협동하기
(C) 더 긴 보고서를 만들기 위해 세부 사용 더 추가하기
(D) 해고에 관한 충분한 정보 제공하기

**해설** 이메일에서 캔버의 월별, 분기별 여객기의 수들을 제공할 것이라고 하 였으므로 (A)가 정답이다.

**어휘** demonstrate 보여주다, 실증하다 | credibility 신뢰성 | qualification 자격 | business owner 사업주 | not a few 적지 않은, 꽤 많은 | typical 전형적인 | run-of-the-mill 평범한 | actively 적극적으로 | deal with ~을 다루다 | on the other hand 다른 한편으로 | appealing 매력적인 | alternative 대안, 대체 | interact 소통하다, 교류하다 | leave a comment 댓글을 달다 | consultant 상담자, 자문위원 | staff writer 전속 기자 | bakery 제과점 | establish 개설하다, 설립하다 | promote 홍보하다 | utilization 활용 | sponsor 후원하다

**186.** 메트릭스 기업은 무엇이겠는가?
(A) 비즈니스 컨설팅 회사
(B) 환경 관련 비정부 기구
(C) 영화 제작 회사
(D) 잡지 출판업체

해설 기사에서 메트릭스 기업이 설문 조사를 하고 비즈니스 관련 컨설팅 회사 사업주들을 위한 강연을 한다고 했으므로 비즈니스 관련 컨설팅 회사임을 알 수 있다. 따라서 정답은 (A)이다.

**187.** run-of-the-mill 주어진 단어, 여덟 번째 줄의 run-of-the-mill과 의미상 가장 가까운 것은 무엇인가?
(A) 평범한
(B) 중요한
(C) 현대의
(D) 위험한

해설 run-of-the-mill은 '특출하지 않은, 평범한'이라는 뜻이다. 따라서 정답은 (A)이다.

**188.** 누가 (귀하의) 사업을 위한 블로그를 발표하겠는가?
(A) 두룽 씨
(B) 드웨 씨
(C) 다얀 씨
(D) 얼턴 씨

해설 일정표에서 〈귀하의 사업을 위한 블로그〉를 처음 수 있는데 누가 발표를 하는지는 나와 있지 않다. 기사의 맘마를 보면 "메트릭스 기업의 자료를 하는지는 대체적인 다연 씨는 라크로 시민문화회관에서 사업추가 무료인 이지 대로인 레퍼러가 대안 씨는 라크로 시민문화회관에서 사업추가 무료 블로그를 사용하는 방법에 대해 써왔으므로, 라크로 시민문화회관에서 발표자가 다얀 씨임을 알 수 있다. 따라서 정답은 (C)이다.

**189.** 두얼 씨에 대해 암시된 것은 무엇인가?
(A) 수년간 문제랑 주간 뉴스를 구독하고 있다.
(B) 라크로 시민문화회관에 일한다.
(C) **홈페이지를 운영할 시간이 없었다.**
(D) 향상 그래픽 디자이너가 되고 싶어 했다.

해설 도얼 씨가 쓴 이메일에서 제과점을 위해 홈페이지를 개설할 여력이 없고 도리 시간을 사용하는 문제가 내용을 보면, 정답이 (C)이다.

**190.** 블로그는 누구를 위한 것이겠는가?
(A) 세계적인 제조회사의 대표 이사
(B) **소규모 사업주**
(C) 노동조합장

---

[191-195]

발신: 베타 에어웨이
수신: 클렌 케인
날짜: 10월 7일
제목: 티켓 확인

클렌 씨께,

| | | | |
|---|---|---|---|
| 베타 에어웨이 210 | | | |

| LAX | —————→ | JFK |
|---|---|---|
| 로스앤젤레스 출발 | | 뉴욕 도착 |
| 10월 29일, 월요일 | | 10월 29일 월요일 |
| 시간: 오전 5시 30분 | | 시간: 오후 1시 50분 |

---

**전화 메시지**

발신자: 매니엘 하딩
연락처: 525-6764 (내선번호: 8)
수신자: 클렌 케인
날짜: 10월 8일 월요일
시간: 오후 1시 05분
세부 내용:

메시지 작성자: 엠마 딘

---

**어휘** itinerary 일정표 | discrepancy 불일치 | in accordance with ~에 따라 | incur 초래하다 | reissue 재발행 | voluntary 임의적인 | be subject to ~의 대상이다 | in the event of ~의 경우에 | toll-free 무료의, 수신자 부담 | originally 원래, 본래 | modification 수정, 변경 | make ~를 변경하다 | sponsor 후원하다

**191.** 이메일의 목적은 무엇인가?
(A) 새 정책에 대해 문의하려고
(B) **예약을 확인하려고**
(C) 공항을 추천하려고
(D) 특별 제안을 재소개하려고

해설 이메일에서 보면 "베타 에어웨이를 통해 항공권을 예매해 주셔서 감사합니다. 이 이메일은 귀하의 여행 일정표로 쓰입니다. 이래 정보를 검토하고 오류 사항이나 일치하지 않는 점이 있으면 베타 에어웨이 예약 센터에 연락주세요." 라고 했다. 따라서 정답은 (B)이다.

**192.** 이메일에서 첫 번째 단락, 첫 번째 줄의 booking과 의미상 가장 가까운 것은 무엇인가?
(A) **예약하다**
(B) 머무르다
(C) 기록하다
(D) 계산하다

해설 book은 reserve와 같이 '예약하다'는 뜻으로 쓰인다. 따라서 정답은 (A)이다.

**193.** 하딩 씨에 대해 암시된 것은 무엇인가?
(A) 10월 29일 회의에 참석할 것이다.
(B) 딘 씨로부터 메시지를 받았다.

**(D) 하청업체가 노동 쟁의를 겪고 있다.**

해설 두 번째 바쁜 사이에 쓴 이메일에서, "귀사의 하청업체 문제로 지체될까 매우 걱정했거든요. 다 잘 됐으면 하고 그들도 파업을 그만하고 복사무실을 나갈 것이라는 내용을 받았으면 해" 부분 씨의 하청업체가 파업으로 노동 쟁의를 겪었던 내용을 알 수 있다. 따라서 정답은 (D)이다.

**(C) 10월 8일에 공장을 방문했다.**

(D) 항공사에서 일한다.

해설 8월에 직원 전화 메시지를 보면 "우리 공장을 직접 확인하기 위해 일찍 사무실을 나갈 것이라 하니 하니라는 내용을 나온다. 전화 메시지의 작성일이 10월 8일이므로 정답은 (C)이다.

**194** 케인 씨가 구매한 비행기표의 현재 가격은 얼마인가?
(A) 20달러
(B) 40달러
(C) 100달러
**(D) 200달러**

해설 연계 문제로 웹 메시[이]지에 보면, "변경으로 인해 발생하는 추가 요금 20달러는 지불하겠습니다"라는 내용이 나온다. 이제 이메일을 보면, "변경 시에는 10%가 추가 부과됩니다"라는 내용이 나온다. 따라서 케인 씨가 원래 구입한 항공편은 20달러의 10배인 (D) 200달러였을 것이다.

**195** N.I.F. 컨퍼런스에 대해 알 수 있는 것은 무엇인가?
(A) 베타 에어[이]가 후원한다.
(B) 로스엔젤레스에서 열린다.
**(C) 몇 시간 앞당겨졌다.**
(D) 2년마다 열린다.

해설 전화 메시[이]지에 보면, "N.I.F. 컨퍼런스 일정에 변화가 있을 수 있어"라는 내용이 나온다. 실제 N.I.F. 컨퍼런스 스케줄이 바꿨던지 이것인으로 알 수 있다. 웹 메시[이]지에서 "제 일정 변경으로 인해" 6시간 빠른 항공편으로 변경했다는 내용이 나온다. 따라서 N.I.F. 컨퍼런스 스케줄이 앞당겨졌음을 알 수 있으므로 (C)가 정답이다.

**[196-200]**

수신: 1559 IBS 기업 부서 부서 팀장들
발신: 제이 브렌든
날짜: 8월 8일
제목: 화물 엘리베이터

구매 부서의 몇몇 직원들이 화물 엘리베이터를 개인적인 이유로 자주 사용한다는 걸 쉽게 됐습니다.

회사 방침에 따라 수용될 수 있는 비즈니스 목적이 아니라면 화물 엘리베이터를 사용해서는 안 됩니다. 화물 엘리베이터는 중장비나 사무용품 같은 제품의 운송 용도입니다. 그래 용무로는 사용할 수 없습니다. 1559 입구 근처 그게 외의 목적으로는 사용할 사람들은 그게 층간 직원들을 수송을 위한 것이나까요. 1569 과적으로 인한 고장 때문에 이번 달에 두 번이나 수리공을 불렀습니다.

마지막으로, 우리 화물 엘리베이터의 적재 하중은 6,000파운드를 초과해서는 안 됩니다. 따라서 그 이상의 무게로 화물 엘리베이터를 사용하지 마세요. 과적으로 인한 고장 때문에 이번 달에 두 번이나 수리공을 불렀습니다.

발신: 블레이크 드윗
수신: 0단 바바
날짜: 8월 9일
제목: 사무용 가구

바바 씨에게,

16A-타입 사무용 가구가 배송을 위해 준비되었다고 하니 정말 다행입니다. 1579 귀사의 하청업체 문제로 지체될까가 매우 걱정했거든요. 다 잘 됐으면 하고 그들도 파업을 그만하고 복배송의 관해 담당드리겠니다, 알아봐서야 할 게 있습니다. 1589 이제 화물용 엘리베이터 귀사가 항상 이용해 왔던 자회 부서 전 직원에게 내려줬어요. 2009 ACE 건물에서 귀사가 이용할 때 다른 화물용 엘리베이터를 사용하시기 바랍니다. 2009 그래서 가구를 배달하실 때 다른 화물용 엘리베이터를 사용하시기 바랍니다.

궁금하신 점이 있으면 언제든 편하게 연락주세요.

1599 블레이크 드윗, IBS 기업

**196** 화물에 따르면, 엘리베이터 고장의 원인은 무엇이라고 설명되었는가?
(A) 승객들의 빈번한 사용
**(B) 화물의 과다 적재**
(C) 기술자들의 부주의한 점검
(D) 뜻하지 않은 정전

해설 화물에서 쓴 이메일에서, "과적으로 인한 고장 때문에 이번 달에 두 번이나 수리공을 불렀다는 내용으로 인한 고장의 원인이 과적으로 인한 것임을 알 수 있다. 따라서 (B)가 정답이다.

**197** 바바 씨에 대해 암시된 것은 무엇인가?
(A) 성공적인 건축가로 경력을 시작했다.
(B) 드윗 씨를 위해 건물 도면을 그렸다.
(C) 브랜드 씨에게 화물 엘리베이터에 대해 조언했다.

**198** 이메일에서 두 번째 단락, 네 번째 줄에 있는 out of order와 의미상 가장 가까운 것은 무엇인가?
(A) 비효율적인
(B) 출시된
(C) 제조된
**(D) 고장 난**

해설 out of order는 '고장 난'이라는 뜻이므로, 같은 뜻을 가진 (D) broken이 정답이다.

**199** 드윗 씨에 대해 알 수 있는 것은 무엇인가?
(A) 사적인 이유로 엘리베이터를 이용하다가 고장 냈다.
(B) 엘리베이터 수리를 위해 수리공에게 연락했다.
**(C) 구매 부서에서 일한다.**
(D) 엘리베이터 기술자로서 일했었다.

해설 드윗 씨가 쓴 이메일에서, "어제 화물 엘리베이터 관련해서 화림이 자회 부서 전 직원에게 내려왔다"라고 썼으므로 그의 부서 전 직원에게 화림이 내려왔음을 알 수 있는데, 이메일 상으로는 그가 어떤 부서에서 일했는지 알 수 없다. 이메일 끝에 IBS 기업이라고만 적혀 있다. 화림에서 수신에 "IBS 기업 구매 부서 직원들"이라고 되어 있으므로, 그는 구매 부서에서 일함을 알 수 있다. 따라서 정답은 (C)이다.

**200** 16A-타입 가구의 배달을 위해 바바 씨는 어떤 엘리베이터를 이용할 것인가?
(A) 엘리베이터 A
(B) 엘리베이터 B
**(C) 엘리베이터 C**
(D) 엘리베이터 D

해설 평면도를 보면 엘리베이터는 총 4개이다. 화림을 보면 두 개의 승객용 엘리베이터를 사용하면서"라는 표현에서 두 개의 엘리베이터 A와 B가 승객용 엘리베이터임을 알 수 있다. 즉, 엘리베이터 C와 D가 화물용인 것이다. 이메일에서 1층 참고 옆에 있는 화물용 엘리베이터가 고장이 났다고 했으므로 참고 옆에 있는 화물용 엘리베이터 D가 고장이 난 것이고, 바바 씨는 다른 화물용 엘리베이터 C를 사용할 것이다. 따라서 (C)가 정답이다.

**ACE 건물 1층 평면도**

| 엘리베이터 C | 사무실 102 | 사무실 101 | 엘리베이터 A | 안내소 |
|---|---|---|---|---|
| | | 통로 | | ⇦ 입구 |
| 엘리베이터 D | 2009 참고 | 사무실 103 | 엘리베이터 B | 경비실 |

**어휘** procurement department 구매 부서   freight elevator 화물용 엘리베이터   frequently 자주   acceptable 받아들일 수 있는, 수용할 수 있는   heavy equipment 중장비   (office) supplies 사무용품   lastly 마지막으로   loading capacity 적재 하중   exceed 초과하다   repairman 수리공   malfunction 고장, 오작동   overloading 과적   shipment 수송, 배송   subcontractor 하청업체   strike 파업   storage room 저장고, 참고   out of order 고장 난   building plan 건축 설계도, 평면도   walkway 통로   security office 경비실   negligent 부주의한   power outage 정전   labor dispute 노동 쟁의

**Actual Test 05**

## 🎧 Listening Comprehension

본책 P182

**PART 1**

| 1 (C) | 2 (B) | 3 (B) | 4 (B) | 5 (A) | 6 (D) | | | | |

**PART 2**

| 7 (B) | 8 (A) | 9 (A) | 10 (C) | 11 (C) | 12 (B) | 13 (B) | 14 (A) | 15 (B) | 16 (C) |
| 17 (A) | 18 (A) | 19 (B) | 20 (C) | 21 (B) | 22 (B) | 23 (C) | 24 (A) | 25 (B) | 26 (C) |
| 27 (B) | 28 (C) | 29 (B) | 30 (C) | 31 (B) | | | | | |

**PART 3**

| 32 (D) | 33 (B) | 34 (D) | 35 (D) | 36 (B) | 37 (A) | 38 (C) | 39 (B) | 40 (B) | 41 (B) |
| 42 (A) | 43 (D) | 44 (D) | 45 (A) | 46 (C) | 47 (A) | 48 (B) | 49 (D) | 50 (D) | 51 (B) |
| 52 (D) | 53 (C) | 54 (B) | 55 (C) | 56 (C) | 57 (B) | 58 (C) | 59 (A) | 60 (C) | 61 (B) |
| 62 (B) | 63 (D) | 64 (A) | 65 (C) | 66 (B) | 67 (C) | 68 (C) | 69 (A) | 70 (B) | |

**PART 4**

| 71 (B) | 72 (D) | 73 (C) | 74 (A) | 75 (B) | 76 (D) | 77 (D) | 78 (A) | 79 (A) | 80 (B) |
| 81 (A) | 82 (B) | 83 (C) | 84 (C) | 85 (C) | 86 (C) | 87 (B) | 88 (C) | 89 (D) | 90 (C) |
| 91 (B) | 92 (D) | 93 (B) | 94 (C) | 95 (B) | 96 (A) | 97 (C) | 98 (C) | 99 (A) | 100 (C) |

## 📖 Reading Comprehension

본책 P194

**PART 5**

| 101 (C) | 102 (A) | 103 (D) | 104 (D) | 105 (C) | 106 (C) | 107 (C) | 108 (D) | 109 (A) | 110 (D) |
| 111 (D) | 112 (A) | 113 (A) | 114 (C) | 115 (B) | 116 (A) | 117 (C) | 118 (B) | 119 (D) | 120 (D) |
| 121 (D) | 122 (D) | 123 (A) | 124 (C) | 125 (B) | 126 (D) | 127 (C) | 128 (B) | 129 (A) | 130 (B) |

**PART 6**

| 131 (C) | 132 (A) | 133 (A) | 134 (C) | 135 (A) | 136 (A) | 137 (C) | 138 (B) | 139 (C) | 140 (C) |
| 141 (A) | 142 (B) | 143 (A) | 144 (B) | 145 (C) | 146 (B) | | | | |

**PART 7**

| 147 (B) | 148 (A) | 149 (A) | 150 (D) | 151 (D) | 152 (D) | 153 (B) | 154 (D) | 155 (A) | 156 (A) |
| 157 (D) | 158 (B) | 159 (C) | 160 (D) | 161 (A) | 162 (B) | 163 (D) | 164 (A) | 165 (D) | 166 (C) |
| 167 (B) | 168 (C) | 169 (A) | 170 (D) | 171 (C) | 172 (D) | 173 (D) | 174 (C) | 175 (B) | 176 (A) |
| 177 (D) | 178 (A) | 179 (C) | 180 (C) | 181 (B) | 182 (B) | 183 (D) | 184 (D) | 185 (A) | 186 (B) |
| 187 (D) | 188 (A) | 189 (A) | 190 (C) | 191 (C) | 192 (A) | 193 (D) | 194 (A) | 195 (B) | 196 (B) |
| 197 (A) | 198 (A) | 199 (B) | 200 (C) | | | | | | |

# PART 1

P182

**1** 미M
(A) The man is examining a car engine.
(B) The man is driving into a garage.
**(C) The man is working on a tire.**
(D) The man is opening a car door.
(A) 남자가 자동차 엔진을 점검하고 있다.
(B) 남자가 차고 안으로 들어오고 있다.
(C) 남자가 타이어 작업을 하고 있다.
(D) 남자가 차 문을 열고 있다.
어휘 examine 살펴보다 garage 차고, 정비소 work on ~에 대한 작업을 하다

**2** 미W
(A) A woman is selling products outside.
**(B) Various merchandise is on display.**
(C) There are some pots on the table.
(D) A store is crowded with customers.
(A) 여자가 야외에서 물건을 팔고 있다.
(B) 다양한 물건들이 진열되어 있다.
(C) 탁자 위에 도자기들이 있다.
(D) 가게가 손님으로 붐빈다.
어휘 merchandise 물건 on display 진열된 pot 도자기, 화분

**3** 영M
(A) The man is standing behind a truck.
**(B) The man is shoveling snow off the sidewalk.**
(C) The man is crossing the street.
(D) The man is putting on a cap.
(A) 남자가 트럭 뒤에 서 있다.
(B) 남자가 인도의 눈을 삽으로 치우고 있다.
(C) 남자가 길을 건너고 있다.
(D) 남자가 모자를 쓰고 있다.
어휘 shovel 삽질하다 sidewalk 인도 put on 쓰다, 입다(동작)

**4** 미W
(A) One of the men is using a cash register.
**(B) One of the men is opening a wallet.**
(C) The men are cleaning a counter.
(D) The men are organizing some items.
(A) 남자 중 한 명이 금전 등록기를 사용하고 있다.
(B) 남자 중 한 명이 지갑을 열고 있다.
(C) 남자들이 카운터를 닦고 있다.
(D) 남자들이 물건을 정리하고 있다.
어휘 cash register 금전 등록기 counter 계산대 organize 정리하다

**5** 미M
**(A) Potted plants are hung on a structure.**
(B) A street lamp is being installed.
(C) A tree casts a shadow over the garden.
(D) People are strolling along the path.
(A) 화분들이 구조물에 걸려 있다.
(B) 가로등이 설치되고 있는 중이다.
(C) 나무는 정원에 그림자를 드리우고 있다.
(D) 사람들이 길을 따라 산책하고 있다...
어휘 potted plant 화분 install 설치하다 cast a shadow 그림자를 드리우다 stroll 산책하다 path 작은 길

**6** 영M
(A) A painting is being put up on the wall.
(B) A man is seated with a hat on.
(C) The café is crowded with talking customers.
**(D) A man is concentrating on his computer.**
(A) 그림 한 점이 벽에 걸리는 중이다.
(B) 남자가 모자를 쓰고 앉아 있다.
(C) 카페는 얘기를 나누는 손님들로 붐빈다.
(D) 한 남자가 컴퓨터에 집중하고 있다.
어휘 be crowded 붐비다 concentrate on ~에 집중하다

# PART 2

P186

**7** 미M / 미W
That play seemed really boring, didn't it?
(A) It's not borrowed.
**(B) Yes, it did.**
(C) I didn't have it.
그 연극은 정말 지루한 것 같았어요, 그렇죠?
(A) 그건 빌린 게 아니에요.
(B) 네, 그랬어요.
(C) 제가 그걸 가지고 있지 않았어요.
어휘 seem ~인 것 같다 boring 지루한

**8** 영M / 미W
How long will the special deals be available?
**(A) For the rest of the month.**
(B) A few miles away.
(C) Yes, the yellow one.
특가는 얼마나 오래 이용 가능한가요?
(A) 이번 달 동안이요.
(B) 몇 마일 떨어졌어요.
(C) 네, 그 노란색이요.
어휘 special deal 특가

**9** 미M / 미W
Can I offer you something to drink?
**(A) Just a glass of water please.**
(B) A new coffee machine.
(C) Yes, from time to time.
마실 것을 드릴까요?
(A) 그냥 물 한 잔 주세요.
(B) 새 커피 기계요.
(C) 네, 기꺼이요.
어휘 offer 제공하다 from time to time 가끔

**10** 미W / 영M
Don't you need a security pass to get into the building?
(A) It's free with an annual pass.
(B) He works at the security office.
**(C) Yes, but I lost it.**
건물 안으로 들어가려면 보안증이 필요하지 않나요?
(A) 연간권이 있으면 무료예요.
(B) 그는 경비실에서 일해요.
(C) 네, 그런데 잃어버렸어요.
어휘 security pass 보안증 annual pass (교통수단) 연간권

**11** 영M / 미M
Which car will you buy tomorrow?
(A) We rented the car in the morning.
(B) Let's go and get some.
**(C) I haven't decided yet.**
내일 어떤 차를 살 건가요?
(A) 우리는 아침에 차를 빌렸어요.
(B) 가서 좀 얻어 오죠.
(C) 아직 결정하지 않았어요.
어휘 rent 빌리다, 세내다

**12** 미M / 미W
Could you let Ms. Cooper know I'm going to leave?
(A) Just leave it on my desk.
**(B) Yes, I'll call her right away.**
(C) About 10 minutes ago.
제가 떠날 거라고 쿠퍼 씨에게 알려 주시겠어요?
(A) 그냥 제 책상 위에 두세요.
(B) 네, 지금 그녀에게 전화할게요.
(C) 약 10분 전에요.
어휘 leave 떠나다; 남겨 두다

**13** 영M / 미W
Why don't we review one more file before we leave?
(A) Because the file is confidential.
**(B) I'll do that after a short break.**
(C) Sure, the view is great from here.
가기 전에 파일 하나만 더 검토하면 어떨까요?
(A) 그 파일은 보안 유지를 해야 하거든요.
(B) 잠깐 쉬고 나서 할게요.
(C) 물론이죠, 경치가 여기서 매우 좋습니다.
어휘 confidential 비밀의 break 휴식 view 경치

**14** 미W / 미M
Are you discussing our budget today or tomorrow?
**(A) Tomorrow at two.**
(B) Thanks for the allocation.
(C) A rather short discussion.
우리의 예산을 오늘 논의할 건가요, 내일 할 건가요?

**(A) 내일 2시예요.**
(B) 할인해 주셔서 고맙습니다.
(C) 상당히 젊은 토론이요.
어휘 allocation 할당(량)  rather 다소

**15** How long will the batteries last?
미W (A) It was the last time I used the machine.
미M **(B) They should be good for a week or so.**
영M (C) He replaced them with bigger batteries.
배터리가 얼마나 오래 갈까요?
(A) 그때가 제가 그 기계를 마지막으로 사용한 때입니다.
**(B) 1주일 정도는 괜찮을 거예요.**
(C) 그가 좀 더 큰 배터리로 길이 끼웠습니다.
어휘 last 지속되다

**16** What are you planning to bring to Warren's retirement party?
미M (A) I'd like the same one as you have.
영M (B) He's tired of the work.
미M **(C) I'm afraid I can't go.**
워런의 은퇴 파티에 무엇 가지고 올 계획이세요?
(A) 당신이 갖고 있는 것과 같은 걸로요.
(B) 그는 그 일에 싫증났어요.
**(C) 저는 못 갈 것 같아요.**
어휘 be tired of 싫증나다

**17** Are there any openings on your company's marketing team?
미W **(A) Yes. Would you like to fill out an application?**
영M (B) Our new product is very popular.
미W (C) They're open until 9 o'clock.
당신 회사 마케팅 팀에 공석이 있나요?
**(A) 네, 지원서를 쓰시겠어요?**
(B) 우리 신상품은 인기가 많아요.
(C) 그들은 9시까지 문을 엽니다.
어휘 opening 일자리 공석  fill out 채우다  application 지원서

**18** I can't get the projector working properly.
영M **(A) Maybe I can help.**
미W (B) I don't work here.
미W (C) On the screen over there.
프로젝터를 제대로 작동시킬 수가 없어요.
**(A) 제가 도와 드릴 수 있겠어요.**
(B) 전 여기서 일하진 않아요.
(C) 저쪽에 있는 화면이요.
어휘 projector 영사기, 프로젝터  property 제대로, 적정하게

**19** When is the article on our new product going to be published?
미W (A) It was a small publishing firm a year ago.
미M **(B) They need to interview our CEO first.**
(C) From Arbor Publishing.
우리 신제품에 관한 기사는 언제 실리나요?
(A) 1년 전에 그 회사는 작은 출판사였어요.
**(B) 그들이 우리 사장님을 먼저 인터뷰해요.**
(C) 아르보 출판사로부터요.
어휘 article 기사, 물품  publish 출간하다  publishing firm 출판사

**20** Are you sure you know how to get to the warehouse?
미W (A) I don't wear suits.
영M (B) That was pretty quick.
**(C) I should after all these visits.**
창고에 어떻게 가는지 확실히 알고 있죠?
(A) 저는 정장을 안 입어요.
(B) 꽤 빨랐네요.
**(C) 그렇게 많이 방문했는데 알아야죠.**
어휘 get to ~에 가다  suit 정장  visit 방문

**21** Where in Sutton does the bus stop?
영M (A) I think so, too.
미M **(B) In the vicinity of City Hall.**
(C) It was certainly July 1st.
서튼에서 버스는 어디에 정차하나요?
(A) 저도 그렇게 생각해요.
**(B) 시청 부근에서요.**
(C) 그건 분명 7월 1일이었어요.
어휘 in the vicinity of ~의 부근

**22** What did the reception staff ask for?
미M (A) All the drawers were stuffed.
미W **(B) My contact details.**
(C) She works for Hopkins Hospital.
프런트 직원이 무엇을 요청했나요?
(A) 모든 서랍들이 가득 채워져 있었어요.
**(B) 제 연락처요.**
(C) 그녀는 홉킨스 병원에서 일합니다.
어휘 ask for 요청하다  stuff ~을 가득 채워 넣다

**23** I ordered five trays of sandwiches for the client meeting at noon today.
영M (A) Current members only.
미W (B) The tables are next to the door.
**(C) I think that should be enough.**
제가 오늘 정오에 있을 고객 회의를 위해 샌드위치 다섯 접시를 주문했어요.
(A) 현재 회원들에게만요.
(B) 탁자들은 문 옆에 있어요.
**(C) 그거면 충분할 거예요.**
어휘 tray 접시  next to ~옆에

**24** Won't you visit the construction site for the factory in Delaware today?
미W **(A) No, but I can check the progress online.**
미M (B) Yes, I plan on applying for a sales job.
(C) New factory layout.
오늘 델라웨어에 있는 공장 건설 현장을 방문하지 않을 건가요?
**(A) 안 갈 테지만, 하지만 진행 상황을 온라인으로 확인할 수 있어요.**
(B) 네, 저는 영업직에 지원하려고요.
(C) 새로운 공장 설계도요.
어휘 construction site 건설 현장  progress 진행  layout 설계도

**25** Wasn't Joan at the pharmaceutical conference in Manchester last week?
미W (A) Where is meeting room 1A?
영M **(B) I didn't see her there.**
(C) Yes, I'm in good condition.
지난주 맨체스터에서 열린 제약 학회에 조안이 있지 않았나요?
(A) 1A 회의실이 어디죠?
**(B) 거기서 그녀를 보지 못했어요.**
(C) 네, 전 정상이요.
어휘 pharmaceutical 약학의, 제약의  be in good condition 몸 상태가 좋다

**26** Did you purchase a one-year limited warranty for your laptop?
미M (A) I'll bring it to you.
미W (B) The software is already installed.
**(C) I bought one for two years.**
당신의 노트북 컴퓨터의 1년짜리 보증서를 구입하셨나요?
(A) 제가 당신께 가져다줄게요.
(B) 그 소프트웨어가 이미 설치되어 있어요.
**(C) 전 2년짜리로 샀어요.**
어휘 warranty 보증서  install 설치하다

**27** Where did you get the discount coupons?
미M (A) Up to 30 percent off.
미W **(B) I downloaded them from a website.**
(C) It hasn't been sent yet.
그 할인 쿠폰들은 어디서 받으셨어요?
(A) 최대 30퍼센트 할인이에요.
**(B) 웹 사이트에서 다운로드 받았어요.**
(C) 그건 아직 발송되지 않았어요.
어휘 up to 최대 ~까지

# PART 3

P187

## Questions 32-34 refer to the following conversation. 미W 영M

W Hello, **32** I would like to place a recruitment advertisement in your local magazine.

M It's lucky you called us today. **33** Our discount package of 30% off a standard advertisement ends at the end of the week.

W Excellent. I want to find an administration clerk. I have a 40-word advertisement that I would like to insert for a month. **34** What is the cost of that?

M It will be $30 for the month. That's with the discount which basically gives you a free week.

여 안녕하세요, 당신의 지역 잡지에 제 채용 광고를 내고 싶습니다.

남 오늘 전화하셔서 다행이네요. 표준 광고의 30퍼센트 할인 상품이 이번 주말에 끝나가든요.

여 정말 잘됐네요. 제가 관리 사원을 찾으려고 하는데요. 한 달 게재하고 싶은 40자 광고가 있거든요. 비용은 얼마인가요?

남 한 달에 30달러입니다. 기본으로 무료로 일주일을 드리는 할인이 포함되어 있어요.

어휘 place an advertisement 광고를 내다 administration clerk 관리 사원 insert 넣다, 삽입하다 basically 기본적으로 special offer 특가품, 특가 판매 subscriber 구독자 format 구성 방식, 판형

### 32 Where does the man work?
(A) At a real estate agency
(B) At a local tourist office
(C) At a radio station
(D) At a recruitment agency

남자가 일하는 장소는 어디인가?
(A) 부동산 중개소
(B) 지역 관광 안내소
(C) 라디오 방송국
(D) 취업 정보업체

### 33 What does the man say about the special offer?
(A) It includes insertion into a website.
(B) It will expire soon.
(C) It is only for subscribers.
(D) It applies only to recruitment advertisements.

특가 판매에 관하여 남자가 말하는 것은 무엇인가?
(A) 웹 사이트에 게재를 포함한다.
(B) 곧 끝날 것이다.
(C) 구독자들만을 위한 것이다.
(D) 채용 광고에만 적용된다.

패러프레이징 ends at the end of the week → expire soon

### 34 What does the woman want to know about the advertisement?
(A) The word count
(B) The format
(C) The color
(D) The cost

광고에 관하여 여자가 알고 싶어 하는 것은 무엇인가?
(A) 단어 수
(B) 판형
(C) 색상
(D) 비용

## Questions 35-37 refer to the following conversation. 미M 미W

M I have a major problem proofreading in this office. **35** The lighting is so bad. Moreover, not much daylight filters through because there are some tall trees just next to the office windows. And every so often, the power fails.

W **36** Maybe you can telecommute. There is no need for you to be physically present in the office. Your predecessor used to work from home. It's a viable option.

M That's a good idea. That would make my work much easier. **37** I will inquire about it.

남 이 사무실에서 교정보는 데 큰 문제가 하나 있어요. 조명이 너무 안 좋아요. 다군다나 큰 나무들이 사무실 창문 바로 옆에 있어서 햇빛이 많이 들어오지 않아요. 그리고 가끔 전기도 나가고요.

여 아마도 재택근무가 가능할 거예요. 꼭 사무실에 계실 필요는 없죠. 당신의 전임자도 재택근무를 했었으요. 가능한 방안이네요.

남 좋은 생각이네요. 그렇게 하면 제 일이 훨씬 더 쉬워질 거예요. 문의를 해야겠어요.

어휘 proofread 교정을 보다 lighting 조명 daylight 햇빛 filter through ~을 스며들게[들어오다] every so often 가끔 power 전기 telecommute 통신 시설을 이용하여 재택 근무하다 physically 육체적으로 present 있는, 참석한 predecessor 전임자 viable 실행 가능한 assemble 모으다, 조립하다 insufficient 불충분한 transplant 옮겨 심다 take on (일 등을) 맡다, 책임지다

### 35 What is the man concerned about?
(A) Background noise
(B) An office closure
(C) Lack of daylight hours
(D) Insufficient light

남자가 걱정하는 것은 무엇인가?
(A) 주변의 소음
(B) 사무실 폐쇄

---

## 28 Would you like to come in for a meeting tomorrow?
영M 미W
(A) No, the restaurant opens every day.
(B) What was the applicant's name again?
**(C) Yes, but it has to be toward the end of the workday.**

내일 회의하러 오시겠습니까?
(A) 아니요, 그 레스토랑은 매일 문을 열어요.
(B) 그 지원자의 이름이 뭐였죠?
(C) 네, 그런데 근무 시간의 후반부 쪽이어야 해요.

어휘 applicant 지원자 toward ~쪽으로 workday 근무 시간

## 29 Didn't you anticipate a lot more people to come to the medical research seminar?
미W 미M
(A) In the main conference room.
**(B) No, this is all I expected.**
(C) I invited them a month ago.

의료 연구 세미나에 훨씬 더 많은 사람들이 올 거라 예상하지 않았었나요?
(A) 본회의장에서요.
(B) 아니요, 이것이 제가 예상했던 전부입니다.
(C) 제가 그들을 한 달 전에 초대했어요.

어휘 anticipate 고대하다, 예상하다

## 30 How many hours will it take to review each financial report?
미W 영M
(A) Report to your supervisor.
(B) It helps solve their financial problems.
**(C) Not long if you focus on the numbers.**

각 재무 보고서를 검토하는 데 얼마나 걸릴까요?
(A) 상사에게 보고하세요.
(B) 그들이 재정 문제를 해결하는 데 도움이 돼요.
(C) 수치에 집중하신다면 오래 걸리지 않아요.

어휘 review 검토하다 financial report 재무 보고서 focus on 집중하다

## 31 I have to stop by the post office on the way to the auditorium.
영M 미M
(A) I'm fine, thanks.
**(B) But the concert is at four.**
(C) Will you continue with it?

공연장에 가는 길에 우체국에 들러야 해요.
(A) 전 괜찮습니다, 고마워요.
(B) 그렇지만 콘서트가 4시예요.
(C) 그걸 계속 해주실래요?

어휘 stop by ~에 들르다 auditorium 강당, 공연장 continue with ~을 계속하다

어휘 rough budget 견적 | road pavement 도로 포장 | small job 간단한 일 | hiring agency 고용업체 | forward 전송하다 | rush 서두르다 | rainy season 장마 | contractor 도급업자 | rough draft 초고 | temporary 일시의 | calculate 계산하다

(C) 일조 시간의 부족
(D) 불충분한 빛

**36** What does the woman suggest?
(A) Using a different office
(B) Working from home
(C) Finding a different employer
(D) Transplanting the trees elsewhere

여자가 제안하는 것은 무엇인가?
(A) 다른 사무실 이용할 것
(B) **재택근무할 것**
(C) 다른 회사를 알아볼 것
(D) 나무들을 다른 곳에 옮겨 심을 것

패러프레이징 telecommute → Working from home

**37** What does the man say he will do?
(A) Ask for information
(B) Leave the company
(C) Assemble a team
(D) Take on extra work

남자는 무엇을 하겠다고 말하는가?
(A) **정보 요청하기**
(B) 회사 떠나기
(C) 팀 구성하기
(D) 추가 업무 맡기

Questions 38-40 refer to the following conversation. 미W 영M

W Mr. Perez, I just got an e-mail from Mr. Wang in the City Office. ❸ ❸ He was asking when the rough budget for the road pavement would be ready. The problem is, I can't work it out until I know the number of people we're planning to hire.

M Well, it's not a small job, but usually it doesn't take more than 20. ❹ I will contact the hiring agency right away and see how many they can send us.

W Okay, please forward the information to me as soon as you get it. Then I'll figure out how much it will cost and send it to Mr. Wang. We have to rush before the rainy season comes.

여 페레즈 씨, 제가 방금 시티 오피스의 왕 씨로부터 이메일을 받았어요. 그는 도로 포장 작업에 대한 견적이 언제 준비되는지 묻네요. 문제는 우리가 몇 명을 고용할지 알기 전까지는 견적을 낼 수가 없어요.

남 음, 간단한 일이 아니지만 그 일은 보통 20명 이상 필요하지는 않아요. 지금 고용업체에 바로 전화해서 우리에게 몇 명을 보내 줄 수 있는지 알아볼게요.

여 네, 그 정보를 받자마자 제게 바로 보내 주세요. 그러면 얼마가 드는지 알아내고 그것을 왕 씨에게 보내야죠. 장마가 오기 전에 서둘러야 해요.

---

Questions 41-43 refer to the following conversation. 미W 미M

W ❹ Carlisle Medical Center. This is Brenda Duggan speaking. How can I help you?

M Hello. I'm calling to make an appointment with Dr. Price. I've been suffering from fevers and muscle aches ever ❷ since I got back from holiday a week ago.

W Oh, I'm sorry to hear that. Please hold on a second while I check our calendar. Well, it looks like there are two openings tomorrow. How does 4 o'clock sound?

M Hmm, [usually work until five.]

W In that case, ❸ we have another opening at 5:30. Does that work for you?

M Yes, I can be there by 5:30.

여 칼리슬 메디컬 센터입니다. 저는 브렌다 듀건입니다. 무엇을 도와 드릴까요?

남 안녕하세요. 저는 프라이스 박사님과 진료 예약을 잡고 싶어요. 일주일 전에 휴가에서 돌아온 이후부터 열과 근육통에 시달리고 있거든요.

여 오, 안타깝네요. 제가 달력을 확인하는 동안 잠시만 기다려 주세요. 음, 내일 비는 시간이 두 곳 있네요. 4시 정각 어떠세요?

남 흠, 저는 보통 5시까지 일을 해요.

여 그런 경우라면, 5시 30분에 다른 비는 시간이 있어요. 그건 괜찮으신가요?

남 네, 5시 30분까지는 갈 수 있습니다.

어휘 suffer from ~로 인해 고생하다 | fever 열 | muscle ache 근육통 | opening (예약 가능한) 시간 | resign 사직하다

**41** Where does the woman most likely work?
(A) At a travel agency
(B) **At a health clinic**
(C) At a restaurant
(D) At an airline

여자는 어디서 일할 것 같은가?
(A) 여행사
(B) **병원**
(C) 레스토랑
(D) 항공사

**42** What does the man say he did a week ago?
(A) Returned from vacation
(B) Started a business overseas
(C) Made an appointment with a doctor
(D) Resigned from a job

남자는 일주일 전에 무엇을 했다고 하는가?
(A) **휴가에서 돌아왔다.**
(B) 해외에서 사업을 시작했다.
(C) 의사와 진료 예약을 잡았다.

**38** Who most likely are the speakers?
(A) City officials
(B) Hiring agents
(C) **Building contractors**
(D) Telephone operators

화자들은 누구인가?
(A) 시 공무원
(B) 고용업체 직원
(C) **건설 도급업자**
(D) 전화 교환원

**39** What are the speakers mainly discussing?
(A) A rough draft of a script
(B) **An estimate for the roadwork**
(C) A budget to prepare for bad weather
(D) A job interview for crew members

화자들은 주로 무엇에 관해 이야기하고 있는가?
(A) 대본 초안
(B) **도로 작업 견적**
(C) 악천후를 대비하기 위한 예산
(D) 직원들을 뽑는 채용 면접

패러프레이징 the rough budget for the road pavement → An estimate for the roadwork

**40** What does Mr. Perez say he will do next?
(A) Hire temporary workers immediately
(B) **Check the number of workers available**
(C) Forward an e-mail to the woman's coworker
(D) Calculate the cost of the repairs

페레즈 씨는 다음에 무엇을 할 거라고 하는가?
(A) 즉각 임시직 직원들을 고용한다.
(B) **일할 수 있는 직원들의 숫자를 알아본다.**
(C) 이메일을 여자의 동료에게 전달한다.
(D) 수리 비용을 계산해 본다.

**43** What does the man imply when he says, "I usually work until five"?
(A) He feels tired after work.
(B) He would like to take a day off.
(C) He is looking for a part-time job.
(D) He would prefer a later appointment.

남자가 "저는 보통 5시까지 일을 해요"라고 말한 의도는 무엇인가?
(A) 퇴근 후에는 피곤함을 느낀다.
(B) 하루 쉬기를 원한다.
(C) 시간제 근무를 찾고 있다.
(D) 더 늦은 예약을 선호한다.

**44** What is the woman asking the man to submit?
(A) Holiday destinations
(B) Confirmation of employment
(C) Revised contact information
(D) Vacation dates

여자가 남자에게 제출하라고 요구한 것은 무엇인가?
(A) 휴가 목적지
(B) 고용 확인
(C) 변경된 연락처
(D) 휴가 일정

**45** What has the woman recently done?
(A) Employ additional staff
(B) Take a vacation
(C) Post new regulations
(D) Organize a company outing

여자는 최근에 무엇을 했는가?
(A) 추가 직원 고용
(B) 휴가 가기
(C) 새 규정 게시
(D) 회사 야유회 준비

패러프레이징 hired some temporary staff → Employ additional staff

**46** What does the man say about his relatives?
(A) They live out of the country.
(B) They work at the same company.
(C) They will be taking some time off.
(D) They just started new jobs.

남자가 자신의 친척에 관하여 말한 것은 무엇인가?
(A) 그들은 외국에서 살고 있다.
(B) 그들은 같은 회사에서 일하고 있다.
(C) 그들은 얼마간 쉴 것이다.
(D) 그들은 막 새로운 일을 시작했다.

Questions 44-46 refer to the following conversation. 미W 영M

W I am sorting out the staff's vacation schedules for the next few months. ④⑤ I have hired some temporary staff to help us out over that period ④④ but I need to know your proposed holiday time so that I can schedule it in.

M Wonderful. Can I let you know tomorrow?

W Tomorrow is fine. I might not be able to schedule the exact dates for everyone but I will do my best to ensure they are all accommodated.

M ④⑥ I am going to visit my relatives in Portland and I will need to find out when they are taking time off work. I'll check with them and get back to you tomorrow.

여 제가 다음 몇 달간의 직원들의 휴가 일정을 짜고 있어요. 제가 그 기간 동안 우리를 도와줄 임시 직원들을 채용했는데, 일정에 넣을 수 있도록 당신의 휴가 계획을 알아야 해요.

남 좋아요, 제가 내일 알려 드려도 될까요?

여 내일이면 괜찮아요. 제가 모든 사람들을 위해 정확한 일정을 잡을 수는 없겠지만 그들이 의견 모두가 꼭 수용되도록 최선을 다할 거예요.

남 저는 포틀랜드에 있는 친척을 방문할 거라서 그들이 언제 쉴지 알아야 하거든요. 제가 그들에게 확인하고 내일 다시 연락드릴게요.

**어휘** sort out 분류하다, 정리하다 ensure 반드시 ~하다 accommodate (의견을) 수용하다[담다] relatives 친척 get back to 다시 연락하다 destination 목적지 employment 고용 outing 견학, 야유회

---

Questions 47-49 refer to the following conversation. 미M

M Now for news on the economy. Our guest this morning is Andrea Fincato. ④⑦ Ms. Fincato is the deputy director of BFD Financial Services, a company that has numerous branches in Dallyville. Ms. Fincato, is it true that you are planning to launch a new service here in town?

W Yes, that's right. We have just purchased new property where we can offer walk-in service for those looking for home loans. ④⑧ We are very excited about this facility as it will make it easier to obtain a loan to buy a property, which is my main aim as a financial provider.

M That's excellent. ④⑨ When will the service become available?

W We are refitting the offices now and they are scheduled to open in November.

남 경제 뉴스를 전해 드립니다. 오늘 아침에 모실 손님은 안드레아 핀카토입니다. 핀카토 씨는 댈리빌에 많은 지점을 가지고 있는 BFD 파이낸셜 서비스사의 부회장입니다. 핀카토 씨, 이곳에서 새로운 서비스를 시작할 계획이라는 게 사실인가요?

여 네, 그렇습니다. 저희는 엄마 전 새 부지를 구입했는데 주택 대출을 찾고 있는 분들을 위한 예약이 필요 없는 서비스를 제공할 수 있게 되었어요. 부동산구매를 위한 대출을 더 쉽게 받을 수 있는 것이 가능해서 금융 서비스 제공업자로서 저의 주된 목표이기도 했고요.

남 훌륭합니다. 서비스는 언제 이용할 수 있게 되나요?

여 지금 사무실을 수리하고 있으며, 11월에 문을 열 계획입니다.

**어휘** deputy director 부회장 numerous 수많은 property 부동산 walk-in 예약이 필요 없는 home loan 주택 대출 aim 목표 refit 수리하다 executive 이사, 중역 official (고위) 공무원 관리 ease 용이하게 하다 refurbish 개조하다, 수리하다 initiative 계획

**47** Who most likely is the woman?
(A) A company executive
(B) A financial consultant
(C) A radio host
(D) A government official

여자는 누구이겠는가?
(A) 회사 간부
(B) 금융 컨설턴트
(C) 라디오 진행자
(D) 정부 관리

**48** What goal does the woman discuss?
(A) Improving working conditions
(B) Easing the process of loan applications

**Questions 53-55 refer to the following conversation.** 미W 미M

W  Brian, I was wondering if you could give me some feedback on my presentation. Do you have a minute?

M  What? Oh, I'm sorry. I was preoccupied with the image editing. What was that again?

W  Ah, you must be working on the new advertisement for Kay Shoes. I'm sorry to bother you. I was going to ask you to look at my presentation slides, but if it's not a good time I'll come back later.

M  No, no. It's fine. I can take a look at them now.

W  Great! I just wanted to make sure all the advertising strategies we discussed with the clients have been incorporated.

M  OK, let me see. Didn't you say you changed the color scheme of the company logo to make it more recognizable? But this one here looks like the old one.

W  Oh, you're right! I'm glad you noticed that.

여  브라이언, 제 발표에 대한 피드백을 주실 수 있을까 해서요. 시간 있으세요?

남  네? 오, 미안해요. 제가 이미지 편집에 정신을 팔고 있었네요. 뭐라고 했었죠?

여  아, 케이 슈즈의 새 광고 작업을 하고 있었군요. 귀찮게 해서 미안해요. 제 발표 슬라이드를 좀 봐달라고 부탁하려고 했는데, 지금이 좋은 때가 아니면 이따가 다시 올게요.

남  아니에요. 괜찮습니다. 지금 볼 수 있어요.

여  잘됐네요! 우리가 고객들과 얘기했던 모든 광고 전략이 다 포함되었는지 확실히 하고 싶어서요.

남  좋아요, 한번 봅시다. 회사 로고를 눈에 더 잘 보이도록 색상 조합을 바꿨다고 하지 않았어요? 그런데 여기 이거는 옛날 것 같은데요.

여  오, 맞아요! 그걸 발견해줘서 정말 기뻐요.

**어휘**  be preoccupied with ~에 정신이 팔리다  bother 귀찮게 하다  incorporate 포함하다  color scheme 색상 조합  recognizable 눈에 잘 띄는  appealing 매력적인  lack ~이 부족하다

53  What industry do the speakers most likely work in?
   (A) Insurance
   (B) Finance
   (C) Advertising
   (D) Construction

화자들은 어떤 산업 분야에서 일하는가?
   (A) 보험
   (B) 금융
   (C) 광고
   (D) 건설

---

**어휘**  depart 출발하다  show around 구경시켜 주다  investment 투자  in person 직접  qualified 자질이 뛰어난  socialize 어울리다, 교제하다

50  What are the speakers mainly discussing?
   (A) Attending a conference
   (B) Going to France on business
   (C) Constructing a factory
   (D) Meeting with foreign investors

화자들이 주로 이야기하는 것은 무엇인가?
   (A) 회의 참석
   (B) 업무 차 프랑스 가기
   (C) 공장 건설
   (D) 외국 투자자들과 만남

51  What is happening today?
   (A) A trip to the airport
   (B) A tour of a facility
   (C) A welcome dinner
   (D) A conference call

오늘 일어나는 일은 무엇인가?
   (A) 공항 가기
   (B) 시설 견학
   (C) 환영 만찬
   (D) 전화 회의

52  What are the speakers looking forward to?
   (A) Hiring qualified employees
   (B) Making a good investment decision
   (C) Arriving in time for a conference
   (D) Socializing with their clients

화자들은 무엇을 기대하는가?
   (A) 자질이 뛰어난 직원 고용하기
   (B) 좋은 투자 결정하기
   (C) 회의에 제시간에 도착하기
   (D) 고객들과 어울리기

**패러프레이징**  get to know each other → Socializing with their clients

---

(C) Creating job opportunities
(D) Refurbishing houses

여자가 말하는 목표는 무엇인가?
   (A) 근무 환경을 개선하는 것
   (B) 대출 신청 과정을 쉽게 하는 것
   (C) 취업 기회를 만드는 것
   (D) 주택을 개조하는 것

49  What does the man ask the woman about?
   (A) A building initiative
   (B) Construction suppliers
   (C) Application forms
   (D) An opening date

남자가 여자에게 물어보는 것은 무엇인가?
   (A) 공사 계획
   (B) 건설 공급 회사
   (C) 신청서 양식
   (D) 개시일

**Questions 50-52 refer to the following conversation.** 미W 영M

W  Jason, do you know when we're meeting with our clients from France? I'm flying to Italy on Friday to attend a conference and I hope to see them before I depart.

M  Oh, you will see them on Thursday. They got here yesterday and Steve Cameron is showing them around our factory in Detroit today before they make an investment decision.

W  I didn't know that. You know, even though we've been doing business with them over the past five years, we only talk on the phone. It's funny because we've never met them in person.

M  That's true. That's why we planned a welcome dinner tomorrow and I'm sure it will allow us to get to know each other.

여  제이슨, 혹시 우리가 프랑스에서 온 고객들과 언제 만나는지 아세요? 제가 회의 때문에 금요일에 이탈리아로 가야 되는데 출발하기 전에 그들을 봤으면 해요.

남  아, 목요일에 그들을 만날 겁니다. 어제 여기 도착했고 스티브 카메론이 오늘 디트로이트에 있는 우리 공장을 견학시켜 주고 나면 그들이 투자 결정을 할 겁니다.

여  그건 몰랐네요. 우리가 지난 5년간 그들과 사업을 해 오고는 있지만 그냥 전화로만 이야기하거든요. 우리가 그들을 직접 만난 적이 없다는 게 좀처럼 없네요.

남  그렇습니다. 그래서 우리가 내일 환영의 저녁 식사를 계획했어요. 그렇게 하면 우리가 서로를 알게 될 겁니다.

**54** Why does the man say, "I was preoccupied with the image editing"?
(A) To explain a new policy
**(B) To offer an excuse**
(C) To request some help
(D) To refuse an offer

남자는 왜 "제가 이미지 편집에 정신을 팔고 있었어요"라고 말하는가?
(A) 새로운 정책을 설명하려고
**(B) 해명을 하려고**
(C) 도움을 요청하려고
(D) 제안을 거절하려고

**55** What is mentioned about the woman's presentation?
(A) An appealing image was used.
(B) It lacks creative advertising strategies.
**(C) A change has not been included.**
(D) Some more research will be needed.

여자의 발표에 대해 무엇이 언급되는가?
(A) 눈길을 끄는 이미지가 사용되었다.
(B) 창의적인 광고 전략이 부족하다.
**(C) 변경 사항이 포함되지 않았다.**
(D) 더 많은 조사가 필요할 것이다.

어휘 unattended 같이 있지 않은, 돌보는 사람이 없는  safe 금고  odd 특별한 홀패가 없는, 다양한  deposit 예치금  storage 보관  identification 신분증

**56** Where most likely are the speakers?
(A) At a storage facility
(B) At an airline check-in counter
**(C) At a hotel reception desk**
(D) At a bus terminal

화자들은 어디에 있겠는가?
(A) 보관 시설
(B) 항공사 체크인 카운터
**(C) 호텔 프런트**
(D) 버스 터미널

**57** What does the woman want to do?
(A) Book a hotel room
**(B) Drop off some papers**
(C) Check out at a later time
(D) Return within a week

여자가 원하는 것은 무엇인가?
(A) 호텔 객실을 예약하는 것
**(B) 서류들을 맡기는 것**
(C) 나중에 체크아웃하는 것
(D) 일주일 내에 돌아오는 것

**58** What does the man ask the woman to do?
(A) Enter a room number
(B) Confirm her departure
**(C) Pay a deposit**
(D) Show her identification

남자가 여자에게 요구하는 것은 무엇인가?
(A) 방 번호를 입력하는 것
(B) 그녀의 출발을 확인하는 것
**(C) 보증금을 지불하는 것**
(D) 그녀의 신분증을 보여 주는 것

Questions 56-58 refer to the following conversation. 미W 영M

W Good morning, 56 I have a room booked for tonight, but I have just been called back to the office. I have a number of important documents that I would prefer not to leave in the room unattended. 57 Do you have a safe place where I can put them?
M It depends on the size of the documents. We have a hotel safe, but it doesn't hold very large items.
W Oh, that will be fine then. I only have business contracts and some odd papers.
M Great. Can I take your room number? 58 I also need your credit card details because we require a deposit on the safe.

여 안녕하세요, 제가 오늘 밤 방을 하나 예약했는데, 방금 사무실에서 다시 호출을 받았어요. 제가 중요한 서류들을 많이 가지고 있는데, 방에 남겨둔 채 자리를 비우고 싶지 않아서요. 제가 그 서류들을 둘 수 있는 안전한 장소가 있나요?
남 서류의 크기에 따라 다릅니다. 저희에게 호텔 금고가 있지만, 아주 큰 물건은 보관하지 않아요.
여 오, 그러면 괜찮을 거예요. 저는 비즈니스 계약서와 몇 장의 서류들만 있어요.
남 좋습니다. 방 번호를 말씀해 주시겠어요? 그리고 금고 사용에 대한 보증금이 필요해서 손님의 신용 카드 정보도 알아야 합니다.

Questions 59-61 refer to the following conversation with three speakers. 미W 영W 영M

W1 Thank you both for coming to discuss the construction of the Greenwood factory. Today's meeting has been very productive.
W2 Yes, 59 I really think that Ian's done an excellent job with the building design. And I'm very excited to take over the project from here.
W1 Ian, is there anything else you want to tell Miranda?
M Oh yes, just one more thing. 60 The client wants to receive written confirmation of every detail about the construction. So, for example, if you discuss some interior materials with the client in person, you need to send him a confirmation e-mail afterwards.
W2 Wow, it sounds like a lot of paperwork. But okay. I got it. So Ian, 61 you're finally taking a much-needed vacation, aren't you?
M Yes, 61 I'm leaving for Berlin tomorrow to see my parents.

여1 그린우드 공장 건설에 대해 논의하려고 둘 다 와 줘서 고마워요. 오늘 회의 는 정말이 생산적이었어요.
여2 네, 이안이 건축 디자인을 정말 훌륭하게 해 준 것 같아요. 제가 여기서부 터 인수인계를 받게 되어서 매우 좋습니다.
여1 이안, 미란다한테 더 얘기할 것이 있나요?
남 아 네, 하나 더 있어요. 고객은 건설에 관한 모든 세부 사항에 대해서 서면 확인을 받기를 원해요. 그러니까 예를 들어서, 고객과 직접 내장재에 대해 논의를 했다면 그 후에 확인 이메일을 보내셔야 해요.
여2 와, 서류 작업이 엄청 많을 것 같네요. 하지만 알겠습니다. 그렇게 할게요. 그나저나 이안, 드디어 그렇게 필요했던 휴가를 가는군요, 그렇죠?
남 네, 내일 부모님을 뵈러 베를린으로 갑니다.

어휘 productive 생산적인  building design 건축 디자인  take over (업무 등) 인계하다  written confirmation 서면 확인  in person 직접  much-needed 매우 필요한  acquire 인수하다  target 목표

**59** What are the speakers mainly discussing?
(A) Changing the leader of a project
(B) Applying for a business loan
(C) Building an office complex
(D) Acquiring a target company

화자들은 무엇에 대해 이야기하는가?
(A) 프로젝트의 책임자를 바꾸는 것
(B) 기업 대출을 신청하는 것
(C) 사무실 단지를 건설하는 것
(D) 목표 회사를 인수하는 것

**60** What is Miranda advised to do?
(A) Negotiate a contract in person
(B) Report to a new manager
(C) Provide written confirmation
(D) Reduce construction costs

미란다는 무엇을 하라는 권고를 받는가?
(A) 직접 만나서 계약을 협상할 것
(B) 새 매니저에게 보고할 것
(C) 서면 확인을 제공할 것
(D) 건설 비용을 줄일 것

**61** What does the man say he will do tomorrow?
(A) Visit a construction site
(B) Go on a vacation
(C) Meet new colleagues
(D) Relocate to another country

남자는 내일 무엇을 할 것이라고 하는가?
(A) 건축 현장을 방문한다.
(B) 휴가를 떠난다.
(C) 새로운 동료를 만난다.
(D) 다른 나라로 이사한다.

---

Questions *62-64* refer to the following conversation and flight schedule. 미M 미W

| Arrivals | | |
|---|---|---|
| From | Status | Estimated Time |
| Moscow | Canceled | 7:00 |
| London | Delayed | 10:40 |
| Munich | On Time | 14:00 |
| Philadelphia | On Time | 15:30 |

M Joni, it looks like **62** Heidi's flight will be delayed for about an hour. **63** I just checked the airline's website.
W I know. A lot of incoming flights were canceled or delayed due to the heavy snowfall last night.
M Should we leave an hour later to pick her up then?
W Well, the traffic is also terrible today. **64** I heard that most of the roads are very slippery. So we ought to leave now. It's better to be early than late, right?
M That's right. Well, I'm ready to go now.

| 도착 | | |
|---|---|---|
| 출발지 | 상태 | 예상 시간 |
| 모스크바 | 취소 | 7:00 |
| 런던 | 지연 | 10:40 |
| 뮌헨 | 정시 도착 | 14:00 |
| 필라델피아 | 정시 도착 | 15:30 |

남 조니, 하이디의 비행기가 한 시간 정도 지연될 것 같은데요. 제가 방금 항공사 웹 사이트에서 확인했어요.
여 알아요. 많은 입국 항공편들이 어젯밤 폭설 때문에 취소되거나 지연되었어요.
남 그럼 그녀를 데리러 한 시간 늦게 출발해야 할까요?
여 음, 오늘은 교통 사정도 안 좋아요. 제가 듣기로는 대부분의 도로가 매우 미끄럽대요. 그러니까 지금 출발해야 해요. 늦는 것보다 이른 게 나으니까요, 그렇죠?
남 맞아요. 전 갈 준비 됐습니다.

**어휘** incoming 입국하는, 들어오는  snowfall 폭설  slippery 미끄러운  status 상태  slick road 미끄러운 도로

---

**62** Look at the graphic. Which city is Heidi traveling from?
(A) Moscow
(B) London
(C) Munich
(D) Philadelphia

시각 자료를 보시오. 하이디는 어느 도시로부터 여행을 오는가?
(A) 모스크바
(B) 런던
(C) 뮌헨
(D) 필라델피아

**63** How did the man learn about the schedule change?
(A) By calling an airline
(B) From a colleague
(C) Through a travel agency
(D) By checking it online

남자는 일정 변경에 대해 어떻게 알았는가?
(A) 항공사에 전화를 해서
(B) 동료로부터
(C) 여행사를 통해서
(D) 온라인으로 확인해서

패러프레이징 checked the airline's website → By checking it online

**64** According to the woman, why should the speakers leave now?
(A) The snow caused slick road conditions.
(B) More snow is expected in the evening.
(C) Several roads have been closed.
(D) An outdoor event is being held.

여자에 의하면, 화자들은 왜 지금 떠나야 하는가?
(A) 눈 때문에 미끄러운 도로가 되었다.
(B) 더 많은 눈이 저녁에 예상된다.
(C) 여러 도로가 폐쇄되었다.
(D) 야외 행사가 열리고 있다.

패러프레이징 roads are very slippery → slick road conditions

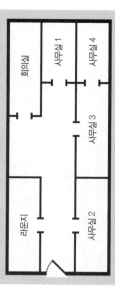

Lounge
Meeting Room
Office 2
Office 1
Office 3
Office 4

W  Hi, Mr. Kenney. Are you leaving the office now?

M  Yes, ⑱ I have a family gathering to go to tonight. What do you want?

W  I'm wondering if you could approve this room assignment before you leave. Here's the layout of our new offices.

M  Okay. It looks good to me. So the sales teams get to use Offices 2 and 3, am I right?

W  Yes. The two biggest rooms have been assigned to our sales people, and ⑲ your office will be the one next to the meeting room. I thought it would be convenient for you because you have a lot of meetings to attend all day long.

M  Okay, that'll work for me. Then your room must be the one in the corner.

W  Yes, that's right.

M  Everything looks good. ⑳ Will you let the sales staff know about the assignments tomorrow?

---

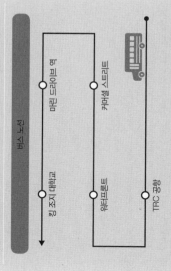

라운지
회의실
사무실 2
사무실 1
사무실 3
사무실 4

여  안녕하세요, 케니 씨. 지금 퇴근하시는 건가요?

남  네, 오늘 밤에 가족 모임이 있어서요. 뭐 필요한 게 있으세요?

여  가시기 전에 이 사무실 배정표를 승인해 주실 수 있나 해서요. 여기 우리의 새로운 사무실 배치도를 보세요.

남  좋아요. 저는 괜찮아 보이는데요. 영업팀이 사무실 2와 3을 쓰는 거죠, 맞나요?

여  네, 가장 큰 두 개의 방이 저희 영업 사원들에게 배정되었고, 당신의 사무실은 회의실 옆이 될 거예요. 하루 종일 참석해야 할 회의가 많으셔서 편리할 것 같다고 생각했어요.

남  좋네요. 그럼 당신의 방은 구석에 있는 거겠네요.

여  네, 맞아요.

남  모두 좋아 보이네요. 내일 영업 직원들에게 배정에 대해 알려주시겠어요?

---

어휘  get off (버스, 기차 등에서) 내리다  approach ~쪽으로 다가가다

**65** What does the woman ask the man about?
(A) Where to go shopping
(B) How much the bus fare is
(C) How to get to her destination
(D) When the next bus leaves

여자는 남자에게 무엇에 대해 묻는가?
(A) 어디로 쇼핑을 갈지
(B) 버스 요금이 얼마인지
(C) 여자의 목적지에 어떻게 가는지
(D) 다음 버스가 언제 떠나는지

**66** Look at the graphic. Which stop will the woman get off at?
(A) Marine Drive Station
(B) Commercial Street
(C) Waterfront
(D) TRC Airport

시각 자료를 보시오. 여자는 어떤 정류장에서 내릴 것인가?
(A) 마린 드라이브 역
(B) 커머셜 스트리트
(C) 워터프론트
(D) TRC 공항

**67** According to the man, how long does it take to walk to the shopping mall?
(A) 5 minutes
(B) 10 minutes
(C) 15 minutes
(D) 30 minutes

남자에 따르면, 쇼핑몰까지 걸어가는 데 얼마나 걸리는가?
(A) 5분
(B) 10분
(C) 15분
(D) 30분

---

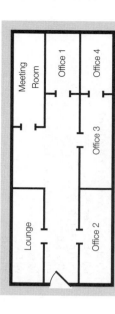

**Bus Route**

Marine Drive Station
King George University
Commercial Street
Waterfront
TRC Airport

W  Excuse me. I'm trying to get to Hastings Shopping Mall. ⑮ Do you know which stop I should get off at?

M  Yes. Let me see… ⑯ We're approaching Waterfront right now. And the next stop is the one where you get off. I can't remember the name of the stop but I'm sure because I catch this bus a lot.

W  Oh, thank you very much for your help.

M  No problem. Once you get off, you can either take a taxi or just walk there. ⑰ It's a 15 minute walk from the stop to the mall. And by taxi, it only takes 5 minutes.

---

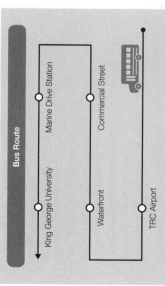

버스 노선

마린 드라이브 역
킹 조지 대학교
커머셜 스트리트
워터프론트
TRC 공항

여  실례합니다. 제가 헤이스팅스 쇼핑몰에 가려고 하는데요. 어느 정류장에서 내려야 하는지 아세요?

남  네. 그러니까… 우리가 지금 워터프론트에 다 와가고 있어요. 그리고 다음 이 정류장이 내려야 할 정류장입니다. 이름이 잘 생각이 안 나지만 이 버스를 많이 타기 때문에 확실합니다.

여  오, 도와주셔서 정말 감사합니다.

남  아니에요. 일단 내리면, 택시를 타거나 걸어서 가시면 됩니다. 정류장에서 쇼핑몰까지 걸어서 15분이에요. 택시를 타면 5분밖에 안 걸리고요.

## PART 4

Questions 71-73 refer to the following advertisement. 영W

⑦ Does your office need a new look? Contact Cranston Office Services. Brad Cranston and his partners are acknowledged for their ergonomic and space-saving designs. ⑦ ⑦ This week only, we are offering a 25% discount on a comprehensive refurbishment of three rooms or more, plus a free initial consultation. ⑦ This offer is good only until the end of the week, so pick up the phone now and call Cranston at 555-1221.

당신의 사무실에 새로운 외관이 필요한가요? 크랜스톤 오피스 서비스에 연락하세요. 브래드 크랜스톤과 그의 파트너들은 인체 공학적이고 공간을 절약하는 디자인으로 인정받고 있습니다. 이번 주에만, 저희는 세 개 이상의 방 전체 수리에 대해 25퍼센트 할인과 함께 무료 첫 상담을 제공합니다. 이 할인은 이번 주말 동안만 이용할 수 있으니 지금 전화기를 들고 555-1221, 크랜스톤으로 전화하세요.

**어휘** acknowledge 인정하다  ergonomic 인체 공학적인  space-saving 공간 절약의  comprehensive 종합적인  refurbishment 수리, 재단장  initial 처음의, 최초의  good 유효한  relocate 이전하다

**71** What is being advertised?
(A) A cleaning company
**(B) A refurbishment service**
(C) A furniture shop
(D) A real estate agency

광고되고 있는 것은 무엇인가?
(A) 청소 회사
**(B) 개조 공사 서비스**
(C) 가구점
(D) 부동산 중개업체

**72** How can customers receive a discount?
(A) By entering a discount code online
(B) By presenting a membership card
(C) By recommending a new customer
**(D) By renovating at least three rooms**

고객들이 할인을 받을 수 있는 방법은 무엇인가?
(A) 온라인에서 할인 코드 입력
(B) 회원 카드 제시
(C) 새로운 고객 추천
**(D) 세 개 이상의 방 수리**

**어휘** refurbishment → renovating  a comprehensive refurbishment → renovating

**73** According to the speaker, what will happen at the end of the week?
(A) A business will relocate.
(B) Additional services will be available.
**(C) A special offer will end.**
(D) A new design will be launched.

화자에 따르면, 이번 주말에 어떤 일이 일어날 것인가?
(A) 업체가 이전할 것이다.
(B) 추가 서비스가 이용 가능할 것이다.
**(C) 특별 판매가 끝날 것이다.**
(D) 새로운 디자인이 출시될 것이다.

Questions 74-76 refer to the following announcement. 호M

⑦ ⑦ Welcome to our 3rd biannual international fair. This year, we have invited publishers and authors from all around the world, from Europe and Asia to Africa and America. We have more than 150 booths opening in the convention center, and hotels near the convention center will hold a variety of events related to this fair. As part of an opening night event, you will receive complimentary mugs and bookmarks. Also, ⑦ if you fill out the back of your admission ticket and put it in the box at the entrance, we will hold a drawing and give prizes such as bookstore gift cards and movie tickets. Check out the details on the back of your tickets.

매년 2번째 열리는 국제 박람회가 세 번째를 맞았습니다. 올해 저희는 유럽, 아시아부터 아프리카, 미국까지 전 세계 출판업자와 저자들을 모셨습니다. 저희는 컨벤션 센터에 150개가 넘는 부스 자리를 마련하고 있으며 컨벤션 센터 근처의 호텔들은 박람회와 관련된 다양한 행사를 개최할 것입니다. 개막일 저녁 행사의 일부로 귀하께서 무료 머그컵과 책갈피를 드립니다. 또한, 입장권 뒷면을 기입하셔서 입구에 있는 박스에 넣으면 추첨을 통해 서점 상품권과 영화 티켓과 같은 선물도 드립니다. 티켓 뒷면의 상세 내용을 확인하세요.

**어휘** biannual 1년에 2번씩  fair 박람회, 전시회  publisher 출판업자  variety of 다양한  bookmark 책갈피  drawing 뽑기

**74** What event is most likely being held?
**(A) A book fair**
(B) A movie preview
(C) A job fair
(D) An international conference on marketing

어떤 행사가 열리는가?
**(A) 도서전**
(B) 영화 시사회
(C) 취업 박람회
(D) 국제 마케팅 회의

---

여  네, 가장 큰 사무실 2개가 영업팀을 위해 배정되었고 캐나 씨의 방은 회의실과 같은 열이 될 거예요. 하루 종일 회의 참석할 일이 많으셔서 그 코너에 있는 방이 되겠어요.
남  네, 그게 좋겠어요. 그럼 당신의 방은 코너에 있는 방이 됩니다.
여  네, 맞아요.
남  모든 게 좋아 보이네요. 내일 영업부 직원들에게 배치에 대해 알려 주실 수 있나요?

**어휘** gathering 모임  approve 승인하다  assignment 배정  layout 배치도  assign 배정하다  all day long 하루 종일  function 행사

**68** What does the man say he will do tonight?
(A) Assign employees new tasks
(B) Design a building
**(C) Attend a family function**
(D) Prepare for a presentation

남자는 오늘 밤에 무엇을 할 것이라고 하는가?
(A) 직원들에게 새 업무를 배정한다.
(B) 빌딩을 설계한다.
**(C) 가족 행사에 참석한다.**
(D) 프레젠테이션을 준비한다.

**패러프레이징** have a family gathering → Attend a family function

**69** Look at the graphic. Which office has been assigned to the man?
**(A) Office 1**
(B) Office 2
(C) Office 3
(D) Office 4

시각 자료를 보시오. 남자에게 어떤 사무실이 배정되었는가?
**(A) 사무실 1**
(B) 사무실 2
(C) 사무실 3
(D) 사무실 4

**70** What does the man ask the woman to do tomorrow?
(A) Hire a moving company
**(B) Inform the sales staff of the assignments**
(C) Attend an anniversary celebration
(D) Give a product demonstration

남자는 여자에게 내일 무엇을 하라고 하는가?
(A) 이사 회사를 고용할 것
**(B) 영업 직원에게 배치에 대해 알릴 것**
(C) 기념일 행사에 참석할 것
(D) 제품 시연을 할 것

**75** According to the speaker, how often is this event held?

(A) Once a year
**(B) Twice a year**
(C) Three times a year
(D) Every three years

화자에 따르면 이 행사는 얼마나 자주 열리는가?
(A) 1년에 한 번
**(B) 1년에 두 번**
(C) 1년에 세 번
(D) 3년마다

패러프레이징 biannual → Twice a year

**76** To have a chance to win the presents, what should the listeners do?

(A) Call the number announced
(B) Buy mugs or bookmarks
(C) Come to the entrance
**(D) Put their tickets in the drawing box**

선물을 탈 수 있는 기회가 있으려면 어떻게 해야 하는가?
(A) 공지된 번호로 전화하기
(B) 머그잔이나 책갈피 사기
(C) 입구로 오기
**(D) 추첨함에 티켓 넣기**

Questions 77-79 refer to the following telephone message. 미M

Hi, It's Gerald. **77** I was wondering if you could meet with the interior designer for me tomorrow morning. **78** We still need to choose a paint color for the walls, but I have another meeting with the event planner at 10. I can't believe the grand opening is in just 7 days. **79** The planner emailed me some ideas for the opening ceremony. So I'll forward them to you right now. After you review them, please give me your opinion. I think we have to decide on the type of event and a budget at tomorrow's meeting. Thanks!

안녕하세요, 제라드예요. 내일 아침에 저 대신 인테리어 디자이너를 만날 수 있나요? 벽에 칠할 페인트 색상을 결정해야 하는데 저는 이벤트 기획자와 또 다른 회의가 10시에 있거든요. 우리 개장일이 일주일 후라는 게 믿기지 않네요. 기획자가 오프닝 행사를 위한 아이디어들을 이메일로 보내왔어요. 그래서 지금 바로 당신에게도 전달하려고 해요. 살펴본 후에 의견 주세요. 내일 회의 때 행사의 종류와 예산을 결정해야만 할 것 같아요. 감사합니다.

어휘 event planner 행사 기획자 forward ~을 전달하다 budget 예산 venue 장소

**77** What is the purpose of the message?

(A) To make a suggestion
(B) To postpone a meeting
(C) To confirm an order
**(D) To ask a favor**

메시지의 목적은 무엇인가?
(A) 제안을 하려고
(B) 회의를 미루려고
(C) 주문을 확인하려고
**(D) 부탁을 하려고**

**78** What does the speaker imply when he says, "the grand opening is in just seven days"?

**(A) He needs to make fast decisions.**
(B) He wants to reschedule an event.
(C) The listener should reserve a venue.
(D) A project is ahead of schedule.

화자가 "개장일이 일주일 후라고"라고 말한 의도는 무엇인가?
**(A) 빠른 결정을 내려야 한다.**
(B) 행사 일정을 바꿔야 한다.
(C) 청자는 장소를 예약해야 한다.
(D) 프로젝트는 일정보다 빠르게 진행되고 있다.

**79** What most likely will the speaker do next?

**(A) Send the listener some information**
(B) Meet with an event planner
(C) Contact some suppliers
(D) Revise a budget plan

화자는 다음에 무엇을 할 것 같은가?
**(A) 청자에게 정보를 보낸다.**
(B) 행사 기획자를 만난다.
(C) 공급업체에 연락한다.
(D) 예산 계획을 수정한다.

Questions 80-82 refer to the following radio broadcast. 영W

This afternoon on SLTW radio's literary hour, we are discussing the latest bestsellers in the Root Booklist. **80** This booklist celebrates its twentieth anniversary this year and to mark this special celebration, a special lifetime achievement award has been presented. **81** We will be joined in the studio by the recipient of this award, bestselling author, Anders Petersen who has written more than 50 novels. **82** We will be talking to him about his prolific career and **82** we will be giving away copies of his latest book to the first five callers. Call us now at 800-292-2288.

오늘 오후 SLTW 라디오 문학의 시간에 저희는 루트 북리스트의 최신 베스트셀러에 대해 토론할 것입니다. 이 북리스트는 올해로 20주년을 기리는 것으로, 이 특별 기념 행사를 축하하기 위해 특별 공로상이 수여되었습니다. 저희는 50권 이상의 소설을 쓴 이 상의 수상자인 베스트셀러 작가, 앤더스 페터슨을 스튜디오에 모실 것입니다. 저희는 그의 다작의 경력에 관하여 그의 얘기가 나올 것이며, 전화를 주시는 선착순 다섯 분에게 그분의 최신작을 무료로 드립니다. 지금 800–292–2288로 전화 주세요.

어휘 literary 문학의, 문학적인　booklist 서적 일람표, 북리스트　anniversary 기념일　mark 기념하다, 축하하다　lifetime achievement award 공로상　recipient 수령인　prolific 다작하는　give away 무료로 나눠 주다　distribute 배포하다, 전파하다　enter 접어들다, 진입하다　broadcast 방송하다　excerpt 발췌, 인용　win 획득하다

**80** Why is this year's booklist special?

(A) It is distributed free of charge.
**(B) It is entering its twentieth year.**
(C) It will be broadcast live on the radio.
(D) It is recommended by well-known authors.

올해의 북리스트가 특별한 이유는 무엇인가?
(A) 무료로 배포된다.
**(B) 20번째 해에 접어든다.**
(C) 라디오에서 라이브로 방송될 것이다.
(D) 유명 작가들이 추천한다.

**81** What will listeners hear next?

**(A) An interview**
(B) A news bulletin
(C) An award announcement
(D) An excerpt from a book

청자들은 다음에 무엇을 듣게 될 것인가?
**(A) 인터뷰**
(B) 뉴스 단신
(C) 수상자 발표
(D) 책의 발췌문

**82** Why should listeners call the station?
(A) To become a member
**(B) To win a free book**
(C) To purchase tickets
(D) To talk to a guest
청자들이 방송국에 전화해야 하는 이유는 무엇인가?
(A) 회원이 되려고
**(B) 무료 책을 받으려고**
(C) 티켓을 구매하려고
(D) 게스트와 얘기하려고
패러프레이징 giving away copies → win a free book

Questions 83-85 refer to the following telephone message. 호M

Hi, Ms. Silber. It's Fredrick. ⑧ I know you're not on duty today, but there's a problem here at the factory. We have hundreds of orders to ship today, but the delivery truck hasn't arrived yet. As you know, the driver always gets here by 7, but it's almost 9 A.M. now. ⑧ I already tried calling the delivery company, but no one answered. I just don't know what to do. Please call me back as soon as you get this message. Thank you.

안녕하세요, 실버 씨. 저는 프레드릭입니다. 오늘 근무가 아닌 건 알지만 공장에 문제가 생겼어요. 오늘 배송해야 할 주문이 수백 개인데 배달 트럭이 아직 도착하지 않았어요. 아시다시피 기사가 항상 7시까지는 여기 오는데 지금 오전 9시가 다 되었어요. 이미 배송 업체에 전화를 해봤지만 아무도 받지 않았어요. 전 어떻게 해야 할지 모르겠어요. 이 메시지를 받자마자 전화해 주세요. 감사합니다.

어휘 on duty 근무인 fill an order 주문을 처리하다

**83** Where most likely does the speaker work?
(A) At an office supply company
(B) At a restaurant
**(C) At a manufacturing plant**
(D) At a delivery company
화자는 어디에서 일할 것 같은가?
(A) 사무용품 회사
(B) 레스토랑
**(C) 생산 공장**
(D) 배달 회사

**84** What is the problem?
(A) Some equipment is out of order.
(B) An invoice was sent incorrectly.
**(C) A delivery vehicle is not available.**
(D) Some orders haven't been filled.
무엇이 문제인가?
(A) 기계가 고장났다.
(B) 청구서가 잘못 발송되었다.
**(C) 배달 차량이 이용 불가능하다.**
(D) 일부 주문이 처리되지 않았다.
패러프레이징 the delivery truck → A delivery vehicle

**85** What does the speaker mean when he says, "I just don't know what to do"?
(A) He cannot respond to an inquiry.
(B) He needs more training.
**(C) The situation is very serious.**
(D) More employees should be hired.
남자가 "전 어떻게 해야 할지 모르겠어요"라고 말한 의미는 무엇인가?
(A) 그는 문의에 답할 수 없다.
(B) 그는 훈련이 더 필요하다.
**(C) 상황이 매우 심각하다.**
(D) 직원이 더 고용되어야 한다.

Questions 86-88 refer to the following announcement. 영W

Before we start today's work, ⑧ I'd like to let you know a few changes to our menu. Today's special is black cod instead of lobster. ⑧ They were caught in the Atlantic Ocean and freshly transported to our restaurant. Please emphasize this point. And ⑧ please do not take orders for clam chowder since we do not have enough clams for the soup today. Also, for the dessert, please recommend our new triple chocolate mousse cake. Tell the customers we imported the finest chocolate from Belgium for this cake. OK. That's about it. Now let's go!

오늘 업무를 시작하기 전에 메뉴에 관해 몇 가지 변화를 알려 드리겠습니다. 오늘의 특별 메뉴는 랍스터 대신 검정 대구 요리입니다. 대서양에서 잡아 신선하게 우리 식당까지 갖고 왔습니다. 이 점을 강조해 주세요. 그리고 오늘 수프에 넣을 대합이 충분치 않아서 클램 차우더 주문을 받지 말아 주세요. 또 디저트는 새로운 트리플 초콜릿 무스 케이크를 추천해 주세요. 고객들에게 이 케이크에 넣을 최상의 초콜릿을 벨기에에서 수입했다는 것도 말씀해 주시고요. 그럼 됐습니다. 자, 시작하죠!

어휘 black cod 은대구 Atlantic Ocean 대서양 transport 수송하다 clam 대합조개 fine 훌륭한 좋은 safety precaution 안전 예방책

**86** Who is this announcement intended for?
(A) Customers
(B) Chefs
**(C) Waiters and waitresses**
(D) Fishermen
누구에게 공지를 하고 있는가?
(A) 고객
(B) 요리사
**(C) 웨이터와 웨이트리스**
(D) 어부

**87** Why is this announcement being made?
(A) To encourage listeners to sell more products
**(B) To describe updates to the restaurant's menu**
(C) To ensure safety precautions are followed
(D) To advertise a new restaurant
왜 이 공지를 하는가?
(A) 청자들이 더 많은 제품을 팔도록 장려하려고
**(B) 식당의 메뉴에 대한 최신 정보를 얘기하려고**
(C) 안전 규정을 꼭 지키도록 하려고
(D) 새 식당을 광고하려고
패러프레이징 a few changes → updates

**88** What would the listeners mention to the customers about today's special?
(A) It was imported from Belgium.
(B) Its price went up.
**(C) It is fresh.**
(D) It was caught in the Pacific.
청자들이 오늘의 특별 메뉴에 대해 고객들에게 말할 내용은 무엇인가?
(A) 벨기에에서 수입했다.
(B) 가격이 올랐다.
**(C) 신선하다.**
(D) 태평양에서 잡혔다.

Questions 89-91 refer to the following telephone message. 미W

Hello, Alfonso. ⑧ This is a message from Huntington Resort regarding the corporate hospitality event you booked online recently. A problem has arisen. The confirmation and details were sent to the e-mail address you provided, ⑩ but we have just received notification that the e-mail was not delivered. It seems that your account is no longer active. As the event is the day after tomorrow, I am telephoning you to confirm your attendance. ⑨ You can call me back to confirm. If you call the Resort number listed and ask for extension 334, you will come straight through to me and I will give you the relevant information.

안녕하세요, 알폰소 씨. 귀하께서 최근에 온라인으로 예약하신 회사 접대 행사에 관하여 헌팅턴 리조트에서 드리는 메시지입니다. 문제가 하나 발생했는데요. 확인 및 세부 사항을 귀하께서 알려 주신 이메일 주소로 보냈으나 저희가 방금 이 메일이 전달되지 않았다는 통지를 받았습니다. 귀하의 계정이 더 이상 활성화되어 있지 않은 것 같습니다. 행사가 내일 모레이기 때문에 귀하가 오시는지 확인 하고자 전화드립니다. 확인을 위해 다시 전화 주시면 됩니다. 기재된 리조트 번호로 전화하셔서 내선 334번을 요청하시면, 제게 바로 연결되며 제가 관련 정보 를 알려드리겠습니다.

**어휘** regarding ~에 관하여  hospitality 환대; 접대  active 활성화된  유효한  relevant 관련된  incorrect 부정확한  misplace 찾지 못하다

**89** Where is the speaker calling from?
(A) A post office
(B) A movie theater
(C) A travel agency
(D) **A hospitality venue**

화자는 어디에서 전화하고 있나?
(A) 우체국
(B) 영화관
(C) 여행사
(D) **접대 장소**

**90** What caused the problem?
(A) A telephone number was incorrect.
(B) A payment was not made.
(C) **An e-mail account was inactive.**
(D) An order form was misplaced.

무엇이 문제를 야기시켰나?
(A) 전화번호가 틀렸다.
(B) 돈이 지불되지 않았다.
(C) **이메일 계정이 활성화되어 있지 않았다.**
(D) 주문서가 분실되었다.

**91** What is the listener advised to do?
(A) Provide a receipt
(B) **Make a call**
(C) Review a contract
(D) Pick up tickets in person

청자가 권고받은 것은 무엇인가?
(A) 영수증 발급하기
(B) **전화하기**
(C) 계약서 검토하기
(D) 티켓 직접 찾아가기

---

**94** What does the speaker suggest?
(A) Redesigning a website
(B) Hiring an industry expert
(C) **Renovating a facility**
(D) Moving to another location

화자는 무엇을 제안하는가?
(A) 웹 사이트를 재설계하는 것
(B) 업계 전문가를 고용하는 것
(C) **시설물을 보수하는 것**
(D) 다른 곳으로 이전하는 것

---

Questions 92-94 refer to the following excerpt from a meeting.
`9W`

**92** Thank you for attending today's board meeting on such short notice. As you all know, we had the lowest earnings ever last year. Despite our efforts to attract meetings and conventions, business at our convention center has decreased dramatically in just a year. And to make the problem even worse, construction of a new convention center has been approved. So it's about time we adopt more aggressive marketing strategies. I know it's a tough call, but **93 94** we need to invest more money in facility renovations at this point to attract more business. As a member of the board, I ask for your support.

감작스러운 공지에도 오늘의 이사회에 참석해 주셔서 감사합니다. 모두 아시듯이, 우리는 작년에 역대 최저의 수익을 기록했습니다. 회의와 컨벤션을 유치하려는 노력에도 불구하고, 우리 컨벤션 센터의 사업은 단 일 년 동안 급격하게 줄어들었습니다. 그리고 설상가상으로 새로운 컨벤션 건축이 승인이 났습니다. 그래서 이제 좀 더 공격적인 마케팅 전략을 취할 때입니다. 어려운 결정이긴 하지만 더 많은 계약을 유치하기 위해 이 시점에서 더 많은 돈을 시설물 보수에 투자해야 합니다. 이사회의 일원으로서, 여러분의 지지를 부탁드립니다.

**어휘** on such short notice 갑작스러운 통보에도  attract 유치하다  earnings 수익  dramatically 급격히  adopt 취하다  aggressive 공격적인  despite ~에도 불구하고

**92** Who most likely are the listeners?
(A) Career counselors
(B) Construction workers
(C) Potential investors
(D) **Board members**

청자들은 누구일 것 같은가?
(A) 직업 상담사
(B) 공사 인부
(C) 잠재 투자자
(D) **임원**

**93** What does the speaker imply when she says, "I know it's a tough call"?
(A) An increase in local tourism is expected.
(B) **It will be a difficult decision for listeners.**
(C) Construction noise will bother customers.
(D) There will be more job opportunities

화자가 "어려운 결정인건 알지만"라고 말한 의도는 무엇인가?
(A) 지역 관광의 증가가 예상된다.
(B) **청자들에게 어려운 결정일 것이다.**
(C) 공사 소음이 고객들에게 불편을 줄 것이다.
(D) 더 많은 일자리가 생길 것이다.

---

Questions 95-97 refer to the following instructions and flowchart.
`9M`

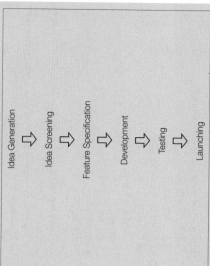

Before we begin today's meeting, I'd like to share some good news. **95** Our new smartphone, the Silverstar 7, has been the bestseller among all our competing lines of mobile phones. **96** Customers seem to really like the exterior design of our new product. It's all because of your hard work in product development. Now, let me explain our revised product development process. Does everyone have a copy of this flowchart? Okay. As you can see, **97** a new step has been added between idea screening and development. At this new stage, detailed specifications for the product and its pricing need to be approved by the executive board. I'm sure this new process will help us work more efficiently.

**알라모 스테이크 하우스**
점심 & 저녁
**10% 할인**

이미 단체 할인을 받은 경우 사용 불가능. 3월 31일까지 사용 가능

안녕하세요, 크리스예요. 우리가 한 씨를 위해 준비하고 있는 승진 파티에 관해 전화합니다. 사무실에서 35명이 오기로 했다는 걸을 들으니 기쁩니다. 이제 알라모 스테이크하우스와 단체 할인에 대해 협상해 볼 수 있겠어요. 제가 알기로 는 그들은 30명 이상의 단체에 대해 최소 20퍼센트 할인을 해주거든요. 그렇지만 안타깝게도 그 레스토랑에서 받은 할인 쿠폰은 못 쓰게 되겠네요. 그리고 타 샤가 동료들에게 돈을 걷어서 한 씨를 위한 선물을 사 올 거예요. 아, 한 가지만 더요, 혹시 카메라 가지고 올 수 있으세요?

0어휘 negotiate 협상하다, 성사시키다 valid 유효한 expiration date 만기일

98  What kind of event is being organized?
(A) A retirement party
(B) A holiday party
**(C) A promotion party**
(D) A theme party

어떤 종류의 행사가 준비되고 있는가?
(A) 은퇴 파티
(B) 연휴 파티
**(C) 승진 파티**
(D) 테마 파티

99  Look at the graphic. Why is the speaker unable to use the coupon for the event?
**(A) The coupon cannot be used with a group discount.**
(B) The venue of the event has been changed.
(C) The restaurant went out of business.
(D) The event will take place after the expiration date.

시각 자료를 보시오. 왜 화자는 쿠폰을 쓸 수 없는가?
**(A) 쿠폰은 단체 할인과 함께 쓸 수 없다.**
(B) 행사의 장소가 변경되었다.
(C) 레스토랑이 폐업했다.
(D) 행사는 쿠폰 만기일 이후에 열리게 된다.

100  What does the speaker ask the listener to do?
(A) Buy a present
(B) Order invitation cards
**(C) Bring a camera**
(D) Hire a band

---

(C) Its new function
(D) Its durability

회자에 의하면, 고객들은 이 신상품의 무엇을 좋아하는가?
**(A) 외형**
(B) 가격
(C) 새 기능
(D) 내구성

0어휘 메뉴프레이징 the exterior design → appearance

97  Look at the graphic. Which step has been added recently?
(A) Idea generation
(B) Idea screening
**(C) Feature specification**
(D) Development

시각 자료를 보시오. 최근에 어떤 단계가 추가되었는가?
(A) 아이디어 생산
(B) 아이디어 검사
**(C) 제품 주요 사항**
(D) 개발

Questions 98-100 refer to the following telephone message and coupon. 호M

**Alamo Steakhouse**
Lunch & Dinner
**10% OFF**

Not valid with already discounted group rates. Valid through March 31.

Hi. It's Chris. 98 I'm calling about the promotion party that we're organizing for Ms. Han. I'm glad to hear that thirty-five people from the office are coming because now I can negotiate a group discount with Alamo Steakhouse. As far as I know, 99 they offer at least a 20% discount for a group of thirty people or more. 99 But unfortunately, we won't be able to use the discount coupon from the restaurant. I'm also letting you know that Tasha will collect money from colleagues and buy a present for Ms. Han. Oh, just one more thing, 100 do you think you can bring your camera with you?

---

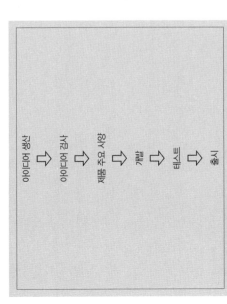

아이디어 생산
⇩
아이디어 검사
⇩
제품 주요 사항
⇩
개발
⇩
테스트
⇩
출시

오늘 회의를 시작하기 전에 좋은 소식을 전하고 싶습니다. 우리의 새 스마트폰 실버스타 7이 우리의 경쟁 스마트폰 사이에서 가장 잘 팔리는 모델이 되었습니 다. 고객들이 우리 신상품의 외형 디자인을 매우 좋아하는 것 같아요. 모두 상품 개발 부서에 있는 여러분들이 열심히 일해준 덕분입니다. 자 이제, 수정된 상품 개발 절차를 설명하도록 할게요. 다음 이 업무 절차표를 한 번씩 갖고 있지요? 좋습니다. 보시다시피, 새로운 단계가 아이디어 검사와 상품 개발 사이에 추가가 되었습니다. 이 새로운 단계에서 세부적인 상품 사양과 가격이 인정되어 의해 승 인되어야 합니다. 이 새로운 과정이 우리가 더 효율적으로 일할 수 있도록 도와줄 것입니다.

0어휘 competing 경쟁하는 exterior 외형의 product development 상품 개발 (부서) flowchart 업무 절차표 screening (걸맞은 것 등을 걸러내는) 검사 specifications (상품의) 사양, 세부 정보 executive board 임원 진 feature 특징으로 다루다 appearance 외형, 겉모습 durability 내구 성

95  What does the speaker say about the Silverstar 7?
(A) It was featured in a technology magazine.
**(B) It has sold better than competing products.**
(C) It has won a design award.
(D) It is the cheapest model on the market.

화자는 실버스타 7에 대해 뭐라고 하는가?
(A) 기술 잡지에 특징으로 실렸다.
**(B) 경쟁 제품들보다 잘 팔린다.**
(C) 디자인 상을 받았다.
(D) 시장에 나온 것 중 가장 싼 모델이다.

96  According to the speaker, what do customers like about the new product?
**(A) Its appearance**
(B) Its price

회자는 장기에게 무엇을 해달라고 하는가?
(A) 선물을 살 것
(B) 초대장을 주문할 것
**(C) 캐러리를 가져갈 것**
(D) 밴드를 고용할 것

## PART 5

P194

**101 해석** 7월 1일 정기적인 점검 때문에 오후 1시에서 5시까지 회사 사이트의 접속이 끊기는 것을 모든 직원들은 알고 있어야 한다.
**해설** 빈칸 뒤에 명사구가 나왔으므로 접속사가 올 수 없다. in case, in that, while은 뒤에 (주어+동사)를 갖춘 절이 나와야 하므로 답이 될 수 없다. 명사구를 받을 수 있는 (C) due to가 정답이다.
**어휘** be advised that ~을 알고 있다, 유의하다 be off-line 접속이 끊기다 scheduled 예정된 maintenance 점검

**102 해석** 외국 투자자들과 오늘 회의는 약간 지연되었지만 곧 시작될 것이다.
**해설** 빈칸이 있는 문장의 시제는 미래 시제이다. 선택지 중에 미래 시제일 때 쓸 수 있는 부사는 (A) shortly뿐이다. 이와 비슷하게 미래 시제일 때 쓸 수 있는 부사로 soon이 있다. (B) 거의 / (D) 공손하게
**어휘** invertor 투자자 be delayed 지연되다 a bit 약간 shortly 곧

**103 해석** 작동하는 서류가 없이는 운전면허증을 받을 수 없습니다.
**해설** 빈칸에 적절한 서류가 없이는 운전면허증을 발급받을 수 없다는 게 자연스러우므로 (D)가 정답이다. 전치사인 without 뒤에는 명사(이나 동명사)가 와야 한다.
**어휘** driver's license 운전면허증 proper 적절한, 알맞은 document 서류

**104 해석** 귀하의 컴퓨터가 보증 기간 내에 고장이 날 경우에는 환불이나 제품 교환 모델을 위해 저희 고객 서비스 부서에 연락해 주세요.
**해설** 문맥상 컴퓨터가 고장이 났을 때 환불이나 교환을 위해 그 객 서비스 부서에 연락하라는 의미가 자연스러우므로 (D)가 정답이다. (B) 불평, 불만 / (C) 승진, 만족
**어휘** malfunction 제대로 작동하지 않다 under warranty 보증 기간 이내에 inquire about 문의하다 replacement 교환, 교체

**105 해석** 매트리스는 건강적으로 말하는 경향이 있어서 매트리스 그녀의 정확한 메시지를 확인하는 것이 필요하다.
**해설** 문맥상 그녀는 생각을 '건강적으로' 말하는 경향이 있다는 의미가 자연스러우므로 (C)가 정답이다. 정확한 메시지가 필요한 이유를 유추하면 쉽게 정답을 찾을 수 있다. (A) 중심적으로 / (B) 거의 / (D) 서로, 상호 간에
**어휘** tendency 경향 confirmation 확인 exact 정확한

**106 해석** 교수들이 그들의 학생들이 휴식 후에 더 재충전되어 보고했으므로 그 대학의 봄방학 도입은 매우 유익하다고 증명되었다.
**해설** as절에서 휴식의 이점에 대해 말하고 있으므로 대학교에 봄 방학이 도입된 것은 '유익한' 것이라는 의미의 (C)가 정답이다. (A) 접근하기 쉬운 / (B) 풍부한 / (D) 알룸 수 있는, 뜨렷한
**어휘** refresh 생기를 되찾다, 재충전하다 introduction 도입 surprisingly 놀랍게 믿을 만큼, 대단히 beneficial 이로운

**107 해석** 시장은 국제 연금 시스템에 관한 연설 후 질문들에 대답하기 위해 기자 회견을 열 것이다.
**해설** 문맥상 그의 연설 '후에' 기자 회견을 열 것이라는 의미가 적절하므로 (C)가 정답이다. (A) except는 전치사 for가 뒤에 붙어 '~을 제외하고'의 의미로 쓰이며 (D) at은 장소 앞에 쓰인다.
**어휘** press conference 기자 회견 pension 연금

**108 해석** 워크숍에 연설가 중 한 분은 우리 회사 부서장님이시고 다른 한 분은 무역 부서의 공무원이다.
**해설** '~ 중 한 명'이라는 의미로 적절한 것은 (D) One이다. (one of the+복수 명사+단수 동사)는 토익에서 자주 나오는 문제이며, 수의 일치를 물어볼 때도 있다.
**어휘** vice president 부사장 government official 관리, 국가 공무원 trade 무역

**109 해석** 우리는 지금 트랜스텔 커뮤니케이션즈 사와 우리 경제 뉴스 프로그램의 전국적인 보급에 대해 협상 중이다.
**해설** 빈칸 앞에 형용사 national이 있기 때문에 빈칸에는 명사가 와야 하고 '보급'이라는 의미의 (A)가 정답이다. (C) 배당금사 / (D) 문제업자
**어휘** be in negotiation with ~와 협상 중이다 distribution 문배, 배급

**110 해석** 체이스 씨는 자녀들에게 성인기를 준비하기 위해 그들 스스로 마지막 학기 등록금을 내게끔 권한다고 알렸다.
**해설** 선택지가 모두 재귀대명사이므로 앞에 있는 재귀대명사를 고르는 문제이다. 빈칸의 oneself의 주체는 them(=his children)이기 때문에 (D) themselves를 써야 한다. 최근 몇 년간 재귀대명사의 관용적 표현은 by oneself라는 의미로, '혼자서, 스스로'라는 숙어로 출제되고 있으므로 참고하자.
**어휘** inform 통지하다, 알리다 semester 학기 tuition fee 등록금 prepare 준비하다 adulthood 성인(기)

**111 해석** 오나타 레지던시스 사는 테니스 코트, 수영장, 헬스장이 완비된 조용한 지역에 위치하고 있다.
**해설** 문맥상 테니스 코트, 수영장, 헬스장이 '완비된' 조용한 단지가 적절한 의미로 (D)가 정답이다.
**어휘** complete with ~이 완비된

**112 해석** 히타 같은 활동용 기기들은 수명을 연장시키기 위해 정기적인 검사를 받아야 한다.

**113 해석** 문맥상 기기의 수명을 '연장시키기' 위해서는 정기적인 검사를 해야 한 다는 의미가 적절하므로 (A)가 정답이다. (B) enlarge는 '크게 하다'의 뜻이며 사진을 확대하다, 처음 증폭하다 등으로 쓰인다. (C) 참다 / (D) 고정하다, 주장하다
**어휘** appliance 기기 undergo 받다, 겪다 prolong 연장하다

**113 해석** 정기적으로 예정됐던 점검 때문에 그 클래규스터의 탐승은 추후 통지가 있을 때까지 중단되었다.
**해설** 문맥상 추후 통지가 있을 때까지 중단됐다는 의미가 적절하므로 (A)가 정답이다. until further notice는 '추후 통지가 있을 때까지'라는 의미이며, 토익에 자주 나오므로 알아 두자.
**어휘** regularly 정기적으로 ride 승차, 탑승 be halted 중단되다

**114 해석** 그 교과서 자료의 일부는 매우 반복적이기 때문에 그 교수는 특정한 색션을 생략했다.
**해설** 형용사를 보어로 취하는 be동사가 있기 때문에 빈칸에는 형용사가 와야 하므로 (C)가 정답이다. (B) 되풀이, 반복
**어휘** material 자료 repetitive 반복적인 certain 특정한

**115 해석** 그 회사의 회의에는 유명한 동기부여 연설자의 발표가 포함되어 있기 때문에 많은 직원들이 참석하고 싶어 했다.
**해설** 출석률이 좋을 수밖에 없는 이유가 먼저 나와 있으므로 well이 적절하며 much와 well은 과거분사 앞에 위치하는데 여기서는 attended를 수식하고 있으므로 (B)가 정답이다.
**어휘** renowned 유명한 motivational 동기를 부여하는

**116 해석** 보드 알리 씨는 식당의 메뉴를 주방장으로 승인했다.
**해설** 시간의 순서상 부사절 접속사 after절의 시제가 과거(완료)이면 주절의 시제는 과거가 와야 하고, after절에 현재 시제가 오면 주절에 과거 시제가 올 수 있으므로 (A)가 정답이다. (조동사(will, may)+동사원형)이 와야 한다. 여기서는 주절에 과거 시제가 있으므로 과거완료 시제인 (A)가 적절하다. after절의 시제를 묻는 문제는 자주 출제되므로 하나의 공식처럼 암기하는 것이 좋다.
**어휘** promote 승진하다 master 익히다 chef 요리사 수업하다

**117 해석** 그 계약 조건들을 담당하고 있는 부장이 예의 잘못 해석된 것으로 보인다.
**해설** 형용사를 목적어를 취하는 2동사 appear to가 있고, 문맥상 경영진에 의해서 잘못 이해되어 있다는 수동의 의미이므로 (C)가 적절하다. (B) 오해, 오역
**어휘** conditions 조건 in charge of ~을 맡아서, 담당하다

**118 해석** 우리는 임요일에 있을 그 회사의 이벤트에 출장 요리 서비스를 제공하고 싶지요. 안타깝게도 우리는 그날 이미 세 개의 다른 파티 약속이 있다.
**해설** 임요일에 있을 그 회사의 이벤트에 서비스를 제공하고 싶지만 '이미' 세 개의 파티가 약속이 돼 있다는 의미가 적절하므로 (B)가 정답이다. (A) well로 동사와 부사를 수식하며, (D) soon은 미래 시제와 잘 어울리는 부사이다.
**어휘** cater 출장 요리 서비스를 제공하다 appointment 약속

# PART 6

**[131-134]**

5월은 IBS 사에서 소중한 직원들 뽑는 시기입니다. 임명 **(131)** 절차는 5월 27일에 있습니다. 그 타이틀에 지원하고 싶어 하는 **(132)** 사람들은 13일까지 신청서를 작성해야 합니다.

**(133)** 많은 직원들에게 있어서 그 타이틀은 여러 방법으로 유익할 것입니다. 첫째, 그 타이틀에 지원하는 직원으로 선택되는 것은 승진에 있어서 가장 강력한 요소들 중 하나입니다. 또한 8월과 9월을 제외하고 1년 중 언제라도 5일간의 휴가를 보장해 줍니다.

위원회는 회사에 최선을 다해 헌신했을 뿐만 아니라 주목할 만한 기여를 한 직원들을 **(134)** 고려할 것입니다. 그 타이틀을 얻는 것은 매우 경쟁적일지라도 지원하는 모든 직원들에게 참가하기를 권장합니다.

**어휘** selection 선택 valuable 가치 있는, 귀중한 nomination 지명, 추천, 임명 take place 열리다, 발생하다 apply for 지원하다 application form 지원서 guarantee 보장하다 fill out 작성하다 committee 위원회 dedication 헌신 noticeable 주목할 만한 contribution 기여 participation 참가 competitive 경쟁적인

**131 해설** 복합 명사를 물어보는 문제로, 뒤의 명사가 핵심을 말해주는 명사이며 앞에 있는 명사의 내용을 수식하여 구체화한다. 문맥상 임명 '절차'는 5월 27일에 열린다는 것 이 적절하므로 단수 동사가 있기 때문에 단수 명사 (C) procedure가 과거형이다. (A) 수익

**131 어휘** president 사장 oversee 감독하다 accounting operations 회계 운영

**132 해설** 관계대명사절의 수식을 받는 대명사를 찾는 문제이다. 대명사 Those는 전치사구 혹은 관계대명사절의 수식을 받기 때문에 정답은 (A) Those이다. (B) Anyone 또한 수식을 받지만 동사 wish와 수일치가 일치하지 않습니다.

**132 어휘** race 경주, 경쟁 continuously 계속해서 platform 플랫폼 developer 개발자 wireless 무선의 division 부서

**133 (A)** 많은 직원들에게 있어서 그 타이틀은 여러 방법으로 유익할 것입니다.
**(B)** 직원들은 그 타이틀로 인해 많은 어려움을 겪을 수 있습니다.
**(C)** 직원들은 그 회사에서 적어도 3년 동안 일했어야 합니다.
**(D)** 지금까지는 많은 직원들은 그 타이틀을 받는 것을 즐기지 않았습니다.

**133 해설** 빈칸은 두 번째 단락의 첫 문장으로, 두 번째 단락의 전체적인 내용과 관련 있는 내용이어야 한다. 빈칸 뒤 줄의 그 다음 줄 각각 부사인 First 와 Also로 시작하고, 승진과 휴가에 대한 내용이므로 타이틀의 여러 장점에 대한 것임을 유추할 수 있다. 따라서 정답은 (A)이다.

**133 어휘** feasibility 가능성 be under way for ~가 진행 중이다 fiber optic cable 광섬유 케이블 remote 먼

**134 해설** 해외 지점의 투자자들이 참석할 수 있도록 하기 위해서 회의 일정이 변경되었다는 것으로 볼 때 반기에 ~할 수 있도록을 의미하는 (B)가 정답이다. (A) 동료로서 / (B) 동료, 관급을 가지다 / (D) 축하하다

**134 어휘** beneficial 유익한

---

**119 해설** 에두아르도 펠렛은 최근까지 파리에서 나온 대부분의 인기 있는 재즈 음악의 뒷모습 지적했다.
문장에 동사가 없으므로 빈칸은 동사 자리이며, '최근까지 ~을 했었던'는 의미로 반과거 과거 시제가 와야 한다는 것을 알 수 있으므로 (D)가 정답이다.

**어휘** write 쓰다, 작성하다 come out of ~에서 나오다

**120 해설** 구매의 증가로 영수증을 5개만 가져 오시면 저렴한 무료 성점 기방을 제공할 것입니다.

**어휘** bring in 가져 오다 complimentary 무료의

**121 해설** 당신의 개인 소유자로부터 중고차를 구입하려고 한다면 정비사를 데리고 가는 것이 바람직하다.

**어휘** advisable 바람직한 bring along ~을 데리고 가다 mechanic 정비사 used car 중고차 private owner 개인 소유자

**122 해설** 정부 기관들도 호수의 대부분을 오염시킨 독극물 유출 이후에 대한 강력한 항의에 응하여 일련의 환경법을 규정하였다.

**어휘** agency 정부 기관 enact (법률 등을) 제정하다, 규정하다, 덤법하다 spill 유출 contaminate 오염시키다 outcry 강력한 항의

**123 해설** 노사는 마침내 일련의 협상 후에 계약 조건들에 동의했다.

**어휘** management and labor 노사 agree on ~에 합의하다 a series of negotiations 일련의 협상 threat of a strike 파업의 위협

**124 해설** membership fee는 '회원 요금'이라는 의미 복합명사이다. 따라서 (C)가 정답이다. (A) 운임, 요금 (B) 가치, 진가 investor 투자자 conference 회의 reschedule 일정을 변경하다

**125 해설** 애니메이션 슬라이드의 적용으로 그 발표를 더욱 재미있고 기억에 남게 만들었다.

**어휘** application 적용, 응용 animated 활기찬, 동영상으로 된 enjoyable 즐거운, 재미있는 memorable 기억할 만한

**126 해설** 그 회사는 90년대 초반에 종이 문서를 디지털 파일로 교체하기 시작했다.

**어휘** cover 포함하다 admittance 입장(허가) locker 개인 사물함

**127 해설** 그 회사의 사장은 회계 운영을 감독하기 위해 세 재정 담당자를 3년마다 임명한다.

**어휘** firm 회사 replace A with B A를 B로 교체하다 in the beginning of the 90s 90년대 초반에

**128 해설** 우리 책임자는 플랫폼을 계속해서 향상시키기 위한 경쟁 때문에 무선 사업부에 몇몇 개발자를 고용하는 것이 필요하다고 생각한다.

[135-138]

**그리핀 감독의 또 하나의 히트작**

하인스 그리핀만은 영화계에서 높이 평가받는 감독 중 한 명으로서 최근 (화젯작) 마스라는 또 하나의 영화를 만들었습니다. 2천만 이상의 관객을 모을 것으로 기대하며 (화젯작)는 단지 두 달 만에 솝 사용하는 사람들에 힘입어 참가하는 기사단이 승마 기를 얻습니다.

각 시저오가 그에게 비밀 음모를 펼치는 것을 모든 체 토너먼트에 참가하는 요한 파발롯을 연기했습니다. 그 영화는 국내 토너먼트의 배후가 누구인지를 딸가지 비밀을 힘으로서 국치 137 효과를 더합니다.

영화의 주목할 만한 점은 시저가 이야기에서 각각의 인물에 복잡함을 묘사하는 데 있어 138 광범위한 기술을 보여 준다는 점입니다.

그 영화는 상업적으로 큰 성공을 거둘 뿐만 아니라 현대 관객에게 만족시키는 역사 드라마의 걸작으로 여겨집니다.

**어휘** respected 훌륭한, 높이 평가되는 director 감독 industry 산업 medieval 중세의 tournament 시합 equestrian 승마의 plot against ~에 반대하여 음모를 꾸미다 notable 주목할 만한 feature 특징 depict 묘사하다 complexity 복잡함 masterpiece 걸작 tale 이야기 commercial 상업적 audience 관객 historical 역사적

convey 전달하다

**135** (A) 이 새로운 영화는 오직 두 달 만에 2천만 이상의 관객을 모을 것으로 기 대합니다.

(B) 감독은 그가 맞이했던 많은 어려움들에서 벗어나려고 투쟁했습니다.

(C) (화젯작)는 현실을 반영하지 않는다는 면에서 대중에게 높이 비판받고 있습니다.

(D) 처음에 (화젯작)의 배우들은 시나리오에 대해 만족하지 않았습니다.

**해설** 빈칸 앞뒤로 (화젯작)에 대한 내용이 나오는데 글의 시작 부분으로 새 영화가 어떤 반응을 불러일으킬지에 대한 (A)가 적절하다.

**어휘** convey 전달하다

**136 해설** 빈칸 뒤에 명사가 있으므로 명사를 수식하는 형용사가 들어가야 한다. 셀택지 중에서 유일한 형용사는 (A)와 (C)뿐이다. fascinating은 감정을 일으키는 주체에 대해 쓰여 '매혹적인, 흥미로운'의 의미이며, fascinated는 감정을 느끼는 주체에 대해 쓰여 '매료된'이라는 뜻이다. story는 감정을 일으키는 주체이므로 (A) fascinating이 적절하다.

**137 해설** 빈칸이 극적인 '효과가 더해진다'라고 적절하므로 (C)가 정답이다. (A) 냄새, 냄 / (B) 비판, 비난 / (D) 명의, 이유

**138 해설** 문맥상 작가가 인물의 복잡함을 묘사하는 데 있어 '광범위한 기술을 수 행했다는 것이 자연스러우므로 (B)가 적절하다. (A) 중은 / (C) 제한적인, 한정된 / (D) 지나친, 과도한

[139-142]

날짜: 6월 10일
발신: DVD 대여점
수신: 휘리 담저
제도: 기한이 지난 대여품

담전 씨, 이 메일은 한 달 전에 귀하께서 대여하신 DVD의 기한이 지났다는 것을 알리기 위해 보내졌습니다. 139 이 DVD들의 일반적인 대여 기간은 오직 2주입니다. 하지만 귀하께서 대여품은 지금 2주보다 더 기한이 지났습니다. 2일 내로 귀하께서 대여품을 반납하지 못하는 대여품이 분실되었다고 2주 뒤마 귀하의 현재 연체료 40달러는 80달러로 두 배가 될 것입니다.

귀하께서 대여품에 대해 기간을 연장하기 위해서 저희 대여점에 연락했다는 것을 압니다. 그러나 이 DVD들은 연장이 140 불가능하다고 귀하에게 알리는 또 하나의 이메일을 보냈던 것을 유감스럽게 생각합니다.

저희가 귀하께서 DVD를 2주 이상 늦게 가질 수 있도록 해주고 141 실물지라도, 대여품 반납이 매우 엄격히고 또한 이 대여품들을 기다리는 사람들에게 공평하지 않습니다. 그러니 가능한 빨리 DVD를 반납해 주세요.

**어휘** overdue 기한이 지난 fine 벌금 rent 빌리다 extend 연장하다, 늘리다 potentially 잠재적으로 account (회계) 장부 strict 엄격한 be exempt from ~에서 면제되다

**139** (A) 만약 하기가 실패 멤버라면, 귀하는 벌금 내는 것을 면제받습니다.

(B) 귀하의 독회에 따르면, 귀하는 주로 공포 영화를 대여하셨습니다.

(C) **이 새로운 정책은 현재 저희 가게 정책에 추가될 것입니다.**

(D) 이 DVD들의 일반적인 대여 기간은 오직 2주입니다.

**해설** 빈칸 뒤에서 기한이 2주보다 더 지났다고 했으므로 빈칸에는 기간에 대한 내용이 적절하다. 따라서 (D)가 정답이다.

**어휘** be exempt from ~에서 면제되다

**140 해설** 빈칸에는 2일 내로 반납해야 하는 DVD를 대신하는 대명사가 들어와야 한다. DVD는 복수이기 때문에 (C) them이 적절하다. (A)는 단수 명사를 대신할 때 쓰이며 뒤에서 수식어구의 수식을 받는다. (B)는 소유격으로 뒤에 명사가 와야 한다. (D)는 단수 명사를 대신할 때 쓰인다.

**141 해설** 문맥상 늦게 DVD를 대여해도 좋을 수 있는 것이 아니라 조건 등이 부합하여야 할 수 있다는 의미다. (B) 할 수 있는 / (C) 할 수 있는 / (D) 노출된

**어휘** eligible for ~할 자격이 있다. eligible for는 자격이나 조건 등이 부합되는 것을 나타낼 때 쓴다.

**142 해설** 빈칸 뒤에 (주어+동사)를 갖은 절이 있으므로 접속사 자리이며, 문맥상 2주 이상 DVD를 즐길 수 있도록 '양보하지도'라는 의미가 되어야 하므로 양보의 부사절을 이끄는 (B) Although가 정답이다. (A)와 (D)는 접속부사이며, (C) 그러므로, 따라서 / (D) 게다가

**어휘** get along with ~와 잘 지내다 culinary 요리의

[143-146]

이사회 회원 여러분께

이사회의 연례 회사 회의이 5월 첫째 주 수요일 6시에 143 열립니다. 행사 장소는 40번 가의 맨해튼 힐로 호텔 연회장이 될 것입니다.

144 평소대로 모든 이사회 구성원들은 가족을 제외하고 통행 손님을 3명까지 초대해도 됩니다. 베타저의 성격을 띤 모임이기 때문에 모든 방문객들은 신분 증을 가져오셔야 합니다.

모임은 회사를 어떻게 개선시킬지에 대해 이사회가 다른 구성원들과 생각을 145 공유하기 위한 시간과 자리입니다. 또한, 음료 우선 음식 요리사들이 준 비한 요리들을 제공하기 위한 것입니다.

저희는 행사에서 여러분 모두를 보기를 바랍니다. 공식적인 행사인 점을 유의해 주시고 그에 맞게 옷을 입고 오기를 권해 드립니다.

감사합니다.

제이콥 타일러
아니스트 앤 영 최고 경영자

**어휘** board of directors 이사회 annual 연례의 exclusive 독점적인, 베타적인 improve 개선하다, 향상시키다 accordingly (상황)에 맞춰, ~에 따라 서 dish 요리

**143 해설** 문맥상 5월 16일 수요일에 연례회가 '열리는 것'이므로 미래 시제가 와 야 한다. 또한, 전목하는 열려지는 것이므로 수동태가 적절하므로 정답은 (A)이다. (B)의 경우 타동사 hold와 뒤에 목적어가 반각 뒤에 나와야 한다. (C)는 과거, (D)는 현재완료 시제다.

**144 해설** 문맥상 매년 전목에 '이전과 같이' 3명이 손님으로 초대 하도 된다는 것이 적절하므로 (B)가 정답이다. (A)와 (C)는 앞 문장과 뒤 문장이 대조를 이룰 때 사용한다. (D) 반면에, 다른 한편으로는

**145 해설** 문맥상 다른 구성원들과 어떻게 하면 회사를 개선시킬지 생각을 '공유 하기' 위해서 전목회가 열린다는 것이 적절하므로 (C)가 정답이다. (A) 강요하다 / (B) 설명하다 / (D) 이해하다

**146** (A) 또한, 음료와 우수한 요리사들이 준비한 요리들을 제공하기 위한 것입니다.

**(B) 스트레스를 받을 때 기족들에게 충고하는 것은 중요합니다.**

(C) 귀하는 회사에 대한 개인적인 견해를 나타내서는 안 됩니다.

(D) 귀하는 모임에 대한 내용이 나오는데 음료와 음식 요리가 제 공된다는 (B)가 정답이다.

**해설** 빈칸 앞에는 모임에 대한 내용이 나오는데 음료와 음식 요리가 제 공된다는 (B)가 정답이다.

**어휘** get along with ~와 잘 지내다 culinary 요리의

## [147-148]

수신: nigel_austell@siglet.org
발신: kala_g27@inttrade.com
날짜: 8월 23일 월요일
제목: 세미나 일정이 변화됨

나이절 씨께

재가 제15일 연례 관광 산업 토론회의 기조 연설자로 임명되어 영광입니다. 저는 참가자들이 강연에서 예상하는 주요 주제들의 이슥합니다. 저는 그 문제의 이 최근에야 비로소 확인된 탐사 관광의 환경적 영향에 대해서 발표할 것입니다. 유일한 문제는 당 전부터 예정되어 있던 조직 위원회가 없다는 것입니다. 또한, 토론회는 하루 전인 9월 1일에 총 예행연습에 참가할 수 없다 때문에 제기 토론회의 센터리스-코렉스 웰러기 때문에 저는 토론회 조직 위원회가 막판 서비스를 울분도 주는 울분도 국제회공이 아닌 국제관광에 도착하는 비행기를 탈 것입니다. 그러므로 저는 조직 위원회와 참여하는 지점을 따로 준비하는 지 저 혼자 investigation 수사 장소

땅습니다. 회의에서 뵙겠습니다. 감사합니다.

카라 가우스
에스페란자 여행사 최고경영자

**어휘** appointed 임명된 keynote speaker 기조 연설자 exploratory 탐사의 complication 상황을 더 복잡하게 만드는 문제 identify 확인하다, 찾다 dress rehearsal 총 예행연습 land 착륙하다 extend 제공하다 by myself 혼자서 investigation 수사 venue 장소

### 147 가우스 씨가 이메일을 예행연습에 참석할 수 없는 이유는 무엇인가?
(A) 그녀는 이른 어머니를 방문해야 한다.
**(B) 그녀는 미리 예정된 회의가 있다.**
(C) 그녀의 어머는 조사를 받고 있다.
(D) 그녀는 마이애미에서 추가 좋다.

**해설** 가우스 씨는 한 달 전부터 정해던 중요한 업무 회의가 있기 때문에 총 예행연습에 감수 없다고 한다. 따라서 정답은 (B)이다.

### 148 가우스 씨는 공항에서 토론회 장소로 어떻게 갈 것인가?
**(A) 아직 결정되지 않았다.**
(B) 조직 위원회에서 가우스 씨에게 택시를 보낼 것이다.
(C) 전용 운전사를 고용할 것이다.
(D) 가까운 기차역에서 기차를 탈 것이다.

**해설** 이메일의 마지막에 가우스 씨는 조직 위원회에서 마이애미 공항까지 픽 업 서비스를 해 줄 것인지, 아니면 자기 자기 가야 하는지 묻고 있다. 따라서 이직 결정되지 않았음을 알 수 있으므로 (A)가 정답이다.

## [149-150]

| | |
|---|---|
| **엘라 노스** | |
| 사만다 씨가 당신이 아직 사무실에 있을 거라고 일러줬어요. 부탁 좀 해도 될까요? | **오후 6시 32분** |
| **타일러 렌트** | |
| 물론이죠. 무슨 일인가요? | **오후 6시 33분** |
| **엘라 노스** | |
| 제가 편집한 주식 자료 사본 좀 가져줄래요? 프로그램에서 필요할 거 같아요. 제 책상 위에 있어요. | **오후 6시 35분** |
| **타일러 렌트** | |
| 오 이런 방송국에 있는 거 아니었어요? 이미 거기 간 좀 있었어요. | **오후 6시 36분** |
| **엘라 노스** | |
| 아니요, 프로그램은 8시에 시작하고요, 여기서 거우 30분밖에 안 걸려요. 주차장 근처 업무에서 기다릴게요. | **오후 6시 37분** |
| **타일러 렌트** | |
| 알았어요. 사본 가지고 곧 내려갈게요. 당신 같은 전문가를 조언했으니 그룹은 운도 좋아요. | **오후 6시 38분** |
| **엘라 노스** | |
| 고마워요. 도움이 되네요. TV 출연은 처음이라 좀 긴장했거든요. | **오후 6시 40분** |

**어휘** sure thing 물론이지 stock data 주식 정보 compile 편집하다 (program) show 프로그램 (broadcast) station 방송국 parking lot 주차장

### 149 오후 6시 33분에, 렌트 씨가 "물론이죠"라고 말할 때, 그 의도로 무엇이겠는가?
**(A) 노스 씨를 기꺼이 도와주겠다.**
(B) 초과 근무 할 필요가 있다는 데 동의한다.
(C) 노스 씨가 무엇을 부탁할지 알고 있다.
(D) 자신도 같이 가야 한다고 생각한다.

**해설** Sure thing은 누군가의 부탁을 받았을 때 기꺼이 하겠다는 의미로 쓸 수 있는 표현이다. 오후 6시 32분에 노스 씨가 "부탁 좀 해도 될까요" 라고 질문을 했고, 이에 대해 기꺼이 도와주겠다는 것이므로 정답은 (A)이다.

### 150 노스 씨는 누구이겠는가?
(A) 뉴스 앵커
(B) 보안 요원
(C) 경찰
**(D) 금융 전문가**

**해설** 오후 6시 35분에 노스 씨는 "제가 편집한 주식 자료", 오후 6시 38분에 렌트 씨는 "당신 같은 전문가를 조언했으니"라는 표현을 보면 노스 씨는 금융 전문가(financial analyst)로서 TV 프로그램에 출연 되는 것임을 알 수 있다. 따라서 정답은 (D)이다.

## [151-152]

**점포 정리 세일**

폴스트 아웃 용품 판매점
94 등록 29번가
뉴욕 시티, 뉴욕

2월 2일부터 10일까지 이월 상품 점포 정리 세일에서 캠핑 용품들에 많은 드릅 잡아하세요. 내구성이 좋은 제로로 만들어진 최고 품질의 텐트와 침낭, 캠핑용 난로, 기타 캠핑 장비들을 보실 수 있습니다. 저년 봄 이월 상품으로 모든 재고 70퍼센트의 가격을 절약하실 수 있고 50퍼센트까지 저렴한 상사를 구매하실 수 있습니다.

유아용 보호 장비를 구매하시는 부모님에게는 기초 전체를 위한 아이 활동 용 양말을 무료로 드립니다. 오셔서 기간 내에 세일 전체를 즐기세요!

**어휘** clearance sale 점포 정리 off-season 이월의, 구시의 gear 정비 durable 내구성이 좋은 outdoor line 야외 상품 first aid kit 구급상자 complimentary 무료의 blowout sale 파격 세일 portable 휴대가 쉬운

### 151 고객들은 작년에 재고 상품에 얼마나 많이 절약할 수 있는가?
(A) 20퍼센트
(B) 40퍼센트
(C) 50퍼센트
**(D) 70퍼센트**

**해설** 작년 봄 상품은 70퍼센트 할인된다고 하므로 정답은 (D)이다.

### 152 고객들이 아이의 보호 장비를 사면 받는 것은 무엇인가?
(A) 추가 할인
(B) 지역 매장의 쿠폰
(C) 휴대용 스파커
**(D) 캠핑 양말**

**해설** 유아용 보호 장비를 구매하면 가족 모두를 위한 아이 활동용 양말을 무료로 준다고 했으므로 정답은 (D)이다.

**[153-154]**

**공인 영양사가 되세요!**

호주 영양사 협회 18번째 정규 설명회

시간: 오전 10:00 - 오후 1:00(정오에 30분간 점심시간 예정)

장소: 29 엘름스우드 애비뉴, 엘버쿨 빅토리아 3205

공인 영양사가 되는 것은 직업에 인기와 수요가 더 증가로 더 경쟁적이 되어 있고 어려워 지게 되었습니다. 영양사들은 종합 병원 general hospital 종합 병원 상급의 치료로 therapeutic 치료로 사립 학교 private school 전지 expertise 전지 식이요법 dietary 식이요법 사이 요 법의 manner 수단, 방법 awareness 의식 aspiring 장차 ~가 되려는 food poisoning 식중독 outbreak 발생 major 전공 전공 높은 급여로 인정을 받습니다. 영양사들은 특별히 사단이 필요한 개인 들을 위해 건강식과 때때로 치료 음식 제공을 할 때 그들이 전문 지식이 인정을 받습니다.

[153] 등록 영양사 18번째 정규 설명회 협회가 되어 요구되는 기술에 관한 새로운 정보를 배우는 곳 인 영양사에 관한 저희 18번째 정규 설명회에 참여하세요. 설명회에 참여하시려 면 www.nsa.au에서 온라인으로 무료로 개별 경력 상담을 해 드립니다. [154] 처음 30명의 등록자 에게 협회원들의 무료로 개별 경력 상담을 해 드립니다. 더 많은 정보는 저희 웹 사이트에서 확인하세요.

**어휘** certified 보증된 nutritionist 영양사 competitive 경쟁력 있는 popularity 인기 be sought after 수요가 있다 prestigious 일류의 appreciate 인정하다

**153** 광고의 목적은 무엇인가?
(A) 균형 잡힌 식사 사이 요법의 중요성에 대한 의사를 증가를 위해
(B) 영양사가 되려는 사람들을 위한 곧 있을 행사를 광고하기 위해
(C) 최근에 발병했던 식중독에 대해 경고하기 위해
(D) 학교 식당의 새로운 영양사를 모집하기 위해

**해설** 공인 영양사에 관한 정규 설명회 행사에 참여하라고 홍보하고 있으므로 로 정답은 (B)이다.

**154** 무료 직업 상담을 받을 사람은 누구인가?
(A) 종류의 일부 등록한 사람들
(B) 상담을 신청한 사람들
(C) 영양 과학을 전공하는 30명의 학생들
(D) 온라인으로 과정에 등록하는 최초 30명

**해설** 먼저 등록한 30명에게 협회원들이 무료로 직업 상담을 해 준다고 하므 로 정답은 (D)이다. (A는 일부 등록한 사람인 것은 맞지만 구체적인 기 준이 제시되어 있지 않다.

---

**[155-157]**

**헤어케어스 인터내셔널 기업**

A4044 캐뷰 서커스

브리스톨 영국

– 렌즈을 위한 가전제품 –

공인 영양사가 되는 것은 직업에 가전이 어디서도 어울리며, 그릇에 저희 제품은 다른 제품과 차별됩니다. [1]- 다섯 개의 갯수가 저장할 수 있는 용기 로 차가운 음료를 쉽게 개별 개별 줍니다. [155] 이쪽 오른쪽 상단의 편리한 것에 있는 온도 조절기는 쉽게 온도를 조절하고 음식을 신선하게 유지시켜 줍니 다. [2]- 세 개의 선반은 정리가 용이하도록 높낮이를 제품하고 특히 위 두 개의 선반은 저장 용도에 맞도록 조정이 가능합니다. [3]- [157] 마지막으로, 저희 제품은 세계적으로 유명한 인증 기관 이피센트 에너지 랩에서 실험된 실험 을 통과했다는 내용 다음에 그 결과 인증 마크를 제품에 붙일 수가 있다는 것입니다.

[156] 크기가 작은 저희 제품은 구하 가정이 어디서도 어울리며, 그릇에 저희 제 품은 다른 제품과 차별됩니다. 용기로 차가운 음료를 쉽게 개별 개별 줍니 다. 이쪽 온도 조절기는 쉽게 온도를 조절하고 음식을 신선하게 유지시켜 줍니 다. 세 개의 선반은 정리가 용이하도록 높낮이를 제품하고 특히 위 두 개의 선반은 저장 용도에 맞도록 조정이 가능합니다. 저희 제품은 세계적으로 유명한 인증 기관 이피센트 에너지 랩에서 실험된 실험을 통과했다는 것입니다.

**어휘** home appliance 가전제품　studio apartment 원룸　compact (길음 종류의 일반적인 제품보다) 소형의 (모양, 크기가 어디에) 맞다 dispenser (손잡이, 단추 등등 돌려 어느 만큼씩 쓸 수 있는) 용기　provide easy access (to) ~에 쉽게 접근을 수 있도록 해주다 conveniently 편리 하게 adjust 조정하다 shelf 선반 adjustable 조정 가능한 fit one's needs ~의 용도에 맞다 last but not least 마지막이지만 역시 중요한 것 은 certification institute 인증 기관 utility bill 전기, 가스, 수도 등 요금 be entitled to ~을 받을 자격이 있다 affix 부착하다

**155** 무엇이 광고되고 있는가?
(A) 냉장고
(B) 전자레인지
(C) 오븐
(D) 에어컨

**해설** 온도 조절기가 쉽게 온도를 조절하고 음식을 신선하게 유지하도록 해 준다는 내용에다 냉장고에 대한 설명임을 알 수 있다. 따라서 (A)가 정 답이다.

**156** 제품의 무엇이 특별한가?
(A) 작은 사이즈
(B) 가벼운 무게
(C) 저렴한 가격
(D) 평생 품질 보증

**해설** 크기가 작은 제품은 가정이 어느 곳이든 맞고, 그릇에 제품이 차별화 된다는 내용에다 작은 사이즈가 장점임을 알 수 있다. 따라서 (A)가 정 답이다.

**157** [1], [2], [3], [4]로 표시된 곳 중에서 다음 문장이 가장 적합한 곳은?
"그 결과, 전기 마크를 제품에 붙일 수 있습니다."
(A) [1]
(B) [2]
(C) [3]
(D) [4]

---

**[158-160]**

**실버튼 고등학교 5월 행사 달력**

| 날짜 | 행사 |
|---|---|
| 5월 3일 ~ 8일 | **중간고사**<br>[158] 학교 일부가 개조 중이고, 이윤에 부착함을 수 있기 때문에 학생들은 신선에 유지하도록 해 선생님에 확인받을 것이 있습니다. |
| 5월 12일 ~ 14일 | **제빵 바자회**<br>[159] 옥성화에서 세일되는 병원에서 최근에 차 사고 로부터 회복 중인 친구 딜라 핫는 이 병 완치 모금을 위한 제빵 바자회를 준비 중입니다. 베이 크 교장 선생님께서는 제빵 바자회에서 실 버튼 바자회에서 개인지 1,000달러 기부을 약속했습니다. 제빵 바자회에서 모든 즐기기를 바랍니다. |
| 5월 25일 | **직장인의 날**<br>[160] 실버튼은 올해 직장인의 날에 기초 연설자로 인 기 동아리 스토리지 씨를 초배해 개별니다. 학생들은 모든 졸리, 노르갈스먼 씨와 같은 유명한 지역이 인사 들을 만날 수 있고 직접 상담에 참여할 수 있습니다. 학생들은 직업 선택을 위해 검사가 있는 108페이지 와 210의 소책자를 위해 1달러를 가져오십시오 |

**어휘** go through 경험하다　unfit 부적합한　bake-sale 빵 바자회　raise 모 으다 bill 청구서 beloved 사랑하는 principal 교장 pledge 약속하다 human right 인권 booklet 소책자 aptitude test 적성 검사 alumni 졸업생, 동창회 refurbish 재단장하다 district school board 교육청 commemorate 기념하다 injured 다친

**158** 실버튼 고등학교에 관해 추론할 수 있는 것은 무엇인가?
(A) 노르갈스먼 씨는 실버튼의 졸업생이다.
(B) 학교의 일부 교실을 새 단장하는 중이다.
(C) 모든 행사는 당일회에 의해서 조직된다.
(D) 직장인의 날 소책자는 교육청에 의해 제공된다.

**해설** 중간고사 일정에서 학교가 현재 학교의 일부가 개조되고 있다고 했으므로 (B) 가 정답이다.

**159** 제빵 바자회를 개최하는 목적은 무엇인가?
(A) 중간고사 종료를 축하하기 위해
(B) 38번째 개교일을 기념하기 위해
(C) 입원한 학생을 위한 돈을 모으기 위해
(D) 학생들의 요리 실력을 높이기 위해

**해설** 제빵 바자회는 차 사고로 병원에서 회복 중인 반 친구를 위해 돈을 모으는 행사임을 알 수 있으므로 정답은 (C)이다.

---

**해설** 세계적으로 유명한 인증 기관 이피센트 에너지 랩에서 실험을 실행한 실험을 통과했다는 내용 다음에 그 결과 인증 마크를 제품에 붙일 수 있다는 문장이 와야 자연스럽다. 따라서 정답은 (D)이다.

**160** 작성자의 날씨에 관하여 사실이 아닌 것은 무엇인가?

(A) 인근 활동가가 행사의 주요 연설자이다.
(B) 지역의 유명 인사가 행사를 축하하러 온다.
(C) 학생들은 1달러로 유한 소책자를 받을 수 있다.
**(D) 교장도 성명자로서 참가한다.**

**해설** 작성의 날 일정에서 인권 활동가 스토로우 씨는 기조 연설자이고, 학생들 지역의 유명 인사들을 만날 수 있으며, 1달러로 소책자를 받을 수 있다. 교장이 성명자로 참가한다는 내용은 없으므로 (D)가 정답이다.

[161-163]

수신: d.forcier@cranmail.net
발신: kelley.cs13@gertschmt.com
날짜: 2017년 2월 3일
제목: 당신 냉방 시스템 미작동

포스이어 씨께

귀하의 냉방 시스템이 지난 이틀간 고장이 났었다니 유감입니다. **161** 저희가 주의깊게 운영했기 않기 때문에 신속하게 귀하의 냉방기를 수리할 수 있었던 것 같습니다. 오늘 이침 귀이가 붙인의 첫 번째로 등록했기 때문에, **162** 저희 정비사가 냉방기 점검 및 수리를 위해 오후 3시에 방문하게 될 것입니다. 정비사가 자동의 경험에 의한 고장이라고 결론을 내리면, 무료로 새 냉방기로 설치할 것이나, **163** 해중 제거와 대응소에서 재정비하는 것까지 모든 관리 서비스의 40퍼센트 할인권을 제공하겠습니다. 고객님은 송수관 동파를 예방하시아 합니다. 모든 물 배판을 단열 처리하는 것이 자동의 우리의 서비를 연동시키는 지 것 같은 간단한 예방 조치를 취하실 수 있습니다.

냉방 문제와 자료 저비 서비스에 관해 더 많은 정보는 www.gertschmt.com으로 방문해 주십시오.

감사합니다.

켈리 피렐리
거스 빌딩 관리 고객 서비스부

**어휘** promptly 즉각적으로 conclude 결론을 내리다 defect 결함 at no charge 무료로 ranging from A to B A부터 B까지의 영역에서 pest 해 충 spring-cleaning 대청소 refurbish 재정비하다 water pipe 송수관 precaution 예방 조치 insulate 단열 처리하다

**161** 어느 요일에 고객 서비스 센터의 직원이 이메일을 읽었는가?

**(A) 월요일**
(B) 화요일
(C) 금요일
(D) 일요일

**해설** 냉방 시스템이 이틀간 고장 났었지만 주말에는 서비스를 운영하지 않 느다고 하였고 오늘 이침에 가장 먼저 포스이어 씨에 붙인을 등록했다고 했으므로 한 직원이 이메일을 읽은 요일은 주말 다음 월요일인 월맞 했으므로 직원이 이메일을 읽은 날은 (A)이다. 따라서 정답은 (A)이다.

**162** 포스이어 씨에 관해 추론할 수 있는 것은 무엇인가?

(A) 과실에 대해 회사를 고소할 것이다.
**(B) 오후에 수리공을 만날 것이다.**
(C) 회사의 본사에 전화할 것이다.
(D) 냉방기를 몇 번 먼 볼 것이다.

**해설** 정비사가 오후 3시에 포스이어 씨의 냉방기 점검 및 수리를 위해 방문할 것이라고 하였으므로 포스이어 씨는 오후에 수리공을 만날 것으로 추 할 수 있다. 따라서 정답은 (B)이다.

**163** 만약 상품에 결함이 발견된다면 고객들은 무엇을 받는가?

(A) 개조 계획에 관한 무료 상담
(B) 수도관 단열
(C) 시우나 지료를 위한 무료 예약
**(D) 관리 서비스에 대한 더 낮은 가격**

**해설** 상품에 결함이 있다면 것이 새로우면 무료로 교체할 것이고 냉방기 관리 서비스를 40퍼센트 음인하는 쿠폰을 준다고 하므로 정답은 (D)이다.

---

**164** 보즈워 씨는 어떤 직책을 갖고 있는가?

**(A) 고객 서비스부 직원**
(B) 기술자
(C) 마케팅 부서 직원
(D) 경영진의 일원

**해설** 고객들이 그룹웨어의 갑작스러운 중단 때문에 그게 고객 서비스부에 전화가 많이 왔지만 보즈워 씨는 적극적으로 상황을 해결했다고 하므 로 그는 고객 서비스부의 직원임을 알 수 있다. 따라서 정답은 (A)이다.

**165** 회사는 보즈워 씨의 아이디어를 어느 정도까지 직업했는가?

(A) 성공 여부 평가
(B) 판매 전략 공식화
(C) 추가 사례 재포장하기
**(D) 견본 제작**

**해설** 자동 정보 시스템에 관한 보즈워 씨의 아이디어가 회사 기술자에 의해 설계되어 예비 시험을 기다리고 하므로 견본이 제작된 상태임 을 알 수 있다. 따라서 정답은 (C)가 정답이다.

**166** 보즈워 씨에게 주어진 보상이 아닌 것은 무엇인가?

(A) 외국의 관광 명소로 가는 무료 휴가
(B) 구내식당에서의 무료 음식
**(C) 더 높은 직책으로의 승진**
(D) 보너스

**해설** 보너스 지급, 입주자의 휴가, 구내식당 식권 10장만 언급되었으므로 나와 있지 않은 (C)가 정답이다.

**167** 보즈워 씨에 관하여 추론할 수 있는 것은 무엇인가?

(A) 기술자의 대표였다.
**(B) 회사의 대표와 만났다.**
(C) 휴가에 자기 가족을 데려갈 것이다.
(D) 그는 10년 넘게 회사에서 일해 왔다.

**해설** 마지막 부분에 보즈워 씨가 지난주 회의에서 직원들의 열정과 사랑 이 기뻐하시는 모습을 보셨다고 하므로 추론할 수 있는 것은 (B)이다.

[164-167]

수신: 놀런 보즈워(nbos@uptoncom.net)
발신: 엘린다 웨이스트(mwgw@uptoncom.net)
날짜: 6월 8일
제목: 당신의 제안에 대해

보즈워 씨께

그룹웨어의 오류나 중단에 관한 정보 시스템 개념이 필요성에 대해 당신의 의미 있는 제안에 감사드립니다. 당신은 데이터 손실의 위험이 있는 갑작스러운 중단 사고 때문에 이 그게 서비스 센에 모의하고 있다고 보고했습니다. 비록 부서에 전화가 무척 많이 오지만 당신은 적극적으로 즉각적이고 재 지 있게 당황스러운 상황을 해결했습니다. 고객과 자사의 서버를 연동시키는 지 동 정보 시스템에 관한 **165** 당신이 생각한 우리의 기술지에 의해 설계되어, 지 금 예비 시험을 기다리는 중입니다.

아시다시피, 회사는 당신이 한 일이 얼마 유용한 한신에 대답해 드리고 감사드리고 **166** 보너스 수여로서 감사의 인정을 표합니다. 또한, 당신의 아이디어는 지사 의 그게 관련 사용들을 향상시킬 중심이 되는 것으로 증명되었기 때문에 회사 는 당신에게 보너스에 추가하여 **166** 회사가 지불하는 바하띠로의 업무상 휴가 를 주기로 결정했습니다. 또한, 당신은 **166** 구내식당에서 이용할 수 있는 10장 의 식권을 받을 것입니다. **167** 당신이 지난주 회의에서 우리 직원들의 열정과 사 정의 기뻐하시는 모습에서 본 대로, 회사 전체가 당신에 한신에 감사드립니다!

보즈워 씨 훌륭했습니다!

**어휘** meaningful 의미 있는 alert 경보 shutdown disconnection 중단 engulf 완전히 에워싸다 address 다루다 resourceful 재치 있게 interlock 서로 맞물리게 하다 pilot test 예비 시험 recognition 인정 grant 수여하다 pivotal 중심이 되는 excitement 기쁨, 흥분 exotic 외의 assess 평가하다 formulate 조직적으로 세우다 prototype 견본 원형

[168-171]

| | |
|---|---|
| 트로이 블룬 [오전 9시 18분] | **168** 콘서트 준비는 어떻게 되어 가고 있나요? |
| 존 페이지 [오전 9시 20분] | 지금까지는 좋아요. 모든 음악 연주자들이 준비됐어요. 이제 하나만 남았네요. |
| 루시 호잉 [오전 9시 21분] | 그게 뭔가요? 서둘러야 해요. |
| 존 페이지 [오전 9시 22분] | **169** 무대 기술자를 고용하는 건데… |
| 루시 호잉 [오전 9시 23분] | **169** 이해가 안 되네요. **170** 이미 몇 명씩 고용한 걸로 아는데요. |
| 존 페이지 [오전 9시 24분] | 그랬죠. **170** 근데, 전자 제어판을 다룰 수 있는 사람이 없어요. |
| 트로이 블룬 [오전 9시 25분] | 이상하네요, 단 한 명도요? |
| 존 페이지 [오전 9시 27분] | **170** 쇼가 진행되는 동안 무대의 모든 조명을 자동으로 조절할 수 있어야 하는데, 아무 나 할 수 있는 게 아니죠. |
| 루시 호잉 [오전 9시 29분] | 그렇다면 이게 끝나고 바로 채용 공고를 낼 게요. 시간이 많지 않아요. |
| 존 페이지 [오전 9시 30분] | 그럼, **171** 저는 음악 연주자들한테 가서 계 약을 체결하게 조금 후 봐요! |

**어휘** preparation for ~을 위한 준비　be lined up 정렬되다, 준비되다　technician 기술자　electronic console 전자식 제어판　weird 이상한　stage light 무대 조명　if that's case 그런 경우라면(=in that case)　advertise a position 채용 공고를 내다　sign (a contract) with ~와 계 약을 체결하다

**168** 블룬 씨는 어떤 회사에서 근무하겠는가?
(A) 텔레비전 제조업체
(B) 조명 장비 소매업체
**(C) 이벤트 기획업체**
(D) 라디오 방송국

**169** 오전 9시 22분에, 호잉 씨가 "이해가 안 되네요"라고 쓸 때, 그 이유는 무엇인가?
**(A) 페이지 씨가 무대 전문가를 고용하는 것에 대해 한 말을 이해할 수 없다.**
(B) 무대 기술자들의 행동을 참을 수가 없다.
(C) 얼마나 많은 음악 연주자들이 오는지 모른다.
(D) 무대 기술자들이 준비될지 예상하지 않았다.

[172-175]

**후레쉬 아로마 주식회사**
신나 파레이드, 뉴캐슬 BT33
뉴잉랜드, 영국
www.fresharoma.co.uk

3월 15일

마이클 마노이
마들러 F & B 기업
1240 독사슨 대로
마들러, 필리핀
마노이 씨께,

이 기회를 빌려 저희 회사를 소개하고 싶습니다. -[1]- **172** 북잉랜드 에서 가장 빠르게 성장하는 음료 회사 중 하나인 저희 후레쉬 아로마 주식 회사는 모든 음료, 특히 북아메 원두로 만든 커피로 특화되어 있습니다.

**172 175** 저희 중간 업체가 직접 우리 아프리카 국가들로부터 커피콩을 수입합니다. -[2]- 물론, 이미 다양한 종류의 커피콩이 있지만, 저 희가 만드는 커피는 다른 커피보다 더 맛이 좋다고 할 것이요. - **173** 저희 전문 구매 이들 덕분에 이프리 커피 라인도 맛을 넣고 - 런던, 파리 - 이런 점 때문에, 저희는 마들러 시에서 가장 큰 음료 도매업체인 마들러 F & B 기업의 파트너가 되고 싶다는 점을 말씀드리고 싶습니다.

(A) [1]
(B) **[2]**
(C) [3]
(D) [4]

해설 중간업체가 커피나무가 널리 경작되는 아프리카 국가들로부터 커피 열매를 수입한다는 내용 다음에 커피 열매들이 거치는 과정이 나와야 자연스럽다. 따라서 정답은 (B)이다; they're coffee seeds를 대신한다.

[176-180]

파리 패션 위크 하이라이트

2017년 6월 3일 　　　　　 파리에서 엘라 화이트

**떠오르는 디자이너의 성공적인 데뷔**

176 디자이너 마이클 휴가사는 6월 1일 파리에서 열린 그의 데뷔 패션쇼에서 인상적인 커미를 드레스 디자인을 선보였습니다. 독일 태생인 휴가사 씨는 10년 동안 네덜란드 자신의 부티크 '니르소스'를 운영하면서 그의 바느질 기술을 완벽히 익혔고 패션 디자인에서 독특한 관점을 키웠습니다. 세련되고 우아한 무드의 드레스에 관한 그의 은자 왕국은 고가 파리에 부티크를 연 후 인기를 끌었습니다. 그의 자연에 대한 사랑은 또한 최소한의 화학적인 가공을 필요로 하는 인조 모피나 자연 직물로 만든 그의 옷에 잘 표현됩니다. 독일 수상이 그의 의류를 입은 후, 177 그는 파리 패션 위크의 조직 위원이며, 쉽게 접할 수 없는 여러 패션 브랜드 그룹으로부터 협조를 받았습니다. 세계 최고의 패션 거물들 중 몇 명과 함께 작업할 것으로 예상되는 것입니다.

수신: 마이클 휴가사(michug@tmail.com)
발신: 반 기우드(vgpersonnel@hmqw.fr)
날짜: 2017년 6월 8일
제목: 일자리 제안

휴가사 씨에게

178 저희는 파리 패션 위크에서 대부 쇼에서 보여줬던 당신의 자신감과 티윌 함에 매우 감명받았습니다. 패션쇼가 끝나고 당신과 나눴던 대화도 정말 즐거웠습니다.

179 저희 HMQW에 더 높은 솜씨 수준을 만들자는 희망으로 저희에게 디자이너로 입사를 제안합니다. 179 저희 제안에 관심이 있으시다면, 6월 14일까지 당신의 작품집과 이력서, 출생증명서 사본을 보내 주세요. 180 당신의 서류를 검토하고 지역 마무리를 위해 당신에게 현지 은행 계좌를 개설하라고 요청할 것입니다. 추가 질문이 있으시면, 저희의 인사부 직원인 장 마리에게 013-681-2017로 인사부에 전화하십시오.

추가 질문이 있으시면, 저희의 인사부 직원인 장 마리에게 연락주십시오.

어휘 couture 유명 디자이너의 제품 sewing 바느질 cultivate 양성하다 perspective 관점 boutique 부티크, 옷 가게 hermit 은둔자 sophisticated 세련된 delicate 우아한 ball gown 무도회 드레스 draw attention 관심을 끌다 faux fur 인조모피 textile 직물, 섬유 chancellor 수상 don 입다 mermaid 인어 thoroughly 철저하게

craftsmanship 솜씨 portfolio 작품집 curriculum vitae 이력서 birth certificate 출생증명서 upon -ing 하자마자

**176 휴가 씨에 관하여 사실인 것은 무엇인가?**
(A) 10년 동안 옷 가게 주인으로 일했다.
(B) 고국에서 교육을 마쳤다.
(C) 작품들이 과하게 화학 처리한 직물에 의존한다.
(D) 파리 패션 위크에 몇 번 참석한 적이 있다.

해설 기사에 의하면 휴가사 씨가 자신이 소유한 '니르소스'를 10년간 운영했다고 하므로 정답은 (A)이다.

**177 오스텔 씨는 누구인가?**
(A) HMQW의 대표
(B) 패션 잡지의 편집장
(C) 독립 수상
(D) 행사 기획자

해설 기사에서 오스텔 씨는 파리 패션 위크의 조직자이며, 그녀가 휴가사 씨를 조대했다고 하므로 정답은 (D)이다.

**178 휴가사 씨는 HMQW의 직원들 처음 만났는가?**
(A) 6월 1일
(B) 6월 3일
(C) 6월 8일
(D) 6월 14일

해설 이메일에서 HMQW의 직원은 패션 위크 대부는 인상적이었으며 패션 소가 끝나고 나눈 대화가 기뻤다고 했으므로, 패션쇼 당일 만났다는 것을 수 있다. 기사에서 휴가사 씨의 패션쇼가 6월 1일에 있었다고 했으므로 정답은 (A)이다.

**179 일자리 제안에서 휴가사 씨에게 요청되지 않은 것은 무엇인가?**
(A) 출생증명서 사본
(B) 작품집
(C) 유효한 건강 보험의 증명
(D) 이력서

해설 이메일에서 일자리 제안에 관심이 있다면 휴가사 씨에게 작품집과 이력서, 출생증명서 사본을 보내 달라고 했으며 (이는 언급되어 있지 않다.

**180 고용 절차를 마무리하기 위해 특별히 요청을 읽은 무엇인가?**
(A) 면접을 위해 HMQW 본사 방문하기
(B) 프랑스의 은행에서 새로운 계좌 신청하기
(C) 현지 은행에서 계좌 만들기
(D) 파리 주체를 제안하기

해설 이메일에서 휴가사 씨가 서류를 보내면 검토 후에, 지역의 은행에서 계좌를 만들라는 요청을 하겠다고 했으므로 (C)가 정답이다.

[181-185]

수신: 그레이스 프레스트(grace29@cooks.com)
발신: 록산나 스테일(roxy_72@vortex.net)
날짜: 8월 11일
제목: 파티, 경품
사랑하는 사촌에게!

지난번에 본 후로 시간이 많이 흘렀네요. 빠른 회답 감사해요. 당신이 새로 태어난 아이의 세례를 축하하러 남패고 아들 준과 함께 할 수 있어서 기뻐요. 친척들을 위해 특별히 준비된 파티 상품을 교회에서 나눠 주기 어렵기 때문에 181 저는 당신의 현지 주소를 확인하고 긍정 안전하게 배달하기로 했어요.

182 일단, 제가 당신의 정확한 주소를 일반 배송을 위해 주소를 등록하려는 소포 수행에 필요한 비밀번호를 드릴 수 있어요 184 저는 6개월 전의 주소인 36 트레비레인 드라이브 라지밀 온타리오 M2O 8F5를 알고 있는데 맞나요? 가능한 한 빨리 답해 주세요. 감사하고, 곧 볼게요!

주소: 183 기족사진을 위해 조대장에 설명된 드레스 코드를 따르시와 해요

수신: 록산나 스테일(roxy_72@vortex.net)
발신: 그레이스 프레스트(grace29@cooks.com)
날짜: 8월 12일
제목: 당신 파티, 경품들

놀랍군요, 파티 선물이 예배 중에 다루기에 그렇게 어려운가요? 그게 무엇인지 정말 궁금하네요. 그리고 우리 가족들은 행사에 입을 정장을 모두 미련했으니 걱정할 필요 없어요. 184 매니얼이 한 달 전에 진즈마 동시에 새로운 지점으로 옮겨서 X3L 9V10에요. 가족들 모두 함께 가서 세례를 기다 새로운 가족을 만나는 것이 매우 기대되네요. 곧 봐요

어휘 party favor 파티 선물 R.S.V.P. 회신 바람 christening 세례 delicate 하기 어려운 distribute 나누어 주다 retrieval 회수 parcel 소포, 꾸러미 portrait 초상화, 사진 transfer 옮기다 branch 지점 come along 함께 가다 verify 확인하다 verification 조회 outfit 옷 pre-ordered 선 주문된 congregate 모이다 pregnant 임신의

**181 첫 번째 이메일의 목적은 무엇인가?**
(A) 가족 행사에 사람들을 초대하기 위해
(B) **주소가 올바른지 확인하기 위해**
(C) 새로운 배달 방법을 소개하기 위해
(D) 파티 주제를 제안하기 위해

해설 첫 번째 이메일에서 파티의 상품을 배송하기로 했다면서 주소를 확인하고 싶다고 했으므로 정답은 (B)이다.

**182 스테일 씨는 올바른 주소를 확인한 후에 무엇을 할 것인가?**
(A) 사촌에게 온라인 배달 개로의 비밀 번호를 준다.
(B) **사촌에게 배달을 받기 위해 필요한 확인 번호를 보낸다.**
(C) 교회품으로 위해 파티 선물을 반송한다.
(D) 사람들 위해 가족들의 옷들을 시러 쇼핑을 간다.

**187** 네이벌린 주식회사는 어떤 회사이겠는가?

(A) 요가 지도 학원
(B) 주간 잡지 출판사
(C) 인테리어 디자인 업체
**(D) 화장품 판매 회사**

해설 네이벌린 주식회사의 "피부가 지성이든 건성이든 얼굴을 더 부드럽게 보이도록 해주는 제품이고 광고문에 '한damp요'라는 내용을 통해 네이벌린 주식회사는 화장품 판매 회사임을 알 수 있다. 따라서 정답은 (D)가 정답이다.

**188** 이메일에서 두 번째 단락, 첫 번째 줄의 단어 get rid of와 의미상 가장 가까운 것은 무엇인가?

**(A) 해소하다**
(B) 강화하다
(C) 샴푸를 넣다
(D) 문제로다

해설 get rid of는 '~을 제거하다'는 뜻으로, get rid of stress는 '스트레스를 해소하다'는 뜻이다. 따라서 '스트레스를 해소하다'라는 뜻의 relieve, (A)가 정답이다.

**189** 포터 씨는 토마스 씨를 어디서 만나겠는가?

**(A) 16번가에서**
(B) 벨리나 로드에서
(C) 프랭클린 로드에서
(D) 이베 애비뉴에서

해설 이메일에서 포터 씨가 "제가 다니는 통제비티 요가 학원의 주소를 보내줄 지에서 토마스 씨가 '제가 다니는 통제비티 요가 학원의 주소를 보내줄게요'라고 했다. 따라서 이들은 요가 건물 안에서 만날 것임을 알 수 있다. 기사에서 요가 학원이 4월 21일에 사우스웨스트 16번 가의 새 지역으로 이사할 전망이다'라는 내용에서 5월 18일에는 16번 가에 위치하고 있음을 유추할 수 있다. 따라서 정답은 (A)이다.

**190** 토마스 씨에 대해 알 수 있는 것은 무엇인가?

(A) 수년간 요가 학원을 다녔다.
(B) 최근 하나 씨를 고용했다.
**(C) 토요일 오후 2시 이후에 쇼핑을 할 것이다.**
(D) 5월 18일 박람회에 참석하지 않았다.

해설 토마스 씨가 쓴 문자 메시지에 "이번 토요일에 저는 오전에 수업이 있고 오후에는 수업이 다 든고 쇼핑하러 갈 거예요'라고 하며, 기사에서 '이상 시간을 오일부터 금요일은 오전 8시부터 오후 6시까지이고, 토요일은 오전 10시부터 오후 2시까지이다'라는 내용에서 요가 수업이 오전 10시에 끝나므로 오전 토요일에는 오후 2시에 끝남을 알 수 있다. 따라서 토요일 오후 2시 이후에 쇼핑을 할 것이라는 (C)가 정답이다.

---

발신: 제니퍼 포터 (jpotter@navelline.com)
수신: 엘라 토마스 (ethomas@navelline.com)
날짜: 5월 18일
제목: A-2 파우더

엘라 씨,

오늘 박람회 어땠어요? 하나 씨가 열라 새로부터 프로그램이 로드 공사 때문에 박람회에 늦을 것 같다는 내용을 문자를 받았다고 해서 걱정했어요. 다 참 해결돼서 잘됐네요. 하나 씨가 지도로 열라 새의 A-2 파우더에 대한 마케팅 홍보를 도와주고 했어요. 하나 씨가 새로운 건성이든 건성이든 얼굴을 더 부드럽게 보이도록 해주는 제품이라고 광고도에야 한다고 새 제품을 출시한다고 했어요. 하나 씨가 지도로 직접 찾아가서 건물 안에서 기다릴게요.

요가를 배우기 시작했고 지도 해도 될까? 전체도 스트레스 좀 해소해야 할 거 같아요. 룸메를 유지하는 데에도 좋고 해서 해볼 만 하다고 생각해요. 주소만 알려주면, 제가 직접 찾아가서 건물 안에서 기다릴게요.

제니퍼
마케팅 팀 네이벌린 주식회사

---

**183** 세러에 관하여 추론할 수 있는 것은 무엇인가?

(A) 손님들은 그룹이 좋아하는 무엇인지 알 수 있다.
(B) 스타일 가족에게 첫 번째 행사다.
(C) 미리 주문한 파티 상품이 개재자 배달되었다.
**(D)사진을 찍기 위하여 친척들이 모일 것이다.**

해설 첫 번째 이메일에서 마지막에 주인으로 가족사진을 찍기 위해 드레스 코드를 따라 입다고 했으므로 정답은 (D)이다.

**184** 지난 6개월 동안 무슨 일이 있었는가?

(A) 포레스트 씨는 파티 계획자로서 일을 시작했다.
(B) 스타일 씨는 온라인으로 파티 상품을 검토를 열었다.
(C) 스타일 씨는 입성했다.
**(D)포레스트 씨는 다른 지역의 새장소로 이사를 했다.**

해설 첫 번째 이메일에서 스타일 씨가 읽고 있는 포레스트 씨의 주소가 두 번째 이메일에서 포레스트 씨가 입하는 집 주소가 다른데, 포레스트 씨는 가족 구성원이 매니얼의 전근 때문에 다른 지역으로 이사했다고 말했다. 따라서 (D)가 정답이다.

**185** 첫 번째 이메일의 4번째 줄 distributed와 의미상 가장 가까운 단어는?

**(A) 나누게 된**
(B) 생산된
(C) 심어진
(D) 기둘고 긴

해설 distributed는 '분배되다, 나누게 되다'이란 표현으로, 의미상 가장 가까운 단어는 '나누게 된'이란 의미의 (A) apportioned이다.

---

벨리지 시 단신                          4월 15일

**벨리지, 도시의 주류로 이동하다!**

189 지난 금요일 공사가 끝남으로써, 통제비티 요가 학원이 4월 21일에 사우스웨스트 16번가의 새로운 지역으로 이사할 전망이다. 개장은 다음 달 초에 하다.
새 지역에서는 벨리지 로드에 있던 예전 장소보다 훨씬 더 큰 주차 구역을 제공한다. 186 "수강생 수 증가를 맞추기 위해 어떤 장소가 필요했습니다."라고 한 위 이사장이 크리스토퍼 케인 씨는 말했다. 또한, "건강 문제에 대한 인식이 늘어나서 대다수의 시민들은 요가를 건강하고 가치가 있는 것으로 봅니다."라고 말했다. 190 증가하는 수요를 맞추기 위해 학원은 토요일에 수업을 추가하고 주말 반으로 수업 시간을 늘릴 예정이다. 190 이상 시간은 월요일부터 금요일은 오전 8시부터 오후 6시까지이고, 토요일은 오전 10시부터 오후 2시까지이다.
한루 출한의 요가는 자기의 마음과 흐름 조절, 간단한 명상, 특정 신체 자세의 선정 등으로 알려져 있다. 요가 운동은 호흡 조절, 명상, 특정 신체 자세에 연습하는 것들이며, 이는 모두 건강과 휴식을 위해 널리 연습되는 것들이다.
블레미크 라믐, 전속 기자

---

어휘 mainstream 주류, 대세   parking space 주차 공간   accommodate 수용하다   awareness 인식, 관심   the majority of 대다수의   worthwhile 보람 있는, 가치 있는   meet consumer demands 소비자 수요를 충족하다   extend 늘리다, 연장하다   meditation 명상   spiritual discipline 정신적 훈련   후식 휴식   bodily posture 신체 자세   relaxation 이완, 휴식   fair 박람회   smooth 매끄러운, 부드러운   launch (제품을)출시하다   keep in a good shape 건강을 유지하다, 좋은 몸매를 유지하다   break 휴식 시간   register 등록하다   take classes 수업을 듣다   go shopping 쇼핑하러 가다   city council 시의회   downsize 축소하다   abolish 폐지하다

**186** 기사에 따르면, 통제비티 요가 학원은 왜 새 지역으로 이사했는가?

(A) 시의회가 개발 계획을 바꿨다.
**(B) 새 요가에 대한 수요가 늘었다.**
(C) 학원이 시설을 축소하기로 결정했다.
(D) 원래 건축 계획이 폐지되었다.

해설 기사에서 "수강생 수 증가를 맞추기 위해 어떤 장소가 필요했습니다. '증가하는 수요를 맞추기 위해' 등의 내용을 통해 이사한 이유가 벨리지 시 내의 요가 수요가 늘었기 때문임을 알 수 있다. 따라서 (B)가 정답이다.

[186-190]

## 다이허 지역 뉴스 6월 2일

### M.O.T. 사진작가들의 모임을 목표로 하다!

M.O.T. 아마추어 사진작가들의 모임을 목표로 하다!

M.O.T. 아마추어 사진작가 대회가 다이허 시의 모네티 예술 센터에서 6월 18일에 열린다. 전 세계 아마추어 사진작가들이 자신의 작품과 영감을 다른 경쟁자들과 공유할 것으로 기대된다.

대회 참여 비용은 무료이다. 경쟁자들은 자유와 사람이라는 각각의 항목에 사진 3개까지 사진을 제출할 수 있다. 사진작가들의 이름은 투표 진행 시 전시되지 않는데, 이는 각 사진을 정정함으로 평가되는 공평한 기회가 주어지록 의미한다. 사진들을 투표자들에게 모두 같은 횟수로 전시된다. "여기서는 작가의 인기나 투표를 위해 대중에 호소하는 것이 아니라 창의성을 구현해 내는 것이 중요하다는 점에서 저희 대회는 특별하다"라고 대회 위원장인 마이클 넬로는 말했다. "지focus는 높이운 상태를 함께 축하하고 다른 작가들도 리 알려주고, 저표 부여 상태를 유지하도록 권장한다. 그들은 자유롭게 서로 다른 관점들을 표현하고 경쟁을 통해 설번한다."라고 대출로 씨는 말했다.

하지만 같은 장소에서 그 다음 날 열리는 M.O.T. 전문 사진작가 대회의 경우에는 위원회가 특별 심사위원단을 준비했다. 화랑 주인, 편집자, 유명한 사진작가들이 특별 심사위원단에게 대회에 대해 권장하기 위한 지역 뉴스임을 알 수 있다.

세계에서 가장 공정한 사진 대회에 예술 작품을 제출할 기한은 6월 16일까지이다. 전시 있는 사진작가들에게 5천 달러의 상금을 받을 기회를 잡을 수 있다. 전화번호 245-5670-3533 / 홈페이지: www.motawards.com.

발신: 엔소니 사이먼
수신: inquiry@motawards.com
날짜: 6월 11일
제목: 사진 응모

담당자 분께,

M.O.T. 아마추어 사진작가 대회에 대해 궁금한 점이 있습니다. 제가 대회에 대한 몇 가지 항목으로 사진을 제출할 수 있는 것으로 알고 있습니다. 저는 '자는 자유'라는 항목에 가능한 한 많이 응모하고 싶습니다. 제가 궁금한 것은 이 항목으로 최대 몇 개까지 응모할 수 있는지입니다. 이 점에 대해 알려주신다면 감사하겠습니다.

좋은 하루 되세요,

엔소니 사이먼

발신: 에런 무디
수신: 네이트 필라
날짜: 6월 14일
제목: 사진 대회

네이트 씨,

다음 주에 열리는 M.O.T. 전문 사진작가 대회를 준비한다고 들었어요. 준비는 잘 되고 있나요? 제가 이런 대회를 성당히 좋아하는 걸 아시겠지만, 대회가 열릴 때쯤 마을 거 같아요. 6월 20과 21일에 중요한 회의가 접혀 있거든요. 생이 기뭄은 지도 네이트 씨처럼 전문 사진작가였으면 하는데, 언제든 열릴 때 출사 나갈 수 있을 테니까요. 성공받으면 크게 혜택 쓰세요.

행운을 빌어요.

에런

**어휘** inspiration 영감 contender 경쟁자, 참가자 enter 응모하다 up to ~까지 display 전시하다 unique 독특한, 특별한 embody 구현하다 popularity 대중성, 인기 appeal 호소하다 accomplish 이루다, 성취해내다 keep up 유지하다 artistic motivation 예술적 동기 부여 freely 자유롭게 thrive 번영하다 the following day 그 다음 날 comprise 구성되다 highly renowned 명망이 높은 (art) gallery 화랑 acclaimed 칭송을 받는, 호평받는 work of art 예술 작품 fair 공정한 cash prize (현금) 상금 maximum 최대한 entry 응모(작) be up for ~에 (상당히) 참여하려고 준비하다 preparation 준비 be (pretty much) into ~에 (상당히) 관심이 있다 outdoors 야외에서 give me a (big) treat (크게) 한턱 쓰세요 criteria 기준 incomparably 비교할 수 없이 prestigious 명망 있는

**191** 기사의 목적은 무엇인가?
(A) 왜 예술 센터가 임대됐는지 설명하려고
(B) 새로 출시된 카메라를 홍보하려고
(C) **사진작가들이 대회에 참여하도록 권장하려고**
(D) 중요한 시 계획을 발표하려고

**해설** 기사는 사진작가 대회에 대한 소식을 전하면서 마지막 부분에서 "전시 있는 사진작가들은 5천 달러의 상금을 받을 기회를 잡을 수 있다"고 했다. 따라서 사진작가들에게 대회에 참여를 권장하기 위한 지역 뉴스임을 알 수 있다. 정답은 (C)이다.

**192** 기사에 따르면 무엇이 M.O.T. 사진작가 대회를 특별하게 하는가?
(A) **공정한 선정 기준**
(B) 비교 불가능한 긴 역사
(C) 잘 훈련된 위원회 회원
(D) 가장 큰 상금

**해설** 기사에서 "사진작가들의 이름은 투표 진행 시 전시되지 않는데, 이는 각 사진들의 정정함으로 평가되는 공평한 기회가 주어짐을 의미한다. 또한, 사진들을 투표자들에게 모두 같은 횟수로 전시된다는 내용을 보면 공정한 선정 기준이 강조되고 있음을 알 수 있다. 따라서 정답은 (A)가 정답이다.

**193** 누가 특별 심사위원단에 포함되지 않겠는가?
(A) 유명한 화랑을 보유하고 있는 사람
(B) 신문의 최종 내용을 책임지는 사람
(C) 전문적으로 사진을 찍는 사람
(D) **명망 있는 대회에서 기준자는 사람**

**해설** 기사에서 "위원회가 특별 심사위원단을 준비했는데, 화랑 사장, 편집자, 유명한 사진작가들 중 영상이 있는 분야 전문가들로 구성되어 있다"는 내용을 보면 교수를 뜻하는 (D)가 정답임을 알 수 있다.

**194** 사이먼 씨는 얼마나 많은 응모작을 내겠는가?
(A) **세 개**
(B) 네 개
(C) 다섯 개
(D) 여섯 개

**해설** 사이먼 씨가 쓴 첫 번째 이메일에서 "저는 '자는 자유' 항목에 가능한 한 많이 응모하고 싶어요"라는 내용이 나온다. 이제 기사를 보면, "경쟁 자들은 자유와 사람이므로 각각의 항목에 3개까지 3개까지 사진을 제출할 수 있다"라고 하였으므로 사이먼 씨는 '자유' 항목에서 최대 3개의 응모작을 낼 것임을 알 수 있다. 따라서 정답은 (A)이다.

**195** 필라 씨는 M.O.T. 사진작가가 대회에 언제 참여하겠는가?
(A) 6월 18일
(B) **6월 19일**
(C) 6월 20일
(D) 6월 21일

**해설** 두 번째 이메일을 보면, "가뭄은 지도 네이트 씨처럼 전문 사진작가였으면 한다"라는 내용에서 네이트 씨가 전문 사진작가임을 알 수 있다. 18일에 열린다"는 내용에서 아마추어를 위한 M.O.T. 아마추어 사진작가 대회가 6월 18일에 열린다는 것을 알 수 있다. 그리고 기사 후반부에 "같은 장소에서 그 다음 날 열리는 M.O.T. 전문 사진작가들을 위한 표현에서 전문 사진작가를 위한 M.O.T. 대회는 그 다음 날인 6월 19일에 열리는 것을 알 수 있다. 따라서 전문 사진작가인 필라 씨는 6월 19일에 열리는 대회에 참석할 것이므로 정답은 (B)이다.

해설 기사에서 "우리는 가격을 제외한 모든 항목에서 아주 높은 점수를 항상 받아왔는데"라고 했고, 이메일에서도 "저는 우리 제품의 품질과 M & S 쇼핑센터의 경쟁력이 경쟁에서 다소 비싸다는 것을 알고 있었고" 등의 표현을 보면 M & S 쇼핑센터의 경쟁력이 가장 약한 부분은 가격임을 알 수 있다. 따라서 (A)가 정답이다.

**198** 메일의 쓴이는 누구이겠는가?
(A) 공동 사장
(B) 마케팅 팀원
(C) 관리 팀 인턴
(D) 하청업자

해설 기사에서 "두 명의 공동 사장의 성에서 각각 첫 글자를 따서 지은 M & S 쇼핑센터"라는 내용이 나오고, "센터의 공동 사장 중 한 명인 작 스미스 씨는 말한다"는 내용을 볼 때, 다른 사장의 성은 M으로 시작함을 알 수 있다. 다른 사장 씨가 쓴 이메일에 보면, "이 문제를 알렉산더 씨에게 계속 보고했는데, 작 스미스 씨에는 달리 너무 인건해서 들으려 하질 않더라고요"라는 내용에서 씨와 또 다른 공동 사장임을 알 수 있다. 따라서 (A)가 정답이다.

어휘 subcontractor 하청업체

**199** 이메일에서 첫 번째 단락 첫 번째 줄의 turned out과 의미상 가장 가까운 것은 무엇인가?
(A) 기대했다
**(B) 판명됐다**
(C) 고백했다
(D) 만료됐다

해설 turn out (to be)은 '~로 판명되다, 드러나다'의 뜻이므로 prove (to be)와 의미가 비슷하다. 따라서 (B)가 정답이다.

어휘 turn out (to be) ~로 판명되다, 드러나다

**200** 포스터에 대해 알 수 있는 것은 무엇인가?
(A) 타사가 씨와 같은 팀에서 일한다.
(B) 바에서 쓰는 높은 의자를 최근 구성했다.
**(C) 그녀의 제안이 받아들여졌다.**
(D) 그녀의 금에는 화사해를 언급했다.

해설 이메일에서 "다른 선택 사항은 제안 씨가 제안한 것처럼 이번 보기 시장 점무용을 유지하기 위해서 담보간 매들 할인 쿠폰을 발급하는 것입니다. 그 내용을 보면, 제안 씨가 내로 무료 담보를 제안한 것을 알 수 있다. 광고에서는 "이달 5월을 시작으로 9월 말까지 M & S 쇼핑센터에서 매달 발급하는 특별 할인 쿠폰의 모든 정식 제품에 적용됩니다"라는 내용에서 그녀의 제안이 받아들여졌음을 알 수 있다. 따라서 (C)가 정답이다.

---

## M & S 쇼핑센터

아래 제품 포함 모든 가정용 가구를 판매합니다.

· 식탁
· 고리버들 의자
· 소파
· 합성수지 의자
· 일광욕 의자
· 술잔용 높은 의자

**200** 이달 5월을 시작으로 9월 말까지 M & S 쇼핑센터에서 매달 발급한 특별 할인 쿠폰의 모든 정식 제품에 적용됩니다! 이 가격에 대해 더 알고 싶으시면, 아래 영업 시간 동안 532-4653로 전화 주시거나 www.afcentre.com을 방문해 주세요.

영업 시간

일요일 – 토요일: 오전 9시 – 오후 7시
일요일: 오전 10시 – 오후 6시

---

## 메이번 트리뷴          4월 15일

시민들은 테이블, 의자, 책상 같은 가구들을 다른 어떤 곳보다 M & S 쇼핑센터에서 더 많이 구매한다. **196** 시의 가구 시장에서 40퍼센트를 점유하고 있는데, 이는 작년보다 10퍼센트 오른 것이다. **197** 두 명의 공동 사장의 성에서 각각 첫 글자를 따서 지은 M & S 쇼핑센터는 식탁만을 파는 작은 소매업체로 시작했지만, 지금은 시에서 가장 큰 쇼핑 장소가 되었다.

더 놀라운 것은 센터에서 고객들에게 최고의 쇼핑 경험을 제공한다는 것이다. 매 이번 트리뷴 3월 15일 판은 메이번 시에 시의 모든 가구들을 대상으로 쇼핑 경험을 제공한 평론을 실었는데, M & S 쇼핑센터는 그 중에서도 1위로 뽑혔다. '놀랍지 않은 뉴스라고 말하는 사람들도 있을 것이다. **197** 우리는 가격을 제외한 모든 항목에서 아주 높은 점수를 항상 받아왔는데,'라고 센터의 공동 사장 중 한 명인 작 스미스 씨는 말했다. **198** '리고 센터의 공동 사장 중 또 한 명인 작 스미스 씨는 말했다.

하지만 다른 의견도 존재한다. 전문가들은 어떤 시점도 빨리 무너질 수 있다고 지적한다. '대부분의 쇼핑객은 사람들에게 실제 장소의 경우 가격이 중요합니다. 소수의 사람들만 고품질을 위해 높은 값을 지불합니다. 다른 사람들에게는 가격이 최우선 오건입니다'라고 L.I.H. 비즈니스 기관의 연구자인 로버트 옐슨 씨는 말했다. M & S 쇼핑센터가 가격 인하를 위해 시업 방향을 바꾸지 않으면 지켜보나라도, 고객 의견을 반영하기 위한 최소한의 노력을 기울이게 보인다.

조수아 콜로스, 전속 기자

---

발신: 브라이언 타나카 (btanaka@mscentre.com)
수신: 윌리엄 리건 (wregan@mscentre.com)
날짜: 4월 19일
제목: 메이번 트리뷴 판

윌리엄 씨,

마케팅 부서에 제안 포스터 씨가 메이번 트리뷴의 3월 판에 대해 알려줬어요. 결과를 예상한 그대로 **197** 저는 우리 제품의 씨가 메이번다 **199** 드러났어요. **197** 이 문제를 알렉산더 씨에게 계속 보고 비싸다는 것을 알고 있었고 **198** 저는 우리 제품의 품질과 M & S 쇼핑센터의 시장에서 매매다 계속 보고 했는데, 작 스미스 씨에는 달리 너무 인건해서 들으려 하질 않더라고요.

메이번 트리뷴에서 언급한 대로, 우리가 이제는 인기를 해야 합니다. 자정부 암박을 견디면서도 고품질을 유지하기 위해서 자는 우리가 파트너에 대해 우연계 해야 한다고 생각해요. 기왕 기능하면 약간 더 값이 싼 원자재를 사용하는 암박을 찾는다든지 않아요. **200** 다른 선택 사항은 제안 씨가 제안한 것처럼 이번 보기 시장 점유율을 유지하기 위해서 담보간 매들 할인 쿠폰을 발급하는 것입니다.

어떻게 생각하는지 알려주세요

브라이언 타나카
관리팀장 M & S 쇼핑센터

---

어휘 occupy 점유하다 | name after ~을 따서 이름을 짓다 | retailer 소매업체 | issue (잡지나 신문 등의) 판 | feature (특징으로) 포함하다 | ratings and reviews 평가와 평론 | reasonable 합리적인 | raw material 원자재 | co-president 공동 사장 | a large portion 대부분의 | matter 중요하다 | when it comes to ~에 대해 얘기하자면 | decoration 장식 | pay a premium 높은 가격을 지불하다 | first priority 우선 사항 | reflect 반영하다 | inevitable 불가피한 | staff writer 전속 기자 | turn out to be ~인 것으로 판명되다 | stubborn 완고한, 고집이 있는 | flexible 유연한 | say 기술(대화 도중 상대의 이목을 끌기 위해 혹은 예를 들 때 쓰는 표현) | slightly 약간 | dining table 식탁 | wicker chair 고리버들 의자 | resin chair 합성수지 의자 | sun lounge 일광욕 등을 위해 따로 둠힘 수 있는 | bar stool 바에 놓는 둥그렇고 높이가 있는 의자 | business hours 영업 시간 | apply to ~에 적용되다 | rate 가격, 요금

**196** M & S 쇼핑센터에 대한 사실로 무엇인가?
(A) 큰 도매업체로 사업을 시작했다.
**(B) 올해 시장 점유율이 10퍼센트 올랐다.**
(C) 오직 사무용 가구만 판매한다.
(D) 시에서 두 번째로 큰 쇼핑센터이다.

해설 기사에서 시의 가구 시장에서 40퍼센트를 점유하고 있는데, 이는 작년보다 10퍼센트 오른 것이라는 내용을 통해 (B)가 정답임을 알 수 있다. 기사에서 작은 소매업체로 시작했다고 했으므로 (A)는 틀렸고, 기사에서 시에서 가장 큰 쇼핑센터라고 했으므로 (D)도 틀렸다.

어휘 wholesaler 도매업체

**197** 기사에 따르면, M & S 쇼핑센터의 경쟁력이 가장 약한 부분은 무엇인가?
**(A) 가격**
(B) 제품 품질
(C) 배달
(D) 보증 서비스

Memo

Memo

Memo

혼자 공부하는 독종을 위한 나혼자 끝내는 新 토익

# 최종 점검 토익 실전 모의고사
# LC+RC 1000제

★ 한 권으로 끝내는 신토익 실전 모의고사 5회분 수록
★ 해설집을 따로 구매할 필요가 없는 LC+RC 합본 실전서
★ 저자의 노하우를 담아 문제의 키워드를 단숨에 파악하는 알짜 해설 수록
★ 토익카들의 답답한 궁금증을 풀어주는 미국식, 영국식, 호주식 발음 완벽 대비
★ 실전용·복습용·고사장 버전의 3종 MP3 무료 다운로드 >> QR코드 & 홈페이지
★ 문제풀이 후 바로 채점할 수 있는 자동 채점 방식 및 받아쓰기 테스트 제공 >> QR코드
★ 신토익 빈출 어휘 리스트 & 테스트 제공 >> www.nexusbook.com

나혼토 1:1 코칭

## RC
저자 홍진걸
>> 네이버 카페(cafe.naver.com/toeicway2)
[나혼토 1:1 코칭] 게시판 이용

## LC
저자 이주은
>> 카카오톡 ID로 찾기(ID: bktellas)
친구 추가 후 1:1 채팅

COLUM BOOKS
스마트폰으로 MP3 파일 다운로드
콜롬북스 APP